Financing *and* Risk Management

FINANCING
and
RISK
MANAGEMENT

RICHARD A. BREALEY

STEWART C. MYERS

with

The Brattle Group

New York   Chicago   San Francisco
Lisbon   London   Madrid   Mexico City   Milan
New Delhi   San Juan   Seoul   Singapore
Sydney   Toronto

The **McGraw·Hill** Companies

1 2 3 4 5 6 7 8 9 0   DOC/DOC   0 8 7 6 5 4 3 2

ISBN 0-07-138378-6

This publication is designed to provide accurate and authoritative information in regard to the subject matter covered. It is sold with the understanding that neither the author nor the publisher is engaged in rendering legal, accounting, or other professional service. If legal advice or other expert assistance is required, the services of a competent professional person should be sought.

—From a Declaration of Principles jointly adopted by a
Committee of the American Bar Association
and a Committee of Publishers

McGraw-Hill books are available at special quantity discounts to use as premiums and sales promotions, or for use in corporate training programs. For more information, please write to the Director of Special Sales, Professional Publishing, McGraw-Hill, Two Penn Plaza, New York, NY 10121-2298. Or contact your local bookstore.

This book is printed on recycled, acid-free paper containing a minimum of 50% recycled de-inked fiber.

CONTENTS

PREFACE

This book describes the theory and practice of corporate finance. We hardly need to explain why financial managers should master the practical aspects of their job, but we should spell out why down-to-earth, red-blooded managers need to bother with theory.

Managers learn from experience how to cope with routine problems. But the best managers are also able to respond to change. To do this you need more than time-honored rules of thumb; you must understand *why* companies and financial markets behave the way they do. In other words, you need the *theory* of finance.

Does that sound intimidating? It shouldn't. Good theory helps you grasp what is going on in the world around you. It helps you to ask the right questions when times change and new problems must be analyzed. It also tells you what things you do *not* need to worry about. Throughout this book we show how managers use financial theory to solve practical problems.

Of course, the theory presented in this book is not perfect and complete—no theory is. There are some famous controversies in which finan-

cial economists cannot agree on what firms ought to do. We have not glossed over these controversies. We set out the main arguments to each side and tell you where we stand.

Once understood, good theory is common sense. Therefore, we have tried to present it at a common sense level, and we have avoided proofs and heavy mathematics. There are no ironclad prerequisites for reading this book except algebra and the English language. An elementary knowledge of accounting, statistics, and microeconomics is helpful, however.

This book has been adapted for business professionals from *Principles of Corporate Finance* by Richard A. Brealey and Stewart C. Myers. For years this book has been the "bible" of corporate finance, and the best selling finance textbook worldwide. Among other changes, the text has been divided into two volumes, this one on corporate financial policy and a companion, *Capital Investment and Valuation*, on corporate investment decisions. We believe that this format will be more useful in an office (as distinct from a classroom) setting. We also have added examples and material not present in the textbook.

ACKNOWLEDGMENTS

This book has benefited from comments and suggestions of many people over the years since the first edition of *Principles of Corporate Finance* was published. We wish to acknowledge those people again here, but trust that it will be satisfactory to do so by reference to the original text (Richard A. Brealey and Stewart C. Myers, *Principles of Corporate Finance,* 7th ed., McGraw-Hill Higher Education, 2003).

The text was adapted from *Principles* by The Brattle Group. A. Lawrence Kolbe and James A. Read, Jr. are the Brattle authors, with Kolbe having primary responsibility for the companion volume and Read having primary responsibility for this volume. Debra A. Paolo provided expert editorial advice and assistance throughout the process.

Financing *and* Risk Management

FINANCING DECISIONS AND MARKET EFFICIENCY

FINANCE AND THE FINANCIAL MANAGER

This book is about financial decisions made by corporations. We should start by saying what these decisions are and why they are important.

Corporations face two broad financial questions: What investments should the firm make? and How should it pay for those investments? The first question involves spending money; the second involves raising it. This book addresses the second topic. A companion volume addresses the first.[1]

The secret of success in financial management is to increase value. That is a simple statement, but not very helpful. It is like advising an investor in the stock market to "Buy low, sell high." The problem is how to do it.

There may be a few activities in which one can read a textbook and then do it, but financial management is not one of them. That is why finance is worth studying. Who wants to work in a field where there is no room for judgment, experience,

creativity, and a pinch of luck? Although this book cannot supply any of these items, it does present the concepts and information on which good financial decisions are based, and it shows you how to use the tools of the trade of finance.

We start in this chapter by explaining what a corporation is and introducing you to its financial manager. We will also take a look at the ocean in which the financial manager swims. Since the manager is the link between the firm's operations and the financial markets, we provide a brief overview of the financial markets and the financial institutions that operate there.

Finance is about money and markets, but it is also about people. The success of a corporation depends on how well it harnesses everyone to work to a common end. The financial manager must appreciate the conflicting objectives often encountered in financial management. Resolving conflicts is particularly difficult when people have different information. This is an important

---

[1]Brealey and Myers on *Corporate Finance: Capital Investment and Valuation*, McGraw-Hill . . .

theme, one which runs through to the last chapter of this book. In this chapter we will start with some definitions and examples.

WHAT IS A CORPORATION?

Not all businesses are corporations. Small ventures can be owned and managed by a single individual. These are called *sole proprietorships*. In other cases several people may join to own and manage a *partnership*.[2] However, this book is about *corporate* finance. So we need to explain what a corporation is.

Almost all large and medium-sized businesses are organized as corporations. For example, General Motors, Chase Manhattan Bank, Microsoft, and General Electric are corporations. So are overseas businesses, such as British Petroleum, Unilever, Nestlé, Volkswagen, and Sony. In each case the firm is owned by stockholders who hold shares in the business.

When a corporation is first established, its shares may all be held by a small group of investors, perhaps the company's managers and a few backers. In this case the shares are not publicly traded and the company is *closely held*. Eventually, when the firm grows and new shares are issued to raise additional capital, its shares will be widely traded. Such corporations are known as *public companies*. Most well-known corporations in the United States are public companies. In many other countries, it's common for large companies to remain in private hands.

By organizing as a corporation, a business can attract a wide variety of investors. Some may hold only a single share worth a few dollars, cast only a single vote, and receive a tiny proportion of profits and dividends. Shareholders may also include giant pension funds and insurance companies whose investment may run to millions of shares and hundreds of millions of dollars, and who are entitled to a correspondingly large number of votes and proportion of profits and dividends.

Although the stockholders own the corporation, they do not manage it. Instead, they vote to elect a *board of directors*. Some of these directors may be drawn from top management, but others are non-executive directors, who are not employed by the firm. The board of directors represents the shareholders. It appoints top management and is supposed to ensure that managers act in the shareholders' best interests.

This *separation of ownership and management* gives corporations permanence.[3] Even if managers quit or are dismissed and replaced, the corporation can survive, and today's stockholders can sell all their shares to new investors without disrupting the operations of the business.

Unlike partnerships and sole proprietorships, corporations have **limited liability,** which means that stockholders cannot be held personally responsible for the firm's debts. If, say, General Motors were to fail, no one could demand that its shareholders put up more money to pay off its debts. The most a stockholder can lose is the amount he or she has invested.

---

[2]Many professional businesses, such as accounting and legal firms, are partnerships. Most large investment banks started as partnerships, but eventually these companies and their financing needs grew too large for them to continue in this form. Goldman Sachs, the last of the leading investment-bank partnerships, announced in 1998 that it planned to issue shares and become a public corporation.

[3]Corporations can be immortal but the law requires partnerships to have a definite end. A partnership agreement must specify an ending date or a procedure for wrapping up the partnership's affairs. A sole proprietorship also will have an end because the proprietor is mortal.

Although a corporation is owned by its stockholders, it is legally distinct from them. It is based on *articles of incorporation* that set out the purpose of the business, how many shares can be issued, the number of directors to be appointed, and so on. These articles must conform to the laws of the state in which the business is incorporated.[4] For many legal purposes, the corporation is considered as a resident of its state. As a legal "person," it can borrow or lend money, and it can sue or be sued. It pays its own taxes (but it cannot vote!).

Because the corporation is distinct from its shareholders, it can do things that partnerships and sole proprietorships cannot. For example, it can raise money by selling new shares to investors and it can buy those shares back. One corporation may make a takeover bid for another and then merge the two businesses.

There are also some *disadvantages* to organizing as a corporation. Managing a corporation's legal machinery and communicating with shareholders can be time-consuming and costly. Furthermore, in the United States there is an important tax drawback. Because the corporation is a separate legal entity, it is taxed separately. So corporations pay tax on their profits, and, in addition, shareholders pay tax on any dividends that they receive from the company. The United States is unusual in this respect. To avoid taxing the same income twice, most other countries give shareholders at least some credit for the tax that the company has already paid.[5]

THE ROLE OF THE FINANCIAL MANAGER

To carry on business, corporations need an almost endless variety of **real assets.** Many of these assets are tangible, such as machinery, factories, and offices; others are intangible, such as technical expertise, trademarks, and patents. All of them need to be paid for. To obtain the necessary money, the corporation sells pieces of paper called **financial assets,** or **securities.** These pieces of paper have value because they are claims on the firm's real assets and the cash that they produce. For example, if the company borrows money from the bank, the bank gets a written promise that the money will be repaid with interest. Thus the bank trades cash for a financial asset. Financial assets include not only bank loans but also shares of stock, bonds, and a dizzying variety of specialized securities.[6]

The financial manager stands between the firm's operations and the **financial markets,** where investors hold the financial assets issued by the firm.[7] The financial manager's role is illustrated in Figure 1.1, which traces the flow of cash from investors to the firm and back to investors again. The flow starts when the firm sells securities to raise cash (arrow 1 in the figure). The cash is used to purchase real assets used in the firm's operations (arrow 2). Later, if the firm does well, the real assets generate cash inflows which more than repay the initial investment (arrow 3). Finally, the cash is either reinvested (arrow 4a) or returned to the investors who purchased the original security

---

[4]Delaware has a well-developed and supportive system of corporate law. Even though they may do little business in that state, a high proportion of United States corporations are incorporated in Delaware.

[5]Or companies may pay a lower rate of tax on profits paid out as dividends.

[6]We review these securities in Chapters 2, 11, and 19.

[7]You will hear financial managers use the terms *financial markets* and *capital markets* almost synonymously. But *capital markets* are, strictly speaking, the source of long-term financing only. Short-term financing comes from the *money market.* We use the term *financial markets* to refer to all sources of financing.

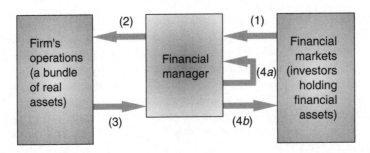

Figure 1.1

Flow of cash between financial markets and the firm's operations. Key: (1) Cash raised by selling financial assets to investors; (2) cash invested in the firm's operations and used to purchase real assets; (3) cash generated by the firm's operations; (4a) cash reinvested; (4b) cash returned to investors.

Source: Adapted from S. C. Myers, ed., *Modern Developments in Financial Management*, New York, Praeger Publishers, Inc., Fig. 1, p. 5.

issue (arrow 4b). Of course, the choice between arrows 4a and 4b is not completely free. For example, if a bank lends money at stage 1, the bank has to be repaid the money plus interest at stage 4b.

Our diagram takes us back to the financial manager's two basic questions. First, what real assets should the firm invest in? Second, how should the cash for the investment be raised? The answer to the first question is the firm's **investment,** or **capital budgeting, decision.** The answer to the second—the focus of this book—is the firm's **financing decision.**

Financial managers of large corporations need to be men and women of the world. They must decide not only *which* assets their firm should invest in but also *where* those assets should be located. Take Nestlé, for example. It is a Swiss company, but only a small proportion of its production takes place in Switzerland. Its 500 or so factories are located in 74 countries. Nestlé's managers must therefore know how to evaluate investments in countries with different currencies, interest rates, inflation rates, and tax systems.

The financial markets in which the firm raises money are likewise international. The stockholders of large corporations are scattered around the globe. Shares are traded around the clock in New York, London, Tokyo, and other financial centers. Bonds and bank loans move easily across national borders. A corporation that needs to raise cash doesn't have to borrow from its hometown bank. Day-to-day cash management also becomes a complex task for firms that produce or sell in different countries. For example, think of the problems that Nestlé's financial managers face in keeping track of the cash receipts and payments in 74 different countries.

We admit that Nestlé is unusual, but few financial managers can close their eyes to international financial issues. So throughout the book we will pay attention to differences in financial systems and examine the problems of investing and raising money internationally.

WHO IS THE FINANCIAL MANAGER?

In this book we will use the term *financial manager* to refer to anyone responsible for a significant investment or financing decision. But only in the smallest firms is a single person responsible for all the decisions discussed in this book. In most cases, responsibility is dispersed. Top management is of course continuously involved in financial decisions. But the engineer who designs a new production facility is also involved: The design determines the kind of real assets the firm will hold. The marketing manager who commits to a major advertising campaign is also making an important investment decision. The campaign is an investment in an intangible asset that is expected to pay off in future sales and earnings.

Nevertheless there are some managers who specialize in finance. Their roles are summarized in Figure 1.2. The **treasurer** is responsible for looking after the firm's cash, raising new capital, and maintaining relationships with banks, stockholders, and other investors who hold the firm's securities.

For small firms, the treasurer is likely to be the only financial executive. Larger corporations also have a **controller,** who prepares the financial statements, manages the firm's internal accounting, and looks after its tax obligations. You can see that the treasurer and controller have different functions: The treasurer's main responsibility is to obtain and manage the firm's capital, whereas the controller ensures that the money is used efficiently.

Still larger firms usually appoint a **chief financial officer (CFO)** to oversee both the treasurer's and the controller's work. The CFO is deeply involved in financial policy and corporate planning. Often he or she will have general managerial responsibilities beyond strictly financial issues and may also be a member of the board of directors.

The controller or CFO is responsible for organizing and supervising the capital budgeting process. However, major capital investment projects are so closely tied to plans for product development, production, and marketing that managers from these areas are inevitably drawn into planning and analyzing the projects. If the firm has staff members specializing in corporate planning, they too are naturally involved in capital budgeting.

Because of the importance of many financial issues, ultimate decisions often rest by law or by custom with the board of directors. For example, only the board has the legal power to declare a dividend or to sanction a public issue of securities. Boards usually delegate decisions for small or medium-sized investment outlays, but the authority to approve large investments is almost never delegated.

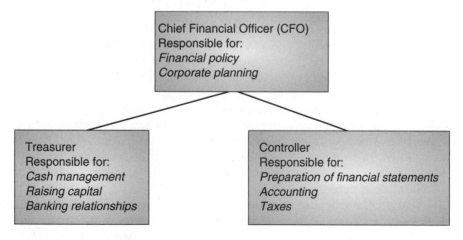

Figure 1.2

The financial managers in large corporations.

SEPARATION OF OWNERSHIP AND MANAGEMENT

In large businesses separation of ownership and management is a practical necessity. Major corporations may have hundreds of thousands of shareholders. There is no way for all of them to be actively involved in management: It would be like running New York City through a series of town meetings for all its citizens. Authority has to be delegated to managers.

The separation of ownership and management has clear advantages. It allows share ownership to change without interfering with the operation of the business. It allows the firm to hire professional managers. But it also brings problems if the managers' and owners' objectives differ. You can see the danger: Rather than attending to the wishes of shareholders, managers may seek a more leisurely or luxurious working lifestyle; they may shun unpopular decisions, or they may attempt to build an empire with their shareholders' money.

Such conflicts between shareholders' and managers' objectives create *principal–agent problems*. The shareholders are the principals; the managers are their agents. Shareholders want management to increase the value of the firm, but managers may have their own axes to grind or nests to feather. **Agency costs** are incurred when (1) managers do not attempt to maximize firm value and (2) shareholders incur costs to monitor the managers and influence their actions. Of course, there are no costs when the shareholders are also the managers. That is one of the advantages of a sole proprietorship. Owner–managers have no conflicts of interest.

Conflicts between shareholders and managers are not the only principal– agent problems that the financial manager is likely to encounter. For example, just as shareholders need to encourage managers to work for the shareholders' interests, so senior management needs to think about how to motivate everyone else in the company. In this case senior management are the principals and junior management and other employees are their agents.

Agency costs can also arise in financing. In normal times, the banks and bondholders who lend the company money are united with the shareholders in wanting the company to prosper, but when the firm gets into trouble, this unity of purpose can break down. At such times decisive changes may be necessary to rescue the firm, but lenders are concerned to get their money back and are reluctant to see the firm taking risks that could imperil the safety of their loans. Squabbles may even break out between different lenders as they see the company heading for possible bankruptcy and jostle for a better place in the queue of creditors.

Think of the company's overall value as a pie that is divided among a number of claimants. These include the management and the shareholders, as well as the company's workforce and the banks and investors who have bought the company's debt. The government is a claimant too, since it gets to tax corporate profits.

All these claimants are bound together in a complex web of contracts and understandings. For example, when banks lend money to the firm, they insist on a formal contract stating the rate of interest and repayment dates, perhaps placing restrictions on dividends or additional borrowing. But you can't devise written rules to cover every possible future event. So written contracts are incomplete and need to be supplemented by understandings and by arrangements that help to align the interests of the various parties.

Principal–agent problems would be easier to resolve if everyone had the same information. That is rarely the case in finance. Managers, shareholders, and lenders may all have different information about the value of a real or financial asset, and it may be many years before all the information is revealed. Financial managers need to recognize these *information asymmetries* and find ways to reassure investors that there are no nasty surprises on the way.

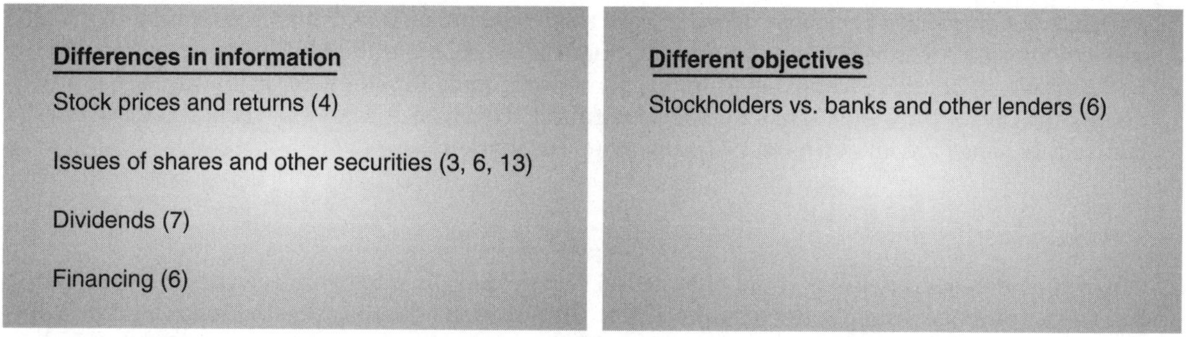

Differences in information	**Different objectives**
Stock prices and returns (4)	Stockholders vs. banks and other lenders (6)
Issues of shares and other securities (3, 6, 13)	
Dividends (7)	
Financing (6)	

Figure 1.3

Differences in objectives and information can complicate financial decisions. We address these issues at several points in this book. (Chapter numbers in parentheses.)

Here is one example. Suppose you are the financial manager of a company that has been newly formed to develop and bring to market a drug for the cure of toetitis. At a meeting with potential investors you present the results of clinical trials, show upbeat reports by an independent market research company, and forecast profits amply sufficient to justify further investment. But the potential investors are still worried that you may know more than they do. What can you do to convince them that you are telling the truth? Just saying "Trust me" won't do the trick. Perhaps you need to *signal* your integrity by putting your money where your mouth is. For example, investors are likely to have more confidence in your plans if they see that you and the other managers have large personal stakes in the new enterprise. Therefore your decision to invest your own money can provide information to investors about the true prospects of the firm.

In later chapters we will look more carefully at how corporations tackle the problems created by differences in objectives and information. Figure 1.3 summarizes the main issues and signposts the chapters where they receive most attention.

FINANCIAL MARKETS

We have seen that corporations raise money by selling financial assets such as stocks or bonds. This increases both the amount of cash held by the company and the amount of stocks or bonds held by the public. Such an issue is known as a *primary issue* and it is sold in the **primary market.** But in addition to helping companies to raise new cash, financial markets also allow investors to trade stocks or bonds between themselves. For example, Ms. Watanabe might decide to raise some cash by selling her Sony stock at the same time that Mr. Hashimoto invests his savings in Sony. So they make a trade. The result is simply a transfer of ownership from one person to another, which has no effect on the company's cash, assets, or operations. Such purchases and sales are known as *secondary transactions* and they take place in the **secondary market.**

Some financial assets have less active secondary markets than others. For example, when a company borrows money from the bank, the bank acquires a financial asset (the company's promise to repay the loan with interest). Banks do sometimes sell packages of loans to other banks, but usually they retain the loan until it is repaid by the borrower. Other financial assets are regularly traded and their prices are shown each day in the newspaper. Some, such as shares of stock, are traded on organized exchanges like the New York, London, or Tokyo Stock Exchanges. In other cases there is no organized exchange and the financial assets are traded by a network of dealers. For example, if General Motors needs to buy foreign currency for an overseas investment, it will do so from one of the major banks that deals regularly in currency. Markets where there is no organized exchange are known as *over-the-counter (OTC)* markets.

Financial Institutions

When corporations raise cash, some of that cash is provided directly by individual investors, but the greater proportion comes from **financial institutions** such as banks, pension funds, and insurance companies. The financial manager is the link between the firm and these institutions and therefore, as a future financial manager, you need to understand their role.

Financial institutions are intermediaries that gather the savings of many individuals and reinvest them in the financial markets. For example, banks raise money by taking deposits or selling debt or stock to investors. They then lend the money to companies or individuals. Of course banks must charge sufficient interest to cover their costs and to compensate their depositors and other investors.

Banks and their immediate relatives, such as savings and loan companies, are the most familiar financial intermediaries. But there are many others, such as insurance companies and mutual funds. In the United States insurance companies are more important than banks for the *long-term* financing of business. They are massive investors in corporate stocks and bonds, and they often make long-term loans directly to corporations. Most of the money to make those loans comes from the sale of insurance policies. Say you buy a fire insurance policy on your home. You pay cash to the insurance company, which it invests in the financial markets. In exchange you get a financial asset (the insurance policy). You receive no interest payments on this financial asset, but if a fire does strike, the company is obliged to cover the damages up to the policy limit. This is the return on your investment. Of course the company will issue not just one policy but thousands. Normally the incidence of fires averages out, leaving the company with a predictable obligation to its policyholders as a group.

Why are these financial intermediaries different from a manufacturing corporation? First, the financial intermediary may raise money in special ways, for example, by taking deposits or selling insurance policies. Second, the financial intermediary invests in *financial* assets, such as stocks, bonds, or loans to businesses or individuals. By contrast, the manufacturing company's main investments are in *real* assets, such as plant and equipment. Thus the intermediary receives cash flows from its investment in one set of financial assets (stocks, bonds, etc.) and repackages those flows for distribution on a different set of financial assets (bank deposits, insurance policies, etc.).

Financial intermediaries contribute in many ways to our individual well-being and the smooth functioning of the economy. Here are some examples.[8]

The Payment Mechanism   Think how inconvenient life would be if all payments had to be made in cash. Fortunately, checking accounts, credit cards, and electronic transfers allow individuals and firms to send and receive payments quickly and safely over long distances. Banks are the obvious providers of payment services, but they are not alone. For example, if you buy shares in a money-

---

[8]Robert Merton gives an excellent overview of these functions in "A Functional Perspective of Financial Intermediation," *Financial Management* 24 (summer 1995), pp. 23–41.

market mutual fund, your money is pooled with that of other investors and is used to buy safe, short-term securities. You can then write checks on this mutual fund investment, just as if you had a bank deposit.

Borrowing and Lending   Almost all financial institutions are involved in channeling savings toward those who can best use them. Thus, if Ms. Jones has more money now than she needs and wishes to save for a rainy day, she can put the money in a bank savings deposit. If Mr. Smith wants to buy a car now and pay for it later, he can borrow money from the bank. Both the lender and borrower are happier than if they were forced to spend cash as it arrived. Of course, individuals are not alone in needing to raise cash by borrowing or selling new shares. Governments often run at a deficit, which they fund by issuing large quantities of debt.

In principle, individuals or firms with cash surpluses could take out newspaper advertisements or surf the Net looking for those with cash shortages. But it is usually cheaper and more convenient to use financial markets or institutions to link up the borrower and lender. For example, banks are equipped to check out the would-be borrower's creditworthiness and to monitor the use of cash lent out. Would you lend money to a stranger contacted over the internet? You would be safer lending the money to the bank and letting the bank decide what to do with it.

Notice that banks promise their checking account customers instant access to their money and at the same time make longer-term loans to companies and individuals. This mismatch between the maturity of their liabilities (the deposits) and most of their assets (the loans) is possible only because the number of depositors is sufficiently large that banks can be fairly sure that they won't all want to withdraw their money simultaneously.

Pooling Risk   Financial markets and institutions allow firms and individuals to pool their risks. For instance, insurance companies make it possible to share the risk of an automobile accident or a household fire. Here is another example. Suppose that you have only a small sum to invest. You could buy the stock of a single company, but then you could be wiped out if that company went belly-up. It's generally better to buy shares in a mutual fund that invests in a diversified portfolio of common stocks or other securities. In this case you are exposed only to the risk that security prices as a whole will fall.[9]

TOPICS COVERED IN THIS BOOK

This book covers long-term financing decisions first, then risk management, and finally financial planning and short-term financial management. It also covers the different types of securities that corporations issue.

Part 1 begins by describing the financial markets where securities are traded. We review the kinds of securities that corporations sell to raise money, and we explain how and when these securities are issued. We conclude by asking whether the company's securities are fairly priced by investors. The answer to this question is crucial for financial decision making.

---

[9]Mutual funds provide other services. For example, they take care of much of the paperwork of holding shares. Investors also hope that the fund's professional managers will be able to outsmart the market and secure higher returns. Can they really beat the market? We'll see in Chapter 4.

Part 2 covers dividend policy and capital structure. There are long-running controversies about these issues, so we will lay them out for you and let you know where we stand. We will also describe what happens when firms land in financial distress because of poor operating performance or excessive borrowing.

Part 3 covers options. The principal reason we devote so much attention to the structure and pricing of vanilla option contracts is that all corporate securities can be viewed as combinations of options and more basic securities. Understanding options is therefore essential for understanding how to price many kinds of securities, including warrants and convertibles, which we analyze in detail.

The subject of Part 4 is debt financing. We single out debt for further analysis because debt comes in many forms. In addition to the variety of debt securities, many financial contracts—leases in particular—are debt equivalents.

An important part of the financial manager's job is to judge which risks the firm should take on and which it should lay off. Part 5 discusses the management of both domestic and international risk exposures.

Part 6 covers financial planning. Financial decisions cannot be reached in isolation. They must be guided by the firm's investment and operating plans, since these are the principal source of value for shareholders.

Finally, in Part 7, we cover short-term financing. Our topics include the channels for short-term borrowing and lending, the management of cash and marketable securities, and the management of accounts receivable.

SUMMARY

Large businesses are usually organized as corporations. Corporations have three important features. First, they are legally distinct from their owners and pay their own taxes. Second, corporations have limited liability, which means that the stockholders who own the corporation cannot be held responsible for the firm's debts. Third, the owners of a corporation are not usually the managers.

The overall task of the financial manager can be broken down into (1) the investment, or capital budgeting, decision and (2) the financing decision. In other words, the firm has to decide (1) what real assets to buy and (2) how to raise the necessary cash.

In small companies there is often only one financial executive, the treasurer. However, most companies have both a treasurer and a controller. The treasurer's job is to obtain and manage the company's financing, while the controller's job is to confirm that the money is used correctly. In large firms there is also a chief financial officer or CFO.

Shareholders want managers to increase the value of the company's stock. Managers may have different objectives. This potential conflict of interest is termed a principal–agent problem. Any loss of value that results is termed an agency cost. Of course there may be other conflicts of interest. For example, the interests of the shareholders may sometimes conflict with those of the firm's banks and bondholders. These and other agency problems become more complicated when agents have more or better information than the principals.

The financial manager plays on an international stage and must understand how international financial markets operate and how to evaluate overseas investments. The investors who hold the company's securities can come from dozens of different countries. These investors include large financial institutions such as banks, insurance companies, and pension funds. Financial institutions play an important role in the economy. For example, they make it easier for firms and individuals to make payments to each other, they channel savings to those firms and individuals who can best use them, and they pool risks.

Further Reading

Financial managers read *The Wall Street Journal (WSJ)*, *The Financial Times (FT)*, or both daily. You should too. *The Financial Times* is published in Britain, but there is a North American edition. *The New York Times* and a few other big-city newspapers have good business and financial sections, but they are no substitute for the *WSJ* or *FT*. The business and financial sections of most United States dailies are, except for local news, nearly worthless for the financial manager.

The Economist, Business Week, Forbes, and *Fortune* contain useful financial sections, and there are several magazines that specialize in finance. These include *Euromoney, Corporate Finance, Journal of Applied Corporate Finance, Risk,* and *CFO Magazine.* This list does not include research journals such as the *Journal of Finance, Journal of Financial Economics, Review of Financial Studies,* and *Financial Management.* In the following chapters we give specific references to pertinent research.

AN OVERVIEW OF CORPORATE FINANCING

W e now begin our analysis of long-term financing decisions—a task we will not complete until Chapter 13. This chapter is an introduction to that material. It reviews with a broad brush topics that will be explored more carefully later on.

We start the chapter by looking at aggregate data on the sources of financing for U.S. corporations. Much of the money for new investment comes from profits that companies retain and reinvest. The remainder comes from selling new equity or debt securities. These financing patterns raise several interesting questions. Do companies rely too heavily on internal financing rather than on new issues of debt or equity? Are debt ratios of U.S. corporations dangerously high? How do patterns of financing differ across the major industrialized countries?

A simple division of sources of cash into debt and equity glosses over many different types of debt securities—and there are several types of equity. Therefore, in this chapter we will canter briefly through the main categories, starting with a detailed look at how stockholders' equity is accounted for. We will also introduce you to *derivatives*. Derivatives do not provide the company with extra cash, but they are widely used to protect the company against major risks.

PATTERNS OF CORPORATE FINANCING

Companies invest in long-term assets (mainly property, plant, and equipment) and net working capital. Table 2.1 shows where they get the cash to pay for these investments. You can see that by far the greater part of the money is generated internally.[1] In other words, it comes from funds that

---

[1]In Table 2.1, internally generated cash was calculated by adding depreciation to retained earnings. Depreciation is a non-cash expense. Thus, retained earnings understate the cash flow available for reinvestment.

Sources and uses of funds in nonfinancial corporations expressed as percentage of each year's total investment

	1988	1989	1990	1991	1992	1993	1994	1995	1996	1997
Uses										
1. Capital expenditures	74	87	87	98	73	81	80	77	81	83
2. Investment in net working capital and other uses[a]	26	13	13	2	27	19	20	23	19	17
3. Total investment	100	100	100	100	100	100	100	100	100	100
Sources										
4. Internally generated cash[b]	81	87	90	112	88	88	86	78	89	85
5. Financial deficit (3 − 4); equals required external financing	19	13	10	−12	12	12	14	22	11	15
Financial deficit covered by[c]										
6. Net stock issues	−26	−27	−14	3	6	4	−7	−8	−9	−14
7. Net increase in debt	45	40	24	−14	7	8	21	30	20	30

[a]Changes in short-term borrowing are shown under net increase in debt. "Other uses" are net of any increase in miscellaneous liabilities and any statistical discrepancy.

[b]Net income plus depreciation less cash dividends paid to stockholders.

[c]Columns may not add up due to rounding.

Source: Board of Governors of the Federal Reserve System, Division of Research and Statistics, *Flow of Funds Accounts,* various issues.

the company has set aside as depreciation and from earnings that are not paid out as dividends. Shareholders are happy for companies to plow this money back into positive-NPV investments because they expect that it will result in a higher price for their shares.

In most years there is a gap between the cash that companies need and the cash that they generate internally. This gap is the financial deficit. To make up the deficit, companies must either sell new equity or borrow. So companies face two basic financing decisions: How much profit should be plowed back into the business rather than paid out as dividends? and What proportion of the deficit should be financed by borrowing rather than by an issue of equity? To answer the first question the firm requires a dividend policy (we discuss this in Chapter 7); and to answer the second it needs to formulate a debt policy (this is the topic of Chapters 5 and 6).

As we will see in Chapters 5–7, the company's dividend and debt policies can be viewed as marketing decisions; the company is packaging and selling its assets, operations, and growth opportunities to outside investors. The company tries to split the cash flows generated by its assets into different streams that will appeal to investors with different tastes, wealth, and tax rates.

Table 2.1 shows dramatic year-to-year variations in the way that firms finance the deficit. For example, during the late 1980s firms borrowed much more than they needed for investment. They used the surplus to buy back their own shares or to purchase and retire *other* companies' shares in the course of mergers and acquisitions.[2] In Table 2.1 the huge volume of repurchases shows up in the negative figure for new equity issues. Apparently in this period companies thought that debt was an attractive form of financing and wanted more of it.

The heavy borrowing and stock repurchases of the late 1980s left many companies with uncomfortably high debt ratios. So the early 1990s were spent paying down debt and replenishing equity. Note in Table 2.1 that debt issues were actually negative in 1991 (firms paid back more debt than they issued). Net stock issues turned positive in the same year. By 1994 the position had reversed once more and firms were again issuing more debt and buying back their stock.

Do Firms Rely Too Heavily on Internal Funds?

We have seen that on average internal funds (depreciation plus retained earnings) make up the bulk of the money that companies need. Some observers worry that this reflects an unjustified reluctance to undertake projects that might require outside finance. For example, Gordon Donaldson, in a field survey of corporate debt policies, encountered several firms which acknowledged "that it was their long-term object to hold to a rate of growth which was consistent with their capacity to generate funds internally." A number of other firms appeared to apply more stringent criteria to expenditure proposals that might require outside finance.[3]

At first glance, this behavior doesn't make sense. Retained earnings are additional capital invested by shareholders, and represent, in effect, a compulsory issue of shares. A firm which retains $1 million could have paid out that cash as dividends and then sold new common shares to raise the same amount of additional capital. Likewise, any reinvestment of dollars labeled "depreciation" amounts to investing money that could have been paid out to investors. The opportunity cost of capital does not depend on whether the project is financed by depreciation, retained earnings, or a new stock issue.

Why, then, do managers have an apparent preference for financing by retained earnings? Some believe that managers are simply taking the line of least resistance and dodging the "discipline of securities markets." But there are other reasons for relying on internally generated funds. The costs of issuing new securities are avoided, for example. Moreover, the announcement of a new equity issue is usually bad news for investors, who worry that the decision signals lower future profits or higher risk.[4] If issues of shares are costly and send a bad-news signal to investors, companies may be justified in looking more carefully at those projects that would require a new stock issue.

Has Capital Structure Changed?

We have seen that in recent years firms have issued more debt than equity. But is there a long-run trend to heavier reliance on debt financing? This is a hard question to answer in general, because

---

[2]We discuss share repurchases in Chapter 7.

[3]See G. Donaldson, *Corporate Debt Capacity*, Division of Research, Graduate School of Business Administration, Harvard University, Boston, 1961, chap. 3, especially pp. 51–56.

[4]Managers do have insiders' insights and naturally are tempted to issue stock when the price looks good to them, i.e., when they are less optimistic than outside investors. The outside investors realize this and will buy a new issue only at a discount from the preannouncement price. More on stock issues in Chapter 3.

financing policy varies so much from industry to industry and from firm to firm. But a few statistics will do no harm as long as you keep these difficulties in mind.

Table 2.2 shows the aggregate balance sheet of all manufacturing corporations in the United States in 1998. If all manufacturing corporations were merged into one gigantic firm, Table 2.2 would be its balance sheet.

Assets and liabilities in Table 2.2 are entered at book, that is, accounting values. These do not generally equal market values. The numbers are nevertheless instructive. The table shows that manufacturing corporations had total book assets of $3,896 billion. On the right-hand side of the balance sheet, we find total long-term liabilities of $1,391 billion and stockholders' equity of $1,508 billion.

So what was the book debt ratio of manufacturing corporations in 1997? It depends on what you mean by *debt*. If all liabilities are counted as debt, the debt ratio is .61:

$$\frac{\text{Debt}}{\text{Total assets}} = \frac{997 + 1,391}{3,896} = .61$$

This measure of debt includes both current liabilities and long-term obligations. Sometimes financial analysts focus on the proportions of debt and equity in *long-term* financing. The proportion of debt in long-term financing is

$$\frac{\text{Long-term liabilities}}{\text{Long-term liabilities} + \text{stockholders' equity}} = \frac{1,391}{1,391 + 1,508} = .48$$

The sum of long-term liabilities and stockholders' equity is called *total capitalization*. Figure 2.1 plots these two ratios from 1954 to 1997. There is a clear upward shift from the 1950s to the 1990s. But before we conclude that industry is becoming weighed down by a crippling debt burden, we need to put these changes in perspective.

1990 versus 1920 Debt ratios in the 1990s, though clearly higher than in the early postwar period, are no higher than in the 1920s and 1930s. You could argue that Figure 2.1 starts from an abnormally low point.

Inflation Some of the upward movement in Figure 2.1 may have reflected inflation, which was especially rapid—by U.S. standards—throughout the 1970s and early 1980s. Rapid inflation means that the *book* value of corporate assets falls behind the actual value of those assets. If corporations were borrowing against *actual* value, it would not be surprising to observe rising ratios of debt-to-book asset values.

To illustrate, suppose that you bought a house 10 years ago for $60,000. You financed the purchase in part with a $30,000 mortgage, 50 percent of the purchase price. Today the house is worth $120,000. Suppose that you repay the remaining balance of your original mortgage and take out a new mortgage of $60,000, which is again 50 percent of current market value. Your *book* debt ratio would be 100 percent. The reason is that the book value of the house is its *original* cost of $60,000 (we assume no depreciation). An analyst having only book values to work with would observe that 10 years ago your book debt ratio was only 50 percent and might conclude that you had decided to "use more debt." But you have no more debt relative to the actual value of your house.

TABLE 2.2

Aggregate balance sheet for manufacturing corporations in the United States, 1998 (figures in $ billions)[a]

Current assets[b]		$1,320	Current liabilities[b]		$997
Fixed assets	$2,181		Long-term debt	$815	
Less depreciation	1,097		Other long-term liabilities[c]	576	
Net fixed assets		1,085	Total long-term liabilities		1,391
Other long-term assets		1,491	Stockholders' equity		1,508
Total assets[d]		$3,896	Total liabilities and stockholders' equity[d]		$3,896

[a]Excludes corporations with less than $250,000 in assets.
[b]See Table 17.1 for a breakdown of current assets and liabilities.
[c]Includes deferred taxes and several miscellaneous categories.
[d]Columns may not add up because of rounding.
Source: U.S. Federal Trade Commission, *Quarterly Financial Report for Manufacturing, Mining and Trade Corporations,* 2nd quarter, 1998.

Figure 2.1

Average debt ratios for manufacturing corporations in the United States have increased in the postwar period. However, note that these ratios compare debt with the *book* value of total assets and total long-term financing. The actual value of corporate assets is higher as a result of inflation.

Source: U.S. Federal Trade Commission, *Quarterly Report for Manufacturing, Mining and Trade Corporations,* various issues.

TABLE 2.3

Median debt-to-total-capital ratios in 1991 for samples of traded companies in the major countries. Debt includes short- and long-term debt. Total capital is defined as the sum of all debt and equity. The adjusted figures correct for some international differences in accounting.

		DEBT TO TOTAL CAPITAL		
	BOOK	BOOK, ADJUSTED	MARKET	MARKET, ADJUSTED
Canada	39%	37%	35%	32%
France	48	34	41	28
Germany	38	18	23	15
Italy	47	39	46	36
Japan	53	37	29	17
United Kingdom	28	16	19	11
United States	37	33	28	23

Source: R. G. Rajan and L. Zingales, "What Do We Know About Capital Structure? Some Evidence from International Data," *Journal of Finance* 50 (December 1995), pp. 1421–1460.

International Comparisons   Corporations in the United States are generally viewed as having less debt than many of their foreign counterparts. That was surely true in the 1950s and 1960s. Now it is not so clear.

Rajan and Zingales examined the balance sheets of a large sample of publicly traded firms in the seven largest industrialized countries. They calculated debt ratios using both book and market values of shareholders' equity. (The book value of debt was assumed to approximate market value.) A taste of their results is given in Table 2.3. Notice that the debt ratios for the United States sample fall in the middle of the pack.

International comparisons of this sort are always muddied by differences in accounting methods. For example, German companies show pension liabilities as a debtlike obligation on their balance sheets, with no offsetting entry for pension assets.[5] They also report "reserves" separately from equity. These reserves do not cover any specific obligations but serve as equity for a rainy day. Reserves might be drawn down to offset a future drop in operating earnings, for example. (This would be unacceptably creative accounting in the United States.) When Rajan and Zingales crossed out the pension liabilities and added back reserves to equity, the *adjusted* debt ratios for German companies dropped to the low levels reported in Table 2.3.

Despite such qualifications, it's still the case that many U.S. corporations are carrying a lot more debt than they used to. Should we be worried? It's true that higher debt ratios mean that more companies will fall into financial distress if a serious recession hits the economy. But all companies live with this risk to some degree, and it does not follow that less risk is better. Finding the optimal debt ratio is like finding the optimal speed limit. We can agree that accidents at 30 miles per hour are generally less dangerous than accidents at 60 miles per hour, but we do not therefore

---

[5]United States companies show a net liability only if the pension plan is underfunded.

TABLE 2.4

Book value of common stockholders' equity of Mobil Corporation, December 31, 1997 (figures in $ millions)

Common shares ($1.00 par value per share)	$ 894
Capital surplus	1,549
Retained earnings	20,661
Foreign exchange translation adjustment	(821)
Treasury shares at cost	(3,158)
Net common equity	$19,125

Note:
Shares:

Authorized	1,200.0
Issued shares, of which:	894.3
Outstanding shares	783.4
Treasury shares	110.9

Source: Mobil Corporation *Annual Reports.*

set the speed limit on all roads at 30. Speed has benefits as well as risks. So does debt, as we will see in Chapter 6.

There is no God-given, correct debt ratio, and if there were, it would change. It may be that some of the new tools that allow firms to manage their risks have made higher debt ratios practicable.

COMMON STOCK

Corporations raise cash in two principal ways—by issuing equity or by issuing debt. The equity consists largely of common stock, but companies may also issue preferred stock. As we shall see, there is a much greater diversity of debt securities. In addition to issuing these securities, companies enter into a variety of side bets, known as *derivative instruments.* These do not raise new cash but they do change the risks the company is exposed to.

We start our tour of corporate securities and derivative instruments by taking a closer look at common stock.

In 1998 Exxon and Mobil announced that they were going to combine their activities through one of the world's largest mergers to date. Table 2.4 shows the common equity of Mobil as it was reported in the company's books at the end of its last year as an independent company.

The maximum number of shares that can be issued is known as the *authorized share capital*; for Mobil it was 1.2 billion shares. This maximum was specified in the firm's articles of incorporation. When in 1997 the company wished to double the number of authorized shares from 600 million to 1.2 billion, it needed the agreement of shareholders to do so. By the end of the year Mobil had already issued 894 million shares, and so it could issue 306 million more without further shareholder approval.

Most of the issued shares were held by investors. These shares are said to be *issued and outstanding*. But Mobil had also bought back about 111 million shares from investors. Repurchased shares are held in a company's treasury until they are either canceled or resold. Treasury shares are said to be *issued but not outstanding*.

The issued shares are entered in the company's books at their par value. Each Mobil share had a par value of $1.00. Thus, the total book value of the issued shares was 894 × $1.00 = $894 million.

Par value has little economic significance.[6] Some companies issue shares with no par value. In this case, the stock is listed in the accounts at an arbitrarily determined figure.

The price of new shares sold to the public almost always exceeds par value. The difference is entered in the company's accounts as additional paid-in capital or capital surplus. Thus, if Mobil had sold an additional 100,000 shares at $70 a share, the common stock account would have increased by 100,000 × $1.00 = $100,000 and the capital surplus account would have increased by 100,000 × ($70 − $1) = $6,900,000.

Mobil distributed about 60 percent of its earnings as dividends. The remainder was retained in the business and used to finance new investment. The cumulative amount of retained earnings was $20,661 million.

The next entry in the common stock account is an adjustment for currency translation losses stemming from Mobil's foreign operations. We'd rather not get into foreign exchange accounting here. Let's move on to the last item, which shows the amount that the company had spent on repurchasing its own stock. The repurchases had *reduced* the stockholders' equity by $3,158 million.

Mobil's net common equity had a book value at the end of 1997 of $19,125 million. That works out at 19,125/783.4 = $24.41 per share. But in December 1997 Mobil shares were priced at $72 each. So the *market value* of the equity was 783.4 × 72 = $56,405 million, more than $37 billion higher than book.

Stockholders' Rights

The common stockholders are the owners of the corporation and therefore have the ultimate control of the company's affairs. In practice this control is limited to a right to vote, either in person or by proxy, on appointments to the *board of directors* and a number of other matters. Mergers, for example, need to be submitted for shareholder approval.

If the corporation's articles specify a *majority voting* system, each director is voted upon separately and stockholders can cast one vote for each share that they own. If the articles permit *cumulative voting,* the directors are voted upon jointly and stockholders can, if they wish, allot all their votes to just one candidate.[7] Cumulative voting makes it easier for a minority group among the stockholders to elect directors representing the group's interests. That is why minority groups devote so much of their efforts to campaigning for cumulative voting.

On many issues a simple majority of votes cast is sufficient to carry the day, but the company charter may specify some decisions that require a *supermajority* of, say, 75 percent of those eligible to vote. For example, a supermajority vote is sometimes needed to approve a merger. This

---

[6]Because some states do not allow companies to sell shares below par value, par value is generally set at a low figure.

[7]For example, suppose there are five directors to be elected and you own 100 shares. You therefore have a total of 5 × 100 = 500 votes. Under the majority voting system, you can cast a maximum of 100 votes for any one candidate. Under a cumulative voting system, you can cast all 500 votes for your favorite candidate.

requirement makes it difficult for the firm to be taken over and therefore helps to protect the incumbent management.

The issues on which stockholders are asked to vote are rarely contested, particularly in the case of large, publicly traded firms. Occasionally, there are *proxy contests* in which the firm's existing management and directors compete with outsiders for control of the corporation. But the odds are stacked against the outsiders, for the insiders can get the firm to pay all the costs of presenting their case and obtaining votes.

Most companies issue just one class of common stock. Occasionally, however, a firm may have two classes outstanding, which differ in their right to vote. Suppose that a firm needs fresh equity capital but its present stockholders do not want to relinquish their control of the firm. The existing shares could be labeled "class A," and then "class B" shares with limited voting privileges could be issued to outsiders.

Shareholders with voting stock may be able to use their votes to toss out bad managers or force management to adopt value-enhancing policies. But, if there are several classes of shares, *all* shareholders reap the benefit of such changes, regardless of whether they are entitled to vote. So here's the question: If everyone gains equally from improved management, why would investors be prepared to pay more for one class of shares than another? It seems as if they can be justified in doing so only if the vote can be used to secure *private* benefits (or perks) that are not available to other shareholders. For example, a company with a controlling vote in another might be able to use its influence to secure a business advantage.

These private benefits of control seem to be much larger in some countries than others. For example, Luigi Zingales has looked at companies in the United States and Italy that have two classes of stock. In the United States investors were on average prepared to pay an extra 11 percent for the shares with the superior voting rights, but in Italy the average premium for a vote was 82 percent.[8]

Equity in Disguise

Common stockholders are the owners of the business. They hold the *equity interest* or *residual claim*, since they receive whatever assets or earnings are left over in the business after all its debts are paid.

Common stocks are, of course, issued by corporations. But a few equity securities are issued not by corporations but by partnerships or trusts. We will give some brief examples.

Partnerships Newhall Land and Farming is a *master limited partnership* which owns large tracts of real estate, mostly in southern California. You can buy "units" in this partnership on the New York Stock Exchange, thus becoming a *limited* partner in Newhall. The most the limited partners can lose is their investment in the company.[9] In this and most other respects, the Newhall partnership units

---

[8]L. Zingales, "What Determines the Value of Corporate Votes?" *Quarterly Journal of Economics*, 110 (1995), pp. 1047–1073, and L. Zingales, "The Value of the Voting Right: A Study of the Milan Stock Exchange," *Review of Financial Studies*, 7 (1994), pp. 125–148. The data for the United States were for the period 1984–1990. This was the height of the leverage buyout boom, when the value of control was likely to have been unusually large. An earlier study that looked at the period 1940–1978 found a premium of only 4 percent. See R. C. Lease, J. J. McConnell, and W. H. Mikkelson, "The Market Value of Control in Publicly-Traded Corporations," *Journal of Financial Economics* 11 (April 1983), pp. 439–471.

[9]A partnership can offer limited liability *only* to its limited partners. The partnership must also have one or more general partners, who have unlimited liability. However, general partners can be corporations. This puts the corporation's shield of limited liability between the partnership and the human beings who ultimately own the general partner.

are just like the shares in an ordinary corporation. They share in the profits of the business and receive cash distributions (like dividends) from time to time.

Partnerships avoid corporate income tax; any profits or losses are passed straight through to the partners' tax returns. Offsetting this tax advantage are various limitations of partnerships. For example, the law regards a partnership merely as a voluntary association of individuals; like its partners, it is expected to have a limited life. A corporation, on the other hand, is an independent legal "person" that can, and often does, outlive all its original shareholders.

Trusts and REITs   Would you like to own a part of the oil in the Prudhoe Bay field on the north slope of Alaska? Just call your broker and buy a few units of the Prudhoe Bay Royalty Trust. British Petroleum (BP) set up this trust and gave it a royalty interest in production from BP's share of the Prudhoe Bay revenues. As the oil is produced, each trust unit gets its share of the revenues.

This trust is the passive owner of a single asset: the right to a share of the revenues from BP's Prudhoe Bay production. Operating businesses, which cannot be passive, are rarely organized as trusts, though there are exceptions, notably *real estate investment trusts,* or *REITs* (pronounced "reets").

REITs were created to facilitate public investment in commercial real estate; there are shopping center REITs, office building REITs, apartment REITs, and REITs that specialize in lending to real estate developers. REIT "shares" are traded just like common stocks.[10] The REITs themselves are not taxed, so long as they pay out at least 95 percent of earnings to the REITs' owners, who must pay whatever taxes are due on the dividends. However, REITs are tightly restricted to real estate investment. You cannot set up a widget factory and avoid corporate taxes by calling it a REIT.

PREFERRED STOCK

Despite its name, **preferred stock** provides only a small proportion of most companies' cash needs and it will occupy less time in later chapters. However, we shall see that it can be a useful method of financing in mergers and certain other special situations.

Preferred stock is legally an equity security. This means that, although it offers a fixed dividend like debt, the directors can choose *not* to pay the dividend. However, all the dividends owed to the preferred *must* be paid before the company can pay a dividend on the common stock. Directors are also aware that failure to pay the preferred dividend earns the company a black mark with investors, so they do not take such a decision lightly.

Like common stock, preferred stock does not have a final repayment date, but in many cases the company agrees to set aside some money each year to buy back stock. If the company goes out of business, the preferred stockholders get in the queue behind all the debtholders but ahead of the common stockholders.

Preferred stockholders have only limited voting rights. However, the consent of the preferred holders must usually be obtained on any matter affecting the security of their claim and most issues also provide the holder with some voting power if the preferred dividend is skipped.

Preferred stock has an important tax advantage. If one corporation buys another's stock, only 30 percent of the dividends received are treated as taxable income to the corporation. This rule

---

[10]There are also some private REITs, whose shares are not publicly traded.

applies to common as well as preferred dividends, but it is most important for preferred issues because preferred stocks have higher dividend yields than most common stocks.

Suppose that your firm has surplus cash to invest. If it buys a bond, interest income will be taxed at the full marginal rate (35 percent). If it buys a preferred share, it owns an asset like a bond (the preferred dividends can be viewed as "interest"), but the effective tax rate is only 30 percent of 35 percent, $.30 \times .35 = .105$, or 10.5 percent. It is no surprise that most preferred shares are held by corporations.[11]

There is also a tax *disadvantage* to preferred stock, for, unlike interest payments on debt, the preferred dividend is not an allowable deduction from taxable profits. Thus the dividend is paid from after-tax income. For most industrial firms this is a serious deterrent to issuing preferred stock. Regulated public utilities, which can take tax payments into account when negotiating the rates they charge customers, can effectively pass the tax disadvantage of preferred stock on to the consumer. As a result, a large fraction of the dollar value of new offerings of nonconvertible preferred stock consists of issues by utilities.

Some companies have discovered the following ingenious way to issue preferred stock *and* make the payments tax-deductible. The company establishes a special-purpose subsidiary in an offshore tax haven, which issues preferred stock, known as MIPs (Monthly Income Preferred Stock).[12] The subsidiary uses the proceeds from the sale to buy a similar quantity of bonds from the parent. The parent company can deduct the interest paid on these bonds from its taxable income, while the subsidiary receives this interest tax-free and uses it to pay the dividend on the preferred stock. Effectively, the company has issued preferred stock and received the deduction for corporate tax.

A FIRST LOOK AT DEBT

When they borrow money, companies promise to make regular interest payments and to repay the principal (i.e., the original amount borrowed). However, this liability is limited. Stockholders have the right to default on the debt if they are willing to hand over the corporation's assets to the lenders. Clearly they will choose to do this only if the value of the assets is less than the amount of the debt. In practice this handover of assets is far from straightforward. Sometimes there may be thousands of lenders with different claims on the firm. Administration of the handover is usually left to the bankruptcy court.

Because lenders are not regarded as proprietors of the firm, they do not normally have any voting power. The company's payments of interest are regarded as a cost and are deducted from taxable income. Thus interest is paid from *before-tax* income, whereas dividends on common and preferred stock are paid from *after-tax* income. Therefore the government provides a tax subsidy on the use of debt which it does not provide on equity. We will cover debt and taxes in detail in Chapter 6.

---

[11]In Chapter 20, we will describe *floating-rate preferreds,* securities designed as temporary parking places for corporations's excess cash. These securities' dividends change with short-term interest rates, in the same way as coupon payments on floating-rate debt.

[12]Alternatively, the parent may establish a limited partnership or a Delaware Business Trust to issue the preferred stock. For a description of MIPs and their near-relations, see A. Khanna and J. J. McConnell, "MIPs, QUIPs and TOPs: Old Wine in New Bottles," *Journal of Applied Corporate Finance* 11 (Summer 1998), pp. 39–44.

TABLE 2.5

Large firms typically issue many different securities. This table shows some of the debt securities on Mobil Corporation's balance sheet at the end of 1996 and 1997 (figures in $ millions).

DEBT SECURITY	1996	1997
6 ½% notes 1997	$148	—
6 ⅜% notes 1998	200	$200
7 ¼% notes 1999	162	148
8 ⅜% notes 2001	200	180
8 ⅝% notes 2006	250	250
8 ⅝% debentures 2021	250	250
7 ⅝% debentures 2033	240	216
8% debentures 2032	250	164
8 ⅛% Canadian dollar eurobonds 1998[a]	110	—
9 % ECU eurobonds 1997[b]	148	—
9 ⅝% sterling eurobonds 1999	187	182
Variable rate notes 1999	110	—
Japanese yen loans 2003–2005	388	347
Variable rate project financing 1998	105	52
Industrial revenue bonds 1998–2030	491	484
Other foreign currencies due 1997–2030	1,090	764
Other long-term debt	660	716
Capital leases	247	335
Commercial paper	1,634	1,097
Bank and other short-term loans	894	1,168

[a]Swapped into 7% U.S. dollar debt.

[b]The ECU was a basket of European currencies. With the formation of the single European currency in 1999 1 ECU became 1 euro.

Source: Mobil Corporation *Annual Reports.*

Debt Comes in Many Forms

The financial manager is faced with an almost bewildering choice of debt securities. Look, for example, at Table 2.5, which shows the many ways that Mobil Corporation borrowed money. In drawing up a borrowing plan, Mobil's financial manager needed to consider the balance between short- and long-term debt, which currencies the company needed to borrow, whether there was a benefit to establishing a project as a separate company which would then borrow directly to finance the investment, and so on. These choices are reflected in the mixture of debt securities that Mobil issued.

Mobil's financial manager also needed to make sure that arrangements were in place if the company needed to borrow more money. The company had already obtained approval from the SEC to issue a further $1.8 billion of bonds in the United States.[13] In addition, it had in place a euro-medium-term note program that would allow it to sell up to $2 billion of additional debt securities

---

[13]This approval was obtained by a *shelf registration.* We explain shelf registrations in Chapter 3.

in the international capital markets and it had similar arrangements in Japan to raise 30 billion yen (about $250 million) by the sale of bonds there. If Mobil needed further short-term loans, it could use a $645 million line of credit; in other words, a group of banks had agreed to lend Mobil up to $645 million on short notice.

You are probably wondering what a "euro-medium-term note program," an ECU eurobond, or a variable rate project financing are. Relax—later in the book we will spend several chapters examining the various features of corporate debt. But here is a preliminary guide to the major distinguishing characteristics.

Maturity   Any obligation payable more than one year from the date of issue is called **funded** debt. Debt due in less than one year is termed **unfunded** and is carried on the balance sheet as a current liability. Unfunded debt is often described as short-term debt and funded debt is described as long-term, although it is clearly artificial to call a 364-day note short-term and a 366-day note long-term (except on leap years).

There are corporate bonds of nearly every conceivable maturity. Walt Disney has issued a 100-year bond. Natwest and several other British banks have issued perpetuities, bonds with no specified maturity. They may survive forever. At the other extreme we find firms literally borrowing overnight. We describe how this is done in Chapter 20.

Large companies often raise short-term debt by selling loans known as **commercial paper.** Smaller companies, which do not have easy access to commercial paper, typically turn to banks for short-term debt financing.

Repayment Provisions   Longer-term loans are commonly repaid in a steady, regular way, perhaps after an initial grace period. For publicly traded bonds this is done by means of a **sinking fund.** Each year the firm pays into the fund a sum of cash which is then used to repurchase and retire the bonds.

Firms may also reserve the right to **call** the debt, that is, to repay and retire the entire issue of debt before the final maturity date. The price at which they can buy back the bonds is specified when the bond is originally issued.

Seniority   Some debt instruments are **subordinated.** In the event of default the subordinated lender gets in line behind the firm's general creditors (but ahead of the preferred and the common stockholders). The subordinated lender holds a *junior claim* and is paid after all *senior* debtholders are satisfied.

When you lend money to a firm, you can assume that you hold a senior claim unless the debt agreement says otherwise. However, this does not always put you at the front of the line, for the firm may have set aside some of its assets specifically for the protection of other creditors. That brings us to our next classification.

Security or Collateral   We have used the word "bond" to refer to all kinds of corporate debt, but in some contexts it means **secured** debt; unsecured long-term claims are called *debentures.* The security for a bond may consist of mortgages on plant and equipment. If the company defaults on its debt, the bondholders have first claim on the mortgaged assets; investors holding debentures have a general claim on the unmortgaged assets but only a junior claim on the mortgaged assets.

An asset pledged to ensure payment of a debt is called **collateral.** Thus a retailer might offer inventory or accounts receivable as collateral to obtain a bank loan. If you start a small business and go to a bank for financing, the bank may ask you to put up your home as collateral until the business accumulates enough assets and earning power to support the loan on its own.

You will see frequent references to *securitization* and to *asset-backed securities*. In this case the collateral is not left with the ultimate borrower but sold to an independent trust, which in turn borrows from investors. For example, suppose a bank wants to finance the money it lends out to its credit-card customers. The rights to a portion of its outstanding credit-card receivables are sold to a trust, which issues a security backed by these balances. Principal and interest payments made by the bank's customers are then given to the trust and paid out to investors. The payments are usually sufficient to pay off and retire the security in a year or two.

Note that the investors are not lending to the bank; they are buying credit-card receivables. They do not have to worry about whether the bank as a whole is creditworthy. If the quality of the receivables is doubtful, the bank may arrange insurance from a third party to guarantee payment.

Sometimes it seems that almost anything can be securitized. There have been securities backed by aircraft leases, royalties from films, auto and home improvement loans, student loans, and property tax liens. By the mid-1990s, issues of asset-backed securities in the United States were running well over $100 billion per year.

Default Risk   Seniority and security do not guarantee payment. A bond can be senior and secured but still be as risky as a vertiginous tightrope walker; it depends on the value and risk of the issuing firm's assets.

A debt security is **investment grade** if it qualifies for one of the top four ratings from Moody's or Standard and Poor's ratings services. (We describe bond ratings in Chapter 10.) Below-investment-grade debt issues are often known as **junk bonds.** The junk bond market took off in the late 1970s, when companies discovered a pool of investors willing to accept unusually high default risks in exchange for high promised yields. Many of these issues were made on short notice to finance mergers and so-called *leveraged buyouts*.

Public versus Privately Placed Debt   A **public issue** of bonds is offered to anyone who wants to buy, and once issued, it can be freely traded. In a **private placement** the issue is sold directly to a small number of qualified lenders, including banks, insurance companies, and pension funds. The securities cannot be resold to individuals; they can be resold only to qualified institutional investors. However, there is increasingly active trading *among* these investors.

The public debt market in the United States is more active than in most other countries. Large U.S. corporations look mostly to the public market for debt financing. Corporations in Germany, Japan, or France generally borrow directly from banks or other financial institutions. Bank debt is by definition privately placed.

Floating versus Fixed Rates   The interest payment, or coupon, on debt is commonly fixed at the time of issue. If a $1,000 bond is issued when long-term interest rates are 10 percent, the firm continues to pay $100 per year regardless of how interest rates fluctuate.

Some bonds offer a variable, or *floating,* rate. For example, the interest rate in each period may be set at 1 percent above **LIBOR** (London interbank offered rate), which is the interest rate at which major international banks in London lend dollars to each other. When LIBOR changes, the interest rate on your loan also changes.

Loan agreements negotiated with banks usually involve a floating interest rate. The rate may be tied to LIBOR or to the **prime rate.** Prime is a benchmark interest rate charged by banks and is adjusted up or down as interest rates change.[14]

---

[14]"Prime" can be misleading, because the *most* creditworthy corporations—large, blue-chip companies—can negotiate bank loans at interest rates *below* prime. The prime rate is a benchmark mostly for loans to smaller or private businesses.

Country and Currency   Many firms in the United States, particularly those with large foreign operations, borrow abroad. The company may borrow dollars abroad (foreign investors have large holdings of dollars), but it may also decide to issue debt in a foreign currency. For example, Mobil issued bonds denominated in Canadian dollars. Mobil could have sold these Canadian dollar bonds in Canada, but instead it decided to market them internationally. They were therefore known as **eurobonds.**

A company may also borrow dollars from a bank outside the United States. Because the bank holds these dollars outside the United States, they are known as **eurodollars.** Alternatively, the company or its foreign subsidiary may finance itself with a bank loan in the foreign country's currency. For example, Mobil might borrow Canadian dollars from a bank in Toronto to finance its Canadian operations.

At this point we should pause to explain some confusing terminology. The term *eurobond* refers to a bond that is marketed internationally, principally by the London branches of international banks. Similarly *eurocurrency* refers to bank deposits held outside the country that issues the currency. Thus, if you were to borrow dollars from the London branch of an international bank, you would be borrowing eurodollars.

That is all fairly straightforward. Unfortunately, when the single European currency was established at the start of 1999, it was called the *euro*. So a "eurobond" could mean a bond that is denominated in euros or a bond that is marketed internationally with payments in dollars, yen, or any other currency. Presumably, bankers will eventually agree on a new set of terms; until they do we will just refer to "international dollar bonds" and "international dollar deposits."

A Debt by Any Other Name

The word "debt" sounds straightforward, but companies enter into a variety of financial arrangements that look suspiciously like debt but are treated differently in the accounts. For example, accounts payable are simply obligations to pay suppliers for goods that they have already delivered. Accounts payable are therefore equivalent to short-term debts. Also, instead of borrowing money to buy equipment, many companies lease or rent it on a long-term basis. As we will show in Chapter 12, such arrangements are equivalent to secured long-term debt.

Convertible Securities

Companies often issue securities that give the owner an option to convert them into other securities. These options may have a substantial effect on value. The most dramatic example is provided by a **warrant,** which is *nothing but* an option.[15] The owner of a warrant can purchase a set number of the company's shares at a set price before a set date. Warrants are often sold as part of a package of other securities. Thus, the firm might make a combination offer of bonds and warrants.

A **convertible bond** gives its owner the option to exchange the bond for a predetermined number of shares. The convertible bondholder hopes that the issuing company's share price will zoom up so that the bond can be converted for a big profit. But, if the shares zoom down, there is no

---

[15]There is an important difference between a warrant and exchange-traded option. An exchange-traded option is a side bet—it has no effect on the value or risk of the corporation that issued the underlying common stock. In contrast, when a warrant is exercised, the strike price is paid to the corporation, thus increasing cash available for investment and other financing purposes.

obligation to convert; the bondholder remains a bondholder. Companies sometimes also issue convertible preferred, usually to finance mergers.

A convertible bond is like a package of a corporate bond and a warrant. There is one principal difference. When the owners of a convertible wish to exercise their option to buy shares, they do not pay cash—they just give up the bond. We cover warrants and convertibles in Chapter 13.

Variety's the Very Spice of Life

We have indicated several dimensions along which corporate securities can be classified. That gives the financial manager plenty of choice in designing securities. As long as you can convince investors of its attractions, you can issue a convertible, subordinated, floating-rate perpetual bond denominated in yen. Rather than combining features of existing securities, you may create an entirely new one. We can imagine a coal mining company issuing preferred shares on which the dividend fluctuates with coal prices. We know of no such security, but it is perfectly legal to issue it and—who knows?—it might generate considerable interest among investors.

DERIVATIVES

Financial innovation in recent years has been unusually fast and extensive. One of the most remarkable developments has been the growth in the use of **derivatives.** These are side bets on interest rates, exchange rates, commodity prices, and so on. Firms do not issue derivatives to raise money; they buy or sell them to protect against adverse changes in various external factors.

Here are four types of derivatives that have experienced rapid growth in the last 20 years.

Traded Options   An option gives the firm the right (but not the obligation) to buy or sell an asset in the future at a price that is agreed upon today. We have already seen that the firm sometimes issues options either on their own (warrants) or tacked onto other securities (convertibles). But, in addition, there is a huge volume of option trading in exchange and over-the-counter (OTC) markets. For example, you can deal in options to buy or sell common stocks, bonds, currencies, and commodities. We describe options and their applications in Chapter 9.

Futures   A futures contract is an order that you place in advance to buy or sell an asset or commodity. The price is fixed when you place the order, but you don't pay for the asset until the delivery date. Futures markets have existed for a long time in commodities such as wheat, soybeans, and copper. The major development in the 1970s occurred when the futures exchanges began to trade contracts on financial assets, such as bonds, currencies, and stock market indexes.

Forwards   Futures are standardized contracts traded on organized exchanges. A forward contract is like a futures in many respects, but it is traded in over-the-counter markets rather than on an exchange. The principal business in forward contracts occurs in the foreign exchange market, where firms that need to protect themselves against a change in the exchange rate buy or sell forward currency through a bank.

Swaps   Table 2.5 shows that Mobil swapped its Canadian dollar debt for U.S. dollar debt. This means that it arranged for a bank to pay it each year the Canadian dollars needed to service its

Canadian dollar debt, and in exchange it agreed to pay the bank the cost of servicing a U.S. dollar loan. Such an arrangement is known as a *currency swap.*

Companies also enter into *interest-rate swaps.* For example, Mobil had arranged for a bank to pay the cost of servicing its fixed-rate loans, while Mobil paid the bank the cost of servicing a similar floating-rate loan.

We discuss swaps, as well as forward and futures contracts, in Chapter 14.

SUMMARY

That completes our tour of corporate securities and derivatives. You may feel like the tourist who has just seen 12 cathedrals in five days. But there will be plenty of time in later chapters for reflection and analysis.

We looked first at the simplest and most important source of finance—common stock. The holders of common stock own the corporation. They are therefore entitled to whatever assets or earnings are left over after all the firm's debts are paid. They also get to vote on important matters, such as membership of the board of directors. Corporations obtain additional finance from the common stockholders either by making a new issue of shares or by plowing back part of the cash that is generated from operations.

The second source of finance is preferred stock. Preferred is like debt in that it promises a fixed dividend, but preferred dividends are within the discretion of the board of directors. However, the firm must pay any dividends on the preferred before it is allowed to pay a dividend on the common stock. Lawyers and tax experts treat preferred as part of the company's equity. That means preferred dividends are not tax-deductible. That is one reason that preferred stock is less popular than debt.

The third important source of finance is debt. Debtholders are entitled to a regular payment of interest and the final repayment of principal. If the company cannot make these payments, it can file for bankruptcy. The usual result is that the debtholders then take over and either sell off the company's assets or continue to operate them under new management.

Note that the tax authorities treat interest payments as a cost and therefore the company can deduct interest when calculating its taxable income. Interest is paid from pretax income, whereas dividends and retained earnings come from after-tax income.

The variety of corporate debt instruments is almost endless. The instruments are classified by maturity, repayment provisions, seniority, security, default risk ("junk" bonds are riskiest), interest rates (fixed or floating), issue procedures (public or private placement), and currency of debt.

The fourth source of finance consists of options. These may not be recorded separately in the company's balance sheet. The simplest option is the warrant which gives its holder the right to buy a share at a set price by a set date. Warrants are often sold as part of a package with debt. Convertible bonds are securities that give their holder the right to convert to shares. They therefore resemble a mixture of straight debt and warrants.

Corporations also buy and sell derivatives to hedge their exposure to external risks, such as fluctuations in commodity prices, interest rates, and foreign exchange rates. Derivatives include traded options, futures, forwards, and swaps.

Financial managers are faced with two broad financing decisions:

1. What proportion of profits should the corporation reinvest in the business rather than distribute as dividends to its shareholders?

2. What proportion of the deficit should be financed by borrowing rather than by an issue of equity?

The answer to the first question depends on the firm's dividend policy and the answer to the second depends on its debt policy.

Table 2.1 summarized the ways that companies raise and spend money. Have another look at it and try to get a feel for the numbers. Notice that

1. Internally generated cash is the principal source of funds. Some people worry about this; they think that if management does not have to go to the trouble of raising the money, it won't think so hard when it comes to spending it.

2. The mix of financing changes from year to year. Sometimes companies prefer to issue equity and pay back part of their debt. At other times, they raise more debt than they need for investment and they use the balance to repurchase equity.

3. Debt ratios in the United States have generally increased over the postwar period. However, they are not appreciably higher than the ratios in the other major industrialized countries.

Further Reading

Here are two useful articles comparing financing in the United States and other major industrialized countries:

W. C. Kester, "Capital and Ownership Structure: A Comparison of United States and Japanese Manufacturing Corporations," *Financial Management*, 15:5–16 (Spring 1986).

R. G. Rajan and L. Zingales, "What Do We Know About Capital Structure? Some Evidence from International Data," *Journal of Finance*, 50:1421–1460 (December 1995).

Taggart describes long-term trends in corporate financing in:

R. A. Taggart, "Secular Patterns in the Financing of Corporations," in B. M. Friedman (ed.), *Corporate Capital Structures in the United States*, University of Chicago Press, 1985.

HOW CORPORATIONS ISSUE SECURITIES

Marvin Enterprises is one of the most remarkable growth companies of the twenty-first century. It was founded by George and Mildred Marvin, two high-school dropouts, together with their chum Charles P. (Chip) Norton. To get the company off the ground the three entrepreneurs relied on their own savings together with personal loans from a bank. However, the company's rapid growth meant that they had soon borrowed to the hilt and needed more equity capital. Equity investment in young private companies is generally known as **venture capital.** Such venture capital may be provided by investment institutions, or by wealthy individuals who are prepared to back an untried company in return for a piece of the action. In the first part of this chapter we will explain how companies like Marvin go about raising venture capital.

Venture capital organizations aim to help growing firms over that awkward adolescent period before they are large enough to go public. For a successful firm such as Marvin, there is

likely to come a time when it needs to tap a wider source of capital and therefore decides to make its first public issue of common stock. The next section of the chapter describes what is involved in such an issue. We will explain the process for registering the offering with the Securities and Exchange Commission and we will introduce you to the underwriters who buy the issue and resell it to the public. We will also see that new issues are generally sold below the price at which they subsequently trade. To understand *why* that is so, we will need to make a brief sortie into the field of auction procedures.

A company's first issue of stock is seldom its last. In Chapter 2 we saw that corporations face a persistent financial deficit which they meet by selling securities. We will therefore look at how established corporations go about raising more capital. In the process we will encounter another puzzle: When companies announce a new issue of stock, the stock price generally falls. We suggest that the explanation lies in the information that investors read into the announcement.

If a stock or bond is sold publicly, it can then be traded on the securities markets. But sometimes investors intend to hold onto their securities and are not concerned about whether they can sell them. In these cases there is little advantage to a public issue, and the firm may prefer to place the securities directly with one or two financial institutions. At the end of this chapter we will explain how companies arrange a private placement.

VENTURE CAPITAL

On April 1, 2013, George and Mildred Marvin met with Chip Norton in their research lab (which also doubled as a bicycle shed) to celebrate the incorporation of Marvin Enterprises. The three entrepreneurs had raised $100,000 from savings and personal bank loans and had purchased one million shares in the new company. At this *zero-stage* investment, the company's assets were $90,000 in the bank ($10,000 had been spent for legal and other expenses of setting up the company), plus the *idea* for a new product, the household gargle blaster. George Marvin was the first to see that the gargle blaster, up to that point an expensive curiosity, could be commercially produced using microgenetic refenestrators.

Marvin Enterprises' bank account steadily drained away as design and testing proceeded. Local banks did not see Marvin's idea as adequate collateral, so a transfusion of equity capital was clearly needed. Preparation of a *business plan* was a necessary first step. The plan was a confidential document describing the proposed product, its potential market, the underlying technology, and the resources (time, money, employees, plant, and equipment) needed for success.

Most entrepreneurs are able to spin a plausible yarn about their company. But it is as hard to convince a venture capitalist that your business plan is sound as to get a first novel published. Marvin's managers were able to point to the fact that they were prepared to put their money where their mouths were. Not only had they staked all their savings in the company but they were mortgaged to the hilt. This *signaled* their faith in the business.[1]

First Meriam Venture Partners was impressed with Marvin's presentation and agreed to buy one million new shares for $1 each. After this *first-stage* financing, the company's market-value balance sheet looked like this:

Marvin Enterprises First-Stage Balance Sheet (Market Values in $ Millions)

Cash from new equity	$1	$1	New equity from venture capital
Other assets, mostly intangible	1	1	Original equity held by entrepreneurs
Value	$2	$2	Value

By accepting a $2 million *after-the-money* valuation, First Meriam implicitly put a $1 million value on the entrepreneurs' idea and their commitment to the enterprise. It also handed the

---

[1]For a formal analysis of how management's investment in the business can provide a reliable signal of the company's value, see H. E. Leland and D. H. Pyle, "Informational Asymmetries, Financial Structure, and Financial Intermediation," *Journal of Finance* 32 (May 1977), pp. 371–387.

entrepreneurs a $900,000 paper gain over their original $100,000 investment. In exchange, the entrepreneurs gave up half their company and accepted First Meriam's representatives to the board of directors.[2]

The success of a new business depends critically on the effort put in by the managers. Therefore venture capital firms try to structure a deal so that management has a strong incentive to work hard. That takes us back to Chapter 1, where we pointed out that the shareholders of a firm (who are the principals) need to provide incentives for the managers (who are their agents) to work to maximize firm value.

If Marvin's management had demanded watertight employment contracts and fat salaries, they would not have found it easy to raise venture capital. Instead the Marvin team agreed to put up with modest salaries. They could cash in only from appreciation of their stock. If Marvin failed they would get nothing, because First Meriam actually bought *preferred* stock designed to convert automatically into common stock when and if Marvin Enterprises succeeded in an initial public offering or consistently generated more than a target level of earnings. But if Marvin Enterprises had failed, First Meriam would have been first in line to claim any salvageable assets. This raised even further the stakes for the company's management.[3]

Venture capitalists rarely give a young company all the money it will need all at once. At each stage they give enough to reach the next major checkpoint. Thus in spring 2015, having designed and tested a prototype, Marvin Enterprises was back asking for more money for pilot production and test marketing. Its *second-stage* financing was $4 million, of which $1.5 million came from First Meriam, its original backers, and $2.5 million came from two other venture capital partnerships and wealthy individual investors. The balance sheet just after the second stage was as follows:

Marvin Enterprises Second-Stage Balance Sheet (Market Values in $ Millions)

Cash from new equity	$4	$4	New equity, second stage
Fixed assets	1	5	Equity from first stage
Other assets, mostly intangible	9	5	Original equity held by entrepreneurs
Value	$14	$14	Value

Now the after-the-money valuation was $14 million. First Meriam marked up its original investment to $5 million, and the founders noted an additional $4 million paper gain.

Does this begin to sound like a (paper) money machine? It was so only with hindsight. At stage one it wasn't clear whether Marvin would ever get to stage two; if the prototype hadn't worked, First Meriam could have refused to put up more funds and effectively closed the business down.[4] Or it could have advanced stage-two money in a smaller amount on less favorable terms.

[2]Venture capital investors do not necessarily demand a majority on the board of directors. Whether they do depends, for example, on how mature the business is and on what fraction they own. A common compromise gives an equal number of seats to the founders and to outside investors; the two parties then agree to one or more additional directors to serve as tie-breakers in case a conflict arises. Regardless of whether they have a majority of directors, venture capital companies are seldom silent partners; their judgment and contacts can often prove useful to a relatively inexperienced management team.

[3]Notice the trade-off here. Marvin's management is being asked to put all its eggs into one basket. That creates pressure for managers to work hard, but it also means that take on risk that could have been diversified away.

[4]If First Meriam had refused to invest at stage two, it would have been an exceptionally hard sell convincing another investor to step in its place. The other outside investors knew they had less information about Marvin than First Meriam and would have read its refusal as a bad omen for Marvin's prospects.

The board of directors could also have fired George, Mildred, and Chip and gotten someone else to try to develop the business.

For every 10 first-stage venture capital investments, only two or three may survive as successful, self-sufficient businesses, and one may pay off big as Marvin Enterprises did.[5] From these statistics come two rules for success in venture capital investment. First, don't shy away from uncertainty; accept a low probability of success. But don't buy into a business unless you can see the *chance* of a big, public company in a profitable market. There's no sense taking a long shot unless it pays off big if you win. Second, cut your losses; identify losers early, and if you can't fix the problem—by replacing management, for example—throw no good money after bad.

For Marvin, fortunately, everything went like clockwork. Third-stage *mezzanine financing* was arranged,[6] full-scale production began on schedule, and gargle blasters were acclaimed by music critics worldwide. Marvin Enterprises went public on February 3, 2019. Once its shares were traded, the paper gains earned by First Meriam and the company's founders turned into fungible wealth.

Before we go on to this initial public offering, let us look briefly at the venture capital markets today.

The Venture Capital Market

Entrepreneurs have generated a continuous flow of successful new corporations for at least a century. Some of the new companies managed to grow by their own bootstraps, by borrowing and generating funds internally. Others sought out equity investment, often from wealthy families or established firms. So venture capital has been around for some time.

But today the United States has a well-developed venture capital *market*, in which specialists set up partnerships, pooling funds from a variety of investors, *seek out* fledgling companies to invest in, and then work with these companies as they try to grow into publicly traded firms. As Figure 3.1 shows, in 1997 these partnerships raised about $10 billion. Note the large amounts contributed by pension funds.

Governments around the world seem to believe that, unless they intervene, profitable new ventures are likely to fail for lack of finance. They therefore look for ways to provide subsidized finance for young companies. In the United States the government provides cheap loans to small-business investment companies (SBICs) that then relend the money to deserving entrepreneurs.[7] SBICs occupy a small, specialized niche in the venture capital markets.

In many countries, such as those of continental Europe, venture capital markets have been slower to develop than in the United States. But this is changing and investment in high-tech ventures in Europe has begun to blossom.[8] At the same time new European exchanges have sprung up

---

[5]One study of venture capital investments between 1960 and 1975 found that about one in six were total failures. On the other hand, thanks to a few outstanding successes the average return after costs was about 19 percent a year. See B. Huntsman and J. P. Hoban, Jr., "Investment in New Enterprise: Some Empirical Observations on Risk, Return, and Market Structure," *Financial Management* 9 (Summer 1980), pp. 44–51.

[6]Mezzanine financing does not necessarily come in the third stage; there may be four or five stages. The point is that mezzanine investors come in late, in contrast to venture capitalists who get in on the ground floor.

[7]SBICs may also buy preferred stock in small businesses.

[8]See "A Survey of Private Equity and Venture Capital in Europe," *1998 Yearbook of the European Private Equity and Venture Capital Association.*

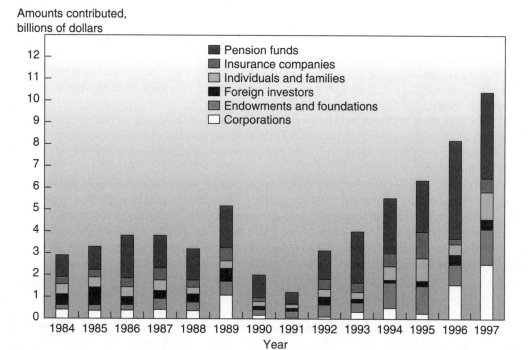

Amounts contributed,
billions of dollars

- Pension funds
- Insurance companies
- Individuals and families
- Foreign investors
- Endowments and foundations
- Corporations

Figure 3.1

Venture capital commitments to independent private firms only.

Source: Venture Economics, Inc., Wellesley, MA. Reproduced with permission.

that model themselves on Nasdaq and specialize in trading the stocks of young, rapidly growing firms. These mini-Nasdaqs include Easdaq, which is a pan-European exchange, as well as national exchanges, such as Aim in London, Neuer Markt in Frankfurt, and Le Nouveau Marché in Paris.

THE INITIAL PUBLIC OFFERING

Very few new businesses make it big, but venture capitalists keep sane by forgetting about the many failures and reminding themselves of the success stories—the investors who got in on the ground floor of firms like Federal Express, Genentech, Compaq, Intel, and Lotus Development Corporation.[9] When First Meriam invested in Marvin Enterprises, it was not looking for a high income stream from its investment; instead it was hoping for rapid growth that would allow Marvin to go public and give First Meriam an opportunity to cash in on some of its gains.

By 2019 Marvin had grown to the point at which it needed substantial new capital to implement its second-generation production technology. At this point it decided to make an initial public offering of stock or **IPO.** This was to be partly a *primary* offering; that is, new shares were to be

---

[9]The founder of Lotus took a finance class from one of the authors. Within five years he had become a multimillionaire. Perhaps that will make you feel better about the cost of this book.

sold to raise additional cash for the company. It was also to be partly a *secondary* offering; that is, the venture capitalists and the company's founders were looking to sell some of their existing shares.

Often when companies go public, the issue is solely intended to raise new capital for the company. But there are also occasions when no new capital is raised and all the shares on offer are being sold as a secondary offering by existing shareholders. For example, in 1998 Dupont sold off a large part of its holding in Conoco for $4.4 billion.[10]

Some of the biggest IPOs occur when governments sell off their shareholdings in companies. For example, the British government raised $9 billion from its sale of British Gas stock, while the secondary offering of Nippon Telegraph and Telephone by the Japanese government brought in nearly $13 billion.

For Marvin there were other benefits from going public. The market value of its stock would provide a readily available measure of the company's performance and would allow Marvin to reward its management team with stock options. Because information about the company would become more widely available, Marvin could diversify its sources of finance and reduce its costs of borrowing. These benefits outweighed the expense of the public issue and the continuing costs of administering a public company and communicating with its shareholders.

Instead of going public, many successful entrepreneurs may decide to sell out to a larger firm or they may continue to operate successfully as private, unlisted companies. Some very large companies in the United States are private. They include Bechtel and Cargill, for example. In other countries it is more common for large companies to remain privately owned. For example, there were only 40 listings of new, independent, nonfinancial companies on the Milan Stock Exchange from 1982 to 1992.[11]

Arranging an Initial Public Offering[12]

Once Marvin had made the decision to go public, the first task was to select the underwriters. Underwriters act as financial midwives to a new issue. Usually they play a triple role: first they provide the company with procedural and financial advice, then they buy the issue, and finally they resell it to the public. After some discussion Marvin settled on Klein Merrick as the lead underwriter. Klein Merrick would be responsible for forming and managing a syndicate of underwriters who would buy and resell the issue.

Together with Klein Merrick and firms of lawyers and accountants, Marvin prepared a **registration statement** for the approval of the Securities and Exchange Commission (SEC).[13] This state-

---

[10]This IPO is dwarfed by the Japanese telecom company NTT DoCoMo, which sold $18 billion of stock in 1998 and handed out $500 million in fees to the underwriters.

[11]The reasons for going public in Italy are analyzed in M. Pagano, F. Panetta, and L. Zingales, "Why Do Companies Go Public? An Empirical Analysis," *Journal of Finance* 53 (February 1998), pp. 27–64.

[12]For an excellent case study of how one company went public, see B. Uttal, "Inside the Deal that Made Bill Gates, $350,000,000," *Fortune*, July 21, 1986.

[13]The rules governing the sale of securities derive principally from the Securities Act of 1933. Some public issues are exempted from the registration requirement. These include issues by small businesses and loans maturing within nine months. Note incidentally that in reviewing the registration statement the SEC's concern is solely with disclosure and it has no power to prevent an issue as long as there has been proper disclosure.

ment is a detailed and sometimes cumbersome document which presents information about the proposed financing and the firm's history, existing business, and plans for the future.[14]

The most important sections of the registration statement are distributed to investors in the form of a **prospectus.** In Appendix B to this chapter we have reproduced the prospectus for Marvin's first public issue of stock. Real prospectuses would go into much more detail on each topic, but this example should serve to give you a feel for the mixture of valuable information and redundant qualification that characterizes these documents. The Marvin prospectus also illustrates how the SEC insists that investors' eyes are opened to the dangers of purchase (see "Certain Considerations" of the prospectus). Some investors have joked that if they read prospectuses carefully, they would never dare buy any new issue.

In addition to registering the issue with the SEC, Marvin also needed to check that the issue complied with the so-called blue-sky laws of each state that regulate sales of securities within the state.[15]

The Sale of Marvin Stock

While Marvin's registration statement was awaiting approval, Marvin and its underwriters began to firm up the issue price. First they looked at the price– earnings ratios of the shares of Marvin's principal competitors. Then they worked through a number of discounted-cash-flow calculations for Marvin itself. Most of the evidence pointed to a market value of $70 a share.

Marvin and Klein Merrick arranged a *road show* to talk to potential investors about the company. These investors gave their reactions to the issue and indicated to the underwriters how much stock they wished to buy. Some stated the maximum price that they were prepared to pay, but others said that they just wanted to invest so many dollars in Marvin at whatever issue price was chosen. Although investors were not bound by these indications, they knew that, if they wanted to keep in the underwriters' good books, they should be careful not to go back on their expressions of interest. The underwriters also were not bound to treat all investors equally. Some who were keen to buy Marvin stock were disappointed in the allotment that they subsequently received.

Immediately after it received clearance from the SEC, Marvin and the underwriters met to fix the issue price. Investors had been enthusiastic about the story that the company had to tell and it was clear that investors were prepared to pay more than $70 for the stock. Marvin's managers were tempted to go for the highest possible price, but the underwriters were more cautious. Not only would they be left with any unsold stock if they overestimated investor demand but they also

---

[14]Fortunately, the amount of detail is considerably less than it used to be. (A registration statement filed by Republic Steel in 1934 comprised 19,897 pages!) Now a complete registration statement might run to 50 pages or so, and some are much shorter. For example, a solid public company may not be required to reprint the standard financial data published in its most recent financial report. These data are incorporated by reference, i.e., by simply referring to them in the registration statement.

The example of the Republic Steel registration statement is cited in P. M. Van Arsdell, *Corporate Finance*, (New York: Ronald Press, 1958).

[15]In 1980, when Apple Computer Inc. made its first public issue, the Massachusetts state government decided the offering was too risky for its residents and therefore barred sale of the shares to individual investors in the state. The state relented later, after the issue was out and the price had risen. Needless to say, this action was not acclaimed by Massachusetts investors.

States do not usually reject security issues by honest firms through established underwriters. We cite the example to illustrate the potential power of state securities laws and to show why underwriters keep careful track of them.

argued that some degree of underpricing was needed to tempt investors to buy the stock. Marvin and the underwriters therefore compromised on an issue price of $80.

Demand for the stock fully lived up to expectations. The underwriters received orders to buy nearly twice the increased number of shares on offer and by the end of the first week the shares were trading at $95.[16] The issue brought the Marvin management team $16 million in cash before their share of the costs, and the 800,000 shares that they retained were worth 800,000 × 95 = $76 million.

The Role of the Underwriter

We have described Marvin's underwriters as providing a triple role—providing advice, buying the new issue, and reselling it to the public. In return they received payment in the form of a *spread*; that is, they were allowed to buy the shares for less than the *offering price* at which the shares were sold on to investors. In the more risky cases the underwriter usually receives some extra noncash compensation, such as warrants to buy additional common stock in the future. Occasionally, where a new issue of common stock is regarded as particularly risky, the underwriter may be unwilling to enter into a fixed commitment and will handle the issue only on a best-efforts or an all-or-none basis. *Best efforts* means that the underwriter promises to sell as much of the issue as possible but does not guarantee the sale of the entire issue. *All-or-none* means that if the entire issue cannot be sold at the offering price, the deal is called off and the issuing company receives nothing.

Since Marvin's issue was relatively large, the sale was handled by a syndicate of underwriters. The names of the members of the syndicate were listed in the prospectus and were also published in the financial press in a tombstone advertisement. (An example of a real *tombstone* advertisement is shown in Figure 3.2.) Klein Merrick acted as syndicate manager for the Marvin issue and for that job kept 20 percent of the spread. A further 25 percent of the spread was used to pay those members of the group who bought the issue. The remaining 55 percent went to the firms that provided the sales force.

As it turned out, investors rushed to buy Marvin's stock, but you can see from the second page of the Marvin prospectus that, if the issue had flopped, the underwriters were permitted to support the price by repurchasing shares in the market. If it became impossible for the underwriters to sell the issue at the offering price, then the syndicate would have dissolved, and the members would have disposed of their securities as best they could.

Most companies raise new capital only occasionally, but underwriters are in the business all the time. Established underwriters are, therefore, careful of their reputation and will not handle a new issue unless they believe the facts have been presented fairly to investors. Thus, in addition to handling the sale of an issue, the underwriters in effect give their seal of approval to it. This implied endorsement may be worth quite a bit to a company like Marvin that is coming to the market for the first time.

Successful underwriting requires financial muscle, considerable experience, and an established reputation. The first columns of Table 3.1 show that underwriting in the United States is dominated by the major investment banks and a few large commercial banks. The largest underwriter in 1997 was Merrill Lynch. As the lead underwriter, Merrill helped to raise $208 billion of debt and equity in the United States.

---

[16]Marvin's issue provides the underwriters with a *greenshoe* option. If demand turns out to be unexpectedly high, the underwriters can increase the number of shares offered.

12,937,500 Shares

The MONY Group Inc.

Common Stock
(par value $0.01 per share)

———

Price $23.50 Per Share

———

Upon request, a copy of the Prospectus describing these securities and the business of the
Company may be obtained within any State from any Underwriter who may legally distribute
it within such State. The securities are offered only by means of the Prospectus, and this
announcement is neither an offer to sell nor a solicitation of an offer to buy.

10,925,000 Shares
This portion of the offering is being offered in the United States by the undersigned.

Goldman, Sachs & Co.   **Donaldson, Lufkin & Jenrette**

Morgan Stanley Dean Witter   **Salomon Smith Barney**

CIBC Oppenheimer   **Conning & Company**   **A.G. Edwards & Sons, Inc.**

Fox-Pitt, Kelton Inc.   **Schroder & Co. Inc.**   **Allen & Company**
Incorporated

Robert W. Baird & Co.   **Chatsworth Securities LLC**   **Doley Securities, Inc.**
Incorporated

Edward D. Jones & Co., L.P.   **Legg Mason Wood Walker**   **Stephens Inc.**
Incorporated

———

2,012,500 Shares
This portion of the offering is being offered outside the United States by the undersigned.

Goldman Sachs International   **Donaldson, Lufkin & Jenrette**

Morgan Stanley Dean Witter **Salomon Smith Barney International**

January 20, 1999

Figure 3.2

Tombstone advertisements such as this list the underwriters to a new issue.

The right-hand side of Table 3.1 shows that, when securities are marketed internationally, the underwriting syndicate generally includes a number of foreign players. Also the London branches of American commercial banks are involved in underwriting international bond issues, whereas their parents in the United States were restricted until recently by the Glass-Steagall Act from underwriting domestic bond issues.[17]

Underwriting is not always fun. On October 15, 1987, the British government finalized arrangements to sell its holding of BP shares at £3.30 a share.[18] This huge issue involved more than $12 billion and was underwritten by an international group of underwriters who marketed it in a number of countries. Four days after the underwriting was agreed, the October crash caused stock prices around the world to nose-dive. The underwriters unsuccessfully appealed to the British government to cancel the issue.[19] By the closing date of the offer, the price of BP stock had fallen to £2.96, and the underwriters had lost more than a billion dollars.

Costs of a New Issue

Marvin's issue entailed substantial administrative costs. Preparation of the registration statement and prospectus involved management, legal counsel, and accountants, as well as the underwriters and their advisers. In addition, the firm had to pay fees for registering the new securities, printing and mailing costs, and so on. You can see from the first page of the Marvin prospectus (Appendix B) that these administrative costs totaled $820,000.

The second major cost of the Marvin issue was underwriting. We have seen that underwriters make their profit by buying the issue from the company at a discount from the price at which they resell it to the public. In Marvin's case this *spread* amounted to $4.5 million, which was equivalent to 6.25 percent of the total amount of the issue.

Marvin's issue was costly in yet another way. Since the offering price was less than the true value of the issued securities, investors who bought the issue got a bargain at the expense of the firm's original stockholders.

These costs of *underpricing* are hidden but nevertheless real. For initial public offerings they generally exceed all other issue costs. Whenever any company goes public, it is very difficult for the underwriters to judge how much investors will be willing to pay for the stock. Sometimes they misjudge demand dramatically. For example, when the prospectus for the initial public offering of Netscape stock was first published, the underwriters indicated that the company would sell 3.5 million shares at a price between $12 and $14 each. However, the enthusiasm for Netscape's Internet browser system was such that underwriters increased the shares available to 5 million and set an issue price of $28. The next morning the volume of orders was so large that trading was delayed by an hour and a half and, when trading did begin, the shares were quoted at $71, over five times the underwriters' initial estimates.

We admit that the Netscape issue was unusual[20] but researchers have found that throughout the world investors who buy at the issue price on average realize very high returns over the fol-

---

[17]The relevant provisions of the Glass-Steagall Act were effectively repealed by the Gramm-Leach Bliley Act of 1999.

[18]The issue was partly a secondary issue (the sale of the British government's shares) and partly a primary issue (BP took the opportunity to raise additional capital by selling new shares).

[19]The government's only concession was to put a floor on the underwriters' losses by giving them the opportunity to resell their stock to the government at £2.80 a share.

[20]However, the performance of Netscape was far from being a record. In 1998 shares in another Internet company, Theglobe.com, were offered at $9 each and closed at $63 1/2 at the end of the first day.

TABLE 3.1

The top managing underwriters in 1997. Values include both debt and equity issues (figures in $ billions)

UNITED STATES		INTERNATIONAL MARKETS	
UNDERWRITER	VALUE OF ISSUES	UNDERWRITER	VALUE OF ISSUES
Merrill Lynch	$ 208	Merrill Lynch	$ 37
Salomon Smith Barney	167	Goldman Sachs	32
Morgan Stanley Dean Witter	140	SBC Warburg Dillon Read	29
Goldman Sachs	137	Deutsche Morgan Grenfell	29
Lehman Brothers	121	Credit Suisse First Boston	27
JP Morgan	104	JP Morgan	24
Credit Suisse First Boston	68	Morgan Stanley Dean Witter	23
Bear, Stearns	58	ABN AMRO Hoare Govett	22
Donaldson Lufkin & Jenrette	46	Lehman Brothers	18
Chase Manhattan	33	Paribas	18
All Underwriters	$1,293	All Underwriters	$496

Source: Securities Data Co.

lowing weeks. For example, a study by Ibbotson, Sindelar, and Ritter of over 10,000 new issues from 1960 to 1992 found average underpricing of 15 percent.[21] But underpricing in the United States is relatively modest by the standards of many countries. For example, the gains from buying initial public offerings in Korea have averaged nearly 80 percent.[22]

You might think that shareholders would prefer not to sell their stock for less than its market price, but many investment bankers and institutional investors argue that underpricing is in the interests of the issuing firm. They say that a low offering price on the initial offer raises the price of the stock when it is subsequently traded in the market and enhances the firm's ability to raise further capital.[23] Skeptics respond that investment bankers push for a low offering price because it reduces the risk that they will be left with unwanted stock and makes them popular with their clients who are allotted stock.

Winner's Curse

Here is another reason that new issues may be underpriced. Suppose that you bid successfully for a painting at an art auction. Should you be pleased? It is true that you now own the painting, which was presumably what you wanted, but everybody else at the auction apparently thought

---

[21]R. G. Ibbotson, J. L. Sindelar, and J. R. Ritter, "The Market's Problems with the Pricing of Initial Public Offerings," *Journal of Applied Corporate Finance* 7 (Spring 1994), pp. 66–74. However, as we will see in Chapter 4, there is some evidence that these early gains are not maintained and in the five years following an initial public offering the shares underperform the market.

[22]For a summary of studies of underpricing in different countries, see T. Loughran, J. R. Ritter, and K. Rydqvist, "Initial Public Offerings: International Insights," *Pacific-Basin Finance Journal* 2 (1994), pp. 165–199.

[23]For an analysis of how a firm could rationally underprice to facilitate subsequent stock issues, see I. Welch, "Seasoned Offerings, Imitation Costs and the Underpricing of Initial Public Offerings," *Journal of Finance* 44 (June 1989), pp. 421–449.

that the picture was worth less than you did. In other words, your success suggests that you may have overpaid.

This problem is known as the *winner's curse*. The highest bidder in an auction is most likely to have overestimated the object's value and, unless bidders recognize this in their bids, the buyer will on average overpay. If bidders are aware of the danger, they are likely to adjust their bids down correspondingly.

When you apply for a new issue of securities, you are likely to suffer from the same problem. For example, suppose that you decide to apply for every new issue of common stock. You will find that you have no problem in getting stock in the issues that no one else wants. But, when the issue is attractive, the underwriters will not have enough stock to go around, and you will receive less stock than you wanted. The result is that your money-making strategy may turn out to be a loser. If you are smart, you will play the game only if there is substantial underpricing on average.

Here then we have a possible rationale for the underpricing of new issues. Uninformed investors who cannot distinguish which issues are attractive are exposed to the winner's curse. Companies and their underwriters are aware of this and need to underprice on average to attract the uninformed investors.[24]

OTHER NEW-ISSUE PROCEDURES

In the case of Marvin's initial public offering, the underwriters used investors' indications of interest to build a book of likely orders and this helped them to set the issue price. A similar book-building procedure is employed for most issues of corporate securities in the United States and in the international capital market. However, firms and governments in different countries employ a wide variety of different techniques for selling their securities.

The two principal methods of selling securities are by means of a fixed price offer or an auction. For example, when a firm in the UK makes an initial public offering, it generally fixes the selling price and then advertises the number of shares on offer. If the price is set too high, investors will not apply for all the shares on offer and the underwriters will be obliged to buy the unsold shares. If the price is set too low, the applications will exceed the number of shares on offer and investors will receive only a proportion of the shares that they applied for.[25] Since the most underpriced offers are likely to be heavily oversubscribed, the fixed price offer leaves investors very exposed to the winner's curse.

The alternative is to sell new securities by auction. In this case investors are invited to submit their bids, stating both how many securities they wish to buy and the price. The securities are then sold to the highest bidders.[26] Most governments, including the U.S. Treasury, sell their bonds by

---

[24]Notice that the winner's curse would disappear if only investors knew what the market price was going to be. One response therefore is to allow trading in a security before it has been issued. This is known as a *grey market* and is most common for debt issues. Investors can observe the price in the grey market and can be more confident that they are not overbidding when the actual issue takes place.

[25]Mario Levis found that, though IPOs in the UK offered an average first-day return of nearly 9 percent in the period 1985–1988, an investor who applied for an equal amount of each IPO would have done little better than break even. See M. Levis, "The Winner's Curse Problem, Interest Costs and the Underpricing of Initial Public Offerings," *Economic Journal* 100 (1990), pp. 76–89.

[26]One advantage of the auction is that you no longer need underwriters to buy any unsold securities. However, the seller might wish to specify a minimum bid price and arrange for underwriters to buy any unsold securities at this reservation price.

auction. In some countries auctions are also used to sell common stocks. For example, initial public offerings in France are sold by an auction.[27] In Singapore IPOs are often sold in two parts: one part is offered for sale at a fixed price, and the other is auctioned to the public.

The bookbuilding method that is used in the United States to sell corporate debt and equity is in some ways like an auction, since potential buyers state how many shares they are ready to buy at given prices. However, the bids are not generally binding and are used only as a guide to fix the price of the issue. Thus, the issue price in such cases is commonly set below the price that is needed to sell the issue, and the underwriters are more likely to allot stock to their favorite clients.[28]

Types of Auctions

Suppose that a government wishes to auction four million bonds and three would-be buyers submit bids. A bids $1,020 each for one million bonds, B bids $1,000 for three million bonds, and C bids $980 for two million bonds. The bids of the two highest bidders (A and B) absorb all the bonds on offer and C is left empty-handed. What price do the winning bidders, A and B, pay?

The answer depends on whether the sale is a *discriminatory-price auction* or a *uniform-price auction.* In a discriminatory-price auction every winner is required to pay the price that he or she bid. In this case A would pay $1,020 and B would pay $1,000. In a uniform-price auction both would pay $1,000, which is the price of the lowest winning bidder (investor B).

It might seem from our example that the proceeds from a uniform-price auction would be lower than from a discriminatory-price auction. But this ignores the fact that the uniform-price auction provides better protection against the winner's curse. Wise bidders know that there is little cost to overbidding in a uniform-price auction, but there is potentially a very high cost to doing so in a discriminatory-price auction.[29] Economists therefore often argue that the uniform-price auction should result in higher proceeds.[30]

Sales of bonds by the U.S. Treasury usually take the form of discriminatory-price auctions so that successful buyers pay their bid. However, governments do occasionally listen to economists, and since 1992 the Treasury has been experimenting with the uniform-price auction for two-year and five-year notes. The Mexican government has also been sufficiently convinced to change from a discriminatory auction to a uniform-price auction.[31]

---

[27]In the case of the French *mise en vente* the sale price for the IPO is usually set somewhat below the maximum price needed to sell the issue. See, for example, B. Biais and A. M. Faugeron-Crouzet, "IPO Auctions," working paper, Université de Toulouse, June 1998.

[28]Underwriters also appear to favor those investors whose bids provide them with the most information about the value of the stock. See F. Cornelli and D. Goldreich, "Bookbuilding and Strategic Allocation," working paper, London Business School, November 1998.

[29]In addition, the price in a uniform-price auction depends not only on the views of B, but also on those of A (for example, if A had bid $990 rather than $1,020, then both A and B would have paid $990 for a bond). Since the uniform-price auction takes advantage of the views of both A and B, it reduces the winner's curse.

[30]Sometimes auctions reduce the winner's curse by allowing uninformed bidders to enter noncompetitive bids, whereby they submit a quantity but not a price. For example, in U.S. Treasury auctions investors may submit noncompetitive bids and receive their full allocation at the average price paid by competitive bidders.

[31]Early experience in the United States and Mexico with uniform-price auctions suggests that they do indeed reduce the winner's curse problem and realize higher prices for the seller. See K. G. Nyborg and S. Sundaresan, "Discriminatory versus Uniform Treasury Auctions: Evidence from When-Issued Transactions," *Journal of Financial Economics* 42 (1996), pp. 63–105, and S. Umlauf, "An Empirical Study of the Mexican Treasury Bill Auction," *Journal of Financial Economics* 33 (1993), pp. 313–340.

GENERAL CASH OFFERS BY PUBLIC COMPANIES

For most companies their first public issue of stock is seldom their last. As they grow, they are likely to make further issues of debt and equity. Public companies can issue securities either by offering them to investors at large or by making a rights issue that is limited to existing stockholders. We will concentrate in this chapter on the mechanics of the general cash offer, which is now used for virtually all debt and equity issues in the United States. However, rights issues are widespread in other countries and you should understand how they work. Therefore in Appendix A to this chapter we describe rights issues and we look at some interesting and controversial questions about their use.

General Cash Offers and Shelf Registration

When a corporation makes a general cash offer of debt or equity, it goes through the same procedure as when it first went public. In other words, it registers the issue with the SEC and then sells the issue to an underwriter (or a syndicate of underwriters), who in turn offers the securities to the public.

In 1982 the SEC issued its Rule 415, which allows large companies to file a single registration statement covering financing plans for up to two years into the future. The actual issue, or issues, can be done with scant additional paperwork, whenever the firm needs the cash or thinks it can issue securities at an attractive price. This is called *shelf registration*—the registration statement is "put on the shelf," to be taken down and used as needed.

Think of how you as a financial manager might use shelf registration. Suppose your company is likely to need up to $200 million of new long-term debt over the next year or so. It can file a registration statement for that amount. It then has prior approval to issue up to $200 million of debt, but it isn't obligated to issue a penny. Nor is it required to work through any particular underwriters; the registration statement may name one or more underwriters the firm thinks it may work with, but others can be substituted later.

Now you can sit back and issue debt as needed, in bits and pieces if you like. Suppose Merrill Lynch comes across an insurance company with $10 million ready to invest in corporate bonds. Your phone rings. It's Merrill Lynch offering to buy $10 million of your bonds, priced to yield, say, 8 1/2 percent. If you think that's a good price, you say "OK" and the deal is done, subject to only a little additional paperwork. Merrill then resells the bonds to the insurance company, it hopes at a slightly higher price than it paid for them, thus earning an intermediary's profit.

Here is another possible deal: Suppose that you perceive a window of opportunity in which interest rates are temporarily low. You invite bids for $100 million of bonds. Some bids may come from large investment banks acting alone; others may come from ad hoc syndicates. But that's not your problem; if the price is right, you just take the best deal offered.

Thus shelf registration gives firms several things that they did not have previously:

1. Securities can be issued in dribs and drabs without incurring excessive transaction costs.

2. Securities can be issued on short notice.

3. Security issues can be timed to take advantage of "market conditions" (although any financial manager who can *reliably* identify favorable market conditions could make a lot more money by quitting and becoming a bond or stock trader instead).

4. The issuing firm can make sure that underwriters compete for its business. It can in effect auction off its securities.

Not all companies eligible for shelf registration actually use it for all their public issues. Sometimes they believe they can get a better deal by making one large issue through traditional channels, especially when the security to be issued has some unusual feature or when the firm believes it needs the investment banker's counsel or stamp of approval on the issue. Consequently shelf registration is less often used for issues of common stock or convertible securities than for garden-variety corporate bonds.

International Security Issues

Well-established companies are not restricted to the capital market in the United States; they can also sell securities in the international capital markets. The procedures for issues are broadly similar to those used in the United States. Here are two points to note:

1. As long as the issue is not publicly offered in the United States, it does not need to be registered with the SEC. However, the company must still provide a prospectus or offering circular.
2. Frequently an international sale of bonds takes the form of a bought deal, in which case one or a few underwriters buy the entire issue. Bought deals allow companies to issue bonds at very short notice.

Large debt issues are now often split, with part sold in the international debt market and part registered and sold in the United States. Likewise with equity issues. For example, in 1992 Wellcome Trust, a British charitable foundation, decided to sell part of its holdings in the Wellcome Group. To handle the sale, it paid about $140 million to a group of 120 underwriters from around the world. These underwriters collected bids from interested investors and forwarded them to Robert Fleming, a London merchant bank, which built up a book of the various bids. Particular classes of investors, such as existing shareholders or those who submitted their bids early, went to the front of the queue, while those who subsequently cut their bids or sold Wellcome stock were demoted.

By the end of the three-week issue period, Wellcome Trust was able to look at a demand curve showing how many shares investors were prepared to buy at each price. In the light of this information it decided to sell 270 million shares, with net proceeds of about $4 billion. About 1,100 institutions and 30,000 individuals ended up buying the shares. About 40 percent of the issue was sold outside the United Kingdom, mainly in the United States, Japan, France, and Germany.

The shares of many companies are now listed and traded on major international exchanges. British Telecom trades on the New York Stock Exchange, as do Sony, Fiat, Telefonos de Mexico, and so on.[32] Several of these companies also trade on overseas exchanges. Citicorp, one of the largest banks in the United States, trades in New York, London, Amsterdam, Tokyo, Zurich, Toronto, and Frankfurt, as well as several smaller exchanges.

Some companies' stocks do not trade at all in their home country. For example, in 1998 Radcom Ltd., an Israeli manufacturer of network test equipment, raised $30 million by an IPO in the United States. Its stock was not traded in Israel. The company thought it could get a better price and more active follow-on trading in New York.[33]

---

[32]Rather than issuing shares directly in the United States, foreign companies generally issue *American depository receipts (ADRs)*. These are simply claims to the shares of the foreign company that are held by a bank on behalf of the ADR owners.

[33]"High-tech firms are much better understood and valued in the U.S." "[The issuers] get a better price, a shareholder base that understands their business, and they can get publicity in a major market for their products." These are representative quotes from M. R. Sesit, "Foreign Firms Flock to U.S. for IPOs," *The Wall Street Journal*, June 23, 1995, p. C1.

TABLE 3.2

Gross underwriting spreads of selected issues, 1998. Costs are given as a percentage of gross proceeds.

TYPE[a]	COMPANY	ISSUE AMOUNT ($ MILLIONS)	UNDERWRITER'S SPREAD (%)
IPO	Hypertension Diagnostics, Inc.	$9.3	8.485%
IPO	Actuate Software Corp.	33.0	7.0
IPO	Enterprise Product Partners	264.0	6.364
IPO	Equant NV	282.2[b]	5.25
IPO	Conoco	4,403.5	3.99
Seasoned	Coulter Pharmaceuticals	60.0	5.48
Seasoned	Stillwater Mining	61.5	5.0
Seasoned	Metronet Communications Corp.	232.6	4.999
Seasoned	Staples, Inc.	446.6	3.25
Seasoned	Safeway, Inc.	1,125	2.75
Seasoned	Media One Group	1,511.3	2.735
Debt:			
2-year notes	General Motors Acceptance Corp.	100	.175
30-year debentures	Bausch & Lomb, Inc.	200	.884
6-year notes	Aramark Corp.	300	.628
15-year subordinated notes	Banque Paribas	400	.753
Convertible zero-coupon bonds	Aspect Telecommunications	490	3.0
10-year notes	Federal Home Loan Mortgage Corp.	1,500	.151

[a]"IPO" refers to initial public offerings of common stock, "seasoned" refers to issues of seasoned stock, and "debt" refers to long-term debt issues.

[b]A further $495 million was offered outside the United States.

Source: Investment Dealer's Digest, various issues, July–October 1998.

The Costs of a General Cash Offer

Whenever a firm makes a cash offer of securities, it incurs substantial administrative costs. Also the firm needs to compensate the underwriters by selling them securities below the price that they expect to receive from investors. Table 3.2 lists underwriting spreads for a few issues in 1998, including what was the largest U.S. IPO ever: Dupont's sale of part of its stake in Conoco. As the table shows, there are economies of scale in issuing securities: the underwriter's spread declines as the size of the issue increases. Spreads for debt securities are lower, less than 1 percent for large issues, but show the same economies of scale.

Figure 3.3 summarizes a study by Lee, Lochhead, Ritter, and Zhao of total issue costs (spreads plus administrative costs) for several thousand issues between 1990 and 1994.

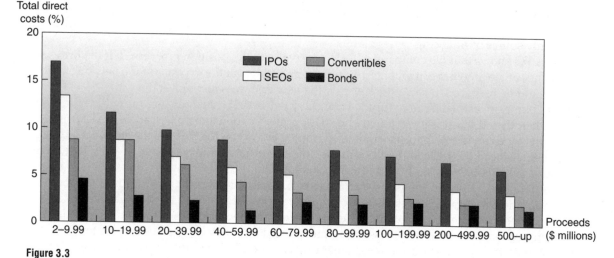

Figure 3.3

Total direct costs as a percentage of gross proceeds. The total direct costs for initial public offerings (IPOs), seasoned equity offerings (SEOs), convertible bonds, and straight bonds are composed of underwriter spreads and other direct expenses.

Market Reaction to Stock Issues

Economists who have studied seasoned issues of common stock have generally found that announcement of the issue results in a decline in the stock price. For industrial issues in the United States this decline amounts to about 3 percent.[34] While this may not sound overwhelming, the fall in market value is equivalent, on average, to nearly a third of the new money raised by the issue.

What's going on here? One view is that the price of the stock is simply depressed by the prospect of the additional supply. On the other hand, there is little sign that the extent of the price fall increases with the size of the stock issue. There is an alternative explanation that seems to fit the facts better.

Suppose that the CFO of a restaurant chain is strongly optimistic about its prospects. From her point of view, the company's stock price is too low. Yet the company wants to issue shares to finance expansion into the new state of Northern California.[35] What is she to do? All the choices have drawbacks. If the chain sells common stock, it will favor new investors at the expense of old shareholders. When investors come to share the CFO's optimism, the share price will rise, and the bargain price to the new investors will be evident.

If the CFO could convince investors to accept her rosy view of the future, then new shares could be sold at a fair price. But this is not so easy. CEOs and CFOs always take care to *sound* upbeat, so just announcing "I'm optimistic" has little effect. But supplying detailed information about business plans and profit forecasts is costly and is also of great assistance to competitors.

---

[34]See, for example, P. Asquith and D. W. Mullins, "Equity Issues and Offering Dilution," *Journal of Financial Economics* 15 (January–February 1986), pp. 61–90.

[35]Northern California seceded from California and became the fifty-second state in 2007.

The CFO could scale back or delay the expansion until the company's stock price recovers. That too is costly, but it may be rational if the stock price is severely undervalued and a stock issue is the only source of financing.

If a CFO knows that the company's stock is *over*valued, the position is reversed. If the firm sells new shares at the high price, it will help existing shareholders at the expense of the new ones. Managers might be prepared to issue stock even if the new cash was just put in the bank.

Of course, investors are not stupid. They can predict that managers are more likely to issue stock when they think it is overvalued and that optimistic managers may cancel or defer issues. Therefore, when an equity issue is announced, they mark down the price of the stock accordingly. Thus the decline in the price of the stock at the time of the new issue may have nothing to do with the increased supply but simply with the information that the issue provides.[36]

Cornett and Tehranian devised a natural experiment which pretty much proves this point.[37] They examined a sample of stock issues by commercial banks. Some of these issues were *involuntary*, since they were mandated by banking authorities to meet regulatory capital standards. The rest were ordinary, voluntary stock issues designed to raise money for various corporate purposes. The involuntary issues caused a much smaller drop in stock prices than the voluntary ones, which makes perfect sense. If the issue is outside the manager's discretion, announcement of the issue conveys no information about the manager's view of the company's prospects.[38]

Most financial economists now interpret the stock price drop on equity issue announcements as an information effect and not a result of the additional supply.[39] But what about an issue of preferred stock or debt? Are they equally likely to provide information to investors about company prospects? A pessimistic manager might be tempted to get a debt issue out before investors become aware of the bad news, but how much profit can you make for your shareholders by selling overpriced debt? Perhaps 1 or 2 percent. Investors know that a pessimistic manager has a much greater incentive to issue equity rather than preferred stock or debt. Therefore, when companies announce an issue of preferred or debt, there is a barely perceptible fall in the stock price.[40]

There is, however, at least one big puzzle left. As we saw in Chapter 4, it appears that the long-run performance of companies that issue shares is substandard. Investors who bought these companies' shares *after* the stock issue earned lower returns than they would have if they had bought into similar companies. This result holds for both IPOs and seasoned issues.[41] It seems that in-

---

[36]This explanation was developed in S. C. Myers and N. S. Majluf, "Corporate Financing and Investment Decisions When Firms Have Information That Investors Do Not Have," *Journal of Financial Economics* 35 (1984), pp. 99–122.

[37]M. M. Cornett and H. Tehranian, "An Examination of Voluntary versus Involuntary Issuances by Commercial Banks," *Journal of Financial Economics* 35 (1994), pp. 99–122.

[38]The fact that regulators found it necessary to force a bank to raise additional capital is probably bad news too. Thus it's no surprise that Cornett and Tehranian found some drop in stock price even for the involuntary issues.

[39]There is another possible information effect. Just as an unexpected increase in the dividend suggests to investors that the company is generating more cash than they thought, the announcement of a new issue may have the reverse implication. However, this effect cannot explain why the announcement of an issue of debt does not result in a similar fall in the stock price.

[40]See L. Shayam-Sunder, "The Stock Price Effect of Risky vs. Safe Debt," *Journal of Financial and Quantitative Analysis* 26 (December 1991), pp. 549–558. Evidence on the price impact of issues of different types of security is summarized in C. Smith, "Investment Banking and the Capital Acquisition Process," *Journal of Financial Economics* 15 (January–February 1986), pp. 3–29.

[41]See, for example, T. Loughran and J. R. Ritter, "The New Issues Puzzle," *Journal of Finance* 50 (March 1995), pp. 23–51. However, not everyone is convinced that the puzzle really exists. See, for example, A. Brav and P. A. Gompers, "Myth or Reality? The Long-Run Underperformance of Initial Public Offerings: Evidence from Venture and Nonventure Capital-backed Companies," *Journal of Finance* 5 (December 1997), pp. 1791–1821.

vestors failed to appreciate fully the issuing companies' information advantage. If so, we have an exception to the efficient-market theory. It will be interesting to see whether the poor relative long-term performance of issuing companies' shares persists. We think the poor performance will disappear now that investors know about it.

PRIVATE PLACEMENTS AND PUBLIC ISSUES

Whenever a company makes a public offering, it is obliged to register the issue with the SEC. It could avoid this costly process by selling the securities privately. There are no hard-and-fast definitions of a private placement, but the SEC has insisted that the security should be sold to no more than a dozen or so knowledgeable investors.

One of the drawbacks of a private placement is that the investor cannot easily resell the security. However, institutions such as life insurance companies invest huge amounts in corporate debt for the long haul and are less concerned about its marketability. Consequently, an active private placement market has evolved for corporate debt. Often this debt is negotiated directly between the company and the lender, but, if the issue is too large to be absorbed by one institution, the company will generally employ an investment bank to draw up a prospectus and identify possible buyers.

As you would expect, it costs less to arrange a private placement than to make a public issue. This is a particular advantage for companies making smaller issues.

In 1990 the SEC relaxed its restrictions on who can buy and trade unregistered securities. The new rule, Rule 144A, allows large financial institutions (known as *qualified institutional buyers*) to trade unregistered securities among themselves. Rule 144A was intended to increase liquidity and reduce interest rates and issue costs for private placements. It was aimed largely at foreign corporations deterred by registration requirements in the United States. The SEC argued that such firms would welcome the opportunity to issue unregistered stocks and bonds which could then be freely traded by large U.S. financial institutions.

Rule 144A issues have proved very popular, particularly with foreign issuers. By 1997 the value of new 144A issues had reached $254 billion and was larger than the traditional private placement market. There has also been an increasing volume of secondary trading in Rule 144A issues.

SUMMARY

In this chapter we have summarized the various procedures for issuing corporate securities. We first looked at how infant companies raise venture capital to carry them through to the point at which they can make their first public issue of stock. We then looked at how companies can make further public issues of securities by a general cash offer. Finally, we reviewed the procedures for a private placement.

It is always difficult to summarize a summary. Instead we will remind you of some of the most important implications for the financial manager who must decide how to issue capital.

Larger is cheaper.   There are economies of scale in issuing securities. It is cheaper to go to the market once for $100 million than to make two trips for $50 million each. Consequently firms bunch security issues. That may often mean relying on short-term financing until a large issue is justified. Or it may mean issuing more than is needed at the moment in order to avoid another issue later.

Watch out for underpricing.   Underpricing is a hidden cost to the existing shareholders. Fortunately, it is usually serious only for companies that are selling stock to the public for the first time.

The winner's curse may be a serious problem with IPOs.   Would-be investors in an initial public offering (IPO) do not know how other investors will value the stock and they worry that they are likely to receive a larger allocation of the overpriced issues. Careful design of issue procedure may reduce the winner's curse.

New stock issues may depress the price.   The extent of this price pressure varies, but for industrial issues in the United States the fall in the value of the existing stock may amount to a significant proportion of the money raised. This pressure is due to the information that the market reads into the company's decision to issue stock.

Shelf registration often makes sense for debt issues by blue-chip firms.   Shelf registration reduces the time taken to arrange a new issue, it increases flexibility, and it may cut underwriting costs. It seems best suited for debt issues by large firms that are happy to switch between investment banks. It seems less suited for issues of unusually risky or complex securities or for issues by small companies that are likely to benefit from a close relationship with an investment bank.

APPENDIX A   THE PRIVILEGED SUBSCRIPTION OR RIGHTS ISSUE

Instead of making an issue of stock to investors at large, companies sometimes give their existing shareholders the right of first refusal. Such issues are known as *privileged subscription*, or *rights issues*. In some countries such as the United States and Japan rights issues have become a rarity and general cash offers are the norm. In Europe equity must generally be sold by rights, though companies have increasingly lobbied for the freedom to make general cash offers. In this appendix we look at how rights issues work and how much they cost.

Here is an example of how rights issues work: In June 1977, American Electric Power Company issued $198 million of common stock by a rights issue. The preliminary stages of the issue, including registration requirements, were the same as those for any other public issue. The only difference lay in selling procedures. Shareholders were sent warrants showing that they owned one "right" for each share that they held. Eleven of these rights entitled a shareholder to buy one additional share at a subscription price of $22 at any time within 24 days of the offer date.[42]

Shareholders could sell, exercise, or throw away these rights. Those who didn't sell should have postponed any exercise decision until the end of the 24-day period. At that point, they should have taken advantage of the opportunity to buy stock at $22 if, and only if, the stock price was at least $22.

To guard against the danger that the price might end up below the subscription price, AEP arranged for the issue to be underwritten. Instead of actually buying the issue as in the cash offer, the underwriters were paid a *standby fee* of $900,000. In return, they stood ready to buy all unsub-

---

[42]A rights issue that gives the shareholder one right for each share held is known as a "New York right." In the United States, almost all issues are New York rights. But in some countries, such as the United Kingdom, you need one right to purchase one new share. This is known as a "Philadelphia right." If AEP were a company in the United Kingdom, the shareholder would need to own 11 shares in order to receive one right and this right would be correspondingly 11 times more valuable.

scribed shares at the subscription price less an additional *take-up fee* of $.287 per share purchased.[43] Most rights issues have standby underwriting, but occasionally companies save the underwriting fee by choosing a low subscription price and crossing their fingers that the market price won't fall below the subscription price.

As it turned out, AEP's stock price was $24 3/8 at the end of the 24 days. Although this was above the $22 subscription price, holders of about 10 percent of the stock failed to exercise their rights. We must attribute this lapse to either ignorance or vacations.[44]

How a Rights Issue Affects the Stock Price

The left-hand portion of Table 3.3 shows the case of a stockholder who owned 11 shares of AEP stock just prior to the rights issue. The price of the stock at that time was about $24, and so this stockholder's total holding was worth $24 × 11, or $264. The AEP offer gave the opportunity to purchase one additional share for $22. Put yourself in the stockholder's shoes. If you buy the new share immediately, your holding increases to 12 shares and, other things being equal, the value of the 12 shares is $264 + $22 = $286. The price per share after the issue would no longer be $24, but $286/12 = $23.83.

The only difference between the old $24 shares and the new $23.83 shares is that the former carried rights to subscribe to the issue. Therefore the old shares are generally termed *rights-on* shares and the new shares are termed *ex-rights* shares. The $.17 difference in price between the two shares represents the price of one right. We can confirm that this is the correct price of the right by imagining a second investor who has no stock in AEP but wishes to acquire some. One way to do this would be to buy 11 rights at $.17 each and then exercise them at a further cost of $22. The total cost of this investor's share would be 11 × $.17 + $22 = $23.87, which, save for rounding error, is the same outlay required to buy one of the new shares directly.

Issue Price Is Irrelevant as Long as the Rights Are Exercised

It should be clear on reflection that AEP could have raised the same amount of money on a variety of terms. For example, instead of a 1-for-11 at $22, it could have made a 1-for-5 1/2 at $11. In this case it would have sold twice as many shares at half the price. If we now work through the arithmetic again in the right-hand portion of Table 3.3, we can see that the issue price is irrelevant in a rights offering. After all, it cannot affect the real plant and equipment owned by the company or the proportion of these assets to which each shareholder is entitled. Therefore the only thing a firm ought to worry about in setting the terms of a rights issue is the possibility that the stock price will fall below the issue price. If that happens, shareholders will not take up their rights and the whole issue will be torpedoed. You can avoid this danger by arranging a standby agreement with the underwriter. But standby agreements tend to be expensive. It may be cheaper just to set the issue price low enough to foreclose the possibility of failure.

---

[43]You can think of standby underwriting as providing shareholders with an option. In return for paying the standby fee, they can sell their stock to the underwriters at the issue price. We will tell you how to value such options in Chapter 9.

[44]Despite this shortfall, AEP did not have to turn to its underwriters. AEP's shareholders had been given an oversubscription privilege, which allowed them to buy unsubscribed shares at the subscription price ($22). As it turned out, AEP had no trouble selling the unsubscribed shares to shareholders who applied for extra shares. Of course, these shareholders profited at the expense of the vacationers and *incognoscenti*.

	TABLE 3.3	
	Issue price in a rights offering does not affect the shareholder's wealth.	

$11	1-FOR-11 AT $22	1-FOR-5 1/2 AT
Before issue:		
Number of shares held	11	11
Share price (rights on)	$24	$24
Value of holding	$264	$264
After issue:		
Number of new shares	1	2
Amount of new investment	$22	$2 \times \$11 = \$22$
Total value of holding	$286	$286
Total number of shares	12	13
New share price (ex-rights)	$286/12 = \$23.83$	$286/13 = \$22$
Value of a right	$24 - 23.83 = \$.17$	$24 - 22 = \$2$

The Choice between the Cash Offer and the Rights Issue

You now know about the two principal forms of public issue—the cash offer to all investors and the rights issue to existing shareholders. The former method is used for almost all debt issues and unseasoned stock issues and many seasoned stock issues. Rights issues are largely restricted to seasoned stock issues.

One essential difference between the two methods is that in a rights offering the issue price is largely irrelevant. Shareholders can sell their new stock or their rights in a free market. Therefore, they can expect to receive a fair price. In a cash offer, however, the issue price may be important. If the company sells stock for less than the market would bear, the buyer has made a profit at the expense of existing shareholders. Although this danger creates a natural presumption in favor of the rights issue, it can be argued that underpricing is a serious problem only in the case of the unseasoned issue of stock in which a rights issue is not a feasible alternative.

APPENDIX B   MARVIN'S NEW-ISSUE PROSPECTUS[45]

PROSPECTUS
900,000 Shares
Marvin Enterprises Inc.
Common Stock ($.10 par value)

Of the 900,000 shares of Common Stock offered hereby, 500,000 shares are being sold by the Company and 400,000 shares are being sold by the Selling Stockholders. See "Principal and Selling

---

[45]Most prospectuses have content similar to that of the Marvin prospectus but go into considerably more detail. Also we have omitted Marvin's financial statements.

Stockholders." The Company will not receive any of the proceeds from the sale of shares by the Selling Stockholders.

Before this offering there has been no public market for the Common Stock. **These securities involve a high degree of risk. See "Certain Considerations."**

THESE SECURITIES HAVE NOT BEEN APPROVED OR DISAPPROVED BY THE SECURITIES AND EXCHANGE COMMISSION NOR HAS THE COMMISSION PASSED ON THE ACCURACY OR ADEQUACY OF THIS PROSPECTUS. ANY REPRESENTATION TO THE CONTRARY IS A CRIMINAL OFFENSE.

	PRICE TO PUBLIC	UNDERWRITING DISCOUNT	PROCEEDS TO COMPANY[1]	PROCEEDS TO SELLING STOCKHOLDERS[1]
Per share	$80.00	$5.00	$75.00	$75.00
Total[2]	$72,000,000	$4,500,000	$37,500,000	$30,000,000

[1]Before deducting expenses payable by the Company estimated at $820,000, of which $455,555 will be paid by the Company and $364,445 will be paid by the Selling Stockholders.

[2]The Company has granted to the Underwriters an option to purchase up to an additional 50,000 shares at the initial public offering price, less the underwriting discount, solely to cover overallotment.

The Common Stock is offered subject to receipt and acceptance by the Underwriters, to prior sale, and to the Underwriters's right to reject any order in whole or in part and to withdraw, cancel, or modify the offer without notice.

Klein Merrick Inc.   **February 3, 2019**

No person has been authorized to give any information or to make any representations, other than as contained therein, in connection with the offer contained in this Prospectus, and, if given or made, such information or representations must not be relied upon. This Prospectus does not constitute an offer of any securities other than the registered securities to which it relates or an offer to any person in any jurisdiction where such an offer would be unlawful. The delivery of this Prospectus at any time does not imply that information herein is correct as of any time subsequent to its date.

IN CONNECTION WITH THIS OFFERING, THE UNDERWRITERS MAY OVERALLOT OR EFFECT TRANSACTIONS WHICH STABILIZE OR MAINTAIN THE MARKET PRICE OF THE COMMON STOCK OF THE COMPANY AT A LEVEL ABOVE THAT WHICH MIGHT OTHERWISE PREVAIL IN THE OPEN MARKET. SUCH STABILIZING, IF COMMENCED, MAY BE DISCONTINUED AT ANY TIME.

Prospectus Summary

The following summary information is qualified in its entirety by the detailed information and financial statements appearing elsewhere in this Prospectus.

The Offering

Common Stock offered by the Company . . . .   500,000 shares

Common Stock offered by the Selling Stockholders. . . . .   400,000 shares

Common Stock to be outstanding after this offering . . . . 4,100,000 shares

Use of Proceeds

For the construction of new manufacturing facilities and to provide working capital.

The Company

Marvin Enterprises Inc. designs, manufactures, and markets gargle blasters for domestic use. Its manufacturing facilities employ integrated microcircuits to control the genetic engineering processes used to manufacture gargle blasters.

The Company was organized in Delaware in 2013.

Use of Proceeds

The net proceeds of this offering are expected to be $37,044,445. Of the net proceeds, approximately $27.0 million will be used to finance expansion of the Company's principal manufacturing facilities. The balance will be used for working capital.

Certain Considerations

Investment in the Common Stock involves a high degree of risk. The following factors should be carefully considered in evaluating the Company:

Substantial Capital Needs   The Company will require additional financing to continue its expansion policy. The Company believes that its relations with its lenders are good, but there can be no assurance that additional financing will be available in the future.

Licensing   The expanded manufacturing facilities are to be used for the production of a new imploding gargle blaster. An advisory panel to the U.S. Food and Drug Administration (FDA) has recommended approval of this product for the U.S. market but no decision has yet been reached by the full FDA committee.

Dividend Policy

The company has not paid cash dividends on its Common Stock and does not anticipate that dividends will be paid on the Common Stock in the foreseeable future.

Management

The following table sets forth information regarding the Company's directors, executive officers, and key employees.

NAME	AGE	POSITION
George Marvin	32	President, Chief Executive Officer, & Director
Mildred Marvin	28	Treasurer & Director
Chip Norton	30	General Manager

George Marvin—George Marvin established the Company in 2013 and has been its Chief Executive Officer since that date. He is a past president of the Institute of Gargle Blasters and has recently been inducted into the Confrèrie des gargarisateurs.

Mildred Marvin—Mildred Marvin has been employed by the Company since 2013.
Chip Norton—Mr. Norton has been General Manager of the Company since 2013. He is a former
vice-president of Amalgamated Blasters, Inc.

Executive Compensation

The following table sets forth the cash compensation paid for services rendered for the year 2018
by the executive officers:

NAME	CAPACITY	CASH COMPENSATION
George Marvin	President and Chief Executive Officer	$300,000
Mildred Marvin	Treasurer	220,000
Chip Norton	General Manager	220,000

Certain Transactions

At various times between 2014 and 2017 First Meriam Venture Partners invested a total of $8.5 mil-
lion in the Company. In connection with this investment, First Meriam Venture Partners was
granted certain rights to registration under the Securities Act of 1933, including the right to have
their shares of Common Stock registered at the Company's expense with the Securities and Exchange Commission.

Principal and Selling Stockholders

The following table sets forth certain information regarding the beneficial ownership of the Company's voting Common Stock as of the date of this prospectus by (i) each person known by the
Company to be the beneficial owner of more than 5 percent of its voting Common Stock, and
(ii) each director of the Company who beneficially owns voting Common Stock. Unless otherwise
indicated, each owner has sole voting and dispositive power over his or her shares.

	COMMON STOCK				
	SHARES BENEFICIALLY OWNED PRIOR TO OFFERING		SHARES TO BE SOLD	SHARES BENEFICIALLY OWNED AFTER OFFER[1]	
NAME OF BENEFICIAL OWNER	NUMBER	PERCENT		NUMBER	PERCENT
George Marvin	375,000	10.4	60,000	315,000	7.7
Mildred Marvin	375,000	10.4	60,000	315,000	7.7
Chip Norton	250,000	6.9	80,000	170,000	4.1
First Meriam Venture Partners	1,700,000	47.2	—	1,700,000	41.5
TFS Investors	260,000	7.2	—	260,000	6.3
Centri-Venture Partnership	260,000	7.2	—	260,000	6.3
Henry Pobble	180,000	5.0	—	180,000	4.4
Georgina Sloberg	200,000	5.6	200,000	—	—

[1]Assuming no exercise of the Underwriters' overallotment option.

Description of Capital Stock

The Company's authorized capital stock consists of 10,000,000 shares of voting Common Stock.

As of the date of this Prospectus, there are 10 holders of record of the Common Stock.

Under the terms of one of the Company's loan agreements, the Company may not pay cash dividends on Common Stock except from net profits without the written consent of the lender.

Underwriting

Subject to the terms and conditions set forth in the Underwriting Agreement, the Company has agreed to sell to each of the Underwriters named below, and each of the Underwriters, for whom Klein Merrick Inc. are acting as Representatives, has severally agreed to purchase from the Company, the number of shares set forth opposite its name below.

UNDERWRITERS	NUMBER OF SHARES TO BE PURCHASED
Klein Merrick, Inc.	400,000
Salomon, Buffett & Co.	150,000
Goldman Stanley, Inc.	150,000
Orange County Securities	100,000
Bank of New England	100,000

In the Underwriting Agreement, the several Underwriters have agreed, subject to the terms and conditions set forth therein, to purchase all shares offered hereby if any such shares are purchased. In the event of a default by any Underwriter, the Underwriting Agreement provides that, in certain circumstances, purchase commitments of the nondefaulting Underwriters may be increased or the Underwriting Agreement may be terminated.

There is no public market for the Common Stock. The price to the public for the Common Stock was determined by negotiation between the Company and the Underwriters and was based on, among other things, the Company's financial and operating history and condition, its prospects and the prospects for its industry in general, the management of the Company, and the market prices of securities for companies in businesses similar to that of the Company.

Legal Matters

The validity of the shares of Common Stock offered by the Prospectus is being passed on for the Company by Thatcher, Kohl, and Lubbers and for the Underwriters by Hawke and Mulroney.

Experts

The consolidated financial statements of the Company have been so included in reliance on the reports of Hooper Firebrand, independent accountants, given on the authority of that firm as experts in auditing and accounting.

Financial Statements

[*Text and tables omitted.*]

Further Reading

A very useful article on investment banking is:

C. W. Smith: "Investment Banking and the Capital Acquisition Process," *Journal of Financial Economics*, 15:3–29 (January–February 1986).

The best sources on venture capital are the specialized journals. See, for example, recent issues of Venture Capital Journal. *A very readable analysis of how venture capital financing is structured to provide the right incentives is contained in:*

W. A. Sahlman: "Aspects of Financial Contracting in Venture Capital," *Journal of Applied Corporate Finance,* 1:23–26 (Summer 1988).

There have been a number of studies of the market for unseasoned issues of common stock. Good articles to start with are:

L. M. Benveniste and W. J. Wilhelm, Jr., "Initial Public Offerings: Going by the Book," *Journal of Applied Corporate Finance,* 98–108 (Spring 1997).

R. G. Ibbotson, J. Sindelar, and J. R. Ritter: "The Market's Problems with Initial Public Offerings," *Journal of Applied Corporate Finance,* 7:66–74 (Spring 1994).

T. Loughran and J. R. Ritter: "The New Issues Puzzle," *Journal of Finance,* 50:23–51 (March 1995).

K. Rock: "Why New Issues Are Underpriced," *Journal of Financial Economics,* 15:187–212 (January–February 1986).

A useful introduction to the design of auction procedures is:

P. Milgrom, "Auctions and Bidding: A Primer," *Journal of Economic Perspectives,* 3:3–22 (1989).

The significant and permanent fall in price after a seasoned stock issue in the United States is documented in the Asquith and Mullins paper. Myers and Majluf relate this price fall to the information associated with security issues:

P. Asquith and D. W. Mullins: "Equity Issues and Offering Dilution," *Journal of Financial Economics,* 15:61–90 (January–February 1986).

S. C. Myers and N. S. Majluf: "Corporate Financing When Firms Have Information That Investors Do Not Have," *Journal of Financial Economics,* 13:187–222 (June 1984).

Lee, Lochhead, Ritter, and Zhao provide some evidence on the costs of issuing securities:

I. Lee, S. Lochhead, J. Ritter, and Q. Zhao, "The Costs of Raising Capital," *Journal of Financial Research,* 19:59–74 (Spring 1996).

Smith argues that the cheapest way to issue stock is by means of a rights issue to existing stockholders; Hansen and Pinkerton and Eckbo and Masulis disagree.

C. W. Smith: "Alternative Methods for Raising Capital: Rights versus Underwritten Offerings," *Journal of Financial Economics,* 5:273–307 (December 1977).

R. S. Hansen and J. M. Pinkerton: "Direct Equity Financing: A Resolution of a Paradox," *Journal of Finance,* 37:651–666 (June 1982).

B. E. Eckbo and R. W. Masulis: "Adverse Selection and the Rights Offer Paradox," *Journal of Financial Economics,* 32:293–332 (December 1992).

CORPORATE FINANCING AND THE SIX LESSONS OF MARKET EFFICIENCY

U p to this point we have described the kinds of securities that corporations issue and how they go about issuing them. Now we turn to a different question: What securities *should* a corporation issue? In other words, what is the best financing strategy? For example,

- Should the firm reinvest most of its earnings in the business, or should it pay them out as dividends?
- If the firm needs more money, should it issue more stock or should it borrow?
- Should it borrow short-term or long-term?
- Should it borrow by issuing a normal long-term bond or a convertible bond (i.e., a bond which can be exchanged for stock by the bondholders)?

There are countless other financing trade-offs, as you will see.

We will take the firm's present portfolio of real assets and its future investment strategy as given. That is, we will separate the investment decision from the financing decision. Strictly speaking, this assumes that capital budgeting and financing decisions are *independent*. In many circumstances this is a reasonable assumption. The firm is generally free to change its capital structure by repurchasing one security and issuing another. In that case there is no need to associate a particular investment project with a particular source of cash. The firm can think, first, about which projects to accept and, second, about how they should be financed.

Sometimes decisions about capital structure depend on project choice or vice versa, and in those cases the investment and financing decisions have to be considered jointly. However, discussion of the interactions of financing and investment decisions is beyond the scope of this book.[1]

---

[1]But see the companion text, **[cite to be filled in by publisher]**

We start this chapter by contrasting investment and financing decisions. The objective in each case is the same—to maximize net present value (NPV). However, it may be harder to find positive-NPV financing opportunities. The reason it is difficult to add value by clever financing decisions is that capital markets are efficient. By this we mean that fierce competition between investors eliminates profit opportunities and causes debt and equity issues to be fairly priced. If you think that sounds like a sweeping statement, you are right. That is why we have devoted this chapter to explaining and evaluating the efficient-market hypothesis.

You may ask why we emphasize this conceptual point. We do it because financing decisions seem overwhelmingly complex if you don't learn to ask the right questions. We are afraid you might flee from confusion to the myths that often dominate popular discussion of corporate financing. You need to understand the efficient-market hypothesis not because it is *universally* true but because it leads you to ask the right questions.

In the balance of this chapter, we define the efficient-market hypothesis more carefully. The hypothesis comes in different strengths, depending on the information available to investors. We also review the evidence for and against efficient markets. The evidence "for" is massive, but over the years a number of puzzling anomalies have accumulated. We close with *the six lessons of market efficiency.*

WE ALWAYS COME BACK TO NPV

Although it is helpful to separate investment and financing decisions, there are basic similarities in the criteria for making them. The decisions to purchase a machine tool and to sell a bond each involve valuation of a risky asset. The fact that one asset is real and the other is financial doesn't matter. In both cases we end up computing net present value.

The phrase net present value of borrowing may seem odd to you. But the following example should help to explain what we mean: As part of its policy of encouraging small business, the government offers to lend your firm $100,000 for 10 years at 3 percent. This means that the firm is liable for interest payments of $3,000 in each of the years 1 through 10 and that it is responsible for repaying the $100,000 in the final year. Should you accept this offer?

We can compute the NPV of the loan agreement in the same way we compute the NPV of an investment project. The one difference is that the first cash flow is *positive* and the subsequent flows are *negative:*

$$\text{NPV} = \text{amount borrowed} - \text{present value of interest payments}$$
$$- \text{present value of loan repayment}$$

$$= +100{,}000 - \sum_{t=1}^{10} \frac{3{,}000}{(1+r)^t} - \frac{100{,}000}{(1+r)^{10}}$$

The only missing variable is r, the opportunity cost of capital. You need that to value the liability created by the loan. We reason this way: The government's loan to you is a financial asset: a piece of paper representing your promise to pay $3,000 per year plus the final repayment of $100,000. How much would that paper sell for if freely traded in the capital market? It would sell for the present value of those cash flows, discounted at r, the rate of return offered by other securities issued by your firm. All you have to do to determine r is to answer the question, "What interest rate would my firm have to pay to borrow money directly from the capital markets rather than from the government?"

Suppose that this rate is 10 percent. Then

$$NPV = +100,000 - \sum_{t=1}^{10} \frac{3,000}{(1.10)^t} - \frac{100,000}{(1.10)^{10}}$$

$$= +100,000 - 56,988 = +\$43,012$$

Of course, you don't need any arithmetic to tell you that borrowing at 3 percent is a good deal when the fair rate is 10 percent. But the NPV calculations tell you just how much that opportunity is worth ($43,012).[2] It also brings out the essential similarity of investment and financing decisions.

Differences between Investment and Financing Decisions

In some ways investment decisions are simpler than financing decisions. The number of different financing decisions (i.e., securities) is continually expanding. You need to learn the major families, genera, and species. You will also need to become familiar with the vocabulary of financing—such matters as tombstones, balloons, strips, and collars.

There are also ways in which financing decisions are much easier than investment decisions. First, financing decisions do not have the same degree of finality as investment decisions. They are easier to reverse. That is, their abandonment value is higher. Second, it's harder to make or lose money by smart or stupid financing strategies. That is, it is difficult to find financing schemes with NPVs significantly different from zero. That reflects the nature of the competition.

When the firm looks at capital investment decisions, it does *not* assume that it is facing perfect, competitive markets. It may have only a few competitors that specialize in the same line of business in the same geographical area. And it may own some unique assets that give it an edge over its competitors. Often these assets are intangible, such as patents, expertise, or reputation. All this opens up the opportunity to make superior profits and find projects with positive NPVs.

In financial markets your competition is all other corporations seeking funds, to say nothing of the state, local, and federal governments that go to New York, London, and other financial centers to raise money. The investors who supply financing are comparably numerous, and they are smart: Money attracts brains. The financial amateur often views capital markets as *segmented*, that is, broken down into distinct sectors. But money moves between those sectors, and it moves fast.

Remember that a good financing decision generates a positive NPV. It is one in which the amount of cash raised exceeds the value of the liability created. But turn that statement around. If selling a security generates a positive NPV for the seller, it must generate a negative NPV for the buyer. Thus, the loan we discussed was a good deal for your firm but a negative NPV from the government's point of view. By lending at 3 percent, it offered a $43,012 subsidy.

---

[2]We ignore here any tax consequences of borrowing. These are discussed in Chapter 6.

What are the chances that your firm could consistently trick or persuade investors into purchasing securities with negative NPVs to them? Pretty low. In general, firms should assume that the securities they issue are fairly priced. That takes us into the main topic of this chapter: efficient capital markets.

WHAT IS AN EFFICIENT MARKET?

A Startling Discovery: Price Changes Are Random

As is so often the case with important ideas, the concept of efficient capital markets stemmed from a chance discovery. In 1953 Maurice Kendall, a British statistician, presented a controversial paper to the Royal Statistical Society on the behavior of stock and commodity prices.[3] Kendall had expected to find regular price cycles, but to his surprise they did not seem to exist. Each series appeared to be "a 'wandering' one, almost as if once a week the Demon of Chance drew a random number . . . and added it to the current price to determine the next week's price." In other words, the prices of stocks and commodities seemed to follow a *random walk*.

If you are not sure what we mean by "random walk," you might like to think of the following example: You are given $100 to play a game. At the end of each week a coin is tossed. If it comes up heads, you win 3 percent of your investment; if it is tails, you lose 2.5 percent. Therefore, your capital at the end of the first week is either $103.00 or $97.50. At the end of the second week the coin is tossed again. Now the possible outcomes are:

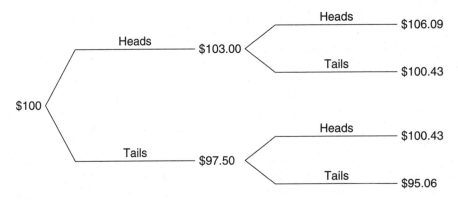

This process is a random walk with a positive drift of .25 percent per week.[4] It is a random walk because successive changes in value are independent. That is, the odds each week are the

[3]See M. G. Kendall, "The Analysis of Economic Time Series, Part I. Prices," *Journal of the Royal Statistical Society* 96 (1953), pp. 11–25. Kendall's idea was not wholly new. It had been proposed in an almost forgotten thesis written 53 years earlier by a French doctoral student, Louis Bachelier. Bachelier's accompanying development of the mathematical theory of random processes anticipated by five years Einstein's famous work on the random Brownian motion of colliding gas molecules. See L. Bachelier, *Theorie de la Speculation*, Gauthiers-Villars, Paris, 1900. Reprinted in English (A. J. Boness, trans.) in P. H. Cootner (ed.), *The Random Character of Stock Market Prices*, M.I.T. Press, Cambridge, MA, 1964, pp. 17–78.

[4]The drift is equal to the expected outcome: $(1/2)(3) + (1/2)(-2.5) = .25\%$.

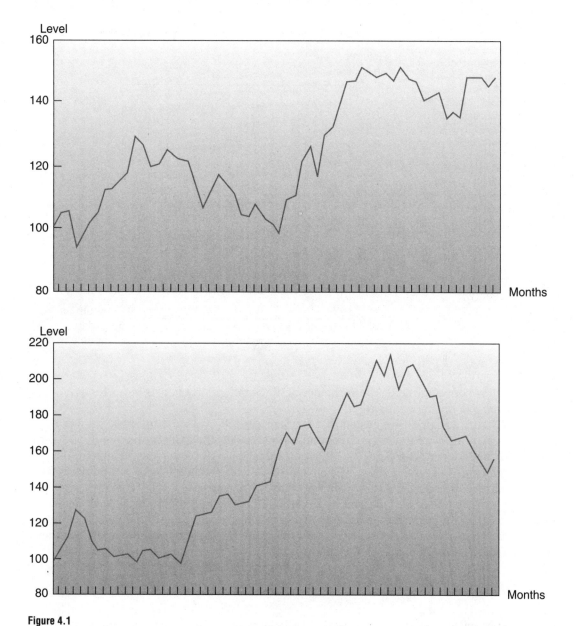

Figure 4.1

One of these charts shows the Standard and Poor's Index for a five-year period. The other shows the results of playing our coin-tossing game for five years. Can you tell which is which?

same, regardless of the value at the start of the week or of the pattern of heads and tails in the previous weeks.

If you find it difficult to believe that there are no patterns in share price changes, look at the two charts in Figure 4.1. One of these charts shows the outcome from playing our game for five

Figure 4.2

Each dot shows a pair of returns for Microsoft stock on two successive days between August 1993 and August 1998. The circled dot records a daily return of +1 percent and then −1 percent on the next day. The scatter diagram shows no significant relationship between returns on successive days.

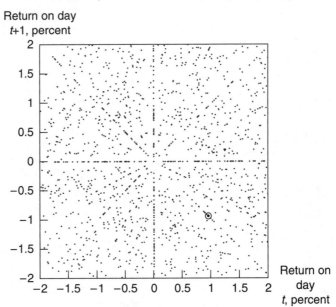

Microsoft return pattern: structure without predictability

Return on day $t+1$, percent

Return on day t, percent

years; the other shows the actual performance of the Standard and Poor's Index for a five-year period. Can you tell which one is which?[5]

When Maurice Kendall suggested that stock prices follow a random walk, he was implying that the price changes are independent of one another just as the gains and losses in our coin-tossing game were independent. Figure 4.2 illustrates this. Each dot shows the change in the price of Microsoft stock on successive days. The circled dot in the southeast quadrant refers to a pair of days in which a 1 percent increase was followed by a 1 percent decrease. If there was a systematic tendency for increases to be followed by decreases, there would be many dots in the southeast quadrant and few in the northeast quadrant. It is obvious from a glance that there is very little pattern in these price movements, but we can test this more precisely by calculating the coefficient of correlation between each day's price change and the next.[6] If price movements persisted, the correlation would be positive; if there was no relationship, it would be 0. In our example, the correla-

[5]The top chart in Figure 4.1 shows the real Standard and Poor's Index for the years 1980 through 1984; the bottom chart is a series of cumulated random numbers. Of course, 50 percent of you are likely to have guessed right, but we bet it was just a guess. A similar comparison between cumulated random numbers and actual price series was first suggested by H. V. Roberts, "Stock Market `Patterns' and Financial Analysis: Methodological Suggestions," *Journal of Finance* 14 (March 1959), pp. 1–10.

[6]Your eye will pick up a pattern of lines radiating out from the center of Figure 4.2. The reason is that stock prices do not change continuously, but in discrete jumps or "ticks." Some days the stock price doesn't change at all, and a return of zero is recorded. This creates the pattern in Figure 4.2, but does not imply predictability. See T. Crack and O. Ledoit, "Robust Structure without Predictability: The 'Compass Rose' Pattern of the Stock Market," *Journal of Finance* 51 (June 1996), pp. 751–762.

Figure 4.3

Cycles self-destruct as soon as they are recognized by investors. The stock price instantaneously jumps to the present value of the expected future price.

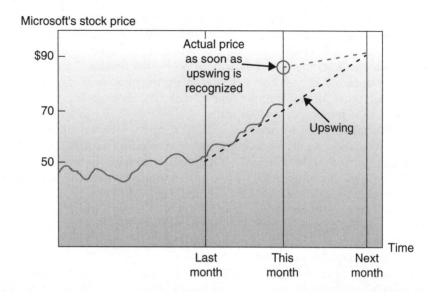

Microsoft's stock price

$90

70

50

Actual price as soon as upswing is recognized

Upswing

Time

Last month   This month   Next month

tion between successive price changes in Microsoft stock was +.054; there was a negligible tendency for price rises to be followed by further price rises.[7]

Figure 4.2 suggests that Microsoft's price changes were effectively uncorrelated. Today's price change gave investors almost no clue as to the likely change tomorrow. Does that surprise you? If so, imagine that it were not the case and that changes in Microsoft's stock price were expected to persist for several months. Figure 4.3 provides an example of such a predictable cycle. You can see that an upswing in Microsoft's stock price started last month, when the price was $70, and it is expected to carry the price to $90 next month. What will happen when investors perceive this bonanza? It will self-destruct. Since Microsoft stock is a bargain at $70, investors will rush to buy. They will stop buying only when the stock offers a normal rate of return. Therefore, as soon as a cycle becomes apparent to investors, they immediately eliminate it by their trading.

Three Forms of Market Efficiency

You should see now why prices in competitive markets must follow a random walk. If past price changes could be used to predict future price changes, investors could make easy profits. But in competitive markets easy profits don't last. As investors try to take advantage of the information in past prices, prices adjust immediately until the superior profits from studying past price movements disappear. As a result, all the information in past prices will be reflected in today's stock price, not tomorrow's. Patterns in prices will no longer exist and price changes in one period will be independent of changes in the next. In other words, the share price will follow a random walk.

In competitive markets today's stock price must already reflect the information in past prices. But why stop there? If markets are competitive, shouldn't today's stock price reflect *all*

---

[7]The correlation coefficient between successive observations is known as the *autocorrelation coefficient*. An autocorrelation of +.054 implies that, if Microsoft stock price rose by 1 percent more than average yesterday, your best forecast of today's price change would be a rise of .054 percent more than average.

the information that is available to investors? If so, securities will be fairly priced and security returns will be unpredictable, whatever information you consider.

Economists often define three levels of market efficiency, which are distinguished by the degree of information reflected in security prices. In the first level, prices reflect the information contained in the record of past prices. This is called the *weak* form of efficiency. If markets are efficient in the weak sense, then it is impossible to make consistently superior profits by studying past returns. Prices will follow a random walk.

The second level of efficiency requires that prices reflect not just past prices but all other published information, such as you might get from reading the financial press. This is known as the *semistrong* form of market efficiency. If markets are efficient in this sense, then prices will adjust immediately to public information such as the announcement of the last quarter's earnings, a new issue of stock, a proposal to merge two companies, and so on.

Finally, we might envisage a *strong* form of efficiency, in which prices reflect all the information that can be acquired by painstaking analysis of the company and the economy. In such a market we would observe lucky and unlucky investors, but we wouldn't find any superior investment managers who can consistently beat the market.

Two types of investment analysts help to make markets efficient. Many analysts study the company's business and try to uncover information about its profitability that will shed new light on the value of the stock. These analysts are called *fundamental analysts*. Competition in fundamental research will tend to ensure that prices reflect all relevant information and that price changes are unpredictable. The other analysts study the past price record and look for trends or cycles. These analysts are called *technical analysts*. Competition in technical research will tend to ensure that current prices reflect all information in the past sequence of prices and that future price changes cannot be predicted from past prices.

Efficient Markets: The Evidence

In the years that followed Maurice Kendall's discovery, financial journals were packed with tests of the efficient-market hypothesis. To test the weak form of the hypothesis, researchers measured the profitability of some of the trading rules used by technical analysts, who claim to find patterns in security prices. They also employed statistical tests such as the one that we described when looking for patterns in the returns on Microsoft stock. For example, in Figure 4.4 we have used the same test to look for relationships between stock market returns in successive weeks. It appears that throughout the world there are few patterns in week-to-week returns.

To analyze the semistrong form of the efficient-market hypothesis, researchers have measured how rapidly security prices respond to different items of news, such as an earnings or dividend announcement, news of a takeover, or macroeconomic news. Figure 4.5 illustrates how the release of such news is immediately reflected in security prices. The graph shows the price run-up of a sample of 194 firms that were targets of takeover attempts. In most takeovers, the acquiring firm is willing to pay a large premium over the current market price of the acquired firm; therefore when a firm becomes the target of a takeover attempt, its stock price increases in anticipation of the takeover premium. Figure 4.5 shows that on the day the public become aware of a takeover attempt (Day 0 in the graph), the stock price of the typical target takes a big upward jump. The adjustment in stock price is immediate: After the big price move on the public announcement day, the run-up is over, and there is no further drift in the stock price, either upward

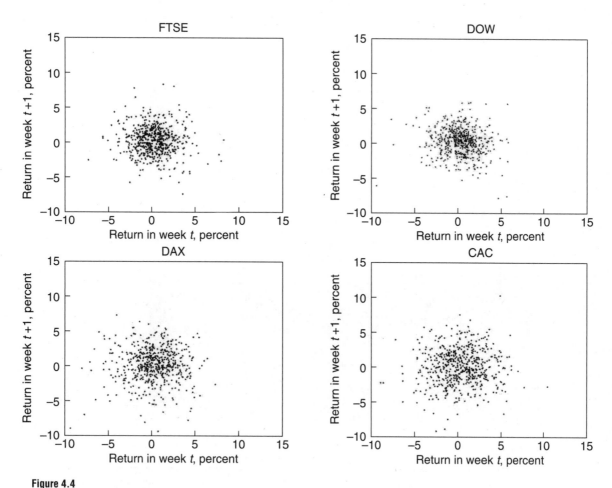

Figure 4.4

Each point in these scatter diagrams shows the return in successive weeks on four stock market indexes between August 1987 and April 1998. The wide scatter of points shows that there is almost no correlation between the return in one week and in the next. The four indexes are FTSE 100 (UK), the Dow Jones Industrial Average (USA), DAX (Germany), and CAC 40 (France).

or downward.[8] Thus within the day, the new stock prices apparently reflect (at least on average) the magnitude of the takeover premium.

A study by Patell and Wolfson shows just how fast prices move when new information becomes available.[9] They found that, when a firm publishes its latest earnings or announces a

---

[8]See A. Keown and J. Pinkerton, "Merger Announcements and Insider Trading Activity," *Journal of Finance* 36 (September 1981), pp. 855–869. Note that prices on the days *before* the public announcement do show evidence of a sustained upward drift. This is evidence of a gradual leakage of information about a possible takeover attempt. Some investors begin to purchase the target firm in anticipation of a public announcement. Consistent with efficient markets, however, once the information becomes public, it is reflected fully and immediately in stock prices.

[9]See J. M. Patell and M. A. Wolfson, "The Intraday Speed of Adjustment of Stock Prices to Earnings and Dividend Announcements," *Journal of Financial Economics* 13 (June 1984), pp. 223–252.

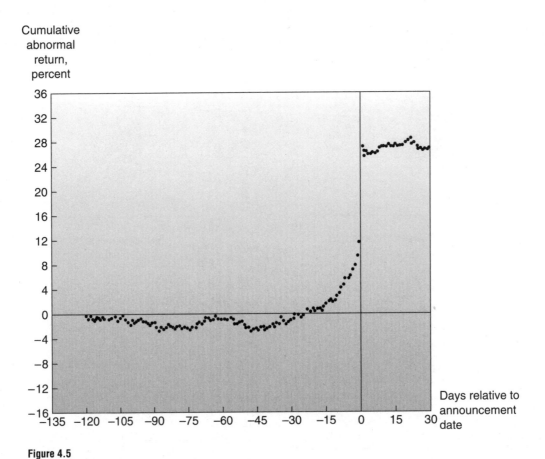

Figure 4.5

The performance of the stocks of target companies compared with that of the market. The prices of target stocks jump up on the announcement day, but from then on, there are no unusual price movements. The announcement of the takeover attempt seems to be fully reflected in the stock price on the announcement day.
Source: A. Keown and J. Pinkerton, "Merger Announcements and Insider Trading Activity," *Journal of Finance* 36 (September 1981); pp. 855–869.

dividend change, the major part of the adjustment in price occurs within 5 to 10 minutes of the announcement.

Tests of the strong form of the hypothesis have examined the recommendations of professional security analysts and have looked for mutual funds or pension funds that could predictably outperform the market. Some researchers have found a slight persistent outperformance, but just as many have concluded that professionally managed funds fail to recoup the costs of management. Look, for example, at Figure 4.6, which is taken from a study by Mark Carhart of the average return on nearly 1,500 U.S. mutual funds. You can see that in some years the mutual funds beat the market, but as often as not it was the other way around. Figure 4.6 provides a fairly crude comparison, for mutual funds have tended to specialize in particular sectors of the market, such as low-beta stocks or large-firm stocks, that may have given below-average returns. To control for such differences, each fund needs to be compared with a benchmark portfolio of similar securities. The study

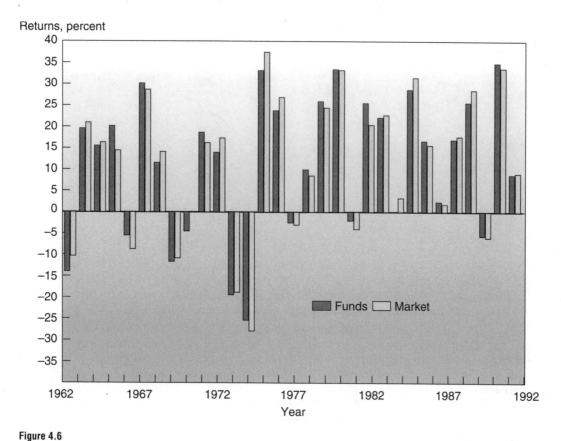

Figure 4.6

Average annual returns on 1,493 U.S. mutual funds and the market index, 1962–1992. Notice that mutual funds underperform the market in approximately half the years.

Source: M. M. Carhart, "On Persistence in Mutual Fund Performance," *Journal of Finance* 52 (March 1997), pp. 57–82.

by Mark Carhart did this, but the message was unchanged: The funds earned a lower return than the benchmark portfolios *after* expenses and roughly matched the benchmarks *before* expenses.

It would be surprising if some managers were not smarter than others and could earn superior returns. But it seems difficult to spot the smart ones, and the top-performing managers one year have about an average chance of falling on their face the next year. For example, *Forbes Magazine*, a widely read investment periodical, has published annually since 1975 an "honor roll" of the most consistently successful mutual funds. Suppose that each year, when Forbes announced its honor roll, you had invested an equal sum in each of these exceptional funds. You would have outperformed the market in only 5 of the following 16 years, and your average annual return before paying any initial fees would have been more than 1 percent below the return on the market.[10]

---

[10]See B. G. Malkiel, "Returns from Investing in Equity Mutual Funds 1971 to 1991," *Journal of Finance* 50 (June 1995), pp. 549–572. It seems to be difficult to measure whether good performance does persist. Some contrary evidence is provided in E. J. Elton, M. J. Gruber, and C. R. Blake, "The Persistence of Risk-Adjusted Mutual Fund Performance," *Journal of Business* 69 (April 1996), pp. 133–157. There is, however, widespread agreement that the worst performing funds continue to underperform. That is not surprising, for they are shrinking and the costs of running them are proportionately higher.

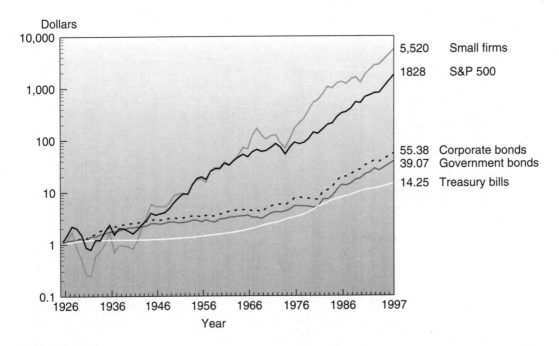

Figure 4.7

How an investment of $1 at the start of 1926 would have grown, assuming reinvestment of all dividend and interest payments.

Source: Ibbotson Associates, Inc., *Stocks, Bonds, Bills, and Inflation, 1998 Yearbook,* Chicago, 1998; cited hereafter in this chapter as the *1998 Yearbook.* © 1998 Ibbotson Associates, Inc.

Such evidence on strong-form efficiency has proved to be sufficiently convincing that many professionally managed funds have given up the pursuit of superior performance. They simply "buy the index," which maximizes diversification and minimizes the costs of managing the portfolio. Corporate pension plans now invest over a quarter of their United States equity holdings in index funds.

PUZZLES AND ANOMALIES—WHAT DO THEY MEAN FOR THE FINANCIAL MANAGER?

Almost without exception, early researchers concluded that the efficient market hypothesis was a remarkably good description of reality. So powerful was the evidence that any dissenting research was regarded with suspicion. But eventually the readers of finance journals grew weary of hearing the same message. The interesting articles became those that turned up some puzzle. Soon the journals were packed with evidence of anomalies that investors have apparently failed to exploit.

We have already referred to one such puzzle—the abnormally high returns on the stocks of small firms. For example, look at Figure 4.7, which shows the results of investing $1 in 1926 in the stocks of either small or large firms. (Notice that the portfolio values are plotted in Figure 4.7 on a logarithmic scale.) By 1997 the $1 invested in small company stocks had appreciated to $5,520, while the investment in large firms was worth only $1,828.[11] Although small firms had higher betas, the difference was not nearly large enough to explain the difference in returns.

Now this may mean one (or more) of three things. First, it could be that investors have demanded a higher expected return from small firms to compensate for some extra risk factor that is not captured in the simple capital asset pricing model. Perhaps the small-firm effect is evidence against the capital asset pricing model (CAPM).

Second, the superior performance of small firms could simply be a coincidence, a finding that stems from the efforts of many researchers to find interesting patterns in the data. There is evidence for and against the coincidence theory. Those who believe that the small-firm effect is a pervasive phenomenon can point to the fact that small-firm stocks have provided a higher return in many other countries. On the other hand, you can see from Figure 4.7 that the superior performance of small-firm stocks in the United States is limited to a relatively short period. Until the early 1960s small-firm and large-firm stocks were neck and neck. A wide gap then opened in the next two decades but it narrowed again in the 1980s when the small-firm effect first became known. If you looked simply at recent years, you might judge that there is a *large-firm* effect.

The third possibility is that we have here an important exception to the efficient-market theory, one that provided investors with an opportunity to make predictably superior profits over a period of two decades. If such anomalies offer easy pickings, you would expect to find a number of investors eager to take advantage of them. It turns out that, while many investors do try to exploit such anomalies, it is surprisingly difficult to get rich by doing so. For example, Professor Richard Roll, who probably knows as much as anyone about market anomalies, confesses

> Over the past decade, I have attempted to exploit many of the seemingly most promising "inefficiencies" by actually trading significant amounts of money according to a trading rule suggested by the "inefficiencies" . . . I have never yet found one that worked in practice, in the sense that it returned more after cost than a buy-and-hold strategy.[12]

Do Investors Respond Slowly to New Information?

We have dwelt on the small-firm effect, but there is no shortage of other puzzles and anomalies. Some of them relate to the short-term behavior of stock prices. For example, returns appear to be higher in January than in other months, they seem to be lower on a Monday than on other days of the week, and most of the daily return comes at the beginning and end of the day.

To have any chance of making money from such short-term patterns, you need to be a professional trader, with one eye on the computer screen and the other on your annual bonus. If you are a corporate financial manager, these short-term patterns in stock prices may be intriguing conundrums, but they are unlikely to change the major financial decisions about which projects to invest in and how they should be financed. The more troubling concern for the corporate financial manager is the possibility that it may be several years before investors fully appreciate the significance of new information. The studies of daily and hourly price movements that we referred to above may not pick up this long-term mispricing, but here are two examples of an apparent long-term delay in the reaction to news.

---

[11]In each case the portfolio values assume that dividends are reinvested.

[12]R. Roll, "What Every CFO Should Know About Scientific Progress in Financial Economics: What Is Known and What Remains to be Resolved," *Financial Management* 23 (Summer 1994), pp. 69–75.

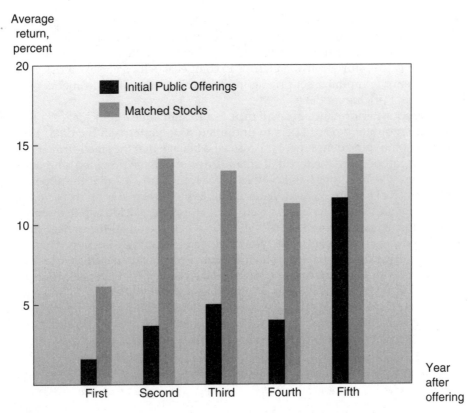

Figure 4.8

Returns on 4,753 initial public offerings from 1970 to 1990 in each of the five years following the issue. Returns on a sample of matching nonissuing firms are shown for comparison.

Source: R. Loughran and J. R. Ritter, "The New Issues Puzzle," *Journal of Finance* 50 (1995), pp. 23–51.

The New Issue Puzzle   When firms first issue stock to the public, investors typically rush to buy. On average, those lucky enough to receive stock realize an immediate capital gain. However, Loughran and Ritter, who studied new issues between 1970 and 1990, found that these early gains turned into losses. Their findings are summarized in Figure 4.8. In total over the five years following an initial public offering the shares performed about 30 percent worse than a portfolio of stocks of firms of similar size.[13] Loughran and Ritter went on to look at issues of stock by firms that were already publicly traded and found similar substandard performance over the five years after the issue.

The Earnings Announcement Puzzle   The earnings announcement puzzle is summarized in Figure 4.9, which shows stock performance following the announcement of unexpectedly good or bad earnings during the years 1974 to 1986.[14] The 10 percent of the stocks of firms with the best earn-

[13]See R. Loughran and J. R. Ritter, "The New Issues Puzzle," *Journal of Finance* 50 (1995), pp. 23–51.

[14]V. L. Bernard and J. K. Thomas, "Post-Earnings-Announcement Drift: Delayed Price Response or Risk Premium?" *Journal of Accounting Research* 27 (Supplement 1989), pp. 1–36.

Figure 4.9

The cumulative abnormal returns of stocks of firms over the 60 days following an announcement of quarterly earnings. The 10 percent of the stocks with the best earnings news (Group 10) outperformed those with the worst news (Group 1) by more than 4 percent.

Source: V. L. Bernard and J. K. Thomas, "Post-Earnings-Announcement Drift: Delayed Price Response or Risk Premium?" *Journal of Accounting Research* 27 (Supplement 1989), pp. 1–36.

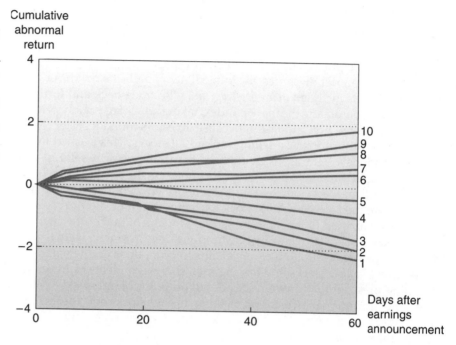

ings news outperformed those with the worst news by more than 4 percent over the two months following the announcement. It seems that investors failed to appreciate immediately the full significance of the earnings announcement and became aware only as further information arrived.

The jury is still out on these studies of longer-term anomalies.[15] In the meantime, some scholars are casting around for an alternative theory that might explain these apparent anomalies. Some argue that the answers lie in behavioral psychology. For example, psychologists have observed that individuals commonly overreact to past information. If that is so, we can understand why the euphoria with which investors greet a company's first issue of stock seems to be followed by a gradual return to reality.

Now this tendency to overreact could be true, but it does not help to explain our other long-term puzzle, the *under*reaction of investors to earnings announcements. Unless we have a theory of human nature that can tell us when investors will underreact and when they will overreact, we are just as well off with the efficient-market theory that tells us that underreactions and overreactions are equally likely.[16]

---

[15]For example, the abnormal returns on new issues largely (but not wholly) disappear if the stocks are value-weighted. See A. Brav and P. A. Gompers, "Myth or Reality? The Long-Run Underperformance of Initial Public Offerings: Evidence from Venture and Nonventure Capital-backed Companies," *Journal of Finance* 5 (December 1997), pp. 1791–1821.

[16]This point is made in E. F. Fama, "Market Efficiency, Long-Term Returns, and Behavioral Finance," *Journal of Financial Economics* 49 (September 1998), pp. 283–306.

The Crash of 1987

On Monday, October 19, 1987, the Dow Jones Industrial Average (the Dow) fell 23 percent in *one day*. Immediately after the crash, everybody started to ask two questions: "Who were the guilty parties?" and "Do prices reflect fundamental values?"

As in most murder mysteries, the immediate suspects are not the ones "who done it." The first group of suspects included *index arbitrageurs,* who trade back and forth between index futures[17] and the stocks comprising the market index, taking advantage of any price discrepancies. On Black Monday futures fell first and fastest because investors found it easier to bail out of the stock market by way of futures than by selling individual stocks. This pushed the futures price below the stock market index.[18] The arbitrageurs tried to make money by selling stocks and buying futures, but they found it difficult to get up-to-date quotes on the stocks they wished to trade. Thus the futures and stock markets were for a time disconnected. Arbitrageurs contributed to the trading volume that swamped the New York Stock Exchange, but they did not cause the crash; they were the messengers who tried to transmit the selling pressure in the futures market back to the exchange.

The second suspects were large institutional investors who were trying to implement *portfolio insurance* schemes. Portfolio insurance aims to put a floor on the value of an equity portfolio by progressively selling stocks and buying safe, short-term debt securities as stock prices fall. Thus the selling pressure that drove prices down on Black Monday led portfolio insurers to sell still more. One institutional investor on October 19 sold stocks and futures totalling $1.7 billion. The immediate cause of the price fall on Black Monday may have been a herd of elephants all trying to leave by the same exit.

Perhaps some large portfolio insurers can be convicted of disorderly conduct, but why did stocks fall *worldwide,*[19] when portfolio insurance was significant only in the United States? Moreover, if sales were triggered mainly by portfolio insurance or trading tactics, they should have conveyed little fundamental information, and prices should have bounced back after Black Monday's confusion had dissipated.

So why did prices fall so sharply? There was no obvious, new fundamental information to justify such a sharp and widespread decline in share values. For this reason, the idea that the market price is the best estimate of intrinsic value seems less compelling than before the crash. It appears that either prices were irrationally high before Black Monday or irrationally low afterward. Could the theory of efficient markets be another casualty of the crash?

The events of October 1987 remind us how exceptionally difficult it is to value common stocks from scratch. For example, suppose that in November 1998 you wanted to check whether common stocks were fairly valued. At least as a first stab, you might have used the constant-growth formula. The annual expected dividend on the Standard and Poor's Industrial Index was about 16.7. Suppose this dividend was expected to grow at a steady rate of 10 percent a year and investors re-

---

[17]An index future provides a way of trading in the stock market as a whole. It is a contract that pays investors the value of the stocks in the index at a specified future date. We discuss futures in Chapter 13.

[18]That is, sellers pushed the futures prices below their *proper relation* to the index (again, see Chapter 13). The proper relation is not exact equality.

[19]Some countries experienced even larger falls than the United States. For example, prices fell by 46 percent in Hong Kong, 42 percent in Australia, and 35 percent in Mexico. For a discussion of the worldwide nature of the crash, see R. Roll, "The International Crash of October 1987," in R. Kamphuis (ed.), *Black Monday and the Future of Financial Markets,* Richard D. Irwin, Inc., Homewood, IL, 1989.

quired an annual return of 11.4 percent a year from common stocks. The constant-growth formula gives a value for the index of

$$PV(\text{index}) = \frac{\text{DIV}}{r - g} = \frac{16.7}{.114 - .10} = 1,193$$

which was the actual level of the index in mid-November 1998. But how confident would you be about any of these figures? Perhaps the likely dividend growth was only 9.6 percent per year. This would produce a 22 percent downward revision in your estimate of the right level of the index, from 1,193 to 928!

$$PV(\text{index}) = \frac{\text{DIV}}{r - g} = \frac{16.7}{.114 - .096} = 928$$

In other words, a price drop like Black Monday's could have occurred in November 1998 if investors had suddenly become 0.4 percentage point less optimistic about future dividend growth.

The extreme difficulty of valuing common stocks from scratch has two important consequences. First, investors almost always price a common stock relative to yesterday's price or relative to today's price of comparable securities. In other words, they generally take yesterday's price as correct, adjusting upward or downward on the basis of today's information. If information arrives smoothly, then as time passes, investors become more and more confident that today's market level is correct. However, when investors lose confidence in the benchmark of yesterday's price, there may be a period of confused trading and volatile prices before a new benchmark is established.

Second, the hypothesis that stock price *always* equals intrinsic value is nearly impossible to test, precisely because it's so difficult to calculate intrinsic value without referring to prices. Thus the crash didn't conclusively disprove the hypothesis, but many people now find it less *plausible*.[20]

However, the crash does not undermine the evidence for market efficiency with respect to *relative* prices. Take for example, Quaker Oats, which sold for $53 per share in June 1998. Could we *prove* that true intrinsic value is $53? No, but we could be more confident that the price of Quaker Oats should be close to that of Heinz ($52) since the two companies had almost the same earnings per share, paid a similar dividend, and had similar prospects. Moreover, if either company announced unexpectedly higher earnings, we could be quite confident that its share price would respond instantly and without bias. In other words, the subsequent price would be set correctly relative to the prior price. The most important lessons of market efficiency for the corporate financial manager are concerned with relative efficiency.

Market Anomalies and the Financial Manager

The financial manager needs to be confident that, when the firm issues new securities, it can do so at a fair price. There are two reasons that this may not be the case. First, the strong form of the efficient-market hypothesis may not be 100 percent true, so that the financial manager may have

---

[20]Some economists believe that the market is prone to "bubbles"—situations in which price grows faster than fundamental value, but investors don't sell because they expect prices to *keep* rising. Of course, all such bubbles pop eventually, but they can, in theory, be self-sustaining for a while. The *Journal of Economic Perspectives* 4 (Spring 1990) contains several nontechnical articles on bubbles.

information that other investors do not have. Alternatively, investors may have the *same* information as management, but be slow to react to it. For example, we described above some evidence that new issues of stock tend to be followed by a prolonged period of low stock returns.

You sometimes hear managers say something along the following lines:

> *Great! Our stock is clearly overpriced. This means we can raise capital cheaply and invest in Project X. Our high stock price gives us a big advantage over our competitors who could not possibly justify investing in Project X.*

But that doesn't make sense. If your stock is truly overpriced, you can help your current shareholders by selling additional stock and using the cash to invest in other capital market securities. But you should *never* issue stock to invest in a project that offers a lower rate of return than you could earn elsewhere in the capital market. Such a project would have a negative NPV. You can always do better than investing in a negative-NPV project: Your company can go out and buy common stocks. In an efficient market, such purchases are always *zero* NPV.

What about the reverse? Suppose you know that your stock is *underpriced.* In that case, it certainly would not help your current shareholders to sell additional "cheap" stock to invest in other fairly priced stocks. If your stock is sufficiently underpriced, it may even pay to forego an opportunity to invest in a positive-NPV project rather than to allow new investors to buy into your firm at a low price. Financial managers who believe that their firm's stock is underpriced may be justifiably reluctant to issue more stock, but they may instead be able to finance their investment program by an issue of debt. In this case the market inefficiency would affect the firm's choice of financing but not its real investment decisions.

THE SIX LESSONS OF MARKET EFFICIENCY

Sorting out the puzzles will take time, but we believe that there is now widespread agreement that capital markets function sufficiently well that opportunities for easy profits are rare. So nowadays when economists come across instances where market prices apparently don't make sense, they don't throw the efficient-market hypothesis onto the economic garbage heap. Instead, they think carefully about whether there is some missing ingredient that their theories ignore.

We suggest therefore that financial managers should assume, at least as a starting point, that security prices are fair and that it is very difficult to outguess the market. This has some important implications for the financial manager.

Lesson 1: Markets Have No Memory

The weak form of the efficient-market hypothesis states that the sequence of past price changes contains no information about future changes. Economists express the same idea more concisely when they say that the market has no memory. Sometimes financial managers seem to act as if this were not the case. For example, studies by Taggart and others in the United States and by Marsh in the United Kingdom show that managers generally favor equity rather than debt financing after an abnormal price rise.[21] The idea is to catch the market while it is high. Similarly, they are often re-

---

[21]R. A. Taggart, "A Model of Corporate Financing Decisions," *Journal of Finance* 32 (December 1977), pp. 1467–1484; P. Asquith and D. W. Mullins, Jr., "Equity Issues and Offering Dilution," *Journal of Financial Economics* 15 (January–February 1986), pp. 16–89; P. R. Marsh, "The Choice between Debt and Equity: An Empirical Study," *Journal of Finance* 37 (March 1982), pp. 121–144.

luctant to issue stock after a fall in price. They are inclined to wait for a rebound. But we know that the market has no memory and the cycles that financial managers seem to rely on do not exist.[22]

Sometimes a financial manager will have inside information indicating that the firm's stock is overpriced or underpriced. Suppose, for example, that there is some good news which the market does not know but you do. The stock price will rise sharply when the news is revealed. Therefore, if the company sold shares at the current price, it would be offering a bargain to new investors at the expense of present stockholders.

Naturally, managers are reluctant to sell new shares when they have favorable inside information. But such information has nothing to do with the history of the stock price. Your firm's stock could be selling at half its price of a year ago, and yet you could have special information suggesting that it is *still* grossly overvalued. Or it may be undervalued at twice last year's price.

Lesson 2: Trust Market Prices

In an efficient market you can trust prices, for they impound all available information about the value of each security. This means that in an efficient market, there is no way for most investors to achieve consistently superior rates of return. To do so, you not only need to know more than *anyone* else, but you also need to know more than *everyone* else. This message is important for the financial manager who is responsible for the firm's exchange-rate policy or for its purchases and sales of debt. If you operate on the basis that you are smarter than others at predicting currency changes or interest-rate moves, you will trade a consistent financial policy for an elusive will-o'-the-wisp.

The company's assets may also be directly affected by management's faith in its investment skills. For example, one company may purchase another simply because its management thinks that the stock is undervalued. On approximately half the occasions the stock of the acquired firm will with hindsight turn out to be undervalued. But on the other half it will be overvalued. On average the value will be correct, so the acquiring company is playing a fair game except for the costs of the acquisition.

Example—Orange County In December 1994, Orange County, one of the wealthiest counties in the United States, announced that it had lost $1.7 billion on its investment portfolio. The losses arose because the county treasurer, Robert Citron, had raised large short-term loans which he then used to bet on a rise in long-term bond prices.[23] The bonds that the county bought were backed by government-guaranteed mortgage loans. However, some of them were of an unusual type known as *reverse floaters,* which means that as interest rates rise, the interest payment on each bond is reduced, and vice versa.

Reverse floaters are riskier than normal bonds. When interest rates rise, prices of all bonds fall, but prices of reverse floaters suffer a double whammy because the interest rate payments decline

---

[22]If high stock prices signal expanded investment opportunities and the need to finance these new investments, we would expect to see firms raise more money *in total* when stock prices are historically high. But this does not explain why firms prefer to raise the extra cash at these times by an issue of equity rather than debt.

[23]Orange County borrowed money in the following way. Suppose it bought bond A and then sold it to a bank with a promise to buy it back at a slightly higher price. The cash from this sale was then invested in bond B. If bond prices fell, the county lost twice over: Its investment in bond B was worth less than the purchase price, and it was obliged to repurchase bond A for more than the bond was now worth. The sale and repurchase of bond A is known as a reverse repurchase agreement, or reverse "repo." We describe repos in Chapter 19.

as the discount rate rises. Thus Robert Citron's policy of borrowing to invest in reverse floaters ensured that when, contrary to his forecast, interest rates subsequently rose, the fund suffered huge losses.

Like Robert Citron, financial managers sometimes take large bets because they believe that they can spot the direction of interest rates, stock prices, or exchange rates, and sometimes their employers may encourage them to speculate.[24] We do not mean to imply that such speculation always results in losses, as in Orange County's case, for in an efficient market speculators win as often as they lose.[25] But corporate and municipal treasurers would do better to trust market prices rather than incur large risks in the quest for trading profits.

Lesson 3: Read the Entrails

If the market is efficient, prices impound all available information. Therefore, if we can only learn to read the entrails, security prices can tell us a lot about the future. For example, in Chapter 15 we will show how information in a company's financial statements can help the financial manager to estimate the probability of bankruptcy. But the market's assessment of the company's securities can also provide important information about the firm's prospects. Thus, if the company's bonds are offering a much higher yield than the average, you can deduce that the firm is probably in trouble.

Here is another example: Suppose that investors are confident that interest rates are set to rise over the next year. In that case, they will prefer to wait before they make long-term loans, and any firm that wants to borrow long-term money today will have to offer the inducement of a higher rate of interest. In other words, the long-term rate of interest will have to be higher than the one-year rate. Differences between the long-term interest rate and the short-term rate tell you something about what investors expect to happen to short-term rates in the future.[26]

Example—Viacom's Bid for Paramount   In September 1993 the entertainment company, Viacom, announced an $8.2 billion friendly bid for Paramount. The following week QVC countered with its own bid for Paramount, worth $9.5 billion. These were the opening salvos in a bidding war that was to continue for five months before Viacom emerged the winner.

But what did investors think of the acquisition? When Viacom announced its bid, its shares fell by 6.8 percent, while the Standard and Poor's Index fell by .4 percent. On past evidence a change in the market index affected Viacom's shares as follows:

$$\text{Expected return on Viacom} = \alpha + \beta \times \text{ return on market}$$

$$= .01 + .78 \times \text{ return on market}$$

---

[24]We don't know why Robert Citron gambled with Orange County's money, but he was under pressure to make up for a shortfall in tax revenues.

[25]Watch out for the speculators who are making very large profits; they are almost certainly taking correspondingly large risks.

[26]We will discuss the relationship between short-term and long-term interest rates in Chapter 9. Notice, however, that in an efficient market the difference between the prices of *any* short-term and long-term contracts always says something about how participants expect prices to move.

The alpha (α) of .01 tells us that, when the market was unchanged, Viacom's shares rose on average by .01 percent a day.[27] The beta (β) of .78 indicates that each 1 percent rise in the market index added an additional .78 percent to Viacom's return. Since the market fell .4 percent at the time of Viacom's bid, we would normally expect the share price to change by $.01 + .78 \times (-.4) = -.3$ percent.[28] So Viacom's shares provided an abnormal return of –6.5 percent:

$$\text{Abnormal return} = \text{actual return} - \text{expected return} = (-6.8) - (-.3) = -6.5\%$$

The total value of Viacom's shares just before the bid was about $7.9 billion. So the abnormal fall in the value of the firm's shares was $.065 \times 7.9$ billion, or $515 million.

To see the performance of Viacom stock over a somewhat longer period, we can accumulate the daily abnormal returns. Thus, if Viacom stock offered an abnormal return of +5 percent on one day and +6 percent on the next, its *cumulative* abnormal return over the two days would be $1.05 \times 1.06 - 1 = .113$ or 11.3 percent. Figure 4.10 shows the cumulative abnormal performance of Viacom's stock both before and after its bid for Paramount. You can see that the abnormal return from just before the initial bid until the final acquisition was about –50 percent. This was equivalent to a $4 billion fall in the value of Viacom's stock. As the stock price fell away, Paramount's investors became less enamored with the Viacom stock that they were offered. To win the bidding war Viacom had to increase the amount of cash on offer and to guarantee to repurchase the stock from Paramount's shareholders if it fell below a specified price.

Notice two things about our example. First, the market's unenthusiastic response to the bid should have suggested to management that investors regarded the proposed acquisition as a poor deal for Viacom. Figure 4.10 shows that, as Viacom battled for control of Paramount, the stock continued to decline and the message for management became correspondingly louder and clearer. Of course, Viacom's managers may have had other information which investors lacked and may have correctly decided to go ahead with the bid anyway. Our point is simply that Viacom's stock price provided a potentially valuable summary of investor opinion.

Second, our example illustrates a very handy way to calculate the abnormal return on a stock. You will come across many instances in the following chapters when we ask how a particular type of financing decision affects the value of the firm. To answer this question, we will focus on that part of the stock's return that is not due to marketwide fluctuations. We refer to this as the abnormal return on the firm's stock. Remember

- Abnormal return = actual return – expected return given the return on the market.

---

[27]It is important when estimating α and β that you choose a period in which you believe that the stock behaved normally. If its performance was abnormal, then estimates of α and β cannot be used to measure the returns that investors expected. As a precaution, ask yourself whether your estimates of expected returns *look* sensible.

[28]You will generally get a fairly similar answer if you use the capital asset pricing model to measure the abnormal returns. This states that the expected return for Viacom stock is

$$\text{Expected return} = r_f + \beta(r_m - r_f)$$

The market return (r_m) was –.4 percent. The interest rate (r_f) was about 3 percent a year, or .01 percent a day. Therefore, the abnormal return for Viacom stock remains at –6.5 percent:

$$\text{Expected return} = .01 + .78(-.4 - .01) = -.3\%$$

$$\text{Abnormal return} = \text{actual return} - \text{expected return} = -6.8 - (-.3) = -6.5\%$$

Figure 4.10

Cumulative abnormal returns from Viacom stock around the time of its takeover battle for Paramount. The negative abnormal return following Viacom's bid suggests that investors regarded the acquisition as a negative-NPV investment.

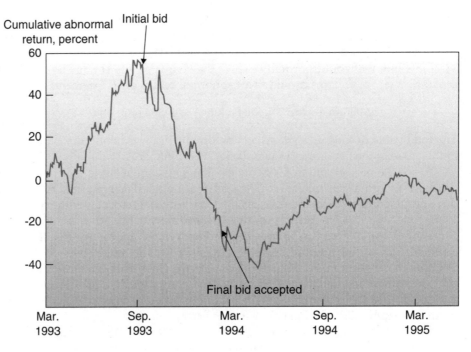

- To measure expected return, we can look at how the firm's stock has responded in the past to market fluctuations.[29]

Lesson 4: There Are No Financial Illusions

In an efficient market there are no financial illusions. Investors are unromantically concerned with the firm's cash flows and the portion of those cash flows to which they are entitled.

Example—Stock Dividends and Splits   We can illustrate our fourth lesson by looking at the effect of stock dividends and splits. Every year hundreds of companies increase the number of shares outstanding either by subdividing the existing shares or by distributing more shares as dividends. This does not affect the company's future cash flows or the proportion of these cash flows attributable to each shareholder. For example, suppose the stock of Chaste Manhattan is selling for $210 per share. A 3-for-1 stock split would replace each outstanding share with three new shares.[30] Chaste would probably arrange this by printing two new shares for each original share and distributing the new shares to its stockholders as a "free gift." After the split we would expect each

---

[29]A little knowledge is a dangerous thing: If you want a good estimate of the abnormal return, you need to know more about how to calculate it than the brief overview that we provide. We suggest that you consult S. J. Brown and J. B. Warner, "Measuring Security Price Performance," *Journal of Financial Economics* 8 (1980), pp. 205–258.

[30]There are some confusing transatlantic differences in terminology. In the United Kingdom such increases usually take the form of a "scrip issue." A 2-for-1 scrip issue (i.e., two new shares in addition to one old) is equivalent to a 3-for-1 stock split.

Figure 4.11

Cumulative abnormal returns at the time of a stock split. (Returns are adjusted for the increase in the number of shares.) Notice the rise before the split and the absence of abnormal changes after the split.

Source: E. Fama, L. Fisher, M. Jensen, and R. Roll, "The Adjustment of Stock Prices to New Information," *International Economic Review* 10 (February 1969), fig. 2b, p. 13.

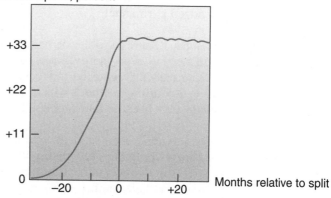

Change in stock price, percent

Months relative to split

share to sell for 210/3 = $70. Dividends per share, earnings per share, and all other per-share variables would be one-third their previous levels.

Figure 4.11 summarizes the results of a classic study of stock splits during the years 1926 to 1960.[31] It shows the cumulative abnormal performance of stocks around the time of the split after adjustment for the increase in the number of shares.[32] Notice the rise in price before the split. The announcement of the split would have occurred in the last month or two of this period. That means the decision to split is both the consequence of a rise in price and the cause of a further rise. It looks as if shareholders are not as hard-headed as we have been making out. They do seem to care about the form as well as the substance. However, during the subsequent year two-thirds of the splitting companies announced above-average increases in cash dividends. Usually such an announcement would cause an unusual rise in the stock price, but in the case of the splitting companies there was no such occurrence at any time after the split. The apparent explanation is that the split was accompanied by an explicit or implicit promise of a dividend increase and the rise in price at the time of the split had nothing to do with a predilection for splits as such but with the information that it was thought to convey.

This behavior does not imply that investors like the dividend increases for their own sake, for companies that split their stocks appear to be unusually successful in other ways. For example, Asquith, Healy, and Palepu found that stock splits are frequently preceded by sharp increases in earnings.[33] Such earnings increases are very often transitory, and investors rightly regard them

[31]See E. F. Fama, L. Fisher, M. Jensen, and R. Roll, "The Adjustment of Stock Prices to New Information," *International Economic Review,* 10 (February 1969), pp. 1–21. Later researchers have discovered that shareholders make abnormal gains both when the split or stock dividend is announced and when it takes place. Nobody has offered a convincing explanation for the latter phenomenon. See, for example, M. S. Grinblatt, R. W. Masulis, and S. Titman, "The Valuation Effects of Stock Splits and Stock Dividends," *Journal of Financial Economics* 13 (December 1984), pp. 461–490.

[32]By this we mean that the study looked at the change in the shareholders' wealth. A decline in the price of Chaste Manhattan stock from $210 to $70 at the time of the split would not affect shareholders' wealth. The authors used the same technique to calculate the abnormal returns that we used when looking at Viacom.

[33]See P. Asquith, P. Healy, and K. Palepu, "Earnings and Stock Splits," *Accounting Review* 64 (July 1989), pp. 387–403.

with suspicion. However, the stock split appears to provide investors with an assurance that in this case the rise in earnings is indeed permanent.

Example—Accounting Changes   There are other occasions on which managers seem to assume that investors suffer from financial illusion. For example, some firms devote considerable ingenuity to the task of manipulating earnings reported to stockholders. This is done by "creative accounting," that is, by choosing accounting methods which stabilize and increase reported earnings. Presumably firms go to this trouble because management believes that stockholders take the figures at face value.[34]

One way that companies can affect their reported earnings is through the way that they cost the goods taken out of inventory. Companies can choose between two methods. Under the FIFO (first-in, first-out) method, the firm deducts the cost of the first goods to have been placed in inventory. Under the LIFO (last-in, last-out) method companies deduct the cost of the latest goods to arrive in the warehouse. When inflation is high, the cost of the goods that were bought first is likely to be lower than the cost of those that were bought last. So earnings calculated under FIFO appear higher than those calculated under LIFO.

Now, if it were just a matter of presentation, there would be no harm in switching from LIFO to FIFO. But the IRS insists that the same method that is used to report to shareholders also be used to calculate the firm's taxes. So the lower immediate tax payments from using the LIFO method also bring lower apparent earnings.

If markets are efficient, investors should welcome a change to LIFO accounting, even though it reduces earnings. Biddle and Lindahl, who studied the matter, concluded that this is exactly what happens, so that the move to LIFO is associated with an abnormal rise in the stock price.[35] It seems that shareholders look behind the figures and focus on the amount of the tax savings.

Lesson 5: The Do-It-Yourself Alternative

In an efficient market investors will not pay others for what they can do equally well themselves. As we shall see, many of the controversies in corporate financing center on how well individuals can replicate corporate financial decisions. For example, companies often justify mergers on the grounds that they produce a more diversified and hence more stable firm. But if investors can hold the stocks of both companies why should they thank the companies for diversifying? It is much easier and cheaper for them to diversify than it is for the firm.

The financial manager needs to ask the same question when considering whether it is better to issue debt or common stock. If the firm issues debt, it will create financial leverage. As a result, the stock will be more risky and it will offer a higher expected return. But stockholders can obtain financial leverage without the firm's issuing debt; they can borrow on their own accounts. The problem for the financial manager is, therefore, to decide whether the company can issue debt more cheaply than the individual shareholder.

---

[34]For a discussion of the evidence that investors are not fooled by earnings manipulation, see R. Watts, "Does It Pay to Manipulate EPS?" in J. M. Stern and D. H. Chew, Jr. (eds.), *The Revolution in Corporate Finance*, Oxford, Basil Blackwell, 1986.

[35]G. C. Biddle and F. W. Lindahl, "Stock Price Reactions to LIFO Adoptions: The Association between Excess Returns and LIFO Tax Savings," *Journal of Accounting Research* 20 (Autumn 1982, Part 2), pp. 551–588.

Lesson 6: Seen One Stock, Seen Them All

The elasticity of demand for any article measures the percentage change in the quantity demanded for each percentage addition to the price. If the article has close substitutes, the elasticity will be strongly negative; if not, it will be near zero. For example, coffee, which is a staple commodity, has a demand elasticity of about –.2. This means that a 5 percent increase in the price of coffee changes sales by $-.2 \times .05 = -.01$; in other words, it reduces demand by only 1 percent. Consumers are likely to regard different *brands* of coffee as much closer substitutes for each other. Therefore, the demand elasticity for a particular brand could be in the region of, say, –2.0. A 5 percent increase in the price of Maxwell House relative to that of Folgers would in this case reduce demand by 10 percent.

Investors don't buy a stock for its unique qualities; they buy it because it offers the prospect of a fair return for its risk. This means that stocks should be like *very* similar brands of coffee, almost perfect substitutes. Therefore, the demand for a company's stock should be highly elastic. If its prospective return is too low relative to its risk, *nobody* will want to hold that stock. If the reverse is true, *everybody* will scramble to buy.

Suppose that you want to sell a large block of stock. Since demand is elastic, you naturally conclude that you need only to cut the offering price very slightly to sell your stock. Unfortunately, that doesn't necessarily follow. When you come to sell your stock, other investors may suspect that you want to get rid of it because you know something they don't. Therefore, they will revise their assessment of the stock's value downward. Demand is still elastic, but the whole demand curve moves down. Elastic demand does not imply that stock prices never change when a large sale or purchase occurs; it *does* imply that you can sell large blocks of stock at close to the market price *as long as you can convince other investors that you have no private information*.

Here is one case that supports this view: In June 1977 the Bank of England offered its holding of BP shares for sale at 845 pence each. The bank owned nearly 67 million shares of BP, so the total value of the holding was £564 million, or about $970 million. It was a huge sum to ask the public to find.

Anyone who wished to apply for BP stock had nearly two weeks within which to do so. Just before the Bank's announcement the price of BP stock was 912 pence. Over the next two weeks the price drifted down to 898 pence, largely in line with the British equity market. Therefore, by the final application date, the discount being offered by the Bank was only 6 percent. In return for this discount, any applicant had to raise the necessary cash, taking the risk that the price of BP would decline before the result of the application was known, and had to pass over to the Bank of England the next dividend on BP.

If Maxwell House coffee is offered at a discount of 6 percent, the demand is unlikely to be overwhelming. But the discount on BP stock was enough to bring in applications for $4.6 billion worth of stock, 4.7 times the amount on offer.

We admit that this case was unusual in some respects, but an important study by Myron Scholes of a large sample of secondary offerings confirmed the ability of the market to absorb blocks of stock. The average effect of the offerings was a slight reduction in the stock price, but the decline was almost independent of the amount offered. Scholes's estimate of the demand elasticity for a company's stock was –3,000. Of course, this figure was not meant to be precise, and some researchers have argued that demand is not as elastic as Scholes's study suggests.[36] However, there

---

[36]For example, see W. H. Mikkelson and M. M. Partch, "Stock Price Effects and Costs of Secondary Distributions," *Journal of Financial Economics* 14 (June 1985), pp. 165–194.

seems to be widespread agreement with the general point that you can sell large quantities of stock at close to the market price as long as other investors do not deduce that you have some private information.

Here again we encounter an apparent contradiction with practice. Many corporations seem to believe not only that the demand elasticity is low but also that it varies with the stock price, so that when the price is relatively low, new stock can be sold only at a substantial discount. State and federal regulatory commissions, which set the prices charged by local telephone companies, electric companies, and other utilities, have sometimes allowed significantly higher earnings to compensate the firm for price "pressure." This pressure is the decline in the firm's stock price that is supposed to occur when new shares are offered to investors. Yet Paul Asquith and David Mullins, who searched for evidence of pressure, found that new stock issues by utilities drove down their stock prices on average by only .9 percent.[37] We will come back to the subject of pressure when we discuss stock issues in Chapter 3.

SUMMARY

The patron saint of the Bolsa (stock exchange) in Barcelona, Spain, is Nuestra Señora de la Esperanza—our Lady of Hope. She is the perfect patroness, for we all hope for superior returns when we invest. But competition between investors will tend to produce an efficient market. In such a market, prices will rapidly impound any new information, and it will be difficult to make consistently superior returns. We may indeed hope, but all we can rationally *expect* in an efficient market is a return just sufficient to compensate us for the time value of money and for the risks we bear.

The efficient-market hypothesis comes in three different flavors. The weak form of the hypothesis states that prices efficiently reflect all the information in the past series of stock prices. In this case it is impossible to earn superior returns simply by looking for patterns in stock prices; in other words, price changes are random. The semistrong form of the hypothesis states that prices reflect all published information. That means it is impossible to make consistently superior returns just by reading the newspaper, looking at the company's annual accounts, and so on. The strong form of the hypothesis states that stock prices effectively impound all available information. It tells us that superior information is hard to find because in pursuing it you are in competition with thousands, perhaps millions, of active, intelligent, and greedy investors. The best you can do in this case is to assume that securities are fairly priced and to hope that one day Nuestra Señora will reward your humility.

While there remain plenty of unsolved puzzles, there seems to be widespread agreement that consistently superior returns are hard to attain. Thirty years ago any suggestion that security investment is a fair game was generally regarded as bizarre. Today it is not only widely discussed in business schools but also permeates investment practice and government policy toward the securities markets.

For the corporate treasurer who is concerned with issuing or purchasing securities, the efficient-market theory has obvious implications. In one sense, however, it raises more questions than it answers. The existence of efficient markets does not mean that the financial manager can let

---

[37]See P. Asquith and D. W. Mullins, "Equity Issues and Offering Dilution," *Journal of Financial Economics* 15 (January–February 1986), pp. 61–89.

financing take care of itself. It provides only a starting point for analysis. It is time now to answer the question: Does financial policy matter? That is the subject of the next three chapters.

Further Reading

The classic review articles on market efficiency are:

E. F. Fama: "Efficient Capital Markets: A Review of Theory and Empirical Work," *Journal of Finance*, 25:383–417 (May 1970).

E. F. Fama: "Efficient Capital Markets: II," *Journal of Finance*, 46:1575–1617 (December 1991).

For evidence on possible exceptions to the efficient-market theory, we suggest:

G. Hawawini and D. B. Keim: "On the Predictability of Common Stock Returns: World-Wide Evidence," in R. A. Jarrow, V. Maksimovic, and W. T. Ziemba (eds.), *Finance*, North-Holland, Amsterdam, Netherlands, 1994.

Martin Gruber's Presidential Address to the American Finance Association is an interesting overview of the performance of mutual fund managers.

M. Gruber, "Another Puzzle: The Growth in Actively Managed Mutual Funds, " *Journal of Finance*, 51:783–810 (July 1996).

A useful collection of papers on behavioral explanations for market anomalies is provided in Richard Thaler's book of readings. Eugene Fama's paper offers a more skeptical view of these behavioral theories.

R. H. Thaler (ed.): *Advances in Behavioral Finance*, Russell Sage Foundation, New York, 1993.

E. F. Fama: "Market Efficiency, Long-Term Returns, and Behavioral Finance," *Journal of Financial Economics*, 49:283–306 (September 1998).

The following book contains an interesting collection of articles on the crash of 1987:

R. W. Kamphuis, Jr., et al. (eds.): *Black Monday and the Future of Financial Markets*, Dow-Jones Irwin, Inc., Homewood, IL, 1989.

PART TWO

DIVIDEND POLICY AND CAPITAL STRUCTURE

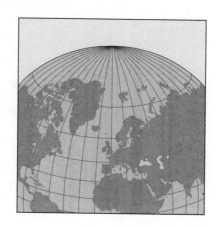

DOES DEBT POLICY MATTER?

A firm's basic resource is the stream of cash flows produced by its assets. When the firm is financed entirely by common stock, all those cash flows belong to the stockholders. When it issues both debt and equity securities, it undertakes to split up the cash flows into two streams, a relatively safe stream that goes to the debtholders and a more risky one that goes to the stockholders.

The firm's mix of different securities is known as its **capital structure.** The choice of capital structure is fundamentally a marketing problem. The firm can issue dozens of distinct securities in countless combinations, but it attempts to find the particular combination that maximizes its overall market value.

Are these attempts worthwhile? We must consider the possibility that *no* combination has any greater appeal than any other. Perhaps the really important decisions concern the company's assets, and decisions about capital structure are mere details—matters to be attended to but not worried about.

Modigliani and Miller (MM) showed that financing decisions don't matter in perfect markets.[1] Their famous "proposition I" states that a firm cannot change the *total* value of its securities just by splitting its cash flows into different streams: The firm's value is determined by its real assets, not by the securities it issues. Thus capital structure is irrelevant as long as the firm's investment decisions are taken as given.

MM's proposition I allows complete separation of investment and financing decisions. It implies that any firm could evaluate investment projects without worrying about where the

---

[1]F. Modigliani and M. H. Miller, "The Cost of Capital, Corporation Finance and the Theory of Investment," *American Economic Review* 48 (June 1958), pp. 261–297. MM's basic argument was anticipated in 1938 by J. B. Williams and to some extent by David Durand. See J. B. Williams, *The Theory of Investment Value,* Harvard University Press, Cambridge, MA, 1938; and D. Durand, "Cost of Debt and Equity Funds for Business: Trends and Problems of Measurement," in *Conference on Research in Business Finance,* National Bureau of Economic Research, New York, 1952.

money for capital expenditures comes from. Managers could assume all-equity financing, for example, to simplify matters. If proposition I holds, that is exactly the right approach.

We believe that in practice capital structure *does* matter, but we nevertheless devote all of this chapter to MM's argument. If you don't fully understand the conditions under which MM's theory holds, you won't fully understand why one capital structure is better than another. The financial manager needs to know what kinds of market imperfection to look for.

In Chapter 6 we will undertake a detailed analysis of the imperfections that are most likely to make a difference, including taxes, the costs of bankruptcy, and the costs of writing and enforcing complicated debt contracts. We will also argue that it is naive to suppose that investment and financing decisions can be completely separated.

But in this chapter we isolate the decision about capital structure by holding the decision about investment fixed. We also assume that dividend policy is irrelevant.

THE EFFECT OF LEVERAGE IN A COMPETITIVE TAX-FREE ECONOMY

We have referred to the firm's choice of capital structure as a *marketing problem*. The financial manager's problem is to find the combination of securities that has the greatest overall appeal to investors—the combination that maximizes the market value of the firm. Before tackling this problem, we ought to make sure that a policy which maximizes firm value also maximizes the wealth of the shareholders.

Let D and E denote the market values of the outstanding debt and equity of the Wapshot Mining Company. Wapshot's 1,000 shares sell for $50 apiece. Thus

$$E = 1,000 \times 50 = \$50,000$$

Wapshot has also borrowed $25,000, and so V, the aggregate market value of all Wapshot's outstanding securities, is

$$V = D + E = \$75,000$$

Wapshot's stock is known as *levered equity*. Its stockholders face the benefits and costs of **financial leverage,** or *gearing*. Suppose that Wapshot "levers up" still further by borrowing an additional $10,000 and paying the proceeds out to shareholders as a special dividend of $10 per share. This substitutes debt for equity capital with no impact on Wapshot's assets.

What will Wapshot's equity be worth after the special dividend is paid? We have two unknowns, E and V:

Old debt	$25,000 }	$35,000 = D
New debt	$10,000 }	
Equity		? = E
Firm value		? = V

If V is $75,000 as before, then E must be $V - D = 75,000 - 35,000 = \$40,000$. Stockholders have suffered a capital loss which exactly offsets the $10,000 special dividend. But if V *increases* to, say, $80,000 as a result of the change in capital structure, then $E = \$45,000$ and the stockholders are $5,000 ahead. In general, any increase or decrease in V caused by a shift in capital structure accrues to the firm's stockholders. We conclude that a policy which maximizes the market value of the firm is also best for the firm's stockholders.

This conclusion rests on two important assumptions: first, that Wapshot can ignore dividend policy and, second, that after the change in capital structure the old and new debt is *worth* $35,000.

Dividend policy may or may not be relevant, but there is no need to repeat the discussion of Chapter 7. We need only note that shifts in capital structure sometimes force important decisions about dividend policy. Perhaps Wapshot's cash dividend has costs or benefits which should be considered in addition to any benefits achieved by its increased financial leverage.

Our second assumption that old and new debt ends up worth $35,000 seems innocuous. But it could be wrong. Perhaps the new borrowing has increased the risk of the old bonds. If the holders of old bonds cannot demand a higher rate of interest to compensate for the increased risk, the value of their investment is reduced. In this case Wapshot's stockholders gain at the expense of the holders of old bonds even though the overall value of the debt and equity is unchanged.

But this anticipates issues better left to Chapter 6. In this chapter we will assume that any issue of debt has no effect on the market value of existing debt.[2]

Enter Modigliani and Miller

Let us accept that the financial manager would like to find the combination of securities that maximizes the value of the firm. How is this done? MM's answer is that the financial manager should stop worrying: in a perfect market any combination of securities is as good as another. The value of the firm is unaffected by its choice of capital structure.

You can see this by imagining two firms that generate the same stream of operating income and differ only in their capital structure. Firm U is unlevered. Therefore the total value of its equity E_U is the same as the total value of the firm V_U. Firm, L, on the other hand, is levered. The value of its stock is, therefore, equal to the value of the firm less the value of the debt: $E_L = V_L - D_L$.

Now think which of these firms you would prefer to invest in. If you don't want to take much risk, you can buy common stock in the unlevered firm U. For example, if you buy 1 percent of firm U's shares, your investment is $.01V_U$ and you are entitled to 1 percent of the gross profits:

DOLLAR INVESTMENT	DOLLAR RETURN
$.01V_U$	.01 Profits

Now compare this with an alternative strategy. This is to purchase the same fraction of both the debt and the equity of firm L. Your investment and return would then be as follows:

---

[2]See E. F. Fama, "The Effects of a Firm's Investment and Financing Decisions," *American Economic Review,* 68 (June 1978), pp. 272–284, for a rigorous analysis of the conditions under which a policy of maximizing the value of the firm is also best for the stockholders.

	DOLLAR INVESTMENT	DOLLAR RETURN
Debt	$.01D_L$	$.01$ Interest
Equity	$.01E_L$	$.01$ (Profits − interest)
Total	$.01(D_L + E_L)$	$.01$ Profits
	$= .01V_L$	

Both strategies offer the same payoff: 1 percent of the firm's profits. In well-functioning markets two investments that offer the same payoff must have the same cost. Therefore $.01V_U$ must equal $.01V_L$: the value of the unlevered firm must equal the value of the levered firm.

Suppose that you are willing to run a little more risk. You decide to buy 1 percent of the outstanding shares in the *levered* firm. Your investment and return are now as follows:

DOLLAR INVESTMENT	DOLLAR RETURN
$.01E_L$	$.01$ (Profits − interest)
$= .01(V_L - D_L)$	

But there is an alternative strategy. This is to borrow $.01D_L$ on your own account and purchase 1 percent of the stock of the *unlevered* firm. In this case, your borrowing gives you an immediate cash *inflow* of $.01D_L$, but you have to pay interest on your loan equal to 1 percent of the interest that is paid by firm L. Your total investment and return are, therefore, as follows:

	DOLLAR INVESTMENT	DOLLAR RETURN
Borrowing	$-.01D_L$	$-.01$ Interest
Equity	$.01V_U$	$.01$ Profits
Total	$.01(V_U - D_L)$	$.01$ (Profits − interest)

Again both strategies offer the same payoff: 1 percent of profits after interest. Therefore, both investments must have the same cost. The quantity $.01(V_U - D_L)$ must equal $.01(V_L - D_L)$ and V_U must equal V_L.

It does not matter whether the world is full of risk-averse chickens or venturesome lions. All would agree that the value of the unlevered firm U must be equal to the value of the levered firm L. As long as investors can borrow or lend on their own account on the same terms as the firm, they can "undo" the effect of any changes in the firm's capital structure. This is the basis for MM's famous proposition I: "The market value of any firm is independent of its capital structure."

The Law of the Conservation of Value

MM's argument that debt policy is irrelevant is an application of an astonishingly simple idea. If we have two streams of cash flow, A and B, then the present value of A + B is equal to the present value of A plus the present value of B. We met this principle of *value additivity* in our discussion of capital budgeting, where we saw that in perfect capital markets the present value of two assets combined is equal to the sum of their present values considered separately.

In the present context we are not combining assets but splitting them up. But value additivity works just as well in reverse. We can slice a cash flow into as many parts as we like; the values of the parts will always sum back to the value of the unsliced stream. (Of course, we have to make sure that none of the stream is lost in the slicing. We cannot say, "The value of a pie is independent of how it is sliced," if the slicer is also a nibbler.)

This is really a *law of conservation of value*. The value of an asset is preserved regardless of the nature of the claims against it. Thus proposition I: Firm value is determined on the *left-hand* side of the balance sheet by real assets—not by the proportions of debt and equity securities issued by the firm.

The simplest ideas often have the widest application. For example, we could apply the law of conservation of value to the choice between issuing preferred stock, common stock, or some combination. The law implies that the choice is irrelevant, assuming perfect capital markets and providing that the choice does not affect the firm's investment, borrowing, and operating policies. If the total value of the equity "pie" (preferred and common combined) is fixed, the firm's owners (its common stockholders) do not care how this pie is sliced.

The law also applies to the *mix* of debt securities issued by the firm. The choices of long-term versus short-term, secured versus unsecured, senior versus subordinated, and convertible versus nonconvertible debt all should have no effect on the overall value of the firm.

Combining assets and splitting them up will not affect values as long as they do not affect an investor's choice. When we showed that capital structure does not affect choice, we implicitly assumed that both companies and individuals can borrow and lend at the same risk-free rate of interest. As long as this is so, individuals can undo the effect of any changes in the firm's capital structure.

In practice corporate debt is not risk-free and firms cannot escape with rates of interest appropriate to a government security. Some people's initial reaction is that this alone invalidates MM's proposition. It is a natural mistake, but capital structure can be irrelevant even when debt is risky.

If a company borrows money, it does not *guarantee* repayment: It repays the debt in full only if its assets are worth more than the debt obligation. The shareholders in the company, therefore, have limited liability.

Many individuals would like to borrow with limited liability. They might, therefore, be prepared to pay a small premium for levered shares *if the supply of levered shares was insufficient to meet their needs.*[3] But there are literally thousands of common stocks of companies that borrow. Therefore it is unlikely that an issue of debt would induce them to pay a premium for *your* shares.[4]

An Example of Proposition I

Macbeth Spot Removers is reviewing its capital structure. Table 5.1 shows its current position. The company has no leverage and all the operating income is paid as dividends to the common stock-

---

[3]Of course, individuals could *create* limited liability if they chose. In other words, the lender could agree that borrowers need repay their debt in full only if the assets of company X are worth more than a certain amount. Presumably individuals don't enter into such arrangements because they can obtain limited liability more simply by investing in the stocks of levered companies.

[4]Capital structure is also irrelevant if each investor holds a fully diversified portfolio. In that case he or she owns *all* the risky securities offered by a company (both debt and equity). But anybody who owns *all* the risky securities doesn't care about how the cash flows are divided between different securities.

TABLE 5.1

Macbeth Spot Removers is entirely equity-financed. Although it *expects* to have an income of $1,500 a year in perpetuity, this income is not certain. This table shows the return to the stockholder under different assumptions about operating income. We assume no taxes.

DATA				
Number of shares	1,000			
Price per share	$10			
Market value of shares	$10,000			
			OUTCOMES	
Operating income ($)	500	1,000	**1,500**	2,000
Earnings per share ($)	.50	1.00	**1.50**	2.00
Return on shares (%)	5	10	**15**	20
			Expected outcome	

holders (we assume still that there are no taxes). The expected earnings and dividends per share are $1.50, but this figure is by no means certain—it could turn out to be more or less than $1.50. The price of each share is $10. Since the firm expects to produce a level stream of earnings in perpetuity, the expected return on the share is equal to the earnings–price ratio, 1.50/10.00 = .15, or 15 percent.

Ms. Macbeth, the firm's president, has come to the conclusion that shareholders would be better off if the company had equal proportions of debt and equity. She therefore proposes to issue $5,000 of debt at an interest rate of 10 percent and use the proceeds to repurchase 500 shares. To support her proposal, Ms. Macbeth has analyzed the situation under different assumptions about operating income. The results of her calculations are shown in Table 5.2.

In order to see more clearly how leverage would affect earnings per share, Ms. Macbeth has also produced Figure 5.1. The solid line shows how earnings per share would vary with operating income under the firm's current all-equity financing. It is, therefore, simply a plot of the data in Table 5.1. The dotted line shows how earnings per share would vary given equal proportions of debt and equity. It is, therefore, a plot of the data in Table 5.2.

Ms. Macbeth reasons as follows: "It is clear that the effect of leverage depends on the company's income. If income is greater than $1,000, the return to the equity holder is *increased* by leverage. If it is less than $1,000, the return is reduced by leverage. The return is unaffected when operating income is exactly $1,000. At this point the return on the market value of the assets is 10 percent, which is exactly equal to the interest rate on the debt. Our capital structure decision, therefore, boils down to what we think about income prospects. Since we expect operating income to be above the $1,000 break-even point, I believe we can best help our shareholders by going ahead with the $5,000 debt issue."

As financial manager of Macbeth Spot Removers, you reply as follows: "I agree that leverage will help the shareholder as long as our income is greater than $1,000. But your argument ignores

TABLE 5.2

Macbeth Spot Removers is wondering whether to issue $5,000 of debt at an interest rate of 10 percent and repurchase 500 shares. This table shows the return to the share-holder under different assumptions about operating income.

	DATA			
Number of shares	500			
Price per share	$10			
Market value of shares	$5,000			
Market value of debt	$5,000			
Interest at 10 percent	$500			

	OUTCOMES			
Operating income ($)	500	1,000	**1,500**	2,000
Interest ($)	500	500	**500**	500
Equity earnings ($)	0	500	**1,000**	1,500
Earnings per share ($)	0	1	**2**	3
Return on shares (%)	0	10	**20**	30
			Expected outcome	

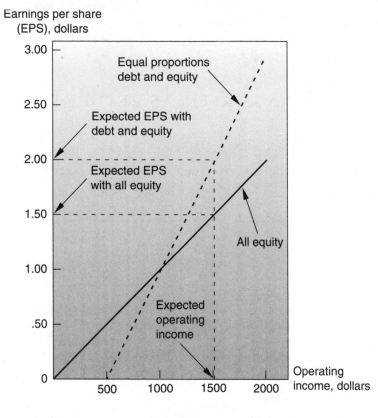

Figure 5.1

Borrowing increases Macbeth's EPS (earnings per share) when operating income is greater than $1,000 and reduces EPS when operating income is less than $1,000. Expected EPS rises from $1.50 to $2.

TABLE 5.3				

Individual investors can replicate Macbeth's leverage.

	OPERATING INCOME ($)			
	500	1,000	1,500	2,000
Earnings on two shares ($)	1	2	3	4
Less interest at 10% ($)	1	1	1	1
Net earnings on investment ($)	0	1	2	3
Return on $10 investment (%)	0	10	**20**	30
			Expected outcome	

the fact that Macbeth's shareholders have the alternative of borrowing on their own account. For example, suppose that an investor borrows $10 and then invests $20 in two unlevered Macbeth shares. This person has to put up only $10 of his or her own money. The payoff on the investment varies with Macbeth's operating income, as shown in Table 5.3. This is exactly the same set of payoffs as the investor would get by buying one share in the levered company. (Compare the last two lines of Tables 5.2 and 5.3.) Therefore a share in the levered company must also sell for $10. If Macbeth goes ahead and borrows, it will not allow investors to do anything that they could not do already, and so it will not increase value."

The argument that you are using is exactly the same as the one MM used to prove proposition I.

HOW LEVERAGE AFFECTS RETURNS

Implications of Proposition I

Consider now the implications of proposition I for the expected returns on Macbeth stock:

	CURRENT STRUCTURE: ALL EQUITY	PROPOSED STRUCTURE: EQUAL DEBT AND EQUITY
Expected earnings per share ($)	1.50	2.00
Price per share ($)	10	10
Expected return on share (%)	15	20

Leverage increases the expected stream of earnings per share but *not* the share price. The reason is that the change in the expected earnings stream is exactly offset by a change in the rate at which the earnings are capitalized. The expected return on the share (which for a perpetuity is equal to the earnings–price ratio) increases from 15 to 20 percent. We now show how this comes about.

The expected return on Macbeth's assets r_A is equal to the expected operating income divided by the total market value of the firm's securities:

$$\text{Expected return on assets} = r_A = \frac{\text{expected operating income}}{\text{market value of all securities}}$$

We have seen that in perfect capital markets the company's borrowing decision does not affect *either* the firm's operating income *or* the total market value of its securities. Therefore the borrowing decision also does not affect the expected return on the firm's assets r_A.

Suppose that an investor holds all of a company's debt and all of its equity. This investor would be entitled to all the firm's operating income; therefore, the expected return on the portfolio would be equal to r_A.

The expected return on a portfolio is equal to a weighted average of the expected returns on the individual holdings. Therefore the expected return on a portfolio consisting of *all* the firm's securities is

$$\begin{matrix} \text{Expected return} \\ \text{on assets} \end{matrix} = \left(\begin{matrix} \text{proportion} \\ \text{in debt} \end{matrix} \times \begin{matrix} \text{expected return} \\ \text{on debt} \end{matrix} \right) + \left(\begin{matrix} \text{proportion} \\ \text{in equity} \end{matrix} \times \begin{matrix} \text{expected return} \\ \text{on equity} \end{matrix} \right)$$

$$r_A = \left(\frac{D}{D+E} \times r_D \right) + \left(\frac{E}{D+E} \times r_E \right)$$

We can rearrange this equation to obtain an expression for r_E, the expected return on the equity of a levered firm:

$$\begin{matrix} \text{Expected return} \\ \text{on equity} \end{matrix} = \begin{matrix} \text{expected return} \\ \text{on assets} \end{matrix} + \begin{matrix} \text{debt–equity} \\ \text{ratio} \end{matrix} \times \left(\begin{matrix} \text{expected return} \\ \text{on assets} \end{matrix} - \begin{matrix} \text{expected return} \\ \text{on debt} \end{matrix} \right)$$

$$r_E = r_A + \frac{D}{E}(r_A - r_D)$$

Proposition II

This is MM's proposition II: The expected rate of return on the common stock of a levered firm increases in proportion to the debt–equity ratio (D/E), expressed in market values; the rate of increase depends on the spread between r_A, the expected rate of return on a portfolio of all the firm's securities, and r_D, the expected return on the debt. Note that $r_E = r_A$ if the firm has no debt.

We can check out this formula for Macbeth Spot Removers. Before the decision to borrow

$$r_E = r_A = \frac{\text{expected operating income}}{\text{market value of all securities}}$$

$$= \frac{1{,}500}{10{,}000} = .15, \text{ or } 15\%$$

If the firm goes ahead with its plan to borrow, the expected return on assets r_A is still 15 percent. The expected return on equity is

$$r_E = r_A + \frac{D}{E}(r_A - r_D)$$

$$= .15 + \frac{5,000}{5,000}(.15 - .10)$$

$$= .20, \text{ or } 20\%$$

The general implications of MM's proposition II are shown in Figure 5.2. The figure assumes that the firm's bonds are essentially risk-free at low debt levels. Thus r_D is independent of D/E, and r_E increases linearly as D/E increases. As the firm borrows more, the risk of default increases and the firm is required to pay higher rates of interest. Proposition II predicts that when this occurs the rate of increase in r_E slows down. This is also shown in Figure 5.2. The more debt the firm has, the less sensitive r_E is to further borrowing.

Why does the slope of the r_E line in Figure 5.2 taper off as D/E increases? Essentially because holders of risky debt bear some of the firm's business risk. As the firm borrows more, more of that risk is transferred from stockholders to bondholders.

The Risk-Return Trade-off

Proposition I says that financial leverage has no effect on shareholders' wealth. Proposition II says that the rate of return they can expect to receive on their shares increases as the firm's debt–equity ratio increases. How can shareholders be indifferent to increased leverage when it increases expected return? The answer is that any increase in expected return is exactly offset by an increase in risk and therefore in shareholders' *required* rate of return.

Look at what happens to the risk of Macbeth shares if it moves to equal debt–equity proportions. Table 5.4 shows how a shortfall in operating income affects the payoff to the shareholders.

Figure 5.2

MM's proposition II. The expected return on equity r_E increases linearly with the debt–equity ratio so long as debt is risk-free. But if leverage increases the risk of the debt, debtholders demand a higher return on the debt. This causes the rate of increase in r_E to slow down.

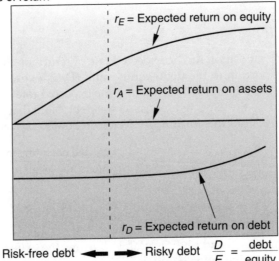

Rates of return

r_E = Expected return on equity

r_A = Expected return on assets

r_D = Expected return on debt

Risk-free debt ⬅➡ Risky debt $\frac{D}{E} = \frac{\text{debt}}{\text{equity}}$

		TABLE 5.4	

Leverage increases the risk of Macbeth shares.

		OPERATING INCOME	
		$500	$1,500
All equity:	Earnings per share ($)	.50	1.50
	Return on shares (%)	5	15
50 percent debt:	Earnings per share ($)	0	2
	Return on shares (%)	0	20

The debt–equity proportion does not affect the *dollar* risk borne by equityholders. Suppose operating income drops from $1,500 to $500. Under all-equity financing, equity earnings drop by $1 per share. There are 1,000 outstanding shares, and so *total* equity earnings fall by $1 × 1,000 = $1,000. With 50 percent debt, the same drop in operating income reduces earnings per share by $2. But there are only 500 shares outstanding, and so total equity income drops by $2 × 500 = $1,000, just as in the all-equity case.

However, the debt–equity choice does amplify the spread of *percentage* returns. If the firm is all-equity-financed, a decline of $1000 in the operating income reduces the return on the shares by 10 percent. If the firm issues risk-free debt with a fixed interest payment of $500 a year, then a decline of $1,000 in the operating income reduces the return on the shares by 20 percent. In other words, the effect of leverage is to double the amplitude of the swings in Macbeth's shares. Whatever the beta of the firm's shares before the refinancing, it would be twice as high afterward.

Just as the expected return on the firm's assets is a weighted average of the expected return on the individual securities, so likewise is the beta of the firm's assets a weighted average of the betas of the individual securities:

$$\frac{\text{Beta of}}{\text{assets}} = \left(\begin{matrix}\text{proportion}\\\text{of debt}\end{matrix} \times \begin{matrix}\text{beta of}\\\text{debt}\end{matrix}\right) + \left(\begin{matrix}\text{proportion}\\\text{of equity}\end{matrix} \times \begin{matrix}\text{beta of}\\\text{equity}\end{matrix}\right)$$

$$\beta_A = \left(\frac{D}{D + E} \times \beta_D\right) + \left(\frac{E}{D + E} \times \beta_E\right)$$

We can rearrange this equation also to give an expression for β_E, the beta of the equity of a levered firm:

$$\text{Beta of equity} = \frac{\text{beta of}}{\text{assets}} + \frac{\text{debt–equity}}{\text{ratio}} \times \left(\frac{\text{beta of}}{\text{assets}} - \frac{\text{beta of}}{\text{debt}}\right)$$

$$\beta_E = \beta_A + \frac{D}{E}(\beta_A - \beta_D)$$

Figure 5.3

If Macbeth is unlevered, the expected return on its equity equals the expected return on its assets. Leverage increases both the expected return on equity (r_E) and the risk of equity (β_E).

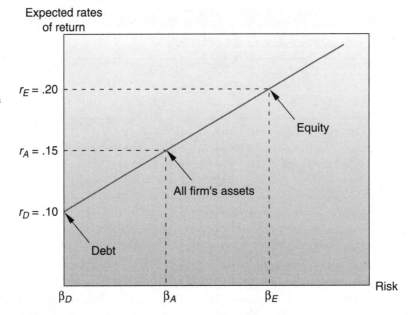

Now you can see why investors require higher returns on levered equity. The required return simply rises to match the increased risk.

In Figure 5.3, we have plotted the expected returns and the risk of Macbeth's securities, assuming that the interest on the debt is risk-free.[5]

THE TRADITIONAL POSITION

What did financial experts think about debt policy before MM? It is not easy to say because with hindsight we see that they did not think too clearly.[6] However, a "traditional" position has emerged in response to MM. In order to understand it, we have to discuss the **weighted-average cost of capital.**

The expected return on a portfolio of all the company's securities is often referred to as the weighted-average cost of capital:[7]

$$\text{Weighted-average cost of capital} = r_A = \left(\frac{D}{V} \times r_D\right) + \left(\frac{E}{V} \times r_E\right)$$

The weighted-average cost of capital is used in capital budgeting decisions to find the net present value of projects that would not change the business risk of the firm.

---

[5]In this case $\beta_D = 0$ and $\beta_E = \beta_A + (D/E)\beta_A$.

[6]Financial economists in 20 years may remark on Brealey and Myers's blind spots and clumsy reasoning. On the other hand, they may not remember us at all.

[7]Remember that in this chapter we ignore taxes. In Chapter 6, we shall see that the weighted-average cost of capital formula needs to be amended when debt interest can be deducted from taxable profits.

For example, suppose that a firm has $2 million of outstanding debt and 100,000 shares selling at $30 per share. Its current borrowing rate is 8 percent, and the financial manager thinks that the stock is priced to offer a 15 percent return. Therefore $r_D = .08$ and $r_E = .15$. (The hard part is estimating r_E, of course.) This is all we need to calculate the weighted-average cost of capital:

$$D = \$2 \text{ million}$$

$$E = 100{,}000 \text{ shares} \times \$30 \text{ per share} = \$3 \text{ million}$$

$$V = D + E = 2 + 3 = \$5 \text{ million}$$

$$\text{Weighted-average cost of capital} = \left(\frac{D}{V} \times r_D\right) + \left(\frac{E}{V} \times r_E\right)$$

$$= \left(\frac{2}{5} \times .08\right) + \left(\frac{3}{5} \times .15\right)$$

$$= .122, \text{ or } 12.2\%$$

Note that we are still assuming that proposition I holds. If it doesn't, we can't use this simple weighted average as the discount rate even for projects that do not change the firm's business "risk class." The weighted-average cost of capital is only a starting point for setting discount rates.

Two Warnings

Sometimes the objective in financing decisions is stated not as "maximize overall market value" but as "minimize the weighted-average cost of capital." If MM's proposition I holds, then these are equivalent objectives. If MM's proposition I does *not* hold, then the capital structure that maximizes the value of the firm also minimizes the weighted-average cost of capital, *provided* that operating income is independent of capital structure. Remember that the weighted-average cost of capital is the expected rate of return on the market value of all of the firm's securities. Anything that increases the value of the firm reduces the weighted-average cost of capital if operating income is constant. But if operating income is varying too, all bets are off.

In Chapter 6 we will show that financial leverage can affect operating income in several ways. Therefore maximizing the value of the firm is *not* always equivalent to minimizing the weighted-average cost of capital.

Warning 1   Shareholders want management to increase the firm's value. They are more interested in being rich than in owning a firm with a low weighted-average cost of capital.

Warning 2   Trying to minimize the weighted-average cost of capital seems to encourage logical short circuits like the following. Suppose that someone says, "Shareholders demand—and deserve—higher expected rates of return than bondholders do. Therefore debt is the cheaper capital source. We can reduce the weighted-average cost of capital by borrowing more." But this doesn't follow if the extra borrowing leads stockholders to demand a still higher expected rate of return. According to MM's proposition II the cost of equity capital r_E increases by just enough to keep the weighted-average cost of capital constant.

Figure 5.4

If the expected rate of return demanded by stockholders r_E is unaffected by financial leverage, then the weighted-average cost of capital r_A declines as the firm borrows more. At 100 percent debt r_A equals the borrowing rate r_D. Of course this is an absurd and totally unrealistic case.

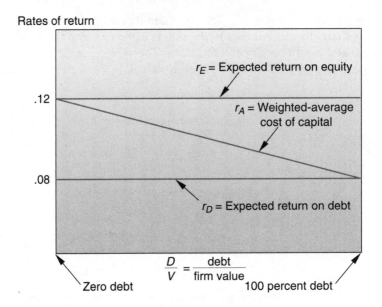

This is not the only logical short circuit you are likely to encounter. Try to explain what's wrong with the following arguments:

(a) "As the firm borrows more and debt becomes risky, both stockholders and bond-holders demand higher rates of return. Thus by reducing the debt ratio we can reduce both the cost of debt and the cost of equity, making everybody better off."

(b) "Moderate borrowing doesn't significantly affect the probability of financial distress or bankruptcy. Consequently moderate borrowing won't increase the expected rate of return demanded by stockholders."

Rates of Return on Levered Equity—The Traditional Position

You may ask why we have even mentioned the aim of minimizing the weighted-average cost of capital if it is often wrong or confusing. We had to because the traditionalists accept this objective and argue their case in terms of it.

The logical short circuit we just described rested on the assumption that r_E, the expected rate of return demanded by stockholders, does not rise as the firm borrows more. Suppose, just for the sake of argument, that this is true. Then r_A, the weighted-average cost of capital, must decline as the debt–equity ratio rises.

Take Figure 5.4, for example, which is drawn on the assumption that shareholders demand 12 percent no matter how much debt the firm has and that bondholders always want 8 percent. The weighted-average cost of capital starts at 12 percent and ends up at 8. Suppose that this firm's operating income is a level, perpetual stream of $100,000 a year. Then firm value starts at

$$V = \frac{100,000}{.12} = \$833,333$$

and ends up at

$$V = \frac{100,000}{.08} = \$1,250,000$$

The gain of \$416,667 falls into the stockholders' pockets.[8]

Of course this is absurd: A firm that reaches 100 percent debt *has to be bankrupt.* If there is *any* chance that the firm could remain solvent, then the equity retains some value, and the firm cannot be 100 percent debt-financed. (Remember that we are working with the *market* values of debt and equity.)

But if the firm is bankrupt and its original shares are worthless pieces of paper, then its *lenders are its new shareholders.* The firm is back to all-equity financing! We assumed that the original stockholders demanded 12 percent—why should the new ones demand any less? They have to bear all of the firm's business risk.[9]

The situation described in Figure 5.4 is just impossible.[10] However, it is possible to stake out a position somewhere *between* Figures 5.3 and 5.4. That is exactly what the traditionalists have done. Their hypothesis is shown in Figure 5.5. They hold that a moderate degree of financial leverage may increase the expected equity return r_E, although not to the degree predicted by MM's proposition II. But irresponsible firms that borrow *excessively* find r_E shooting up faster than MM predict. Consequently, the weighted-average cost of capital r_A declines at first, then rises. Its minimum point is the point of optimal capital structure. Remember that minimizing r_A is equivalent to maximizing overall firm value if, as the traditionalists assume, operating income is unaffected by borrowing.

Two arguments might be advanced in support of the traditional position. First, it could be that investors don't notice or appreciate the financial risk created by "moderate" borrowing, although they wake up when debt is "excessive." If so, investors in moderately leveraged firms may accept a lower rate of return than they really should.

That seems naive.[11] The second argument is better. It accepts MM's reasoning as applied to perfect capital markets but holds that actual markets are imperfect. Imperfections may allow firms that borrow to provide a valuable service for investors. If so, levered shares might trade at premium prices compared to their theoretical values in perfect markets.

Suppose that corporations can borrow more cheaply than individuals. Then it would pay investors who want to borrow to do so indirectly by holding the stock of levered firms. They would

---

[8]Note that Figure 5.4 relates r_E and r_D to D/V, the ratio of debt to firm value, rather than to the debt–equity ratio D/E. In this figure we wanted to show what happens when the firm is 100 percent debt-financed. At that point $E = 0$ and D/E is infinite.

[9]We ignore the costs, delays, and other complications of bankruptcy. They are discussed in Chapter 6.

[10]This case is often termed the *net-income* (NI) approach because investors are assumed to capitalize income *after* interest at the same rate regardless of financial leverage. In contrast, MM's approach is a net-operating-income (NOI) approach because the value of the firm is fundamentally determined by operating income, the total dollar return to *both* bondholders and stockholders. This distinction was emphasized by D. Durand in his important, pre-MM paper, "Cost of Debt and Equity Funds for Business: Trends and Problems of Measurement," in *Conference on Research in Business Finance,* National Bureau of Economic Research, New York, 1952.

[11]This first argument may reflect a confusion between financial risk and the risk of default. Default is not a serious threat when borrowing is moderate; stockholders worry about it only when the firm goes "too far." But stockholders bear financial risk—in the form of increased volatility of rate of return and higher beta—even when the chance of default is nil. We demonstrated this in Figure 5.3.

Figure 5.5

The dashed lines show MM's view of the effect of leverage on the expected return on equity r_E and the weighted-average cost of capital r_A. (See Figure 5.2.) The solid lines show the traditional view. Traditionalists say that borrowing at first increases r_E more slowly than MM predict but that r_E shoots up with excessive borrowing. If so, the weighted-average cost of capital can be minimized if you use just the right amount of debt.

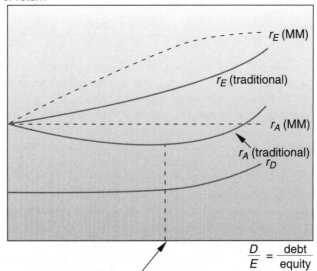

Rates of return

Traditionalists believe there is an optimal debt-equity ratio that minimizes r_A.

be willing to live with expected rates of return that do not fully compensate them for the business and financial risk they bear.

Is corporate borrowing really cheaper? It's hard to say. Interest rates on home mortgages are not too different from rates on high-grade corporate bonds.[12] Rates on margin debt (borrowing from a stockbroker with the investor's shares tendered as security) are not too different from the rates firms pay banks for short-term loans.

There are some individuals who face relatively high interest rates, largely because of the costs lenders incur in making and servicing small loans. There are economies of scale in borrowing. A group of small investors could do better by borrowing via a corporation, in effect pooling their loans and saving transaction costs.[13]

But suppose that this class of investors is large, both in number and in the aggregate wealth it brings to capital markets. Shouldn't the investors' needs be fully satisfied by the thousands of levered firms already existing? Is there really an unsatisfied clientele of small investors standing ready to pay a premium for one more firm that borrows?

Maybe the market for corporate leverage is like the market for automobiles. Americans need millions of automobiles and are willing to pay thousands of dollars apiece for them. But that doesn't mean that you could strike it rich by going into the automobile business. You're at least 50 years too late.

---

[12]One of the authors once obtained a home mortgage at a rate ½ percentage point *less* than the contemporaneous yield on long-term AT&T bonds.

[13]Even here there are alternatives to borrowing on personal account. Investors can draw down their savings accounts or sell a portion of their investment in bonds. The impact of reductions in lending on the investor's balance sheet and risk position is exactly the same as increases in borrowing.

Where to Look for Violations of MM's Propositions

MM's propositions depend on perfect capital markets. Here we are using the phrase *perfect capital markets* a bit loosely, for scholars have argued about the *degree* of perfection necessary for proposition I. (We remember an off-the-cuff comment made many years ago by Ezra Solomon: "A perfect capital market should be *defined* as one in which the MM theory holds.")

We believe capital markets are generally well-functioning, but they are not 100 percent perfect 100 percent of the time. Therefore, MM must be wrong some times in some places. The financial manager's problem is to figure out when and where.

That is not easy. Just finding market imperfections is insufficient.

Consider the traditionalists' claim that imperfections make borrowing costly and inconvenient for many individuals. That creates a clientele for whom corporate borrowing is better than personal borrowing. That clientele would, in principle, be willing to pay a premium for the shares of a levered firm.

But maybe it doesn't *have* to pay a premium. Perhaps smart financial managers long ago recognized this clientele and shifted the capital structures of their firms to meet its needs. The shifts would not have been difficult or costly to make. But if the clientele is now satisfied, it is no longer willing to pay a premium for levered shares. Only the financial managers who *first* recognized the clientele extracted any advantage from it.

Today's Unsatisfied Clienteles Are Probably Interested in Exotic Securities

So far we have made little progress in identifying cases where firm value might plausibly depend on financing. But our examples illustrate what smart financial managers look for. They look for an *unsatisfied* clientele, investors who want a particular kind of financial instrument but because of market imperfections can't get it or can't get it cheaply.

MM's proposition I is violated when the firm, by imaginative design of its capital structure, can offer some *financial service* that meets the needs of such a clientele. Either the service must be new and unique or the firm must find a way to provide some old service more cheaply than other firms or financial intermediaries can.

Now, is there an unsatisfied clientele for garden-variety debt or levered equity? We doubt it. But perhaps you can invent an exotic security and uncover a latent demand for it.

In several subsequent chapters we will encounter a number of new securities that have been invented by companies and advisers. These securities take the company's basic cash flows and repackage them in ways that are thought to be more attractive to investors. However, while inventing these new securities is easy, it is more difficult to find investors who will rush to buy them.[14]

Imperfections and Opportunities

The most serious capital market imperfections are often those created by government. An imperfection which supports a violation of MM's proposition I *also* creates a money-making opportunity. Firms and intermediaries will find some way to reach the clientele of investors frustrated by the imperfection.

---

[14]We return to the topic of security innovation in Chapter 11.

For many years the United States government imposed a limit on the rate of interest that could be paid on savings accounts. It did so in order to protect savings institutions by limiting competition for their depositors' money. The fear was that depositors would run off in search of higher yields, causing a cash drain that savings institutions would not be able to meet. This would cut off the supply of funds from those institutions for new real estate mortgages and knock the housing market for a loop. The savings institutions could not have afforded to offer higher interest rates on deposits—even if the government had allowed them to—because most of their past deposits had been locked up in fixed-rate mortgages issued when interest rates were much lower.

These regulations created an opportunity for firms and financial institutions to design new savings schemes that were not subject to the interest-rate ceilings. One invention was the *floating-rate note*, first issued on a large scale and with terms designed to appeal to individual investors by Citicorp in July 1974. Floating-rate notes are medium-term debt securities whose interest payments "float" with short-term interest rates. On the Citicorp issue, for example, the coupon rate used to calculate each semiannual interest payment was set at 1 percentage point above the contemporaneous yield on Treasury bills. The holder of the Citicorp note was therefore protected against fluctuating interest rates, because Citicorp sent a larger semiannual check when interest rates rose (and, of course, a smaller check when rates fell).

Citicorp evidently found an untapped clientele of investors, for it was able to raise $650 million in the first offering. The success of the issue suggests that Citicorp was able to add value by changing its capital structure. However, other companies were quick to jump on Citicorp's bandwagon, and within five months an additional $650 million of floating-rate notes were issued by other companies. By the mid-1980s about $43 billion of floating-rate securities were outstanding, though by that time the interest-rate ceiling was no longer a motive.[15]

Interest-rate regulation also provided financial institutions with an opportunity to create value by offering money-market funds. These are mutual funds invested in Treasury bills, commercial paper, and other high-grade, short-term debt instruments. Any saver with a few thousand dollars to invest can gain access to these instruments through a money-market fund and can withdraw money at any time by writing a check against his or her fund balance. Thus the fund resembles a checking or savings account which pays close to market interest rates.[16] These money-market funds have become enormously popular. By 1998, their assets had increased to $600 billion.

As floating-rate notes, money-market funds, and other instruments became more easily available, the protection given by government restrictions on savings account rates became less and less helpful. Finally the restrictions were lifted, and savings institutions met their competition head-on.

Long before interest-rate ceilings were finally removed, most of the gains had gone out of issuing the new securities to individual investors. Once the clientele was finally satisfied, MM's proposition I was restored (until the government creates a new imperfection). The moral of the story is this: If you ever find an unsatisfied clientele, do something right away, or capital markets will evolve and steal it from you.

---

[15]A good review of the development of the floating-rate note market is by R. S. Wilson, "Domestic Floating-Rate and Adjustable Rate Debt Securities," in F. J. Fabozzi and T. D. Fabozzi (eds.), *Handbook of Fixed Income Securities*, 4th ed., Dow-Jones Irwin, Homewood, IL, 1995.

[16]Money-market funds offer rates slightly lower than those on the securities they invest in. This spread covers the fund's operating costs and profits.

SUMMARY

At the start of this chapter we characterized the firm's financing decision as a marketing problem. Think of the financial manager as taking all of the firm's real assets and selling them to investors as a package of securities. Some financial managers choose the simplest package possible: all-equity financing. Some end up issuing dozens of debt and equity securities. The problem is to find the particular combination that maximizes the market value of the firm.

Modigliani and Miller's (MM's) famous proposition I states that no combination is better than any other—that the firm's overall market value (the value of all its securities) is independent of capital structure. Firms that borrow do offer investors a more complex menu of securities, but investors yawn in response. The menu is redundant. Any shift in capital structure can be duplicated or "undone" by investors. Why should they pay extra for borrowing indirectly (by holding shares in a levered firm) when they can borrow just as easily and cheaply on their own accounts?

MM agree that borrowing increases the expected rate of return on shareholders' investments. But it also increases the risk of the firm's shares. MM show that the risk increase exactly offsets the increase in expected return, leaving stockholders no better or worse off.

Proposition I is an extremely general result. It applies not just to the debt–equity trade-off but to *any* choice of financing instruments. For example, MM would say that the choice between long-term and short-term debt has no effect on firm value.

The formal proofs of proposition I all depend on the assumption of perfect capital markets.[17] MM's opponents, the "traditionalists," argue that market imperfections make personal borrowing excessively costly, risky, and inconvenient for some investors. This creates a natural clientele willing to pay a premium for shares of levered firms. The traditionalists say that firms should borrow to realize the premium.

But this argument is incomplete. There may be a clientele for levered equity, but that is not enough; the clientele has to be *unsatisfied*. There are already thousands of levered firms available for investment. Is there still an unsatiated clientele for garden-variety debt and equity? We doubt it.

Proposition I is violated when financial managers find an untapped demand and satisfy it by issuing something new and different. The argument between MM and the traditionalists finally boils down to whether this is difficult or easy. We lean toward MM's view: Finding unsatisfied clienteles and designing exotic securities to meet their needs is a game that's fun to play but hard to win.

APPENDIX MM AND THE CAPITAL ASSET PRICING MODEL

We showed earlier in this chapter that, as the firm increases its leverage, the expected equity return goes up in lockstep with beta of the equity. Given this, it should be no surprise to find that we can use the capital asset pricing model to derive MM's proposition I. The following demonstration has been simplified by assuming that the firm can issue risk-free debt.

---

[17]Proposition I can be proved umpteen different ways. The references at the end of this chapter include several more abstract and general proofs. Our formal proofs have been limited to MM's own arguments and (in the appendix to this chapter) a proof based on the capital asset pricing model.

The firm is initially all-equity-financed. Its expected end-of-period value is V_1, which we take to include any operating income for the initial period. We now draw on the certainty-equivalent form of the capital asset pricing model which states that the present value of the firm is

$$V = E = \frac{V_1 - \lambda \, \text{Cov}(\tilde{V}_1, \tilde{r}_m)}{1 + r_f}$$

where λ is the market price of risk $(r_m - r_f)/\sigma^2_m$.

Now suppose that the firm borrows D at the risk-free rate of interest and distributes the proceeds to stockholders. They get D dollars now but next year they will have to repay the debt with interest. Therefore instead of receiving V_1 at the end of the year, they can expect to receive only $V_1 - (1 + r_f)D$. The present value of their levered equity is

$$E = \frac{V_1 - (1 + r_f)D - \lambda \, \text{Cov}[\tilde{V}_1 - (1 + r_f)D, \tilde{r}_m]}{1 + r_f}$$

But since $(1 + r_f)D$ is known, it has no effect on the covariance. When debt is risk-free, stockholders have to bear *all* the risk associated with V_1. Therefore, we substitute $\text{Cov}(\tilde{V}_1, \tilde{r}_m)$ for $\text{Cov}[\tilde{V}_1 - (1 + r_f)D, \tilde{r}_m]$. This gives us

$$E = \frac{V_1 - (1 + r_f)D - \lambda \, \text{Cov}(\tilde{V}_1, \tilde{r}_m)}{1 + r_f}$$

$$= \frac{V_1 - \lambda \, \text{Cov}(\tilde{V}_1, \tilde{r}_m)}{1 + r_f} - D$$

To calculate the value of the *firm* we add the value of the debt D. This gives

$$V = \frac{V_1 - \lambda \, \text{Cov}(\tilde{V}_1, \tilde{r}_m)}{1 + r_f}$$

The value of the levered firm is identical to the value of the unlevered firm.

Further Reading

The pioneering work on the theory of capital structure is:
F. Modigliani and M. H. Miller: "The Cost of Capital, Corporation Finance and the Theory of Investment," *American Economic Review*, 48:261–297 (June 1958).

However, Durand deserves credit for setting out the issues that MM later solved:
D. Durand: "Cost of Debt and Equity Funds for Business: Trends and Problems in Measurement," in *Conference on Research in Business Finance*, National Bureau of Economic Research, New York, 1952, pp. 215–247.

MM provided a shorter and clearer proof of capital structure irrelevance in:
F. Modigliani and M. H. Miller: "Reply to Heins and Sprenkle," *American Economic Review*, 59:592–595 (September 1969).

A somewhat difficult article which analyzes capital structure in the context of capital asset pricing theory is:
R. S. Hamada: "Portfolio Analysis, Market Equilibrium and Corporation Finance," *Journal of Finance*, 24:13–31 (March 1969).

More abstract and general theoretical treatments can be found in:

J. E. Stiglitz: "On the Irrelevance of Corporate Financial Policy," *American Economic Review,* 64:851–866 (December 1974).

E. F. Fama: "The Effects of a Firm's Investment and Financing Decisions," *American Economic Review,* 68:272–284 (June 1978).

The fall 1988 issue of the Journal of Economic Perspectives *contains an anniversary collection of articles, including one by Modigliani and Miller, which review and assess the MM propositions. The summer 1989 issue of* Financial Management *contains three more articles under the heading "Reflections on the MM Propositions 30 Years Later."*

HOW MUCH SHOULD A FIRM BORROW?

In Chapter 5 we found that debt policy rarely matters in well-functioning capital markets. Few financial managers would accept that conclusion as a practical guideline. If debt policy doesn't matter, then they shouldn't worry about it—financing decisions should be delegated to underlings. Yet financial managers do worry about debt policy. This chapter explains why.

If debt policy were *completely* irrelevant, then actual debt ratios should vary randomly from firm to firm and industry to industry. Yet almost all airlines, utilities, banks, and real estate development companies rely heavily on debt. And so do many firms in capital-intensive industries like steel, aluminum, chemicals, petroleum, and mining. On the other hand, it is rare to find a drug company or advertising agency that is not predominantly equity-financed. Glamorous growth companies like Genentech, Hewlett-Packard, and Merck rarely use much debt despite rapid expansion and often heavy requirements for capital.

The explanation of these patterns lies partly in the things we left out of the last chapter. We

ignored taxes. We assumed bankruptcy was cheap, quick, and painless. It isn't, and there are costs associated with financial distress even if legal bankruptcy is ultimately avoided. We ignored potential conflicts of interest between the firm's security holders. For example, we did not consider what happens to the firm's "old" creditors when new debt is issued or when a shift in investment strategy takes the firm into a riskier business. We ignored the information problems that favor debt over equity when cash must be raised from new security issues. We ignored the incentive effects of financial leverage on management's investment and payout decisions.

Now we will put all these things back in: taxes first, then the costs of bankruptcy and financial distress. This will lead us to conflicts of interest and to information and incentive problems. In the end we will have to admit that debt policy *does* matter.

However, we will not throw away the MM theory we developed so carefully in Chapter 5. We're shooting for a theory combining MM's insights *plus* the effects of taxes, costs of bankruptcy and financial distress, and various other complications. We're not dropping back to the traditional view based on imperfections in the capital market. Instead, we want to see how well-functioning capital markets respond to taxes and the other things covered in this chapter.

CORPORATE TAXES

Debt financing has one important advantage under the corporate income tax system in the United States. The interest that the company pays is a tax-deductible expense. Dividends and retained earnings are not. Thus the return to bondholders escapes taxation at the corporate level.

Table 6.1 shows simple income statements for firm U, which has no debt, and firm L, which has borrowed $1,000 at 8 percent. The tax bill of L is $28 less than that of U. This is the *tax shield* provided by the debt of L. In effect the government pays 35 percent of the interest expense of L. The total income that L can pay out to its bondholders and stockholders increases by that amount.

Tax shields can be valuable assets. Suppose that the debt of L is fixed and permanent. (That is, the company commits to refinance its present debt obligations when they mature and to keep rolling over its debt obligations indefinitely.) It looks forward to a permanent stream of cash flows of $28 per year. The risk of these flows is likely to be less than the risk of the operating assets of L. The tax shields depend only on the corporate tax rate[1] and on the ability of L to earn enough to cover interest payments. The corporate tax rate has been pretty stable. (It did fall from 46 to 34 percent after the Tax Reform Act of 1986, but that was the first material change since the 1950s.) And the ability of L to earn its interest payments must be reasonably sure; otherwise it could not have borrowed at 8 percent.[2] Therefore we should discount the interest tax shields at a relatively low rate.

But what rate? One common assumption is that the risk of the tax shields is the same as that of the interest payments generating them. Thus we discount at 8 percent, the expected rate of return demanded by investors who are holding the firm's debt:

$$\text{PV(tax shield)} = \frac{28}{.08} = \$350$$

In effect the government itself assumes 35 percent of the $1,000 debt obligation of L.

Under these assumptions, the present value of the tax shield is independent of the return on the debt r_D. It equals the corporate tax rate T_c times the amount borrowed D:

---

[1]Always use the marginal corporate tax rate, not the average rate. Average rates are often much lower than marginal rates because of accelerated depreciation and other tax adjustments. For large corporations, the marginal rate is usually taken as the statutory rate, which was 35 percent when this chapter was written (1999). However, effective marginal rates can be less than the statutory rate, especially for smaller, riskier companies which cannot be sure that they will earn taxable income in the future. See J. R. Graham, "Debt and the Marginal Tax Rate," *Journal of Financial Economics* 41 (May 1996), pp. 41–73.

[2]If the income of L does not cover interest in some future year, the tax shield is not necessarily lost. L can carry back the loss and receive a tax refund up to the amount of taxes paid in the previous three years. If L has a string of losses, and thus no prior tax payments that can be refunded, then losses can be carried forward and used to shield income in subsequent years.

| | TABLE 6.1 | |

The tax deductibility of interest increases the total income that can be paid out to bondholders and stockholders.

	INCOME STATEMENT OF FIRM U	INCOME STATEMENT OF FIRM L
Earnings before interest and taxes	$1,000	$1,000
Interest paid to bondholders	0	80
Pretax income	1,000	920
Tax at 35%	350	322
Net income to stockholders	$650	$598
Total income to both bondholders and stockholders	$0 + 650 = $650	$80 + 598 = $678
Interest tax shield (.35 × interest)	$0	$28

$$\text{Interest payment} = \text{return on debt} \times \text{amount borrowed}$$

$$= r_D \times D$$

$$\text{PV(tax shield)} = \frac{\text{corporate tax rate} \times \text{expected interest payment}}{\text{expected return on debt}}$$

$$= \frac{T_c(r_D D)}{r_D} = T_c D$$

Of course, PV(tax shield) is less if the firm does not plan to borrow permanently, or if it may not be able to use the tax shields in the future.

How Do Interest Tax Shields Contribute to the Value of Stockholders' Equity?

MM's proposition I amounts to saying that the value of a pie does not depend on how it is sliced. The pie is the firm's assets, and the slices are the debt and equity claims. If we hold the pie constant, then a dollar more of debt means a dollar less of equity value.

But there is really a third slice, the government's. Look at Table 6.2. It shows an *expanded* balance sheet with *pretax* asset value on the left and the value of the government's tax claim recognized as a liability on the right. MM would still say that the value of the pie—in this case *pretax* asset value—is not changed by slicing. But anything the firm can do to reduce the size of the government's slice obviously makes stockholders better off. One thing it can do is borrow money, which reduces its tax bill and, as we saw in Table 6.1, increases the cash flows to debt and equity investors. The *after-tax* value of the firm (the sum of its debt and equity values as shown in a normal market value balance sheet) goes up by PV(tax shield).

Recasting Merck's Capital Structure

Merck & Company is a large, successful firm that uses essentially no long-term debt. Table 6.3(*a*) shows simplified book and market value balance sheets for Merck as of year-end 1997.

TABLE 6.2

Normal and expanded market value balance sheets. In a normal balance sheet, assets are valued after tax. In the expanded balance sheet, assets are valued pretax, and the value of the government's tax claim is recognized on the right-hand side. Interest tax shields are valuable because they reduce the government's claim.

Normal Balance Sheet (Market Values)

Asset value (present value of after-tax cash flows)	Debt
Total assets	Equity
	Total value

Expanded Balance Sheet (Market Values)

Pretax asset value (present value of *pretax* cash flows)	Debt
	Government's claim (present value of future taxes)
Total pretax assets	Equity
	Total value

Suppose that you were Merck's financial manager in 1997 with complete responsibility for its capital structure. You decide to borrow $1 billion on a permanent basis and use the proceeds to repurchase shares.

Table 6.3(*b*) shows the new balance sheets. The book version simply has $1,000 million more long-term debt and $1,000 million less equity. But we know that Merck's assets must be worth more, for its tax bill has been reduced by 35 percent of the interest on the new debt. In other words, Merck has an increase in PV(tax shield), which is worth $T_c D = .35 \times 1,000 = \$350$ million. If the MM theory holds *except* for taxes, firm value must increase by $350 million to $134,506 million. Merck's equity ends up worth $125,877 million.

Now you have repurchased $1,000 million worth of shares, but Merck's equity value has dropped by only $650 million. Therefore Merck's stockholders must be $350 million ahead. Not a bad day's work.[3]

MM and Taxes

We have just developed a version of MM's proposition I as "corrected" by them to reflect corporate income taxes.[4] The new proposition is

---

[3]Notice that as long as the bonds are sold at a fair price, all the benefits from the tax shield go to the shareholders.

[4]Interest tax shields are recognized in MM's original article, F. Modigliani and M. H. Miller, "The Cost of Capital, Corporation Finance and the Theory of Investment," *American Economic Review* 48 (June 1958), pp. 261–297. The valuation procedure used in Table 6.3(*b*) is presented in their 1963 article "Corporate Income Taxes and the Cost of Capital: A Correction," *American Economic Review* 53 (June 1963), pp. 433–443.

TABLE 6.3(*a*)

Simplified balance sheets for Merck & Co., December 31, 1997

Book Values			
Net working capital	$ 2,644	$ 1,347	Long-term debt
Long-term assets	17,599	6,282	Other long-term liabilities
		12,614	Equity
Total assets	$20,243	$20,243	Total value
Market Values			
Net working capital	$ 2,644	$ 1,347	Long-term debt
Market value of long-term assets	131,512	6,282	Other long-term liabilities
		126,527	Equity
Total assets	$134,156	$134,156	Total value

Notes:

1. Market value is equal to book value for net working capital, long-term debt, and other long-term liabilities. Equity is entered at actual market value: number of shares times closing price on December 31, 1997. The difference between the market and book values of long-term assets is equal to the difference between the market and book values of equity.

2. The market value of the long-term assets includes the tax shield on the existing debt. This tax shield is worth .35 × 1,347 = $471 million.

$$\text{Value of firm} = \text{value if all-equity-financed} + \text{PV(tax shield)}$$

In the special case of permanent debt,

$$\text{Value of firm} = \text{value if all-equity-financed} + T_c D$$

Our imaginary financial surgery on Merck provides the perfect illustration of the problems inherent in this "corrected" theory. That $350 million windfall came too easily; it seems to violate the law that there is no such thing as a money machine. And if Merck's stockholders would be richer with $2,347 million of corporate debt, why not $3,347 or $13,961 million?[5] Our formula implies that firm value and stockholders' wealth continue to go up as D increases. The implied optimal debt policy is embarrassingly extreme: All firms should be 100 percent debt-financed.

MM were not that fanatical about it. No one would expect the formula to apply at extreme debt ratios. There are several reasons why our calculations overstate the value of interest tax shields. First, it's wrong to think of debt as fixed and perpetual; a firm's ability to carry debt changes over time as profits and firm value fluctuate.[6] Second, many firms face marginal tax rates

---

[5]The last figure would correspond to a 100 percent book debt ratio. But Merck's *market* value would be $138,571 million according to our formula for firm value. Merck's common shares would have an aggregate value of $118,328 million.

[6]Our calculation here assumes that debt is repaid on a fixed schedule regardless of future performance of the project or the firm.

TABLE 6.3(*b*)

Balance sheets for Merck & Co. with additional $1 billion of long-term debt substituted for stockholders' equity (figures in millions)

	Book Values		
Net working capital	$ 2,644	$ 2,347	Long-term debt
Long-term assets	17,599	6,282	Other long-term liabilities
		11,614	Equity
Total assets	$20,243	$20,243	Total value

	Market Values		
Net working capital	$ 2,644	$ 2,347	Long-term debt
Market value of long-term assets	131,512	6,282	Other long-term liabilities
Additional tax shields	350	125,877	Equity
Total assets	$134,506	$134,506	Total value

Notes:

1. The figures in Table 6.3(*b*) for net working capital, long-term assets, and other long-term liabilities are identical to those in Table 6.3(*a*).

2. Present value of tax shields assumed equal to corporate tax rate (35 percent) times additional long-term debt.

less than 35 percent.[7] Third, you can't use interest tax shields unless there will be future profits to shield—and no firm can be absolutely sure of that.

But none of these qualifications explains why firms like Merck not only exist but also thrive with no debt at all. It is hard to believe that the management of Merck is simply missing the boat.

Therefore we have argued ourselves into a corner. There are just two ways out:

1. Perhaps a fuller examination of the U.S. system of corporate *and personal* taxation will uncover a tax disadvantage of corporate borrowing, offsetting the present value of the corporate tax shield.

2. Perhaps firms that borrow incur other costs—bankruptcy costs, for example—offsetting the present value of the tax shield.

We will now explore these two escape routes.

CORPORATE AND PERSONAL TAXES

When personal taxes are introduced, the firm's objective is no longer to minimize the *corporate* tax bill; the firm should try to minimize the present value of *all* taxes paid on corporate income. "All taxes" include *personal* taxes paid by bondholders and stockholders.

---

[7]See J. R. Graham, "Debt and the Marginal Tax Rate," *Journal of Financial Economics* 41 (May 1996), pp. 41–73.

Figure 6.1

The firm's capital structure determines whether operating income is paid out as interest or equity income. Interest is taxed only at the personal level. Equity income is taxed at both the corporate and the personal levels. However, T_{pE}, the personal tax rate on equity income, can be less than T_p, the personal tax rate on interest income.

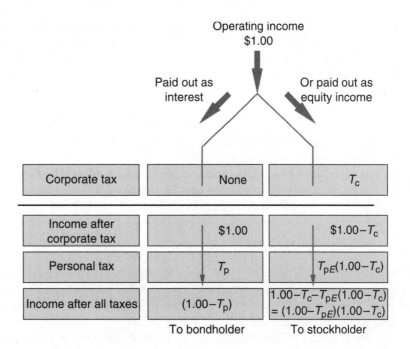

Figure 6.1 illustrates how corporate and personal taxes are affected by leverage. Depending on the firm's capital structure, a dollar of operating income will accrue to investors either as debt interest or equity income (dividends or capital gains). That is, the dollar can go down either branch of Figure 6.1.

Notice that Figure 6.1 distinguishes between T_p, the personal tax rate on interest, and T_{pE}, the effective personal rate on equity income. The two rates are equal if equity income comes entirely as dividends. But T_{pE} can be less than T_p if equity income comes as capital gains. By 1999, the top rate on ordinary income, including interest and dividends, was 39.6 percent. The rate on realized capital gains was 28 percent.[8] However, capital gains taxes can be deferred until shares are sold, so the top effective capital gains rate can be less than 28 percent.

The firm's objective should be to arrange its capital structure so as to maximize after-tax income. You can see from Figure 6.1 that corporate borrowing is better if $1 - T_p$ is more than $(1 - T_{pE}) \times (1 - T_c)$; otherwise, it is worse. The *relative* tax advantage of debt over equity is

$$\text{Relative tax advantage of debt} = \frac{1 - T_p}{(1 - T_{pE})(1 - T_c)}$$

This suggests two special cases. First, suppose all equity income comes as dividends. Then debt and equity income are taxed at the same effective personal rate. But with $T_{pE} = T_p$, the relative advantage depends only on the *corporate* rate:

$$\text{Relative advantage} = \frac{1 - T_p}{(1 - T_{pE})(1 - T_c)} = \frac{1}{1 - T_c}$$

---

[8]See Chapter 7 for details. Note that we are simplifying by ignoring *corporate* investors, for example, banks, that pay top rates of 35 percent. Of course, banks shield their interest income by paying interest to lenders and depositors.

In this case, we can forget about personal taxes. The tax advantage of corporate borrowing is exactly as MM calculated it.[9] They do not have to assume away personal taxes. Their theory of debt and taxes requires only that debt and equity be taxed at the same rate.

The second special case occurs when corporate and personal taxes cancel to make debt policy irrelevant. This requires

$$1 - T_p = (1 - T_{pE})(1 - T_c)$$

This case can happen only if T_c, the corporate rate, is less than the personal rate T_p *and* if T_{pE}, the effective rate on equity income, is small.

In any event we seem to have a simple, practical decision rule. Arrange the firm's capital structure to shunt operating income down that branch of Figure 6.1 where the tax is least. We will now try a couple of back-of-the-envelope calculations to see what that rule could imply.

Debt Policy before and after Tax Reform

Before the 1986 Tax Reform Act, the corporate tax rate was 46 percent, and interest and dividends were taxed at rates up to 50 percent. The top capital gains rate was 20 percent. The *effective* rate was less than 20 percent because capital gains taxes can be deferred until shares are sold.

You can see the two opposing tax effects. Corporate tax rules subsidized debt—the government in effect paid $.46 for every dollar of interest. But the personal tax rules favored equity because of the low tax rate on capital gains. For companies with low-dividend payouts, the two effects roughly canceled.

Consider a firm paying no dividends, and suppose that deferral of capital gains cuts the effective personal tax rate on equity income to half the pre-1986 statutory capital gains rate, that is, T_{pE} = .10. If T_p, the tax rate on interest, is .50, then

	INTEREST	EQUITY INCOME
Income before tax	$1.00	$1.00
Less corporate tax		
at $T_c = .46$	0	.46
Income after corporate tax	1.00	.54
Personal tax at $T_p = .5$		
and $T_{pE} = .10$	.50	.054
Income after all taxes	$ .50	$ .496

Advantage to debt = $.004

---

[9]Of course, personal taxes reduce the dollar amount of corporate interest tax shields, but the appropriate discount rate for cash flows after personal tax is also lower. If investors are willing to lend at a prospective return *before* personal taxes of r_D, then they must also be willing to accept a return *after* personal taxes of $r_D(1 - T_p)$, where T_p is the marginal rate of personal tax. Thus we can compute the value after personal taxes of the tax shield on permanent debt:

$$PV(\text{tax shield}) = \frac{T_c \times (r_D D) \times (1 - T_p)}{r_D \times (1 - T_p)} = T_c D$$

This brings us back to our previous formula for firm value:

$$\text{Value of firm} = \text{value if all-equity-financed} + T_c D$$

For any practical purpose this is a dead heat. It's worth paying the 46 percent corporate tax on equity income to avoid the 50 percent personal tax on interest income.

The 1986 Tax Reform Act reduced the corporate tax rate to 34 percent, reduced the top personal rate on interest and dividends to 28 percent, and increased the tax on realized capital gains to 28 percent. By 1999, the corporate rate had edged up to 35 percent, and the top rate on interest and dividends had jumped to 39.6 percent. The capital gains rate remained at 28 percent.

Here is a second numerical example, using 1999 rates, and again assuming zero dividends and an effective capital gains rate of one-half the statutory rate on realized gains, that is, $28/2 = 14$ percent:

	INTEREST	EQUITY INCOME
Income before tax	$1.00	$1.00
Less corporate tax		
at $T_c = .35$	0	.35
Income after corporate tax	1.00	.65
Personal tax at $T_p = .396$		
and $T_{pE} = .14$	.396	.091
Income after all taxes	$ .604	$ .559

Advantage to debt = $.045

Here debt takes the lead. Moreover, the lead lengthens when we consider companies that pay dividends. Suppose half of equity income comes as dividends and half comes as capital gains. Capital gains are deferred for long enough that their effective rate is half the statutory rate, that is one-half of 28, or 14 percent. Thus the effective rate on equity income is the average of the dividend and capital gains rates, or $(.396 + .14)/2 = .268$.

	INTEREST	EQUITY INCOME
Income before tax	$1.00	$1.00
Less corporate tax		
at $T_c = .35$	0	.35
Income after corporate tax	1.00	.65
Less personal tax at $T_p = .396$		
and $T_{pE} = .268$	.396	.174
Income after all taxes	$ .604	$ .476

Advantage to debt = $.128

The advantage to debt financing is about $.13 on the dollar.

As these back-of-the-envelope calculations show, the current (1999) U.S. tax system clearly favors debt over equity financing. But the magnitude of debt's tax advantage is not so clear. Which investors' tax rates should be used? What's T_{pE}, for example? The shareholder roster of a large corporation may include tax-exempt investors (such as pension funds or university endowments) as well as millionaires. All possible tax brackets will be mixed together. And it's the same with T_p, the personal tax rate on interest. The large corporation's "typical" bondholder might be a tax-exempt pension fund, but many taxpaying investors also hold corporate debt.

Merton Miller's "Debt and Taxes"

How does capital structure affect firm value when investors have different tax rates? There is one model that may help us think through that question. It was put forward in "Debt and Taxes," Merton Miller's 1976 presidential address to the American Finance Association.[10]

Miller was considering debt policy before the 1986 Tax Reform Act. He started by assuming that all equity income comes as unrealized capital gains and nobody pays any tax on equity income; T_{pE} is zero for all investors. But the rate of tax on interest depends on the investor's tax bracket. Tax-exempt institutions do not pay any tax on interest; for them T_p is zero. At the other extreme, millionaires paid tax at a rate of 50 percent on bond interest; for them T_p was .50. Most investors fell somewhere between these two extremes.

Consider a simple world with these tax rates. Suppose that companies are initially financed entirely by equity. If financial managers are on their toes, this cannot represent a stable situation. Think of it in terms of Figure 6.1. If every dollar goes down the equity branch, there are no taxes paid at the personal level (remember $T_{pE} = 0$). Thus the financial manager need consider only corporate taxes, which we know create a strong incentive for corporate borrowing.

As companies begin to borrow, some investors have to be persuaded to hold corporate debt rather than common stock. There should be no problem in persuading tax-exempt investors to hold debt. They do not pay any personal taxes on bonds or stocks. Thus, the initial impact of borrowing is to save corporate taxes and to leave personal taxes unchanged.

But as companies borrow more, they need to persuade taxpaying investors to migrate from stocks to bonds. Therefore they have to offer a bribe in the form of a higher interest rate on their bonds. Companies can afford to bribe investors to migrate as long as the corporate tax saving is greater than the personal tax loss. But there is no way that companies can bribe millionaires to hold their bonds. The corporate tax saving cannot compensate for the extra personal tax that those millionaires would need to pay. Thus the migrations stop when the corporate tax saving *equals* the personal tax loss. This point occurs when T_p, the personal tax rate of the migrating investor, equals the corporate tax rate T_c.

Let us put some numbers on this. The corporate tax rate T_c was 46 percent. We continue to assume that T_{pE}, the effective rate of tax on equity income, is zero for all investors. In this case, companies will bribe investors with tax rates below 46 percent to hold bonds. But there is nothing to be gained (or lost) by persuading investors with tax rates *equal* to 46 percent to hold bonds. In the case of these investors $1 of operating income will produce income after all taxes of $.54, regardless of whether the dollar is interest or equity income:

	INCOME REMAINING AFTER ALL TAXES
Income paid out as interest	$1 - T_p = 1 - .46 = \$.54$
Income paid out as equity income	$(1 - T_{pE})(1 - T_c) = (1 - 0)(1 - .46) = \$.54$

In this equilibrium taxes determine the aggregate amount of corporate debt but not the amount issued by any particular firm. The debt–equity ratio for corporations as a whole depends on the corporate tax rate and the funds available to individual investors in the various tax

---

[10]M. H. Miller, "Debt and Taxes," *Journal of Finance* 32 (May 1977), pp. 261–276.

brackets. If the corporate tax rate is increased, migration starts again, leading to a higher debt–equity ratio for companies as a whole. If personal tax rates are increased, the migration reverses, leading to a lower debt–equity ratio. If *both* personal and corporate tax rates are increased by the same amount—10 percentage points, say—there is no migration and no change. That could explain why there was no substantial increase in the debt–equity ratio when the corporate income tax rose drastically at the start of World War II. Personal tax rates were simultaneously increased by about the same amount.

In our example the companies that first sold bonds to tax-exempt investors may have gained an advantage. But once the "low-tax" investors have bought bonds and the migrations have stopped, no single firm can gain an advantage by borrowing more or suffer any penalty by borrowing less. Therefore there is no such thing as an optimal debt–equity ratio *for any single firm.* The market is interested only in the *total* amount of debt. No single firm can influence that.

One final point about Miller's tax equilibrium: Because he assumes equity returns escape personal tax ($T_{pE} = 0$), investors are willing to accept lower rates of return on low-risk common stocks than on debt. Consider a safe (zero-beta) stock. The standard capital asset pricing model would give an expected return of $r = r_f$, the risk-free interest rate. But the investor migrating from equity to debt gives up r and earns $r_f(1 - T_p)$, the *after-tax* interest rate. In equilibrium, the migrating investor is content with either debt or equity, so $r = r_f(1 - T_p)$. Moreover, that investor's T_p equals the corporate rate T_c. Therefore, $r = r_f(1 - T_c)$. If we accept Miller's argument lock, stock, and barrel, the security market line should pass through the after-tax risk-free interest rate.

The Bottom Line on Debt and Taxes

Miller's model was intended not as a detailed description of the U.S. tax system but as a way of illustrating how corporate and personal taxes could cancel out and leave firm value independent of capital structure. Nevertheless, the model's predictions are plausible only if the effective tax rate on equity income is substantially lower than that on interest, enough lower to offset the corporate interest tax shield. Under today's tax system, it's hard to see how Miller's model could work out as he originally intended. Even if there were no tax advantage to borrowing before the 1986 tax law changes, there ought to be one now.

The majority of financial managers and economists believe our tax system favors corporate borrowing. But it's easy to overestimate the advantage. Analyses like Tables 6.3(*a*) and 6.3(*b*), which calculate the present value of a safe, perpetual stream of corporate interest tax shields, must overestimate debt's net value added. As Miller's paper shows, the aggregate supplies of corporate debt and equity should adjust to minimize the sum of corporate and personal taxes; at the resulting equilibrium the higher personal tax rate on debt income should partially offset the tax deductibility of interest at the corporate level.

We should also remember that the corporate tax shield on debt is not constant regardless of the amount borrowed. In practice few firms can be *sure* they will show a taxable profit in the future. If a firm shows a loss and cannot carry the loss back against past taxes, its interest tax shield must be carried forward with the hope of using it later. The firm loses the time value of money while it waits. If its difficulties are deep enough, the wait may be permanent and the interest tax shield may be lost forever.

Notice also that borrowing is not the only way to shield income against tax. Firms have accelerated write-offs for plant and equipment. Investment in many intangible assets can be expensed immediately. So can contributions to the firm's pension fund. The more that firms shield income in these other ways, the lower is the expected tax shield from borrowing.[11]

Thus corporate tax shields are worth more to some firms than to others. Firms with plenty of noninterest tax shields and uncertain future prospects should borrow less than consistently profitable firms with lots of taxable profits to shield. Firms with large accumulated tax-loss carry-forwards shouldn't borrow at all. Why should such a firm "bribe" taxpaying investors to hold debt when it can't use interest tax shields?

We believe there is a moderate tax advantage to corporate borrowing, at least for companies that are reasonably sure they can use the corporate tax shields. For companies that do not expect to be able to use the corporate tax shields we believe there is a moderate tax disadvantage.

COSTS OF FINANCIAL DISTRESS

Financial distress occurs when promises to creditors are broken or honored with difficulty. Sometimes financial distress leads to bankruptcy. Sometimes it only means skating on thin ice.

As we will see, financial distress is costly. Investors know that levered firms may fall into financial distress, and they worry about it. That worry is reflected in the current market value of the levered firm's securities. Thus, the value of the firm can be broken down into three parts:

$$\begin{array}{c} \text{Value} \\ \text{of firm} \end{array} = \begin{array}{c} \text{value if} \\ \text{all-equity-financed} \end{array} + \text{PV(tax shield)} - \begin{array}{c} \text{PV(costs of} \\ \text{financial distress)} \end{array}$$

The costs of financial distress depend on the probability of distress and the magnitude of costs encountered if distress occurs.

Figure 6.2 shows how the trade-off between the tax benefits and the costs of distress determines optimal capital structure. PV(tax shield) initially increases as the firm borrows more. At moderate debt levels the probability of financial distress is trivial, and so PV(cost of financial distress) is small and tax advantages dominate. But at some point the probability of financial distress increases rapidly with additional borrowing; the costs of distress begin to take a substantial bite out of firm value. Also, if the firm can't be sure of profiting from the corporate tax shield, the tax advantage of debt is likely to dwindle and eventually disappear. The theoretical optimum is reached when the present value of tax savings due to additional borrowing is just offset by increases in the present value of costs of distress. This is called the *trade-off theory* of capital structure.

Costs of financial distress cover several specific items. Now we identify these costs and try to understand what causes them.

Bankruptcy Costs

You rarely hear anything nice said about corporate bankruptcy. But there is some good in almost everything. Corporate bankruptcies occur when stockholders exercise their *right to default*. That

---

[11]For a discussion of the effect of these other tax shields on company borrowing, see H. DeAngelo and R. Masulis, "Optimal Capital Structure under Corporate and Personal Taxation," *Journal of Financial Economics* 8 (March 1980), pp. 5–29. For some evidence on the average marginal tax rate of U.S. firms, see J. R. Graham, "Debt and the Marginal Tax Rate," *Journal of Financial Economics* 41 (May 1996), pp. 41–73 and "Proxies for the Corporate Marginal Tax Rate," *Journal of Financial Economics* 42 (October 1996), pp. 187–221.

Figure 6.2

The value of the firm is equal to its value if all-equity-financed plus PV(tax shield) minus PV(costs of financial distress). According to the trade-off theory of capital structure, the manager should choose the debt ratio that maximizes firm value.

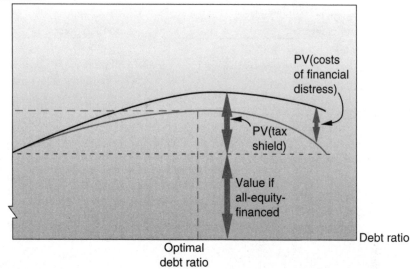

Market value

PV(costs of financial distress)

PV(tax shield)

Value if all-equity-financed

Debt ratio

Optimal debt ratio

right is valuable; when a firm gets into trouble, limited liability allows stockholders simply to walk away from it, leaving all its troubles to its creditors. The former creditors become the new stockholders, and the old stockholders are left with nothing.

In our legal system all stockholders in corporations automatically enjoy limited liability. But suppose that this were not so. Suppose that there are two firms with identical assets and operations. Each firm has debt outstanding, and each has promised to repay $1,000 (principal and interest) next year. But only one of the firms, Ace Limited, enjoys limited liability. The other firm, Ace Unlimited, does not; its stockholders are personally liable for its debt.

Figure 6.3 compares next year's possible payoffs to the creditors and stockholders of these two firms. The only differences occur when next year's asset value turns out to be less than $1,000. Suppose that next year the assets of each company are worth only $500. In this case Ace Limited defaults. Its stockholders walk away; their payoff is zero. Bondholders get the assets worth $500. But Ace Unlimited's stockholders can't walk away. They have to cough up $500, the difference between asset value and the bondholders' claim. The debt is paid whatever happens.

Suppose that Ace Limited does go bankrupt. Of course, its stockholders are disappointed that their firm is worth so little, but that is an operating problem having nothing to do with financing. Given poor operating performance, the right to go bankrupt—the right to default—is a valuable privilege. As Figure 6.3 shows, Ace Limited's stockholders are in better shape than Unlimited's are.

The example illuminates a mistake people often make in thinking about the costs of bankruptcy. Bankruptcies are thought of as corporate funerals. The mourners (creditors and especially shareholders) look at their firm's present sad state. They think of how valuable their securities used to be and how little is left. Moreover, they think of the lost value as a cost of bankruptcy. That is the mistake. The decline in the value of assets is what the mourning is really about. That has no necessary connection with financing. The bankruptcy is merely a legal mechanism for allowing creditors to take over when the decline in the value of assets triggers a default. Bankruptcy is not the cause of the decline in value. It is the result.

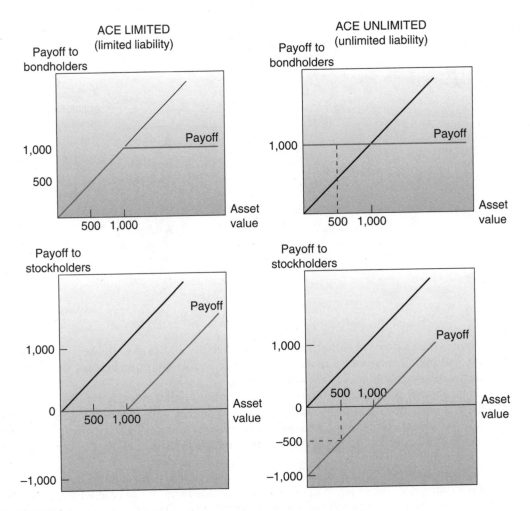

Figure 6.3

Comparison of limited and unlimited liability for two otherwise identical firms. If the two firms' asset values are less than $1,000, Ace Limited stockholders default and its bondholders take over the assets. Ace Unlimited stockholders keep the assets, but they must reach into their own pockets to pay off its bondholders. The total payoff to both stockholders and bondholders is the same for the two firms.

Be careful not to get cause and effect reversed. When a person dies, we do not cite the implementation of his or her will as the cause of death.

We said that bankruptcy is a legal mechanism allowing creditors to take over when a firm defaults. Bankruptcy costs are the costs of using this mechanism. There are no bankruptcy costs at all shown in Figure 6.3. Note that only Ace Limited can default and go bankrupt. But, regardless of what happens to asset value, the *combined* payoff to the bondholders and stockholders of Ace Limited is always the same as the *combined* payoff to the bondholders and stockholders of Ace Unlimited. Thus the overall market values of the two firms now (this year) must be identical. Of course, Ace Limited's stock is worth more than Ace Unlimited's stock because of Ace Limited's right to default. Ace Limited's *debt* is worth correspondingly less.

Figure 6.4

Total payoff to Ace Limited security holders. There is a $200 bankruptcy cost in the event of default (shaded area).

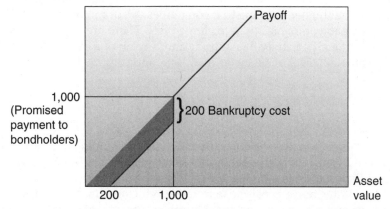

Our example was not intended to be strictly realistic. Anything involving courts and lawyers cannot be free. Suppose that court and legal fees are $200 if Ace Limited defaults. The fees are paid out of the remaining value of Ace's assets. Thus if asset value turns out to be $500, creditors end up with only $300. Figure 6.4 shows next year's *total* payoff to bondholders and stockholders net of this bankruptcy cost. Ace Limited, by issuing risky debt, has given lawyers and the court system a claim on the firm if it defaults. The market value of the firm is reduced by the present value of this claim.

It is easy to see how increased leverage affects the present value of the costs of financial distress. If Ace Limited borrows more, it must promise more to bondholders. This increases the probability of default and the value of the lawyers' claim. It increases PV (costs of financial distress) and reduces Ace's present market value.

The costs of bankruptcy come out of stockholders' pockets. Creditors foresee the costs and foresee that *they* will pay them if default occurs. For this they demand compensation in advance in the form of higher payoffs when the firm does not default; that is, they demand a higher promised interest rate. This reduces the possible payoffs to stockholders and reduces the present market value of their shares.

Evidence on Bankruptcy Costs

Bankruptcy costs can add up fast. Manville, which declared bankruptcy in 1982 because of expected liability for asbestos-related health claims, spent $200 million on fees before it emerged from bankruptcy in 1988.[12] While Eastern Airlines was in bankruptcy, it spent $114 million on professional fees.[13] Daunting as such numbers may seem, they are not a large fraction of the companies' asset values. For example, the fees incurred by Eastern amounted to only 3.5 percent of its assets when it entered bankruptcy, or about the equivalent of one jumbo jet.

---

[12]S. P. Sherman, "Bankruptcy's Spreading Blight," *Fortune*, June 3, 1991, pp. 123–132.

[13]L. Gibbs and A. Boardman, "A Billion Later, Eastern's Finally Gone," *American Lawyer Newspaper Groups*, February 6, 1995.

Lawrence Weiss, who studied 31 firms that went bankrupt between 1980 and 1986, found average costs of about 3 percent of total book assets and 20 percent of the market value of equity in the year prior to bankruptcy. A study by Edward Altman found that costs were similar for retail companies but higher for industrial companies. Also, bankruptcy eats up a larger fraction of asset value for small companies than for large ones. There are significant economies of scale in going bankrupt.[14] Finally, a study by Andrade and Kaplan of a sample of troubled and highly leveraged firms estimated costs of financial distress amounting to 10 to 20 percent of predistress market value.[15]

Direct versus Indirect Costs of Bankruptcy

So far we have discussed the *direct* (that is, legal and administrative) costs of bankruptcy. There are indirect costs too, which are nearly impossible to measure. But we have circumstantial evidence indicating their importance.

Some of the indirect costs arise from the reluctance to do business with a firm that may not be around for long. Customers worry about the continuity of supplies and the difficulty of obtaining replacement parts if the firm ceases production. Suppliers are disinclined to put effort into servicing the firm's account and demand cash on the nail for their goods. Potential employees are unwilling to sign on and the existing staff keep slipping away from their desks for job interviews.

Managing a bankrupt firm is not easy. Consent of the bankruptcy court is required for many routine business decisions, such as the sale of assets or investment in new equipment. At best this involves time and effort; at worst the proposals are thwarted by the firm's creditors, who have little interest in the firm's long-term prosperity and would prefer the cash to be paid out to them.

Sometimes the problem is reversed: the bankruptcy court is so anxious to maintain the firm as a going concern that it allows the firm to engage in negative-NPV activities. When Eastern Airlines entered the "protection" of the bankruptcy court in 1989, it still had some valuable, profit-making routes and saleable assets such as planes and terminal facilities. The creditors would have been best served by a prompt liquidation, which probably would have generated enough cash to pay off all debt and preferred stockholders. But the bankruptcy judge was keen to keep Eastern's planes flying at all costs, so he allowed the company to sell many of its assets to fund hefty operating losses. When Eastern finally closed down after two years, it was not just bankrupt, but *administratively* insolvent: there was almost nothing for creditors, and the company was running out of cash to pay legal expenses.[16]

We do not know what the sum of direct and indirect costs of bankruptcy amounts to. We suspect it is a significant number, particularly for large firms for which proceedings would be lengthy and complex. Perhaps the best evidence is the reluctance of creditors to force bankruptcy. In prin-

---

[14]The pioneering study of bankruptcy costs is J. B. Warner, "Bankruptcy Costs: Some Evidence," *Journal of Finance* 26 (May 1977), pp. 337–348. The Weiss and Altman papers are L. A. Weiss, "Bankruptcy Resolution: Direct Costs and Violation of Priority of Claims," *Journal of Financial Economics* 27 (October 1990), pp. 285–314, and E. I. Altman, "A Further Investigation of the Bankruptcy Cost Question," *Journal of Finance* 39 (September 1984), pp. 1067–1089.

[15]G. Andrade and S. N. Kaplan, "How Costly is Financial (not Economic) Distress? Evidence from Highly Leveraged Transactions that Became Distressed," *Journal of Finance* 53 (October 1998), pp. 1443–1493.

[16]The bankruptcy of Eastern Airlines is analyzed in L. A. Weiss and K. H. Wruck, "Information Problems, Conflicts of Interest, and Asset Stripping: Chapter 11's Failure in the Case of Eastern Airlines," *Journal of Financial Economics* 48 (1998), pp. 55–97.

TABLE 6.4

Texaco's stock price dropped by $3.375 when its bankruptcy filing was announced. Pennzoil was Texaco's largest creditor; its stock price dropped too, by $15.125. The combined market value of the two firms' stock fell $1,445 million.

	SHARE PRICE			NUMBER OF SHARES, MILLIONS	CHANGE IN VALUE, MILLIONS
	FRIDAY APRIL 10, 1987	MONDAY APRIL 13, 1987	CHANGE		
Texaco	$31.875	$28.50	–$ 3.375	242	–$ 817
Pennzoil	92.125	77.00	–15.125	41.5	–628
Total					–$1,445

ciple, they would be better off to end the agony and seize the assets as soon as possible. Instead, creditors often overlook defaults in the hope of nursing the firm over a difficult period. They do this in part to avoid costs of bankruptcy.[17] There is an old financial saying, "Borrow $1,000 and you've got a banker. Borrow $10,000,000 and you've got a partner."

Here is one final piece of evidence on the direct plus indirect costs of bankruptcy: On April 10, 1987, Texaco filed for bankruptcy, surprising most investors and financial analysts. Texaco's biggest creditor was Pennzoil, to whom it owed $10.5 billion in damages stemming from Texaco's 1984 takeover of Getty Oil.[18] Texaco had been negotiating with Pennzoil, trying to cut a deal in which Pennzoil would give up its claim—which Texaco was contesting—in exchange for an immediate cash settlement. When these negotiations broke down, Texaco turned to the bankruptcy court.

Table 6.4 reports that Texaco stock fell from $31.875 to $28.50 after the announcement, a fall of $817 million in Texaco's equity value. At the same time Pennzoil's equity value fell by $628 million. We do not know how Texaco's other creditors fared, but the value of their claims cannot have increased. Therefore, bankruptcy reduced the market value of (the claims on) Texaco's assets by at least $817 plus $628, or $1,445 million, roughly $1.5 billion. We can take this loss as the stock market's estimate of the present value of the direct and indirect costs of the Texaco bankruptcy.

But how could bankruptcy cost $1.5 *billion*? Texaco's business operations were healthy and profitable, thus unlikely to encounter the sort of problems that plagued Eastern Airlines. We are at a loss to explain how a stock market could rationally forecast bankruptcy costs as large as those implied by Table 6.4.[19]

---

[17]There is another reason. Creditors are not always given absolute priority in bankruptcy. *Absolute priority* means that creditors must be paid in full before stockholders receive a cent. Sometimes reorganizations are negotiated which provide something for everyone, even though creditors are *not* paid in full. Thus creditors can never be sure how they will fare in bankruptcy.

[18]Pennzoil thought it had struck a deal to buy Getty when Texaco arrived with a higher bid. Texaco finally won, but Pennzoil sued, arguing that Texaco had broken up a valid contract between Pennzoil and Getty. The court agreed and ordered Texaco to pay over $11.1 billion. This amount was reduced on appeal, but with interest the damages still amounted to $10.5 billion by April 1987.

[19]The Texaco bankruptcy is discussed by L. Summers and D. M. Cutler, "The Costs of Conflict and Financial Distress: Evidence from the Texaco-Pennzoil Litigation," *RAND Journal of Economics* 19 (Summer 1988), pp. 157–172.

In all this discussion of bankruptcy costs we have said very little about bankruptcy *procedures*. These are described in the appendix at the end of this chapter.

Financial Distress without Bankruptcy

Not every firm which gets into trouble goes bankrupt. As long as the firm can scrape up enough cash to pay the interest on its debt, it may be able to postpone bankruptcy for many years. Eventually the firm may recover, pay off its debt, and escape bankruptcy altogether.

When a firm is in trouble, both bondholders and stockholders want it to recover, but in other respects their interests may be in conflict. In times of financial distress the security holders are like many political parties—united on generalities but threatened by squabbling on any specific issue.

Financial distress is costly when these conflicts of interest get in the way of proper operating, investment, and financing decisions. Stockholders are tempted to forsake the usual objective of maximizing the overall market value of the firm and to pursue narrower self-interest instead. They are tempted to play games at the expense of their creditors. We will now illustrate how such games can lead to costs of financial distress.

Here is the Circular File Company's book balance sheet:

Circular File Company (Book Values)

Net working capital	$ 20	$ 50	Bonds outstanding
Fixed assets	80	50	Common stock
Total assets	$100	$100	Total value

We will assume there is only one share and one bond outstanding. The stockholder is also the manager. The bondholder is somebody else.

Here is its balance sheet in market values—a clear case of financial distress, since the face value of Circular's debt ($50) exceeds the firm's total market value ($30):

Circular File Company (Market Values)

Net working capital	$20	$25	Bonds outstanding
Fixed assets	10	5	Common stock
Total assets	$30	$30	Total value

If the debt matured today, Circular's owner would default, leaving the firm bankrupt. But suppose that the bond actually matures one year hence, that there is enough cash for Circular to limp along for one year, and that the bondholder cannot "call the question" and force bankruptcy before then.

The one-year grace period explains why the Circular share still has value. Its owner is betting on a stroke of luck that will rescue the firm, allowing it to pay off the debt with something left over. The bet is a long shot—the owner wins only if firm value increases from $30 to more than $50.[20] But the owner has a secret weapon: he controls investment and operating strategy.

---

[20]We are not concerned here with how to work out whether $5 is a fair price for stockholders to pay for the bet. We will come to that in Chapter 8 when we discuss the valuation of options.

Risk Shifting: The First Game

Suppose that Circular has $10 cash. The following investment opportunity comes up:

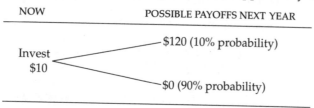

NOW	POSSIBLE PAYOFFS NEXT YEAR
Invest $10	$120 (10% probability)
	$0 (90% probability)

This is a wild gamble and probably a lousy project. But you can see why the owner would be tempted to take it anyway. Why not go for broke? Circular will probably go under anyway, so the owner is essentially betting with the bondholder's money. But the owner gets most of the loot if the project pays off.

Suppose that the project's NPV is –$2 but that it is undertaken anyway, thus depressing firm value by $2. Circular's new balance sheet might look like this:

Circular File Company (Market Values)

Net working capital	$10	$20	Bonds outstanding
Fixed assets	18	8	Common stock
Total assets	$28	$28	Total value

Firm value falls by $2, but the owner is $3 ahead because the bond's value has fallen by $5.[21] The $10 cash that used to stand behind the bond has been replaced by a very risky asset worth only $8.

Thus a game has been played at the expense of Circular's bondholder. The game illustrates the following general point: Stockholders of levered firms gain when business risk increases. Financial managers who act strictly in their shareholders' interests (and *against* the interests of creditors) will favor risky projects over safe ones. They may even take risky projects with negative NPVs.

This warped strategy for capital budgeting clearly is costly to the firm and to the economy as a whole. Why do we associate the costs with financial distress? Because the temptation to play is strongest when the odds of default are high. Exxon would never invest in our negative-NPV gamble. Its creditors are not vulnerable to this type of game.

Refusing to Contribute Equity Capital: The Second Game

We have seen how stockholders, acting in their immediate, narrow self-interest, may take projects which reduce the overall market value of their firm. These are errors of commission. Conflicts of interest may also lead to errors of omission.

Assume that Circular cannot scrape up any cash, and therefore cannot take that wild gamble. Instead a *good* opportunity comes up: a relatively safe asset costing $10 with a present value of $15 and NPV = +$5.

---

[21]We are not calculating this $5 drop. We are simply using it as a plausible assumption. The tools necessary for a calculation come in Chapter 8.

This project will not in itself rescue Circular, but it is a step in the right direction. We might therefore expect Circular to issue $10 of new stock and to go ahead with the investment. Suppose that two new shares are issued to the original owner for $10 cash. The project is taken. The new balance sheet might look like this:

Circular File Company (Market Values)

Net working capital	$20	$33	Bonds outstanding
Fixed assets	25	12	Common stock
Total assets	$45	$45	Total value

The total value of the firm goes up by $15 ($10 of new capital and $5 NPV). Notice that the Circular bond is no longer worth $25, but $33. The bondholder receives a capital gain of $8 because the firm's assets include a new, safe asset worth $15. The probability of default is less, and the payoff to the bondholder if default occurs is larger.

The stockholder loses what the bondholder gains. Equity value goes up not by $15 but by $15 − $8 = $7. The owner puts in $10 of fresh equity capital but gains only $7 in market value. Going ahead is in the firm's interest but not the owner's.

Again, our example illustrates a general point. If we hold business risk constant, any increase in firm value is shared among bondholders and stockholders. The value of any investment opportunity to the firm's *stockholders* is reduced because project benefits must be shared with bondholders. Thus it may not be in the stockholders' self-interest to contribute fresh equity capital even if that means forgoing positive-NPV investment opportunities.

This problem theoretically affects all levered firms, but it is most serious when firms land in financial distress. The greater the probability of default, the more bondholders have to gain from investments which increase firm value.

And Three More Games, Briefly

As with other games, the temptation to play the next three games is particularly strong in financial distress.

Cash In and Run   Stockholders may be reluctant to put money into a firm in financial distress, but they are happy to take the money out—in the form of a cash dividend, for example. The market value of the firm's stock goes down by less than the amount of the dividend paid, because the decline in *firm* value is shared with creditors. This game is just "refusing to contribute equity capital" run in reverse.

Playing for Time   When the firm is in financial distress, creditors would like to salvage what they can by forcing the firm to settle up. Naturally, stockholders want to delay this as long as they can. There are various devious ways of doing this, for example, through accounting changes designed to conceal the true extent of trouble, by encouraging false hopes of spontaneous recovery, or by cutting corners on maintenance, research and development, and so on, in order to make this year's operating performance look better.

Bait and Switch   This game is not always played in financial distress, but it is a quick way to get *into* distress. You start with a conservative policy, issuing a limited amount of relatively safe debt.

Then you suddenly switch and issue a lot more. That makes all your debt risky, imposing a capital loss on the "old" bondholders. Their capital loss is the stockholders' gain.

The most dramatic example of bait and switch occurred in October 1988, when the management of RJR Nabisco announced its intention to acquire the company in a *leveraged buy-out* (LBO). This put the company "in play" for a transaction in which existing shareholders would be bought out and the company would be "taken private." The cost of the buy-out would be almost entirely debt-financed. The new private company would start life with an extremely high debt ratio.

RJR Nabisco had debt outstanding with a market value of about $2.4 billion. The announcement of the coming LBO drove down this market value by $298 million.[22]

What the Games Cost

Why should anyone object to these games so long as they are played by consenting adults? Because playing them means poor decisions about investments and operations. These poor decisions are *agency costs* of borrowing.

The more the firm borrows, the greater is the temptation to play the games (assuming the financial manager acts in the stockholders' interest). The increased odds of poor decisions in the future prompt investors to mark down the present market value of the firm. The fall in value comes out of stockholders' pockets. Potential lenders, realizing that games may be played at their expense, protect themselves by demanding better terms.

Therefore it is ultimately in the stockholders' interest to avoid temptation. The easiest way to do this is to limit borrowing to levels at which the firm's debt is safe or close to it.

But suppose that the tax advantages of debt spur the firm on to a high debt ratio and a significant probability of default or financial distress. Is there any way to convince potential lenders that games will not be played? The obvious answer is to give lenders veto power over potentially dangerous decisions.

There we have the ultimate economic rationale for all that fine print backing up corporate debt. Debt contracts almost always limit dividends or equivalent transfers of wealth to stockholders; the firm may not be allowed to pay out more than it earns, for example. Additional borrowing is almost always limited. For example, many companies are prevented by existing bond indentures from issuing any additional long-term debt unless their ratio of earnings to interest charges exceeds 2.0.[23]

Sometimes firms are restricted from selling assets or making major investment outlays except with the lenders' consent. The risks of playing for time are reduced by specifying accounting procedures and by giving lenders access to the firm's books and its financial forecasts.

Of course, fine print cannot be a complete solution for firms that insist on issuing risky debt. The fine print has its own costs; you have to spend money to save money. Obviously a complex debt contract costs more to negotiate than a simple one. Afterward it costs the lender more to monitor the firm's performance. Lenders anticipate monitoring costs and demand compensation in the

---

[22]We thank Paul Asquith for these figures. RJR Nabisco was finally taken private not by its management but by another LBO partnership.

[23]RJR Nabisco bondholders might have done better if they had effective covenants to protect them against drastic increases in financial leverage. We discuss covenants and the rest of the fine print in debt contracts in Chapter 11.

form of higher interest rates; thus the monitoring costs—another agency cost of debt—are ultimately paid by stockholders.

Perhaps the most severe costs of the fine print stem from the constraints it places on operating and investment decisions. For example, an attempt to prevent the risk-shifting game may also prevent the firm from pursuing good investment opportunities. At the minimum there are delays in clearing major investments with lenders. In some cases lenders may veto high-risk investments even if net present value is positive. Lenders can lose from risk shifting even when the firm's overall market value increases. In fact, the lenders may try to play a game of their own, forcing the firm to stay in cash or low-risk assets even if good projects are forgone.

Thus, debt contracts cannot cover every possible manifestation of the games we have just discussed. Any attempt to do so would be hopelessly expensive and doomed to failure in any event. Human imagination is insufficient to conceive of all the possible things that could go wrong. We will always find surprises coming at us on dimensions we never thought to think about.

We hope we have not left the impression that managers and stockholders always succumb to temptation unless restrained. Usually they refrain voluntarily, not only from a sense of fair play but also on pragmatic grounds: A firm or individual that makes a killing today at the expense of a creditor will be coldly received when the time comes to borrow again. Aggressive game playing is done only by out-and-out crooks and by firms in extreme financial distress. Firms limit borrowing precisely because they don't wish to land in distress and be exposed to the temptation to play.

Costs of Distress Vary with Type of Asset

Suppose your firm's only asset is a large downtown hotel, mortgaged to the hilt. The recession hits, occupancy rates fall, and the mortgage payments cannot be met. The lender takes over and sells the hotel to a new owner and operator. You use your firm's stock certificates for wallpaper.

What is the cost of bankruptcy? In this example, probably very little. The value of the hotel is, of course, much less than you hoped, but that is due to the lack of guests, not to the bankruptcy. Bankruptcy doesn't damage the hotel itself. The direct bankruptcy costs are restricted to items such as legal and court fees, real estate commissions, and the time the lender spends sorting things out.[24]

Suppose we repeat the story of Heartbreak Hotel for Fledgling Electronics. Everything is the same, except for the underlying real assets—not real estate but a high-tech going concern, a growth company whose most valuable assets are technology, investment opportunities, and its employees' human capital.

If Fledgling gets into trouble, the stockholders may be reluctant to put up money to cash in on its growth opportunities. Failure to invest is likely to be much more serious for Fledgling than for a company like Heartbreak Hotel.

If Fledgling finally defaults on its debt, the lender will find it much more difficult to cash in by selling off the assets. Many of them are intangibles which have value only as a part of a going concern.

---

[24]In 1989 the Rockefeller family sold 80 percent of Rockefeller Center—several acres of extremely valuable Manhattan real estate—to Mitsubishi Estate Company for $1.4 billion. A REIT, Rockefeller Center Properties, held a $1.3 billion mortgage loan (the REIT's only asset) secured by this real estate. But rents and occupancy rates did not meet forecasts, and by 1995 Mitsubishi had incurred losses of about $600 million. Then Mitsubishi quit, and Rockefeller Center was bankrupt. That triggered a complicated series of maneuvers and negotiations. But did this damage the value of the Rockefeller Center properties? Was Radio City Music Hall, one of the properties, any less valuable because of the bankruptcy? We doubt it.

Could Fledgling be kept as a going concern through default and reorganization? It may not be as hopeless as putting a wedding cake through a car wash, but there are a number of serious difficulties. First, the odds of defections by key employees are higher than they would be if the firm had never gotten into financial trouble. Special guarantees may have to be given to customers who have doubts about whether the firm will be around to service its products. Aggressive investment in new products and technology will be difficult; each class of creditors will have to be convinced that it is in their interest for the firm to invest new money in risky ventures.

Some assets, like good commercial real estate, can pass through bankruptcy and reorganization largely unscathed; the values of other assets are likely to be considerably diminished. The losses are greatest for the intangible assets that are linked to the health of the firm as a going concern—for example, technology, human capital, and brand image. That may be why debt ratios are low in the pharmaceutical industry, where value depends on continued success in research and development, and in many service industries where value depends on human capital. We can also understand why highly profitable growth companies, such as Microsoft or Hewlett Packard, use mostly equity finance.[25]

The moral of these examples is this: *Do not think only about the probability that borrowing will bring trouble. Think also of the value that may be lost if trouble comes.*

The Trade-off Theory of Capital Structure

Financial managers often think of the firm's debt–equity decision as a trade-off between interest tax shields and the costs of financial distress. Of course, there is controversy about how valuable interest tax shields are and what kinds of financial trouble are most threatening, but these disagreements are only variations on a theme. Thus, Figure 6.2 illustrates the debt–equity trade-off.

This *trade-off theory* of capital structure recognizes that target debt ratios may vary from firm to firm. Companies with safe, tangible assets and plenty of taxable income to shield ought to have high target ratios. Unprofitable companies with risky, intangible assets ought to rely primarily on equity financing.

If there were no costs of adjusting capital structure, then each firm should always be at its target debt ratio. However, there are costs, and therefore delays, in adjusting to the optimum. Firms cannot immediately offset the random events that bump them away from their capital structure targets, so we should see random differences in actual debt ratios among firms having the same target debt ratio.

All in all, this trade-off theory of capital structure choice tells a comforting story. Unlike MM's theory, which seemed to say that firms should take on as much debt as possible, it avoids extreme predictions and rationalizes moderate debt ratios.

But what are the facts? Can the trade-off theory of capital structure explain how companies actually behave?

The answer is "yes and no." On the "yes" side, the trade-off theory successfully explains many industry differences in capital structure. High-tech growth companies, for example, whose assets

---

[25]Empirical research confirms that firms holding largely intangible assets borrow less. See, for example, M. Long and I. Malitz, "The Investment-Financing Nexus: Some Empirical Evidence," *Midland Corporate Finance Journal* 3 (Fall 1985), pp. 53–59.

are risky and mostly intangible, normally use relatively little debt. Airlines can and do borrow heavily because their assets are tangible and relatively safe.[26]

The trade-off theory also helps explain what kinds of companies "go private" in leveraged buy-outs (LBOs). LBOs are acquisitions of public companies by private investors who finance a large fraction of the purchase price with debt. The target companies for LBO takeovers are usually mature, cash-cow businesses with established markets for their products but little in the way of high-NPV growth opportunities. That makes sense by the trade-off theory, because these are exactly the kind of companies that *ought* to have high debt ratios.

The trade-off theory also says that companies saddled with extra heavy debt—too much to pay down with a couple of years' internally generated cash—should issue stock, constrain dividends, or sell off assets to raise cash to rebalance capital structure. Here again, we can find plenty of confirming examples. When Texaco bought Getty Petroleum in January 1984, it borrowed $8 billion from a consortium of banks to help finance the acquisition. (The loan was arranged and paid over to Texaco within two weeks!) By the end of 1984, it had raised about $1.8 billion to pay down this debt, mostly by selling assets and forgoing dividend increases. Chrysler, when it emerged from near-bankruptcy in 1983, sold $432 million of new common stock to help regain a conservative capital structure.[27] In 1991, after a second brush with bankruptcy, it again sold shares to replenish equity, this time for $350 million.[28]

On the "no" side, there are a few things the trade-off theory cannot explain. It cannot explain why some of the most successful companies thrive with little debt, thereby giving up valuable interest tax shields. Think of Merck, which as Table 6.3(a) shows, is basically all-equity-financed. Granted, Merck's most valuable assets are intangible, the fruits of its pharmaceutical research and development. We know that intangible assets and conservative capital structures tend to go together. But Merck also has a very large corporate income tax bill ($1.8 billion in 1997) and the highest possible credit rating. It could borrow enough to save tens of millions of tax dollars without raising a whisker of concern about possible financial distress.

Merck illustrates an odd fact about real-life capital structures: Within an industry, the most profitable companies generally borrow the least.[29] Here the trade-off theory fails, for it predicts exactly the reverse: Under the trade-off theory, high profits should mean more debt-servicing capacity and more taxable income to shield and should give a *higher* target debt ratio.[30]

---

[26]We are not suggesting that all airline companies are safe; many are not. But air*craft* can support debt where air*lines* cannot. If Fly-by-Night Airlines fails, its planes retain their value in another airline's operations. There's a good secondary market in used aircraft, so a loan secured by aircraft can be well protected even if made to an airline flying on thin ice (and in the dark). [2]

[27]Note that Chrysler issued stock *after* it emerged from financial distress. It did not *prevent* financial distress by raising equity money when trouble loomed on its horizon. Why not? Refer back to "Refusing to Contribute Equity Capital: The Second Game" or forward to the analysis of asymmetric information below.

[28]Chrysler simultaneously contributed $300 million of newly issued shares to its underfunded pension plans.

[29]For example, Carl Kester, in a study of the financing policies of firms in the United States and in Japan, found that in each country, high book profitability was the most statistically significant variable distinguishing low- from high-debt companies. See "Capital and Ownership Structure: A Comparison of United States and Japanese Manufacturing Corporations," *Financial Management* 15 (Spring 1986), pp. 5–16.

[30]Here we mean debt as a fraction of the book or replacement value of the company's assets. Profitable companies might not borrow a greater fraction of their market value. Higher profits imply higher market value as well as stronger incentives to borrow.

In general it appears that public companies rarely make major shifts in capital structure just because of taxes,[31] and it is hard to detect the present value of interest tax shields in firms' market values.[32]

A final point on the "no" side for the trade-off theory: Debt ratios in the early 1900s, when income tax rates were low (or zero), were just as high as those in the 1990s. Debt ratios in other industrialized countries are equal to or higher than those in the United States. Many of these countries have imputation tax systems, which should eliminate the value of the interest tax shields.[33]

None of this disproves the trade-off theory. As George Stigler emphasized, theories are not rejected by circumstantial evidence; it takes a theory to beat a theory. So we now turn to a completely different theory of financing.

THE PECKING ORDER OF FINANCING CHOICES

The pecking-order theory starts with *asymmetric information*—a fancy term indicating that managers know more about their companies' prospects, risks, and values than do outside investors.

Managers obviously know more than investors. We can prove that by observing stock price changes caused by announcements by managers. When a company announces an increased regular dividend, stock price typically rises, because investors interpret the increase as a sign of management's confidence in future earnings. In other words, the dividend increase transfers information from managers to investors. This can happen only if managers know more in the first place.

Asymmetric information affects the choice between internal and external financing and between new issues of debt and equity securities. This leads to a *pecking order*, in which investment is financed first with internal funds, reinvested earnings primarily; then by new issues of debt; and finally with new issues of equity. New equity issues are a last resort when the company runs out of debt capacity, that is, when the threat of costs of financial distress brings regular insomnia to existing creditors and to the financial manager.

We will take a closer look at the pecking order in a moment. First, you must appreciate how asymmetric information can force the financial manager to issue debt rather than common stock.

---

[31]Mackie-Mason found that tax-paying companies are more likely to issue debt (vs. equity) than nontaxpaying companies. This shows that taxes do affect financing choices. However, it is not necessarily evidence for the static trade-off theory. Miller's "Debt and Taxes" theory would make the same prediction. Under that theory, tax-paying firms would see no net tax advantage to debt: corporate interest tax shields would be offset by the taxes paid by investors in the firm's debt. But the balance would tip in favor of equity for a firm that was losing money and reaping no benefits from interest tax shields. See J. Mackie-Mason, "Do Taxes Affect Corporate Financing Decisions?" *Journal of Finance* 45 (December 1990), pp. 1471–1493.

[32]A recent empirical study by E. F. Fama and K. R. French, covering over 2,000 firms from 1965 to 1992, failed to find any evidence that interest tax shields contributed to firm value. See "Taxes, Financing Decisions and Firm Value," *Journal of Finance* 53 (June 1998), pp. 819–843.

[33]We describe the Australian imputation tax system in Chapter 7. Look at Table 7.4, supposing that an Australian corporation pays $A10 of interest. This reduces the corporate tax by $A3.30; it also reduces the tax credit taken by the shareholders by $A3.30. The final tax does not depend on whether the corporation or the shareholder borrows.

You can check this by redrawing Figure 6.1 for the Australian system. The corporate tax rate T_c will cancel out. Since income after all taxes depends only on investors' tax rates, there is no special advantage to corporate borrowing.

Debt and Equity Issues with Asymmetric Information

To the outside world Smith & Company and Jones, Inc., our two example companies, are identical. Each runs a successful business with good growth opportunities. The two businesses are risky, however, and investors have learned from experience that current expectations are frequently bettered or disappointed. Current expectations price each company's stock at $100 per share, but the true values could be higher or lower:

	SMITH & CO.	JONES, INC.
True value could be higher, say	$120	$120
Best current estimate	100	100
True value could be lower, say	80	80

Now suppose that both companies need to raise new money from investors to fund capital investment. They can do this either by issuing bonds or by issuing new shares of common stock. How would the choice be made? One financial manager—we will not tell you which one—might reason as follows:

> *Sell stock for $100 per share? Ridiculous! It's worth at least $120. A stock issue now would hand a free gift to new investors. I just wish those stupid, skeptical shareholders would appreciate the true value of this company. Our new factories will make us the world's lowest-cost producer. We've painted a rosy picture for the press and security analysts, but it just doesn't seem to be working. Oh well, the decision is obvious: we'll issue debt, not underpriced equity. A debt issue will save underwriting fees too.*

The other financial manager is in a different mood:

> *Beefalo burgers were a hit for a while, but it looks like the fad is fading. The fast-food division's gotta find some good new products or it's all downhill from here. Export markets are OK for now, but how are we going to compete with those new Siberian ranches? Fortunately the stock price has held up pretty well—we've had some good short-run news for the press and security analysts. Now's the time to issue stock. We have major investments under way, and why add increased debt service to my other worries?*

Of course, outside investors can't read the financial managers' minds. If they could, one stock might trade at $120 and the other at $80.

Why doesn't the optimistic financial manager simply educate investors? Then the company could sell stock on fair terms, and there would be no reason to favor debt over equity or vice versa.

This is not so easy. (Note that both companies are issuing upbeat press releases.) Investors can't be told what to think; they have to be convinced. That takes a detailed layout of the company's plans and prospects, including the inside scoop on new technology, product design, marketing plans, and so on. Getting this across is expensive for the company and also valuable to its competitors. Why go to the trouble? Investors will learn soon enough, as revenues and earnings evolve. In the meantime the optimistic financial manager can finance growth by issuing debt.

Now suppose there are two press releases:

> *Jones, Inc., will issue $120 million of five-year senior notes.*

> *Smith & Co. announced plans today to issue 1.2 million new shares of common stock. The company expects to raise $120 million.*

As a rational investor, you immediately learn two things. First, Jones's financial manager is optimistic and Smith's is pessimistic. Second, Smith's financial manager is also stupid to think that investors would pay $100 per share. The attempt to sell stock shows that it must be worth less. Smith might sell stock at $80 per share, but certainly not at $100.[34]

Smart financial managers think this through ahead of time. The end result? Both Smith and Jones end up issuing debt. Jones, Inc., issues debt because its financial manager is optimistic and doesn't want to issue undervalued equity. A smart, but pessimistic, financial manager at Smith issues debt because an attempt to issue equity would force the stock price down and eliminate any advantage from doing so. (Issuing equity also reveals the manager's pessimism immediately. Most managers prefer to wait. A debt issue lets bad news come out later through other channels.)

The story of Smith and Jones illustrates how asymmetric information favors debt issues over equity issues. If managers are better informed than investors and both groups are rational, then any company that can borrow will do so rather than issuing fresh equity. In other words, debt issues will be higher in the pecking order.

Taken literally this reasoning seems to rule out any issue of equity. That's not right, because asymmetric information is not always important and there are other forces at work. For example, if Smith had already borrowed heavily, and would risk financial distress by borrowing more, then it would have a good reason to issue common stock. In this case announcement of a stock issue would not be entirely bad news. The announcement would still depress the stock price—it would highlight managers' concerns about financial distress—but the fall in price would not necessarily make the issue unwise or infeasible.

High-tech, high-growth companies can also be credible issuers of common stock. Such companies' assets are mostly intangible, and bankruptcy or financial distress would be especially costly. This calls for conservative financing. The only way to grow rapidly and keep a conservative debt ratio is to issue equity. If investors see equity issued for these reasons, problems of the sort encountered by Jones's financial manager become much less serious.

With such exceptions noted, asymmetric information can explain the dominance of debt financing over new equity issues in practice. Debt issues are frequent; equity issues, rare. The bulk of external financing comes from debt, even in the United States, where equity markets are highly information-efficient. Equity issues are even more difficult in countries with less well developed stock markets.

None of this says that firms ought to strive for high debt ratios—just that it's better to raise equity by plowing back earnings than issuing stock. In fact, a firm with ample internally generated funds doesn't have to sell any kind of security and thus avoids issue costs and information problems completely.[35]

Implications of the Pecking Order

The pecking-order theory of corporate financing goes like this.[36]

1. Firms prefer internal finance.

---

[34]A Smith stock issue might not succeed even at $80. Persistence in trying to sell at $80 could convince investors that the stock is worth even less!

[35]Even debt issues can create information problems if the odds of default are significant. A pessimistic manager may try to issue debt quickly, before bad news gets out. An optimistic manager will delay pending good news, perhaps arranging a short-term bank loan in the meantime. Rational investors will take this behavior into account in pricing the risky debt issue.

[36]The description is paraphrased from S. C. Myers, "The Capital Structure Puzzle," *Journal of Finance* 39 (July 1984), pp. 581–582. For the most part, this section follows Myers's arguments.

2. They adapt their target dividend payout ratios to their investment opportunities, while trying to avoid sudden changes in dividends.

3. Sticky dividend policies, plus unpredictable fluctuations in profitability and investment opportunities, mean that internally generated cash flow is sometimes more than capital expenditures and other times less. If it is more, the firm pays off debt or invests in marketable securities. If it is less, the firm first draws down its cash balance or sells its marketable securities.

4. If external finance is required, firms issue the safest security first. That is, they start with debt, then possibly hybrid securities such as convertible bonds, then perhaps equity as a last resort.

In this theory, there is no well-defined target debt–equity mix, because there are two kinds of equity, internal and external, one at the top of the pecking order and one at the bottom. Each firm's observed debt ratio reflects its cumulative requirements for external finance.

The pecking order explains why the most profitable firms generally borrow less—not because they have low target debt ratios but because they don't need outside money. Less profitable firms issue debt because they do not have internal funds sufficient for their capital investment programs and because debt financing is first on the pecking order of *external* financing.

In the pecking-order theory, the attraction of interest tax shields is assumed to be a second-order effect. Debt ratios change when there is an imbalance of internal cash flow, net of dividends, and real investment opportunities. Highly profitable firms with limited investment opportunities work down to low debt ratios. Firms whose investment opportunities outrun internally generated funds are driven to borrow more and more.

This theory explains the inverse intraindustry relationship between profitability and financial leverage. Suppose firms generally invest to keep up with the growth of their industries. Then rates of investment will be similar within an industry. Given sticky dividend payouts, the least profitable firms will have less internal funds and will end up borrowing more.

The pecking order seems to predict changes in many mature firms' debt ratios to a T. These companies' debt ratios increase when the firms have financial deficits and decline when they have surpluses.[37] If asymmetric information makes major equity issues or retirements rare, this behavior is nearly inevitable.

The pecking order is less successful in explaining *inter*industry differences in debt ratios. For example, debt ratios tend to be low in high-tech, high-growth industries, even when the need for external capital is great. There are also mature, stable industries—electric utilities, for example—in which ample cash flow is *not* used to pay down debt. High dividend payout ratios give the cash flow back to investors instead.

Financial Slack

Other things equal, it's better to be at the top of the pecking order than at the bottom. Firms that have worked down the pecking order and need external equity may end up living with excessive debt or passing by good investments because shares can't be sold at what managers consider a fair price.

In other words, *financial slack* is valuable. Having financial slack means having cash, marketable securities, readily saleable real assets, and ready access to the debt markets or to bank

---

[37]See L. Shyam Sunder and S. C. Myers, "Testing Static Tradeoff Against Pecking Order Models of Capital Structure," *Journal of Financial Economics* 51 (February 1999), pp. 219–244.

financing. Ready access basically requires conservative financing so that potential lenders see the company's debt as a safe investment.

In the long run, a company's value rests more on its capital investment and operating decisions than on financing. Therefore, you want to make sure your firm has sufficient financial slack so that financing is quickly available for good investments. Financial slack is most valuable to firms with plenty of positive-NPV growth opportunities. That is another reason why growth companies usually aspire to conservative capital structures.

Free Cash Flow and the Dark Side of Financial Slack[38]

There is also a dark side to financial slack. Too much of it may encourage managers to take it easy, expand their perks, or empire-build with cash that should be paid back to stockholders. In other words, slack can make agency problems worse.

Michael Jensen has stressed the tendency of managers with ample free cash flow (or unnecessary financial slack) to plow too much cash into mature businesses or ill-advised acquisitions. "The problem," Jensen says, "is how to motivate managers to disgorge the cash rather than investing it below the cost of capital or wasting it in organizational inefficiencies."[39]

If that's the problem, then maybe debt is an answer. Scheduled interest and principal payments are contractual obligations of the firm. Debt forces the firm to pay out cash. Perhaps the best debt level would leave just enough cash in the bank, after debt service, to finance all positive-NPV projects, with not a penny left over.

We do not recommend this degree of fine-tuning, but the idea is valid and important. Debt can discipline managers who are tempted to invest too much. It can also provide the pressure to force improvements in operating efficiency.

THE AFTER-TAX WEIGHTED-AVERAGE COST OF CAPITAL

Think back to Chapter 5 and Modigliani and Miller's (MM's) proposition I. MM showed that, without taxes or financial market imperfections, the cost of capital does not depend on financing. In other words, the weighted average of the expected returns to debt and equity investors equals the opportunity cost of capital, regardless of the debt ratio:

$$\text{Weighted-average return to debt and equity} = r_D \frac{D}{V} + r_E \frac{E}{V}$$

$$= r, \text{a constant, independent of } D/V$$

Here r is the opportunity cost of capital, the expected rate of return investors would demand if the firm had no debt at all; r_D and r_E are the expected rates of return on debt and equity, the "cost of

---

[38]Some of the following is drawn from S. C. Myers, "Still Searching for Optimal Capital Structure," *Journal of Applied Corporate Finance* 6 (Spring 1993), pp. 4–14.

[39]M. C. Jensen, "Agency Costs of Free Cash Flow, Corporate Finance and Takeovers," *American Economic Review* 26 (May 1986), p. 323.

debt" and "cost of equity." The weights D/V and E/V are the fractions of debt and equity, based on market values; V, the total market value of the firm, is the sum of D and E.

But you can't look up r, the opportunity cost of capital, in *The Wall Street Journal* or find it on the Internet. So financial managers turn the problem around: They start with the estimates of r_D and r_E and then infer r. Under MM's assumptions,

$$r = r_D \frac{D}{V} + r_E \frac{E}{V}$$

This formula calculates r, the opportunity cost of capital, as the expected rate of return on a portfolio of all the firm's outstanding securities.

We have discussed this weighted-average cost of capital formula in Chapter 5. However, the formula misses a crucial difference between debt and equity: interest payments are tax-deductible. Therefore we move on to the *after-tax* weighted-average cost of capital, nicknamed WACC:

$$\text{WACC} = r_D(1 - T_c)\frac{D}{V} + r_E \frac{E}{V}$$

Here T_c is the marginal corporate tax rate.

Notice that the after-tax WACC is less than the opportunity cost of capital (r), because the "cost of debt" is calculated after tax as $r_D(1 - T_c)$. Thus the tax advantages of debt financing are reflected in a lower discount rate. Notice too that all the variables in the weighted-average formula refer to the firm as a whole. As a result, the formula gives the right discount rate only for projects that are just like the firm undertaking them. The formula works for the "average" project. It is incorrect for projects that are safer or riskier than the average of the firm's existing assets. It is incorrect for projects whose acceptance would lead to an increase or decrease in the firm's debt ratio.

Several questions about how to calculate the weighted-average cost of capital arise with sufficient frequency that we will address them here:

How Does the Formula Change when There are More Than Two Sources of Financing?   Easy: There is one cost for each element. The weight for each element is proportional to its market value. For example, if the capital structure includes both preferred and common shares,

$$\text{WACC} = r_D(1 - T_c)\frac{D}{V} + r_P \frac{P}{V} + r_E \frac{E}{V}$$

where r_P is investors' expected rate of return on preferred stocks.

What about Short-term Debt?   Many companies consider only long-term financing when calculating WACC. They leave out the cost of short-term debt. In principle this is incorrect. The lenders who hold short-term debt are investors who can claim their share of operating earnings. A company that ignores this claim will misstate the required return on capital investments.

But "zeroing out" short-term debt is not a serious error if the debt is only temporary, seasonal, or incidental financing or if it is offset by holdings of cash and marketable securities.[40] Suppose, for

---

[40]Financial practitioners have rules of thumb for deciding whether short-term debt is worth including in the weighted-average cost of capital. Suppose, for example, that short-term debt is 10 percent of total liabilities and that net working capital is negative. Then short-term debt is almost surely being used to finance long-term assets and should be explicitly included in WACC.

example, that your company's Italian subsidiary takes out a six-month loan from an Italian bank to finance its inventory and accounts receivable. The dollar equivalent of this loan will show up as a short-term debt on the parent's balance sheet. At the same time headquarters may be lending money by investing surplus dollars in short-term securities. If lending and borrowing offset, there is no point in including the cost of short-term debt in the weighted-average cost of capital, because the company is not a *net* short-term borrower.

What about Other Current Liabilities?   Current liabilities are usually "netted out" by subtracting them from current assets. The difference is entered as net working capital on the left-hand side of the balance sheet. The sum of long-term financing on the right is called *total capitalization*.

Net working capital
  = current assets
  – current liabilities
Plant and equipment
Growth opportunities
	
	Long-term debt (D)
	Preferred stock (P)
	Equity (E)
	Total capitalization (V)

When net working capital is treated as an asset, forecasts of cash flows for capital investment projects must treat increases in net working capital as a cash outflow and decreases as an inflow.

Since current liabilities include short-term debt, netting them out against current assets excludes the cost of short-term debt from the weighted-average cost of capital. We have just explained why this can be an acceptable approximation. But when short-term debt is an important, permanent source of financing—as is common for small firms and firms outside the United States—it should be shown explicitly on the right side of the balance sheet, not netted out against current assets. The interest cost of short-term debt is then one element of the weighted-average cost of capital.

How are the Costs of the Financing Elements Calculated?   You can often use stock market data to get an estimate of r_E, the expected rate of return demanded by investors in the company's stock. With that estimate, WACC is not too hard to calculate, because the borrowing rate r_D and the debt and equity ratios D/V and E/V can be directly observed or estimated without too much trouble.[41] Estimating the value and required return for preferred shares is likewise usually not too complicated.

Estimating the required return on other security types can be troublesome. Convertible debt, where the investors' return comes partly from an option to exchange the debt for the company's stock, is one example. We will leave convertibles to Chapter 9.

Junk debt, where the risk of default is high, is likewise difficult. The higher the odds of default, the lower the market price of the debt and the higher the *promised* rate of interest. But the weighted-average cost of capital is an *expected*, that is, average, rate of return, not a promised one. For example, in January 1999, TWA bonds maturing in 2006 sold at only 65 percent of face value and offered a 17.5 percent promised yield, more than 10 percentage points above yields on the

---

[41]Most corporate debt is not actively traded, so its market value cannot be observed directly. But you can usually value a nontraded debt security by looking to securities which *are* traded and which have approximately the same default risk and maturity. See Chapter 10.

For healthy firms the market value of debt is usually not too far from book value, so many managers and analysts use book value for D in the weighted-average cost of capital formula. However, be sure to use *market*, not book, values for E.

highest-quality debt issues maturing at the same time. The price and yield on the TWA bond demonstrated investors' concern about TWA's chronic financial ill-health. But the 17.5 percent yield was not an expected return, because it did not average in the losses to be incurred if TWA defaults. Including 17.5 percent as a "cost of debt" in a calculation of WACC would therefore overstate TWA's true cost of capital.

This is bad news: There is no easy or tractable way of estimating the expected rate of return on most junk debt issues.[42] The good news is that for most debt the odds of default are small. That means the promised and expected rates of return are close, and the promised rate can be used as an approximation in the weighted-average cost of capital.

SUMMARY

Our task in this chapter was to show why capital structure matters. We did not throw away MM's proposition I, that capital structure is irrelevant; we added to it. However, we did not arrive at any simple, satisfactory theory of optimal capital structure.

The traditional trade-off theory emphasizes taxes and financial distress. The value of the firm is broken down as

Value if all-equity-financed + PV(tax shield) − PV(costs of financial distress)

According to this theory, the firm should increase debt until the value from PV(tax shield) is just offset, at the margin, by increases in PV(costs of financial distress).

The costs of financial distress can be broken down as follows:

1. Bankruptcy costs
   (a) Direct costs such as court fees.
   (b) Indirect costs reflecting the difficulty of managing a company undergoing liquidation or reorganization.

2. Costs of financial distress short of bankruptcy
   (a) Conflicts of interest between bondholders and stockholders of firms in financial distress may lead to poor operating and investment decisions. Stockholders acting in their narrow self-interest can gain at the expense of creditors by playing "games" which reduce the overall value of the firm.
   (b) The fine print in debt contracts is designed to prevent these games. But fine print increases the costs of writing, monitoring, and enforcing the debt contract.

The value of the tax shield is more controversial. It would be easy to compute if we had only corporate taxes to worry about. In that case the net tax saving from borrowing would be just the marginal corporate tax rate T_c times $r_D D$, the interest payment. This tax shield is usually valued by discounting at the borrowing rate r_D. In the special case of fixed, permanent debt

$$\text{PV(tax shield)} = \frac{T_c(r_D D)}{r_D} = T_c D$$

---

[42]When betas can be estimated for the junk issue or for a sample of similar issues, the expected return can be calculated from the capital asset pricing model. Otherwise, the yield should be adjusted for the probability of default. Evidence on historical default rates on junk bonds is described in Chapter 11.

· Most economists have become accustomed to thinking only of the corporate tax advantages of debt. But many firms seem to thrive with no debt at all despite the strong tax inducement to borrow.

Miller has presented an alternative theory which may explain this. He argued that the net tax saving from corporate borrowing can be zero when personal taxes as well as corporate taxes are considered. Interest income is not taxed at the corporate level but is taxed at the personal level. Equity income is taxed at the corporate level but may largely escape personal taxes if it comes in the form of capital gains. Thus T_pE, the effective personal rate on equity income, is usually less than T_p, the regular personal rate which applies to interest income. This reduces the relative tax advantage of debt:

$$\text{Relative advantage} = \frac{1 - T_p}{(1 - T_{pE})(1 - T_c)}$$

Note that the relative advantage is $1/(1 - T_c)$ if interest and equity income are taxed at the same personal rates.

In Miller's theory, the supply of corporate debt expands as long as the corporate tax rate exceeds the personal tax rate of the investors absorbing the increased supply. The supply which equates these two tax rates establishes an optimal debt ratio for the aggregate of corporations. But, if the total supply of debt suits investors' needs, any single taxpaying firm must find that debt policy does not matter.

The Tax Reform Act of 1986 undercut Miller's argument by cutting back the extra personal taxes paid on interest income versus taxes paid on equity income (dividends and capital gains). But there is probably still a personal tax disadvantage to debt which to some degree offsets its corporate tax advantage.

We suggest that borrowing may make sense for some firms but not for others. If a firm can be fairly sure of earning a profit, there is likely to be a net tax saving from borrowing. However, for firms that are unlikely to earn sufficient profits to benefit from the corporate tax shield, there is little, if any, net tax advantage to borrowing. For these firms the net tax saving could even be negative.

The trade-off theory balances the tax advantages of borrowing against the costs of financial distress. Corporations are supposed to pick a target capital structure that maximizes firm value. Firms with safe, tangible assets and plenty of taxable income to shield ought to have high targets. Unprofitable companies with risky, intangible assets ought to rely primarily on equity financing.

This theory of capital structure successfully explains many industry differences in capital structure, but it does not explain why the most profitable firms *within* an industry generally have the most conservative capital structures. Under the trade-off theory, high profitability should mean high debt capacity *and* a strong corporate tax incentive to use that capacity.

There is a competing, pecking-order theory, which states that firms use internal financing when available and choose debt over equity when external financing is required. This explains why the less profitable firms in an industry borrow more—not because they have higher target debt ratios but because they need more external financing and because debt is next on the pecking order when internal funds are exhausted.

The pecking order is a consequence of asymmetric information. Managers know more about their firms than outside investors do, and they are reluctant to issue stock when they believe the price is too low. They try to time issues when shares are fairly priced or overpriced. Investors understand this, and interpret a decision to issue shares as bad news. That explains why stock price usually falls when a stock issue is announced.

Debt is better than equity when these information problems are important. Optimistic managers will prefer debt to undervalued equity, and pessimistic managers will be pressed to follow suit. The pecking-order theory says that equity will be issued only when debt capacity is running out and financial distress threatens.

The pecking-order theory is clearly not 100 percent right. There are many examples of equity issued by companies that could easily have borrowed. But the theory does explain why most external financing comes from debt, and it explains why changes in debt ratios tend to follow requirements for external financing.

The pecking-order theory stresses the value of financial slack. Without sufficient slack, the firm may be caught at the bottom of the pecking order and be forced to choose between issuing undervalued shares, borrowing and risking financial distress, or passing up positive-NPV investment opportunities.

There is, however, a dark side to financial slack. Surplus cash or credit tempts managers to overinvest or to indulge an easy and glamorous corporate lifestyle. When temptation wins, or threatens to win, a high debt ratio can help: it forces the company to disgorge cash and prods managers and organizations to try harder to be more efficient.

APPENDIX BANKRUPTCY PROCEDURES

Each year roughly 100,000 businesses file for bankruptcy. Most are small private firms, but about 1 percent of listed firms also go under each year.

Occasionally bankruptcy proceedings are initiated by the creditors, but usually it is the firm itself that decides to file. It can choose one of two procedures, which are set out in Chapters 7 and 11 of the 1978 Bankruptcy Reform Act. The purpose of Chapter 7 is to oversee the firm's death and dismemberment, while Chapter 11 seeks to nurse the firm back to health.

Most small firms make use of Chapter 7. In this case the bankruptcy judge appoints a trustee, who then closes the firm down and auctions off the assets. The proceeds from the auction are used to pay off the creditors. There is a pecking order of unsecured creditors. The U.S. Treasury, court officers, and the trustee have first peck. Wages come next, followed by taxes and debts to some government agencies such as the Pension Benefit Guarantee Corporation. Frequently the trustee will need to prevent some creditors from trying to jump the gun and collect on their debts, and sometimes the trustee will retrieve property that a creditor has recently seized.

Instead of agreeing to a liquidation, large public companies generally attempt to rehabilitate the business. This is in the shareholders' interests; they have nothing to lose if things deteriorate further and everything to gain if the firm recovers.

The procedures for rehabilitation are set out in Chapter 11 of the 1978 act. Their purpose is to keep the firm alive and operating and to protect the value of its assets[43] while a plan of reorganization is worked out. During this period, other proceedings against the firm are halted, and the company usually continues to be run by its existing management.[44] The responsibility for devel-

---

[43]In order to keep the firm alive, it may be necessary to continue to use assets that were offered as collateral, but this denies secured creditors access to their collateral. In order to resolve this problem, the Bankruptcy Reform Act makes it possible for firms operating under Chapter 11 to keep such assets as long as the creditors who have a claim on those assets are compensated for any decline in their value. Thus, the firm might make cash payments to the secured creditors to cover economic depreciation of the assets.

[44]Occasionally the court will appoint a trustee to manage the firm.

oping the plan falls on the debtor firm. If it cannot devise an acceptable plan, the court may invite anyone to do so—for example, a committee of creditors.

The plan goes into effect if it is accepted by the creditors and confirmed by the court. Acceptance requires approval by at least one-half of the creditors voting, and the creditors voting "aye" must represent two-thirds of the value of the creditors' aggregate claim against the firm. The plan also needs to be approved by two-thirds of the shareholders. Once the creditors and shareholders have accepted the plan, the court normally approves it, provided that each class of creditors is in favor and that the creditors will be no worse off under the plan than they would be if the firm's assets were liquidated and distributed. Under certain conditions the court may confirm a plan even if one or more classes of creditors vote against it,[45] but the rules for a "cram-down" are complicated, and we will not attempt to cover them here.

The reorganization plan is basically a statement of who gets what; each class of creditors gives up its claim in exchange for new securities or a mixture of securities and cash. The problem is to design a new capital structure for the firm that will (1) satisfy the creditors and (2) allow the firm to solve the *business* problems that got the firm into trouble in the first place.[46] Sometimes satisfying these two requirements requires a plan of baroque complexity. When the Penn Central Corporation was finally reorganized in 1978 (seven years after the largest railroad bankruptcy ever), more than a dozen new securities were created and parceled out among 15 classes of creditors.

The Securities and Exchange Commission (SEC) plays a role in many reorganizations, particularly for large, public companies. Its interest is to ensure that all relevant and material information is disclosed to the creditors before they vote on a proposed plan of reorganization. The SEC may take part in a hearing before court approval of a plan, for example.

Chapter 11 proceedings are often successful, and the patient emerges fit and healthy. But in other cases rehabilitation proves impossible, and the assets are liquidated. Sometimes the firm may emerge from Chapter 11 for a brief period before it is once again submerged by disaster and back in the bankruptcy court. For example, TWA came out of Chapter 11 bankruptcy at the end of 1993 and was back again less than two years later, prompting jokes about "Chapter 22."[47]

Is Chapter 11 Efficient?

Here is a simple view of the bankruptcy decision: Whenever a payment is due to creditors, management checks the value of the equity. If the value is positive, the firm pays the creditors (if necessary, raising the cash by an issue of shares). If the equity is valueless, the firm defaults on its debt and petitions for bankruptcy. If the assets of the bankrupt firm can be put to better use elsewhere, the firm is liquidated and the proceeds are used to pay off the creditors. Otherwise, the creditors simply become the new owners, and the firm continues to operate.[48]

---

[45]But at least one class of creditors must vote for the plan; otherwise, the court cannot approve it.

[46]Although Chapter 11 is designed to keep the firm in business, the reorganization plan often involves the sale or closure of large parts of the business.

[47]One study found that after emerging from Chapter 11 bankruptcy about one in three firms again reentered bankruptcy or privately restructured their debt. See E. S. Hotchkiss, "Postbankruptcy Reform and Management Turnover," *Journal of Finance* 50 (March 1995), pp. 3–21.

[48]If there are several classes of creditors, the junior creditors initially become the owners of the company and are responsible for paying off the senior debt. They now face exactly the same decision as the original owners. If their equity is valueless, they will also default and turn over ownership of the company to the next class of creditors.

In practice, matters are rarely so simple. For example, we observe that firms often petition for bankruptcy even when the equity has a positive value. And firms are often reorganized even when the assets could be used more efficiently elsewhere. The problems in Chapter 11 usually arise because the goal of paying off the creditors conflicts with the goal of maintaining the business as a going concern. We described earlier how the assets of Eastern Airlines seeped away as the court attempted to keep the airline flying. When the company filed for bankruptcy, its assets were more than sufficient to repay in full its liabilities of $3.7 billion. When it finally became clear that the airline was a terminal case, it was liquidated and the creditors received less than $.9 billion. The creditors would clearly have been better off if Eastern had been liquidated immediately; the unsuccessful attempt at resuscitation cost the creditors $2.8 billion.[49]

Here are some reasons that Chapter 11 proceedings do not always achieve an efficient solution:

1. Although the reorganized firm is legally a new entity, it is entitled to the tax-loss carry-forwards belonging to the old firm. If the firm is liquidated rather than reorganized, the tax-loss carry-forwards disappear. Thus there is a tax incentive to continue operating the firm even when its assets could be sold and put to better use elsewhere.

2. If the firm's assets are sold off, it is easy to determine what is available to pay the creditors. However, when the company is reorganized, it needs to conserve cash. Therefore, claimants are generally paid in a mixture of cash and securities. This makes it less easy to judge whether they receive a fair shake. For example, each bondholder may be offered $300 in cash and $700 in a new bond which pays no interest for the first two years and a low rate of interest thereafter. A bond of this kind in a company that is struggling to survive may not be worth much, but the bankruptcy court usually looks at the face value of the new bonds and may therefore regard the bondholders as paid off in full.

   Senior creditors who know they are likely to get a raw deal in a reorganization are likely to press for a liquidation. Shareholders and junior creditors prefer a reorganization. They hope that the court will not interpret the pecking order too strictly and that they will receive some crumbs when the firm's remaining value is sliced up. In the majority of cases their hopes are realized; often they receive a substantial portion of the equity of the reorganized company even though the unsecured creditors receive less than they are owed.[50]

3. Although shareholders and junior creditors are at the bottom of the pecking order, they have a secret weapon—they can play for time. On average it takes two to three years before a plan is presented to the court and agreed to by each class of creditor. (The bankruptcy proceedings of the Missouri Pacific Railroad took a total of 22 years.) When they use delaying tactics, the junior claimants are betting on a stroke of luck that will rescue their investment. On the other hand, the senior claimants know that time is working against them, so they may be prepared to accept a smaller payoff as part of the price for getting a plan accepted. Also, prolonged bankruptcy cases are costly (the bankruptcy proceedings of Wickes Corporation involved about $250 million in legal and administrative costs). Senior claimants may see their money seeping into lawyers' pockets and therefore decide to settle quickly.

---

[49]These estimates of creditor losses are taken from L. A. Weiss and K. H. Wruck, "Information Problems, Conflicts of Interest, and Asset Stripping: Chapter 11's Failure in the Case of Eastern Airlines," *Journal of Financial Economics* 48 (1998), pp. 55–97.

[50]Franks and Torous found that stockholders received some payoff—usually securities—in two-thirds of Chapter 11 reorganizations. See J. R. Franks and W. N. Torous, "An Empirical Investigation of U.S. Firms in Reorganization," *Journal of Finance* 44 (July 1989), pp. 747–770. A similar study concluded that in a third of the cases shareholders received more than 25 percent of the equity in the new firm. See L. A. Weiss, "Bankruptcy Resolution: Direct Costs and Violation of Priority of Claims," *Journal of Financial Economics* 27 (October 1990), pp. 285–314.

4. While a reorganization plan is being drawn up, the company is likely to need additional working capital. It is therefore allowed to buy goods on credit and borrow money. The new creditors have priority over the old creditors, and their debt may even be secured by assets that are already mortgaged to existing debtholders. This also gives the old creditors an incentive to settle quickly, before their claims are diluted by the new debt.

5. While the firm is in Chapter 11, secured debt receives interest but unsecured debt does not. For unsecured debtholders that is another reason for a fast settlement.

6. Sometimes profitable companies have filed for Chapter 11 bankruptcy to protect themselves against burdensome suits.[51] For example, Continental Airlines, which was bedeviled by a costly labor contract, filed for Chapter 11 in 1982 and immediately cut pay by up to 50 percent.[52] In 1995 Dow Corning was threatened with costly litigation for damage allegedly caused by its silicone-gel breast implants. Dow filed for bankruptcy under Chapter 11, and the bankruptcy judge agreed to stay the damage suits. Needless to say, lawyers and legislators worry that these actions were contrary to the original intent of the bankruptcy acts.

Workouts

If Chapter 11 reorganizations are not efficient, why don't firms bypass the bankruptcy courts and get together with their creditors to work out a solution?

Many firms that are in distress do first seek a negotiated settlement. For example, they can seek to delay repayment of the debt or negotiate an interest-rate holiday. However, shareholders and junior creditors know that senior creditors are anxious to avoid formal bankruptcy proceedings. So they are likely to be tough negotiators, and senior creditors generally need to make concessions to reach agreement.[53] The larger the firm, and the more complicated its capital structure, the less likely it is that everyone will agree to any proposal. For example, Wickes Corporation tried—and failed—to reach a negotiated settlement with its 250,000 creditors.

Sometimes the firm does agree to an informal workout with its creditors and then files under Chapter 11 to obtain the approval of the bankruptcy court.[54] Such *prepackaged bankruptcies* reduce the likelihood of subsequent litigation and allow the firm to gain the special tax advantages of Chapter 11.

Alternative Bankruptcy Procedures

The United States bankruptcy system is often described as a debtor-oriented system: its principal focus is on rescuing firms in distress. But this comes at a cost, for there are many instances in which the firm's assets would be better redeployed in other uses. One critic of Chapter 11, Michael Jensen, has argued that "the U.S. bankruptcy system is fundamentally flawed. It is

---

[51]See, for example, A. Cifelli, "Management by Bankruptcy," *Fortune*, October 1983, pp. 69–73.

[52]The pay cut enabled Continental to reduce fares aggressively and improve its load factors, but it did not solve Continental's problems. Shortly after emerging from bankruptcy, it was back in the bankruptcy court.

[53]Franks and Torous show that creditors make even greater concessions to junior claimholders in informal workouts than in Chapter 11 reorganizations. See J. R. Franks and W. N. Torous, "How Shareholders and Creditors Fare in Workouts and Chapter 11 Reorganizations," *Journal of Financial Economics* 35 (May 1994), pp. 349–370.

[54]For example, when TWA reentered Chapter 11 in 1995, it had already agreed to a *prepack* with its creditors.

expensive, it exacerbates conflicts of interest among different classes of creditors, and it often takes years to resolve individual cases."[55] Jensen's proposed solution is to require that any bankrupt company be put immediately on the auction block and the proceeds be distributed to claimants in accordance with the priority of their claims.[56]

In other countries the main purpose of bankruptcy law is not to rehabilitate the business but to recover as much as possible for the lenders and to ensure that the senior claimants get first peck. For example, in the United Kingdom creditors can apply for the appointment of a *liquidator* or a *receiver*, whose principal responsibility is to sell enough of the firm's assets to pay off its debts.[57] Similarly, in Germany an administrator (called a *konkursverwalter*) is appointed to sell the firm for cash, though he or she may decide that it is preferable not to do so immediately. In principle these procedures should help to ensure that assets are quickly and efficiently transferred to their best use. However, the arguments are not one-sided. Many observers worry that assets are sold off at fire-sale prices just to satisfy the senior creditors.

Further Reading

Modigliani and Miller's analysis of the present value of interest tax shields at the corporate level is in:
F. Modigliani and M. H. Miller: "Corporate Income Taxes and the Cost of Capital: A Correction," *American Economic Review,* 53:433–443 (June 1963).

F. Modigliani and M. H. Miller: "Some Estimates of the Cost of Capital to the Electric Utility Industry, 1954–57," *American Economic Review,* 56:333–391 (June 1966).

Miller extends the MM model to personal as well as corporate taxes; DeAngelo and Masulis argue that firms with plenty of noninterest tax shields, for example, shields from depreciation, should borrow less:
M. H. Miller: "Debt and Taxes," *Journal of Finance,* 32:261–276 (May 1977).

H. DeAngelo and R. Masulis: "Optimal Capital Structure under Corporate Taxation," *Journal of Financial Economics,* 8:5–29 (March 1980).

The following articles analyze the conflicts of interest between bondholders and stockholders and their implications for financing policy (do not read the last article until you have read Chapter 8):
M. C. Jensen and W. H. Meckling: "Theory of the Firm: Managerial Behavior, Agency Costs and Ownership Structure," *Journal of Financial Economics,* 3:305–360 (October 1976).

S. C. Myers: "Determinants of Corporate Borrowing," *Journal of Financial Economics,* 5:146–175 (1977).

D. Galai and R. W. Masulis: "The Option Pricing Model and the Risk Factor of Stock," *Journal of Financial Economics,* 3:53–82 (January–March 1976).

Myers describes the pecking-order theory, which is in turn based on work by Myers and Majluf; Baskin surveys some of the evidence for that theory:
S. C. Myers: "The Capital Structure Puzzle," *Journal of Finance,* 39:575–592 (July 1984).

---

[55]M. C. Jensen, "Corporate Control and the Politics of Finance," *Journal of Applied Corporate Finance* 4 (Summer 1991), pp. 13–33.

[56]An ingenious alternative set of bankruptcy procedures is proposed in P. Aghion, O. Hart, and J. Moore, "The Economics of Bankruptcy Reform," *Journal of Law, Economics and Organization* 8 (1992), pp. 523–546.

[57]A *receiver* is appointed by secured creditors and a *liquidator* is appointed by unsecured creditors. For more information on the UK and German systems, see J. R. Franks, K. Nyborg, and W. N. Torous, "A Comparison of US, UK and German Insolvency Codes," *Financial Management* 25 (Autumn 1996), pp. 86–101.

S. C. Myers and N. S. Majluf: "Corporate Financing and Investment Decisions When Firms Have Information Investors Do Not Have," *Journal of Financial Economics*, 13:187–222 (June 1984).

J. Baskin: "An Empirical Investigation of the Pecking Order Hypothesis," *Financial Management*, 18:26–35 (Spring 1989).

Two useful reviews of theory and evidence on optimal capital structure are:
M. J. Barclay, C. W. Smith, and R. L. Watts: "The Determinants of Corporate Leverage and Dividend Policies," *Journal of Applied Corporate Finance*, 7:4–19 (Winter 1995).

M. Harris and A. Raviv: "The Theory of Optimal Capital Structure," *Journal of Finance*, 48:297–356 (March 1991).

Altman's book is a general survey of the bankruptcy decision; also listed below are several good studies of the conflicting interests of different security holders and the costs and consequences of reorganization:
E. A. Altman: *Corporate Financial Distress: A Complete Guide to Predicting, Avoiding and Dealing with Bankruptcy*, John Wiley & Sons, New York, 1983.

M. White: "The Corporate Bankruptcy Decision," *Journal of Economic Perspectives*, 3:129–152 (Spring 1989).

J. R. Franks and W. N. Torous: "An Empirical Analysis of U.S. Firms in Reorganization," *Journal of Finance*, 44:747–770 (July 1989).

J. R. Franks and W. N. Torous: "How Shareholders and Creditors Fare in Workouts and Chapter 11 Reorganizations," *Journal of Financial Economics*, 35:349–370 (May 1994).

L. A. Weiss, "Bankruptcy Resolution: Direct Costs and Violation of Priority of Claims," *Journal of Financial Economics*, 27:285–314 (October 1990).

The Summer 1991 issue of the Journal of Applied Corporate Finance *contains several articles on bankruptcy and reorganizations.*

The Spring 1993 and Winter 1995 issues of the Journal of Applied Corporate Finance *contain several articles on the incentive effects of capital structure.*

The January–February 1986 issue of the Journal of Financial Economics *(vol. 15, no. 1/2) collects a series of empirical studies on the stock price impacts of debt and equity issues and capital structure changes.*

THE DIVIDEND CONTROVERSY

In this chapter we explain how companies set their dividend payments and we discuss the controversial question of how dividend policy affects value.

Why should you care about the answer to this question? Of course, if you are responsible for deciding on your company's dividend payment, you will want to know how it affects value. But there is a more general reason than that. If dividend policy does not affect value, then the company's investment decision is independent of its financing policy. In that case a good project is a good project is a good project, no matter who undertakes it or how it is ultimately financed. But perhaps it *does* affect value. In that case the attractiveness of a new project may depend on where the money is coming from. For example, if investors prefer companies with high payouts, companies might be reluctant to take on investments financed by retained earnings.

The first step toward understanding dividend policy is to recognize that the phrase means different things to different people. Therefore we must start by defining what *we* mean by it.

A firm's decisions about dividends are often mixed up with other financing and investment decisions. Some firms pay low dividends because management is optimistic about the firm's future and wishes to retain earnings for expansion. In this case the dividend is a by-product of the firm's capital budgeting decision. Suppose, however, that the future opportunities evaporate, that a dividend increase is announced, and that the stock price falls. How do we separate the impact of the dividend increase from the impact of investors' disappointment at the lost growth opportunities?

Another firm might finance capital expenditures largely by borrowing. This releases cash for dividends. In this case the firm's dividend is a by-product of the borrowing decision.

We must isolate dividend policy from other problems of financial management. The precise question we should ask is, What is the effect of a change in cash dividends paid, *given the firm's capital budgeting and borrowing decisions?* Of course the cash used to finance a dividend increase has to come from somewhere. If we fix the firm's investment outlays and borrowing, there is only one possible source—an issue of stock. Thus we define *dividend policy* as the trade-off between retaining earnings on the one hand and paying out cash and issuing new shares on the other.

This trade-off may seem artificial at first, for we do not observe firms scheduling a stock issue with every dividend payment. But there are many firms that pay dividends and also issue stock from time to time. They could avoid the stock issues by paying lower dividends. Many other firms restrict dividends so that they do not have to issue shares. They could issue stock occasionally and increase the dividend. Both groups of firms are facing the dividend policy trade-off.

Companies can hand back cash to their shareholders either by paying a dividend or by buying back their stock. So we start the chapter with some basic institutional material on dividends and stock repurchases. We then look at how companies decide on dividend payments and we show how both dividends and stock repurchases provide information to investors about company prospects. We then come to the central question, How does dividend policy affect firm value? You will see why we call this chapter "The Dividend Controversy."

HOW DIVIDENDS ARE PAID

The dividend is set by the firm's board of directors. The announcement of the dividend states that the payment will be made to all those stockholders who are registered on a particular *record date*. Then about two weeks later dividend checks are mailed to stockholders.

Shares are normally bought and sold *with dividend* or *cum dividend* until a few days before the record date, at which point they trade *ex dividend*. Investors who buy with dividend need not worry if their shares are not registered in time. The dividend must be paid over to them by the seller.

The company is not free to declare whatever dividend it chooses. Some restrictions may be imposed by lenders, who are concerned that excessive dividend payments would not leave enough in the kitty to pay the company's debts. State law also helps to protect the company's creditors against excessive dividend payments. For example, companies are not allowed to pay a dividend out of *legal capital*, which is generally defined as the par value of outstanding shares.[1]

Dividends Come in Different Forms

Most companies pay a *regular cash dividend* each quarter,[2] but occasionally this regular dividend is supplemented by a one-off *extra* or *special dividend*.

---

[1]Where there is no par value, legal capital is defined as part or all of the receipts from the issue of shares. Companies with wasting assets, such as mining companies, are sometimes permitted to pay out legal capital.

[2]In 1999 Disney changed to paying dividends once a year rather than quarterly. Disney has an unusually large number of investors with only a handful of shares. By making an annual payment, Disney reduced the substantial cost of mailing dividend checks to these investors.

Dividends are not always in the form of cash. Frequently companies also declare *stock dividends*. For example, Archer Daniels Midland has paid a yearly stock dividend of 5 percent for over 20 years. That means it sends each shareholder 5 extra shares for every 100 shares currently owned. You can see that a stock dividend is very much like a stock split. Both increase the number of shares, but the company's assets, profits, and total value are unaffected. So both reduce value *per share*. The distinction between the two is technical. A stock dividend is shown in the accounts as a transfer from retained earnings to equity capital, whereas a split is shown as a reduction in the par value of each share.

There are also other types of noncash dividend. For example, companies sometimes send shareholders a sample of their product. The British company Dundee Crematorium once offered its more substantial shareholders a discount cremation. Needless to say, they were not *required* to receive this dividend.

Many companies have automatic dividend reinvestment plans (DRIPs). Often the new shares are issued at a 5 percent discount from the market price; the firm offers this sweetener because it saves the underwriting costs of a regular share issue.[3] Sometimes 10 percent or more of total dividends will be reinvested under such plans.

Share Repurchase

When a firm wants to pay cash to its shareholders, it usually declares a cash dividend. The alternative is to repurchase its own stock. The reacquired shares are usually kept in the company's treasury and can be resold if the company needs money.

There is an important difference in the taxation of dividends and stock repurchases. Dividends are taxed as ordinary income, but stockholders who sell shares back to the firm pay tax only on capital gains realized in the sale. However, the Internal Revenue Service is on the lookout for companies that disguise dividends as repurchases, and it may decide that regular or proportional repurchases should be taxed as dividend payments.

There are three main ways to repurchase stock. The most common method is for the firm to announce that it plans to buy its stock in the open market, just like any other investor.[4] However, sometimes companies offer to buy back a stated number of shares at a fixed price, which is typically set at about 20 percent above the current market level. Shareholders can then choose whether to accept this offer. Finally, repurchase may take place by direct negotiation with a major shareholder. The most notorious instances are greenmail transactions, in which the target of a takeover attempt buys off the hostile bidder by repurchasing any shares that it has acquired. "Greenmail" means that these shares are repurchased by the target at a price which makes the bidder happy to leave the target alone. This price does not always make the target's shareholders happy, however.

---

[3]Sometimes companies not only allow shareholders to reinvest dividends, but also allow them to buy additional shares at a discount. In some cases substantial amounts of money have been invested. For example, AT&T has raised over $400 million a year through DRIPs. For an amusing and true rags-to-riches story, see M. S. Scholes and M. A. Wolfson, "Decentralized Investment Banking: The Case of Dividend-Reinvestment and Stock-Purchase Plans," *Journal of Financial Economics* 24 (September 1989), pp. 7–36.

[4]An alternative procedure is to employ a *Dutch auction*. In this case the firm states a series of prices at which it is prepared to repurchase stock. Shareholders submit offers declaring how many shares they wish to sell at each price and the company then calculates the lowest price at which it can buy the desired number of shares. This is another example of the uniform-price auction described in Chapter 3.

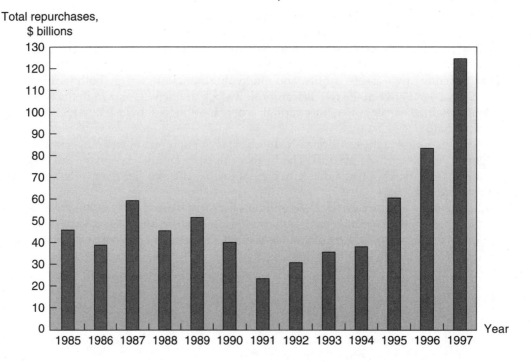

Figure 7.1

Stock repurchases in the United States 1985–1997. (Figures in $ billions.)
Source: Compustat 1998.

Stock repurchase plans were big news in October 1987. On Monday, October 19, stock prices in the United States nose-dived more than 20 percent. The next day the board of Citicorp approved a plan to repurchase $250 million of the company's stock. Citicorp was soon joined by a number of other corporations whose managers were equally concerned about the market crash. Altogether, over a two-day period these firms announced plans to buy back a total of $6.2 billion of stock. News of these huge buyback programs helped to stem the slide in stock prices.

Figure 7.1 shows that since the 1980s repurchases have become an everyday event. As we write this chapter in August 1998, new repurchase programs have been announced in the last two weeks by CBS Corporation ($2 billion), Sara Lee ($3 billion), Columbia/HCA ($1 billion), ITT industries ($1 billion), and Merck ($5 billion). The biggest and most dramatic repurchases have been in the oil industry, where cash resources for a long time outran good capital investment opportunities. Exxon is in first place, having spent about $21 billion on repurchasing shares through year-end 1997.

All these repurchases were like bumper dividends; they caused large amounts of cash to be paid to investors. But they did not *substitute* for dividends; none of the companies just mentioned reduced its dividend when it undertook a large repurchase program. If a company has accumulated large amounts of unwanted cash or if it wishes to change its capital structure by replacing equity with debt, it generally repurchases stock. Dividends are seldom used for these purposes.

Consider the example of U.S. banks. In 1997 large bank holding companies paid out just under 40 percent of their earnings as dividends. There were few profitable investment opportunities for the remaining income, but the banks did not want to commit themselves in the long run to any larger dividend payments. They therefore returned the cash to shareholders not by upping the dividend rate, but by repurchasing $16 billion of stock.[5]

Buybacks are far less common outside the United States. Some countries such as Austria and Norway ban them entirely. In many other European countries they are taxed as dividends, often at very high rates. So companies that have amassed large mountains of cash may prefer to invest it to earn low rates of interest rather than to hand it back to their shareholders, who could reinvest it in other companies that are short of cash.

HOW DO COMPANIES DECIDE ON DIVIDEND PAYMENTS?

Lintner's Model

In the mid-1950s John Lintner conducted a classic series of interviews with corporate managers about their dividend policies.[6] His description of how dividends are determined can be summarized in four "stylized facts":[7]

1. Firms have long-run target dividend payout ratios. Mature companies with stable earnings generally pay out a high proportion of earnings; growth companies have low payouts.

2. Managers focus more on dividend changes than on absolute levels. Thus, paying a $2.00 dividend is an important financial decision if last year's dividend was $1.00, but no big deal if last year's dividend was $2.00.

3. Dividend changes follow shifts in long-run, sustainable earnings. Managers "smooth" dividends. Transitory earnings changes are unlikely to affect dividend payouts.

4. Managers are reluctant to make dividend changes that might have to be reversed. They are particularly worried about having to rescind a dividend increase.

Lintner developed a simple model which is consistent with these facts and explains dividend payments well. Here it is: Suppose that a firm always stuck to its target payout ratio. Then the dividend payment in the coming year (DIV1) would equal a constant proportion of earnings per share (EPS1):

$$DIV_1 = \text{target dividend}$$

$$= \text{target ratio} \times EPS_1$$

The dividend *change* would equal

$$DIV_1 - DIV_0 = \text{target change}$$

$$= \text{target ratio} \times EPS_1 - DIV_0$$

---

[5]B. Hirtle, "Bank Holding Company Capital Ratios and Shareholder Payouts," *Federal Reserve Bank of New York: Current Issues in Economics and Finance*, 4 (September 1998).

[6]J. Lintner, "Distribution of Incomes of Corporations among Dividends, Retained Earnings, and Taxes," *American Economic Review* 46 (May 1956), pp. 97–113.

[7]The stylized facts are given by Terry A. Marsh and Robert C. Merton, "Dividend Behavior for the Aggregate Stock Market," *Journal of Business* 60 (January 1987), pp. 1–40. See pp. 5–6. We have paraphrased and embellished.

A firm that always stuck to its target payout ratio would have to change its dividend whenever earnings changed. But the managers in Lintner's survey were reluctant to do this. They believed that shareholders prefer a steady progression in dividends. Therefore, even if circumstances appeared to warrant a large increase in their company's dividend, they would move only partway toward their target payment. Their dividend changes therefore seemed to conform to the following model:

$$DIV_1 - DIV_0 = \text{adjustment rate} \times \text{target change}$$

$$= \text{adjustment rate} \times (\text{target ratio} \times EPS_1 - DIV_0)$$

The more conservative the company, the more slowly it would move toward its target and, therefore, the *lower* would be its adjustment rate.

Lintner's simple model suggests that the dividend depends in part on the firm's current earnings and in part on the dividend for the previous year, which in turn depends on that year's earnings and the dividend in the year before. Therefore, if Lintner is correct, we should be able to describe dividends in terms of a weighted average of current and past earnings.[8] The probability of an increase in the dividend rate should be greatest when *current* earnings have increased; it should be somewhat less when only the earnings from the previous year have increased; and so on. An extensive study by Fama and Babiak confirmed this hypothesis.[9] Their tests of Lintner's model suggest that it provides a fairly good explanation of how companies decide on the dividend rate, but it is not the whole story. We would expect managers to take future prospects as well as past achievements into account when setting the payment. As we shall see in the next section, that is indeed the case.

THE INFORMATION IN DIVIDENDS AND STOCK REPURCHASES

In some countries you cannot rely on the information that companies provide. Passion for secrecy and a tendency to construct multilayered corporate organizations produce asset and earnings figures that are next to meaningless. Some people say that, thanks to creative accounting, the situation is little better for some companies in the United States.

How does an investor in such a world separate marginally profitable firms from the real money makers? One clue is dividends. Investors can't read managers' minds, but they can learn

---

[8]This can be demonstrated as follows: Dividends per share in time t are

(1) $$DIV_t = aT(EPS_t) + (1-a)DIV_{t-1}$$

where a is the adjustment rate and T is the target payout ratio. But the same relationship holds in $t-1$:

(2) $$DIV_{t-1} = aT(EPS_{t-1}) + (1-a)DIV_{t-2}$$

Substitute for DIV_{t-1} in (1):

$$DIV_t = aT(EPS_t) + aT(1-a)(EPS_{t-1}) + (1-a)^2 DIV_{t-2}$$

We can make similar substitutions for DIV_{t-2}, DIV_{t-3}, etc., thereby obtaining

$$DIV_t = aT(EPS_t) + aT(1-a)(EPS_{t-1}) + aT(1-a)^2(EPS_{t-2}) + \cdots + aT(1-a)^n(EPS_{t-n})$$

[9]E. F. Fama and H. Babiak, "Dividend Policy: An Empirical Analysis," *Journal of the American Statistical Association* 63 (December 1968), pp. 1132–1161.

from managers' actions. They know that a firm which reports good earnings and pays a generous dividend is putting its money where its mouth is. We can understand, therefore, why investors would value the information content of dividends and would refuse to believe a firm's reported earnings unless they were backed up by an appropriate dividend policy.

Of course, firms can cheat in the short run by overstating earnings and scraping up cash to pay a generous dividend. But it is hard to cheat in the long run, for a firm that is not making enough money will not have enough cash to pay out. If a firm chooses a high dividend payout without the cash flow to back it up, that firm will ultimately have to reduce its investment plans or turn to investors for additional debt or equity financing. All of these consequences are costly. Therefore, most managers don't increase dividends until they are confident that sufficient cash will flow in to pay them.

There is plenty of evidence that managers do look to the future when they set the dividend payment. For example, Healy and Palepu report that on average earnings jumped 43 percent in the year that companies paid a dividend for the first time.[10] If managers thought that this was a temporary windfall, they might have been cautious about committing themselves to paying out cash. But it looks as if they had good reason to be confident about prospects, for over the next four years earnings grew on average by a further 164 percent.

Since dividends anticipate future earnings, it is no surprise to find that announcements of dividend cuts are usually taken by investors as bad news (stock price typically falls) and that dividend increases are good news (stock price rises). In the case of the dividend initiations studied by Healy and Palepu, the announcement of the dividend resulted in an abnormal rise of 4 percent in the stock price.[11]

When dividends change unexpectedly, the stock price can bounce back and forth as investors struggle to interpret the significance of the change. In 1994 FPL Group, the parent company of Florida Power and Light Company, announced a reduction in its quarterly dividend from $.62 a share to $.42. This was the first-ever dividend cut for a healthy utility, so the company did its best to spell out to investors why it had taken such an unusual step. FPL pointed to the prospect of increased competition in the electric utility industry, and argued that the company's historically high payout ratio was no longer in shareholders' best interests. The company also felt that it would be prudent to reduce debt, and that part of the cash savings from the dividend cut would be used for this purpose. At the same time, the company announced plans to return part of the cash saved by the dividend cut by repurchasing up to 10 million shares of stock over the next three years. FPL explained that this would reduce shareholders' taxes.

All this sounded logical, but investors' first reaction was dismay. On the day of the announcement the company's stock price fell nearly 14 percent. However, as analysts considered FPL's reason for the dividend cut, they concluded that the action was not an indication of financial weakness. Within a month of the announcement the stock price had more than recovered its initial loss.[12]

---

[10]See P. Healy and K. Palepu, "Earnings Information Conveyed by Dividend Initiations and Omissions," *Journal of Financial Economics* 21 (1988), pp. 149–175. Not everyone agrees that dividend changes predict future earnings. See, for example, S. Benartzi, R. Michaely, and R. Thaler, "Do Changes in Dividends Signal the Future or the Past?" *Journal of Finance* 52 (July 1997), pp. 1007–1034.

[11]Healy and Palepu also looked at companies that *stopped* paying a dividend. In this case the stock price on average declined by an abnormal 9.5 percent on the announcement and earnings fell over the next four quarters.

[12]The events surrounding FPL's dividend cut are described in D. Soter, E. Brigham, and P. Evanson, "The Dividend Cut `Heard Round the World': The Case of FPL," *Journal of Applied Corporate Finance* 9 (Spring 1996), pp. 4–15.

If FPL had always paid a dividend of $.42, you could be sure that the 1994 dividend decision would not have caused consternation. Investors were not worried about the *level* of FPL's dividend but about the *change*, which they saw as providing important information about future profitability.

It seems that in some other countries investors are less preoccupied with dividend changes. For example, in Japan there is a much closer relationship between corporations and major stockholders, and therefore information may be more easily shared with investors. Consequently, Japanese corporations are more prone to cut their dividends when there is a drop in earnings, but investors do not mark the stocks down as sharply as in the United States.[13]

The Information Content of Share Repurchase

Share repurchases, like dividends, are a way to hand cash back to shareholders. But unlike dividends, share repurchases are frequently a one-off event. So a company that announces a repurchase program is not making a long-term commitment to earn and distribute more cash. The information in the announcement of a share repurchase program is therefore likely to be different from the information in a dividend payment.

Companies repurchase shares when they have accumulated more cash than they can invest profitably or when they wish to increase their debt levels. Neither circumstance is good news in itself, but shareholders are frequently relieved to see companies paying out the excess cash rather than frittering it away on unprofitable investments. Shareholders also know that firms with large quantities of debt to service are less likely to squander cash. A study by Comment and Jarrell, who looked at the announcements of open-market repurchase programs, found that on average they resulted in an abnormal price rise of 2 percent.[14]

Stock repurchases may also be used to signal a manager's confidence in the future. Suppose that you, the manager, believe that your stock is substantially undervalued. You announce that the company is prepared to buy back a fifth of its stock at a price that is 20 percent above the current market price. But (you say) you are certainly not going to sell any of your own stock at that price. Investors jump to the obvious conclusion—you must believe that the stock is a good value even at 20 percent above the current price.

When companies offer to repurchase their stock at a premium, senior management and directors usually commit to hold onto their stock. So it is not surprising that researchers have found that announcements of offers to buy back shares above the market price have prompted a larger rise in the stock price, averaging about 11 percent.[15]

THE CONTROVERSY ABOUT DIVIDEND POLICY

We have seen that a dividend increase indicates management's optimism about earnings and thus affects the stock price. But the jump in stock price that accompanies an unexpected dividend in-

---

[13]The dividend policies of Japanese *keiretsus* are analyzed in K. L. Dewenter and V. A. Warther, "Dividends, Asymmetric Information, and Agency Conflicts: Evidence from a Comparison of the Dividend Policies of Japanese and U.S. Firms," *Journal of Finance* 53 (June 1998), pp. 879–904.

[14]See R. Comment and G. Jarrell, "The Relative Signalling Power of Dutch-Auction and Fixed Price Self-Tender Offers and Open-Market Share Repurchases," *Journal of Finance* 46 (September 1991), pp. 1243–1271.

[15]See R. Comment and G. Jarrell, *op. cit.*

crease would happen eventually anyway as information about future earnings comes out through other channels. We now ask whether the dividend decision *changes* the value of the stock, rather than simply providing a *signal* of stock value.

One endearing feature of economics is that it can always accommodate not just two but three opposing points of view. And so it is with the controversy about dividend policy. On the right there is a conservative group which believes that an increase in dividend payout increases firm value. On the left, there is a radical group which believes that an increase in payout reduces value. And in the center there is a middle-of-the-road party which claims that dividend policy makes no difference.

The middle-of-the-road party was founded in 1961 by Miller and Modigliani (always referred to as "MM" or "M and M"), when they published a theoretical paper showing the irrelevance of dividend policy in a world without taxes, transaction costs, or other market imperfections.[16] By the standards of 1961 MM were leftist radicals, because at that time most people believed that even under idealized assumptions increased dividends made shareholders better off.[17] But now MM's proof is generally accepted as correct, and the argument has shifted to whether taxes or other market imperfections alter the situation. In the process MM have been pushed toward the center by a new leftist party which argues for low dividends. The leftists' position is based on MM's argument modified to take account of taxes and costs of issuing securities. The conservatives are still with us, relying on essentially the same arguments as in 1961.

We begin our discussion of dividend policy with a presentation of MM's original argument. Then we will undertake a critical appraisal of the positions of the three parties. Perhaps we should warn you before we start that our own position was for many years marginally leftist. But after the 1986 Tax Reform Act we joined the middle-of-the-roaders.

Dividend Policy Is Irrelevant in Perfect Capital Markets

In their classic 1961 article MM argued as follows: Suppose your firm has settled on its investment program. You have worked out how much of this program can be financed from borrowing, and you plan to meet the remaining funds requirement from retained earnings. Any surplus money is to be paid out as dividends.

Now think what happens if you want to increase the dividend payment without changing the investment and borrowing policy. The extra money must come from somewhere. If the firm fixes its borrowing, the only way it can finance the extra dividend is to print some more shares and sell them. The new stockholders are going to part with their money only if you can offer them shares that are worth as much as they cost. But how can the firm do this when its assets, earnings, investment opportunities, and, therefore, market value are all unchanged? The answer is that there must be a *transfer of value* from the old to the new stockholders. The new ones get the newly printed shares, each one worth less than before the dividend change was announced, and the old ones

---

[16]M. H. Miller and F. Modigliani: "Dividend Policy, Growth and the Valuation of Shares," *Journal of Business* 34 (October 1961), pp. 411–433.

[17]Not *everybody* believed dividends make shareholders better off. MM's arguments were anticipated in 1938 in J. B. Williams, *The Theory of Investment Value*, Harvard University Press, Cambridge, MA, 1938. Also, a proof very similar to MM's was developed by J. Lintner in "Dividends, Earnings, Leverage, Stock Prices and the Supply of Capital to Corporations," *Review of Economics and Statistics* 44 (August 1962), pp. 243–269.

Figure 7.2

This firm pays out a third of its worth as a dividend and raises the money by selling new shares. The transfer of value to the new stockholders is equal to the dividend payment. The total value of the firm is unaffected.

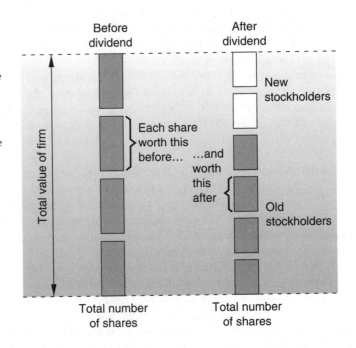

suffer a capital loss on their shares. The capital loss borne by the old shareholders just offsets the extra cash dividend they receive.

Figure 7.2 shows how this transfer of value occurs. Our hypothetical company pays out a third of its total value as a dividend and it raises the money to do so by selling new shares. The capital loss suffered by the old stockholders is represented by the reduction in the size of the shaded boxes. But that capital loss is exactly offset by the fact that the new money raised (the white boxes) is paid over to them as dividends.

Does it make any difference to the old stockholders that they receive an extra dividend payment plus an offsetting capital loss? It might if that were the only way they could get their hands on cash. But as long as there are efficient capital markets, they can raise the cash by selling shares. Thus the old shareholders can cash in either by persuading the management to pay a higher dividend or by selling some of their shares. In either case there will be a transfer of value from old to new shareholders. The only difference is that in the former case this transfer is caused by a dilution in the value of each of the firm's shares, and in the latter case it is caused by a reduction in the number of shares held by the old shareholders. The two alternatives are compared in Figure 7.3.

Because investors do not need dividends to get their hands on cash, they will not pay higher prices for the shares of firms with high payouts. Therefore firms ought not to worry about dividend policy. They should let dividends fluctuate as a by-product of their investment and financing decisions.

Dividend Irrelevance—An Illustration

Consider the case of Rational Demiconductor, which at this moment has the following balance sheet:

Rational Demiconductor's Balance Sheet (Market Values)

Cash ($1,000 held for investment)	1,000	0	Debt
Fixed assets	9,000	10,000 + NPV	Equity
Investment opportunity ($1,000 investment required)	NPV		
Total asset value	$10,000 + NPV	$10,000 + NPV	Value of firm

Rational Demiconductor has $1,000 cash earmarked for a project requiring $1,000 investment. We do not know how attractive the project is, and so we enter it at NPV; after the project is undertaken it will be worth $1,000 + NPV. Note that the balance sheet is constructed with market values; equity equals the market value of the firm's outstanding shares (price per share times number of shares outstanding). It is not necessarily equal to book net worth.

Now Rational Demiconductor uses the cash to pay a $1,000 dividend to its stockholders. The benefit to them is obvious: $1,000 of spendable cash. It is also obvious that there must be a cost. The cash is not free.

Where does the money for the dividend come from? Of course, the immediate source of funds is Rational Demiconductor's cash account. But this cash was earmarked for the investment project. Since we want to isolate the effects of dividend policy on shareholders' wealth, we assume that the company *continues* with the investment project. That means that $1,000 in cash must be raised by new financing. This could consist of an issue of either debt or stock. Again, we just want to look at dividend policy for now. Thus Rational Demiconductor ends up financing the dividend with a $1,000 stock issue.

Now we examine the balance sheet after the dividend is paid, the new stock is sold, and the investment is undertaken. Because Rational Demiconductor's investment and borrowing policies are unaffected by the dividend payment, its overall market value must be unchanged at

Figure 7.3

Two ways of raising cash for the firm's original shareholders. In each case the cash received is offset by a decline in the value of the old stockholders' claim on the firm. If the firm pays a dividend, each share is worth less because more shares have to be issued against the firm's assets. If the old stockholders sell some of their shares, each share is worth the same but the old stockholders have fewer shares.

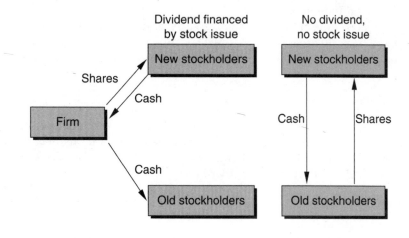

$10,000 + NPV.[18] We know also that if the new stockholders pay a fair price, their stock is worth $1,000. That leaves us with only one missing number—the value of the stock held by the original stockholders. It is easy to see that this must be

$$\text{Value of original stockholders' shares} = \text{value of company} - \text{value of new shares}$$

$$= (10{,}000 + \text{NPV}) - 1{,}000$$

$$= \$9{,}000 + \text{NPV}$$

The old shareholders have received a $1,000 cash dividend and incurred a $1,000 capital loss. Dividend policy doesn't matter.

By paying out $1,000 with one hand and taking it back with the other, Rational Demiconductor is recycling cash. To suggest that this makes shareholders better off is like advising a cook to cool the kitchen by leaving the refrigerator door open.

Of course, our proof ignores taxes, issue costs, and a variety of other complications. We will turn to those items in a moment. The really crucial assumption in our proof is that the new shares are sold at a fair price. The shares sold to raise $1,000 must actually be *worth* $1,000.[19] In other words, we have assumed efficient capital markets.

Calculating Share Price

We have assumed that Rational Demiconductor's new shares can be sold at a fair price, but what is that price and how many new shares are issued?

Suppose that before this dividend payout the company had 1,000 shares outstanding and that the project had an NPV of $2,000. Then the old stock was worth in total $10,000 + NPV = $12,000, which works out at $12,000/1,000 = $12 per share. After the company has paid the dividend and completed the financing, this old stock is worth $9,000 + NPV = $11,000. That works out at $11,000/1,000 = $11 per share. In other words, the price of the old stock falls by the amount of the $1 per share dividend payment.

Now let us look at the new stock. Clearly, after the issue this must sell at the same price as the rest of the stock. In other words, it must be valued at $11. If the new stockholders get fair value, the company must issue $1,000/$11 or 91 new shares in order to raise the $1,000 that it needs.

Share Repurchase

We have seen that any increased cash dividend payment must be offset by a stock issue if the firm's investment and borrowing policies are held constant. In effect the stockholders finance the extra dividend by selling off part of their ownership of the firm. Consequently, the stock price falls by just enough to offset the extra dividend.

---

[18]All other factors that might affect Rational Demiconductor's value are assumed constant. This is not a necessary assumption, but it simplifies the proof of MM's theory.

[19]The "old" shareholders get all the benefit of the positive NPV project. The new shareholders require only a fair rate of return. They are making a zero-NPV investment.

This process can also be run backward. With investment and borrowing policy given, any *reduction* in dividends must be balanced by a reduction in the number of shares issued or by repurchase of previously outstanding stock. But if the process has no effect on stockholders' wealth when run forward, it must likewise have no effect when run in reverse. We will confirm this by another numerical example.

Suppose that a technical discovery reveals that Rational Demiconductor's new project is not a positive-NPV venture but a sure loser. Management announces that the project is to be discarded, and that the $1,000 earmarked for it will be paid out as an extra dividend of $1 per share. After the dividend payout, the balance sheet is

Rational Demiconductor's Balance Sheet (Market Values)

Cash	$ 0	$ 0	Debt
Existing	9,000	9,000	Equity
fixed assets			
New project	0		
Total asset value	$9,000	$9,000	Total firm value

Since there are 1,000 shares outstanding, the stock price is $10,000/1,000 = $10 before the dividend payment and $9,000/1,000 = $9 *after* the payment.

What if Rational Demiconductor uses the $1,000 to repurchase stock instead? As long as the company pays a fair price for the stock, the $1,000 buys $1,000/$10 = 100 shares. That leaves 900 shares worth 900 × $10 = $9,000.

As expected, we find that switching from cash dividends to share repurchase has no effect on shareholders' wealth. They forgo a $1 cash dividend but end up holding shares worth $10 instead of $9.

Note that when shares are repurchased the transfer of value is in favor of those stockholders who do not sell. They forgo any cash dividend but end up owning a larger slice of the firm. In effect they are using their share of Rational Demiconductor's $1,000 distribution to buy out some of their fellow shareholders.

Stock Repurchase and Valuation

Valuing the equity of a firm that repurchases its own stock can be confusing. Let's work through a simple example.

Company X has 100 shares outstanding. It earns $1,000 a year, all of which is paid out as a dividend. The dividend per share is, therefore, $1,000/100 = $10. Suppose that investors expect the dividend to be maintained indefinitely and that they require a return of 10 percent. In this case the value of each share is $PV_{share} = \$10/.10 = \$100$. Since there are 100 shares outstanding, the *total* market value of the equity is $PV_{equity} = 100 \times \$100 = \$10,000$. Note that we could reach the same conclusion by discounting the *total* dividend payments to shareholders ($PV_{equity} = \$1,000/.10 = \$10,000$).[20]

Now suppose the company announces that instead of paying a cash dividend in year 1, it will spend the same money repurchasing its shares in the open market. The total expected cash flows

---

[20]When valuing the entire equity, remember that if the company is expected to issue additional shares in the future, we should include the dividend payments on these shares only if we also include the amount that investors pay for them.

to shareholders (dividends and cash from stock repurchase) are unchanged at $1,000. So the total value of the equity also remains at $1,000/.10 = $10,000. This is made up of the value of the $1,000 received from the stock repurchase in year 1 ($PV_{repurchase}$ = $1,000/1.1 = $909.1) and the value of the $1,000-a-year dividend starting in year 2 [$PV_{dividends}$ = $1,000/(.10 × 1.1) = $9,091]. Each share continues to be worth $10,000/100 = $100 just as before.

Think now about those shareholders who plan to sell their stock back to the company. They will demand a 10 percent return on their investment. So the price at which the firm buys back shares must be 10 percent higher than today's price, or $110. The company spends $1,000 buying back its stock, which is sufficient to buy $1,000/$110 = 9.09 shares.

The company starts with 100 shares, it buys back 9.09, and therefore 90.91 shares remain outstanding. Each of these shares can look forward to a dividend stream of $1,000/90.91 = $11 per share. So after the repurchase shareholders have 10 percent fewer shares, but earnings and dividends per share are 10 percent higher. An investor who owns one share today that is not repurchased will receive no dividends in year 1 but can look forward to $11 a year thereafter. The value of each share is therefore 11/(.1 × 1.1) = $100.

Our example illustrates several points. First, other things equal, company value is unaffected by the decision to repurchase stock rather than to pay a cash dividend. Second, when valuing the entire equity you need to include both the cash that is paid out as dividends and the cash that is used to repurchase stock. Third, when calculating the cash flow *per share*, it is double counting to include both the forecasted dividends per share *and* the cash received from repurchase (if you sell back your share, you don't get any subsequent dividends). Fourth, a firm that repurchases stock instead of paying dividends reduces the number of shares outstanding but produces an offsetting increase in earnings and dividends per share.

THE RIGHTISTS

Much of traditional finance literature has advocated high payout ratios. Here, for example, is a statement of the rightist position made by Graham and Dodd in 1951:

> . . . the considered and continuous verdict of the stock market is overwhelmingly in favor of liberal dividends as against niggardly ones. The common stock investor must take this judgment into account in the valuation of stock for purchase. It is now becoming standard practice to evaluate common stock by applying one multiplier to that portion of the earnings paid out in dividends and a much smaller multiplier to the undistributed balance.[21]

This belief in the importance of dividend policy is common in the business and investment communities. Stockholders and investment advisers continually pressure corporate treasurers for increased dividends. When we had wage-price controls in the United States in 1974, it was deemed necessary to have dividend controls as well. As far as we know, no labor union objected that "dividend policy is irrelevant." After all, if wages are reduced, the employee is worse off. Dividends are the shareholders' wages, and so if the payout ratio is reduced the shareholder is worse off. Therefore fair play requires that wage controls be matched by dividend controls. Right?

---

[21]These authors later qualified this statement, recognizing the willingness of investors to pay high price–earnings multiples for growth stocks. But otherwise they stuck to their position. We quoted their 1951 statement because of its historical importance. Compare B. Graham and D. L. Dodd, *Security Analysis: Principles and Techniques*, 3d ed., McGraw-Hill Book Company, New York, 1951, p. 432, with B. Graham, D. L. Dodd, and S. Cottle, *Security Analysis: Principles and Techniques*, 4th ed., McGraw-Hill Book Company, New York, 1962, p. 480.

Wrong! You should be able to see through that kind of argument by now. But let us turn to some of the more serious arguments for a high-payout policy.

Do MM Ignore Risk?

One of the most common and immediate objections to MM's argument about the irrelevance of dividends is that dividends are cash in hand while capital gains are at best in the bush. It may be true that the recipient of an extra cash dividend forgoes an equal capital gain, but if the dividend is safe and the capital gain is risky, isn't the stockholder ahead?

It's true that dividends are more predictable than capital gains. Managers can stabilize dividends but they cannot control stock price. From this it seems a small step to conclude that increased dividends make the firm less risky.[22] But the important point is, once again, that as long as investment policy and borrowing are held constant, a firm's *overall* cash flows are the same regardless of payout policy. The risks borne by *all* the firm's stockholders are likewise fixed by its investment and borrowing policies and are unaffected by dividend policy.[23]

A dividend increase creates a transfer of ownership between "old" and "new" stockholders. The old stockholders—those who receive the extra dividend and do not buy their part of the stock issue undertaken to finance the dividend—find their stake in the firm reduced. They have indeed traded a safe receipt for an uncertain future gain. But the reason their money is safe is not because it is special "dividend money" but because it is in the bank. If the dividend had not been increased, the stockholders could have achieved an equally safe position just by selling shares and putting the money in the bank.

If we really believed that old stockholders are better off by trading a risky asset for cash, then we would also have to argue that the new stockholders—those who trade cash for the newly issued shares—are worse off. But this doesn't make sense: The new stockholders are bearing risk, but they are getting paid for it. They are willing to buy because the new shares are priced to offer a return adequate to cover the risk.

MM's argument for the irrelevance of dividend policy does not assume a world of certainty: It assumes an efficient capital market. Market efficiency means that the transfers of value created by shifts in dividend policy are carried out on fair terms. And since the *overall* value of (old and new) stockholders' equity is unaffected, nobody gains or loses.

Market Imperfections

We believe—and it is widely believed—that MM's conclusions follow from their assumption of perfect and efficient capital markets. Nobody claims their model is an exact description of the

---

[22]By analogy one could presumably argue that interest payments are even more predictable, so that a company's risk would be diminished by increasing the proportion of receipts paid out as interest.

[23]There are a number of variations of the bird-in-the-hand argument. Perhaps the most persuasive is found in M. J. Gordon, "Dividends, Earnings and Stock Prices," *Review of Economics and Statistics* 41 (May 1959), pp. 99–105. He reasoned that investors run less risk if the firm pays them cash now rather than retaining and reinvesting it in the hope of paying higher future dividends. But careful analysis of Gordon's argument shows that he was really talking about changes in *investment* policy, not dividend policy. See M. J. Brennan, "A Note on Dividend Irrelevance and the Gordon Valuation Model," *Journal of Finance* 26 (December 1971), pp. 1115–1122.

so-called real world. Thus the dividend controversy finally boils down to arguments about imperfections, inefficiencies, or whether stockholders are fully rational.[24]

There is a natural clientele for high-payout stocks. For example, some financial institutions are legally restricted from holding stocks lacking established dividend records. Trusts and endowment funds may prefer high-dividend stocks because dividends are regarded as spendable "income," whereas capital gains are "additions to principal."[25]

There is also a natural clientele of investors who look to their stock portfolios for a steady source of cash to live on. In principle this cash could be easily generated from stocks paying no dividends at all; the investor could just sell off a small fraction of his or her holdings from time to time. But it is simpler and cheaper for AT&T to send a quarterly check than for its stockholders to sell, say, one share every three months. AT&T's regular dividends relieve many of its shareholders of transaction costs and considerable inconvenience.[26]

Dividends and Investment Policy

If it is true that nobody gains or loses from shifts in dividend policy, why do shareholders often clamor for higher dividends? One possible explanation is that they don't trust managers to spend retained earnings wisely and they fear that the money will be plowed back into building a larger empire rather than a more profitable one. In this case the dividend decision is mixed up with the firm's investment and operating decisions. The dividend increase may lead to a rise in the stock price not because investors like dividends but because they want management to run a tighter ship.

TAXES AND THE RADICAL LEFT

The left-wing dividend creed is simple: Whenever dividends are taxed more heavily than capital gains, firms should pay the lowest cash dividend they can get away with. Available cash should be retained or used to repurchase shares.

By shifting their distribution policies in this way, corporations can transmute dividends into capital gains. If this financial alchemy results in lower taxes, it should be welcomed by any taxpaying investor. That is the basic point made by the leftist party when it argues for low-dividend payout.

If dividends are taxed more heavily than capital gains, investors should pay more for stocks with low dividend yields. In other words, they should accept a lower *pretax* rate of return from securities offering returns in the form of capital gains rather than dividends. Table 7.1 illustrates this.

---

[24]Psychologists' experiments show that human beings are not 100-percent rational decision makers. Shefrin and Statman use some of the psychologists' results to argue that investors may have an irrational preference for cash dividends. See H. Shefrin and M. Statman, "Explaining Investor Preference for Cash Dividends," *Journal of Financial Economics* 13 (June 1984), pp. 253–282.

[25]Most colleges and universities are legally free to spend capital gains from their endowments, but they usually restrict spending to a moderate percentage which can be covered by dividends and interest receipts.

[26]Those advocating generous dividends might go on to argue that a regular cash dividend relieves stockholders of the risk of having to sell shares at "temporarily depressed" prices. Of course, the firm will have to issue shares eventually to finance the dividend, but (the argument goes) the firm can pick the *right time* to sell. If firms really try to do this and if they are successful—two big *ifs*—then stockholders of high-payout firms might indeed get something for nothing.

TABLE 7.1

Effects of a shift in dividend policy when dividends are taxed more heavily than capital gains. The high-payout stock (firm B) must sell at a lower price in order to provide the same after-tax return.

	FIRM A (NO DIVIDEND)	FIRM B (HIGH DIVIDEND)
Next year's price	$112.50	$102.50
Dividend	$0	$10.00
Total pretax payoff	$112.50	$112.50
Today's stock price	$100	$96.67
Capital gain	$12.50	$5.83
Before-tax rate of return, percent	$\frac{12.5}{100} \times 100 = 12.5$	$\frac{15.83}{96.67} \times 100 = 16.4$
Tax on dividend at 50%	$0	$.50 \times 10 = \$5.00$
Tax on capital gains at 20%	$.20 \times 12.50 = \$2.50$	$.20 \times 5.83 = \$1.17$
Total after-tax income (dividends plus capital gains less taxes)	$(0 + 12.50)$ $-2.50 = \$10.00$	$(10.00 + 5.83)$ $-(5.00 + 1.17) = \$9.66$
After-tax rate of return	$\frac{10}{100} \times 100 = 10.0\%$	$\frac{9.66}{96.67} \times 100 = 10.0\%$

The stocks of firms A and B are equally risky. Investors expect A to be worth $112.50 per share next year. The share price of B is expected to be only $102.50, but a $10 dividend is also forecasted, and so the total pretax payoff is the same, $112.50.

Yet we find B's stock selling for less than A's and therefore offering a higher pretax rate of return. The reason is obvious: Investors prefer A because its return comes in the form of capital gains. Table 7.1 shows that A and B are equally attractive to investors who pay a 50 percent tax on dividends and a 20 percent tax on capital gains (the maximum marginal rates before 1986). Each offers a 10 percent return after all taxes. The difference between the stock prices of A and B is exactly the present value of the extra taxes the investors face if they buy B.[27]

The management of B could save these extra taxes by eliminating the $10 dividend and using the released funds to repurchase stock instead. Its stock price should rise to $100 as soon as the new policy is announced.

Why Pay Any Dividends at All?

It is true that when companies make very large one-off distributions of cash to shareholders, they generally choose to do so by share repurchase than by a large temporary hike in dividends. But if

---

[27]Michael Brennan has modeled what happens when you introduce taxes into an otherwise perfect market. He found that the capital asset pricing model continues to hold, but on an *after-tax* basis. Thus, if A and B have the same beta, they should offer the same after-tax rate of return. The spread between pretax and post-tax returns is determined by a weighted average of investors' tax rates. See M. J. Brennan, "Taxes, Market Valuation and Corporate Financial Policy," *National Tax Journal* 23 (December 1970), pp. 417–427.

dividends attract more tax than capital gains, why should any firm ever pay a cash dividend? If cash is to be distributed to stockholders, isn't share repurchase always the best channel for doing so? The leftist position seems to call not just for low payouts but for zero payouts whenever capital gains have a tax advantage.

Few leftists would go quite that far. A firm which eliminates dividends and starts repurchasing stock on a regular basis may find that the Internal Revenue Service recognizes the repurchase program for what it really is and taxes the payments accordingly. That is why financial managers do not usually announce that they are repurchasing shares to save stockholders taxes; they give some other reason.[28]

The low-payout party has nevertheless maintained that the market rewards firms which have low-payout policies. They have claimed that firms which paid dividends and as a result had to issue shares from time to time were making a serious mistake. Any such firm was essentially financing its dividends by issuing stock; it should have cut its dividends at least to the point at which stock issues were unnecessary. This would not only have saved taxes for shareholders but it would also have avoided the transaction costs of the stock issues.[29]

Empirical Evidence on Dividends and Taxes

It is hard to deny that taxes are important to investors. You can see that in the bond market. Interest on municipal bonds is not taxed, and so municipals sell at low pretax yields. Interest on federal government bonds is taxed, and so these bonds sell at higher pretax yields. It does not seem likely that investors in bonds just forget about taxes when they enter the stock market. Thus, we would expect to find a historical tendency for high-dividend stocks to sell at lower prices and therefore to offer higher yields, just as in Table 7.1.

Unfortunately, there are difficulties in measuring this effect. For example, suppose that stock A is priced at $100 and is expected to pay a $5 dividend. The *expected* yield is, therefore, 5/100 = .05, or 5 percent. The company now announces bumper earnings and a $10 dividend. Thus with the benefit of hindsight, A's *actual* dividend yield is 10/100 = .10, or 10 percent. If the unexpected increase in earnings causes a rise in A's stock price, we will observe that a high actual yield is accompanied by a high actual return. But that would not tell us anything about whether a high *expected* yield was accompanied by a high *expected* return. In order to measure the effect of dividend policy, we need to estimate the dividends that investors expected.

A second problem is that nobody is quite sure what is meant by high dividend yield. For example, utility stocks have generally offered high yields. But did they have a high yield all year, or only in months or on days that dividends were paid? Perhaps for most of the year, they had zero yields and were perfect holdings for the highly taxed individuals.[30] Of course, high-tax investors did not want to hold a stock on the days dividends were paid, but they could sell their

---

[28]They might say, "Our stock is a good investment," or, "We want to have the shares available to finance acquisitions of other companies." What do you think of these rationales?

[29]These costs can be substantial. Refer back to Chapter 3, especially Figure 3.3.

[30]Suppose there are 250 trading days in a year. Think of a stock paying quarterly dividends. We could say that the stock offers a high dividend yield on 4 days but a zero dividend yield on the remaining 246 days.

stock temporarily to a security dealer. Dealers are taxed equally on dividends and capital gains and therefore should not have demanded any extra return for holding stocks over the dividend period.[31] If shareholders could pass stocks freely between each other at the time of the dividend payment, we should not observe any tax effects at all.

Given these difficulties in measuring the relationship between expected yield and return, it is not surprising that different researchers have come up with different results. Table 7.2 summarizes some of the findings. Notice that in each of these tests the estimated tax rate was positive. In other words, high-yielding stocks appeared to have lower prices and to offer higher returns. However, while the dividends-are-bad school could claim that the weight of evidence is on its side, the contest is by no means over. Many respected scholars, including Merton Miller and Myron Scholes, were unconvinced. They stressed the difficulty of measuring dividend yield properly and proving the link between dividend yield and expected return.[32]

The Taxation of Dividends and Capital Gains

But all this evidence has more historical than current interest, for it precedes the Tax Reform Act of 1986. Before reform there was a dramatic difference between the taxation of dividends and capital gains: Investors paid up to 50 percent tax on dividends versus a maximum 20 percent on capital gains. However, the 1986 Tax Reform Act equalized the tax rates on dividends and capital gains and so largely undercut the leftists' arguments and left the center party in the ascendancy. More recently, a gap has begun to open up again, though it is much smaller than it once was. As we write this chapter, the tax rate on capital gains for most shareholders is 28 percent, while for taxable incomes above $61,400 the tax rate on dividends ranges from 31 percent to 39.6 percent.[33]

Tax law favors capital gains in another way. Taxes on dividends have to be paid immediately, but taxes on capital gains can be deferred until shares are sold and capital gains are realized.

---

[31]The stock could also be sold to a corporation, which could "capture" the dividend and then resell the shares. Corporations are natural buyers of dividends, because they pay tax only on 30 percent of dividends received from other corporations. (We say more on the taxation of intercorporate dividends later in this section.)

[32]Miller reviews several of the studies cited in Table 7.2 in "Behavioral Rationality in Finance: The Case of Dividends," *Journal of Business* 59 (October 1986), pp. S451–S468.

[33]Here are two examples of 1998 marginal tax rates by income bracket:

	INCOME BRACKET	
MARGINAL TAX RATE	SINGLE	MARRIED, JOINT RETURN
15%	$0–$25,350	$0–$42,350
28	$25,351–$61,400	$42,351–$102,300
31	$61,401–$128,100	$102,301–$155,950
36	$128,101–$278,450	$155,951–$278,450
39.6	Over $278,450	Over $278,450

There are different schedules for married taxpayers filing separately and for single taxpayers who are heads of households.

TABLE 7.2

Some tests of the effect of yield on returns: A positive implied tax rate on dividends means that investors require a higher pretax return from high-dividend stocks, but the standard errors show the difficulty of estimating this tax rate.

TEST	TEST PERIOD	IMPLIED TAX RATE	STANDARD ERROR OF TAX RATE
Brennan	1946–1965	34%	12
Black & Scholes (1974)	1936–1966	22	24
Litzenberger & Ramaswamy (1979)	1936–1977	24	3
Litzenberger & Ramaswamy (1982)	1940–1980	14–23	2–3
Rosenberg & Marathe (1979)	1931–1966	40	21
Bradford & Gordon (1980)	1926–1978	18	2
Blume (1980)	1936–1976	52	25
Miller & Scholes (1982)	1940–1978	4	3
Stone & Bartter (1979)	1947–1970	56	28
Morgan (1982)	1946–1977	21	2
Ang & Peterson (1985)	1973–1983	57	27

Sources: M. J. Brennan: "Dividends and Valuation in Imperfect Markets: Some Empirical Tests," unpublished paper, not dated.

F. Black and M. Scholes: "The Effects of Dividend Yield and Dividend Policy on Common Stock Prices and Returns," *Journal of Financial Economics* 1 (May 1974), pp. 1–22.

R. H. Litzenberger and K. Ramaswamy: "The Effect of Personal Taxes and Dividends on Capital Asset Prices: Theory and Empirical Evidence," *Journal of Financial Economics* 7 (June 1979), pp. 163–195.

R. H. Litzenberg and K. Ramaswamy: "The Effects of Dividends on Common Stock Prices: Tax Effects or Information Effects," *Journal of Finance* 37 (May 1982), pp. 429–443.

B. Rosenberg and V. Marathe: "Tests of Capital Asset Pricing Model Hypotheses," in H. Levy (ed.), *Research in Finance I*, JAI Press, Greenwich, CT, 1979.

D. F. Bradford and R. H. Gordon: "Taxation and the Stock Market Valuation of Capital Gains and Dividends," *Journal of Public Economics* 14 (1980), pp. 109–136.

M. E. Blume: "Stock Returns and Dividend Yields: Some More Evidence," *Review of Economics and Statistics* 62 (November 1980), pp. 567–577.

M. H. Miller and M. Scholes: "Dividends and Taxes: Some Empirical Evidence," *Journal of Political Economy* 90 (1982), pp. 1118–1141.

B. K. Stone and B. J. Bartter: "The Effect of Dividend Yield on Stock Returns: Empirical Evidence on the Relevance of Dividends," W.P.E.-76-78, Georgia Institute of Technology, Atlanta, GA, 1979.

I. G. Morgan: "Dividends and Capital Asset Prices," *Journal of Finance* 37 (September 1982), pp. 1071–1086.

J. S. Ang and D. R. Peterson: "Return, Risk and Yield: Evidence from Ex Ante Data," *Journal of Finance* 40 (June 1985), pp. 537–548.

Stockholders can choose when to sell their shares and thus when to pay the capital gains tax. The longer they wait, the less the present value of the capital gains tax liability.[34]

The distinction between capital gains and dividends is less important for financial institutions, many of which operate free of all taxes and therefore have no tax reason to prefer capital gains to dividends or vice versa. Pension funds are untaxed, for example. Only corporations have a tax reason to *prefer* dividends. They pay corporate income tax on only 30 percent of any dividends received. Thus the effective tax rate on dividends received by large corporations is 30 percent of 35 percent (the marginal corporate tax rate), or 10.5 percent. But they have to pay a 35 percent tax on the full amount of any realized capital gain.

Although the dividend affects the shareholder's tax liability, it does not in general alter the taxes that must be paid by the company itself. Corporate income tax has to be paid regardless of whether the company distributes or retains its profits. There is one exception: If the Internal Revenue Service (IRS) can prove that earnings are retained solely to avoid any taxes on dividends, it can levy an additional tax on the excess retentions. However, public companies are almost always able to justify their retentions to the IRS.

The implications of these tax rules for dividend policy are pretty simple. Capital gains have advantages to many investors, but they are far less advantageous than they were before the passage of the 1986 Tax Reform Act. Thus, the leftist case for minimizing cash dividends is weaker than it used to be. At the same time, the middle-of-the-road party has increased its share of the vote.

THE MIDDLE-OF-THE-ROADERS

The middle-of-the-road party, principally represented by Miller, Black, and Scholes, maintains that a company's value is not affected by its dividend policy.[35] We have already seen that this would be the case if there were no impediments such as transaction costs or taxes. The middle-of-the-roaders are aware of these phenomena but nevertheless raise the following disarming question: If companies could increase their share price by distributing more or less cash dividends, why have they not already done so? Perhaps dividends are where they are because no company believes that it could increase its stock price simply by changing its dividend policy.

This "supply effect" is not inconsistent with the existence of a clientele of investors who demand low-payout stocks. Firms recognized that clientele long ago. Enough firms may have

---

[34]When securities are sold capital gains tax is paid on the difference between the selling price and the initial purchase price or *basis*. Thus, shares purchased in 1993 for $20 (the basis) and sold for $30 in 1998 would generate $10 per share in capital gains and a tax of $2.80 at a 28 percent marginal rate.

Suppose the investor now decides to defer sale for one year. Then, if the interest rate is 8 percent, the present value of the tax, viewed from 1998, falls to 2.80/1.08 = $2.59. That is, the *effective* capital gains rate is 25.9 percent. The longer sale is deferred, the lower the effective rate will be.

The effective rate falls to zero if the investor dies before selling, because the investor's heirs get to "step up" the basis without recognizing any taxable gain. Suppose the price is still $30 when the investor dies. The heirs could sell for $30 and pay no tax, because they could claim a $30 basis. The $10 capital gain would escape tax entirely.

[35]F. Black and M. S. Scholes, "The Effects of Dividend Yield and Dividend Policy on Common Stock Prices and Returns," *Journal of Financial Economics* 1 (May 1974), pp. 1–22; M. H. Miller and M. S. Scholes, "Dividends and Taxes," *Journal of Financial Economics* 6 (December 1978), pp. 333–364; and M. H. Miller, "Behavioral Rationality in Finance: The Case of Dividends," *Journal of Business* 59 (October 1986), pp. S451–S468.

switched to low-payout policies to satisfy fully the clientele's demand. If so, there is no incentive for *additional* firms to switch to low-payout policies.

Miller, Black, and Scholes similarly recognize possible high-payout clienteles but argue that they are satisfied also. If all clienteles are satisfied, their demands for high or low dividends have no effect on prices or returns. It doesn't matter which clientele a particular firm chooses to appeal to. If the middle-of-the-road party is right, we should not expect to observe any general association between dividend policy and market values, and the value of any individual company would be independent of its choice of dividend policy.

The middle-of-the-roaders stress that companies would not have generous payout policies unless they believed that this was what investors wanted. But this does not answer the question, Why *should* so many investors want high payouts?

Before the Tax Reform Act, this was the chink in the armor of the middle-of-the-roaders. If high dividends bring high taxes, it's difficult to believe that investors got what they wanted. The response of the middle-of-the-roaders was to argue that there were plenty of wrinkles in the tax system which determined stockholders could use to avoid paying taxes on dividends. For example, instead of investing directly in common stocks, they could do so through a pension fund or insurance company, which received more favorable tax treatment.

Since 1986, the tax disadvantage of dividends has diminished in the United States, so it is easier to suppose that there is a substantial clientele of investors who are content to receive high dividends. That is why there have been many new converts to the middle-of-the-road cause.

Has this Tax Reform Act led to a change in corporate and investor attitudes to dividends? Corporations *believe* that it has led to a pressure for higher payouts, but we still need to wait before we can be confident that there has been a shift in payouts or investors' required returns. Meanwhile, we may gain some clues from the experience of other countries that have changed tax rates on dividends relative to capital gains. In Canada, for example, dividend payouts increased after a capital gains tax was introduced and dividend tax rates were cut for many investors.[36]

Alternative Tax Systems

In the United States shareholders' returns are taxed twice. They are taxed at the corporate level (corporate tax) and in the hands of the shareholder (income tax or capital gains tax). These two tiers of tax are illustrated in Table 7.3, which shows the after-tax return to the shareholder if the company distributes all its income as dividends. We assume the company earns $100 a share before tax and therefore pays corporate tax of $.35 \times 100 = \$35$. This leaves $65 a share to be paid out as a dividend, which is then subject to a second layer of tax. For example, a shareholder who is taxed at the top marginal rate of 39.6 percent pays tax on this dividend of $.396 \times 65 = \$25.7$. Only a tax-exempt pension fund or charity would retain the full $65.

Of course, dividends are regularly paid by companies that operate under very different tax systems. In fact, the two-tier United States system is relatively rare. Some countries, such as Germany, tax investors at a higher rate on dividends than on capital gains, but they offset this by having a split-rate system of corporate taxes. Profits that are retained in the business attract a higher rate of corporate tax than profits that are distributed. Under this split-rate system, tax-exempt in-

---

[36]The Canadian experience is summarized in our Canadian edition, especially pp. 409–415. See R. Brealey, S. Myers, G. Sick, and R. Giammarino, *Principles of Corporate Finance*, 2d Canadian ed., McGraw-Hill Ryerson, Ltd., Toronto, 1992.

TABLE 7.3		

In the United States returns to shareholders are taxed twice (figures in dollars per share)

	RATE OF INCOME TAX	
	0%	39.6%
Operating income	100	100
Corporate tax ($T_c = .35$)	35	35
After-tax income (paid out as dividends)	65	65
Income tax	0	25.7
Available to shareholder	65	39.3

vestors prefer that the company pay high dividends, whereas millionaires might vote to retain profits.

In some other countries, shareholders' returns are not taxed twice. For example, in Australia shareholders are taxed on dividends, but they may deduct from this tax bill their share of the corporate tax that the company has paid. This is known as an *imputation tax system*. Table 7.4 shows how the imputation system works. Suppose that an Australian company earns pretax profits of $A100 a share. After it pays corporate tax at 33 percent, the profit is $A67 a share. The company now declares a net dividend of $A67 and sends each shareholder a check for this amount. This dividend is accompanied by a tax credit saying that the company has already paid $A33 of tax on the shareholder's behalf. Thus shareholders are treated as if each received a total, or gross, dividend of 67 + 33 = $A100 and paid tax of $A33. If the shareholder's tax rate is 33 percent, there is no more tax to pay and the shareholder retains the net dividend of $A67. If the shareholder pays tax at the top personal rate of 47 percent, then he or she is required to pay an additional $14 of tax; if the tax rate is 15 percent (the rate at which Australian pension funds are taxed), then the shareholder receives a refund of 33 − 15 = $A18.[37]

Under an imputation tax system, millionaires have to cough up the extra personal tax on dividends. If this is more than the tax that they would pay on capital gains, then millionaires would prefer that the company does not distribute earnings. If it is the other way around, they would prefer dividends.[38] Investors with low tax rates have no doubts about the matter. If the company pays a dividend, these investors receive a check from the revenue service for the excess tax that the company has paid, and therefore they prefer high payout rates.

Look once again at Table 7.4 and think what would happen if the corporate tax rate was zero. The shareholder with a 15 percent tax rate would still end up with $A85, and the shareholder with the 47 percent rate would still receive $A53. Thus, under an imputation tax system, when a

---

[37]In Australia and New Zealand, shareholders receive a credit for the full amount of corporate tax that has been paid on their behalf. In other countries such as Spain, the tax credit is less than the corporate tax rate. You can think of the tax system in these countries as lying between the Australian and United States systems.

[38]In the case of Australia the tax rate on capital gains is the same as the tax rate on dividends. However, investors are taxed only on the real (i.e., inflation-adjusted) value of capital gains.

TABLE 7.4

Under imputation tax systems, such as that in Australia, shareholders receive a tax credit for the corporate tax that the firm has paid (figures in Australian dollars per share)

	RATE OF INCOME TAX		
	15%	33%	47%
Operating income	100	100	100
Corporate tax ($T_c = .33$)	33	33	33
After-tax income	67	67	67
Grossed-up dividend	100	100	100
Income tax	15	33	47
Tax credit for corporate payment	−33	−33	−33
Tax due from shareholder	−18	0	14
Available to shareholder	85	67	53

company pays out all its earnings, there is effectively only one layer of tax—the tax on the shareholder. The revenue service collects this tax through the company and then sends a demand to the shareholder for any excess tax or makes a refund for any overpayment.[39]

SUMMARY

Dividends come in many forms. The most common is the regular cash dividend, but sometimes companies pay an extra or special cash dividend, and sometimes they pay a dividend in the form of stock.

When managers decide on the dividend, their primary concern seems to be to give shareholders a "fair" level of dividends. Most managers have a conscious or subconscious long-term target payout rate. If firms simply applied the target payout rate to each year's earnings, dividends could fluctuate wildly. Managers therefore try to smooth dividend payments by moving only partway toward the target payout in each year. Also they don't just look at past earnings performance: They try to look into the future when they set the payment. Investors are aware of this and they know that a dividend increase is often a sign of optimism on the part of management.

As an alternative to dividend payments, the company can repurchase its own stock. Although this has the same effect of distributing cash to shareholders, the Internal Revenue Service taxes shareholders only on the capital gains that they may realize as a result of the repurchase.

In recent years many companies have bought back their stock in large quantities, but repurchases do not generally substitute for dividends. Instead, they are used to return unwanted cash to

---

[39]This is only true for earnings that are paid out as dividends. Retained earnings are subject to corporate tax. Shareholders get the benefit of retained earnings in the form of capital gains.

shareholders or to retire equity and replace it with debt. Investors usually interpret stock repurchases as an indication of managers' optimism.

If we hold the company's investment policy constant, then dividend policy is a trade-off between cash dividends and the issue or repurchase of common stock. Should firms retain whatever earnings are necessary to finance growth and pay out any residual as cash dividends? Or should they increase dividends and then (sooner or later) issue stock to make up the shortfall of equity capital? Or should they reduce dividends below the "residual" level and use the released cash to repurchase stock?

If we lived in an ideally simple and perfect world, there would be no problem, for the choice would have no effect on market value. The controversy centers on the effects of dividend policy in our flawed world. A common—though by no means universal—view in the investment community is that high payout enhances share price. There are natural clienteles for high-payout stocks. But we find it difficult to explain a *general* preference for dividends other than in terms of an irrational prejudice. The case for "liberal dividends" depends largely on a wealth of tradition.

The most obvious and serious market imperfection has been the different tax treatment of dividends and capital gains. Before the Tax Reform Act of 1986, dividends were taxed at rates up to 50 percent, but capital gains rates topped out at only 20 percent. Thus investors should have required a higher before-tax return on high-payout stocks to compensate for their tax disadvantage. High-income investors should have held mostly low-payout stocks.

This view has a respectable theoretical basis. It is supported by some evidence that gross returns have, on the average, reflected the tax differential. The weak link is the theory's silence on the question of why companies continued to distribute such large sums contrary to the preferences of investors.

The third view of dividend policy starts with the notion that the actions of companies *do* reflect investors' preferences; the fact that companies pay substantial dividends is the best evidence that investors want them. If the supply of dividends exactly meets the demand, no single company could improve its market value by changing its dividend policy. Although this explains corporate behavior, it is at a cost, for we cannot explain why dividends are what they are and not some other amount.

These theories are too incomplete and the evidence is too sensitive to minor changes in specification to warrant any dogmatism. Our sympathies, however, lie with the third, middle-of-the-road view. Our recommendations to companies would emphasize the following points: First, there is little doubt that sudden shifts in dividend policy can cause abrupt changes in stock price. The principal reason is the information that investors read into the company's actions. Given such problems, there is a clear case for smoothing dividends, for example, by defining the firm's target payout and making relatively slow adjustments toward it. If it is necessary to make a sharp dividend change, the company should provide as much forewarning as possible and take care to ensure that the action is not misinterpreted.

Subject to these strictures, we believe that, at the very least, a company should adopt a target payout that is sufficiently low as to minimize its reliance on external equity. Why pay out cash to stockholders if that requires issuing new shares to get the cash back? It's better to hold on to the cash in the first place.

If dividend policy doesn't affect firm value, then you don't need to worry about it when estimating the cost of capital. But if (say) you believe that tax effects are important, then in principle you should recognize that investors demand higher returns from high-payout stocks. Some financial managers do take dividend policy into account, but most become de facto middle-of-the-roaders when estimating the cost of capital. It seems that the effects of dividend policy are too uncertain to justify fine-tuning such estimates.

Further Reading

Lintner's classic analysis of how companies set their dividend payments is provided in:
J. Lintner: "Distribution of Incomes of Corporations among Dividends, Retained Earnings, and Taxes," *American Economic Review,* 46:97–113 (May 1956).

There have been a number of tests of how well Lintner's model describes dividend changes. One of the best known is:
E. F. Fama and H. Babiak: "Dividend Policy: An Empirical Analysis," *Journal of the American Statistical Association,* 63:1132–1161 (December 1968).

Marsh and Merton have reinterpreted Lintner's findings and used them to explain the aggregate dividends paid by United States corporations:
T. A. Marsh and R. C. Merton: "Dividend Behavior for the Aggregate Stock Market," *Journal of Business,* 60:1–40 (January 1987).

The pioneering article on dividend policy in the context of a perfect capital market is:
M. H. Miller and F. Modigliani: "Dividend Policy, Growth and the Valuation of Shares," *Journal of Business,* 34:411–433 (October 1961).

There are several interesting models explaining the information content of dividends. Two influential examples are:
S. Bhattacharya: "Imperfect Information, Dividend Policy and the Bird in the Hand Fallacy," *Bell Journal of Economics and Management Science,* 10:259–270 (Spring 1979).

M. H. Miller and K. Rock: "Dividend Policy Under Asymmetric Information," *Journal of Finance,* 40:1031–1052 (September 1985).

Financial Management *published a special issue on dividend policy in Autumn 1998. It includes four articles on the information content of dividends.*

The effect of differential rates of tax on dividends and capital gains is analyzed rigorously in the context of the capital asset pricing model in:
M. J. Brennan: "Taxes, Market Valuation and Corporate Financial Policy," *National Tax Journal,* 23:417–427 (December 1970).

The argument that dividend policy is irrelevant even in the presence of taxes is presented in:
F. Black and M. S. Scholes: "The Effects of Dividend Yield and Dividend Policy on Common Stock Prices and Returns," *Journal of Financial Economics,* 1:1–22 (May 1974).

M. H. Miller and M. S. Scholes: "Dividends and Taxes," *Journal of Financial Economics,* 6:333–364 (December 1978).

A brief review of some of the empirical evidence is contained in:
R. H. Litzenberger and K. Ramaswamy: "The Effects of Dividends on Common Stock Prices: Tax Effects or Information Effects," *Journal of Finance,* 37:429–443 (May 1982).

Merton Miller reviews research on the dividend controversy in:
M. H. Miller: "Behavioral Rationality in Finance: The Case of Dividends," *Journal of Business,* 59:S451–S468 (October 1986).

PART THREE

OPTIONS

SPOTTING AND VALUING OPTIONS

Figure 8.1(*a*) shows your payoff if you buy Pfluegel Corp. stock at $85. You gain dollar-for-dollar if the stock price goes up and you lose dollar-for-dollar if it falls. That's trite; it doesn't take a genius to draw a 45-degree line.

Look now at panel (*b*), which shows the payoffs from an investment strategy that retains the upside potential of Pfluegel stock but gives complete downside protection. In this case your payoff stays at $85 even if Pfluegel stock price falls to $70, $60, or zero. Panel (*b*)'s payoffs are clearly better than panel (*a*)'s. If a financial alchemist could turn panel (*a*) into (*b*), you'd be willing to pay for the service.

Of course alchemy has its dark side. Panel (*c*) shows an investment strategy for masochists. You lose if the stock price falls, but you give up any chance of profiting from a rise in the stock price. If you *like* to lose, or if somebody pays you enough to take the strategy on, this is the strategy for you.

Now, as you have probably suspected, all this financial alchemy is for real. You really can do all the transmutations shown in Figure 8.1. You do them with options, and we will show you how.

But why should the financial manager of an industrial company be interested in such matters? One reason is that companies regularly use commodity, currency, and interest-rate options to reduce risk. For example, a meatpacking company that wishes to put a ceiling on the cost of beef might take out an option to buy live cattle. A company that wishes to limit its future borrowing costs might take out an option to sell long-term bonds. And so on. In Chapter 13 we will explain how firms employ options to limit their risk.

Another important reason why financial managers need to understand options is that they are often tacked on to an issue of corporate securities and so provide the investor or the company with the flexibility to change the terms of the issue. For example, in Chapter 9 we will show how warrants and convertibles give their holders an option to buy common stock in exchange for cash or bonds. Then in Chapter 11 we will see how corporate bonds may give the issuer or the investor the option of early repayment.

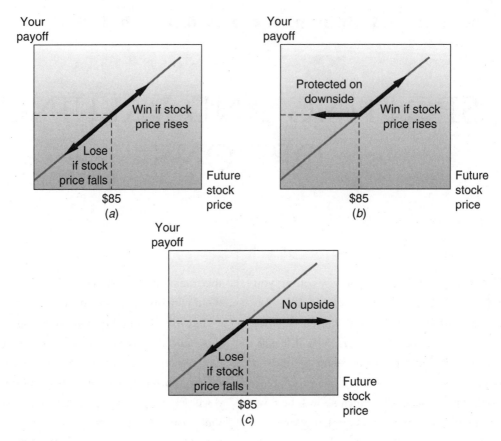

Figure 8.1

Payoffs to three investment strategies for Intel stock. (*a*) You buy one share for $85. (*b*) No downside. If stock price falls, your payoff stays at $85. (*c*) A strategy for masochists? You lose if stock price falls, but you don't gain if it rises.

In fact, we shall see that whenever a company borrows, it creates an option. The reason is that the borrower is not *compelled* to repay the debt at maturity. If the value of the company's assets is less than the amount of the debt, the company will choose to default on the payment and the bondholders will get to keep the company's assets. Thus, when the firm borrows, the lender effectively acquires the company and the shareholders obtain the option to buy it back by paying off the debt. This is an extremely important insight. It means that anything that we can learn about traded options applies equally to corporate liabilities.[1]

---

[1] This relationship was first recognized by Fischer Black and Myron Scholes, in "The Pricing of Options and Corporate Liabilities," *Journal of Political Economy* 81 (May–June 1973), pp. 637–654.

In this chapter we use traded stock options to explain how options work and how they are valued. But we hope that our brief survey has convinced you that the interest of financial managers in options goes far beyond traded stock options. That is why we are asking you here to invest to acquire several important ideas. The return to this investment comes primarily in later chapters.

Our first task in the chapter is to understand how call and put options work and how the payoff on an option depends on the price of the underlying asset. We will then return to the topic of financial alchemy and show how options can be combined to produce the interesting strategies that we depicted in Figure 8.1(*b*) and (*c*).

The second half of the chapter looks at how options are valued. We first identify the variables that determine option values. We will then describe a simple way to value options, known as the binomial model. Finally, we will introduce you to the famous Black–Scholes formula for valuing options.

CALLS, PUTS, AND SHARES

The Chicago Board Options Exchange (CBOE) was founded in 1973 to allow investors to buy and sell options on individual shares. The CBOE was an almost instant success and a number of other exchanges have since copied its example. In addition to options on individual common stocks, investors can now trade options on stock indexes, bonds, commodities, and foreign exchange.

Table 8.1 is an extract from the table of option prices in a daily newspaper for July 1998. It shows the prices for two types of options on Intel stock—calls and puts. We will explain each in turn.

A **call option** gives its owner the right to buy stock at a specified *exercise* or *strike* price on or before a specified exercise date. In some cases, the option can be exercised only on one particular day, and it is then conventionally known as a *European call*; in other cases (such as the Intel options shown in Table 8.1), the option can be exercised on or at any time before that day, and it is then known as an *American call*.

TABLE 8.1

The prices of call and put options on Intel stock in July 1998. Intel stock was trading at around $85 per share.

EXERCISE DATE	EXERCISE PRICE	PRICE OF CALL OPTIONS	PRICE OF PUT OPTIONS
October 1998	$80	$8.875	$3.25
January 1999	80	11.375	4.75
January 1999	**85**	**8.625**	**6.875**

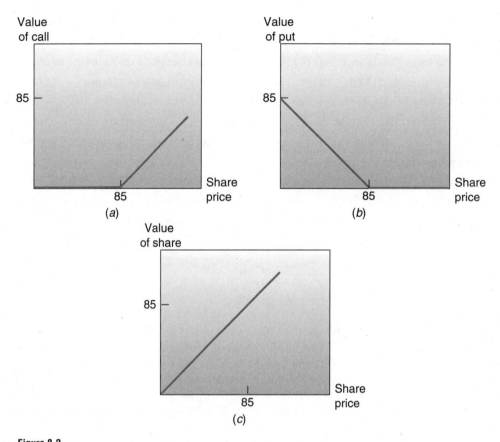

Figure 8.2

Payoffs to owners of Intel calls, puts, and shares (shown by the colored lines) depend on the share price. (*a*) Result of buying Intel call exercisable at $85. (*b*) Result of buying Intel put exercisable at $85. (*c*) Result of buying Intel share.

The third column of Table 8.1 sets out the prices of Intel call options with different exercise prices and exercise dates. The first entry shows that for $8.875 you could acquire an option to buy a share of Intel stock for $80 on or before October 1998. Moving down to the next row, you can see that for a price of $11.375 you could extend your option to buy Intel stock until January 1999. The third row also shows the price of a January call option, but this one has an exercise price of $85.

In Chapter 4 we met Louis Bachelier, who in 1900 first suggested that security prices follow a random walk. Bachelier also devised a very convenient shorthand to illustrate the effects of investing in different options.[2] We will use this shorthand to compare three possible investments in Intel—a call option, a put option, and the stock itself.

The *position diagram* in Figure 8.2(*a*) shows the possible consequences of investing in Intel January call options with an exercise price of $85 (boldfaced in row 3 of Table 8.1). The outcome from

---

[2]L. Bachelier, *Théorie de la Speculation*, Gauthier-Villars, Paris, 1900. Reprinted in English in P. H. Cootner (ed.), *The Random Character of Stock Market Prices*, M.I.T. Press, Cambridge, MA, 1964.

investing in Intel calls depends on what happens to the stock price. If the stock price at the end of this six-month period turns out to be less than the $85 exercise price, nobody will pay $85 to obtain the share via the call option. Your call will in that case be valueless, and you will throw it away. On the other hand, if the stock price turns out to be greater than $85, it will pay to exercise your option to buy the share. In this case the call will be worth the market price of the share minus the $85 that you must pay to acquire it. For example, suppose that the price of Intel stock rises to $100. Your call will then be worth $100 – $85 = $15. That is your payoff, but of course it is not all profit. Table 8.1 shows that you had to pay $8.625 to buy the call.

Now let us look at the Intel **put options** in the right-hand column of Table 8.1. Whereas the call option gives you the right to *buy* a share for a specified exercise price, the comparable put gives you the right to sell the share. For example, the boldfaced entry in the right-hand column of Table 8.1 shows that for $6.875 you could acquire an option to sell Intel stock for a price of $85 anytime within the next six months. The circumstances in which the put turns out to be profitable are just the opposite of those in which the call is profitable. You can see this from the position diagram in Figure 8.2(*b*). If Intel's share price immediately before expiration turns out to be *greater* than $85, you won't want to sell stock at that price. You would do better to sell the share in the market, and your put option will be worthless. Conversely, if the share price turns out to be less than $85, it will pay to buy stock at the low price and then take advantage of the option to sell it for $85. In this case, the value of the put option on the exercise date is the difference between the $85 proceeds of the sale and the market price of the share. For example, if the share is worth $65, the put is worth $20:

$$\text{Value of put option at expiration = exercise price – market price of the share}$$

$$= \$85 - \$65$$

$$= \$20$$

Our third investment consists of Intel stock itself. Figure 8.2(*c*) betrays few secrets when it shows that the value of this investment is always exactly equal to the market value of the share.

Selling Calls, Puts, and Shares

Let us now look at the position of an investor who *sells* these investments. If you sell, or "write," a call, you promise to deliver shares if asked to do so by the call buyer. In other words, the buyer's asset is the seller's liability. If by the exercise date the share price is below the exercise price, the buyer will not exercise the call and the seller's liability will be zero. If it rises above the exercise price, the buyer will exercise and the seller will give up the shares. The seller loses the difference between the share price and the exercise price received from the buyer. Notice that it is the buyer who always has the option to exercise; the seller simply does as he or she is told.

Suppose that the price of Intel stock turns out to be $120, which is above the option's exercise price of $85. In this case the buyer will exercise the call. The seller is forced to sell stock worth $120 for only $85 and so has a payoff of –$35.[3] Of course, that $35 loss is the buyer's gain. Figure 8.3(*a*) shows how the payoffs to the seller of the Intel call option vary with the stock price. Notice that for

---

[3]The seller has some consolation for he or she was paid $8.625 in July for selling the call.

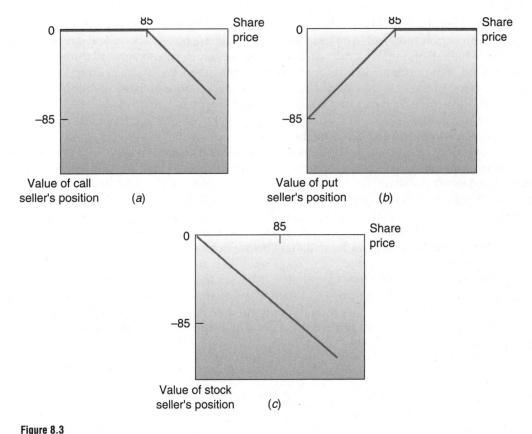

Figure 8.3

Payoffs to sellers of Intel calls, puts, and shares (shown by the colored lines) depend on the share price. (*a*) Result of selling Intel call exercisable at $85. (*b*) Result of selling Intel put exercisable at $85. (*c*) Result of selling Intel share short.

every dollar the buyer makes, the seller loses a dollar. Figure 8.3(*a*) is just Figure 8.2(*a*) drawn up-side down.

In just the same way we can depict the position of an investor who sells, or writes, a put by standing Figure 8.2(*b*) on its head. The seller of the put has agreed to pay the exercise price of $85 for the share if the buyer of the put should request it. Clearly the seller will be safe as long as the share price remains above $85 but will lose money if the share price falls below this figure. The worst thing that can happen is that the stock becomes worthless. The seller would then be obliged to pay $85 for a stock worth $0. The "value" of the option position would be –$85.

Finally, Figure 8.3(*c*) shows the position of someone who sells Intel stock short. Short sellers sell stock which they do not yet own. As they say on Wall Street:

> *He who sells what isn't his'n*
> *Buys it back or goes to prison.*

Eventually, therefore, the short seller will have to buy the stock back. The short seller will make a profit if it has fallen in price and a loss if it has risen.[4] You can see that Figure 8.3(c) is simply an up-side-down Figure 8.2(c).

FINANCIAL ALCHEMY WITH OPTIONS

Now that you understand the possible payoffs from calls and puts, we can return to the investment strategies that we illustrated in the introduction to this chapter. It is time to start practicing some financial alchemy by conjuring up the strategies shown in Figure 8.1. Let's start with the strategy for masochists.

Look at row 1 of Figure 8.4. The first diagram shows the payoffs from buying a share of Intel stock, while the second shows the payoffs from *selling* a call option with an $85 exercise price. The third diagram shows what happens if you combine these two positions. The result is the no-win strategy that we depicted in panel (c) of Figure 8.1. You lose if the stock price declines below $85, but, if the stock price rises above $85, the owner of the call option will demand that you hand over your stock for the $85 exercise price. So you lose on the downside and give up any chance of a profit. That's the bad news. The good news is that you get paid for taking on this liability. In July 1998 you would have been paid $8.625, the price of a six-month call option.

Now look at row 2 of Figure 8.4. The first diagram again shows the payoff from buying a share of Intel stock, while the next diagram in row 2 shows the payoffs from buying a Intel put option with an exercise price of $85. The third diagram shows the effect of combining these two positions. You can see that, if Intel's stock price rises above $85, your put option is valueless, so you simply receive the gains from your investment in the share. However, if the stock price falls below $85, you can exercise your put option and sell your stock for $85. Thus, by adding a put option to your investment in the stock, you have protected yourself against loss.[5] This is the strategy that we depicted in panel (b) of Figure 8.1. Of course, there is no gain without pain. The cost of insuring yourself against loss is the amount that you pay for a put option on Intel stock with an exercise price of $85. In July 1998 the price of this put was $6.875. This was the going rate for financial alchemists.

We have just seen how put options can be used to provide downside protection. We will now show you how call options can be used to get the same result. This is illustrated in row 3 of Figure 8.4. The first diagram shows the payoff from placing the present value of $85 in a bank deposit. Regardless of what happens to the price of Intel stock, your bank deposit will pay off $85. The second diagram in row 3 shows the payoff from a call option on Intel stock with an exercise price of $85, and the third diagram shows the effect of combining these two positions. Notice that, if the price of Intel stock falls, your call is worthless, but you still have your $85 in the bank. For every dollar that Intel stock price rises above $85, your investment in the call option pays off an extra dollar. For example, if the stock price rises to $100, you will have $85 in the bank and a call worth $15. Thus you participate fully in any rise in the price of the stock, while being fully pro-

---

[4]Selling short is not as simple as we have described it. For example, a short seller usually has to put up margin, that is, deposit cash or securities with the broker. This assures the broker that the short seller will be able to repurchase the stock when the time comes to do so.

[5]This combination of a stock and a put option is known as a *protective put*.

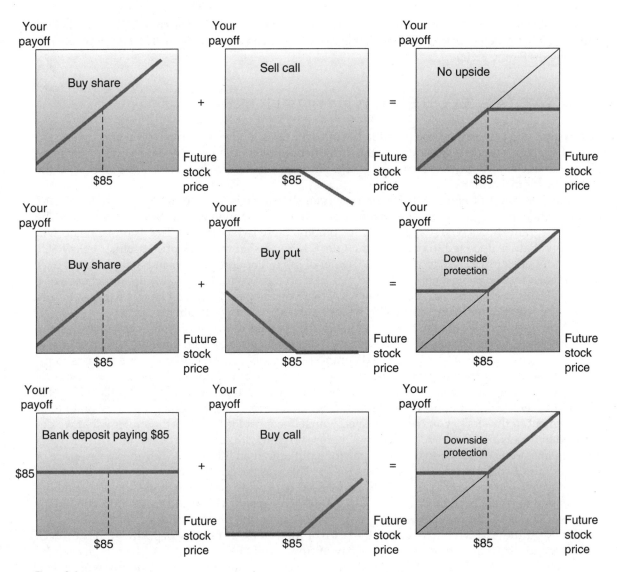

Figure 8.4

The first row shows how options can be used to create a strategy where you lose if the stock price falls but do not gain if it rises [(strategy (c) in Figure 8.1]. The second and third rows show how to create the reverse strategy where you gain on the upside but are protected on the downside [strategy (b) in Figure 8.1].

tected against any fall. So we have just found another way to provide the downside protection that we depicted in panel (b) of Figure 8.1.

These last two rows of Figure 8.4 tell us something about the relationship between a call option and a put option. Regardless of the future stock price, both investment strategies provide identical payoffs. In other words, if you buy the share and a put option to sell it after six months for $85, you receive the same payoff as from buying a call option and setting enough money aside to pay the $85 exercise price. Therefore, if you are committed to holding the two packages until the end of six months, the two packages should sell for the same price today. This gives us a fundamental relationship for European options:[6]

Value of call + present value of exercise price = value of put + share price

To repeat, this relationship holds because the payoff of

[Buy call, invest present value of exercise price in safe asset[7]]

is identical to the payoff from

[Buy put, buy share]

There are many other ways to express this basic relationship between share price, call and put values, and the present value of the exercise price. Each expression implies two investment strategies that give identical results. For example, suppose that you want to solve for the value of a put. You simply need to twist the formula around to give

Value of put = value of call + present value of exercise price − share price

From this expression you can deduce that

[buy put]

is identical to

[Buy call, invest present value of exercise price in safe asset, sell share]

In other words, if puts are not available, you can create them by buying calls, putting cash in the bank, and selling shares.

The Difference between Safe and Risky Bonds

In Chapter 6 we discussed the plight of Circular File Company, which borrowed $50 per share. Unfortunately the firm fell on hard times and the market value of its assets fell to $30. Circular's bond and stock prices fell to $25 and $5, respectively. Circular's *market* value balance sheet is now

Circular File Company (Market Values)

Asset value	$30	$25	Bonds
		5	Stock
	$30	$30	Firm value

---

[6]This relationship is known as *put–call parity*. It holds only if you are committed to holding the options until the final exercise date. It therefore does not hold for American options, which you can exercise *before* the final date. If the stock makes a dividend payment before the final exercise date, you need to recognize that the investor who buys the call misses out on this dividend. In this case the relationship is

Value of call + present value of exercise price = value of put + share price − present value of dividend.

[7]The present value is calculated at the *risk-free* rate of interest. It is the amount that you would have to invest today in a bank deposit or Treasury bills to realize the exercise price on the option's expiration date.

If Circular's debt were due and payable now, the firm could not repay the $50 it originally borrowed. It would default, bondholders receiving assets worth $30 and shareholders receiving nothing. The reason Circular stock is worth $5 is that the debt is *not* due now but rather is due a year from now. A stroke of good fortune could increase firm value enough to pay off the bondholders in full, with something left over for the stockholders.

Let us go back to a statement that we made at the start of the chapter. Whenever a firm borrows, the lender effectively acquires the company and the shareholders obtain the option to buy it back by paying off the debt. The stockholders have in effect purchased a call option on the assets of the firm. The bondholders have sold them this call option. Thus the balance sheet of Circular File can be expressed as follows:

Circular File Company (Market Values)

Asset value	$30	$25	Bond value = asset value – value of call
		5	Stock value = value of call
	$30	$30	Firm value = asset value

If this still sounds like a strange idea to you, try drawing one of Bachelier's position diagrams for Circular File. It should look like Figure 8.5. If the future value of the assets is less than $50, Circular will default and the stock will be worthless. If the value of the assets exceeds $50, the stockholders will receive asset value less the $50 paid over to the bondholders. The payoffs in Figure 8.5 are identical to a call option on the firm's assets, with an exercise price of $50.

Now look again at the basic relationship between calls and puts:

Value of call + present value of exercise price = value of put + value of share

To apply this to Circular File, we have to interpret "value of share" as "asset value," because the common stock is a call option on the firm's assets. Also, "present value of exercise price" is the present value of receiving the promised payment of $50 to bondholders *for sure* next year. Thus

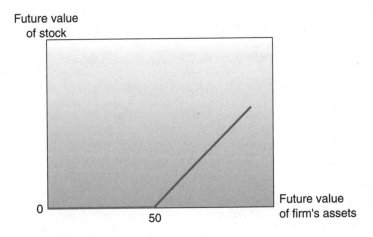

Figure 8.5

The value of Circular's common stock is the same as the value of a call option on the firm's assets with an exercise price of $50.

Value of call + present value of promised payment to bondholders

= value of put + asset value

Now we can solve for the value of Circular's bonds. This is equal to the firm's asset value less the value of the shareholders' call option on these assets:

Bond value = asset value − value of call

= present value of promised payment to bondholders − value of put

Circular's bondholders have in effect (1) bought a safe bond and (2) given the shareholders the option to sell them the firm's assets for the amount of the debt. You can think of the bondholders as receiving the $50 promised payment, but they have given the shareholders the option to take the $50 back in exchange for the assets of the company. If firm value turns out to be less than the $50 that is promised to bondholders, the shareholders will exercise their put option.

Circular's risky bond is equal to a safe bond less the value of the shareholders' option to default. To value this risky bond we need to value a safe bond and then subtract the value of the default option. The default option is equal to a put option on the firm's assets.

In the case of Circular File the option to default is extremely valuable because default is likely to occur. At the other extreme, the value of GE's option to default is trivial compared to the value of GE's assets. Default on GE bonds is possible but extremely unlikely. Option traders would say that for Circular File the put option is "deep in the money" because today's asset value ($30) is well below the exercise price ($50). For GE the put option is well "out of the money" because the value of GE's assets substantially exceeds the value of GE's debt.

We know that Circular's stock is equivalent to a call option on the firm's assets. It is also equal to (1) owning the firm's assets, (2) borrowing the present value of $50 with the obligation to repay regardless of what happens, but also (3) buying a put on the firm's assets with an exercise price of $50.

We can sum up by presenting Circular's balance sheet in terms of asset value, put value, and the present value of a sure $50 payment:

Circular File Company (Market Values)

Asset value	$30	$25	Bond value = present value of promised payment − value of put
		5	Stock value = asset value − present value of promised payment + value of put
	$30	$30	Firm value = asset value

Again you can check this with a position diagram. The colored line in Figure 8.6 shows the payoffs to Circular's bondholders. If the firm's assets are worth more than $50, the bondholders are paid off in full; if the assets are worth less than $50, the firm defaults and the bondholders receive the value of the assets. You could get an identical payoff pattern by buying a safe bond (the upper black line) and selling a put option on the firm's assets (the lower black line).

Spotting the Option

Options rarely come with a large label attached. Often the trickiest part of the problem is to identify the option. For example, we suspect that until it was pointed out, you did not realize that every

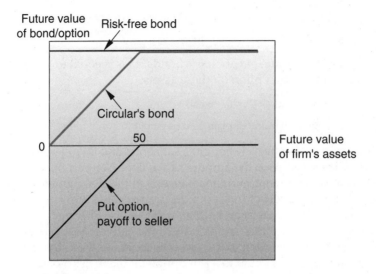

Figure 8.6

You can also think of Circular's bond (the colored line) as equivalent to a
risk-free bond (the upper black line) *less* a put option on the firm's assets
with an exercise price of $50 (the lower black line).

risky bond contains a hidden option. When you are not sure whether you are dealing with a put or
a call or a complicated blend of the two, it is a good precaution to draw a position diagram. Here
is an example.

The Flatiron and Mangle Corporation has offered its president, Ms. Higden, the following incentive scheme: At the end of the year Ms. Higden will be paid a bonus of $50,000 for every dollar
that the price of Flatiron stock exceeds its current figure of $120. However, the maximum bonus
that she can receive is set at $2 million.

You can think of Ms. Higden as owning 50,000 tickets, each of which pays nothing if the stock
price fails to beat $120. The value of each ticket then rises by $1 for each dollar rise in the stock
price up to the maximum of $2,000,000/50,000 = $40. Figure 8.7 shows the payoffs from just one of
these tickets. The payoffs are not the same as those of the simple put and call options that we drew
in Figure 8.2, but it is possible to find a combination of options that exactly replicates Figure 8.7.
Before going on to read the answer, see if you can spot it yourself. (If you are someone who enjoys
puzzles of the make-a-triangle-from-just-two-matchsticks type, this one should be a walkover.)

The answer is in Figure 8.8. The solid black line represents the purchase of a call option with
an exercise price of $120, and the dotted line shows the sale of another call option with an exercise
price of $160. The colored line shows the payoffs from a combination of the purchase and the
sale—exactly the same as the payoffs from one of Ms. Higden's tickets.

Thus, if we wish to know how much the incentive scheme is costing the company, we need to
calculate the difference between the value of 50,000 call options with an exercise price of $120 and
the value of 50,000 calls with an exercise price of $160.

We could have made the incentive scheme depend in a much more complicated way on the
stock price. For example, the bonus could peak at $2 million and then fall steadily back to zero as

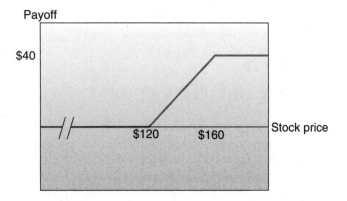

Figure 8.7

The payoff from one of Ms. Higden's "tickets" depends on Flatiron's stock price.

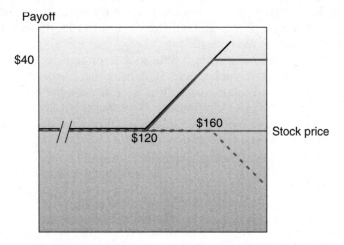

Figure 8.8

The solid black line shows the payoff from buying a call with an exercise price of $120. The dotted line shows the *sale* of a call with an exercise price of $160. The combined purchase and sale (shown by the colored line) is identical to one of Ms. Higden's "tickets."

the stock price climbs above $160. (Don't ask why anyone would want to offer such an arrangement—perhaps there's some tax angle.) You could still have represented this scheme as a combination of options. In fact, we can state a general theorem:

Any set of contingent payoffs—that is, payoffs which depend on the value of some other asset—can be valued as a mixture of simple options on that asset.

For instance, if you needed to value a capital project that would pay off $2 million if the price of copper was less than $1,500 per ton but only $1 million if the price was greater than $1,500, you could use option theory to do so.

WHAT DETERMINES OPTION VALUES?

So far we have said nothing about how the market value of an option is determined. We do know what an option is worth when it matures, however. Consider, for instance, our earlier example of an option to buy Intel stock at $85. If Intel's stock price is below $85 on the exercise date, the call will be worthless; if the stock price is above $85, the call will be worth $85 less than the value of the stock. In terms of Bachelier's position diagram, the relationship is depicted by the heavy, lower line in Figure 8.9.

Even before maturity the price of the option can never remain below the heavy line in Figure 8.9. For example, if our option were priced at $5 and the stock were priced at $100, it would pay any investor to sell the stock and then buy it back by purchasing the option and exercising it for an additional $85. That would give a money machine with a profit of $10. The demand for options from investors using the money machine would quickly force the option price up at least to the heavy line in the figure. For options that still have some time to run, the heavy line is therefore a lower limit on the market price of the option.

The diagonal line in Figure 8.9 is the *upper* limit to the option price. Why? Because the stock gives a higher ultimate payoff, whatever happens. If at the option's expiration the stock price ends up above the exercise price, the option is worth the stock price less the exercise price. If the stock price ends up below the exercise price, the option is worthless, but the stock's owner still has a valuable security. Let P be the stock price at the option's expiration date, and assume the option's exercise price is $85. Then the extra dollar returns realized by stockholders are

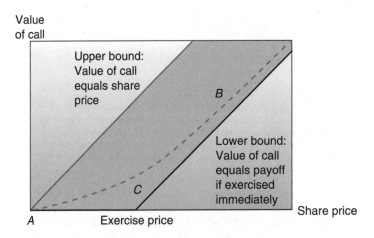

Figure 8.9

Value of a call before its expiration date (dashed line). The value depends on the stock price. It is always worth more than its value if exercised now (heavy line). It is never worth more than the stock price itself.

	STOCK PAYOFF	OPTION PAYOFF	EXTRA PAYOFF FROM HOLDING STOCK INSTEAD OF OPTION
Option exercised (*P* greater than $85)	*P*	*P* – 85	$85
Option expires unexercised (*P* less than or equal to $85)	*P*	0	*P*

If the stock and the option have the same price, everyone will rush to sell the option and buy the stock. Therefore, the option price must be somewhere in the shaded region of Figure 8.9. In fact, it will lie on a curved, upward-sloping line like the dashed curve shown in the figure. This line begins its travels where the upper and lower bounds meet (at zero). Then it rises, gradually becoming parallel to the upward-sloping part of the lower bound. This line tells us an important fact about option values: *The value of an option increases as stock price increases,* if the exercise price is held constant.

That should be no surprise. Owners of call options clearly hope for the stock price to rise, and are happy when it does. But let us look more carefully at the shape and location of the dashed line. Three points, A, B, and C, are marked on the dashed line. As we explain each point you will see why the option price has to behave as the dashed line predicts.

Point A. *When the stock is worthless, the option is worthless:* A stock price of zero means that there is no possibility the stock will ever have any future value.[8] If so, the option is sure to expire unexercised and worthless, and it is worthless today.

Point B. *When the stock price becomes large, the option price approaches the stock price less the present value of the exercise price:* Notice that the dashed line representing the option price in Figure 8.9 eventually becomes parallel to the ascending heavy line representing the lower bound on the option price. The reason is as follows: The higher the stock price is, the higher is the probability that the option will eventually be exercised. If the stock price is high enough, exercise becomes a virtual certainty; the probability that the stock price will fall below the exercise price before the option expires becomes trivially small.

If you own an option which you know will be exchanged for a share of stock, you effectively own the stock now. The only difference is that you don't have to pay for the stock (by handing over the exercise price) until later, when formal exercise occurs. In these circumstances, buying the call is equivalent to buying the stock but financing part of the purchase by borrowing. The amount implicitly borrowed is the present value of the exercise price. The value of the call is therefore equal to the stock price less the present value of the exercise price.

This brings us to another important point about options. Investors who acquire stock by way of a call option are buying on credit. They pay the purchase price of the option today, but they do not pay the exercise price until they actually take up the option. The delay in payment is particularly valuable if interest rates are high and the option has a long maturity. *Thus, the value of an option increases with both the rate of interest and the time to maturity.*

---

[8]If a stock *can* be worth something in the future, then investors will pay *something* for it today, although possibly a very small amount.

Point C. *The option price always exceeds its minimum value* (except when stock price is zero): We have seen that the dashed and heavy lines in Figure 8.9 coincide when stock price is zero (point *A*), but elsewhere the lines diverge; that is, the option price must exceed the minimum value given by the heavy line. The reason for this can be understood by examining point *C*.

At point *C*, the stock price exactly equals the exercise price. The option is therefore worthless if exercised today. However, suppose that the option will not expire until three months hence. Of course we do not know what the stock price will be at the expiration date. There is roughly a 50 percent chance that it will be higher than the exercise price, and a 50 percent chance that it will be lower. The possible payoffs to the option are therefore

OUTCOME	PAYOFF
Stock price rises (50 percent probability)	Stock price less exercise price (option is exercised)
Stock price falls (50 percent probability)	Zero (option expires worthless)

If there is a positive probability of a positive payoff, and if the worst payoff is zero, then the option must be valuable. That means the option price at point *C* exceeds its lower bound, which at point *C* is zero. In general, the option prices will exceed their lower-bound values as long as there is time left before expiration.

One of the most important determinants of the *height* of the dashed curve (i.e., of the difference between actual and lower-bound value) is the likelihood of substantial movements in the stock price. An option on a stock whose price is unlikely to change by more than 1 or 2 percent is not worth much; an option on a stock whose price may halve or double is very valuable.

Panels (*a*) and (*b*) in Figure 8.10 illustrate this point. The panels compare the payoffs at expiration of two options with the same exercise price and the same stock price. The panels assume that stock price equals exercise price (like point *C* in Figure 8.9), although this is not a necessary assumption. The only difference is that the price of stock Y at its option's expiration date [Figure 8.10(*b*)] is much harder to predict than the price of stock X at its option's expiration date. You can see this from the probability distributions superimposed on the figures.

In both cases there is roughly a 50 percent chance that the stock price will decline and make the options worthless, but if the prices of stocks X and Y rise, the odds are that Y will rise more than X. Thus there is a larger chance of a big payoff from the option on Y. Since the chance of a zero payoff is the same, the option on Y is worth more than the option on X. Figure 8.11 illustrates this: The higher curved line belongs to the option on Y.

The probability of large stock price changes during the remaining life of an option depends on two things: (1) the variance (i.e., volatility) of the stock price *per period* and (2) the number of periods until the option expires. If there are t remaining periods, and the variance per period is σ^2, the value of the option should depend on cumulative variability $\sigma^2 t$.[9] Other things equal, you would

---

[9] Here is an intuitive explanation: If the stock price follows a random walk (see Chapter 4), successive price changes are statistically independent. The cumulative price change before expiration is the sum of t random variables. The variance of a sum of independent random variables is the sum of the variances of those variables. Thus, if σ^2 is the variance of the daily price change, and there are t days until expiration, the variance of the cumulative price change is $\sigma^2 t$.

Payoff to call
option on firm
X's shares

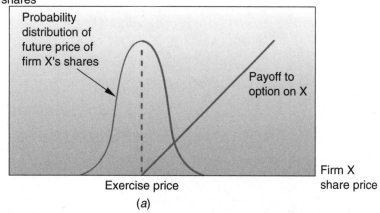

(a)

Payoff to call
option on firm
Y's shares

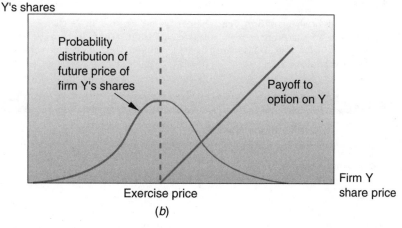

(b)

Figure 8.10

Call options are written against the shares of (a) firm X and (b) firm Y. In each case, the current share price equals the exercise price, so each option has a 50 percent chance of ending up worthless (if the share price falls) and a 50 percent chance of ending up "in the money" (if the share price rises). However, the chance of a *large* payoff is *greater* for the option on firm Y's share because Y's stock price is more volatile and therefore has more upside potential.

like to hold an option on a volatile stock (high σ^2). Given volatility, you would like to hold an option with a long life ahead of it (large t). Thus the value of an option increases *with both the variability of the share and the time to maturity.*

It's a rare person who can keep all these properties straight at first reading. Therefore, we have summed them up in Table 8.2.

Values of calls
on shares of
firms X and Y

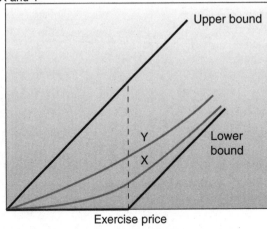

Figure 8.11

Values of calls on shares of firm X and shares of firm Y. The call on Y's shares is worth more because Y's shares are more volatile (see Figure 8.10). The higher curved line describes the value of a call on Y's shares; the lower curved line describes the value of a call on X's shares.

TABLE 8.2

What the price of a call option depends on

1. Increases in variables:

If there is an *increase* in:	The changes in the call option price are:
Stock price (P)	Positive
Exercise price (EX)	Negative
Interest rate (r_f)	Positive*
Time to expiration (t)	Positive
Volatility of stock price (σ)	Positive*

2. Other properties:
   a. *Upper bound.* The option price is always less than the stock price.
   b. *Lower bound.* The option price never falls below the payoff to immediate exercise (P – EX or zero, whichever is larger).
   c. If the stock is worthless, the option is worthless.
   d. As the stock price becomes very large, the option price approaches the stock price less the present value of the exercise price.

---

*The *direct* effects of increases in r_f or σ on option price are positive. There may also be *indirect* effects. For example, an increase in r_f could reduce stock price P. This in turn could reduce option price.

AN OPTION-VALUATION MODEL

We would now like to replace the qualitative statements of Table 8.2 with an exact option-valuation model—a formula we can plug numbers into and get a definite answer. The search for that formula went on for years before Fischer Black and Myron Scholes finally found it. Before we show you what they found, we should say a few words to explain why the search was so difficult.

Why Discounted Cash Flow Won't Work for Options

Our standard operating procedure of (1) forecasting expected cash flow and (2) discounting at the opportunity cost of capital is not helpful for options. The first step is messy but feasible. Finding *the* opportunity cost of capital is impossible, because the risk of an option changes every time the stock price moves,[10] and we know it *will* move along a random walk through the option's lifetime.

When you buy a call, you are *taking a position* in the stock but putting up less of your own money than if you had bought the stock directly. Thus an option is always riskier than the underlying stock. It has a higher beta and a higher standard deviation of return.

How much riskier the option is depends on the stock price relative to the exercise price. An option that is in the money (stock price greater than exercise price) is safer than one that is out of the money (stock price less than exercise price). Thus a stock price increase raises the option's price *and* reduces its risk. When the stock price falls, the option's price falls *and* its risk increases. That is why the expected rate of return investors demand from an option changes day by day, or hour by hour, every time the stock price moves.

We repeat the general rule: The higher the stock price is relative to the exercise price, the safer the options, although the option is always riskier than the stock. The option's risk changes every time the stock price changes.

Constructing Option Equivalents from Common Stocks and Borrowing

If you've digested what we've said so far, you can appreciate why options are hard to value by standard discounted-cash-flow formulas and why a rigorous option-valuation technique eluded economists for many years. The breakthrough came when Black and Scholes exclaimed, "Eureka! We have found it![11] The trick is to set up an *option equivalent* by combining common stock investment and borrowing. The net cost of buying the option equivalent must equal the value of the option."

We will show you how this works with a simple numerical example. In Table 8.1 we saw that in July 1998 you could have bought six-month call options on Intel stock with an exercise price of $85. Intel's stock price at that time was also $85, so the options were *at the money*.[12] The interest rate was 2.5 percent for six months, or just over 5 percent a year. To keep matters simple, we will assume that Intel stock can do only two things over the six months—either the price will fall by 20 percent to $68 or it will rise by 25 percent to $106.25.

---

[10]It also changes over time even with the stock price constant.

[11]We do not know whether Black and Scholes, like Archimedes, were sitting in bathtubs at the time.

[12]We ignore here the fact that Intel stockholders receive a small quarterly dividend of $.03 a share, while the optionholders do not. We discuss how to handle dividends later in this chapter.

If Intel's stock price falls to $68, the call option will be worthless, but if the price rises to $106.25, the option will be worth $106.25 - 85 = \$21.25$. The possible payoffs to the option are therefore

	STOCK PRICE = $68	STOCK PRICE = $106.25
1 call option	$0	$21.25

Now compare these payoffs with what you would get if you bought 5/9 of a share and borrowed $36.86 from the bank:[13]

	STOCK PRICE = $68	STOCK PRICE = $106.25
5/9 of a share	$37.78	$59.03
Repayment of loan + interest	− 37.78	− 37.78
Total payoff	$ 0	$21.25

Notice that the payoffs from the levered investment in the stock are identical to the payoffs from the call option. Therefore, both investments must have the same value:

$$\text{Value of call} = \text{value of 5/9 of a share} - \$36.86 \text{ bank loan}$$

$$= (85 \times 5/9) - 36.86 = \$10.36$$

Presto! You've valued a call option.

To value the Intel option, we borrowed money and bought stock in such a way that we exactly replicated the payoff from a call option. The number of shares needed to replicate one call is often called the **hedge ratio** or **option delta**. In our Intel example one call is replicated by a levered position in 5/9 of a share. The option delta is, therefore, 5/9, or about .56.

How did we know that Intel's call option was equivalent to a levered position in 5/9 of a share? We used a simple formula that says

$$\text{Option delta} = \frac{\text{spread of possible option prices}}{\text{spread of possible share prices}} = \frac{21.25 - 0}{106.25 - 68} = \frac{5}{9}$$

You have learned not only to value a simple option but also that you can replicate an investment in the option by a levered investment in the underlying asset. Thus, if you can't buy or sell an option on an asset, you can create a homemade option by a replicating strategy—that is, you buy or sell delta shares and borrow or lend the balance.

Risk-Neutral Valuation   Notice why the Intel call option should sell for $10.36. If the option price is higher than $10.36, you could make a certain profit by buying 5/9 of a share of stock, selling a call option, and borrowing $36.86. Similarly, if the option price is less than $10.36, you could make an equally certain profit by selling 5/9 of a share, buying a call, and lending the balance. In either case there would be a money machine.[14]

---

[13]The amount that you need to borrow from the bank is simply the present value of the difference between the payoffs from the option and the payoffs from the 5/9 share.

[14]Of course, you don't get seriously rich by dealing in 5/9 of a share. But if you multiply each of our transactions by a million, it begins to look like real money.

If there's a money machine, everyone scurries to take advantage of it. So when we said that the option price should be $10.36 or there would be a money machine, we did not have to know anything about investor attitudes to risk. The price cannot depend on whether investors detest risk or do not care a jot.

This suggests an alternative way to value the option. We can *pretend* that all investors are *indifferent* about risk, work out the expected future value of the option in such a world, and discount it back at the risk-free interest rate to give the current value. Let us check that this method gives the same answer.

If investors are indifferent to risk, the expected return on the stock must be equal to the rate of interest:

$$\text{Expected return on Intel stock} = 2.5\% \text{ per six months}$$

We know that Intel stock can either rise by 25 percent to $106.25 or fall by 20 percent to $68. We can, therefore, calculate the probability of a price rise in our hypothetical risk-neutral world:

$$\text{Expected return} = [\text{probability of rise} \times 25]$$
$$+ [(1 - \text{probability of rise}) \times (-20)]$$
$$= 2.5 \text{ percent}$$

Therefore,

$$\text{Probability of rise} = .50 \text{ or } 50\%$$

Notice that this is not the *true* probability that Intel stock will rise. Since investors dislike risk, they will almost surely require a higher expected return than the interest rate from Intel stock. Therefore the true probability is greater than .5.

We know that if the stock price rises, the call option will be worth $21.25; if it falls, the call will be worth nothing. Therefore, if investors are risk-neutral, the expected value of the call option is

$$[\text{Probability of rise} \times 21.25] + [(1 - \text{probability of rise}) \times 0]$$
$$= (.5 \times 21.25) + (.5 \times 0)$$
$$= \$10.625$$

And the current value of the call is

$$\frac{\text{Expected future value}}{1 + \text{interest rate}} = \frac{10.625}{1.025} = \$10.36$$

Exactly the same answer that we got earlier!

We now have two ways to calculate the value of an option:

1. Find the combination of stock and loan that replicates an investment in the option. Since the two strategies give identical payoffs in the future, they must sell for the same price today.
2. Pretend that investors do not care about risk, so that the expected return on the stock is equal to the interest rate. Calculate the expected future value of the option in this hypothetical risk-neutral world and discount it at the interest rate.

Valuing the Intel Put Option

Valuing the Intel call option may well have seemed like pulling a rabbit out of a hat. To give you a second chance to watch how it is done, we will use the same method to value another option—this time, the six-month Intel put option with an $85 exercise price.[15] We continue to assume that the stock price will either rise to $106.25 or fall to $68.

If Intel's stock price rises to $106.25, the option to sell for $85 will be worthless. If the price falls to $68, the put option will be worth $85 − 68 = $17. Thus the payoffs to the put are

	STOCK PRICE = $68	STOCK PRICE = $106.25
1 put option	$17	$0

We start by calculating the option delta using the formula that we presented above:[16]

$$\text{Option delta} = \frac{\text{spread of possible option prices}}{\text{spread of possible stock prices}} = \frac{0-17}{106.25-68} = -\frac{4}{9}$$

Notice that the delta of a put option is always negative; that is, you need to *sell* delta shares of stock to replicate the put. In the case of the Intel put you can replicate the option payoffs by *selling* $4/9$ of an Intel share and *lending* $46.07. Since you have sold the share short, you will need to lay out money at the end of six months to buy it back, but you will have money coming in from the loan. Your net payoffs are exactly the same as the payoffs you would get if you bought the put option:

	STOCK PRICE = $68	STOCK PRICE = $106.25
Sale of $4/9$ of a share	− $30.22	− $47.22
Repayment of loan + interest	+ 47.22	+ 47.22
Total payoff	$17	$ 0

Since the two investments have the same payoffs, they must have the same value:

$$\text{Value of put} = -4/9 \text{ of a share} + \$46.07 \text{ bank loan}$$

$$= \$8.29$$

Valuing the Put Option by the Risk-Neutral Method   Valuing the Intel put option with the risk-neutral method is a cinch. We already know that the probability of a rise in the stock price is .5. Therefore the expected value of the put option in a risk-neutral world is

---

[15]When valuing *American* put options, you need to recognize the possibility that it will pay to exercise early. We discuss how to handle the possibility of early exercise later in this chapter.

[16]The delta of a put option is always equal to the delta of a call option with the same exercise price minus one. In our example, delta of put = $5/9 - 1 = -4/9$.

$$[\text{Probability of rise} \times 0] + [(1 - \text{probability of rise}) \times 17]$$

$$= (.5 \times 0) + (.5 \times 17)$$

$$= \$8.50$$

And therefore the current value of the put is

$$\frac{\text{Expected future value}}{1 + \text{interest rate}} = \frac{8.50}{1.025} = \$8.29$$

The Relationship between Call and Put Prices We pointed out earlier that for European options there is a simple relationship between the value of the call and that of the put:[17]

$$\text{Value of put} = \text{value of call} - \text{share price} + \text{present value of exercise price}$$

Since we had already calculated the value of the Intel call, we could also have used this relationship to find the value of the put:

$$\text{Value of put} = 10.36 - 85 + \frac{85}{1.025} = \$8.29$$

Everything checks.

THE BLACK–SCHOLES FORMULA

The essential trick in pricing any option is to set up a package of investment in the stock and a loan that will exactly replicate the payoffs from the option. If we can price the stock and the loan, then we can also price the option.

This *concept* is completely general. But so far all our *examples* use a simplified version of a special approach, called the **binomial method**. This method starts by reducing the possible changes in next period's stock price to two, an "up" move and a "down" move. This simplification is OK if the time period is very short, so that a large number of small moves is accumulated over the life of the option. But it was fanciful to assume just two possible prices for Intel stock at the end of six months.

We could make the problem slightly more realistic by assuming that there were two possible changes in the stock price in each three-month period. That would give a wider range of six-month prices. It would still be possible to construct a series of levered investments in the stock that would give exactly the same prospects as the option.

There is no reason to stop at three-month periods. We could go on to take shorter and shorter intervals, with each interval showing two possible changes in Intel's stock price. Eventually we would reach a situation in which the stock price was changing continuously and generating a continuum of possible six-month prices. We could still replicate the call option by a levered investment in the stock, but we would need to adjust the degree of leverage continuously as the year went by.

---

[17]*Reminder:* This formula applies only when the two options have the same exercise price and exercise date.

Calculating the value of this levered investment may sound like a hopelessly tedious business, but Black and Scholes derived a formula that does the trick. It is an unpleasant-looking formula, but on closer acquaintance you will find it exceptionally elegant and useful. The formula is

Value of call option = [delta × share price] – [bank loan]

$\uparrow$ $\uparrow$ $\uparrow$

$[N(d_1) \quad \times \quad P] \quad - [N(d_2) \times PV(EX)]$

where

$$d_1 = \frac{\log [P / PV(EX)]}{\sigma\sqrt{t}} + \frac{\sigma\sqrt{t}}{2}$$

$$d_2 = d_1 - \sigma\sqrt{t}$$

$N(d)$ = cumulative normal probability density function[18]

EX = exercise price of option; PV(EX) is calculated by discounting at the risk-free interest rate r_f

t = number of periods to exercise date

P = price of stock now

σ = standard deviation per period of (continuously compounded) rate of return on stock

Notice that the value of the call in the Black–Scholes formula has the same properties that we identified earlier. It increases with the level of the stock price P and decreases with the present value of the exercise price PV(EX), which in turn depends on the interest rate and time to maturity. It also increases with the time to maturity and the stock's variability ($\sigma\sqrt{t}$).

To derive their formula Black and Scholes assumed that there is a continuum of stock prices, and therefore to replicate an option investors must continuously adjust their holding in the stock. Of course this is not literally possible, but even so the formula performs remarkably well in the real world, where stocks trade only intermittently and prices jump from one level to another. The Black–Scholes model has also proved very flexible; it can be adapted to value options on a variety of assets with special features, such as foreign currency, bonds, and futures. It is not surprising therefore that it has been extremely influential and has become the standard model for valuing options. Every day dealers on the options exchanges use this formula to make huge trades. These dealers are not for the most part trained in the formula's mathematical derivation; they just use a computer or a specially programmed calculator to find the value of the option.

Using the Black–Scholes Formula

The Black–Scholes formula may look difficult, but it is very straightforward to apply. Let us practice using it to value the Intel call.

---

[18]That is, $N(d)$ is the probability that a normally distributed random variable $\bar{x}$ will be less than or equal to d. $N(d_1)$ in the Black–Scholes formula is the option delta. Thus the formula tells us that the value of a call is equal to an investment of $N(d_1)$ in the common stock less borrowing of $N(d_2) \times PV(EX)$.

Here are the data that you need:

- Price of stock now = $P = 85$.
- Exercise price = EX = 85.
- Standard deviation of continuously compounded annual returns = $\sigma = .32$.
- Years to maturity = $t = .5$.
- Interest rate per annum = $r = 5.0625$ percent (equivalent to 2.5 percent for six months).

Remember that the Black–Scholes formula for the value of a call is

$$[N(d_1) \times P] - [N(d_2) \times \mathrm{PV(EX)}]$$

where

$$d_1 = \frac{\log\,[P/\mathrm{PV(EX)}]}{\sigma\sqrt{t}} + \frac{\sigma\sqrt{t}}{2}$$

$$d_2 = d_1 - \sigma\sqrt{t}$$

$N(d)$ = cumulative normal probability function

There are three steps to using the formula to value the Intel call:

Step 1.   Calculate d_1 and d_2. This is just a matter of plugging numbers into the formula (noting that "log" means *natural* log):

$$d_1 = \frac{\log\,[P/\mathrm{PV(EX)}]}{\sigma\sqrt{t}} + \frac{\sigma\sqrt{t}}{2}$$

$$= \log[85/(85/1.025)]/(.32 \times \sqrt{.5}) + (.32 \times \sqrt{.5})/2$$

$$= .2223$$

$$d_2 = d_1 - \sigma\sqrt{t} = .2223 - (.32 \times \sqrt{.5}) = -.004$$

Step 2.   Find $N(d_1)$ and $N(d_2)$. $N(d_1)$ is the probability that a normally distributed variable will be less than d_1 standard deviations above the mean. If d_1 is large, $N(d_1)$ is close to 1.0 (i.e., you can be almost certain that the variable will be less than d_1 standard deviations above the mean). If d_1 is zero, $N(d_1)$ is .5 (i.e., there is a 50 percent chance that a normally distributed variable will be below the average).

The simplest way to find $N(d_1)$ is to use the Excel function NORMSDIST. For example, if you enter NORMSDIST(.2223) into an Excel spreadsheet, you will see that there is a .5879 probability that a normally distributed variable will be less than .2223 standard deviations above the mean. Alternatively, you can use a set of normal probability tables such as those in Appendix Table 1, in which case you need to interpolate between the cumulative probabilities for $d_1 = .22$ and $d_1 = .23$.

Again you can use the Excel function to find $N(d_2)$. If you enter NORMSDIST(–.004) into an Excel spreadsheet, you should get the answer .4984. In other words, there is a probability of .4984 that a normally distributed variable will be less than .004 standard deviations *below* the mean. Alternatively, if you use Appendix Table 1, you need to look up the value for +.004 and subtract it from 1.0:

$$N(d_2) = N(-.004) = 1 - N(+.004)$$

$$= 1 - .5016 = .4984$$

Step 3. Plug these numbers into the Black–Scholes formula. You can now calculate the value of the Intel call:

$$[\text{Delta} \times \text{price}] - [\text{bank loan}]$$

$$= [N(d_1) \times P] - [N(d_2) \times PV(EX)]$$

$$= [.5879 \times 85) - [.4984 \times 85 / 1.025] = 8.64$$

The Black-Scholes formula gives the values of European call options written on stocks that do not pay dividends. Of course, the same formula can be used in conjunction with the put-call parity theorem to find the value of European puts. For example, the value of the corresponding European put on Intel (with six months to expiration and an exercise price of $85) is:

$$\text{Value of put} = \text{value of call} - \text{share price} + \text{present value of exercise price}$$

$$= 8.64 - 85 + 85/1.025 = 6.57$$

In fact, there is a version of the Black-Scholes formula that allows you to compute the value of put options directly:

$$\text{Value of put} = \left[N(-d_2) \times PV(EX)\right] - \left[N(-d_1) \times P\right]$$

where d_1 and d_2 are defined as before. You can use Appendix Table 1 to find cumulative probabilities for values less than zero (i.e., below the mean) if you recognize that $N(-d) = 1-N(d)$. Since we have already computed $N(d_1)$ and $N(d_2)$, it is easy to check that we get the same answer when we use the put valuation formula:

$$\text{Value of put} = \left[(1-N(d_2)) \times PV(EX)\right] - \left[(1-N(d_1)) \times P\right]$$

$$= [(0.5016) \times 85/1.025] - [(0.4121) \times 85] = 6.57$$

What if the underlying stock pays dividends? We can still use the Black-Scholes formulas with one modification: subtract from the share price the present value of dividends the stock will pay prior to the option expiration date. The modified formulas are:

$$\text{Value of put} = \left[N(d_1) \times (P-PV(div))\right] - \left[N(d_2) \times PV(EX)\right]$$

$$\text{Value of put} = \left[N(-d_2) \times PV(EX)\right] - \left[N(-d_1) \times (P-PV(div))\right]$$

where

$$d_1 = \frac{\log[(P - PV(div)) / PV(EX)]}{\sigma\sqrt{}} + \frac{\sigma\sqrt{t}}{2}$$

$$d_2 = d_1 - \sigma\sqrt{t}$$

In many cases we can forecast near-term dividends with a high degree of confidence, so for options with a short time to expiration it is often reasonable to discount a dividend forecast to the present at the risk-free rate.

In general, there are not exact closed-form solutions for the values of American options. An American call on a non-dividend paying stock is a special case because we know that it will never pay to exercise early. Therefore, the value of an American call is exactly equal to the value of an otherwise identical European call. But what about American puts and American calls on dividend paying stocks? We may be able to obtain a reasonable approximation to the value of an American option by treating it *as if* it were European. This will be a conservative estimate of value because the holder of an American option has the same rights as the holder of an otherwise identical European option *plus* the right to exercise "early." The value of that right is related to both the spread between the risk-free interest rate and the dividend yield on the underlying stock and the time remaining to expiration. The larger the spread and the longer the time to expiration, the greater the value of the early exercise feature, other things equal.

American options are harder to evaluate than Europeans. The holder of a European option has only one decision to make—whether or not to strike on the expiration date. The holder of an American option, in contrast, has to decide *when* as well as whether to exercise. Suppose, for example, you hold a deep in-the-money call option with one month to expiration. Should you strike now or continue to hold the option in the hopes of an even larger gain later? To solve this problem you need to consider how the price of the stock might evolve over the time remaining to expiration. You also need to determine the conditions under which you would exercise the option in the future. A rigorous solution to this problem entails the application of numerical approximation methods. These methods boil down to approximating the risk-neutral probability distribution for the price of the underlying security and then solving simultaneously for the value and optimal exercise strategy. The binomial approximation scheme described earlier is one way to implement this idea.[19]

SUMMARY

There are two basic types of option. An American call is an option to buy an asset at a specified exercise price on or before a specified exercise date. Similarly, an American put is an option to sell the asset at a specified price on or before a specified date. European calls and puts are exactly the same except that they cannot be exercised before the specified exercise date. Calls and puts are the basic building blocks that can be combined to give any pattern of payoffs.

What determines the value of a call option? Common sense tells us that it ought to depend on three things:

1. In order to exercise an option you have to pay the exercise price. Other things being equal, the less you are obliged to pay, the better. Therefore, the value of an option increases with the ratio of the asset price to the exercise price.

2. You do not have to pay the exercise price until you decide to exercise the option. Therefore, an option gives you a free loan. The higher the rate of interest and the longer the time to maturity, the more this free loan is worth. Therefore the value of an option increases with the interest rate and time to maturity.

3. If the price of the asset falls short of the exercise price, you won't exercise the option. You will, therefore, lose 100 percent of your investment in the option no matter how far the asset depreciates below the exercise price. On the other hand, the more the price rises *above* the exercise price, the more profit you will make. Therefore the option holder does not lose from increased variability if things go wrong, but gains if they go right. The value of an option increases with the variance per period of the stock return multiplied by the number of periods to maturity.

---

[19]For more on these numerical methods, see the textbooks by Hull and Jarrow and Turnbull listed in the references.

We explained how to value an option on a stock when there are only two possible changes in the stock price in each subperiod. Black and Scholes have also derived a formula that gives the value of an option when there is a continuum of possible future stock prices. We showed you how to apply this formula to a simple option problem.

Further Reading

The classic articles on option valuation are:

F. Black and M. Scholes: "The Pricing of Options and Corporate Liabilities," *Journal of Political Economy,* 81:637–654 (May–June 1973).

R. C. Merton: "Theory of Rational Option Pricing," *Bell Journal of Economics and Management Science,* 4:141–183 (Spring 1973).

There are also a number of good texts on option valuation. They include:

J. Hull: *Options, Futures and Other Derivatives,* 3rd ed., Prentice-Hall, Inc., Englewood Cliffs, NJ, 1997.

R. Jarrow and S. Turnbull: *Derivative Securities,* South-Western College Publishing, Cincinnati, OH, 1996.

M. Rubinstein: *Derivatives: A PowerPlus Picture Book,* 1998.[20]

The magazine Risk *contains regular articles on the valuation of more complex options.*

---

[20]This book is published by the author and is listed on *www.in-the-money.com.*

WARRANTS AND CONVERTIBLES

Many debt issues are either packages of bonds and warrants or convertibles. The warrant gives its owner the right to buy other company securities. A convertible bond gives its owner the right to exchange the bond for other securities.

There is also convertible preferred stock—it is often used to finance mergers, for example. Convertible preferred gives its owner the right to exchange the preferred share for other securities.

What are these strange hybrids, and how should you value them? Why are they issued? We will answer each of these questions in turn.

WHAT IS A WARRANT?

A significant proportion of private placement bonds and a smaller proportion of public issues are sold with warrants. In addition, warrants are sometimes sold with issues of common or preferred stock; they are also often given to investment bankers as compensation for underwriting services or used to compensate creditors in the case of bankruptcy.[1]

In April 1995 B.J. Services, a firm servicing the oil industry, issued 4.8 million warrants as partial payment for an acquisition. Each of these warrants allows the holder to buy one share of B.J. Services for $30 at any time before April 2000. When the warrants were issued, the shares were priced at $19, so that the price needed to rise by more than 50 percent to make it worthwhile to exercise the warrants.

The warrant holders are not entitled to vote or to receive dividends. But the exercise price of the warrant is automatically adjusted for any stock dividends or stock splits. So, when in 1998

---

[1]The term *warrant* usually refers to a long-term option issued by a company on its own stock or bonds, but investment banks and other financial institutions also issue "warrants" to buy the stock of another firm. For example, in October 1994 the French bank Credit Lyonnais sold one million warrants that entitled their holders to buy shares in three German automobile firms.

B.J. Services split its stock 2 for 1, it also split the warrants 2 for 1 and reduced the exercise price to $30 \div 2 = \$15.00$. As we write this in January 1999 the share price is \$16 and the price of the warrants is \$9.[2]

Valuing Warrants

As a trained option spotter (having read Chapter 8), you have probably already classified the B.J. Services warrant as a five-year American call option exercisable at \$15 (after adjustment for the 1998 stock split). You can depict the relationship between the value of the warrant and the value of the common stock with our standard option shorthand, as in Figure 9.1. The lower limit on the value of the warrant is the heavy line in the figure.[3] If the price of B.J. Services stock is less than \$15, the lower limit on the warrant price is zero; if the price of the stock is greater than \$15, the lower limit is equal to the stock price minus \$15. Investors in warrants sometimes refer to this lower limit as the *theoretical* value of the warrant. It is a misleading term, because both theory and practice tell us that before the final exercise date the value of the warrant should lie *above* the lower limit, on a curve like the one shown in Figure 9.1.

The height of this curve depends on two things. As we explained in Chapter 8, it depends on the variance of the stock returns per period (σ^2) times the number of periods before the option expires ($\sigma^2 t$). It also depends on the rate of interest (r_f) times the length of the option period (t). Of course as time runs out on a warrant, its price snuggles closer and closer to the lower bound. On the final day of its life, its price hits the lower bound.

Two Complications: Dividends and Dilution

If the warrant has no unusual features and the stock pays no dividends, then the value of the option can be estimated from the Black–Scholes formula described in Chapter 8.

But there is a problem when warrants are issued against dividend-paying stocks. The warrant holder is not entitled to dividends. In fact the warrant holder loses every time a cash dividend is paid because the dividend reduces stock price and thus reduces the value of the warrant. It may pay to exercise the warrant before maturity in order to capture the extra income.[4]

Remember that the Black–Scholes option-valuation formula assumes that the stock pays no dividends. Thus it will not give the theoretically correct value for a warrant issued by a dividend-paying firm. However, the value can be found by applying numerical approximation methods of the sort referred to at the end of Chapter 8.

Another complication is that exercise of the warrants increases the number of shares. Therefore, exercise means that the firm's assets and profits are spread over a larger number of shares. Firms with significant amounts of warrants or convertibles outstanding are required to report earnings on a "fully diluted" basis, which recognizes the potential increase in the number of shares.

This problem of *dilution* never arises with call options. If you buy or sell an option on the Chicago Board Options Exchange, you have no effect on the number of shares outstanding.

---

[2]The B.J. Services warrant is fairly standard, but you do occasionally encounter "funnies," such as "income warrants" that make a regular interest payment.

[3]Do you remember why this is a lower limit? What would happen if, by some accident, the warrant price was *less* than the stock price minus \$15? (See Chapter 8.)

[4]This cannot make sense unless the dividend payment is larger than the interest that could be earned on the exercise price. By *not* exercising, the warrant holder keeps the exercise price and can put this money to work.

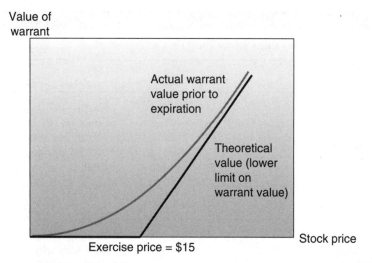

Value of warrant

Actual warrant value prior to expiration

Theoretical value (lower limit on warrant value)

Stock price

Exercise price = $15

Figure 9.1

Relationship between the value of the B.J. Services warrant and stock price. The heavy line is the lower limit for warrant value. Warrant value falls to the lower limit just before the option expires. Before expiration, warrant value lies on a curve like the one shown here.

Example: Valuing United Glue's Warrants

United Glue has just issued a $2 million package of debt and warrants. Here are some basic data that we can use to value the warrants:

- Number of shares outstanding (N):   1 million
- Current stock price (P): $12
- Number of warrants issued per share outstanding (q):   .10
- Total number of warrants issued (Nq):   100,000
- Exercise price of warrants (EX): $10
- Time to expiration of warrants (t):   4 years
- Annual standard deviation of stock price changes (σ):   .40
- Rate of interest (r):   10%
- United stock pays no dividends.

Suppose that without the warrants the debt is worth $1.5 million. Then investors must be paying $.5 million for the warrants:

$$\text{Costs of warrants} = \text{total amount of financing} - \text{value of loan without warrants}$$

$$500,000 = \quad\quad 2,000,000 \quad\quad - \quad\quad 1,500,000$$

$$\text{Each warrant costs investors } \frac{500,000}{100,000} = \$5$$

Table 9.1 shows the market value of United's assets and liabilities both before and after the issue.

TABLE 9.1

United Glue's market value balance sheet (in $ millions)

BEFORE THE ISSUE			
Existing assets	$16	$ 4	Existing loans
		12	Common stock
			(1 million shares
			at $12 a share)
Total	$16	$16	Total

AFTER THE ISSUE			
Existing assets	$16	$ 4	Existing loans
New assets financed		1.5	New loan without warrants
by debt and warrants	2	5.5	Total debt
		.5	Warrants
		12	Common stock
		12.5	Total equity
Total	$18	$18.0	Total

Now let us take a stab at checking whether the warrants are really worth the $500,000 that investors are paying for them. Since the warrant is a call option to buy the United stock, we can use the Black–Scholes formula to value the warrant. It turns out that a four-year call to buy United stock at $10 is worth $6.15.[5] Thus the warrant issue looks like a good deal for investors and a bad deal for United. Investors are paying $5 a share for warrants that are worth $6.15.

How the Value of United Warrants Is Affected by Dilution

Unfortunately, our calculations for United warrants do not tell the whole story. Remember that when investors exercise a traded call or put option, there is no change in either the company's assets or the number of shares outstanding. But, if United's warrants are exercised, the number of

---

[5]In Chapter 8 we saw that the Black–Scholes formula for the value of a call is

$$[N(d_1) \times P] - [N(d_2) \times PV(EX)]$$

where $d_1 = \log[P/PV(EX)]/\sigma\sqrt{t} + \sigma\sqrt{t}/2$

$d_2 = d_1 - \sigma\sqrt{t}$

$N(d_1)$ = cumulative normal probability function

Plugging the data for United into this formula gives

$d_1 = \log[12/(10/1.1^4)]/(.40 \times \sqrt{4}) + .40 \times \sqrt{4}/2 = 1.104$ and $d_2 = 1.104 - .40 \times \sqrt{4}/2 = .704$. Appendix Table 1 shows that $N(d_1) = .865$, and $N(d_2) = .620$. Therefore, estimated warrant value = $.865 \times 12 - .620 \times (10/1.1^4) = \$6.15$.

shares outstanding will increase by $Nq = 100,000$. Also the assets will increase by the amount of the exercise money ($Nq \times EX = 100,000 \times \$10 = \$1$ million). In other words, there will be dilution. We need to allow for this dilution when we value the warrants.

Let us call the value of United's equity V:

$$\text{Value of equity} = V = \text{value of United's total assets} - \text{value of debt}$$

If the warrants are exercised, equity value will increase by the amount of the exercise money to $V + NqEX$. At the same time the number of shares will increase to $N + Nq$. So the share price after the warrants are exercised will be

$$\text{Share price after exercise} = \frac{V + NqEX}{N + Nq}$$

At maturity the warrant holder can choose to let the warrants lapse or to exercise them and receive the share price less the exercise price. Thus the value of the warrants will be the share price minus the exercise price or zero, whichever is the higher. Another way to write this is

$$\text{Warrant value at maturity} = \text{maximum (share price} - \text{exercise price, zero)}$$

$$= \text{maximum} \left(\frac{V + NqEX}{N + Nq} - EX, 0 \right)$$

$$= \text{maximum} \left(\frac{V/N - EX}{1 + q}, 0 \right)$$

$$= \frac{1}{1 + q} \text{ maximum} \left(\frac{V}{N} - EX, 0 \right)$$

This tells us the effect of dilution on the value of United's warrants. The warrant value is the value of $1/(1 + q)$ call options written on the stock of an alternative firm with the same total equity value V, *but with no outstanding warrants*. The alternative firm's stock price would be equal to V/N—that is, the total value of United's equity (V) divided by the number of shares outstanding (N).[6] The stock price of this alternative firm is more variable than United's stock price. So when we value the call option on the alternative firm, we must remember to use the standard deviation of the changes in V/N.

Now we can recalculate the value of United's warrants allowing for dilution. First we find the stock price of the alternative firm:

$$\text{Current equity value of alternative firm} = V = \text{value of United's total assets} - \text{value of loans}$$

$$= 18 - 5.5 = \$12.5 \text{ million}$$

$$\text{Current share price of alternative firm} = \frac{V}{N} = \frac{12.5 \text{ million}}{1 \text{ million}} = \$12.50$$

---

[6]The modifications to allow for dilution when valuing warrants were originally proposed in F. Black and M. Scholes, "The Pricing of Options and Corporate Liabilities," *Journal of Political Economy* 81 (May–June 1973), pp. 637–654. Our exposition follows a discussion in D. Galai and M. I. Schneller, "Pricing of Warrants and the Valuation of the Firm," *Journal of Finance* 33 (December 1978), pp. 1333–1342.

Also, suppose the standard deviation of the share price changes of this alternative firm is $\sigma^* = .41.$[7]

The Black–Scholes formula gives a value of $6.64 for a call option on a stock with a price of $12.50 and a standard deviation of .41. The value of United warrants is equal to the value of $1/(1 + q)$ call options on the stock of this alternative firm. Thus warrant value is

$$\frac{1}{1+q} \times \text{value of call on alternative firm} = \frac{1}{1.1} \times 6.64 = \$6.03$$

This is a somewhat lower value than the one we computed when we ignored dilution but still a bad deal for United.

It may sound from all this as if you need to know the value of United warrants to compute their value. This is not so. The formula does not call for warrant value but for V, the value of United's equity (that is, the shares *plus* warrants). Given equity value, the formula calculates how the overall value of equity should be split up between stock and warrants. Thus, suppose that United's underwriter advises that $500,000 extra can be raised by issuing a package of bonds and warrants rather than bonds alone. Is this a fair price? You can check using the Black–Scholes formula with the adjustment for dilution.

Finally, notice that these modifications are necessary to apply the Black– Scholes formula to value a warrant. They are not needed by the warrant holder, who must decide whether to exercise at maturity. If at maturity the price of the stock exceeds the exercise price of the warrant, the warrant holder will of course exercise.

---

[7]How in practice could we compute σ^*? It would be easy if we could wait until the warrants had been trading for some time. In that case σ^* could be computed from the returns on a package of *all* the company's shares and warrants. In the present case we need to value the warrants *before* they start trading. We argue as follows: The standard deviation of the *assets* before the issue is equal to the standard deviation of a package of the common stock and the existing loans. For example, suppose that the company's debt is risk-free and that the standard deviation of stock returns *before* the bond–warrant issue is 38 percent. Then we calculate the standard deviation of the initial assets as follows:

$$\frac{\text{Standard deviation}}{\text{of initial assets}} = \frac{\text{proportion in}}{\text{common stock}} \times \frac{\text{standard deviation}}{\text{of common stock}}$$

$$= \frac{12}{16} \times 38 = 28.5\%$$

Now suppose that the assets after the issue are equally risky. Then

$$\frac{\text{Standard deviation of}}{\text{assets after issue}} = \frac{\text{proportion of equity}}{\text{after issue}} \times \frac{\text{standard deviation}}{\text{of equity } (\sigma^*)}$$

$$28.5 = \frac{12.5}{18} \times \frac{\text{standard deviation}}{\text{of equity } (\sigma^*)}$$

$$\text{Standard deviation of equity } (\sigma^*) = 41\%$$

Notice that in our example the standard deviation of the stock returns *before* the warrant issue was slightly lower than the standard deviation of the package of stock and warrants. However, the warrant holders bear proportionately more of this risk than do the stockholders; so the bond–warrant package could either increase or reduce the risk of the stock.

WHAT IS A CONVERTIBLE BOND?

The convertible bond is a close relative of the bond–warrant package. Also, many companies choose to issue convertible preferred as an alternative to issuing packages of preferred stock and warrants. We will concentrate on convertible bonds, but almost all our comments apply to convertible preferred issues.

In 1996 ALZA, a pharmaceutical company, issued $500 million of 5 percent convertible bonds due in 2006.[8] These could be converted at any time to 26.2 shares of common stock. In other words, the owner had a 10-year option to return the bond to the company and receive 26.2 shares of stock in exchange. The number of shares into which each bond can be converted is called the bond's *conversion ratio*. The conversion ratio of the ALZA bond was 26.2.

In order to receive 26.2 shares of ALZA stock, the owner has to surrender bonds with a face value of $1,000. Therefore to receive one share, the owner has to surrender a face amount of $1,000/26.2 = $38.17. This figure is called the *conversion price*. Anybody who bought the bond at $1,000 in order to convert it into 26.2 shares paid the equivalent of $38.17 per share.

At the time of issue the price of ALZA stock was about $28. Therefore the conversion price was 36 percent higher than the stock price.

Convertibles are usually protected against stock splits or stock dividends. If ALZA split its stock 2 for 1, the conversion ratio would be increased to 52.4 and the conversion price would drop to $1,000/52.4 = $19.08.

The Convertible Managerie

ALZA's convertible issue is typical, but you may come across more complicated cases. One of the most unusual types of convertible is the *LYON* (liquid yield option note). This is a callable and putable, zero-coupon bond (and you can't get much more complicated than that). LYONs have been issued by a number of firms, including ALZA.

ALZA issued its LYON in 1994 at a price of 35.47 percent. It was a 20-year zero-coupon bond that was convertible at any time into 12.99 shares, though the company could instead pay out the cash equivalent of these shares. When ALZA issued the convertible, corporate bonds yielded roughly 10 percent. So if investors were to convert immediately, they would be giving up a bond worth $1,000/1.10^{20} = $149. If they were to wait 20 years to convert, they would be relinquishing a bond worth $1,000 (as long as the firm is solvent). So the value of the bond that they give up increases each year.

The ALZA LYON contains two other options. Starting in 1999 the company has the right to call the bond for cash. The exercise price of this call option starts at 46 percent and increases each year until it reaches 100 percent in 2014. The bondholders also have an option, for they can put the bond back to the company in 1999 at a price of 46 percent, or they can do so in 2004 at 60 percent, or in 2009 at 77 percent. These put options help to provide a somewhat more solid floor to the issue. Even if interest rates rise and prices of other bonds fall, LYON holders have a guaranteed price in these three

---

[8]The ALZA issue was a convertible subordinated debenture. The term *subordinated* indicates that the bond is a junior debt; its holders will be at the bottom of the heap of creditors in the event of default. A *debenture* is simply an unsecured bond. Therefore there are no specific assets that have been reserved to pay off the holders in the event of default. There is more about these terms in Chapter 8.

years at which they can sell their bonds.[9] Obviously investors who exercise the put would be giving up the opportunity to convert their bonds into stock; it would be worth taking advantage of the guarantee only if the conversion price of the bonds was well below the exercise price of the put.[10]

Mandatory Convertibles

In recent years a number of companies have issued preferred stock or debt which is *automatically* converted into equity after several years. Investors in mandatory convertibles receive the benefit of a higher current income than common stockholders, but there is a limit on the value of the common stock that they ultimately receive. Thus they share in the appreciation of the common stock only up to this limit. As the stock price rises above this limit, the number of shares that the convertible holder receives is reduced proportionately.[11]

Valuing Convertible Bonds

The owner of a convertible owns a bond and a call option on the firm's stock. So does the owner of a bond–warrant package. There are differences, of course, the most important being the requirement that a convertible owner give up the bond in order to exercise the call option. The owner of a bond–warrant package can (generally) exercise the warrant for cash and keep the bond. Nevertheless, understanding convertibles is easier if you analyze them first as bonds and then as call options.

Imagine that Eastman Kojak has issued convertible bonds with a total face value of $1 million and that these can be converted at any stage to one million shares of common stock. The price of Kojak's convertible bond depends on its *bond value* and its *conversion value*. The bond value is what each bond would sell for if it could not be converted. The conversion value is what the bond would sell for if it had to be converted immediately.

Value at Maturity   Figure 9.2(*a*) shows the possible *bond values* when the Kojak convertible matures. As long as the value of the firm's assets does not fall below $1 million, the bond will pay off in full. But if the firm value is *less* than $1 million, there will not be enough to pay off the bondholders. In the extreme case that the assets are worthless, the bondholders will receive nothing. Thus the horizontal line in Figure 9.2(*a*) shows the payoff if the bond is repaid in full, and the sloping line shows the payoffs if the firm defaults.[12]

---

[9]Of course, this guarantee would not be worth much if the company was in financial distress and *couldn't* buy the bonds back.

[10]The reasons for issuing LYONs are discussed in J. J. McConnell and E. S. Schwartz, "The Origin of LYONs: A Case Study in Financial Innovation," *Journal of Applied Corporate Finance* 4 (Winter 1992), pp. 40–47. For a discussion of how to value an earlier LYON issue by Waste Management see J. McConnell and E. S. Schwartz, "Taming LYONs," *Journal of Finance* 41 (July 1986), pp. 561–576.

[11]These mandatory convertibles are known as PERCS, YES, and CHIPS. Sometimes mandatory convertibles specify that if the price of the common stock rises sufficiently high, the cap on the value of the convertible is removed and holders receive a proportion of any further gain in the value of the common. These convertibles are known as PRIDES, DECS, ACES, or SAILS. Mandatory convertibles are described in E. R. Arzac, "PERCs, DECs, and Other Mandatory Convertibles," *Journal of Applied Corporate Finance* 10 (Spring 1997), pp. 54–63

[12]You may recognize this as the position diagram for a default-free bond *minus* a put option on the assets with an exercise price equal to the face value of the bonds. See Chapter 8.

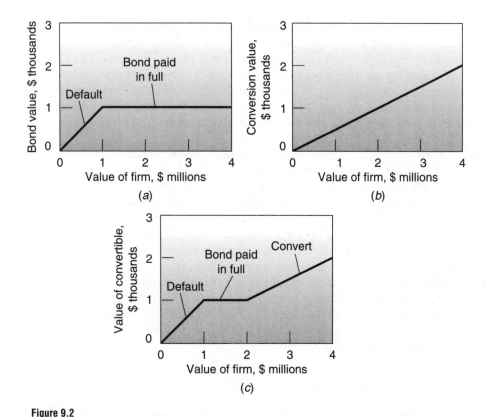

Figure 9.2

(*a*) The bond value when Eastman Kojak's convertible bond matures. If firm value is at least $1 million, the bond is paid off in full; if it is less than $1 million, the bondholders receive the value of the firm's assets. (*b*) The conversion value at maturity. If converted, the value of the convertible bond rises in proportion to firm value. (*c*) At maturity the convertible bondholder can choose to receive the principal repayment on the bond or convert to common stock. The value of the convertible bond is therefore the higher of its bond value and its conversion value.

You can think of the bond value as a lower bound, or "floor," to the price of the convertible. But that floor has a nasty slope and, when the company falls on hard times, the bonds may not be worth much. For example, in 1997 Boston Chicken issued a seven-year $7\frac{3}{4}$ percent convertible bond. But in the following months Boston Chicken fell out of bed. One year after the convertible was issued, its price had fallen 75 percent below the issue price and its promised yield to maturity was about 60 percent. Shortly afterwards the company filed for Chapter 11 bankruptcy.

Figure 9.2(*b*) shows the possible *conversion values* at maturity. We assume that Kojak already has one million shares of common stock outstanding, so the convertible holders will be entitled to half the value of the firm. For example, if the firm is worth $2 million,[13] the one million shares obtained by conversion would be worth $1 each. Each convertible bond can be exchanged for 1,000 shares of stock and therefore would have a conversion value of $1,000 × 1 = $1,000$.

---

[13]Firm value is equal to the value of Kojak's common stock *plus* the value of its convertible bonds.

Kojak's convertible also cannot sell for less than its conversion value. If it did, smart investors would buy the convertible, exchange it rapidly for stock, and sell the stock. Their profit would be equal to the difference between the conversion value and the price of the convertible.

Therefore, there are *two* lower bounds to the price of the convertible: its bond value and its conversion value. Investors will not convert if bond value exceeds conversion value; they will do so if conversion value exceeds bond value. In other words, the price of the convertible at maturity is represented by the higher of the two lines in Figure 9.2(*a*) and (*b*). This is shown in Figure 9.2(*c*).

Value before Maturity   We can also draw a picture similar to Figure 9.2 when the convertible is *not* about to mature. Because even healthy companies may subsequently fall sick and default on their bonds, other things equal, the bond value will be lower when the bond has some time to run. Thus bond value before maturity is represented by the curved line in Figure 9.3(*a*).[14]

Figure 9.3(*b*) shows that the lower bound to the price of a convertible before maturity is again the higher of the bond value and conversion value. However, before maturity the convertible bondholders *do not have to make a now-or-never choice for or against conversion*. They can wait and then, with the benefit of hindsight, take whatever course turns out to give them the highest payoff. Thus before maturity a convertible is always worth more than its lower-bound value. Its actual selling price will behave as shown by the top line in Figure 9.3(*c*). The difference between the top line and the lower bound is the value of a call option on the firm. Remember, however, that this option can be exercised only by giving up the bond. In other words, the option to convert is a call option with an exercise price equal to the bond value.

Dilution and Dividends Revisited

If you want to value a convertible, it is easiest to break the problem down into two parts. First estimate bond value; then add the value of the conversion option.

When you value the conversion option, you need to look out for the same things that make warrants more tricky to value than traded options. For example, dilution may be important. If the bonds are converted, the company saves on its interest payments and is relieved of having eventually to repay the loan; on the other hand, net profits have to be divided among a larger number of shares.[15] Companies are obliged to show in their financial statements how earnings would be affected by conversion.[16]

Also, you must remember that the convertible owner is missing out on the dividends on the common stock. If these dividends are higher than the interest on the bonds, it may pay to convert before the final exercise date in order to pick up the extra cash income.

---

[14]Remember, the value of a risky bond is the value of a safe bond *less* the value of a put option on the firm's assets. The value of this option increases with maturity.

[15]In practice investors often ignore dilution and calculate conversion value as the share price times the number of shares into which the bonds can be converted. A convertible bond actually gives an option to acquire a fraction of the "new equity"— the equity *after* conversion. When we calculated the conversion value of Kojak's convertible, we recognized this by multiplying the proportion of common stock that the convertible bondholders would receive by the total value of the firm's assets (i.e., the value of the common stock plus the value of the convertible).

[16]These "diluted" earnings take into account the extra shares but not the savings in interest payments.

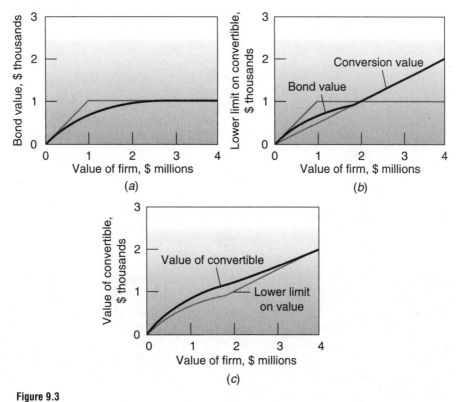

Figure 9.3

(*a*) Before maturity the bond value of Eastman Kojak's convertible bond is close to that of a similar default-free bond when firm value is high, but it falls sharply if firm value falls to a very low level. (*b*) If investors were obliged to make an immediate decision for or against conversion, the value of the convertible would be equal to the higher of bond value or conversion value. (*c*) Since convertible bondholders do not have to make a decision until maturity, (*b*) represents a lower limit. The value of the convertible bond is worth *more* than either bond value or conversion value.

Forcing Conversion

Companies usually retain an option to buy back or "call" the convertible bond at a preset price. If the company calls the bond, the owner has a brief period, usually about 30 days, within which to convert the bond or surrender it.[17] If a bond is surrendered, the investor receives the call price in cash. But if the share price is higher than the call price, the investor will convert the bond instead of surrendering it. Thus a call can *force conversion* if the stock price is high enough.

Most convertible bonds provide for two or more years of *call protection*. During this period the company is not permitted to call the bonds. However, many convertibles can be called early, before the end of the call protection, if the stock price has risen enough to provide a nice conversion profit. For example, a convertible with a call price of $40 might be callable early if the stock price trades above $65 for at least two weeks.

---

[17]Companies may also reserve the right to force conversion of warrants.

Value of convertible

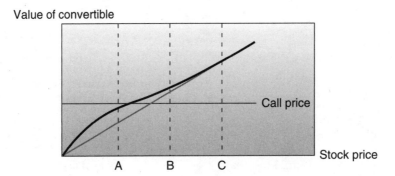

Figure 9.4

The decision to call a convertible. The financial manager should call at price C but wait at prices A and B. (*Note:* The conversion price is the straight upward-sloping line.)

Calling the bond obviously does not affect the total size of the company pie, but it can affect the size of the individual slices. In other words, conversion has no effect on the total value of the firm's assets, but it does affect how asset value is *distributed* among the different classes of security holders. Therefore, if you want to maximize your shareholders' slice of the pie, you must minimize the convertible bondholders' slice. That means you must not call the bonds if they are worth *less* than the call price, for that would be giving the bondholders an unnecessary present. Similarly, you must not allow the bonds to remain uncalled if their value is *above* the call price, for that would not be minimizing the value of the bonds.

Let's apply this reasoning to specific cases. Refer to Figure 9.4, which matches Figure 9.3(*c*) but has the call price drawn in as a horizontal line. Consider the firm values corresponding to three stock prices, marked A, B, and C:

- At price A, the convertible is "out of the money." Calling the bond leads to redemption for cash and hands bondholders a free gift equal to the difference between the call price and the convertible value. Therefore the company should not call.

- Suppose call protection ends with price at level C. Then the financial manager should call immediately, forcing the convertible value down to the call price.[18]

- What if call protection ends with price at level B, barely above the call price? In this case the financial manager will probably wait. Remember, if a call is announced, bondholders have a 30-day period in which to decide whether to convert or redeem. The stock price could easily fall below the call price during this period, forcing the company to redeem for cash. Usually calls are not announced until the stock price is about 20 percent above the call price. This provides a safety margin to ensure conversion.[19]

---

[18]The financial manager might delay calling for a time at price C if interest payments on the convertible debt are less than the extra dividends that would be paid after conversion. This delay would reduce cash payments to bondholders. Nothing is lost if the financial manager always calls "on the way down" if stock price subsequently falls toward level B. Note that investors may convert voluntarily if dividends after conversion exceed interest on the convertible bond.

[19]See P. Asquith and D. Mullins, "Convertible Debt: Corporate Call Policy," *Journal of Finance* 46 (September 1991), pp. 1273–1290.

Do companies follow these simple guidelines? On the surface they don't, for there are many instances of convertible bonds selling well above the call price. But the explanation seems to lie in the call-protection period, during which companies are not allowed to call their bonds. Paul Asquith found that most convertible bonds that are worth calling are called as soon as possible after this period ends.[20] The typical delay for bonds that can be called is slightly less than four months after the conversion value first exceeds the call price.

THE DIFFERENCE BETWEEN WARRANTS AND CONVERTIBLES

We have dwelt on the basic similarity between warrants and convertibles. Now let us look at some of the differences:

1. *Warrants are usually issued privately.* Packages of bonds with warrants or preferred stock with warrants tend to be more common in private placements. By contrast most convertible bonds are issued publicly.

2. *Warrants can be detached.* When you buy a convertible, the bond and the option are bundled up together. You cannot sell them separately. This may be inconvenient. If your tax position or attitude to risk inclines you to bonds, you may not want to hold options as well. Sometimes warrants are also "nondetachable," but usually you can keep the bond and sell the warrant.

3. *Warrants may be issued on their own.* Warrants do not have to be issued in conjunction with other securities. Often they are used to compensate investment bankers for underwriting services. Many companies also give their executives long-term options to buy stock. These executive stock options are not usually called warrants, but that is exactly what they are. Companies can also sell warrants on their own directly to investors, though they rarely do so.

4. *Warrants are exercised for cash.* When you convert a bond, you simply exchange your bond for common stock. When you exercise warrants, you generally put up extra cash, though occasionally you have to surrender the bond or can choose to do so. This means that bond–warrant packages and convertible bonds usually have different effects on the company's cash flow and on its capital structure.

5. *A package of bonds and warrants may be taxed differently.* There are some tax differences between warrants and convertibles. Suppose that you are wondering whether to issue a convertible bond at 100. You can think of this convertible as a package of a straight bond worth, say, 90 and an option worth 10. If you issue the bond and option separately, the IRS will note that the bond is issued at a discount and that its price will rise by 10 points over its life. The IRS will allow you, the issuer, to spread this prospective price appreciation over the life of the bond and deduct it from your taxable profits. The IRS will also allocate the prospective price appreciation to the taxable income of the bondholder. Thus, by issuing a package of bonds and warrants rather than a convertible, you may reduce the tax paid by the issuing company and increase the tax paid by the investor.[21]

---

[20]See P. Asquith, "Convertible Bonds Are Not Called Late," *Journal of Finance* 50 (September 1995), pp. 1275–1289.

[21]See J. D. Finnerty, "The Case for Issuing Synthetic Convertible Bonds," *Midland Corporate Finance Journal* 4 (Fall 1986), pp. 73–82.

WHY DO COMPANIES ISSUE WARRANTS AND CONVERTIBLES?

You hear many arguments for issuing warrants and convertibles, but most of them have a "Heads I win, tails you lose" flavor. For example, here is one such argument:[22]

> *A company that wishes to sell common stock must usually offer the new stock at 10 percent to 20 percent below the market price for the flotation to be a success.[23] However, if warrants are sold for cash, exercisable at 20 percent to 50 percent above the market price of the common, the result will be equivalent to selling common stock at a premium rather than a discount; and if the warrants are never exercised, the proceeds from their sale will become a clear profit to the company.*

There is something immediately suspicious about an argument like this. If the shareholder inevitably wins, the warrant holder must inevitably lose. But that doesn't make sense. Surely there must be some price at which it pays to buy warrants.

Suppose that your company's stock is priced at $100 and that you are considering an issue of warrants exercisable at $120. You believe that you can sell these warrants at $10. If the stock price subsequently fails to reach $120, the warrants will not be exercised. You will have sold warrants for $10 each, which with the benefit of hindsight proved to be worthless to the buyer. If the stock price reaches $130, say, the warrants will be exercised. Your firm will have received the initial payment of $10 *plus* the exercise price of $120. On the other hand, it will have issued to the warrant holders stock worth $130 per share. The net result is a standoff. You have received a payment of $130 in exchange for a liability worth $130.

Think now what happens if the stock price rises above $130. Perhaps it goes to $200. In this case the warrant issue will end up producing a loss of $70. This is not a cash outflow but an opportunity loss. The firm receives $130, but in this case it could have sold stock for $200. On the other hand, the warrant holders gain $70: They invest $130 in cash to acquire stock that they can sell, if they like, for $200.

Our example is oversimplified—for instance, we have kept quiet about the time value of money and risk—but we hope it has made the basic point. When you sell warrants, you are selling options and getting cash in exchange. Options are valuable securities. If they are properly priced, this is a fair trade; in other words, it is a zero-NPV transaction.

You can see why the quotation is misleading. When it refers to "selling stock at a premium," the implicit comparison is with the market value of the stock today. The relevant comparison is with what it may be worth tomorrow.

Managers often use similar arguments to justify the sale of convertibles. Some managers look on convertibles as "cheap debt." Others regard them as a deferred sale of stock at an attractive price.

We have seen that a convertible is like a package of a straight bond and an option. The difference between the market value of the convertible and that of the straight bond is therefore the price investors place on the call option. The convertible is "cheap" only if this price overvalues the option.

---

[22]See S. T. Kassouf: *Evaluation of Convertible Securities* (New York: *Analytical Investors* 1966), p. 6.

[23]This is an overestimate of the discount associated with seasoned issues. See Chapter 3.

What then of the other managers—those who regard the issue as a deferred sale of common stock? A convertible bond gives you the right to buy stock by giving up a bond.[24] Bondholders may decide to do this, but then again they may not. Thus issue of a convertible bond *may* amount to a deferred stock issue. But if the firm *needs* equity capital, a convertible issue is an unreliable way of getting it.

Taken at their face value the motives of these managers are irrational. Convertibles are not just cheap debt, nor are they a deferred sale of stock. But we suspect that these simple phrases encapsulate some more complex and rational motives.

Notice that convertibles tend to be issued by the smaller and more speculative firms. They are almost invariably unsecured and generally subordinated.[25] Now put yourself in the position of a potential investor. You are approached by a small firm with an untried product line that wants to issue some junior unsecured debt. You know that if things go well, you will get your money back, but if they do not, you could easily be left with nothing. Since the firm is in a new line of business, it is difficult to assess the chances of trouble. Therefore you don't know what the fair rate of interest is. Also, you may be worried that once you have made the loan, management will be tempted to run extra risks. It may take on additional senior debt, or it may decide to expand its operations and go for broke on your money. In fact, if you charge a very high rate of interest, you could be encouraging this to happen.

What can management do to protect you against a wrong estimate of the risk and to assure you that its intentions are honorable? In crude terms, it can give you a piece of the action. You don't mind the company running unanticipated risks as long as you share in the gains as well as the losses.[26]

Convertible securities and warrants make sense whenever it is unusually costly to assess the risk of debt or whenever investors are worried that management may not act in the bondholders' interest.[27]

You can also think of a convertible issue as a *contingent* issue of equity. If a company's investment opportunities expand, its stock price is likely to increase, allowing the financial manager to call and force conversion of a convertible bond into equity. Thus the company gets fresh equity when it is most needed for expansion. Of course, it is also stuck with debt if the company does not prosper.[28]

---

[24]That is much the same as already having the stock together with the right to sell it for the convertible's bond value. In other words, instead of thinking of a convertible as a bond plus a call option, you could think of it as the stock plus a put option. Now you see why it is wrong to think of a convertible as equivalent to the sale of stock; it is equivalent to the sale of both stock *and* a put option. If there is any possibility that investors will want to hold onto their bond, the put option will have some value.

[25]The ALZA convertible was a subordinated debenture. See footnote 8.

[26]See M. J. Brennan and E. S. Schwartz, "The Case for Convertibles," *Journal of Applied Corporate Finance* 1 (Summer 1988), pp. 55–64.

[27]Changes in risk ought to be more likely when the firm is small and its debt is low-grade. If so, we should find that the convertible bonds of such firms offer their owners a larger potential ownership share. This is indeed the case. See C. M. Lewis, R. J. Rogalski, and J. K. Seward, "Understanding the Design of Convertible Debt," *Journal of Applied Corporate Finance* 11 (Spring 1998), pp. 45–53.

[28]Jeremy Stein points out that an issue of a convertible sends a better signal to investors than a straight equity issue. As we explained in Chapter 3, announcement of a common stock issue prompts worries of overvaluation and usually depresses stock price. Convertibles are hybrids of debt and equity and send a less negative signal. If the company is likely to need equity, its willingness to issue a convertible, and to take the chance that stock price will rise enough to allow forced conversion, also signals management's confidence. See J. Stein, "Convertible Bonds as Backdoor Equity Financing," *Journal of Financial Economics* 32 (1992), pp. 3–21.

The relatively low coupon rate on convertible bonds may also be a convenience for rapidly growing firms facing heavy capital expenditures. They may be willing to give up the conversion option to reduce immediate cash requirements for debt service. Without the conversion option, lenders might demand extremely high (promised) interest rates to compensate for the probability of default. This would not only force the firm to raise still more capital for debt service but also increase the risk of financial distress. Paradoxically, lenders' attempts to protect themselves against default may actually increase the probability of financial distress by increasing the burden of debt service on the firm.[29]

SUMMARY

Instead of issuing straight bonds, companies may sell either packages of bonds and warrants or convertible bonds.

A warrant is just a long-term call option issued by the company. You already know a good deal about valuing call options. You know from Chapter 8 that call options must be worth at least as much as the stock price less the exercise price. You know that their value is greatest when they have a long time to expiration, when the underlying stock is risky, and when the interest rate is high.

Warrants are somewhat trickier to value than call options traded on the options exchanges. First, because they are long-term options, it is important to recognize that the warrant holder does not receive any dividends. Second, dilution must be allowed for.

A convertible bond gives its holder the right to swap the bond for common stock. The rate of exchange is usually measured by the *conversion ratio*—that is, the number of shares that the investor gets for each bond. Sometimes the rate of exchange is expressed in terms of the *conversion price*—that is, the face value of the bond that must be given up in order to receive one share.

Convertibles are like a package of a bond and a call option. When you evaluate the conversion option, you must again remember that the convertible holder does not receive dividends and that conversion results in dilution of the common stock. There are two other things to watch out for. One is the problem of default risk. If the company runs into trouble, you may have not only a worthless conversion option but also a worthless bond. Second, the company may be able to force conversion by calling the bond. It should do this when the market price of the convertible exceeds the call price.

You hear a variety of arguments for issuing warrants or convertibles. Convertible bonds and bonds with warrants are almost always junior bonds and are frequently issued by risky companies. We think that this says something about the reasons for their issue. Suppose that you are lending to an untried company. You are worried that the company may turn out to be riskier than you thought or that it may issue additional senior bonds. You can try to protect yourself against such eventualities by imposing very restrictive conditions on the debt, but it is often simpler to allow some extra risk as long as you get a piece of the action. The convertible and bond–warrant package give you a chance to participate in the firm's successes as well as its failures. They diminish the possible conflicts of interest between bondholder and stockholder.

---

[29]This fact led to an extensive body of literature on "credit rationing." A lender rations credit if it is irrational to lend more to a firm regardless of the interest rate the firm is willing to *promise* to pay. Whether this can happen in efficient, competitive capital markets is controversial. We give an example of credit rationing in Chapter 19. For a review of this literature, see E. Baltensperger, "Credit Rationing: Issues and Questions," *Journal of Money, Credit and Banking* 10 (May 1978), pp. 170–183.

Further Reading

The items listed in Chapter 8 under "Further Reading" are also relevant to this chapter, in particular Black and Scholes's discussion of warrant valuation.

Ingersoll's work represents the "state of the art" in valuing convertibles:

J. E. Ingersoll: "A Contingent Claims Valuation of Convertible Securities," *Journal of Financial Economics*, 4:289–322 (May 1977).

Ingersoll also examines corporate call policies on convertible bonds in:

J. E. Ingersoll: "An Examination of Corporate Call Policies on Convertible Securities," *Journal of Finance*, 32:463–478 (May 1977).

Brennan and Schwartz's paper was written about the same time as Ingersoll's and reaches essentially the same conclusions; they also present a general procedure for valuing convertibles:

M. J. Brennan and E. S. Schwartz: "Convertible Bonds: Valuation and Optimal Strategies for Call and Conversion," *Journal of Finance*, 32:1699–1715 (December 1977).

Two useful articles on warrants are:

E. S. Schwartz: "The Valuation of Warrants: Implementing a New Approach," *Journal of Financial Economics*, 4:79–93 (January 1977).

D. Galai and M. A. Schneller: "Pricing of Warrants and the Value of the Firm," *Journal of Finance*, 33:1333–1342 (December 1978).

Asquith's analysis of the effect of call protection provides evidence that firms' decisions on calling convertibles are more rational than was previously believed:

P. Asquith: "Convertible Bonds Are Not Called Late," *Journal of Finance*, 50:1275–1289 (September 1995).

For nontechnical discussions of the pricing of convertibles and the reasons for their use, see:

M. J. Brennan and E. S. Schwartz: "The Case for Convertibles," *Journal of Applied Corporate Finance*, 1:55–64 (Summer 1988).

C. M. Lewis, R. J. Rogalski, and J. K. Seward, "Understanding the Design of Convertible Debt," *Journal of Applied Corporate Finance*, 11:45–53 (Spring 1998).

DEBT
FINANCING

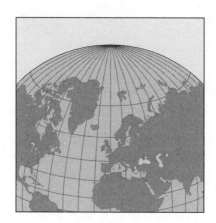

VALUING DEBT

H ow do you estimate the present value of a company's bonds? The answer is simple. You take the cash flows and discount them at the opportunity cost of capital. Therefore, if a bond produces cash flows of C dollars per year for N years and is then repaid at its face value ($1,000), the present value is

$$PV = \frac{C}{1 + r_1} + \frac{C}{(1 + r_2)^2} + \cdots$$
$$+ \frac{C}{(1 + r_N)^N} + \frac{\$1,000}{(1 + r_N)^N}$$

where $r_1, r_2, \ldots, r_N$ are the appropriate discount rates for the cash flows to be received by the bond owners in periods $1, 2, \ldots, N$.

That is correct as far as it goes but it does not tell us anything about what *determines* the discount rates. For example,

1. In 1945 U.S. Treasury bills offered a return of .4 percent: At their 1981 peak they offered a return of over 17 percent. Why does the same security offer radically different yields at different times?

2. In December 1998 the U.S. Treasury could borrow for one year at an interest rate of 4.5 percent, but it had to pay over 5 percent for a 30-year loan. Why do bonds maturing at different dates offer different rates of interest? In other words, why is there a *term structure* of interest rates?

3. In December 1998 the United States government could issue long-term bonds at a rate of about 5 percent. But even the most blue-chip corporate issuers had to pay at least 50 basis points (.5 percent) more on their long-term borrowing. What explains the premium that firms have to pay?

These questions lead to deep issues which will keep economists simmering for years. But we can give general answers and at the same time present some fundamental ideas.

Why should the financial manager care about these ideas? Who needs to know how bonds are priced as long as the bond market is active and efficient? Efficient markets protect the ignorant trader. If it is necessary to know whether the price is right for a proposed bond issue, you can check the prices of similar bonds. There is no need to worry about the historical behavior of interest rates, about the term structure, or about the other issues discussed in this chapter.

We do not believe that ignorance is desirable even when it is harmless. At least you ought to be able to read *The Wall Street Journal* and talk to investment bankers. More important, you will encounter many problems of bond pricing where there are no similar instruments already traded. How do you evaluate a private placement with a custom-tailored repayment schedule? How about financial leases? In Chapter 12 we will see that they are essentially debt contracts, but often extremely complicated ones, for which traded bonds are not close substitutes. You will find that the terms, concepts, and facts presented in this chapter are essential to the analysis of these and other practical problems in financing covered in later chapters.

We start the chapter with our first question: "Why does the general level of interest rates change over time?" Next we turn to the relationship between short- and long-term interest rates, and we consider three issues:

1. Each period's cash flow on a bond potentially needs to be discounted at a different interest rate, but bond investors often calculate the yield to maturity as a summary measure of the interest rate on the bond. We first explain how these measures are related.

2. Second, we show why a change in interest rates has a greater impact on the price of long-term loans than on short-term loans.

3. Finally, we look at some theories that explain why short- and long-term interest rates may differ.

To close the chapter we focus on corporate bonds and examine the risk of default and its effect on bond prices.

REAL AND NOMINAL RATES OF INTEREST

Indexed Bonds and the Real Rate of Interest

There is a distinction between the real and nominal rate of interest. Most bonds promise a fixed *nominal* rate of interest. The *real* interest rate that you receive depends on the inflation rate. For example, if a one-year bond promises you a return of 10 percent and the expected inflation rate is 4 percent, the expected real return on your bond is $1.10/1.04 - 1 = .058$, or 5.8 percent. Since future inflation rates are uncertain, the real rate on a bond is also uncertain. For example, if inflation turns out to be higher than the expected 4 percent, the real return will be *lower* than 5.8 percent.

You *can* nail down a real return; you do so by buying an indexed bond whose payments are linked to inflation. Indexed bonds have been around in many countries for decades, but they were almost unknown in the United States until 1997 when the U.S. Treasury began to issue inflation-indexed bonds known as TIPs (Treasury Inflation-Protected Securities).[1] The real cash flows on

---

[1] In 1988 Franklin Savings Association had issued a 20-year bond whose interest (but not principal) was tied to the rate of inflation. Since then a trickle of companies have also issued indexed bonds.

TIPs are fixed, but the nominal cash flows (interest and principal) are increased as the Consumer Price Index increases.

As we write this at the end of 1998, 3.625 percent TIPs of 2028 are priced at $98\,^{24}/_{32}$ and offer a yield of 3.69 percent. This yield is a *real* yield: It measures how much extra goods your investment would allow you to buy. The 3.69 percent yield on TIPs was about $1^{1}/_{2}$ percent less than on nominal Treasury bonds. If the annual inflation rate proves to be higher than $1^{1}/_{2}$ percent, you will earn a higher return by holding TIPs; if the inflation rate is lower than $1^{1}/_{2}$ percent, the reverse will be true.

What determines the real interest rate that investors demand? The classical economist's answer to this question is summed up in the title of Irving Fisher's great book: *The Theory of Interest: As Determined by Impatience to Spend Income and Opportunity to Invest It.*[2] The real interest rate, according to Fisher, is the price which equates the supply and demand for capital. The supply depends on people's willingness to save, that is, to postpone consumption.[3] The demand depends on the opportunities for productive investment.

For example, suppose that investment opportunities generally improve. Firms have more good projects, so they are willing to invest more at any interest rate. Therefore, the rate has to rise to induce individuals to save the additional amount that firms want to invest.[4] Conversely, if investment opportunities deteriorate, there will be a fall in the real interest rate.

Fisher's theory emphasizes that the required real rate of interest depends on real phenomena. A high aggregate willingness to save may be associated with such factors as high aggregate wealth (because wealthy people usually save more), an uneven distribution of wealth (an even distribution would mean fewer rich people, who do most of the saving), and a high proportion of middle-aged people (the young don't need to save and the old don't want to—"You can't take it with you"). Correspondingly, a high propensity to invest may be associated with a high level of industrial activity or major technological advances.

Real interest rates do change, but they do so gradually. We can see this by looking at the UK, where the government has issued indexed bonds since 1982. The colored line in Figure 10.1 shows that the (real) yield on these bonds has fluctuated within a relatively narrow range, while the yield on nominal government bonds has declined dramatically.

Inflation and Nominal Interest Rates

Now let us see what Irving Fisher had to say about inflation and interest rates. Suppose that consumers are equally happy with 100 apples today or 105 apples in a year's time. In this case the real or "apple" interest rate is 5 percent. Suppose also that I know the price of apples will increase over the year by 10 percent. Then I will part with $100 today if I am repaid $115 at the end of the year. That $115 is needed to buy me 5 percent more apples than I can get for my $100 today. In other words, the nominal, or "money," rate of interest must equal the required real, or "apple,"

---

[2]New York: Augustus M. Kelley, 1965; originally published in 1930.

[3]Some of this saving is done indirectly. For example, if you hold 100 shares of GM stock, and GM retains earnings of $1 per share, GM is saving $100 on your behalf.

[4]We assume that investors save more as interest rates rise. It doesn't have to be that way; here is an example of how a higher interest rate could mean *less* saving: Suppose that 20 years hence you will need $50,000 at current prices for your children's college expenses. How much will you have to set aside today to cover this obligation? The answer is the present value of a real expenditure of $50,000 after 20 years, or $50,000/(1 + \text{real interest rate})^{20}$. The higher the real interest rate, the lower the present value and the less you have to set aside.

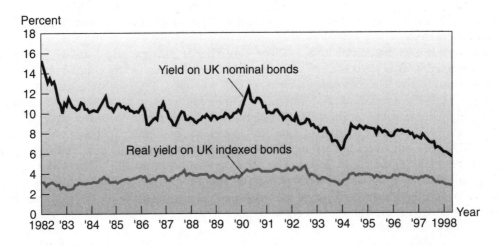

Figure 10.1

The colored line shows the real yield on long-term indexed bonds issued by the UK government. The black line shows the yield on UK government long-term nominal bonds. Notice that the real yield has been much more stable than the nominal yield.

rate plus the prospective rate of inflation.[5] A change of 1 percent in the expected inflation rate produces a change of 1 percent in the nominal interest rate. That is Fisher's theory: A change in the expected inflation rate will cause the same change in the *nominal* interest rate; it has no effect on the required *real* interest rate.[6]

Nominal interest rates cannot be negative; if they were, everyone would prefer to hold cash, which pays zero interest.[7] But what about *real* rates? For example, is it possible for the money rate of interest to be 5 percent and the expected rate of inflation to be 10 percent, thus giving a negative real interest rate? If this happens, you may be able to make money in the following way:

---

[5]We oversimplify. If apples cost $1.00 apiece today and $1.10 next year, you need $1.10 \times 105 = \$115.50$ next year to buy 105 apples. The money rate of interest is 15.5 percent, not 15. Remember, the exact formula relating real and money rates is

$$1 + r_{\text{money}} = (1 + r_{\text{real}})(1 + i)$$

where i is the expected inflation rate. Thus

$$r_{\text{money}} = r_{\text{real}} + i + i(r_{\text{real}})$$

In our example, the money rate should be

$$r_{\text{money}} = .05 + .10 + .10(.05) = .155$$

When we said the money rate should be 15 percent, we ignored the cross-product term $i(r_{\text{real}})$. This is a common rule of thumb because the cross-product term is usually small. But there are countries where i is large (sometimes 100 percent or more). In such cases it pays to use the full formula.

[6]The apple example was taken from R. Roll, "Interest Rates on Monetary Assets and Commodity Price Index Changes," *Journal of Finance* 27 (May 1972), pp. 251–278.

[7]There seems to be an exception to almost every statement. In late 1998 concern about the solvency of some Japanese banks led to a large volume of yen deposits with Western banks. Some of these banks *charged* their customers interest on these deposits; the nominal interest rate was negative.

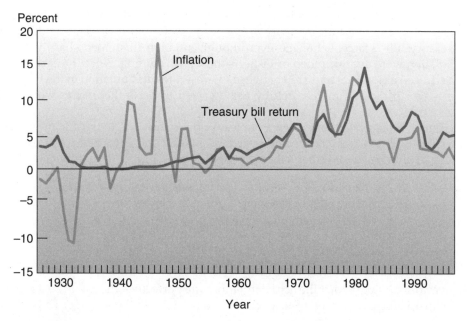

Figure 10.2

The return on U.S. Treasury bills and the rate of inflation 1926–1997.

Source: Ibbotson Associates, *1998 Yearbook,* Ibbotson Associates, Inc., Chicago, 1998.

You borrow $100 at an interest rate of 5 percent and you use the money to buy apples. You store the apples and sell them at the end of the year for $110, which leaves you enough to pay off your loan plus $5 for yourself.

Since easy ways to make money are rare, we can conclude that if it doesn't cost anything to store goods, the money rate of interest can't be less than the expected rise in prices. But many goods are even more expensive to store than apples, and others can't be stored at all (you can't store haircuts, for example). For these goods, the money interest rate can be less than the expected price rise.

How Well Does Fisher's Theory Explain Interest Rates?

Not all economists would agree with Fisher that the real rate of interest is unaffected by the inflation rate. For example, if changes in prices are associated with changes in the level of industrial activity, then in inflationary conditions I might want more or less than 105 apples in a year's time to compensate me for the loss of 100 today.

We wish we could show you the past behavior of interest rates and *expected* inflation. Instead, we have done the next best thing and plotted in Figure 10.2 the return on U.S. Treasury bills against *actual* inflation. Notice that between 1926 and 1997 the return on Treasury bills has been below the inflation rate about as often as it has been above. The average real interest rate during this period was .7 percent. Since 1981 the return on bills has been significantly higher than inflation.

Fisher's theory states that changes in anticipated inflation produce corresponding changes in the rate of interest. But there is little evidence of this in the 1930s and 1940s. During this period, the return on Treasury bills scarcely changed even though inflation fluctuated sharply. Either these changes in inflation were unanticipated or Fisher's theory was wrong. Since the early 1950s, there appears to have been a closer relationship between interest rates and inflation in the United States.[8] Therefore, it is worth looking more carefully at how well Fisher's theory has worked in these recent years.

Eugene Fama has suggested that one way to test Fisher's theory is to twist it around and measure whether the inflation rate can be forecasted by subtracting a constant real rate from the observed nominal rate. That is, if Fisher's theory is right,

$$\text{Nominal interest rate} = \text{real interest rate} + \text{inflation rate forecasted by investors}$$

or

$$\text{Inflation rate forecasted by investors} = \text{nominal interest rate} - \text{real interest rate}$$

Of course, investors cannot predict the actual inflation rate perfectly—there will be a random forecast error. But in an efficient market, we expect them to be right on the average. Thus, the forecast error should be zero on the average.

Suppose that we observe the nominal returns on Treasury bills and the *actual* rates of inflation. We fit the following equation to these data:

$$\text{Actual inflation rate} = a + b \text{ (nominal interest rate)} + \text{random forecasting error}$$

If Fisher is correct, the coefficient b should be close to 1.0 and the constant term a should be equal to minus the real interest rate. For 1953 to mid-1998, b was .80, a little less than we should expect if Fisher is right *and* if the real interest rate is constant.[9]

Before leaving this topic, we must add two qualifications. First, the real interest rate is really an *expected* rate. When you buy a Treasury bill and hold it to maturity, you know what the dollar payoff will be, but the *real* payoff is uncertain because future inflation is not wholly predictable. Thus, to be perfectly precise, we should define the short-term real interest rate as follows:

$$\text{Real interest rate} = expected \text{ real rate of return from U.S. Treasury bills}$$

$$= \text{nominal rate of return on Treasury bills} - expected \text{ rate of inflation}$$

---

[8]This probably reflects government policy, which before 1951 stabilized nominal interest rates. The 1951 "accord" between the Treasury and the Federal Reserve System permitted more flexible nominal interest rates after 1951.

[9]Fama fitted his equation to quarterly data for the period 1953 to 1971. His estimate of b was .98, which is almost identical to the figure that Fisher would predict. See E. F. Fama, "Short-Term Interest Rates as Predictors of Inflation," *American Economic Review* 65 (June 1975), pp. 269–282.

Second, Nelson and Schwert, and Hess and Bicksler, have pointed out that the (expected) real interest rate *does* vary over time. Indeed we have seen that the real rate appears to have been unusually high since 1981. If that is so, Fama's test may be inappropriate.[10]

Until these problems have been resolved, we recommend that you look on Fisher's theory simply as a useful rule of thumb. Thus, if the expected inflation rate changes, your best bet is that there will be a corresponding change in the interest rate.

TERM STRUCTURE AND YIELDS TO MATURITY

We turn now to the relationship between short- and long-term rates of interest. Suppose that we have a simple loan which pays $1 at time 1. The present value of this loan is

$$PV = \frac{1}{1 + r_1}$$

Thus we discount the cash flow at r_1, the rate appropriate for a one-period loan. This rate is fixed today; it is often called today's one-period **spot rate.**

If we have a loan which pays $1 at both time 1 and time 2, present value is

$$PV = \frac{1}{1 + r_1} + \frac{1}{(1 + r_2)^2}$$

Thus the first period's cash flow is discounted at today's one-period spot rate and the second period's flow is discounted at today's two-period spot rate. The series of spot rates r_1, r_2, etc., is one way of expressing the **term structure** of interest rates.

Yield to Maturity

Rather than discounting each of the payments at a different rate of interest, we could find a single rate of discount that would produce the same present value. Such a rate is known as the **yield to maturity,** though it is in fact no more than our old acquaintance, the internal rate of return (IRR), masquerading under another name. If we call the yield to maturity y, we can write the present value as

$$PV = \frac{1}{1 + y} + \frac{1}{(1 + y)^2}$$

All you need to calculate y is the price of a bond, its annual payment, and its maturity. You can then rapidly work out the yield with the aid of a preprogrammed calculator.

---

[10]C. R. Nelson and G. Schwert, "Short-Term Interest Rates as Predictors of Inflation: On Testing the Hypothesis that the Real Rate of Interest Is Constant," *American Economic Review,* 67 (June 1977), pp. 478–486; P. Hess and J. Bicksler, "Capital Asset Prices versus Time Series Models as Predictors of Inflation," *Journal of Financial Economics* 2 (December 1975), pp. 341–360. In response to these criticisms, Fama and Gibbons subsequently recognized that the real interest rate is not constant. They found that *b* was still close to 1.0. See E. F. Fama and M. Gibbons, "Inflation, Real Returns and Capital Investment," *Journal of Monetary Economics* 9 (1982), pp. 297–323.

Example The yield to maturity is unambiguous and easy to calculate. It is the stock-in-trade of any bond dealer. However, you should treat any internal rate of return with suspicion. The more closely we examine the yield to maturity, the less informative it is seen to be. Here is an example.

It is 2003. You are contemplating an investment in U.S. Treasury bonds and come across the following quotations for two bonds:[11]

BOND	PRICE	YIELD TO MATURITY (IRR)
5s of '08	85.21%	8.78%
10s of '08	105.43	8.62

The phrase "5s of '08" refers to a bond maturing in 2008 paying annual interest amounting to 5 percent of the bond's face value. The interest payment is called the *coupon* payment. Bond investors would say that such bonds have a 5 percent coupon. Face value plus interest is paid back at maturity, 2008. The price of each bond is quoted as a percent of face value. Therefore, if face value is $1,000, you would have to pay $852.11 to buy the bond and your yield would be 8.78 percent. Letting 2003 be $t = 0$, 2004 be $t = 1$, etc., we have the following discounted-cash-flow calculation:[12]

			CASH FLOWS				
BOND	C_0	C_1	C_2	C_3	C_4	C_5	YIELD
5s of '08	−852.11	+50	+50	+50	+50	+1,050	8.78%
10s of '08	−1,054.29	+100	+100	+100	+100	+1,100	8.62

Although the two bonds mature at the same date, they presumably were issued at different times—the 5s when interest rates were low and the 10s when interest rates were high.

Are the 5s of '08 a better buy? Is the market making a mistake by pricing these two issues at different yields? The only way you will know for sure is to calculate the bonds' present values by using spot rates of interest: r_1 for 2004, r_2 for 2005, etc. This is done in Table 10.1.

The important assumption in Table 10.1 is that long-term interest rates are higher than short-term interest rates. We have assumed that the one-year interest rate is $r_1 = .05$, the two-year rate is $r_2 = .06$, and so on. When each year's cash flow is discounted at the rate appropriate to that year, we see that each bond's present value is exactly equal to the quoted price. Thus each bond is *fairly priced*.

Why do the 5s have a higher yield? Because for each dollar that you invest in the 5s you receive relatively little cash inflow in the first four years and a relatively high cash inflow in the final year. Therefore, although the two bonds have identical maturity dates, the 5s provide a greater proportion of their cash flows in 2008. In this sense the 5s are a longer-term investment than the 10s. Their higher yield to maturity just reflects the fact that long-term interest rates are higher than short-term rates.

[11]The quoted bond price is known as the *flat* (or *clean*) price. The price that the bond buyer pays (sometimes called the *dirty* price) is equal to the flat price *plus* the interest that the seller has already earned on the bond since the last interest payment date. You need to use the flat price to calculate yields to maturity.

[12]Coupon payments in the United States are actually made semiannually; the owners of the 5s of '08 would receive $25 every six months. Thus our calculations are not exact. We have also rounded to two decimal places.

TABLE 10.1

Calculating present value of two bonds when long-term interest rates are higher than short-term rates

		PRESENT VALUE CALCULATIONS			
		5s OF '08		10s OF '08	
PERIOD	INTEREST RATE	C_t	PV AT r_t	C_t	PV AT r_t
$t = 1$	$r_1 = .05$	$ 50	$ 47.62	$ 100	$ 95.24
$t = 2$	$r_2 = .06$	50	44.50	100	89.00
$t = 3$	$r_3 = .07$	50	40.81	100	81.63
$t = 4$	$r_4 = .08$	50	36.75	100	73.50
$t = 5$	$r_5 = .09$	1,050	682.43	1,100	714.92
	Totals	$1,250	$852.11	$1,500	$1,054.29

Problems with Yield to Maturity

With this in mind, we can sum up the problems with the yield to maturity.

First, when a bond's yield to maturity is calculated, the *same* rate is used to discount *all* payments to the bondholder. The bondholder may actually demand different rates of return (r_1, r_2, etc.) for different periods. Unless two bonds offer exactly the same pattern of cash flows, they are likely to have different yields to maturity. Therefore the yield to maturity on one bond can offer only a rough guide to the appropriate yield on another.

Second, yields to maturity do not determine bond prices. It is the other way around. The demand by companies for capital and the supply of savings by individuals combine to determine the spot rates r_1, r_2, etc. These rates then determine the value of any package of future cash flows. Finally, *given* the value, we can compute the yield to maturity. We cannot, however, derive the appropriate yield to maturity without first knowing the value. We cannot, for example, assume that the yield should be the same for two bonds with the same maturity unless they also happen to have the same coupon.

Thus it is dangerous to rely on yield to maturity—like most averages, it hides much of the interesting information.[13]

Measuring the Term Structure

Financial managers who want just a quick, summary measure of interest rates look in the financial press at the yields to maturity on government bonds. Thus managers will make broad generalizations such as "If we borrow money today, we will have to pay an interest rate of 8 percent." But if you wish to understand why different bonds sell at different prices, you must dig deeper and look at the separate rates of interest for one-year cash flows, for two-year cash flows, and so on. In other words, you must look at the spot rates of interest.

---

[13]For a good analysis of the relationship between the yield to maturity and spot interest rates, see S. M. Schaefer, "The Problem with Redemption Yields," *Financial Analysts Journal* 33 (July–August 1977), pp. 59–67.

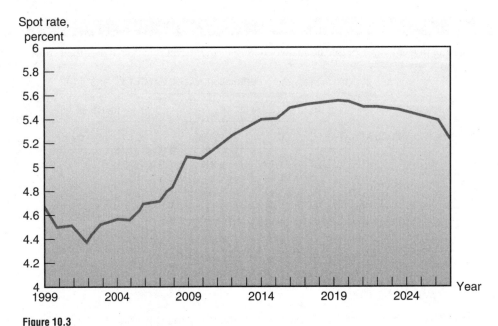

Figure 10.3

Spot rates on U.S. Treasury strips, October 1998.

To find the spot interest rate, you need the price of a bond that simply makes one future pay-ment. Fortunately, such bonds do exist. They are known as *stripped bonds* or *strips*. Strips originated in 1982 when several investment bankers came up with a novel idea. They bought U.S. Treasury bonds and reissued their own separate mini-bonds, each of which made only one payment. The idea proved to be popular with investors, who welcomed the opportunity to buy the mini-bonds rather than the complete package.

If you've got a smart idea, you can be sure that others will soon clamber onto your band-wagon. It was therefore not long before the Treasury issued its own mini-bonds.[14] The prices of these bonds are shown each day in the daily press. For example, in October 1998, a 20-year strip cost $340.79 and gave the investor a single payment of $1,000 20 years later. Thus the 20-year spot rate was $(1{,}000/340.79)^{1/20} - 1 = .0553$, or 5.53 percent.[15]

In Figure 10.3 we have used the prices of strips with different maturities to plot the term struc-ture of spot rates from 1 to 20 years. You can see that investors required an interest rate of 4.7 per-cent from a bond that made a payment only at the end of year 1 and a rate of 5.5 percent from a bond that paid off only in year 2019.

---

[14]The Treasury continued to auction coupon bonds in the normal way, but investors could exchange them at the Federal Reserve Bank for stripped bonds.

[15]This is an annually compounded rate. The yields quoted by investment dealers are semiannually compounded rates.

TABLE 10.2

The first four columns show that the cash flow in year 6 accounts for only 58.4 percent of the present value of the 13 3/4s of 2004. The final column shows how to calculate a weighted average of the time to each cash flow. This average is the bond's duration.

YEAR	C_t	PV(C_t) AT 5.5%	PROPORTION OF TOTAL VALUE [PV(C_t)/V]	PROPORTION OF TOTAL VALUE × TIME
1	137.5	130.33	.092	.092
2	137.5	123.54	.087	.175
3	137.5	117.10	.083	.249
4	137.5	110.99	.079	.314
5	137.5	105.21	.075	.373
6	1137.5	824.97	.584	3.505
		V = 1,412.13	1.000	Duration = 4.708 years

DURATION AND VOLATILITY

Long-term government bonds have provided a higher average rate of return than short-term bills, but the returns on long bonds have also been more variable.[16] The standard deviation of annual returns on a portfolio of long-term bonds was 9.2 percent compared with a standard deviation of 3.2 percent for bills.

We now need to look more carefully at the variability of long-term and short-term bonds. But what do we mean by these phrases? For example, a bond that matures in year 6 also makes interest payments in each of years 1 through 5. Therefore, it is somewhat misleading to describe the bond as a six-year bond; the average time to each cash flow is less than six years.

In July 1998 Treasury $13^3/_4$s of 2004 had a present value of 141.21 (percent of par) and yielded 5.5 percent. Table 10.2 shows where this present value comes from. Notice that the cash flow in year 6 accounts for only 58.4 percent of value. About 40 percent of the value comes from earlier cash flows.

Bond analysts often use the term **duration** to describe the average time to each payment. If we call the total value of the bond V, then duration is calculated as follows:[17]

$$\text{Duration} = \left[\frac{1 \times PV(C_1)}{V}\right] + \left[\frac{2 \times PV(C_2)}{V}\right] + \left[\frac{3 \times PV(C_3)}{V}\right] + \cdots$$

For the $13^3/_4$s of 2004,

$$\text{Duration} = (1 \times .092) + (2 \times .087) + (3 \times .083) + \cdots = 4.708 \text{ years}$$

---

[16]See Ibbotson Associates, Inc., *Stocks, Bonds, Bills, and Inflation, 1998 Yearbook,* Chicago, 1998.

[17]We assume annual interest payments. Actual payments are semiannual.

The Treasury $7^{1}/_{4}$s of 2004 have the same maturity as the $13^{3}/_{4}$s, but the first five years' coupon payments account for a smaller fraction of the bonds' value. In this sense the $7^{1}/_{4}$s are longer bonds than the $13^{3}/_{4}$s. The duration of the $7^{1}/_{4}$s is 5.115 years.

Consider now what happens to the prices of our two bonds as interest rates change:

	$13^{3}/_{4}$s OF 2004		$7^{1}/_{4}$s OF 2004	
	NEW PRICE	CHANGE	NEW PRICE	CHANGE
Yield falls .5%	144.41	+ 2.26%	111.42	+2.46%
Yield rises .5%	138.11	− 2.20	106.15	−2.39
Difference	6.30	4.46%	5.27	4.85%

Thus a 1 percent variation in yield causes the price of the $13^{3}/_{4}$s to change by 4.46 percent. We can say that the $13^{3}/_{4}$s have a **volatility** of 4.46 percent.

Notice that the $7^{1}/_{4}$ percent bonds have the greater volatility and that they also have the longer duration. In fact, a bond's volatility is directly related to its duration:

$$\text{Volatility (percent)} = \frac{\text{duration}}{1 + \text{yield}}$$

In the case of the $13^{3}/_{4}$s,

$$\text{Volatility (percent)} = \frac{4.708}{1.055} = 4.46$$

Volatility is a useful summary measure of the likely effect of a change in interest rates on the value of a bond. The longer a bond's duration, the greater its volatility. In Chapter 13 we will make use of this relationship between duration and volatility to describe how firms can protect themselves against interest-rate changes. Here is an example that should give you a flavor of things to come.

Suppose your firm has promised to make pension payments to retired employees. The discounted value of these pension payments is $1 million, and therefore the firm puts aside $1 million in the pension fund and invests that money in government bonds. So the firm has a liability of $1 million and (through the pension fund) an offsetting asset of $1 million. But, as interest rates fluctuate, the value of the pension liability will change and so will the value of the bonds in the pension fund. How can the firm ensure that the value of the bonds is always sufficient to meet the liabilities? Answer: By making sure that the duration of the bonds is always the same as the duration of the pension liability.

EXPLAINING THE TERM STRUCTURE

The term structure in Figure 10.3 is for the most part upward-sloping. In other words, long rates of interest are higher than short rates. This is the more common pattern but sometimes it is the other way around, with short rates higher than long rates. Why do we get these shifts in term structure?

TABLE 10.3

Two investment strategies for Ms. Long, who wants to invest $1,000 for two years

STRATEGY	NOW	YEAR 1	YEAR 2 (FINAL PAYOFF)
L1: Invest in two one-year bonds	$1,000 $\longrightarrow$	$1,000(1 + r_1)$ $\longrightarrow$	$1,000(1 + r_1)(1 + {_1}r_2)$
		Invest in first bond yielding r_1 — Invest in second bond yielding ${_1}r_2$	
L2: Invest in one two-year bond	$1,000$ $\longrightarrow$	Invest in bond yielding r_2	$1,000(1 + r_2)^2$
Strategy L2 can be expressed as	$1,000$ $\longrightarrow$	$1,000(1 + r_1)$ $\longrightarrow$	$1,000(1 + r_1)(1 + f_2)$
		Invest for 1 year at r_1 — Invest for second year at implicit forward rate f_2	

Ms. Long's Problem

Let us look at a simple example. Ms. Long wants to invest $1,000 for two years. Two strategies open to her are described in Table 10.3. Strategy L1 is to put the money in a one-year bond at an interest rate of r_1. At the end of the year she must then take her money and find another one-year bond. Let us call the rate of interest on this second bond ${_1}r_2$—that is, the spot rate of interest at time 1 on a loan maturing at time 2.[18] As Table 10.3 shows, the final payoff to this strategy is $1,000(1 + r_1)(1 + {_1}r_2)$.

Of course Ms. Long cannot know for sure what the one-period spot rate of interest ${_1}r_2$ will be next year. Suppose that she *expects* it to be 11 percent. That is, $E({_1}r_2) = .11$. The current one-period spot rate is 10 percent. The expected final payoff is

$$1,000(1 + r_1)[1 + E({_1}r_2)] = 1,000(1.10)(1.11) = \$1,221$$

Instead of making two separate investments of one year each, Ms. Long could invest her money today in a bond that pays off in year 2 (strategy L2 in Table 10.3). That is, she would invest at the two-*year* spot rate r_2 and receive a final payoff of $1,000(1 + r_2)^2$. If $r_2 = .105$, the payoff is $1,000(1.105)^2 = \$1,221$.

Now look below the dashed line in Table 10.3. The table shows that strategy L2 can be reinterpreted as investing for one year at the spot rate r_1 and for the second year at a **forward rate** f_2.

---

[18]Be careful to distinguish ${_1}r_2$ from r_2, the spot interest rate on a two-year bond held from time 0 to time 2. The quantity ${_1}r_2$ is a one-year spot rate established at time 1.

The forward rate is the extra return that Ms. Long gets by lending for two years rather than one. This forward rate is *implicit* in the two-year spot rate r_2. It is also *guaranteed:* By buying the two-year bond, Ms. Long can "lock in" an interest rate of f_2 for the second year.

Suppose that the two-year spot rate is 10.5 percent as before. Then the forward rate f_2 must be 11 percent. By definition, this forward rate is the implicit interest rate in the second year of the two-year loan:

$$(1 + r_2)^2 = (1 + r_1)(1 + f_2)$$

$$(1.105)^2 = (1.10)(1 + f_2)$$

$$f_2 = \frac{(1.105)^2}{1.10} - 1 = .11$$

or 11 percent.[19] The two-year spot rate of 10.5 percent is an average of the 10 percent one-year spot rate and the 11 percent forward rate.

What should Ms. Long do? One possible answer is that she should follow the strategy that gives the highest *expected* payoff. That is, she should compare

EXPECTED PAYOFF TO STRATEGY L1	TO	(CERTAIN) PAYOFF TO STRATEGY L2
$1,000(1 + r_1)[1 + E(_1r_2)]$	to or to	$1,000(1 + r_2)^2$ $1,000(1 + r_1)(1 + f_2)$

Strategy L1 gives the higher expected return if $E(_1r_2)$, the expected future spot rate, exceeds the forward rate f_2 implicit in the two-year spot rate r_2. In our numerical example, with $r_1 = .10$, $r_2 = .105$, and $E(_1r_2) = .11$, the two strategies give the same expected return:

STRATEGY	PAYOFF
L1	$1,000(1.10)(1.11) = \$1,221$ (expected)
L2	$1,000(1.105)^2 = \$1,221$ (certain)

Mr. Short's Problem

Now let us look at the decision faced by Mr. Short. He also has $1,000 to invest, but he wants it back in one year. An obvious strategy is to invest in a one-year bond. In this case his payoff is $1,000(1 + r_1)$. This is strategy S1 in Table 10.4. A second strategy (S2 in the table) is to buy a two-year bond and sell it after one year. The sale price will be the bond's present value in year 1. At that time, the bond will have one year to maturity. Its present value will be equal to its year-2 payoff $1,000(1 + r_2)^2$ discounted at $_1r_2$, the one-period spot rate prevailing in year 1:

---

[19]Actually 11.002 percent. We rounded.

TABLE 10.4

Two investment strategies for Mr. Short, who wants to invest $1,000 for one year

STRATEGY	NOW		YEAR 1 (FINAL PAYOFF)
S1: Invest in one-year bond	$1,000	$\xrightarrow{\text{Invest at } r_1}$	$1,000(1 + r_1)$
S2: Invest in two-year bond, but sell in year 1	$1,000	$\xrightarrow{\text{Invest, sell for PV at year 1}}$	$\dfrac{1,000(1 + r_2)^2}{1 + {}_1r_2}$

$$\text{PV of two-year bond at year 1} = \frac{1,000(1 + r_2)^2}{1 + {}_1r_2}$$

We know from Ms. Long's problem that the two-period rate r_2 can be expressed in terms of the one-period spot rate r_1 and the forward rate f_2. Thus

$$\text{PV of two-year bond at year 1} = \frac{1,000(1 + r_1)(1 + f_2)}{1 + {}_1r_2}$$

Of course Mr. Short cannot predict the future spot rate, and therefore he cannot predict the price at year 1 of the two-year bond. But if $r_2 = .105$, and he expects the spot rate to be ${}_1r_2 = .11$, then the expected price is[20]

$$\frac{1,000(1.105)^2}{1.11} = \frac{1,221}{1.11} = \$1,100$$

---

[20]Here we are making an approximation, because the expected payoff of S2 in $t = 1$ is not exactly equal to $[1,000(1 + r_2)^2]/[1 + E({}_1r_2)]$. We should calculate the expected price of the two-year bond at $t = 1$. Call this $\tilde{P}$. By definition

$$\tilde{P} = \frac{1,000(1 + r_2)^2}{1 + {}_1\tilde{r}_2}$$

and

$$E(\tilde{P}) = E\left[\frac{1,000(1 + r_2)^2}{1 + {}_1\tilde{r}_2}\right]$$

But

$$E\left[\frac{1,000(1 + r_2)^2}{1 + {}_1\tilde{r}_2}\right]$$

is only approximately equal to

$$\frac{1,000(1 + r_2)^2}{1 + E({}_1\tilde{r}_2)}$$

In general, for any positive random variable $\tilde{x}$, $E(1/\tilde{x})$ is greater than $1/E(\tilde{x})$. This is called *Jensen's inequality*. Ignoring Jensen's inequality can be dangerous if the variance of $\tilde{x}$ is large.

What should Mr. Short do? Suppose that he prefers the strategy that gives the highest expected payoff. Then he should compare

(CERTAIN) PAYOFF TO STRATEGY S1	TO	EXPECTED PAYOFF TO STRATEGY S2
$1,000(1 + r_1)$	to	$\dfrac{1,000(1 + r_2)^2}{1 + E(_1r_2)}$
	or to	$\dfrac{1,000(1 + r_1)(1 + f_2)}{1 + E(_1r_2)}$

Strategy S2 is better if the forward rate f_2 exceeds the expected future spot rate $E(_1r_2)$. If Mr. Short faces the same interest rates as Ms. Long [$r_1 = .10$, $r_2 = .105$, $E(_1r_2) = .11$, $f_2 = .11$], the two strategies give the same expected return:

STRATEGY	PAYOFF
S1	$1,000(1.10) = \$1,100$ (certain)
S2	$\dfrac{1,000(1.105)^2}{1.11} = \dfrac{1,000(1.10)(1.11)}{1.11} = \$1,100$ (expected)

The Expectations Hypothesis

If the world is made up of people like Ms. Long and Mr. Short, all trying to maximize their expected return, then one-year and two-year bonds can exist side by side only if

$$f_2 = E(_1r_2)$$

This condition was satisfied in our numerical example—both f_2 and $E(_1r_2)$ equaled 11 percent. But what happens if the forward rate exceeds the expected future spot rate? Then both Long and Short prefer investing in two-year bonds. If the world were entirely made up of expected-return maximizers, and f_2 exceeds $E(_1r_2)$, no one would be willing to hold one-year bonds. On the other hand, if the forward rate were *less* than the expected future spot rate, no one would be willing to hold two-year bonds. Since investors *do* hold both one-year and two-year bonds, it follows that forward rates of interest must equal expected future spot rates (providing that investors are interested only in expected return).

This is the **expectations hypothesis** of the term structure.[21] It says that the *only* reason for an upward-sloping term structure is that investors expect future spot rates to be higher than current spot rates; the *only* reason for a declining term structure is that investors expect spot rates to fall below current levels. The expectations hypothesis also implies that investing in short-term bonds (as in strategies L1 and S1) gives exactly the same expected return as investing in long-term bonds (as in strategies L2 and S2).

---

[21]The expectations hypothesis is usually attributed to Lutz and Lutz. See F. A. Lutz and V. C. Lutz, *The Theory of Investment in the Firm,* (Princeton, NJ: Princeton University Press, 1951).

The Liquidity-Preference Theory

Unfortunately the expectations theory says nothing about risk. Look back for a moment at our two simple cases. Ms. Long wants to invest for two years. If she buys a two-year bond, she can nail down her final payoff today. If she buys a one-year bond, she knows her return for the first year but she does not know at what rate she will be able to reinvest her money. If she does not like this uncertainty, she will tend to prefer the two-year bond, and she will hold the one-year bond only if

$$E(_1r_2) \text{ is greater than } f_2$$

What about Mr. Short? He wants to invest for one year. If he invests in a one-year bond, he can nail down his payoff today. If he buys the two-year bond, he will have to sell it next year at an unknown price. If he does not like this uncertainty, he will prefer the one-year investment, and he will hold the two-year bond only if

$$E(_1r_2) \text{ is less than } f_2$$

Here we have the basis for the **liquidity-preference** theory of term structure.[22] Other things equal, Ms. Long will prefer to invest in two-year bonds and Mr. Short in one-year bonds. If more companies want to issue two-year bonds than there are Ms. Longs to hold them, they will need to offer a bonus to tempt some of the Mr. Shorts to hold them. Conversely, if more companies want to issue one-year bonds than there are Mr. Shorts to hold them, they will need to offer a bonus to tempt some of the Ms. Longs to hold them.

Any bonus shows up as a difference between forward rates and expected future spot rates. This difference is usually called the **liquidity premium.**

The liquidity-preference theory assumes that there is a shortage of lenders like Ms. Long. In this case the liquidity premium is positive and the forward rate will exceed the expected spot rate. A positive liquidity premium rewards investors for lending long by offering them higher long-term rates of interest. Thus, if this view is right, the term structure should be upward-sloping more often than not. Of course, if future spot rates are expected to fall, the term structure could be downward-sloping and *still* reward investors for lending long. But the liquidity-preference hypothesis would predict a less dramatic downward slope than the expectations hypothesis.

Introducing Inflation

We argued above that Ms. Long could nail down her return by investing in two-year bonds. What do we mean by that? If the bonds are issued by the U.S. Treasury, she can be virtually certain that she will be paid the promised number of dollars. But she cannot be certain what that money will buy. The expectations theory and the liquidity-preference theory of term structure implicitly assume that future inflation rates are known. Let us consider the opposite case in which the *only* uncertainty about interest rates stems from uncertainty about inflation.[23]

---

[22]The liquidity-preference hypothesis is usually attributed to Hicks. See J. R. Hicks, *Value and Capital: An Inquiry into Some Fundamental Principles of Economic Theory,* 2d ed. (Oxford: Oxford University Press, 1946). For a theoretical development, see R. Roll, *The Behavior of Interest Rates: An Application of the Efficient Market Model to U.S. Treasury Bills* (New York: Basic Books, Inc., 1970).

[23]The following is based on R. A. Brealey and S. M. Schaefer, "Term Structure and Uncertain Inflation," *Journal of Finance* 32 (May 1977), pp. 277–290.

Suppose that Irving Fisher is right and short rates of interest always incorporate fully the market's latest views about inflation. Suppose also that the market learns more as time passes about the likely inflation rate in a particular year. Perhaps today it has only a very hazy idea about inflation in year 2, but in a year's time it expects to be able to make a much better prediction.

Because future inflation rates are never known with certainty, neither Ms. Long nor Mr. Short can make a completely risk-free investment. But since they expect to learn a good deal about the inflation rate in year 2 from experience in year 1, next year they will be in a much better position to judge the appropriate interest rate in year 2. It is therefore more risky for either of them to make a forward commitment to lend in year 2. Even Ms. Long, who wants to invest for two years, would be incurring unnecessary risk by buying a two-year bond. Her least risky strategy is to invest in successive one-year bonds. She does not know what her reinvestment rate will be, but at least she knows that it will incorporate the latest information about inflation in year 2.

Of course this means that borrowers must offer some incentive if they want investors to lend long. Therefore the forward rate of interest f_2 must be greater than the expected spot rate $E(_1r_2)$ by an amount that compensates investors for the extra inflation risk.

Example   Suppose that the real interest rate is always 2 percent. Nominal interest rates therefore equal 2 percent plus the expected rate of inflation. Suppose that the *expected* inflation rate is 8 percent for both year 1 and year 2. However, inflation may accelerate to 10 percent in year 1, or it may decrease to 6 percent. To keep things simple, assume that the actual inflation rate for year 1 continues for year 2:

	ACTUAL INFLATION IN YEAR 1	ACTUAL INFLATION IN YEAR 2
Expected inflation rate = .08	.10	.10
	.08	.08
	.06	.06

Each outcome has a probability of $1/3$.

Now reconsider Ms. Long's problem. Suppose that she can lend for either one or two years at 10 percent (the 2 percent real rate plus the 8 percent expected inflation rate). If she invests in a one-year bond, she will get $1,000(1.1) = \$1,100$ in year 1. This amount is reinvested, but at what rate? The answer is that the future spot rate $_1r_2$ will be 2 percent plus the inflation rate experienced in year 1 and projected for year 2:

ACTUAL INFLATION RATE	SPOT INTEREST RATE IN YEAR 1
.10	.12
.08	.10
.06	.08

Thus the final payoffs to lending short are

	YEAR 1	REINVEST AT	FINAL PAYOFF IN YEAR 2
	$1,100	$_1r_2 = .12$	$1,232
Invest for first year at $r_1 = .10$	1,100	$_1r_2 = .10$	1,210
	1,100	$_1r_2 = .08$	1,188

Note that this strategy gives high payoffs when inflation turns out high.

Now Ms. Long could lock in a $1,210 payoff in year 2 by purchasing a two-year bond at 10 percent $[1,000(1 + r_2)^2 = 1,000(1.1)^2 = \$1,210]$. But this would not lock in her *real* return. In fact, lending short is the *safer* strategy when the final payoffs are converted back to current dollars:

STRATEGY	FINAL PAYOFFS	INFLATION RATE	INFLATION-ADJUSTED PAYOFFS*
Buy two-year bond	$1,210	.10	$1,000
	1,210	.08	1,037
	1,210	.06	1,077
Buy one-year bond	1,232	.10	1,018
	1,210	.08	1,037
	1,188	.06	1,057

*The inflation-adjusted payoffs are calculated by dividing by $(1 + i)^2$. In this case i is the actual inflation rate.

A Comparison of Theories of Term Structure

We have described three views about why long and short interest rates differ. The first view, the expectations theory, is somewhat extreme and not fully supported by the facts. For example, if we look back over the period 1926–1997, we find that the return on long-term U.S. Treasury bonds has been on average 1.8 percent higher than the return on short-term Treasury bills.[24] Perhaps short-term interest rates did not go up as much as investors expected, but it seems more likely that investors wanted a higher expected return for holding long bonds and that on the average they got it. If so, the expectations theory is wrong.

The expectations theory states that if the forward rate of interest is 1 percent above the spot rate of interest—a forward premium—then your best estimate is that the spot rate of interest will rise by 1 percent. In a study of the U.S. Treasury bill market between 1959 and 1982, Eugene Fama found that a forward premium *does* on average precede a rise in the spot rate but the rise is less than the expectations theory would predict.[25]

---

[24]See Ibbotson Associates, *1998 Yearbook,* (Chicago: Ibbotson Associates, Inc., 1998).

[25]See E. F. Fama, "The Information in the Term Structure," *Journal of Financial Economics* 13 (December 1984), pp. 509–528.

The expectations theory has few strict adherents, but Fama's study confirms that long-term interest rates do reflect, in part, investors' expectations about future short-term rates.

Our other two theories both suggest that long-term bonds ought to offer some additional return to compensate for their additional risk. The liquidity-preference theory supposes that risk comes solely from uncertainty about the underlying real rates. This may be a fair approximation in periods of price stability such as the early 1990s. The inflation-premium theory supposes that the risk comes solely from uncertainty about the inflation rate, which may be a fair approximation in periods of fluctuating inflation such as the 1970s and 1980s.

If short-term rates of interest are significantly lower than long-term rates, it is often tempting to borrow short-term rather than long-term. Our discussion of term structure theories should serve to warn against such naive strategies. One reason for higher long rates could be that short rates are expected to rise in the future. Also, investors who buy long bonds may be accepting liquidity or inflation risks for which they correctly want compensation. You should borrow short when the term structure is upward-sloping only if you feel that investors are *overestimating* future increases in interest rates or *overestimating* the risks of lending long.

If the risk of bond investment comes primarily from uncertainty about the real rate, then the safest strategy for investors is to hold bonds that match their liabilities. For example, the firm's pension fund generally has long-term liabilities. The liquidity-preference theory, therefore, implies that the pension fund should favor long-term bonds. If the risk comes from uncertainty about the inflation rate, then the safest strategy is to hold short bonds. For example, most pension funds have real liabilities that depend on the level of wage inflation. The inflation-premium theory implies that, if a pension fund wants to minimize risk, it should favor short-term bonds.

Some New Theories of Term Structure

These term structure theories tell us how bond prices may be determined at a point in time. More recently, financial economists have proposed some important theories of how price *movements* are related. These new theories take advantage of the fact that the returns on bonds with different maturities tend to move together. For example, if short-term interest rates are high, it is a good bet that long-term rates will also be high. If short-term rates fall, long-term rates usually keep them company. These linkages between interest-rate movements can tell us something about relationships between bond prices.

Suppose, for example, that you can invest in three possible government loans: a three-month Treasury bill, a medium-term bond, and a long-term bond. The return on the Treasury bill over the next three months is certain; we will assume it yields a 2 percent quarterly rate. But the return on each of the other bonds depends on what happens to interest rates. Suppose that you foresee only two possible outcomes—a sharp rise in interest rates or a sharp fall. Table 10.5 summarizes how the prices of the three investments would be affected. Notice that the long-term bond has a longer duration and therefore a wider range of possible outcomes.

Now suppose that you start with $100. You invest half of this money in the Treasury bill and half in the long-term bond. In this case the change in the value of your portfolio will be $(.5 \times 2) + [.5 \times (-15)] = -\$6.5$ if interest rates rise and $(.5 \times 2) + (.5 \times 18) = +\$10$ if interest rates fall. Thus, regardless of whether interest rates rise or fall, your portfolio will provide exactly the same payoffs as an investment in the medium-term bond. Since the two investments provide identical payoffs, they must sell for the same price or there will be a money machine. So, the value of the medium-term bond must be halfway between the value of a three-month bill and that of the long-term

TABLE 10.5				

Illustrative payoffs from three government securities. Note the wider range of outcomes from the longer-duration loans. We don't know what the medium-term bond sells for, but we can figure it out from how its value *changes* when interest rates rise or fall.

		CHANGE IN VALUE		
	BEGINNING PRICE	INTEREST RATES RISE	INTEREST RATES FALL	ENDING VALUE
Treasury bill	98	+2	+2	100
Medium- term bond	?	−6.5	+10	?
Long-term bond	105	−15	+18	90 or 123

bond, that is, (98 + 105)/2 = 101.5. Knowing this, you can calculate what the yield to maturity on the medium-term bond has to be. You can also calculate its value next year, either 101.5 − 6.5 = 95 or 101.5 + 10 = 111.5.

Our example is grossly oversimplified, but you have probably already noticed that the basic idea is the same that we used when valuing an option. In order to value an option on a share, we constructed a portfolio of a risk-free loan and the common stock that would exactly replicate the payoffs from the option. That allowed us to price the option *given* the price of the risk-free loan and the share. Here we value a bond by constructing a portfolio of two or more other bonds that will provide exactly the same payoffs. That allows us to value one bond *given* the prices of the other bonds.

In practice bond traders use extremely intricate and complex models, but the underlying idea is the same as in Table 10.5: First identify how changes in the prices of bonds of different maturities are related, then calculate the proper relationships between yields and prices.

ALLOWING FOR THE RISK OF DEFAULT

You should by now be familiar with some of the basic ideas about why interest rates change and why short rates may differ from long rates. It only remains to consider our third question: "Why do some borrowers have to pay a higher rate of interest than others?"

The answer is obvious: "Bond prices go down, and interest rates go up, when the probability of default increases." But when we say "interest rates go up," we mean *promised* interest rates. If the borrower defaults, the *actual* interest rate paid to the lender is less than the promised rate. The *expected* interest rate may go up with increasing probability of default, but this is not a logical necessity.

These points can be illustrated by a simple numerical example. Suppose that the interest rate on one-year, *risk-free* bonds is 9 percent. Backwoods Chemical Company has issued 9 percent notes with face values of $1,000, maturing in one year. What will the Backwoods notes sell for?

The answer is easy—if the notes are risk-free, just discount principal ($1,000) and interest ($90) at 9 percent:

$$\text{PV of notes} = \frac{\$1,000 + 90}{1.09} = \$1,000$$

Suppose instead that there is a 20 percent chance that Backwoods will default. If default does occur, holders of its notes receive nothing. In this case, the possible payoffs to the noteholders are

	PAYOFF	PROBABILITY
Full payment	$1,090	.8
No payment	0	.2

The expected payment is .8($1,090) + .2($0) = $872.

We can value the Backwoods notes like any other risky asset, by discounting their expected payoff ($872) at the appropriate opportunity cost of capital. We might discount at the risk-free interest rate (9 percent) if Backwoods's possible default is totally unrelated to other events in the economy. In this case the default risk is wholly diversifiable, and the beta of the notes is zero. The notes would sell for

$$\text{PV of notes} = \frac{\$872}{1.09} = \$800$$

An investor who purchased these notes for $800 would receive a *promised* yield of about 36 percent:

$$\text{Promised yield} = \frac{\$1,090}{\$800} - 1 = .363$$

That is, an investor who purchased the notes for $800 would earn a 36.3 percent rate of return *if* Backwoods does not default. Bond traders therefore might say that the Backwoods notes "yield 36 percent." But the smart investor would realize that the notes' *expected* yield is only 9 percent, the same as on risk-free bonds.

This of course assumes that risk of default with these notes is wholly diversifiable, so that they have no market risk. In general, risky bonds do have market risk (that is, positive betas) because default is more likely to occur in recessions when all businesses are doing poorly. Suppose that investors demand a 2 percent risk premium and an 11 percent expected rate of return. Then the Backwoods notes will sell for 872/1.11 = $785.59 and offer a promised yield of (1,090/785.59) − 1 = .388, or about 39 percent.

You rarely see traded bonds offering 39 percent yields, although we will soon encounter an example of one company's bonds that had a promised yield of 50 percent.

Bond Ratings

The relative quality of most traded bonds can be judged from bond ratings given by Moody's and Standard and Poor's. Table 10.6 summarizes these ratings. For example, the highest quality bonds are rated triple-A (Aaa) by Moody's, then come double-A (Aa) bonds, and so on. Bonds rated Baa or

TABLE 10.6

Key to Moody's and Standard and Poor's bond ratings. The highest quality bonds are rated triple-A. Then come double-A bonds, and so on. Investment-grade bonds have to be triple-B or higher. Bonds that don't make this cut are called junk bonds.

MOODY'S	STANDARD AND POOR'S	
Aaa	AAA	
Aa	AA	Investment
A	A	grade
Baa	BBB	
Ba	BB	
B	B	
Caa	CCC	Junk
Ca	CC	bonds
C	C	

above are known as *investment grade* bonds. Commercial banks, many pension funds, and other financial institutions are not allowed to invest in bonds unless they are investment grade.[26]

Bond ratings are judgments about firms' financial and business prospects. There is no fixed formula by which ratings are calculated. Nevertheless, investment bankers, bond portfolio managers, and others who follow the bond market closely can get a fairly good idea of how a bond will be rated by looking at a few key numbers such as the firm's debt–equity ratio, the ratio of earnings to interest, and the return on assets.[27]

Table 10.7 shows that bond ratings do reflect the probability of default. Since 1971 no bond that was initially rated triple-A by Standard and Poor's has defaulted in the year after issue and fewer than one in a thousand has defaulted within 10 years of issue. At the other extreme, over 2 percent of CCC bonds have defaulted in their first year and by year 10 almost half have done so. Of course, bonds rarely fall suddenly from grace. As time passes and the company becomes progressively more shaky, the agencies revise downward the bond's rating to reflect the increasing probability of default.

Since bond ratings reflect the probability of default, it is not surprising that there is also a close correspondence between a bond's rating and its promised yield. For example, in the postwar period the promised yield on Moody's Baa corporate bonds has been on average about .9 percent more than on Aaa's.

---

[26]Investment-grade bonds can usually be entered at face value on the books of banks and life insurance companies.

[27]See, for example, R. S. Kaplan, and G. Urwitz, "Statistical Models of Bond Ratings: A Methodological Inquiry," *Journal of Business* 52 (April 1979), pp. 231–261.

TABLE 10.7

Default rates of corporate bonds 1971–1997 by Standard and Poor's rating at date of issue

RATING AT TIME OF ISSUE	PERCENTAGE DEFAULTING WITHIN		
	1 YEAR AFTER ISSUE	5 YEARS AFTER ISSUE	10 YEARS AFTER ISSUE
AAA	.00	.06	.06
AA	.00	.67	.74
A	.00	.22	.64
BBB	.03	1.64	2.80
BB	.37	8.32	16.37
B	1.47	21.95	33.01
CCC	2.28	35.42	47.46

Source: R. A. Waldman, E. I. Altman, and A. R. Ginsberg, "Defaults and Returns on High Yield Bonds: Analysis Through 1997," Salomon Smith Barney, New York, January 30, 1998.

Firms and governments, having noticed the link between bond ratings and yields, worry that a reduction in rating will result in higher interest charges.[28] When the Asian currency crisis in 1998 led Moody's to downgrade the Malaysian government's risk rating, the government immediately canceled a much-needed $2 billion bond issue. "Going to the market now would mean having to offer paper at near junk bond status," complained one official. "It makes no sense to go to the market now," said another, who described the Moody's rating at "grossly unfair."[29]

Junk Bonds

Bonds rated below Baa are known as **junk bonds.** Most junk bonds used to be *fallen angels,* i.e., bonds of companies that had fallen on hard times. But during the 1980s new issues of junk bonds multiplied tenfold as more and more companies issued large quantities of low-grade debt to finance takeovers or to defend themselves against being taken over.

The development of this market for low-grade corporate bonds was largely the brainchild of the investment banking firm Drexel Burnham Lambert. The result was that for the first time corporate midgets were able to take control of corporate giants, and they could finance this activity by issues of debt. However, issuers of junk bonds often had debt ratios of 90 or 95 percent. Many worried that these high levels of leverage resulted in undue risk and pressed for legislation to ban junk bonds.

Between 1986 and 1988 Campeau Corporation amassed a huge retailing empire by acquiring major department store chains such as Federated Department Stores and Allied Stores. Unfortu-

---

[28]They almost certainly exaggerate the influence of the rating agencies, who are as much following investor opinion as leading it.

[29]*The Wall Street Journal Europe,* July 27, 1998, p. 24.

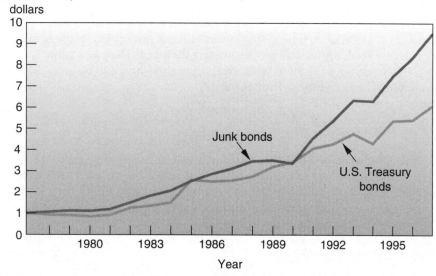

Figure 10.4

Cumulative value of investments in junk and Treasury bonds, 1978–1997. The plot assumes investment of $1 in 1977.

Source: R. A. Waldman, E. I. Altman, and A. R. Ginsberg, "Defaults and Returns on High Yields
Bonds: Analysis through 1997," Salomon Smith Barney, New York, January 30, 1998.

nately, it also amassed $10.9 billion in debt, which was supported by just $.9 billion of book equity.
So when in September 1989 Campeau announced that it was having difficulties meeting the interest
payments on its debt, the junk bond market took a nosedive and worries about the riskiness of junk
bonds intensified. Campeau's own bonds fell to the point at which they offered a promised yield of
nearly 50 percent. Campeau eventually filed for bankruptcy, and investors with large holdings of
junk bonds took large losses.

In 1990 and 1991 the default rate for junk bonds climbed to over 10 percent and the market for
new issues of these bonds dried up. But later in the decade the market began to boom again and
with increasing economic prosperity the annual default rate fell to 1–2 percent.

Junk bonds promise a higher yield than U.S. Treasuries. When junk bonds were out of favor,
the yield spread was nearly 9 percent, but the gap has since narrowed. Of course, companies can't
always keep their promises. Many junk bonds have defaulted, while some of the more successful
issuers have called their bonds, thus depriving their holders of the prospect of a continuing stream
of high coupon payments. Figure 10.4 shows the performance since 1977 of a portfolio of junk
bonds and 10-year Treasury bonds. On average, the *promised yield* on junk bonds was 4.4 percent
higher than that on Treasuries, but the annual *realized return* was only 2.3 percent higher.[30]

---

[30]See R. A. Waldman, E. I. Altman, and A. R. Ginsberg, "Defaults and Returns on High Yield Bonds: Analysis Through
1997," Salomon Smith Barney, New York, January 30, 1998.

Option Pricing and Risky Debt

In Chapter 8 we showed that holding a corporate bond is equivalent to lending money with no chance of default *but* at the same time giving stockholders a put option on the firm's assets. When a firm defaults, its stockholders are in effect exercising their put. The put's value is the value of limited liability—of stockholders' right to walk away from their firm's debts in exchange for handing over the firm's assets to its creditors. To summarize,

$$\text{Bond value} = \begin{array}{c} \text{bond value} \\ \text{assuming no chance} \\ \text{of default} \end{array} - \text{value of put}$$

Thus, valuing bonds should be a two-step process. The first step is easy: Calculate the bond's value assuming no default risk. (Discount promised interest and principal payments at the rates offered by Treasury issues.) Second, calculate the value of a put written on the firm's assets, where the maturity of the put equals the maturity of the bond and the exercise price of the put equals the promised payments to bondholders.

Owning a corporate bond is also equivalent to owning the firm's assets *but* giving a call option on these assets to the firm's stockholders:

$$\text{Bond value} = \text{asset value} - \text{value of call on assets}$$

Thus you can also calculate a bond's value, given the value of the firm's assets, by valuing a call on these assets and subtracting the call value from the asset value. (The call value is just the value of the firm's common stock.) Therefore, if you can value puts and calls on a firm's assets, you can value its debt.[31]

Figure 10.5 shows a simple application of option theory to pricing corporate debt. It takes a company with average operating risk and shows how the promised interest rate on its debt should vary with its leverage and the maturity of the debt. For example, if the company has a 20 percent debt ratio and all its debt matures in 25 years, then it should pay about one-half percentage point above the government borrowing rate to compensate for default risk. Companies with more leverage ought to pay higher premiums. Notice that at relatively modest levels of leverage, promised yields increase with maturity. This makes sense, for the longer you have to wait for repayment, the greater is the chance that things will go wrong. However, if the company is already in distress and its assets are worth less than the face value of the debt, then promised yields are higher at low maturities. (In our example, they run off the top of the graph for maturities of less than four years.) This also makes sense, for in these cases the longer that you wait, the greater is the chance that the company will recover and avoid default.[32]

In practice, interest-rate differentials tend to be greater than those shown in Figure 10.5. High-grade corporate bonds typically offer promised yields about 1 percentage point greater than U.S.

---

[31]However, option valuation procedures cannot value the *assets* of the firm. Puts and calls must be valued as a proportion of asset value. For example, note that the Black–Scholes formula (Chapter 8) requires stock price in order to compute the value of a call option.

[32]Sarig and Warga plot the difference between corporate bond yields and the yield on U.S. Treasuries. They confirm that the yield difference increases with maturity for high-grade bonds and declines for low-grade bonds. See O. Sarig and A. Warga, "Bond Price Data and Bond Market Liquidity," *Journal of Financial and Quantitative Analysis* 44 (1989), pp. 1351–1360. Incidentally, the shape of the curves in Figure 10.5 depends on how leverage is defined. If we had plotted curves for constant ratios of the *market* value of debt to debt plus equity, the curves would all have started from zero.

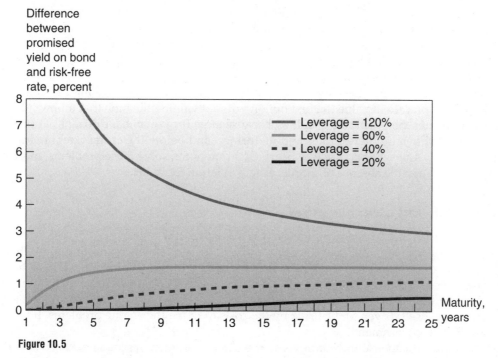

Figure 10.5

How the interest rate on risky corporate debt changes with leverage and maturity. These curves are calculated using option pricing theory under the following simplifying assumptions: (1) the risk-free interest rate is constant for all maturities; (2) the standard deviation of the returns on the company's assets is 25 percent per annum; (3) debt is in the form of zero-coupon bonds; and (4) leverage is the ratio $D/(D + E)$, where E is the market value of equity and D is the face value of the debt discounted at the risk-free interest rate.

Treasury bonds. Does this mean that these companies are paying too much for their debt? Probably not; there are a number of possible other explanations. One possibility is that corporate bonds have other disadvantages in addition to their risk of default. They are less liquid than Treasury bonds, for example. Notice also that Figure 10.5 makes several artificial assumptions. One assumption is that the company does not pay dividends. If it does regularly pay out part of its assets to stockholders, there may be substantially fewer assets to protect the bondholder in the event of trouble. In this case, the market may be quite justified in requiring a higher yield on the company's bonds.

There are other complications; in practice the valuation of corporate debt and equity's a good bit more difficult than it sounds. For example, in constructing Figure 10.5 we assumed that the company made only a single issue of zero-coupon debt. But suppose instead that it issues a 10-year bond which pays interest annually. We can still think of the company's stock as a call option which can be exercised by making the promised payments. But in this case there are 10 payments rather than just 1. To value the stock, we would have to value 10 sequential call options. The first option can be exercised by making the first interest payment when it comes due. By exercise the stockholders obtain a second call option, which can be exercised by making the second interest payment. The reward to exercising is that the stockholders get a third call option, and so on. Finally, in year 10 the stockholders can exercise the tenth option. By paying off both the principal and the last year's interest, the stockholders regain unencumbered ownership of the company's assets.

Of course, if the firm does not make any of these payments when due, bondholders take over and stockholders are left with nothing. In other words, by not exercising one call option, stockholders give up all subsequent call options.

Valuing the equity when the 10-year bond is issued is equivalent to valuing the first of the 10 call options. But you cannot value the first option without valuing the nine that follow.[33] Even this example understates the practical difficulties, because large firms may have dozens of outstanding debt issues with different interest rates and maturities, and before the current debt matures they may make further issues. But do not lose heart. Computers can solve these problems, more or less by brute force, even in the absence of simple, exact valuation formulas.

Valuing Government Loan Guarantees

In the summer of 1971 Lockheed Corporation was in trouble. It was nearly out of cash after absorbing heavy cost overruns on military contracts and, at the same time, committing more than $800 million[34] to the development of the L1011 TriStar airliner. Introduction of the TriStar had been delayed by unexpected problems with its Rolls-Royce engines, and it would be many years before the company could recoup its investment in the plane. Lockheed was on the brink of bankruptcy. (Rolls-Royce was itself driven to the brink by the costs of fixing the engine problems. It was taken over by the British government.)

After months of suspense and controversy, the U.S. government rescued Lockheed by agreeing to guarantee up to $250 million of new bank loans. If Lockheed had defaulted on these loans, the banks could have gotten their money back directly from the government.

From the banks' point of view, these loans were as safe as Treasury notes. Thus, Lockheed was assured of being able to borrow up to $250 million at a favorable rate.[35] This assurance in turn gave Lockheed's banks the confidence to advance the rest of the money the firm needed.

The loan guarantee was a helping hand—a subsidy—to bring Lockheed through a difficult period. What was it worth? What did it cost the government?

This loan guarantee did not turn out to cost the government anything, because Lockheed survived, recovered, and paid off the loans the government guaranteed. Does that mean that the value of the guarantee to Lockheed was also zero? Does it mean the government absorbed no risks when it gave the guarantee in 1971, when Lockheed's survival was still uncertain? Of course not. The government absorbed the risk of default. Obviously the banks' loans to Lockheed were worth more with the guarantee than they would have been without it.

The present value of a loan guarantee is the amount lenders would be willing to pay to relieve themselves of all risk of default on an otherwise equivalent unguaranteed loan. It is the difference between the present value of the loan with the guarantee and its present value without the guarantee. A guarantee can clearly have substantial value on a large loan when the chance of default by the firm is high.

---

[33]The other approach to valuing the company's debt (subtracting put value from risk-free bond value) is no easier. The analyst would be confronted by not one simple put but a package of 10 sequential puts.

[34]See U. Reinhardt, "Break-Even Analysis for Lockheed's TriStar: An Application of Financial Theory," *Journal of Finance* 28 (September 1973), pp. 821–838.

[35]Lockheed paid the current Treasury bill rate plus a fee of roughly 2 percent to the government.

It turns out that a loan guarantee can be valued as a put on the firm's assets, where the put's maturity equals the loan's maturity and its exercise price equals the interest and principal payments promised to lenders. We can easily show the equivalence by starting with the definition of the value of the guarantee.

$$\begin{array}{ccc} \text{Value of} \\ \text{guarantee} \end{array} = \begin{array}{c} \text{value of} \\ \text{guaranteed loan} \end{array} - \begin{array}{c} \text{loan value} \\ \text{without the} \\ \text{guarantee} \end{array}$$

Without a guarantee, the loan becomes an ordinary debt obligation of the firm. We know from Chapter 8 that

$$\begin{array}{c} \text{Value of} \\ \text{ordinary loan} \end{array} = \begin{array}{c} \text{value assuming} \\ \text{no chance of} \\ \text{default} \end{array} - \text{value of put}$$

The loan's value, assuming no chance of default, is exactly its guaranteed value. Thus the put value equals the difference between the values of a guaranteed and an ordinary loan. This is exactly the value of the loan guarantee.

Thus option pricing theory should lead to a way of calculating the actual cost of the government's many loan guarantee programs. This will be a healthy thing. The government's possible liability under existing guarantee programs has been enormous. In 1987, for example, $4 billion in loans to shipowners had been guaranteed under the so-called Title IX program to support shipyards in the United States.[36] This program is one of dozens. Yet the true cost of these programs is not widely recognized. Because loan guarantees involve no immediate outlay, they do not appear in the federal budget. Members of Congress sponsoring loan guarantee programs do not, as far as we know, present careful estimates of the value of the programs to business and the present value of the programs' cost to the public.

Calculating the Probability of Default

Banks and other financial institutions not only want to know the value of the loans that they have made but they also need to know the risk that they are incurring. Suppose that the assets of Backwoods Chemical have a current market value of $100 and its debt has a face value of $60 (i.e., 60 percent leverage), all of which is due to be repaid at the end of five years. Figure 10.6 shows the range of possible values of Backwoods's assets when the loan becomes due. The expected value of the assets is $120, but this value is by no means certain. There is a probability of 20 percent that the asset value could fall below $60, in which case the company will default on its debt. This probability is shown by the shaded area in Figure 10.6.

To calculate the probability that Backwoods will default, we need to know the expected growth in the market value of its assets, the face value and maturity of the debt, and the variability of future asset values. Real world cases are likely to be more complex than our Backwoods example. For example, firms may have several classes of debt maturing on different dates. If so, shareholders have an option on an option. It may be worth their while to put up more money to pay off the short-term

---

[36]The actual figure on March 31, 1987, was $4,497,365,297.98. Since 1987 these government guarantees to shipowners have been substantially reduced.

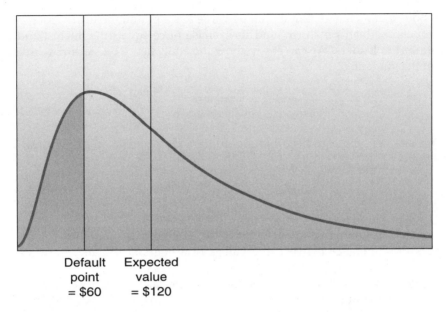

Default   Expected
point   value
= $60   = $120

Figure 10.6

Backwoods Chemical has issued five-year debt with a face value of $60. The shaded area shows that there is a 20 percent probability that the value of the company's assets in year five will be less than $60, in which case the company will choose to default.

debt and thus keep alive the chance that the firm's fortunes will recover before the rest of the debt becomes due.

However, banks and consulting firms are now finding that they can use these ideas to measure the risk of actual loans.[37] For example, look at Figure 10.7. The colored line shows the market value of the assets of Venture Stores, a retailer with 93 stores in the Midwest. The solid line shows the asset value at which the company would choose to default on its debts. Between 1993 and 1998 the market value of Venture's assets crept closer and closer to the default point, until eventually in January 1998 the company filed for bankruptcy. At this point the market value of assets and the firm's liabilities were essentially identical and the equity was valueless.

Of course, nobody had a crystal ball that could foresee ahead of time what would happen to Venture Stores, but KMV, a consulting firm specializing in the assessment of credit risk, estimated the *probability* at each point that Venture Stores would default in the next year. The colored line in Figure 10.8 shows how KMV progressively increased its assessment of the probability of default. The black line also shows how the bond rating was periodically revised to reflect the company's deteriorating prospects.

---

[37]Banks are not just interested in the risk of individual loans; they would also like to know the risk of their entire portfolio. Therefore specialists in credit risk also need to recognize the correlation between the outcomes. A portfolio of loans, all of which are to factory outlets in suburban Hicksville, is likely to be more risky than a portfolio with a wide variety of different borrowers.

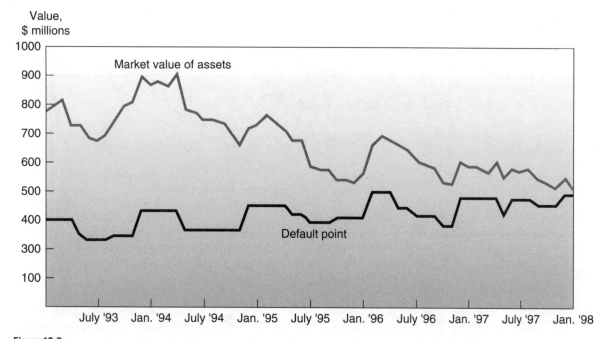

Figure 10.7

The figure shows how the market value of the assets of Venture Stores crept toward the point at which the firm would choose to default.

Source: KMV Credit Monitor.

SUMMARY

Efficient debt management presupposes that you understand how bonds are valued. That means you need to consider three problems:

1. What determines the general level of interest rates?
2. What determines the difference between long-term and short-term rates?
3. What determines the difference between the interest rates on company and government debt?

Here are some things to remember.

The rate of interest depends on the demand for savings and the supply. The *demand* comes from firms who wish to invest in new plant and equipment. The supply of savings comes from individuals who are willing to consume tomorrow rather than today. The equilibrium interest rate is the rate which produces a *balance* between the demand and supply.

The best-known theory about the effect of inflation on interest rates was suggested by Irving Fisher. He argued that the nominal, or money, rate of interest is equal to the expected real rate plus the expected inflation rate. If the expected inflation rate increases by 1 percent, so too will the money rate of interest. During the past 40 years Fisher's simple theory has not done a bad job of explaining changes in short-term interest rates in the United States.

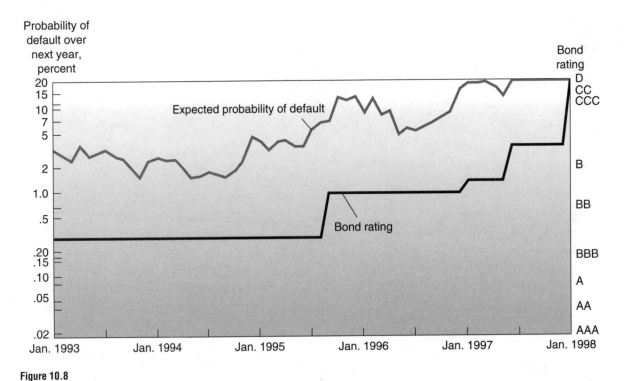

Figure 10.8

The figure shows estimates by *KMV Credit Monitor* of the probability that Venture Stores would default on its debt within a year (left-hand scale) together with the company's bond rating (right-hand scale).

The value of any bond is equal to the cash payments discounted at the spot rates of interest. For example, the value of a 10-year bond with a 5 percent coupon equals

$$PV(\text{percent of face value}) = \frac{5}{1 + r_1} + \frac{5}{(1 + r_2)^2} + \cdots + \frac{105}{(1 + r_{10})^{10}}$$

Bond dealers generally look at the yield to maturity on a bond. This is simply the internal rate of return y, the discount rate at which

$$\text{Bond price} = \frac{5}{1 + y} + \frac{5}{(1 + y)^2} + \cdots + \frac{105}{(1 + y)^{10}}$$

The yield to maturity y is a complex average of the spot interest rates r_1, r_2, etc. Like most averages it can be a useful summary measure, but it can also hide a lot of interesting information. We suggest you refer to yields on stripped bonds as measures of the spot rates of interest.

When you invest in a bond you usually receive a regular interest payment and then the final principal payment. Duration measures the *average* time to each payment. It is a useful summary measure of the length of a loan. It is also important because there is a direct relationship between the duration of a bond and its volatility. A change in interest rates has a greater effect on the price of a bond with a longer duration.

The one-period spot rate r_1 may be very different from the two-period spot rate r_2. In other words, investors often want a different annual rate of interest for lending for one year than for two years. Why is this? The *expectations theory* says that bonds are priced so that the expected rate of return from investing in bonds over any period is independent of the maturity of the bonds held by the investor. The expectations theory predicts that r_2 will exceed r_1 only if *next* year's one-period interest rate is expected to rise.

The *liquidity-preference* theory points out that you are not exposed to risks of changing interest rates and changing bond prices if you buy a bond that matures exactly when you need the money. However, if you buy a bond that matures *before* you need the money, you face the risk that you may have to reinvest your savings at a low rate of interest. And if you buy a bond that matures *after* you need the money, you face the risk that the price will be low when you come to sell it. Investors don't like risk and they need some compensation for taking it. Therefore when we find that r_2 is generally higher than r_1, it may mean that investors have relatively short horizons and have to be offered an inducement to hold long bonds.

No bonds are risk-free in real terms. If inflation rates are uncertain, the safest strategy for an investor is to keep investing in short bonds and to trust that the rate of interest on the bonds will vary as inflation varies. Therefore another reason why r_2 may be higher than r_1 is that investors have to be offered an inducement to accept additional inflation risk.

Finally, we come to our third question: "What determines the difference between interest rates on company and government debt?" Company debt sells at a lower price than government debt. This discount represents the value of the company's option to default. We showed you how the value of this option varies with the degree of leverage and the time to maturity.

Ratings are widely used as a guide to the risk of loans. However, banks and consulting firms also recognize that the option to default is a put option and they have been developing models to estimate the probability that the borrower will exercise its option to default.

Further Reading

A good general text on debt markets is:
S. Sundaresan: *Fixed Income Markets and Their Derivatives,* South-Western College Publishing, Cincinnati, Ohio, 1997.

Reviews of some of the standard theories of the term structure literature may be found in Nelson and Roll:
C. R. Nelson: "The Term Structure of Interest Rates: Theories and Evidence," in J. L. Bicksler (ed.), *Handbook of Financial Economics,* North-Holland Publishing Company, Amsterdam, 1980.

R. Roll: *The Behavior of Interest Rates: An Application of the Efficient Market Model to U.S. Treasury Bills,* Basic Books, Inc., New York, 1970.

Dobson, Sutch, and Vanderford review some of the early empirical tests of term structure theories; more recent tests are provided by Fama and Shiller, Campbell, and Schoenholtz:
S. Dobson, R. Sutch, and D. Vanderford: "An Evaluation of Alternative Empirical Models of the Term Structure of Interest Rates," *Journal of Finance,* 31:1035–1066 (September 1976).

E. F. Fama: "The Information in the Term Structure," *Journal of Financial Economics,* 13:509– 528 (December 1984).

E. F. Fama: "Term Premiums in Bond Returns," *Journal of Financial Economics,* 13:529–546 (December 1984).

R. J. Shiller, J. Y. Campbell, and K. L. Schoenholtz: "Forward Rates and Future Policy: Interpreting the Term Structure of Interest Rates," *Brookings Papers on Economic Activity,* 1:173– 217 (1983).

The following paper by Schaefer is a good review of duration and of how it is used to hedge fixed liabilities:
S. M. Schaefer: "Immunisation and Duration: A Review of Theory, Performance and Application," *Midland Corporate Finance Journal,* 3:41–58 (Autumn 1984).

The Cox, Ingersoll, and Ross paper was the first to use no-arbitrage conditions to derive a rigorous model of the term structure. Ho provides a survey of such models. Brown and Schaefer provide a test of the Cox, Ingersoll, Ross model.
J. C. Cox, J. E. Ingersoll, and S. A. Ross: "A Theory of the Term Structure of Interest Rates," *Econometrica,* 53:385–407 (May 1985).

T. S. Y. Ho: "Evolution of Interest Rate Models: A Comparison," *Journal of Derivatives,* 2:9–20 (Summer 1995).

R. H. Brown and S. M. Schaefer: "The Term Structure of Real Interest Rates and the Cox, Ingersoll, Ross Model," *Journal of Financial Economics,* 35:3–42 (1994).

The classic paper on the valuation of the option to default on corporate debt is:
R. Merton: "On the Pricing of Corporate Debt: The Risk Structure of Interest Rates," *Journal of Finance,* 29:449–470 (May 1974).

THE MANY DIFFERENT KINDS OF DEBT

In Chapters 5 and 6 we discussed how much a company should borrow. But companies also need to think about what *type* of debt to issue. They must decide whether to issue short- or long-term debt, whether to issue straight bonds or convertible bonds, whether to issue in the United States or in the international debt market, and whether to sell the debt publicly or place it privately with a few large investors.

Large companies are almost continuously facing these decisions. Take, for example, ICI, a large British chemical company.[1] In January 1997 ICI negotiated a *revolving credit*, which allowed the company to borrow up to $2.1 billion from a group of banks. The interest rate on this debt was linked to LIBOR, the rate at which major international banks lend dollars to each other.

In May of the same year ICI agreed to buy Unilever's specialty chemicals business for $8.5 billion. The company's financial manager had

seven days to come up with the money. Again the manager turned to a syndicate of banks, which agreed to provide ICI with a straight five-year *term loan* of $4.5 billion plus a $4 billion revolving credit. The interest rate on the debt was also not fixed but was set at 55 basis points (.55 percent) above LIBOR. If interest rates rose sharply, this could have landed ICI with some hefty interest charges. So the company protected itself by buying *caps*. The banks that sold the caps agreed to pay part of the interest charges above an agreed amount.

The bank loans provided ICI with the cash that it needed for the acquisition, but they did not come cheaply. Therefore the company set about selling off some of its existing businesses to repay part of the debt, and at the same time it began to replace the remaining bank loans with cheaper and more flexible forms of debt. ICI's first step in July was to sell $2 billion of short-

---

[1] ICI's 1997 debt issues are described in J. Adams, "A Case Study in Capital Raising," *Corporate Finance* (December 1997), pp. 27–32.

term debt, known as *commercial paper*, to investors in the United States. By selling its debt directly to investors rather than borrowing from a bank, ICI was able to reduce its annual interest bill by $8 million.

Later that month ICI set up a $4 billion *euro medium-term note* (EMTN) program that allowed it to sell a variety of medium- and long-term loans directly to investors. ICI had to decide whether it was better to issue sterling or dollar debt. Since the strong pound was reducing the profitability of ICI's exports, the company resolved to reduce its risk by borrowing dollars. ICI's treasurer reasoned that, if the pound appreciated further, the lower cost of buying dollars to service the debt would offset the reduced profits on the company's exports.

The first deal under the medium-term note program was the sale of a $500 million five-year *fixed-rate bond*. This was followed within a couple of weeks by the issue of a £300 million 10-year bond which was then converted into dollar debt by a *swap*. Next ICI sold $1.25 billion of *floating-rate notes* (FRN). These notes consisted of three series; one matured in one year, one matured in 15 months, and one matured in 18 months.

ICI had sold its commercial paper in the United States, but the subsequent issues of debt had all been sold in Europe. The company, therefore, decided it was time to turn to the United States market for its next issue. This consisted of a $1.25 billion *yankee bond* with maturities of 5 to 10 years. Finally, ICI closed the year by replacing the $2.1 billion arrangement that it had negotiated in January. It did so by establishing a new 364-day revolving credit with a group of banks.

This huge borrowing program allowed ICI to complete successfully a major program of acquisitions and disposals. Asked about the barrage of debt issues in 1997, ICI's treasurer commented, "We wanted every investor with money burning a hole in his pocket to have ICI's name right in front of him. And for two months we did exactly that."

Later we will explain these different types of loan.[2] We cite the example of ICI at this point simply to illustrate the wide choice of debt that is available. As a financial manager, you need to choose the type that makes sense for your company. For example, foreign currency debt may be best suited for firms with a substantial overseas business. Short-term debt is generally used when the firm has only a temporary need for funds.[3] Sometimes competition between lenders opens a window of opportunity in a particular sector of the debt market. The effect may be only a few basis-points reduction in yield, but on a large issue that can translate into a saving of several million dollars. Remember the saying, "A million dollars here and a million there—pretty soon it begins to add up to real money."[4]

Our focus in this chapter is on straight long-term debt. We begin our discussion by looking at the different types of bonds. We examine the differences between senior and junior bonds and between

---

[2]In this chapter we concentrate on longer-term loans. Short-term debt is discussed in Chapter 19.

[3]For example, Stohs and Mauer show that firms with a preponderance of short-term assets tend to issue short-term debt. See M. H. Stohs and D. C. Mauer, "The Determinants of Corporate Debt Maturity Structure," *Journal of Business* 69 (July 1996), pp. 279–312.

[4]The remark was made by the late Senator Everett Dirksen. However, he was talking billions.

secured and unsecured bonds. Then we describe how bonds may be repaid by means of a sinking fund and how the borrower or the lender may have an option for early repayment. We also look at some of the restrictive provisions that deter the company from taking actions that would damage the bonds' value. We not only describe the different features of corporate debt but also try to explain *why* sinking funds, repayment options, and the like exist. They are not simply matters of custom; there are generally good economic reasons for their use.

Debt may be sold to the public or placed privately with large financial institutions. Because privately placed bonds are broadly similar to public issues, we will not discuss them at length. However, we will discuss another form of private debt known as project finance. This is the glamorous part of the debt market. The words *project finance* conjure up images of multimillion-dollar loans to finance huge ventures in exotic parts of the world. You'll find there's something to the popular image, but it's not the whole story.

We conclude the chapter by looking at a few unusual bonds and considering the reasons for innovation in the debt markets.

DOMESTIC BONDS AND INTERNATIONAL BONDS

A firm can issue a bond either in its home country or in another country. Of course, any firm that raises money abroad is subject to the rules of the country in which it does so. For example, any issue in the United States of publicly traded bonds needs to be registered with the SEC. Since the cost of registration can be particularly large for foreign firms, these firms often avoid registration by complying with the SEC's Rule 144A for bond issues in the United States. Rule 144A bonds can be bought and sold only by large financial institutions.[5]

Bonds that are sold to local investors in another country's bond market are known as *foreign bonds*. The United States is by far the largest market for foreign bonds, but Japan and Switzerland are also important. These bonds have a variety of nicknames: A bond sold publicly by a foreign company in the United States is known as a *yankee bond* (ICI's bond issue in the United States was a yankee bond); a bond sold by a foreign firm in Japan is a *samurai*.

There is also a large international market for long-term bonds. These international bond issues are sold throughout the world by syndicates of underwriters. The underwriters are mainly located in London. They include the London branches of large U.S., European, and Japanese banks and security dealers. International issues are usually made in one of the major currencies. The U.S. dollar has been the most popular choice, but the yen and British pound are often used. Almost certainly, a high proportion of international bond issues will be made in the euro, the new currency of the European Monetary Union.

The international bond market arose during the 1960s because the U.S. government imposed an interest-equalization tax on the purchase of foreign securities and discouraged American corpo-

---

[5]We described Rule 144A in Chapter 3.

rations from exporting capital. Therefore both European and American multinationals were forced to tap an international market for capital.[6] This market came to be known as the *eurobond market*, but be careful not to confuse a eurobond (which may be in any currency) with a bond denominated in euros.

The interest-equalization tax was removed in 1974, and there are no longer any controls on capital exports from the United States. Since U.S. firms can now choose whether to borrow in New York or London, the interest rates in the two markets are usually similar. However, the international bond market is not directly subject to regulation by the U.S. authorities, and therefore the financial manager needs to be alert to small differences in the cost of borrowing in one market rather than another.

THE BOND CONTRACT

To give you some feel for the bond contract (and for some of the language in which it is couched), we have summarized in Table 11.1 the terms of an issue of 30-year bonds by Ralston Purina Company. We will look at each of the principal items in turn.

Indenture, or Trust Deed

The Ralston Purina offering was a public issue of bonds, which was registered with the SEC and listed on the New York Stock Exchange. In the case of a public issue, the bond agreement is in the form of an **indenture**, or **trust deed**, between the borrower and a trust company.[7] Continental Bank, which is the trust company for the Ralston Purina bond, represents the bondholders. It must see that the terms of the indenture are observed and look after the bondholders in the event of default. A copy of the bond indenture is included in the registration statement. It is a turgid legal document.[8] Its main provisions are summarized in the prospectus to the issue.

Moving down Table 11.1, you will see that the Ralston Purina bonds are *registered*. This means that the company's registrar records the ownership of each bond and the company pays the interest and the final principal amount directly to each owner.[9]

Almost all bonds issued in the United States are issued in registered form, but in many countries bonds may be issued in *bearer* form. In this case, the certificate constitutes the primary evidence of ownership so the bondholder must send in coupons to claim interest and must send the certificate itself to claim the final repayment of principal. International bonds almost invariably

---

[6]Also, until 1984 the United States imposed a withholding tax on interest payments to foreign investors. Investors could avoid this tax by buying an international bond issued in London rather than a similar bond issued in New York.

[7]In the case of international bond issues, there is a *fiscal agent* who carries out broadly similar functions to a bond trustee.

[8]For example, the indenture for one J.C. Penney bond states: "In any case where several matters are required to be certified by, or covered by an opinion of, any specified Person, it is not necessary that all such matters be certified by, or covered by the opinion of, only one such Person, or that they be certified or covered by only one document, but one such Person may certify or give an opinion with respect to some matters and one or more such other Persons as to other matters, and any such Person may certify or give an opinion as to such matters in one or several documents." Try saying that three times fast.

[9]Often, investors do not physically hold the security; instead, their ownership is represented by a book entry. The "book" is in practice a computer.

TABLE 11.1

Summary of terms of 9½ percent sinking fund debenture 2016 issued by Ralston Purina Company

Listed	New York Stock Exchange
Trustee	Continental Bank, Chicago
Rights on default	The trustee or 25% of the debentures outstanding may declare interest due and payable.
Indenture modification	Indenture may not be modified except as provided with the consent of two-thirds of the debentures outstanding.
Registered	Fully registered
Denomination	$1,000
To be issued	$86.4 million
Issue date	June 4, 1986
Offered	Issued at a price of 97.60% plus accrued interest (proceeds to Company 96.725%) through First Boston Corporation, Goldman Sachs and Company, Shearson Lehman Brothers, Stifel Nicolaus and Company, and associates.
Interest	At a rate of 9½% per annum, payable June 1 and December 1 to holders registered on May 15 and November 15.
Security	Not secured. Company will not permit to have any lien on its property or assets without equally and ratably securing the debt securities.
Sale and lease-back	Company will not enter into any sale and lease-back transaction unless the Company within 120 days after the transfer of title to such principal property applies to the redemption of the debt securities at the then-applicable option redemption price an amount equal to the net proceeds received by the Company upon such sale.
Maturity	June 1, 2016
Sinking fund	Annually between June 2, 1996, and June 2, 2015, sufficient to redeem not less than $13.5 million principal amount, plus similar optional payments. Sinking fund is designed to redeem 90% of the debentures prior to maturity.
Callable	At whole or in part at any time at the option of the Company with at least 30, but not more than 60, days' notice on each May 31 as follows:

1989	106.390	1990	106.035	1991	105.680
1992	105.325	1993	104.970	1994	104.615
1995	104.260	1996	103.905	1997	103.550
1998	103.195	1999	102.840	2000	102.485
2001	102.130	2002	101.775	2003	101.420
2004	101.065	2005	100.710	2006	100.355

and thereafter at 100 plus accrued interest; provided, however, that prior to June 1, 1996, the Company may not redeem the bonds from, or in anticipation of, moneys borrowed having an effective interest cost of less than 9.748%.

allow the owner to hold them in bearer form. However, since the ownership of such bonds cannot be traced, the IRS has tried to deter U.S. residents from holding them.[10]

The Bond Terms

Like most dollar bonds, the Ralston Purina bonds have a face value of $1,000. Notice, however, that the bond price is shown as a percentage of face value. Also, the price is stated net of *accrued interest*. This means that the bond buyer must pay not only the quoted price but also the amount of any future interest that may have accrued. For example, an investor who bought bonds for delivery on (say) June 11, 1986, would be receiving them 10 days into the first interest period. Therefore, accrued interest would be $10/360 \times 9.5 = .26$ percent, and the investor would pay a price of 97.60 plus .26 percent of accrued interest.[11]

The Ralston Purina bonds were offered to the public at a price of 97.60 percent, but the company received only 96.725 percent. The difference represents the underwriters' spread. Of the $86.4 million raised, about $85.6 million went to the company and $.8 million went to the underwriters.

Since the bonds were issued at a price of 97.60 percent, investors who hold the bonds to maturity receive a capital gain over the 30 years of 2.40 percent.[12] However, the bulk of their return is provided by the regular interest payment. The annual interest or *coupon* payment on each bond is 9.50 percent of $1,000, or $95. This interest is payable semiannually, so every six months investors receive interest of $95/2 = \$47.50$. Most U.S. bonds pay interest semiannually, but a comparable international bond would generally pay interest annually.[13]

The regular interest payment on a bond is a hurdle that the company must keep jumping. If the company ever fails to pay the interest, lenders can demand their money back instead of waiting until matters may have deteriorated further.[14] Thus interest payments provide added protection for lenders.[15]

Sometimes bonds are sold with a lower interest payment but at a larger discount on their face value, so investors receive a significant part of their return in the form of capital appreciation.[16]

---

[10]U.S. residents cannot generally deduct capital losses on bearer bonds. Also, payments on such bonds cannot be made to a bank account in the United States.

[11]In the U.S. corporate bond market accrued interest is calculated on the assumption that a year is composed of twelve 30-day months; in some other markets (such as the U.S. Treasury bond market) calculations recognize the actual number of days in each calendar month.

[12]This gain is not taxed as income as long as it amounts to less than .25 percent a year. We discuss later the taxation of bonds that are sold at a deep discount on their face value.

[13]If a bond pays interest semiannually, investors usually calculate a *semiannually* compounded yield to maturity on the bond. In other words, the yield is quoted as twice the six-month yield. Because international bonds pay interest annually, it is conventional to quote their yields to maturity on an *annually* compounded basis. Remember this when comparing yields.

[14]There is one type of bond on which the borrower is obliged to pay interest only if it is covered by the year's earnings. These so-called *income bonds* are rare and have largely been issued as part of railroad reorganizations. For a discussion of the attraction of income bonds, see J. J. McConnell and G. G. Schlarbaum, "Returns, Risks, and Pricing of Income Bonds, 1956–1976 (Does Money Have an Odor?)," *Journal of Business* 54 (January 1981), pp. 33–64.

[15]See F. Black and J. C. Cox, "Valuing Corporate Securities: Some Effects of Bond Indenture Provisions," *Journal of Finance* 31 (May 1976), pp. 351–367. Black and Cox point out that the interest payment would be a trivial hurdle if the company could sell assets to make the payment. Such sales are, therefore, restricted.

[16]Any bond that is issued at a discount is known as an *original issue discount* (OID) bond. A zero coupon is often called a "pure discount bond."

The ultimate is the zero-coupon bond, which pays no interest at all; in this case the entire return consists of capital appreciation.[17]

The Ralston Purina interest payment is fixed for the life of the bond, but in some issues the payment varies with the general level of interest rates. For example, the payment may be tied to the U.S. Treasury bill rate or (more commonly) to the London interbank offered rate (LIBOR), which is the rate at which international banks lend to one another. Often these floating-rate notes specify a minimum (or floor) interest rate or they may specify a maximum (or cap) on the rate.[18] You may also come across "collars," which stipulate both a maximum and a minimum payment, or "drop-locks," which provide that if the rate falls to a specified trigger point, the payment is then fixed for the remainder of the bond's life.

SECURITY AND SENIORITY

Almost all debt issues by industrial and financial companies are general unsecured obligations. Longer-term unsecured issues like the Ralston Purina bond are usually called **debentures**; shorter-term issues are usually called **notes**.

Utility company bonds are commonly secured. This means that if the company defaults on the debt, the trustee or lender may take possession of the relevant assets. If these are insufficient to satisfy the claim, the remaining debt will have a general claim, alongside any unsecured debt, against the other assets of the firm.

The majority of secured debt consists of **mortgage bonds**. These sometimes provide a claim against a specific building, but they are more often secured on all the firm's property.[19] Of course, the value of any mortgage depends on the extent of alternative uses of the property. A custom-built machine for producing buggy whips will not be worth much when the market for buggy whips dries up.

Companies that own securities may use them as collateral for a loan. For example, holding companies are firms whose main assets consist of common stock in a number of subsidiaries. So, when holding companies wish to borrow, they generally use these investments as collateral. The problem for the lender is that this stock is junior to *all* other claims on the assets of the subsidiaries, and so these *collateral trust bonds* usually include detailed restrictions on the freedom of the subsidiaries to issue debt or preferred stock.

A third form of secured debt is the **equipment trust certificate**. This is most frequently used to finance new railroad rolling stock but may also be used to finance trucks, aircraft, and ships. Under this arrangement a trustee obtains formal ownership of the equipment. The company makes a down payment on the cost of the equipment, and the balance is provided by a package of equipment trust

---

[17]The ultimate of ultimates was an issue of a perpetual zero-coupon bond on behalf of a charity.

[18]Instead of issuing a capped floating-rate loan, a company will sometimes issue an uncapped loan and at the same time buy a cap from a bank. The bank pays the interest in excess of the specified level. Earlier in the chapter we saw how ICI purchased a separate cap on its interest payments.

[19]If a mortgage is *closed*, no more bonds may be issued against the mortgage. However, usually there is no specific limit to the amount of bonds that may be secured (in which case the mortgage is said to be *open*). Many mortgage bonds are secured not only by existing property but also by "after-acquired" property. However, if the company buys only property that is already mortgaged, the bondholder would have only a junior claim on the new property. Therefore, mortgage bonds with after-acquired property clauses also limit the extent to which the company can purchase additional mortgaged property.

certificates with different maturities that might typically run from 1 to 15 years. Only when all these debts have finally been paid off does the company become the formal owner of the equipment. Bond rating agencies such as Moody's or Standard and Poor's usually rate equipment trust certificates one grade higher than the company's regular debt.

Bonds may be senior claims or they may be subordinated to the senior bonds or to *all* other creditors.[20] If the firm defaults, the senior bonds come first in the pecking order. The subordinated lender gets in line behind the firm's general creditors (but ahead of the preferred stockholder and the common stockholder).

If default does occur, it pays to hold senior secured debt. On average banks with senior secured loans can expect to recover over 60 percent of the amount of the loan. At the other extreme, the recovery rate for subordinated bondholders is less than a third of the face value of their debt.[21]

ASSET-BACKED SECURITIES

Instead of borrowing money directly, companies sometimes bundle up a group of assets and then sell the cash flows from these assets. These securities are known as **asset-backed** securities.

Suppose your company has made a large number of mortgage loans to buyers of homes or commercial real estate. However, you don't want to wait until the loans are paid off; you would like to get your hands on the money now. Here is what you do.

You establish a separate company that buys a package of the mortgage loans. To finance this purchase, the company sells *mortgage pass-through certificates*.[22] The holders of these certificates simply receive a share of the mortgage payments. For example, if interest rates fall and the mortgages are repaid early, holders of the pass-through certificates are also repaid early. That's not generally popular with these holders, for they get their money back just when they don't want it—when interest rates are low.[23]

Real estate companies are not unique in wanting to turn future receipts into up-front cash. Investment bankers seem to be able to repackage almost any set of cash flows into a loan. In 1997 David Bowie, the British rock star, established a company that then purchased the royalties from his current albums. The company financed the purchase by selling $55 million of 10-year notes at an interest rate of 7.9 percent. The royalty receipts were used to make the interest and principal payments on the notes. When asked about the singer's reaction to the idea, his manager replied, "He kind of looked at me cross-eyed and said 'What?'"[24]

---

[20]If a bond does not specifically state that it is junior, you can assume that it is senior.

[21] Recovery rates for bank loans are estimated in E. Asarnow and D. Edwards, "Measuring Loss on Defaulted Bank Loans: a 24-Year Study," *Journal of Commercial Lending* 78 (March 1995), pp. 11–19. Recovery rates for defaulting public bond issues are given in R. A. Waldman, E. I. Altman, and A. R. Ginsberg, "Defaults and Returns on High Yield Bonds: Analysis Through 1997," Salomon Smith Barney, New York, January 30, 1998.

[22]Mortgage-backed loans for commercial real estate are called (not surprisingly) *commercial mortgage backed securities* or *CMBS*.

[23]Sometimes, instead of issuing one class of pass-through certificates, the company will issue several different classes of security, known as *collateralized mortgage obligations* or *CMOs*. For example, any mortgage prepayments might be used first to pay off one class of security holders and only then will other classes start to be repaid.

[24]See J. Mathews, "David Bowie Reinvents Self, This Time as a Bond Issue," *Washington Post*, February 7, 1997.

REPAYMENT PROVISIONS

Sinking Funds

The maturity date of the Ralston Purina bond is June 1, 2016, but part of the issue is repaid on a regular basis before maturity. To do this, the company makes a regular repayment into a *sinking fund*. If the payment is in the form of cash, the trustee selects bonds by lottery and uses the cash to redeem them at their face value.[25] Instead of paying cash, the company can buy bonds in the marketplace and pay these into the fund.[26] This is a valuable option for the company. If the price of the bond is low, the firm will buy bonds in the market and hand them to the sinking fund; if the price is high, it will call the bonds by lottery.

Generally, there is a mandatory fund which *must* be satisfied and an optional fund which can be satisfied if the borrower chooses.[27] For example, Ralston Purina *must* contribute at least $13.5 million each year to the sinking fund but has the option to contribute a further $13.5 million.

As in the case of Ralston Purina, most "sinkers" begin to operate after about 10 years. For lower-quality issues the payments are usually sufficient to redeem the entire issue in equal installments over the life of the bond. In contrast, high-quality bonds often have light sinking fund requirements with large balloon payments at maturity.

We saw earlier that interest payments provide a regular test of the company's solvency. Sinking funds provide an additional hurdle that the firm must keep jumping. If it cannot pay the cash into the sinking fund, the lenders can demand their money back. That is why long-dated, low-quality issues usually involve larger sinking funds.

Unfortunately, a sinking fund is a weak test of solvency if the firm is allowed to repurchase bonds in the market. Since the *market* value of the debt must always be less than the value of the firm, financial distress reduces the cost of repurchasing debt in the market. The sinking fund, then, is a hurdle that gets progressively lower as the hurdler gets weaker.

Call Provisions

Corporate bonds sometimes include a call option that allows the company to pay back the debt early. Occasionally, you come across bonds that give the *investor* the repayment option. Retractable (or putable) bonds give investors the option to demand early repayment, and extendible bonds give them the option to extend the bond's life.

These days, issues of straight bonds are much less likely to include a call provision.[28] However, Ralston Purina had the option to buy back the entire bond issue. The company was subject to two

---

[25]Every investor dreams of buying up the entire supply of a sinking-fund bond that is selling way below face value and then forcing the company to buy the bonds back at face value. Cornering the market in this way is fun to dream about but difficult to do. For a discussion, see K. B. Dunn and C. S. Spatt, "A Strategic Analysis of Sinking Fund Bonds," *Journal of Financial Economics* 13 (September 1984), pp. 399–424.

[26]If the bonds are privately placed, the company cannot repurchase them in the marketplace; it must call them at their face value.

[27]A number of private placements (particularly those in extractive industries) require a payment only when net income exceeds some specified level.

[28]See, for example, L. Crabbe, "Callable Corporate Bonds: A Vanishing Breed," Board of Governors of the Federal Reserve System, Washington, D.C., 1991.

limitations on the use of this call option: Until 1989 the company was prohibited from calling the bond in any circumstances and from 1989 to 1996 it was not allowed to call the bond in order to replace it with new debt yielding less than the 9.748 percent yield on the original bond.

If interest rates fall and bond prices rise, the option to buy back the bond at a fixed price can be very attractive. The company can buy back the bond and issue another at a higher price and a lower interest rate. And so it proved with the Ralston Purina bond. By the time that the restrictions on calling the bonds were removed in 1996, interest rates had declined. The company was therefore able to repurchase the bond at the call price of 103.905, which was below the bond's potential value.

How does a company know when to call its bonds? The answer is simple: Other things equal, if it wishes to maximize the value of its stock, it must minimize the value of its bonds. Therefore, the company should never call the bond if its market value is less than the call price, for that would just be giving a present to the bondholders. Equally, a company *should* call the bond if it's worth *more* than the call price.

Of course, investors take the call option into account when they buy or sell the bond. They know that the company will call the bond as soon as it is worth more than the call price, so no investor will be willing to pay more than the call price for the bond. The market price of the bond may, therefore, reach the call price, but it will not rise above it. This gives the company the following rule for calling its bonds: *Call the bond when, and only when, the market price reaches the call price.*[29]

If we know how bond prices behave over time, we can modify the basic option-valuation model of Chapter 8 to find the value of the callable bond, *given* that investors know that the company will call the issue as soon as the market price reaches the call price. For example, look at Figure 11.1. It illustrates the relationship between the value of a straight 8 percent five-year bond and the value of a callable 8 percent five-year bond. Suppose that the value of the straight bond is very low. In this case there is little likelihood that the company will ever wish to call its bonds. (Remember that it will call the bonds only when their price equals the call price.) Therefore the value of the callable bond will be almost identical to the value of the straight bond. Now suppose that the straight bond is worth exactly 100. In this case there is a good chance that the company will wish at some time to call its bonds. Therefore the value of our callable bond will be slightly less than that of the straight bond. If interest rates decline further, the price of the straight bond will continue to rise, but nobody will ever pay more than the call price for the callable bond.

A call provision is not a free lunch. It provides the issuer with a valuable option, but that is recognized in a lower issue price. So why do companies bother with call provisions? One reason is that bond indentures often place a number of restrictions on what the company can do. Companies are happy to agree to these restrictions as long as they know they can escape from them if the restrictions prove too inhibiting. The call provision provides the escape route.

We mentioned earlier that some bonds also provide the investor with an option to demand early repayment. *Putable* bonds exist largely because bond indentures cannot anticipate every action that the company may take which could harm the bondholder. If the value of the bonds is reduced, the put option allows bondholders to demand their money back.

---

[29]See M. J. Brennan and E. S. Schwartz, "Savings Bonds, Retractable Bonds, and Callable Bonds," *Journal of Financial Economics* 5 (1997), pp. 67–88. Of course, this assumes that the bond is correctly priced, that investors are behaving rationally, and that investors expect the *firm* to behave rationally. Also, we ignore some complications. First, you may not wish to call a bond if you are prevented by a nonrefunding clause from issuing new debt. Second, the call premium is a tax-deductible expense for the company but is taxed as a capital gain to the bondholder. Third, there are other possible tax consequences to both the company and the investor from replacing a low-coupon bond with a higher-coupon bond. Fourth, there are costs to calling and reissuing debt.

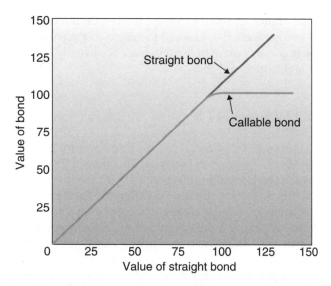

Figure 11.1

Relationship between the value of a callable bond and that of a straight
(non-callable) bond. Assumptions: (1) Both bonds have an 8 percent coupon
and a five-year maturity; (2) the callable bond may be called at face value
any time before maturity; (3) the short-term interest rate follows a random
walk, and the expected returns on bonds of all maturities are equal.

Source: M. J. Brennan and E. S. Schwartz, "Savings Bonds, Retractable Bonds,
and Callable Bonds," *Journal of Financial Economics* 5 (1977), pp. 67–88.

Defeasance

In 1985 U.S. Steel retired its issue of $4\frac{5}{8}$ percent subordinated debentures and thereby added
almost $70 million to pretax income. The method that it used to retire the bonds is known as *defea-
sance*. This works as follows: The firm transfers the debt to a trust fund which is then responsible
for making all payments of interest and principal to the bondholders. To provide the trust fund
with the wherewithal to make these payments, the firm also contributes to the trust a package of
U.S. Treasury bonds. The cash flows on these Treasury bonds are designed to match the payments
on the firm's debt.

When U.S. Steel retired its debentures, interest rates were relatively high and the debentures
were selling well below their face value of $168 million. Thus it cost the company less than $168 million to buy the matching portfolio of Treasury bonds. This difference between the face value of the
debt and the cost of the matching portfolio was reported by the company as extraordinary income.

As interest rates rose in the 1980s, the prices of many company bonds fell below their face values, and this led to a flurry of interest in defeasance. Firms found that defeasance increased their
reported income and removed debt from the balance sheet.[30] But how did investors respond? The
bondholders were understandably delighted, since they now had a bond that was backed by

---

[30]There are two forms of defeasance. With *in-substance defeasance* the debt is no longer shown on the balance sheet but the
firm is still obliged to observe the terms of the indenture. With *legal defeasance* (or *novation*) all the firm's obligations are
extinguished.

U.S. Treasuries. Despite the higher reported earnings, the shareholders were *less* pleased. The Treasury bonds that the firms bought were risk-free and therefore cost more than the risky bonds that the firm retired. As a result, an announcement of bond defeasance usually led to a rise in the price of the defeased bonds but a fall in the price of the stock.[31]

RESTRICTIVE COVENANTS

The difference between a corporate bond and a comparable Treasury bond is that the company has the option to default whereas the government supposedly doesn't. That is a valuable option. If you don't believe us, think about whether (other things equal) you would prefer to be a shareholder in a company with limited liability or in a company with unlimited liability. Of course you would prefer to have the option to walk away from your company's debts. Unfortunately, every silver lining has its cloud, and the drawback to having a default option is that corporate bondholders expect to be compensated for giving it to you. That is why corporate bonds sell at lower prices and therefore higher yields than government bonds.[32]

Investors know there is a risk of default when they buy a corporate bond. But they still want to make sure that the company plays fair. They don't want it to gamble with their money or to take unreasonable risks. Therefore the bond indenture may include a number of restrictive covenants to prevent the company from purposely increasing the value of its default option.[33]

After Ralston Purina had issued its bonds, the company had a total market value of $7.6 billion and total long-term debt of $2.1 billion. This meant that the company value would need to fall by over 70 percent before it would pay Ralston Purina to default. But suppose that after issuing the 9.5 percent bonds, Ralston Purina announced a bumper $3 billion bond issue. The company would have a market value of $10.6 billion and long-term debt of $5.1 billion. It would now pay the company to default if its value fell by little more than 50 percent ($1 - 5.1/10.6 = .52$, or 52 percent). The original bondholders would be worse off. If they had known about the new issue, they would not have been willing to pay such a high price for their bonds.

A new issue hurts the original bondholders because it increases the *ratio* of senior debt to company value. The bondholders would not object to an issue if the company kept the ratio the same by simultaneously issuing common stock. Therefore, the bond agreement often states that the company may issue more senior debt only if the ratio of senior debt to the value of net book assets is within a specified limit.

Why don't senior lenders demand limits on *subordinated* debt? The answer is that the subordinated lender does not get *any* money until the senior bondholders have been paid in full.[34] The senior bondholders, therefore, view subordinated bonds in much the same way that they view equity: They would be happy to see an issue of either. Of course, the converse is not true. Holders of subordinated debt *do* care both about the total amount of debt and the proportion that is senior to

---

[31]See, for example, J. R. Hand, P. J. Hughes, and S. E. Sefcik, "In-Substance Defeasances: Security Price Reactions and Motivations," *Journal of Accounting and Economics* 13 (May 1990), pp. 47–89.

[32]In Chapters 8 and 10 we showed that this option to default is equivalent to a put option on the assets of the firm.

[33]We described in Chapter 6 some of the games that managers can play at the expense of bondholders.

[34]In practice the courts do not always observe the strict rules of precedence (see the appendix to Chapter 6). Therefore the subordinated debtholder may receive *some* payment even when the senior debtholder is not fully paid off.

their claim. As a result, the indenture for an issue of subordinated debt generally includes a restriction on both total debt and senior debt.

All bondholders worry that the company may issue more secured debt. An issue of mortgage bonds usually imposes a limit on the amount of secured debt. This is not necessary when you are issuing unsecured debentures. As long as the debenture holders are given equal protection, they do not care how much you mortgage your assets. Therefore, the Ralston Purina debenture includes a so-called *negative pledge clause,* in which the debenture holders simply say, "Me, too."[35]

Instead of borrowing money to buy an asset, companies may enter into a long-term agreement to rent or lease it. For the debtholder this is very similar to secured borrowing. Therefore indentures also include limitations on leasing.

We have talked about how an unscrupulous borrower can try to increase the value of the default option by issuing more debt. But that is not the only way that such a company can exploit its existing bondholders. For example, we know that the value of an option is affected by dividend payments. If the company pays out large dividends to its shareholders and doesn't replace the cash by an issue of stock, there are fewer assets available to cover the debt. Therefore most bond issues restrict the amount of dividends that the company may pay.[36]

Changes in Covenant Protection

Before 1980 most bonds had covenants limiting further issues of debt and payments of dividends. But then institutions relaxed their requirements for lending to large public companies and accepted bonds with no such restrictions. This was the case with RJR Nabisco, the food and tobacco giant, which in 1988 had $5 billion of A-rated debt outstanding. In that year the company was taken over, and $19 billion of additional debt was substituted for equity. As soon as the first plans for the takeover were announced, the value of the existing debt fell by about 12 percent, and it was downrated to BB. For one of the bondholders, Metropolitan Life Insurance, this meant a $40 million loss. Metropolitan sued the company, arguing that the bonds contained an *implied* covenant preventing major financing changes that would undercut existing bondholders.[37] However, Metropolitan lost: The courts held that only the written covenants count.

Restrictions on debt issues and dividend payments quietly returned to fashion.[38] Bond analysts and lawyers started to look more closely at *event risks* like the debt-financed takeover that

---

[35]"Me too" is not acceptable legal jargon. Instead the Ralston Purina bond agreement states that the company will not consent to any lien on its assets without securing the debentures "equally and ratably."

[36]See A. Kalay, "Stockholder-Bondholder Conflict and Dividend Constraints," *Journal of Financial Economics* 10 (1982), pp. 211–233. A dividend restriction might typically prohibit the company from paying dividends if their cumulative amount would exceed the sum of (1) cumulative net income, (2) the proceeds from the sale of stock or conversion of debt, and (3) a dollar amount equal to one year's dividend.

[37]*Metropolitan Life Insurance Company* (plaintiff) *v. RJR Nabisco, Inc., and F. Ross Johnson* (defendants), Supreme Court of the State of New York, County of New York, Complaint, Nov. 16, 1988.

[38]A study by Paul Asquith and Thierry Wizman suggests that better covenants would have protected Metropolitan Life and other bondholders against loss. On average, the announcement of a leveraged buyout led to a fall of 5.2 percent in the value of the bond if there were no restrictions on further debt issues, dividend payments, or mergers. However, if the bond was protected by strong covenants, announcement of a leveraged buyout led to a *rise* in the bond price of 2.6 percent. See P. Asquith and T. A. Wizman, "Event Risk, Bond Covenants, and the Return to Existing Bondholders in Corporate Buyouts," *Journal of Financial Economics* 27 (September 1990), pp. 195–213.

socked Metropolitan. Some companies agreed to *poison-put* clauses that oblige the borrower to repay the bonds if a large quantity of stock is bought by a single investor and the firm's bonds are downrated.

Unfortunately, there are always nasty surprises around the next corner. One such surprise came in 1992, when the hotel chain, Marriott, announced its intention to divide its operations into two separate businesses. One, Host Marriott, was to own the hotels and the rest of the real estate, while the other, Marriott International, was to manage the hotel chain and get most of the profits. What shocked bond investors was the fact that almost all of the company's $3 billion of debt was to be loaded onto Host Marriott. Marriott's stock jumped 12 percent on the news, but Moody's downrated the company's bonds to the junk bond category and the price of the bonds fell by as much as 30 percent. Once again bondholders and their lawyers began to scrutinize the fine print.

PRIVATE PLACEMENTS AND PROJECT FINANCE

The Ralston Purina debenture was registered with the SEC and sold to the public. However, debt is often placed privately with a small number of financial institutions. As we saw in Chapter 3, it costs less to arrange a private placement than to make a public debt issue. But there are three other ways in which the private placement bond may differ from its public counterpart.

First, if you place an issue privately with one or two financial institutions, it may be necessary to sign only a simple promissory note. This is just an IOU which lays down certain conditions that the borrower must observe. However, when you make a public issue of debt, you must worry about who is to represent the bondholders in any subsequent negotiations and what procedures are needed for paying interest and principal. Therefore the contractual arrangement has to be that much more complicated.

The second characteristic of publicly issued bonds is that they are highly standardized products. They *have* to be—investors are constantly buying and selling without checking the fine print in the agreement. This is not so necessary in private placements and so the debt contract can be custom-tailored for firms with special problems or opportunities. The relationship between borrower and lender is much more intimate. Imagine a $20 million debt issue privately placed with an insurance company, and compare it with an equivalent public issue held by 200 anonymous investors. The insurance company can justify a more thorough investigation of the company's prospects and therefore may be more willing to accept unusual terms or conditions.[39]

All bond agreements seek to protect the lender by imposing a number of conditions on the borrower. These conditions tend to be more severe in the case of privately placed debt. The borrowers are willing to agree to these conditions because they know that, when the debt is privately placed, the conditions can be modified later if it makes sense. However, in the case of a public issue it can be extremely cumbersome to get the permission of all the existing bondholders.

These features give private placements a particular niche in the corporate debt market, namely, loans to small and medium-sized firms. These are the firms that face the highest issue costs in public issues, that require the most detailed investigation, and that may require specialized, flexible loan arrangements. However, many large companies also use private placements.

---

[39]Of course debt with the same terms could be offered publicly, but then 200 separate investigations would be required—a much more expensive proposition.

Of course, the advantages of private placements are not free, for the lenders demand a higher rate of interest to compensate them for holding an illiquid asset. It is difficult to generalize about the differences in interest rates between private placements and public issues, but a typical differential is on the order of 50 basis points or .50 percentage points.

Project Finance

We are not going to dwell further on the topic of private placement bonds, because the greater part of what we have had to say about public issues is also true of private placements. However, we do need to discuss a different form of private loan, one that is tied as closely as possible to the fortunes of a particular project and that minimizes the exposure of the parent. Such a loan is usually referred to as **project finance** and is a specialty of large international banks.

Project finance means debt supported by the project, not by the project's sponsoring companies. Debt ratios are nevertheless very high. They can be high because the debt is supported not just by the project's assets but also by a variety of contracts and guarantees provided by customers, suppliers, and local governments, as well as by the project's owners.

Example   Here is how project finance was used to construct a large new oil-fired power plant in Pakistan. First, a separate firm, the Hub Power Company (Hubco), was established to own the power station. Hubco then engaged a consortium of companies, headed by the Japanese company, Mitsui & Co., to build the power station, while the British company, National Power, became responsible for managing and running it. Hubco agreed to buy the fuel from the Pakistan State Oil Company and to sell the power station's output to another government body, the Water and Power Development Authority (WAPDA).

Hubco's lawyers drew up a complex series of contracts to make sure that each of these parties came up to scratch. For example, the contractors guaranteed to deliver the plant on time and to ensure that it would operate to specifications. National Power, the plant manager, agreed to maintain the plant and operate it efficiently. Pakistan State Oil Company entered into a long-term contract to supply oil to Hubco and WAPDA agreed to buy Hubco's output for the next 30 years.[40] Since WAPDA would pay for the electricity with rupees, Hubco was concerned about the possibility of a fall in the value of the rupee. The State Bank of Pakistan, therefore, arranged to provide Hubco with foreign exchange at guaranteed exchange rates.

The effect of these contracts was to ensure that each risk was borne by the party that was best able to measure and control it. For example, the contractors were best placed to ensure that the plant was completed on time, so it made sense to ask them to bear the risk of construction delays. Similarly, the plant operator was best placed to operate the plant efficiently and would be penalized if it failed to do so. The contractors and the plant manager were prepared to take on these risks because the project involved an established technology and there was relatively little chance of unpleasant surprises.

---

[40]WAPDA entered into a *take-or-pay* agreement with Hubco; if it did not take the electricity, it still had to pay for it. In the case of pipeline projects the contract with the customer is often in the form of a *throughput* agreement, whereby the customer agrees to make a minimum use of the pipeline. Another arrangement for transferring revenue risk to a customer is the tolling contract, whereby the customer agrees to deliver to the project company materials that it is to process and to return to the customer. One purpose of transferring revenue risk to customers is to encourage them to estimate their demand for the project's output thoroughly.

While these contracts sought to be as precise as possible about each party's responsibilities, they could not cover every eventuality; inevitably the contracts were incomplete. Therefore, to buttress the formal legal agreements, the contractors and the plant manager became major shareholders in Hubco. This meant that if they cut corners in building and running the plant, they would share in the losses.

The equity in Hubco was highly levered. Over 75 percent of the $1.8 billion investment in the project was financed by debt. Some of this was junior debt provided by a fund that was set up by the World Bank and western and Japanese government aid agencies. The bulk of the debt was senior debt and was provided by a group of major international banks.[41] The banks were encouraged to invest because they knew that the World Bank and several governments were in the frontline and would take a hit if the project were to fail. But they were still concerned that the government of Pakistan might prevent Hubco from paying out foreign currency or it might impose a special tax or prevent the company bringing in the specialist staff it needed. Therefore, to protect Hubco against these political risks, the government promised to pay compensation if it interfered in such ways with the operation of the project. Of course, the government could not be prevented from tearing up that agreement, but, if it did, Hubco was able to call on a $360 million guarantee by the World Bank and the Export–Import Bank of Japan. This was supposed to keep the Pakistan government honest once the plant was built and operating. Governments can be surprisingly relaxed in the face of the wrath of a private corporation but are usually reluctant to break an agreement that lands the World Bank with a large bill.

The arrangements for the Hubco project were complex, costly, and time-consuming. Not everything was plain sailing. The project was suspended for over a year by the Gulf War and it looked at one time as if it would be spiked by a Pakistani court ruling that the interest on the loans contravened Islamic law. Ten years after the start of discussions the final agreement on financing the project was signed and within a short time Hubco was producing a fifth of all Pakistan's electricity.

However, that was not the end of the Hubco story. After the fall of Benazir Bhutto's government in Pakistan, the new government terminated the contract with Hubco and announced a 30 percent cut in electricity tariffs. This inevitably led to a dispute with the World Bank, which spelled out that, until the dispute could be resolved, nothing could move on new loans.[42]

Project Finance—Some Common Features

No two project financings are alike, but they have some common features:

- The project is established as a separate company.

- The contractors and the plant manager become major shareholders in the project and thus share in the risk of the project's failure.

- The project company enters into a complex series of contracts that distributes risk among the contractors, the plant manager, the suppliers, and the customers.

---

[41] Notice that the project was not financed by a public bond issue. The concentrated ownership of bank debt induces the lenders to evaluate the project carefully and to monitor its subsequent progress. It also facilitates the renegotiation of the debt if the project company runs into difficulties.

[42] The World Bank was particularly concerned that a clear separation should be made between the issue of electricity tariffs and investigations into alleged corruption by Hubco officials.

- The government may guarantee that it will provide the necessary permits, allow the purchase of foreign exchange, and so on.

- The detailed contractual arrangements and government guarantees allow a large part of the capital for the project to be provided in the form of bank debt or other privately placed borrowing.

The Role of Project Finance

Project finance is widely used in developing countries to fund power, telecommunication, and transportation projects, but it is also used in the major industrialized countries. In the United States project finance is most commonly used to fund power plants. For example, an electric utility company may get together with an industrial company to construct a cogeneration plant which provides electricity to the utility and waste heat to a nearby industrial plant. The utility stands behind the cogeneration project and guarantees its revenue stream. Banks are happy to lend as much as 90 percent of the cost of the project because they know that, once the project is up and running, the cash flow is insulated from most of the risks facing normal businesses.[43]

There are some interesting regulatory implications, however. When a utility builds a power plant, it is entitled to a fair return on its investment: Regulators are supposed to set customer charges that will allow the utility to earn its cost of capital. Unfortunately, the cost of capital is not easily measured and is a natural focus for argument in regulatory hearings. But when a utility buys electric power, the cost of capital is rolled into the contract price and treated as an operating cost. In this case the pass-through to customers may be less controversial.

INNOVATION IN THE BOND MARKET

Domestic and international bonds, fixed- and floating-rate bonds, coupon bonds and zeros, callable and putable bonds, secured and unsecured bonds, senior and junior bonds, privately placed bonds and project finance—you might think that all this would give you as much choice as you need. Yet almost every day some new type of bond seems to be issued.

We have already encountered a number of the more exotic bonds. For example, you may remember from Chapter 9 the convertible LYONs and the bonds that turn automatically into equity. In this chapter we cited the "Bowie bonds" as an example of asset-backed bonds. In Chapter 13 we will also come across catastrophe bonds whose payoffs are linked to the occurrence of natural disasters.

Here are a couple more examples of unusual bonds. The first was an issue of a three-year Japanese yen bond by the Norwegian Christiania Bank. The issue came in two parts or *tranches*. Tranche A paid interest equal to the prime rate but subject to a maximum (or *cap*) of 12.8 percent. Tranche B paid interest of 12.8 percent *less* the prime rate. Thus, if the general level of interest rates rose, the interest payment on tranche B fell[44] but it was not allowed to fall below zero. If you had invested an equal amount in each tranche, the average interest rate on your two holdings would have been 6.4 percent.

---

[43]Such extremely high debt ratios must rest on the utility's creditworthiness. In a sense, the utility has borrowed money "off balance sheet."

[44]Bonds whose interest payments move in the opposite direction to the general level are called *reverse floaters* or *yield-curve notes*. We encountered them in Chapter 4 where we saw how they contributed to the financial problems of Orange County.

That was not the end of tranche B's complications, since the principal payment was not fixed at 100 percent. Instead, it declined if the Japanese stock market index fell. If the index fell by about 50 percent, the bondholder did not receive any principal repayment at all. Thus investing in tranche B was like buying an unusual floating-rate note and also selling a put option on the Japanese stock market. To compensate for the possible capital loss, the bonds offered a relatively high rate of interest.

For several years the majority of international issues of yen bonds involved similar options. Why? One reason is that life insurance companies in Japan cannot distribute capital gains to policyholders and therefore had a powerful appetite for high-yielding bonds even if such investments involved the risk of a capital loss. Christiania Bank paid a high interest rate on the package, but it got a put option in exchange. If it did not want to hold on to this put option, it could easily sell it to foreign investors who were worried that the Japanese equity market was overpriced and wanted to protect themselves against a fall in that market.

Our second example is the *pay-in-kind* bond (or *PIK*). This makes regular interest payments, but in the early years of the bond's life the issuer can choose to pay interest in the form of either cash or more bonds with an equivalent face value.[45] That can be a valuable option. If the company falls on hard times and bond prices drop, it can hand over low-priced bonds instead of hard cash.[46] Many of the companies that have issued PIKs were leveraged buyouts. Such firms are typically short of cash in their initial years and therefore find the option to pay interest in the form of bonds particularly attractive. For example, when Kohlberg, Kravis, and Roberts took over RJR Nabisco, the shareholders were partly paid off in PIKs.[47]

The Causes of Financial Innovation

It is often difficult to foresee which new securities will become popular and which will never get off the ground. Sometimes a new financial instrument is designed to widen investor choice. For example, the unusual weather in 1997–1998 resulting from El Niño encouraged a number of firms to market financial contracts that would pay off in unfavorable weather conditions. These firms hoped that *weather derivatives* would prove popular with the newly deregulated energy companies, the agricultural community, and many other businesses that might wish to protect themselves against the vagaries of the weather. It is too early to tell whether these derivatives will succeed. If they do, they will form an additional item in the armory of weapons for managing risk.

Merton Miller believes that the government also plays a crucial role in fostering innovation. He compares government regulation and tax with the grain of sand that irritates the oyster and

---

[45]For a discussion of PIKs, see L. S. Goodman and A. H. Cohen, "Pay-in-Kind Debentures: An Innovation," *Journal of Portfolio Management* 15 (Winter 1989), pp. 9–16.

[46]To complicate matters, most PIKs are callable. So if interest rates fall and bond prices rise, the firm may buy the bonds back at the call price.

[47]The use of PIKs to finance highly leveraged buyouts earned them a bad reputation. Ross Johnson, the president of RJR Nabisco, was reported to have marveled at the potential for PIKs. " 'I mean,' Johnson went on, 'we have found something better than the U.S. printing press. And they've got it all down here on Wall Street. And nobody knows it's going on. I wonder if the World Bank knows about it. You could solve the third-world debt crisis with this stuff. It's a brand new currency.' " [Quoted in B. Burrough and J. Helyar, *Barbarians at the Gate: The Fall of RJR Nabisco* (New York: Harper & Row, 1990), p. 489.]

TABLE 11.2			

GMAC's original issue discount bonds were expected to appreciate by an increasing percentage amount each year, but the IRS allowed GMAC to deduct the same *dollar* amount each year from taxable income.

YEAR	(1) PV AT START OF YEAR	(2) CHANGE IN PV DURING YEAR	(3) ALLOWABLE TAX WRITE-OFF
1	$252.5	$ 37.3	$ 74.75
2	289.8	42.8	74.75
3	332.5	49.1	74.75
4	381.6	56.3	74.75
5	437.9	64.6	74.75
6	502.5	74.1	74.75
7	576.6	85.1	74.75
8	661.7	97.6	74.75
9	759.4	112.0	74.75
10	871.4	128.6	74.75
		$747.5	$747.50

produces the pearl.[48] We have seen how one unusual bond, the option-linked yen bond, was a consequence of Japanese insurance regulation. Let us also look at how a quirk in the tax rules brought about a new type of bond in the United States.

Example   In June 1981 General Motors Acceptance Corporation (GMAC) issued $750 million of 10-year zero-coupon notes. The issue price was $252.50 for each note. Thus the investor faced a prospective fourfold increase in value over 10 years, which is equivalent to a compound return of about 14.8 percent a year.

Table 11.2 shows the expected yearly change in the value of the GMAC notes. In year 1, the prospective appreciation is .148 × 252.5 = $37.3. At the start of year 2, the expected value of the notes is 252.5 + 37.3 = $289.8. Thus the appreciation in year 2 is .148 × 289.8 = $42.8. And so on. Of course, the total appreciation over the 10 years is 1,000 − 252.5 = $747.5.

The attraction to GMAC of zero-coupon debt arose from an IRS mistake. The IRS correctly recognized that even if debt does not pay interest, it is still costly to the issuer. Therefore, it allowed the company to deduct a portion of the original issue discount from taxable income. But in calculating this deduction, the IRS employed simple, rather than compound, interest. Thus GMAC was permitted to deduct the same amount in each year, 747.5/10 = $74.75.

If you compare columns 2 and 3 of Table 11.2, you will see that in the early years of the loan's life, GMAC could deduct more than the cost of the loan from its taxable income. For example, in

---

[48]See M. H. Miller, "Financial Innovation: The Last Twenty Years and the Next," *Journal of Financial and Quantitative Analysis* 21 (December 1986), pp. 459–471.

year 1 each note cost GMAC $37.3, or 14.8 percent of the amount of the loan. However, when calculating taxable profits, GMAC was allowed to deduct $74.75, or 29.6 percent of the amount of the loan. From year 7 onward, the deduction is less than the cost of the loan, but, other things equal, GMAC benefited from having the extra tax shield in the early years.

Of course, this is not the whole story. Just as the IRS pretended that GMAC paid interest of $74.75 a year, so it pretended that the noteholders received interest of $74.75 a year. But as long as GMAC notes were bought by tax-exempt investors, this was no disadvantage.[49]

The tax advantage of zero-coupon bonds led to a flurry of issues in 1981. By 1982, the IRS had become sufficiently concerned about the loss of revenue that it began to use compound interest to calculate the tax deduction. From that point on, the tax incentive to issue zero-coupon debt disappeared. Yet zeros survived, and companies continued to issue them, though at a slower rate than before.[50]

Initially the benefits of zero-coupon debt went to those investment banks that were smart enough to devise and market the idea and to issuers such as GMAC.[51] But remember, there was an advantage to zero-coupon debt only as long as the marginal investor had a lower tax rate than the borrower. This takes us back to the capital structure controversy of Chapter 6. As long as only a few companies issued zero-coupon bonds, there were enough tax-exempt investors who were happy to hold them. But as more such debt was issued, those companies that came late on the scene faced a higher rate of interest. Thus, as soon as everyone had cottoned on to the idea, all the benefits went to the tax-exempt investors in the form of this higher interest rate.

The lesson is a simple one: Investment banks and companies can be sure of benefiting from an innovation only if they are early in the field. Once the market is in equilibrium, all the benefits go to the players that are in short supply (in our example, the tax-exempt investors).

SUMMARY

Now that you have read this chapter, you should have a fair idea of what you are letting yourself in for when you make a public issue of bonds. You can issue the bonds in the domestic U.S. market, in a foreign bond market, or in the international bond market. International bonds (also called eurobonds) are marketed simultaneously in a number of foreign countries, usually by the London branches of international banks and security dealers.

The detailed bond agreement is set out in the indenture between your company and a trustee, but the main provisions are summarized in the prospectus to the issue.

The indenture states whether the bonds are senior or subordinated and whether they are secured or unsecured. Most bonds are unsecured debentures or notes. This means that they are general claims on the corporation. The principal exceptions are utility mortgage bonds, collateral trust bonds, and equipment trust certificates. In the event of a default, the trustee to these issues can repossess the company's assets in order to pay off the debt.

---

[49]Zero-coupon bonds were popular with the Japanese since the Japanese tax authorities treated the price appreciation as a capital gain. This ruling was changed in 1985.

[50]For a discussion of the tax incentives for OID debt, see D. Pyle, "Is Deep Discount Debt Financing a Bargain?" *Chase Financial Quarterly* 1 (1981), pp. 39–61.

[51]We may oversimplify: If investors foresaw that further issues were going to force up the interest rate on zero-coupon bonds, they might have been reluctant to buy the early issues at the lower interest rate.

Most long-term bond issues have a sinking fund. This means that the company must set aside enough money each year to retire a specified number of bonds. A sinking fund reduces the average life of the bond, and it provides a yearly test of the company's ability to service its debt. It therefore protects the bondholders against the risk of default.

Long-dated bonds may be callable before maturity. The company usually has to pay a call premium, which is initially equal to the coupon and which declines progressively to zero. The option to call the bond may be very valuable: If interest rates decline and bond values rise, you may be able to call a bond that would be worth substantially more than the call price. Of course, if investors know that you may call the bond, the call price will act as a ceiling on the market price. Your best strategy, therefore, is to call the bond as soon as the market price hits the call price. You are unlikely to do better than that.

The bond indenture also imposes certain conditions on the borrower. Here are some examples of *negative covenants:*

1. Issues of senior bonds prohibit the company from issuing further senior debt if the ratio of senior debt to net tangible assets is too high.

2. Issues of subordinated bonds may also prohibit the company from issuing further senior or junior debt if the ratio of *all* debt to net tangible assets is too high.

3. Unsecured bonds incorporate a negative pledge clause, which prohibits the company from securing additional debt without giving equal treatment to the existing unsecured bonds.

4. Most bonds place a limit on the company's dividend payments.

The indenture may also include *affirmative covenants* that oblige the company to take positive steps to protect the bondholders. The really important affirmative covenants are those that give the bondholder the chance to claim a default and get money out while the company still has substantial value. For example, some privately placed bonds require that the company maintain a minimum level of working capital or net worth. Since a deficiency in either is a good indication of financial weakness, this condition is tantamount to giving the bondholders the right to demand their money back as soon as life appears hazardous.

Private placements are less standardized than public issues, and they impose more stringent covenants. Otherwise, they are generally close counterparts of publicly issued bonds. Sometimes private debt takes the form of project finance. In this case the loan is tied to the fortunes of a particular project.

There is an enormous variety of bond issues, and new forms of bonds are spawned almost daily. By a principle of natural selection, some of these new instruments become popular and may even replace existing species. Others are ephemeral curiosities. Some innovations succeed because they widen investor choice and allow investors to manage their risks better. Others owe their origin to tax rules and government regulation.

Further Reading

A useful general work on debt securities is:
F. J. Fabozzi: *Fixed Income Securities*, Frank J. Fabozzi Associates, New Hope, PA, 1997.

The articles by Brennan and Schwartz and by Kraus are general discussions of call provisions:
M. J. Brennan and E. S. Schwartz: "Savings Bonds, Retractable Bonds and Callable Bonds," *Journal of Financial Economics*, 5:67–88 (1977).

A. Kraus: "An Analysis of Call Provisions and the Corporate Refunding Decision," *Midland Corporate Finance Journal*, 1:46–60 (Spring 1983).

Smith and Warner provide an extensive survey and analysis of covenants:
C. W. Smith and J. B. Warner: "On Financial Contracting: An Analysis of Bond Covenants," *Journal of Financial Economics*, 7:117–161 (June 1979).

Discussions of project finance include:
R. A. Brealey, I. A. Cooper, and M. Habib: "Using Project Finance to Fund Infrastructure Investments," *Journal of Applied Corporate Finance*, 9:25–38 (Fall 1996).

P. K. Nevitt and F. J. Fabozzi, *Project Financing*, Euromoney Publications, London, 6th ed., 1995.

Chapter Twelve

LEASING

Most of us occasionally rent a car, bicycle, or boat. Usually such personal rentals are short-lived; we may rent a car for a day or week. But in corporate finance longer-term rentals are common. A rental agreement that extends for a year or more and involves a series of fixed payments is called a **lease**.

Firms lease as an alternative to buying capital equipment. Computers are often leased; so are trucks, railroad cars, aircraft, and ships. Just about every kind of asset has been leased sometime by somebody, including electric power plants, nuclear fuel, handball courts, and zoo animals.

Every lease involves two parties. The *user* of the asset is called the *lessee*. The lessee makes periodic payments to the *owner* of the asset, who is called the *lessor*. For example, if you sign an agreement to rent an apartment for a year, you are the lessee and the owner is the lessor.

You often see references to the *leasing industry*. This refers to lessors. (Almost all firms are lessees to at least a minor extent.) Who are the lessors?

Some of the largest lessors are equipment manufacturers. For example, IBM is a large

lessor of computers, and Xerox is a large lessor of copiers.

The other two major groups of lessors are banks and independent leasing companies. Leasing companies play an enormous role in the airline business. For example, in 1998 GE Capital Aviation Services, a subsidiary of GE Capital, owned and leased out about 900 commercial aircraft. A large fraction of the world's airlines rely entirely on leasing to finance their fleets.

Leasing companies offer a variety of services. Some act as lease brokers (arranging lease deals) as well as lessors. Others specialize in leasing automobiles, trucks, and standardized industrial equipment; they succeed because they can buy equipment in quantity, service it efficiently, and if necessary resell it at a good price.

We begin this chapter by cataloging the different kinds of leases and some of the reasons for their use. Then we show how short-term, or cancelable, lease payments can be interpreted as equivalent annual costs. The remainder of the chapter analyzes long-term leases used as alternatives to debt financing.

285

WHAT IS A LEASE?

Leases come in many forms, but in all cases the lessee (user) promises to make a series of payments to the lessor (owner). The lease contract specifies the monthly or semiannual payments, with the first payment usually due as soon as the contract is signed. The payments are usually level, but their time pattern can be tailored to the user's needs. For example, suppose that a manufacturer leases a machine to produce a complex new product. There will be a year's "shakedown" period before volume production starts. In this case, it might be possible to arrange for lower payments during the first year of the lease.

When a lease is terminated, the leased equipment reverts to the lessor. However, the lease agreement often gives the user the option to purchase the equipment or take out a new lease.

Some leases are short-term or cancelable during the contract period at the option of the lessee. These are generally known as *operating leases*. Others extend over most of the estimated economic life of the asset and cannot be canceled or can be canceled only if the lessor is reimbursed for any losses. These are called *capital, financial,* or *full-payout leases*.[1]

Financial leases are a *source of financing*. Signing a financial lease contract is like borrowing money. There is an immediate cash inflow because the lessee is relieved of having to pay for the asset. But the lessee also assumes a binding obligation to make the payments specified in the lease contract. The user could have borrowed the full purchase price of the asset by accepting a binding obligation to make interest and principal payments to the lender. Thus the cash-flow consequences of leasing and borrowing are similar. In either case, the firm raises cash now and pays it back later. A large part of this chapter will be devoted to comparing leasing and borrowing as financing alternatives.

Leases also differ in the services provided by the lessor. Under a *full-service*, or *rental*, lease, the lessor promises to maintain and insure the equipment and to pay any property taxes due on it. In a *net* lease, the lessee agrees to maintain the asset, insure it, and pay any property taxes. Financial leases are usually net leases.

Most financial leases are arranged for brand new assets. The lessee identifies the equipment, arranges for the leasing company to buy it from the manufacturer, and signs a contract with the leasing company. This is called a *direct* lease. In other cases, the firm sells an asset it already owns and leases it back from the buyer. These *sale and lease-back* arrangements are common in real estate. For example, firm X may wish to raise cash by selling a factory but still retain use of the factory. It could do this by selling the factory for cash to a leasing company and simultaneously signing a long-term lease contract for the factory. Legal ownership of the factory passes to the leasing company, but the right to use it stays with firm X.

You may also encounter *leveraged* leases. These are financial leases in which the lessor borrows part of the purchase price of the leased asset, using the lease contract as security for the loan. This does not change the lessee's obligations, but it can complicate the lessor's analysis considerably.

---

[1]In the shipping industry, a financial lease is called a *bareboat charter* or a *demise hire*.

WHY LEASE?

You hear many suggestions about why companies should lease equipment rather than buy it. Let us look at some sensible reasons and then at four more dubious ones.

Sensible Reasons for Leasing

Short-Term Leases Are Convenient   Suppose you want the use of a car for a week. You could buy one and sell it seven days later, but that would be silly. Quite apart from the fact that registering ownership is a nuisance, you would spend some time selecting a car, negotiating purchase, and arranging insurance. Then at the end of the week you would negotiate resale and cancel the registration and insurance. When you need a car only for a short time, it clearly makes sense to rent it. You save the trouble of registering ownership, and you know the effective cost. In the same way, it pays a company to lease equipment that it needs for only a year or two. Of course, this kind of lease is always an operating lease.

Sometimes the cost of short-term rentals may seem prohibitively high, or you may find it difficult to rent at any price. This can happen for equipment that is easily damaged by careless use. The owner knows that short-term users are unlikely to take the same care they would with their own equipment. When the danger of abuse becomes too high, short-term rental markets do not survive. Thus, it is easy enough to buy a Lamborgini Diablo, provided your pockets are deep enough, but nearly impossible to rent one.

Cancellation Options Are Valuable   Some leases that *appear* expensive really are fairly priced once the option to cancel is recognized. We return to this point in the next section.

Maintenance Is Provided   Under a full-service lease, the user receives maintenance and other services. Many lessors are well equipped to provide efficient maintenance. However, bear in mind that these benefits will be reflected in higher lease payments.

Standardization Leads to Low Administrative and Transaction Costs   Suppose that you operate a leasing company which specializes in financial leases for trucks. You are effectively lending money to a large number of firms (the lessees) which may differ considerably in size and risk. But, because the underlying asset is in each case the same saleable item (a truck), you can safely "lend" the money (lease the truck) without conducting a detailed analysis of each firm's business. You can also use a simple, standard lease contract. This standardization makes it possible to "lend" small sums of money without incurring large investigative, administrative, or legal costs.

For these reasons leasing is often a relatively cheap source of cash for the small company. It offers financing on a flexible, piecemeal basis, with lower transaction costs than in a private placement or a public bond or stock issue.

Tax Shields Can Be Used   The lessor owns the leased asset and deducts its depreciation from taxable income. If the lessor can make better use of depreciation tax shields than an asset's user can, it may make sense for the leasing company to own the equipment and pass on some of the tax benefits to the lessee in the form of low lease payments.

Avoiding the Alternative Minimum Tax   Red-blooded financial managers want to earn lots of money for their shareholders but *report* low profits to the tax authorities. Tax law in the United

States allows this. A firm may use straight-line depreciation in its annual report but choose accelerated depreciation (and the shortest possible asset life) for its tax books. By this and other perfectly legal and ethical devices, profitable companies have occasionally managed to escape tax entirely. Almost all companies pay less tax than their public income statements suggest.[2]

But the 1986 Tax Reform Act has a trap for companies that shield too much income: the alternative minimum tax (*AMT*). Corporations must pay the AMT whenever it is higher than their tax computed in the regular way.

Here is how the AMT works: It requires a second calculation of taxable income, in which part of the benefit of accelerated depreciation and other tax-reducing items[3] is added back. The AMT is 20 percent of the result.

Suppose Yuppytech Services would have $10 million in taxable income but for the AMT, which forces it to add back $9 million of tax privileges:

	REGULAR TAX	ALTERNATIVE MINIMUM TAX
Income	$10	$10 + 9 = 19$
Tax rate	.35	.20
Tax	$ 3.5	$3.8

Yuppytech must pay $3.8 million, not $3.5.[4]

How can this painful payment be avoided? How about leasing? Lease payments are *not* on the list of items added back in calculating the AMT. If you lease rather than buy, tax depreciation is less and the AMT is less. There is a net gain if the *lessor* is not subject to the AMT and can pass back depreciation tax shields in the form of lower lease payments.

Some Dubious Reasons for Leasing

Leasing Avoids Capital Expenditure Controls   In many companies lease proposals are scrutinized as carefully as capital expenditure proposals, but in others leasing may enable an operating manager to avoid the elaborate approval procedures needed to buy an asset. Although this is a dubious reason for leasing, it may be influential, particularly in the public sector. For example, city hospitals have sometimes found it politically more convenient to lease their medical equipment than to ask the city government to provide funds for purchase. Another example is provided by the United States Navy, which once leased a fleet of new tankers and supply ships instead of asking Congress for the money to buy them.

---

[2]Year-by-year differences between reported tax expense and taxes actually paid are explained in footnotes to the financial statements. The cumulative difference is shown on the balance sheet as a deferred tax liability. (Note that accelerated depreciation *postpones* taxes; it does not eliminate taxes.)

[3]Other items include some interest receipts from tax-exempt municipal securities and taxes deferred by use of completed contract accounting. (The completed contract method allows a manufacturer to postpone reporting taxable profits until a production contract is completed. Since contracts may span several years, this deferral can have a substantial positive NPV.)

[4]But Yuppytech can carry forward the $.3 million difference. If later years' AMTs are *lower* than regular taxes, the difference can be used as a tax credit. Suppose the AMT next year is $4 million and the regular tax is $5 million. Then Yuppytech pays only $5 - .3 = \$4.7$ million.

Leasing Preserves Capital   Leasing companies provide "100 percent financing"; they advance the full cost of the leased asset. Consequently, they often claim that leasing preserves capital, allowing the firm to save its cash for other things.

But the firm can also "preserve capital" by borrowing money. If Greymare Bus Lines leases a $100,000 bus rather than buying it, it does conserve $100,000 cash. It could also (1) buy the bus for cash and (2) borrow $100,000, using the bus as security. Its bank balance ends up the same whether it leases or buys and borrows. It has the bus in either case, and it incurs a $100,000 liability in either case. What's so special about leasing?

Leases May Be Off-Balance-Sheet Financing   In some countries, such as Germany, financial leases are off-balance-sheet financing; that is, a firm can acquire an asset, finance it through a financial lease, and show neither the asset nor the lease contract on its balance sheet.

In the United States, the Financial Accounting Standards Board (FASB) requires that all *capital* (i.e., financial) leases be capitalized. This means that the present value of the lease payments must be calculated and shown alongside debt on the right-hand side of the balance sheet. The same amount must be shown as an asset on the left-hand side.[5]

The FASB defines capital leases as leases which meet *any one* of the following requirements:

1. The lease agreement transfers ownership to the lessee before the lease expires.
2. The lessee can purchase the asset for a bargain price when the lease expires.
3. The lease lasts for at least 75 percent of the asset's estimated economic life.
4. The present value of the lease payments is at least 90 percent of the asset's value.

All other leases are operating leases as far as the accountants are concerned.

Many financial managers have tried to take advantage of this arbitrary boundary between operating and financial leases. Suppose that you want to finance a computer-controlled machine tool costing $1 million. The machine tool's life is expected to be 12 years. You could sign a lease contract for 8 years, 11 months (just missing requirement 3) with lease payments having a present value of $899,000 (just missing requirement 4). You could also make sure the lease contract avoids requirements 1 and 2. Result? You have off-balance-sheet financing. This lease would not have to be capitalized, although it is clearly a long-term, fixed obligation.

Now we come to the $64,000 question: "Why should anyone *care* whether financing is off balance sheet or on balance sheet?" Shouldn't the financial manager worry about substance rather than appearance?

When a firm obtains off-balance-sheet financing, the conventional measures of financial leverage, such as the debt–equity ratio, understate the true degree of financial leverage. Some believe that financial analysts do not always notice off-balance-sheet lease obligations (which are still referred to in footnotes) or the greater volatility of earnings that results from the fixed lease payments. They may be right, but we would not expect such an imperfection to be widespread.

When a company borrows money, it must usually consent to certain restrictions on future borrowing. Early bond indentures did not include any restrictions on financial leases. Therefore leasing was seen as a way to circumvent restrictive covenants. Loopholes such as these are easily stopped, and most bond indentures now include limits on leasing.

---

[5]This "asset" is then amortized over the life of the lease. The amortization is deducted from book income, just as depreciation is deducted for a purchased asset.

Long-term lease obligations ought to be regarded as debt whether or not they appear on the balance sheet. Financial analysts may overlook moderate leasing activity, just as they overlook minor debts. But major lease obligations are generally recognized and taken into account.

Leasing Affects Book Income   Leasing can make the firm's balance sheet and income statement *look* better by increasing book income or decreasing book asset value, or both.

A lease which qualifies as off-balance-sheet financing affects book income in only one way: The lease payments are an expense. If the firm buys the asset instead and borrows to finance it, both depreciation and interest expense are deducted. Leases are usually set up so that payments in the early years are less than depreciation plus interest under the buy-and-borrow alternative. Consequently, leasing increases book income in the early years of an asset's life. The book rate of return can increase even more dramatically, because the book value of assets (the denominator in the book-rate-of-return calculation) is understated if the leased asset never appears on the firm's balance sheet.

Leasing's impact on book income should in itself have no effect on firm value. In efficient capital markets investors will look through the firm's accounting results to the true value of the asset and the liability incurred to finance it.

OPERATING LEASES

Suppose you decide to lease a machine tool for one year. What will the rental payment be in a competitive leasing industry? The lessor's *equivalent annual cost*, which is the annual rental payment sufficient to cover the present value of all the costs of owning and operating the underlying asset.

Example of an Operating Lease

The boyfriend of the daughter of the CEO of Establishment Industries takes her to the senior prom in a pearly white stretch limo. The CEO is impressed. He decides Establishment Industries ought to have one for VIP transportation. Establishment's CFO prudently suggests a one-year operating lease instead and approaches Acme Limolease for a quote.

Table 12.1 shows Acme's analysis. Suppose it buys a new limo for $75,000 which it plans to lease out for seven years (years 0 through 6). The table gives Acme's forecasts of operating, maintenance, and administrative costs, the latter including the costs of negotiating the lease, keeping track of payments and paperwork, and finding a replacement lessee when Establishment's year is up. For simplicity we assume zero inflation and use a 7 percent real cost of capital. We also assume that the limo will have zero salvage value at the end of year 6. The present value of all costs, partially offset by the value of depreciation tax shields,[6] is $98,150. Now, how much does Acme have to charge in order to break even?

Acme can afford to buy and lease out the limo only if the rental payments forecasted over six years have a present value of at least $98,150. The problem, then, is to calculate a six-year annuity

---

[6]The depreciation tax shields are safe cash flows if the tax rate does not change and Acme is sure to pay taxes. If 7 percent is the right discount rate for the other flows in Table 12.1, the depreciation tax shields deserve a lower rate. A more refined analysis would discount safe depreciation tax shields at an after-tax borrowing or lending rate. See the next section of this chapter.

TABLE 12.1

Calculating the zero-NPV rental rate (or equivalent annual cost) for Establishment Industries' pearly white stretch limo (figures in $ thousands)

	YEAR						
	0	1	2	3	4	5	6
Initial cost	−75						
Maintenance, insurance, selling, and administrative costs	−12	−12	−12	−12	−12	−12	−12
Tax shield on costs	+4.2	+4.2	+4.2	+4.2	+4.2	+4.2	+4.2
Depreciation tax shield[a]		+5.25	+8.40	+5.04	+3.02	+3.02	+1.51
Total	−82.80	−2.55	.60	−2.76	−4.78	−4.78	−6.29
PV at 7% = −$98.15[b]							
Break-even rent (level)	26.18	26.18	26.18	26.18	26.18	26.18	26.18
Tax	−9.16	−9.16	−9.16	−9.16	−9.16	−9.16	−9.16
Break-even rent after tax	17.02	17.02	17.02	17.02	17.02	17.02	17.02
PV at 7% = $98.15[b]							

Note: We assume no inflation and a 7 percent real cost of capital. The tax rate is 35 percent.

[a]Depreciation tax shields are calculated using the five-year schedule under the modified accelerated cost recovery system (MACRS).

[b]Note that the first payment of these annuities comes immediately. The standard annuity formula must be multiplied by $1 + r = 1.07$.

with a present value of $98,150. We will follow common leasing practice and assume rental payments in advance rather than in arrears.

As Table 12.1 shows, the required annuity is $26,180, that is, about $26,000.[7] This annuity's present value (after taxes) exactly equals the present value of the after-tax costs of owning and operating the limo. The annuity provides Acme with a competitive expected rate of return (7 percent) on its investment. Acme could try to charge Establishment Industries more than $26,000, but if the CFO is smart enough to ask for bids from Acme's competitors, the winning lessor will end up receiving this amount.

Remember that Establishment Industries is not obligated to continue using the limo for more than one year. Acme may have to find several new lessees over the limo's economic life. Even if Establishment continues, it can renegotiate a new lease at whatever rates prevail in the future. Thus Acme does not know what it can charge in year 1 or afterward. If pearly white falls out of favor with teenagers and CEOs, Acme is probably out of luck.

---

[7]This is a level annuity because we are assuming that (1) there is no inflation and (2) the services of a six-year-old limo are no different than a brand-new limo's. If users of aging limos see them as obsolete or unfashionable, or if new limos are cheaper, then lease rates for older limos would have to be cut. This would give a *declining* annuity: initial users would pay more than the amount shown in Table 12.1, later users, less.

In real life Acme would have several further things to worry about. For example, how long will the limo stand idle when it is returned at year 1? If idle time is likely before a new lessee is found, then lease rates have to be higher to compensate.[8]

In an operating lease, the *lessor* absorbs these risks, not the lessee. The discount rate used by the lessor must include a premium sufficient to compensate its shareholders for the risks of buying and holding the leased asset. In other words, Acme's 7 percent real discount rate must cover the risks of investing in stretch limos. (As we will see in the next section, risk bearing in *financial* leases is fundamentally different.)

Lease or Buy?

If you need a car or limo for only a day or a week you will surely rent it; if you need one for five years you will probably buy it. In between there is a gray region in which the choice of lease or buy is not obvious. The decision rule should be clear in concept, however: If you need an asset for your business, *buy it if the equivalent annual cost of ownership and operation is less than the best lease rate you can get from an outsider*. In other words, buy if you can "rent to yourself" cheaper than you can rent from others. (Again we stress that this rule applies to *operating* leases.)

If you plan to use the asset for an extended period, your equivalent annual cost of owning the asset will usually be less than the operating lease rate. The lessor has to mark up the lease rate to cover the costs of negotiating and administering the lease, the foregone revenues when the asset is off-lease and idle, and so on. These costs are avoided when the company buys and rents to itself.

There are two cases in which operating leases may make sense even when the company plans to use an asset for an extended period. First, the lessor may be able to buy and manage the asset at less expense than the lessee. For example, the major truck leasing companies buy thousands of new vehicles every year. That puts them in an excellent bargaining position with truck manufacturers. These companies also run very efficient service operations, and they know how to extract the most salvage value when trucks wear out and it is time to sell them. A small business, or a small division of a larger one, cannot achieve these economies and often finds it cheaper to lease trucks than to buy them.

Second, operating leases often contain useful options. Suppose Acme offers Establishment Industries the following two leases:

1. A one-year lease for $26,000.
2. A six-year lease for $28,000, *with the option to cancel the lease* at any time from year 1 on.[9]

The second lease has obvious attractions. Suppose Establishment's CEO becomes fond of the limo and wants to use it for a second year. If rates increase, lease 2 allows Establishment to continue at the old rate. If rates decrease, Establishment can cancel lease 2 and negotiate a lower rate with Acme or one of its competitors.

---

[8]If, say, limos were off-lease and idle 20 percent of the time, lease rates would have to be 25 percent above those shown in Table 12.1.

[9]Acme might also offer a one-year lease for $28,000 but give the lessee an option to *extend* the lease on the same terms for up to five additional years. This is, of course, identical to lease 2. It doesn't matter whether the lessee has the (put) option to cancel or the (call) option to continue.

Of course, lease 2 is a more costly proposition for Acme: In effect it gives Establishment an insurance policy protecting it from increases in future lease rates. The difference between the costs of leases 1 and 2 is the annual insurance premium. But lessees may happily pay for insurance if they have no special knowledge of future asset values or lease rates. A leasing company acquires such knowledge in the course of its business and can generally sell such insurance at a profit.

Computers are frequently leased on a short-term, cancelable basis. It is difficult to estimate how soon such equipment will become obsolete, because the technology of computers is advancing rapidly and somewhat unpredictably. Leasing with an option to cancel passes the risk of premature obsolescence from the user to the lessor. Usually the lessor is a computer manufacturer or a computer leasing specialist and therefore knows more about the risks of obsolescence than the user does. Thus the lessor is better equipped than the user to bear these risks. It makes sense for the user to pay the lessor for the option to cancel.

Be sure to check out the options before you sign (or reject) an operating lease.[10]

VALUING FINANCIAL LEASES

For operating leases the decision centers on "lease versus buy." For *financial* leases the decision amounts to "lease versus borrow." Financial leases extend over most of the economic life of the leased equipment. They are *not* cancelable. The lease payments are fixed obligations equivalent to debt service.

Financial leases make sense when the company is prepared to take on the business risks of owning and operating the leased asset. If Establishment Industries signs a *financial* lease for the stretch limo, it is stuck with that asset. The financial lease is just another way of borrowing money to pay for the limo.

Financial leases do offer special advantages to some firms in some circumstances. However, there is no point in further discussion of these advantages until you know how to value financial lease contracts.

Example of a Financial Lease

Imagine yourself in the position of Thomas Pierce III, president of Greymare Bus Lines. Your firm was established by your grandfather, who was quick to capitalize on the growing demand for transportation between Widdicombe and nearby townships. The company has owned all its vehicles from the time the company was formed; you are now reconsidering that policy. Your operating manager wants to buy a new bus costing $100,000. The bus will last only eight years before going to the scrap yard. You are convinced that investment in the additional equipment is worthwhile. However, the representative of the bus manufacturer has pointed out that her firm would also be willing to lease the bus to you for eight annual payments of $16,900 each. Greymare would remain responsible for all maintenance, insurance, and operating expenses.

---

[10]McConnell and Schallheim calculate the value of options in operating leases under various assumptions about asset risk, depreciation rates, etc. See J. J. McConnell and J. S. Schallheim, "Valuation of Asset Leasing Contracts," *Journal of Financial Economics* 12 (August 1983), pp. 237–261.

TABLE 12.2

Cash-flow consequences of the lease contract offered to Greymare Bus Lines (figures in $ thousands; some columns do not add due to rounding)

	YEAR							
	0	1	2	3	4	5	6	7
Cost of new bus	+100							
Lost depreciation tax shield		−7.00	−11.20	−6.72	−4.03	−4.03	−2.02	0
Lease payment	−16.9	−16.9	−16.9	−16.9	−16.9	−16.9	−16.9	−16.9
Tax shield of lease payment	+5.92	+5.92	+5.92	+5.92	+5.92	+5.92	+5.92	+5.92
Cash flow of lease	+89.02	−17.99	−22.19	−17.71	−15.02	−15.02	−13.00	−10.98

Table 12.2 shows the direct cash-flow consequences of signing the lease contract. (An important indirect effect is considered later.) The consequences are

1. Greymare does not have to pay for the bus. This is equivalent to a cash inflow of $100,000.

2. Greymare no longer owns the bus, and so it cannot depreciate it. Therefore it gives up a valuable depreciation tax shield. In Table 12.2, we have assumed depreciation would be calculated using five-year tax depreciation schedules.

3. Greymare must pay $16,900 per year for eight years to the lessor. The first payment is due immediately.

4. However, these lease payments are fully tax-deductible. At a 35 percent marginal tax rate, the lease payments generate tax shields of $5,920 per year. You could say that the after-tax cost of the lease payment is $16,900 − $5,920 = $10,980.

We must emphasize that Table 12.2 assumes that Greymare will pay taxes at the full 35 percent marginal rate. If the firm were sure to lose money, and therefore pay no taxes, lines 2 and 4 would be left blank. The depreciation tax shields are worth nothing to a firm that pays no taxes, for example.

Table 12.2 also assumes the bus will be worthless when it goes to the scrap yard at the end of year 7. Otherwise there would be an entry for salvage value lost.

Who Really Owns the Leased Asset?

To a lawyer or a tax accountant, that would be a silly question: The lessor is clearly the *legal* owner of the leased asset. That is why the lessor is allowed to deduct depreciation from taxable income.

From an *economic* point of view, you might say that the *user* is the real owner, because in a *financial* lease, the user faces the risks and receives the rewards of ownership. Greymare cannot cancel a financial lease. If the new bus turns out to be hopelessly costly and unsuited for Greymare's routes, that is Greymare's problem, not the lessor's. If it turns out to be a great success, the profit goes to Greymare, not the lessor. The success or failure of the firm's business operations does not depend on whether the buses are financed by leasing or some other financial instrument.

In many respects, a financial lease is equivalent to a secured loan. The lessee must make a series of fixed payments; if the lessee fails to do so, the lessor can repossess the asset. Thus we can think of a balance sheet like this

Greymare Bus Lines (Figures in $ Thousands)

Bus	100	100	Loan secured by bus
All other assets	1,000	450	Other loans
		550	Equity
Total assets	1,100	1,100	Total liabilities

as being economically equivalent to a balance sheet like this

Greymare Bus Lines (Figures in $ Thousands)

Bus	100	100	Financial lease
All other assets	1,000	450	Other loans
		550	Equity
Total assets	1,100	1,100	Total liabilities

Having said this, we must immediately add two qualifications. First, legal ownership can make a big difference when a financial lease expires because the lessor gets the salvage value of the asset. Once a secured loan is paid off, the user owns the asset free and clear.

Second, lessors and secured creditors may be treated differently in bankruptcy. If a company defaults on a lease payment, you might think that the lessor could pick up the leased asset and take it home. But if the bankruptcy court decides the asset is "essential" to the lessee's business, it "affirms" the lease. Then the bankrupt firm can continue to use the asset, *but* it must also continue to make the lease payments. This can be *good* news for the lessor: It is paid cash while other creditors cool their heels. Even secured creditors are not paid until the bankruptcy process works itself out.

If the lease is not affirmed but "rejected," the lessor can of course recover the leased asset. If it is worth less than the future payments the lessee had promised, the lessor can try to recoup this loss. But in this case the lender must get in line with the unsecured creditors.

Of course, neither the lessor nor the secured lender can be sure it will come out whole. Our point is that lessors and secured creditors have different rights when the asset user gets into trouble.

Leasing and the Internal Revenue Service

We have already noted that the lessee loses the tax depreciation of the leased asset but can deduct the lease payment in full. The *lessor*, as legal owner, uses the depreciation tax shield but must report the lease payments as taxable rental income.

However, the Internal Revenue Service is suspicious by nature and will not allow the lessee to deduct the entire lease payment unless it is satisfied that the arrangement is a genuine lease and not a disguised installment purchase or secured loan agreement. Here are examples of lease provisions that will arouse its suspicion:

1. Designating any part of the lease payment as "interest."
2. Giving the lessee the option to acquire the asset for, say, $1 when the lease expires. Such a provision would effectively give the asset's salvage value to the lessee.

3. Adopting a schedule of payments such that the lessee pays a large proportion of the cost over a short period and thereafter is able to use the asset for a nominal charge.

4. Including a so-called hell-or-high-water clause that obliges the lessee to make payments regardless of what subsequently happens to the lessor or the equipment.

5. Limiting the lessee's right to issue debt or pay dividends while the lease is in force.

6. Leasing "limited use" property—for example, leasing a machine or production facility which is custom-designed for the lessee's operations and which therefore will have scant secondhand value.

Some leases are designed *not* to qualify as a true lease for tax purposes. Suppose a manufacturer finds it convenient to lease a new computer but wants to keep the depreciation tax shields. This is easily accomplished by giving the manufacturer the option to purchase the computer for $1 at the end of the lease. Then the Internal Revenue Service treats the lease as an installment sale, and the manufacturer can deduct depreciation and the interest component of the lease payment for tax purposes. But the lease is still a lease for all other purposes.

A First Pass at Valuing a Lease Contract

When we left Thomas Pierce III, president of Greymare Bus Lines, he had just set down in Table 12.2 the cash flows of the financial lease proposed by the bus manufacturer.

These cash flows are typically assumed to be about as safe as the interest and principal payments on a secured loan issued by the lessee. This assumption is reasonable for the lease payments because the lessor is effectively lending money to the lessee. But the various tax shields might carry enough risk to deserve a higher discount rate. For example, Greymare might be confident that it could make the lease payments but not confident that it could earn enough taxable income to use these tax shields. In that case the cash flows generated by the tax shields would probably deserve a higher discount rate than the borrowing rate used for the lease payments.

A lessee might, in principle, end up using a separate discount rate for each line of Table 12.2, each rate chosen to fit the risk of that line's cash flow. But established, profitable firms usually find it reasonable to simplify by discounting the types of flows shown in Table 12.2 at a single rate based on the rate of interest the firm would pay if it borrowed rather than leased. We will assume Greymare's borrowing rate is 10 percent.

At this point we need to review the valuation of debt-equivalent flows. When a company lends money, it pays tax on the interest it receives. Its net return is the after-tax interest rate. When a company borrows money, it can *deduct* interest payments from its taxable income. The net cost of borrowing is the after-tax interest rate. Thus the after-tax interest rate is the effective rate at which a company can transfer debt-equivalent flows from one time period to another. Therefore, to value the incremental cash flows stemming from the lease, we need to discount them at the after-tax interest rate.

Since Greymare can borrow at 10 percent, we should discount the lease cash flows at $r_D(1 - T_c)$ = .10(1 − .35) = .065, or 6.5 percent. This gives

$$\text{NPV lease} = +89.02 - \frac{17.99}{1.065} - \frac{22.19}{(1.065)^2} - \frac{17.71}{(1.065)^3} - \frac{15.02}{(1.065)^4}$$

$$- \frac{15.02}{(1.065)^5} - \frac{13.00}{(1.065)^6} - \frac{10.98}{(1.065)^7}$$

$$= -.70, \text{ or } -\$700$$

Since the lease has a negative NPV, Greymare is better off buying the bus.

A positive or negative NPV is not an abstract concept; in this case Greymare's shareholders really are $700 poorer if the company leases. Let us now check how this situation comes about.

Look once more at Table 12.2. The lease cash flows are

	YEAR							
	0	1	2	3	4	5	6	7
Lease cash flows, thousands	+89.02	−17.99	−22.19	−17.71	−15.02	−15.02	−13.00	−10.98

The lease payments are contractual obligations like the principal and interest payments on secured debt. Thus you can think of the incremental lease cash flows in years 1 through 7 as the "debt service" of the lease. Table 12.3 shows a loan with *exactly* the same debt service as the lease. The initial amount of the loan is 89.72 thousand dollars. If Greymare borrowed this sum, it would need to pay interest in the first year of $.10 \times 89.72 = 8.97$ and would *receive* a tax shield on this interest of $.35 \times 8.97 = 3.14$. Greymare could then repay 12.15 of the loan, leaving a net cash outflow of 17.99 (exactly the same as for the lease) in year 1 and an outstanding debt at the start of year 2 of 60.42.

As you walk through the calculations in Table 12.3, you see that it costs exactly the same to service a loan that brings an immediate inflow of 89.72 as it does to service the lease, which brings in only 89.02. That is why we say that the lease has a net present value of $89.02 – 89.72 = –.7$, or –$700. If Greymare leases the bus rather than raising an *equivalent loan*,[11] there will be $700 less in Greymare's bank account.

Our example illustrates two general points about leases and equivalent loans. First, if you can devise a borrowing plan that gives the same cash flow as the lease in every future period but a higher immediate cash flow, then you should not lease. If, however, the equivalent loan provides the same future cash outflows as the lease but a lower immediate inflow, then leasing is the better choice.

Second, our example suggests two ways to value a lease:

1. *Hard way.* Construct a table like Table 12.3 showing the equivalent loan.
2. *Easy way.* Discount the lease cash flows at the *after-tax* interest rate that the firm would pay on an equivalent loan. Both methods give the same answer—in our case an NPV of –$700.

The Story So Far

We concluded that the lease contract offered to Greymare Bus Lines was *not* attractive because the lease provided $700 less financing than the equivalent loan. The underlying principle is as follows: A financial lease is superior to buying and borrowing if the financing provided by the lease exceeds the financing generated by the equivalent loan.

The principle implies this formula:

$$\begin{array}{c} \text{Net value} \\ \text{of lease} \end{array} = \begin{array}{c} \text{initial financing} \\ \text{provided} \end{array} - \sum_{t=1}^{N} \frac{\text{lease cash flow}}{[1 + r_D(1 - T_c)]^t}$$

---

[11]When we compare the lease to its equivalent loan, we do not mean to imply that the bus alone could support all of that loan. Some part of the loan would be supported by Greymare's other assets. Some part of the lease would likewise be supported by the other assets.

TABLE 12.3

Details of the equivalent loan to the lease offered to Greymare Bus Lines (figures in $ thousands; cash outflows shown with negative sign)

	YEAR							
	0	1	2	3	4	5	6	7
Amount borrowed at year-end	89.72	77.56	60.42	46.64	34.66	21.89	10.31	0
Interest paid at 10%		−8.97	−7.76	−6.04	−4.66	−3.47	−2.19	−1.03
Interest tax shield at 35%		+3.14	+2.71	+2.11	+1.63	+1.21	+.77	+.36
Interest paid after tax		−5.83	−5.04	−3.93	−3.03	−2.25	−1.42	−.67
Principal repaid		−12.15	−17.14	−13.78	−11.99	−12.76	−11.58	−10.31
Net cash flow of equivalent loan	89.72	−17.99	−22.19	−17.71	−15.02	−15.02	−13.00	−10.98

where N is the length of the lease. Initial financing provided equals the cost of the leased asset minus any immediate lease payment or other cash outflow attributable to the lease.

Notice that the value of the lease is its incremental value relative to borrowing via an equivalent loan. A positive lease value means that *if* you acquire the asset, lease financing is advantageous. It does not prove you should acquire the asset.

However, sometimes favorable lease terms rescue a capital investment project. Suppose that Greymare had decided *against* buying a new bus because the NPV of the $100,000 investment was −$5,000 assuming normal financing. The bus manufacturer could rescue the deal by offering a lease with a value of, say, +$8,000. By offering such a lease, the manufacturer would in effect cut the price of the bus to $92,000, giving the bus-lease package a positive value to Greymare. We could express this more formally by treating the lease's NPV as a favorable financing side effect which adds to project adjusted present value (APV):

$$APV = NPV \text{ of project} + NPV \text{ of lease}$$

$$= -5,000 + 8,000 = +\$3,000$$

Notice also that our formula applies to net financial leases. Any insurance, maintenance, and other operating costs picked up by the lessor have to be evaluated separately and added to the value of the lease. If the asset has salvage value at the end of the lease, that value should be taken into account also.

Suppose, for example, that the bus manufacturer offers to provide routine maintenance that would otherwise cost $2,000 per year after tax. However, Mr. Pierce reconsiders and decides that the bus will probably be worth $10,000 after eight years. (Previously he assumed the bus would be worthless at the end of the lease.) Then the value of the lease increases by the present value of the maintenance savings and decreases by the present value of the lost salvage value.

Maintenance and salvage value are harder to predict than the cash flows shown in Table 12.2, and so they normally deserve a higher discount rate. Suppose that Mr. Pierce uses 12 percent. Then the maintenance savings are worth

$$\sum_{t=0}^{7} \frac{2000}{(1.12)^t} = \$11,100$$

The lost salvage value is worth $\$10,000/(1.12)^8 = \$4,000$.[12] Remember that we previously calculated the value of the lease as –$700. The revised value is therefore $-700 + 11,100 - 4,000 = \$6,400$. Now the lease looks like a good deal.

WHEN DO FINANCIAL LEASES PAY?

We have examined the value of a lease from the viewpoint of the lessee. However, the lessor's criterion is simply the reverse. As long as lessor and lessee are in the same tax bracket, every cash outflow to the lessee is an inflow to the lessor, and vice versa. In our numerical example, the bus manufacturer would project cash flows in a table like Table 12.2, but with the signs reversed. The value of the lease to the bus manufacturer would be

$$\begin{aligned} \text{Value of} \\ \text{lease to} &= -89.02 + \frac{17.99}{1.065} + \frac{22.19}{(1.065)^2} + \frac{17.71}{(1.065)^3} + \frac{15.02}{(1.065)^4} + \frac{15.02}{(1.065)^5} \\ \text{lessor} \end{aligned}$$

$$+ \frac{13.00}{(1.065)^6} + \frac{10.98}{(1.065)^7}$$

$$= +.70, \text{ or } \$700$$

In this case, the values to lessee and lessor exactly offset (–$700 + $700 = 0). The lessor can win only at the lessee's expense.

But both lessee and lessor can win if their tax rates differ. Suppose that Greymare paid no tax ($T_c = 0$). Then the only cash flows of the bus lease would be

	YEAR							
	0	1	2	3	4	5	6	7
Cost of new bus	+100							
Lease payment	–16.9	–16.9	–16.9	–16.9	–16.9	–16.9	–16.9	–16.9

These flows would be discounted at 10 percent, because $r_D(1 - T_c) = r_D$ when $T_c = 0$. The value of the lease is

$$\text{Value of lease} = +100 - \sum_{t=0}^{7} \frac{16.9}{(1.10)^t}$$

$$= +100 - 99.18 = +.82, \text{ or } \$820$$

In this case there is a net gain of $700 to the lessor (who has the 35 percent tax rate) *and* a net gain of $820 to the lessee (who pays zero tax). This mutual gain is at the expense of the government.

---

[12]For simplicity, we have assumed that maintenance expenses are paid at the start of the year and that salvage value is measured at the *end* of year 8.

On one hand, the government gains from the lease contract because it can tax the lease payments. On the other hand, the contract allows the lessor to take advantage of depreciation and interest tax shields which are of no use to the lessee. However, because the depreciation is accelerated and the interest rate is positive, the government suffers a net loss in the present value of its tax receipts as a result of the lease.

Now you should begin to understand the circumstances in which the government incurs a loss on the lease and the other two parties gain. Other things being equal, the potential gains to lessor and lessee are highest when

- The lessor's tax rate is substantially higher than the lessee's.
- The depreciation tax shield is received early in the lease period.
- The lease period is long and the lease payments are concentrated toward the end of the period.
- The interest rate r_D is high—if it were zero, there would be no advantage in present value terms to postponing tax.

SUMMARY

A lease is just an extended rental agreement. The owner of the equipment (the *lessor*) allows the user (the *lessee*) to operate the equipment in exchange for regular lease payments.

There is a wide variety of possible arrangements. Short-term, cancelable leases are known as *operating leases*. In these leases the lessor bears the risks of ownership. Long-term, noncancelable leases are called *full-payout, financial,* or *capital* leases. In these leases the lessee bears the risks. Financial leases are *sources of financing* for assets the firm wishes to acquire and use for an extended period.

Many vehicle or office equipment leases include insurance and maintenance. They are *full-service* leases. If the lessee is responsible for insurance and maintenance, the lease is a *net* lease.

Frequently the lessor acquires the asset directly from the manufacturer. This is a *direct* lease. Sometimes the lessor acquires the asset from the user and then leases it back to the user. This is a *sale and lease back*.

Most leases involve only the lessee and the lessor. But if the asset is very costly, it may be convenient to arrange a *leveraged* lease, in which the cost of the leased asset is financed by issuing debt and equity claims against the asset and the future lease payments.

The key to understanding operating leases is equivalent annual cost. In a competitive leasing market, the annual operating lease payment will be forced down to the lessor's equivalent annual cost. Operating leases are attractive to equipment users if the lease payment is less than the *user's* equivalent annual cost of buying the equipment. Operating leases make sense when the user needs the equipment only for a short time, when the lessor is better able to bear the risks of obsolescence, or when the lessor can offer a good deal on maintenance. Remember too that operating leases often have valuable options attached.

A financial lease extends over most of the economic life of the leased asset and cannot be canceled by the lessee. Signing a financial lease is like signing a secured loan to finance purchase of the leased asset. With financial leases, the choice is not "lease versus buy" but "lease versus borrow."

Many companies have sound reasons for financing via leases. For example, companies that are not paying taxes can usually strike a favorable deal with a taxpaying lessor. Also, it may be less costly and time-consuming to sign a standardized lease contract than to negotiate a long-term secured loan.

When a firm borrows money, it pays the after-tax rate of interest on its debt. Therefore, the opportunity cost of lease financing is the after-tax rate of interest on the firm's bonds. To value a financial lease, we need to discount the incremental cash flows from leasing by the after-tax interest rate.

An equivalent loan is one that commits the firm to exactly the same future cash flows as a financial lease. When we calculate the net present value of the lease, we are measuring the difference between the amount of financing provided by the lease and the financing provided by the equivalent loan:

$$\frac{\text{Value}}{\text{of lease}} = \frac{\text{financing provided}}{\text{by lease}} - \frac{\text{value of}}{\text{equivalent loan}}$$

We can also analyze leases from the lessor's side of the transaction, using the same approaches we developed for the lessee. If lessee and lessor are in the same tax bracket, they will receive exactly the same cash flows but with signs reversed. Thus, the lessee can gain only at the lessor's expense, and vice versa. However, if the lessee's tax rate is lower than the lessor's, then both can gain at the federal government's expense.

Further Reading

A useful general reference on leasing is:

J. S. Schallheim, *Lease or Buy? Principles for Sound Decisionmaking*, Harvard Business School Press, Boston, Mass., 1994.

The approach to valuing financial leases presented in this chapter is based on:

S. C. Myers, D. A. Dill, and A. J. Bautista: "Valuation of Financial Lease Contracts," *Journal of Finance*, 31:799–819 (June 1976).

J. R. Franks and S. D. Hodges: "Valuation of Financial Lease Contracts: A Note," *Journal of Finance*, 33:647–669 (May 1978).

Other useful works include Nevitt and Fabozzi's book and the theoretical discussions of Miller and Upton and of Lewellen, Long, and McConnell:

P. K. Nevitt and F. J. Fabozzi: *Equipment Leasing*, 3d ed., Dow Jones–Irwin, Inc., Homewood, Ill., 1988

M. H. Miller and C. W. Upton: "Leasing, Buying and the Cost of Capital Services," *Journal of Finance*, 31:761–786 (June 1976).

W. G. Lewellen, M. S. Long, and J. J. McConnell: "Asset Leasing in Competitive Capital Markets," *Journal of Finance*, 31:787–798 (June 1976).

Harold Bierman gives a detailed account of leasing and the AMT in:

H. Bierman: "Buy versus Lease with an Alternative Minimum Tax," *Financial Management*, 17:87–92 (Winter 1988).

The options embedded in many operating leases are discussed in:

T. E. Copeland and J. E. Weston: "A Note on the Evaluation of Cancellable Operating Leases," *Financial Management*, 11:68–72 (Summer 1982).

J. J. McConnell and J. S. Schallheim: "Valuation of Asset Leasing Contracts," *Journal of Financial Economics*, 12:237–261 (August 1983).

S. R. Grenadier, "Valuing Lease Contracts: A Real Options Approach," *Journal of Financial Economics*, 38:297–331 (July 1995).

RISK MANAGEMENT

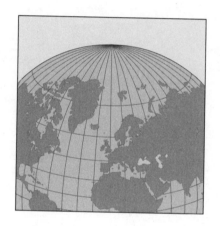

MANAGING RISK

Most of the time we take risk as God-given. An asset or business has its beta, and that's that. Its cash flow is exposed to unpredictable changes in raw material costs, tax rates, technology, and a long list of other variables. There's nothing the manager can do about it.

That's not wholly true. To some extent managers can choose the risks that the business takes. For example, companies reduce risk by building flexibility into their operations. A company that uses standardized machine tools rather than specialized equipment lowers the cost of bailing out if things go wrong. A petrochemical plant that is designed to use either oil or natural gas as a feedstock reduces the impact of an unfavorable shift in relative fuel prices. And so on.

In this chapter we shall explain how companies also enter into financial contracts that insure against or hedge (i.e., offset) a variety of business hazards. But first we should give some reasons *why* they do so.

Insurance and hedging are seldom free: At best they are zero-NPV transactions.[1] Most businesses insure or hedge to reduce risk, not to make money. Why, then, bother to reduce risk in this way? For one thing, it makes financial planning easier and reduces the odds of an embarrassing cash shortfall. A shortfall might mean only an unexpected trip to the bank, but if financing is hard to obtain on short notice, the company might need to cut back its capital expenditure program. In extreme cases an unhedged setback could trigger financial distress or even bankruptcy. Banks and bondholders are aware of this possibility, and, before lending to your firm, they will often insist that it is properly insured.

In some cases hedging also makes it easier to decide whether an operating manager deserves

---

[1]Hedging transactions are zero-NPV when trading is costless and markets are completely efficient. In practice the firm has to pay small trading costs at least.

a stern lecture or a pat on the back. Suppose your confectionery division shows a 60 percent profit increase in a period when cocoa prices decline by 12 percent. How much of the increase is due to the change in cocoa prices and how much to good management? If cocoa prices were hedged, it's probably good management. If they were not, things have to be sorted out with hindsight by asking, "What would profits have been *if* cocoa prices had been hedged?"[2]

Finally, hedging extraneous events can help focus the operating manager's attention. It's naive to expect the manager of the confectionery division *not* to worry about cocoa prices if her bottom line and bonus depend on them. That worrying time would be better spent if the prices were hedged.[3]

Of course, managers are not paid to avoid all risks, but if they can reduce their exposure to risks for which there are no compensating rewards, they can afford to place larger bets when the odds are in their favor.

INSURANCE

Most businesses buy insurance against a variety of hazards—the risk that their plant will be damaged by fire; that their ships, planes, or vehicles will be involved in accidents; that the firm will be held liable for environmental damage; and so on.

When a firm takes out insurance, it is simply transferring the risk to the insurance company. Insurance companies have some advantages in bearing risk. First, they may have considerable experience in insuring similar risks, so they are well placed to estimate the probability of loss and price the risk accurately. Second, they may be skilled at providing advice on measures that the firm can take to reduce the risk, and they may offer lower premiums to firms that take this advice. Third, an insurance company can *pool* risks by holding a large, diversified portfolio of policies. The claims on any individual policy can be highly uncertain, yet the claims on a portfolio of policies may be very stable. Of course, insurance companies cannot diversify away macroeconomic risks; firms use insurance policies to reduce their specific risk, and they find other ways to avoid macro risks.

Insurance companies also suffer some *disadvantages* in bearing risk, and these are reflected in the prices they charge. Suppose your firm owns a $1 billion offshore oil platform. A meteorologist has advised you that there is a 1-in-10,000 chance that in any year the platform will be destroyed as a result of a storm. Thus the *expected* loss from storm damage is $1 billion/10,000 = $100,000.

The risk of storm damage is almost certainly not a macroeconomic risk and can potentially be diversified away. So you might expect that an insurance company would be prepared to insure the platform against such destruction as long as the premium was sufficient to cover the expected loss.

---

[2]Many large firms insure or hedge away operating divisions' risk exposures by setting up internal, make-believe markets between each division and the treasurer's office. Trades in the internal markets are at real (external) market prices. The object is to relieve the operating managers of risks outside their control. The treasurer makes a separate decision on whether to offset the *firm's* exposure.

[3]A Texas oilman who lost hundreds of millions in ill-fated deals protested, "Why should I worry? Worry is for strong minds and weak characters." If there are any financial managers with weak minds and strong characters, we especially advise them to hedge whenever they can.

In other words, a fair premium for insuring the platform should be $100,000 a year.[4] Such a premium would make insurance a zero-NPV deal for your company. Unfortunately, no insurance company would offer a policy for only $100,000. Why not?

- *Reason 1: Administrative costs.* An insurance company, like any other business, incurs a variety of costs in arranging the insurance and handling any claims. For example, disputes about the liability for environmental damage can eat up millions of dollars in legal fees. Insurance companies need to recognize these costs when they set their premiums.

- *Reason 2: Adverse selection.* Suppose that an insurer offers life insurance policies with "no medical needed, no questions asked." There are no prizes for guessing who will be most tempted to buy this insurance. Our example is an extreme case of the problem of *adverse selection.* Unless the insurance company can distinguish between good and bad risks, the latter will always be most eager to take out insurance. Insurers increase premiums to compensate.

- *Reason 3: Moral hazard.* Two farmers met on the road to town. "George," said one, "I was sorry to hear about your barn burning down." "Shh," replied the other, "that's tomorrow night." The story is an example of another problem for insurers, known as *moral hazard.* Once a risk has been insured, the owner may be less careful to take proper precautions against damage. Insurance companies are aware of this and factor it into their pricing.

When these extra costs are small, insurance may be close to a zero-NPV transaction. When they are large, insurance may be a costly way to protect against risk.

Many insurance risks are *jump risks*; one day there is not a cloud on the horizon and the next day the hurricane hits. The risks can also be huge. For example, Hurricane Andrew, which devastated Florida, cost insurance companies $17 billion; the Northridge earthquake in California cost $12 billion.

The losses from a major natural disaster could wipe out a large proportion of the $290 billion of capital of the U.S. insurance industry. But these losses would amount to only a small fraction of the value of securities owned by U.S. investors. Therefore, insurance companies have been looking for ways to share these risks with investors. One solution is for the insurance company to issue *catastrophe bonds* (or *CAT bonds*). The payments on a CAT bond depend on whether a catastrophe occurs and how much is lost. For example, if an earthquake hits California, and claims on the insurance industry exceed some minimum, the interest or principal payments on the bond are reduced. In effect, owners of CAT bonds coinsure the insurance companies' risks.[5]

How British Petroleum (BP) Changed Its Insurance Strategy[6]

Major public companies typically buy insurance against large potential losses and self-insure against routine ones. The idea is that large losses can trigger financial distress. On the other hand,

---

[4]This is imprecise. If the premium is paid at the beginning of the year and the claim is not settled until the end, then the zero-NPV premium equals the discounted value of the expected claim or $100,000/(1 + r)$.

[5]For a discussion of CAT bonds and other techniques to spread insurance risk, see M. S. Canter, J. B. Cole, and R. L. Sandor, "Insurance Derivatives: A New Asset Class for the Capital Markets and a New Hedging Tool for the Insurance Industry," *Journal of Applied Corporate Finance* 10 (Fall 1997), pp. 69–83, and N. A. Doherty, "Financial Innovation in the Management of Catastrophe Risk," *Journal of Applied Corporate Finance* 10 (Fall 1997), pp. 84–95.

[6]Our description of BP's insurance strategy draws heavily on N. A. Doherty and C. W. Smith, Jr., "Corporate Insurance Strategy: The Case of British Petroleum," *Journal of Applied Corporate Finance* 6 (Fall 1993), pp. 4–15.

routine losses for a corporation are predictable, so there is little point paying premiums to an insurance company and receiving back a fairly constant proportion as claims.

BP has challenged this conventional wisdom. Like all oil companies, BP is exposed to a variety of potential losses. Some arise from routine events such as vehicle accidents and industrial injuries. At the other extreme, they may result from catastrophes such as a major oil spill or the loss of an offshore oil rig. In the past BP purchased considerable external insurance.[7] During the 1980s it paid out an average of $115 million a year in insurance premiums and recovered $25 million a year in claims.

Recently BP took a hard look at its insurance strategy. It decided to allow local managers to insure against routine risks, for in those cases insurance companies have an advantage in assessing and pricing risk and compete vigorously against one another. However, it decided not to insure against most losses above $10 million. For these larger, more specialized risks BP felt that insurance companies had less ability to assess risk and were less well placed to advise on safety measures. As a result, BP concluded, insurance against large risks was not competitively priced.

How much extra risk does BP assume by its decision not to insure against major losses? BP estimated that large losses of above $500 million could be expected to occur once in 30 years. But BP is a huge company with equity worth about $85 billion. So even a $500 million loss, which could throw most companies into bankruptcy, would translate after tax into a fall of less than 1 percent in the value of BP's equity. BP concluded that this was a risk worth taking. In other words, it concluded that for large, low-probability risks the stock market was a more efficient risk-absorber than the insurance industry.

BP is not the only company that has looked at the package of risks that it faces and the way that these risks should be managed. Here is how *The Economist* summarized risk management in Duke Energy:[8]

> Duke's risk managers are currently designing a model that examines different types of risk together: movements in exchange rates, changes in raw material prices, downtime caused by distribution failures, and so on. This is supposed to produce an "aggregate loss distribution," which estimates the likelihood that several events could happen at once and sink the company. With this better understanding of the company's aggregate risk, Duke's managers can make a more informed decision about how much of this potential loss should be absorbed by shareholders, how much hedged in the financial markets, and how much transferred to insurers.

HEDGING WITH FUTURES

Hedging involves taking on one risk to offset another. We will explain shortly how to set up a hedge, but first we will give some examples and describe some tools that are specially designed for hedging. These are futures, forwards, and swaps. Together with options, they are known as *derivative instruments* or *derivatives* because their value depends on the value of another asset. You can think of them as side bets on the value of the underlying asset.[9]

We start with the oldest actively traded derivative instruments, **futures contracts**. Futures were originally developed for agricultural and other commodities. For example, suppose that a wheat farmer expects to have 100,000 bushels of wheat to sell next September. If he is worried that

---

[7]However, with one or two exceptions insurance has not been available for the very largest losses of $500 million or more.

[8]"Meet the Riskmongers," *The Economist*, July 18, 1998, p. 93.

[9]"Side bet" conjures up an image of wicked speculators. Derivatives attract their share of speculators, some of whom may be wicked, but they are also used by sober and prudent businesspeople to reduce risk.

the price may decline in the interim, he can hedge by selling 100,000 bushels of September wheat futures. In this case he agrees to deliver 100,000 bushels of wheat in September at a price that is set today. Do not confuse this futures contract with an option, in which the holder has a choice whether or not to make delivery; the farmer's futures contract is a firm promise to deliver wheat.

A miller is in the opposite position. She needs to *buy* wheat after the harvest. If she would like to fix the price of this wheat ahead of time, she can do so by *buying* wheat futures. In other words, she agrees to take delivery of wheat in the future at a price that is fixed today. The miller also does not have an option; if she holds the contract to maturity, she is obliged to take delivery.

Both the farmer and the miller have less risk than before.[10] The farmer has hedged risk by *selling* wheat futures; this is termed a *short hedge*. The miller has hedged risk by *buying* wheat futures; this is known as a *long hedge*.

The price of wheat for immediate delivery is known as the *spot price*. When the farmer sells wheat futures, the price that he agrees to take for his wheat may be very different from the spot price. But as the date for delivery approaches, a futures contract becomes more and more like a spot contract and the price of the future snuggles up to the spot price.

The farmer may decide to wait until his futures contract matures and then deliver wheat to the buyer. In practice such delivery is very rare, for it is more convenient for the farmer to buy back the wheat futures just before maturity.[11] If he is properly hedged, any loss on his wheat crop will be exactly offset by the profit on his sale and subsequent repurchase of wheat futures.

Commodity and Financial Futures

Futures contracts are bought and sold on organized futures exchanges. Table 13.1 lists the principal commodity futures contracts and the exchanges on which they are traded. Notice that our farmer and miller are not the only businesses that can hedge risk with commodity futures. The lumber company and the builder can hedge against changes in lumber prices, the copper producer and the cable manufacturer can hedge against changes in copper prices, the oil producer and the trucker can hedge against changes in gasoline prices, and so on.[12]

For many firms the wide fluctuations in interest rates and exchange rates have become at least as important a source of risk as changes in commodity prices. Financial futures are similar to commodity futures, but instead of placing an order to buy or sell a commodity at a future date, you place an order to buy or sell a financial asset at a future date. Table 13.2 lists some important financial futures. It is far from complete. You can trade futures on the Thailand stock market index, the Russian rouble, Finnish government bonds, and many other financial assets.

Financial futures have been a remarkably successful innovation. They were invented in 1972; within a few years, trading in financial futures significantly exceeded trading in commodity futures.

---

[10]We oversimplify. For example, the miller won't reduce risk if bread prices vary in proportion to the postharvest wheat price. In this case the miller is in the hazardous position of having fixed her cost but not her selling price. This point is discussed in A. C. Shapiro and S. Titman, "An Integrated Approach to Corporate Risk Management," *Midland Corporate Finance Journal* 3 (Summer 1985), pp. 41–56.

[11]In the case of some of the financial futures described below, you *cannot* deliver the asset. At maturity the buyer simply receives (or pays) the difference between the spot price and the price at which he or she agreed to purchase the asset.

[12]By the time you read this, the list of futures contracts will almost certainly be out of date. Unsuccessful contracts are regularly dropped, and at any time the exchanges may be seeking approval for literally dozens of new contracts.

TABLE 13.1

The most active commodity futures and the principal exchanges on which they are traded

FUTURE	EXCHANGE	FUTURE	EXCHANGE
Barley	WPG	Orange juice	CTN
Canola	WPG	Sugar	CSCE, LIFFE
Corn	CBT, MCE		
Oats	CBT, WPG	Aluminum	LME
Rice	CBT	Copper	COMEX, LME, MCE
Wheat	CBT, KC, MCE, MPLS	Gold	COMEX
		Lead	LME
Flaxseed	WPG	Nickel	LME
Soybeans	CBT	Palladium	NYMEX
Soybean meal	CBT	Platinum	NYMEX
Soybean oil	CBT, MCE	Silver	COMEX, CBT
		Tin	LME
		Zinc	LME
Cattle	CME	California Oregon Border Electricity	NYMEX
Live hogs	CME	Crude oil	IPE, NYMEX
Pork bellies	CME	Gas oil	IPE
		Heating oil	NYMEX
Cocoa	CSCE, LIFFE	Natural gas	NYMEX
Coffee	CSCE, LIFFE	Unleaded gasoline	NYMEX
Cotton	CTN		
Lumber	CME	Freight rates	LIFFE

Key to abbreviations:

CBT	Chicago Board of Trade	LIFFE	London International Financial
CME	Chicago Mercantile Exchange		Futures and Options Exchange
COMEX	Commodity Exchange Division of NYMEX	LME	London Metal Exchange
CSCE	Coffee, Sugar and Cocoa Exchange, New York	MCE	MidAmerica Commodity Exchange
CTN	New York Cotton Exchange	MPLS	Minneapolis Grain Exchange
IPE	International Petroleum Exchange of London	NYMEX	New York Mercantile Exchange
KC	Kansas City Board of Trade	WPG	Winnipeg Commodity Exchange

The Mechanics of Futures Trading

When you buy or sell a futures contract, the price is fixed today but payment is not made until later. You will, however, be asked to put up margin in the form of either cash or Treasury bills to demonstrate that you have the money to honor your side of the bargain. As long as you earn interest on the margined securities, there is no cost to you.

In addition, futures contracts are *marked to market*. This means that each day any profits or losses on the contract are calculated; you pay the exchange any losses and receive any profits. For example,

TABLE 13.2				

Some financial futures contracts and the principal exchanges on which they are traded

U.S. Treasury bonds	CBT	3-month euro deposits	LIFFE
U.S. Treasury notes	CBT	Short sterling deposits	LIFFE
U.S. Municipal bonds	CBT	Canadian bankers' acceptances	ME
German government bonds (Bunds)	Eurex		
Japanese government bonds (JGBs)	SIMEX, TSE	Dow Jones Industrial Average	CBT
British government bonds (gilts)	LIFFE	S&P 500 Index	CME
		French equity index (CAC)	MATIF
U.S. Treasury bills	CME	German equity index (DAX)	Eurex
30-day Federal funds	CBT	Japanese equity index (Nikkei)	OSE, SIMEX
1-month LIBOR	LIFFE	UK equity index (FTSE)	LIFFE
Eurodollar deposits	CME		
Euroyen deposits	CME, SIMEX, TIFFE	Euro	CME
		Japanese yen	CME

Key to abbreviations:

CBT	Chicago Board of Trade
CME	Chicago Mercantile Exchange
LIFFE	London International Financial Futures and Options Exchange
MATIF	Marché à Terme d'Instruments Financiers
ME	Montreal Exchange
OSE	Osaka Securities Exchange
SIMEX	Singapore International Monetary Exchange
TIFFE	Tokyo International Financial Futures Exchange
TSE	Tokyo Stock Exchange

suppose that our farmer agreed to deliver 100,000 bushels of wheat at $2.80 a bushel. The next day the price of wheat futures declines to $2.75 a bushel. The farmer now has a profit on his sale of 100,000 × $.05 = $5,000. The exchange's clearinghouse therefore pays this $5,000 to the farmer. You can think of the farmer as closing out his position every day and then opening up a new position. Thus after the first day the farmer has realized a profit of $5,000 on his trade and now has an obligation to deliver wheat for $2.75 a bushel. The $.05 that the farmer has already been paid *plus* the $2.75 that remains to be paid equals the $2.80 selling price at which the farmer originally agreed to deliver wheat.

Of course, our miller is in the opposite position. The fall in the futures price leaves her with a *loss* of $.05 a bushel. She must, therefore, pay over this loss to the exchange's clearinghouse. In effect the miller closes out her initial purchase at a $.05 loss and opens a new contract to take delivery at $2.75 a bushel.[13]

---

[13]Notice that neither the farmer nor the miller need be concerned about whether the other party will honor his or her side of the bargain. The futures exchange guarantees the contract and protects itself by settling up profits and losses each day.

Spot and Futures Prices—Financial Futures

If you want to buy a security, you have a choice. You can buy it for immediate delivery at the spot price. Alternatively, you can place an order for later delivery; in this case you buy at the futures price. When you buy a financial future, you end up with exactly the same security that you would have if you bought in the spot market. However, there are two differences. First, you don't pay for the security up front, and so you can earn interest on its purchase price. Second, you miss out on any dividend or interest that is paid in the interim. This tells us something about the relationship between the spot and futures prices:[14]

$$\frac{\text{Futures price}}{(1 + r_f)^t} = \frac{\text{spot}}{\text{price}} - \text{PV}\left(\begin{array}{c}\text{dividends or}\\ \text{interest payments}\\ \text{forgone}\end{array}\right)$$

Here r_f is the t-period risk-free interest rate. An example will show how and why this formula works.

Example: Stock Index Futures Suppose six-month stock index futures trade at 1,235 when the index is 1,212. The six-month interest rate is 5 percent, and the average dividend yield of stocks in the index is 1.2 percent per year. Are these numbers consistent?

Suppose you buy the futures contract and set aside the money to exercise it. At a 5 percent annual rate, you'll earn about 2.5 percent interest over the next six months. Thus you invest

$$\frac{\text{Futures price}}{(1 + r_f)^t} = \frac{1,235}{1.025} = 1,204.9$$

What do you get in return? Everything you would have gotten by buying the index now at the spot price, except for the dividends paid over the next six months. If we assume, for simplicity, that a half-year's dividends are paid in month six (rather than evenly over six months), your payoff is

$$\text{Spot price} - \text{PV(dividends)} = 1,212 - \frac{1,212\,(.006)}{1.025} = 1,204.9$$

You get what you pay for.

Spot and Futures Prices—Commodities

The difference between buying *commodities* today and buying commodity futures is more complicated. First, because payment is again delayed, the buyer of the future earns interest on her money. Second, she does not need to store the commodities and, therefore, saves warehouse costs, wastage, and so on. On the other hand, the futures contract gives no *convenience yield*, which is the value of being able to get your hands on the real thing. The manager of a supermarket can't burn heating oil futures if there's a sudden cold snap, and he can't stock the shelves with orange juice futures if he runs out of inventory at 1 P.M. on a Saturday. All this means that for commodities,

---

[14]This relationship is strictly true only if the contract is not marked to market. Otherwise, the value of the future depends on the path of interest rates up to the delivery date. In practice this qualification is usually unimportant. See J. C. Cox, J. E. Ingersoll, and S. A. Ross, "The Relationship between Forward and Futures Prices," *Journal of Financial Economics* 9 (1981), pp. 321–346.

$$\frac{\text{Futures price}}{(1 + r_f)^t} = \text{spot price} + \text{PV}\binom{\text{storage}}{\text{costs}} - \text{PV}\binom{\text{convenience}}{\text{yield}}$$

No one would be willing to hold the futures contract at a higher futures price or to hold the commodity at a lower futures price.[15]

It's interesting to compare the formulas for futures prices of commodities to the formulas for securities. PV(convenience yield) plays the same role as PV(dividends or interest payments forgone). But financial assets cost nothing to store, so PV(storage costs) does not appear in the formula for financial futures.

You can't observe PV(convenience yield) or PV(storage) separately, but you can infer the difference between them by comparing the spot price to the discounted futures price. This difference—that is, convenience yield less storage cost—is called *net convenience yield*.

Here is an example using quotes for December 1998: At that time the spot price of wheat was about 287.5 cents per bushel. The futures price for December 1999 was 339.0 cents. Of course, if you bought and held the futures, you would pay after one year. The present value of this outlay in December 1998 was 339.0/(1.05) = 322.9 cents, using a one-year risk-free rate of 5 percent. So PV (net convenience yield) is negative at –35.4 cents per bushel:

$$\text{PV (net convenience yield)} = \text{spot price} - \frac{\text{futures price}}{1 + r_f}$$

$$= 287.5 - 322.9 = -35.4 \text{ cents}$$

Sometimes the net convenience yield is expressed as a percentage of the spot price, in this case as –35.4/287.5 = –.123, or –12.3 percent. Evidently, warehouses were full, storage costs were high, and users had no worries that they would run short of wheat in the months ahead.

Figure 13.1 plots percentage net convenience yields for copper and heating oil. Notice the seasonal pattern for oil: high net convenience yields in the winter (in the Northern Hemisphere). The spread between the spot and futures price of copper bounces around and can rise to very high levels when there are shortages or fears of an interruption of supply.[16]

FORWARD CONTRACTS

Each day billions of dollars of futures contracts are bought and sold. This liquidity is possible only because futures contracts are standardized and mature on a limited number of dates each year.

Fortunately there is usually more than one way to skin a financial cat. If the terms of futures contracts do not suit your particular needs, you may be able to buy or sell a **forward contract**. Forward contracts are simply tailor-made futures contracts. The main forward market is in foreign currency. We will discuss forward exchange rates in the next chapter.

---

[15]Our formula could overstate the futures price if no one is willing to hold the commodity, that is, if inventories fall to zero or some absolute minimum.

[16]For evidence that the net convenience yield is related to the level of inventories, see M. J. Brennan, "The Price of Convenience and the Valuation of Commodity Contingent Claims," in D. Lund and B. Øksendal (eds.), *Stochastic Models and Option Values*, North-Holland Publishing Company, Amsterdam, 1991.

Monthly convenience
yield, percent

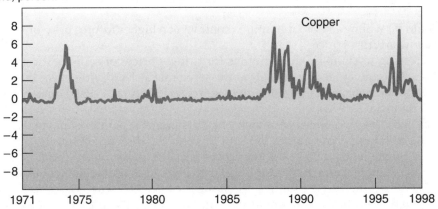

Monthly convenience
yield, percent

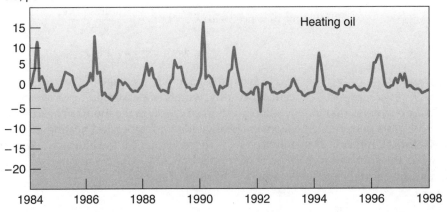

Figure 13.1

Monthly percentage net convenience yield (convenience yield *less* storage costs) for two commodities. Note the different vertical scales.

Source: R. S. Pindyck, "The Present Value Model of Rational Commodity Pricing," *Economic Journal* 103 (May 1993), pp. 511–530. We thank Li Jin for updating these plots.

It is also possible to enter into a forward interest rate contract. For example, suppose that you know that at the end of six months you are going to need a three-month loan. You worry that interest rates will rise over the six-month period. You can lock in the interest rate on that loan by buying a *forward rate agreement (FRA)* from a bank.[17] For example, the bank might offer to sell you a six-month

---

[17]Note that the party which profits from a rise in rates is described as the "buyer." In our example you would be said to "buy six against nine months" money, meaning that the forward rate agreement is for a three-month loan in six months' time.

forward rate agreement on three-month LIBOR at 7 percent.[18] If at the end of six months the three-month LIBOR rate is greater than 7 percent, the bank will pay you the difference; if three-month LIBOR is less than 7 percent, you pay the bank the difference.[19] The total principal amount of FRAs outstanding is several trillion dollars.

Homemade Forward Contracts

Suppose that you borrow $90.91 for one year at 10 percent and lend $90.91 for two years at 12 percent. These interest rates are for loans made today; therefore, they are spot interest rates.

The cash flows on your transactions are as follows:

	YEAR 0	YEAR 1	YEAR 2
Borrow for 1 year at 10%	+90.91	−100	
Lend for 2 years at 12%	−90.91		+114.04
Net cash flow	0	−100	+114.04

Notice that you do not have any net cash outflow today but you have contracted to pay out money in year 1. The interest rate on this forward commitment is 14.04 percent. To calculate this forward interest rate, we simply worked out the extra return for lending for two years rather than one:

$$\text{Forward interest rate} = \frac{(1 + 2\text{-year spot rate})^2}{1 + 1\text{-year spot rate}} - 1$$

$$= \frac{(1.12)^2}{1.10} - 1 = .1404, \text{ or } 14.04\%$$

In our example you manufactured a forward loan by borrowing short-term and lending long. But you can also run the process in reverse. If you wish to fix today the rate at which you borrow next year, you borrow long and lend the money until you need it next year.

SWAPS

Suppose that the Possum Company wishes to borrow euros to help finance its European operations. Since Possum is better known in the United States, the financial manager believes that the company can obtain more attractive terms on a dollar loan than on a euro loan. Therefore, the company issues $10 million of five-year 8 percent notes in the United States. At the same time Possum arranges with a bank to **swap** its future dollar liability for euros. Under this arrangement the bank agrees to pay Possum sufficient dollars to service its dollar loan; in exchange Possum agrees to make a series of annual payments in euros to the bank. Possum and the bank are referred to as *counterparties*.

---

[18]LIBOR (London interbank offered rate) is the interest rate at which major international banks in London lend each other dollars.

[19]Unlike futures contracts, forwards are not marked to market. Thus all profits or losses are settled when the contract matures.

Here are Possum's cash flows (in millions):

	YEAR 0		YEARS 1–4		YEAR 5	
	DOLLARS	EUROS	DOLLARS	EUROS	DOLLARS	EUROS
1. Issue dollar loan	+10		−.8		−10.8	
2. Swap dollars for euros	−10	+8.5	+.8	−.5	+10.8	−9.0
3. Net cash flow	0	+8.5	0	−.5	0	−9.0

The combined effect of Possum's two steps (line 3) is to convert an 8 percent dollar loan into a 5.9 percent euro loan. The device that makes this possible is the *currency swap*. You can think of the cash flows for the swap (line 2) as a series of forward currency contracts. In each of years 1 through 4 Possum agrees to purchase $.8 million at a cost of .5 million euros; in year 5 it agrees to buy $10.8 million at a cost of 9.0 million euros.[20]

The bank's cash flows from the swap are the reverse of Possum's. It has undertaken to pay out dollars in the future and receive euros. Since the bank is now exposed to the risk that the euro will weaken unexpectedly against the dollar, it will try to hedge this risk by engaging in a series of futures or forward contracts or by swapping euros for dollars with another counterparty. As long as Possum and the other counterparty honor their promises, the bank is fully protected against risk. The recurring nightmare for swap managers is that one party will default, leaving the bank with a large unmatched position. This is called *counterparty risk.*

Swaps are not new. For many years the British government limited purchases of foreign currency to invest abroad. These restrictions led many British firms to arrange so-called back-to-back loans. The firm would lend sterling to a company in the United States and simultaneously borrow dollars, which could then be used for foreign investment. In taking out the back-to-back loan, the British firm agreed to make a series of future dollar payments in exchange for receiving a flow of sterling income.

In 1979 these limits on overseas investment were removed, and British firms no longer needed to take out back-to-back loans. However, during the 1980s the banks did a respray job on the back-to-back loan and relaunched it as a swap. Swaps turned out to be very popular with corporate customers; in recent years some two-thirds of international dollar bond issues have been accompanied by a swap.

Swaps are not limited to future exchanges of currency. The most common form of swap is actually an *interest rate swap*, in which counterparties swap fixed-interest-rate loans for floating-rate loans. In this case one party promises to make a series of fixed annual payments in return for receiving a series of payments that are linked to the level of short-term interest rates. Sometimes swaps are used to convert between floating-rate loans that are tied to different base rates. For example, a firm might wish to swap a series of payments that are linked to the prime rate for a series of payments that are linked to the Treasury bill rate.

---

[20]Usually in a currency swap the two parties make an initial payment to each other (i.e., Possum pays the bank $10 million and receives 8.5 million euros). However, this is not necessary, and in the case of interest rate swaps that are in the *same* currency, no initial payments occur and there are no final principal repayments. Interest rate swaps are explained below.

Do-It-Yourself Interest Rate Swaps

Before we leave swaps, one more example may be helpful. We begin with a homemade fixed-to-floating interest rate swap.

Friendly Bancorp has made a five-year, $50 million loan to fund part of the construction cost of a large cogeneration project. The loan carries a fixed interest rate of 8 percent. Annual interest payments are therefore $4 million. Interest payments are made annually, and all the principal will be repaid at year 5. The bank wants to swap the $4 million, five-year annuity (the fixed interest payments) into a floating-rate annuity.

The bank could borrow at a 6 percent fixed rate for five years.[21] Therefore, the $4 million interest it receives could support a fixed-rate loan of 4/.06 = $66.67 million. This will be the *notional principal* amount of the swap.

The bank can construct the homemade swap as follows: It borrows $66.67 million at a fixed interest rate of 6 percent for five years and simultaneously lends the same amount at LIBOR. We assume that LIBOR is now 5 percent.[22] LIBOR is a short-term interest rate, so future interest receipts will fluctuate as the bank's investment is rolled over.

The net cash flows to this strategy are shown in the top panel of Table 13.3. Notice that there is no net cash flow in year 0 and that in year 5 the principal amount of the short-term investment is used to pay off the $66.67 million loan. What's left? A cash flow equal to the *difference* between the interest earned (LIBOR × 66.67) and the $4 million outlay on the fixed loan. The bank also has $4 million per year coming in from the project financing, so it has transformed that fixed payment into a floating payment keyed to LIBOR.

Of course, there's an easier way to do this, shown in the bottom panel of Table 13.3. The bank can just call a swap dealer and agree to a five-year, fixed-to-LIBOR swap on a notional principal of $66.67 million.[23] Naturally, Friendly Bancorp takes the easier route and enters the swap. Let's see what happens.

The starting payment is based on the starting LIBOR rate of 5 percent:

Bank	$\longrightarrow$	$4	$\longrightarrow$	Counterparty
Bank	$\longleftarrow$	.05 × $66.67 = $3.33	$\longleftarrow$	Counterparty
Bank	$\longrightarrow$	Net = $.67	$\longrightarrow$	Counterparty

The second payment is based on LIBOR at year 1. Suppose it increases to 6 percent:

Bank	$\longrightarrow$	$4	$\longrightarrow$	Counterparty
Bank	$\longleftarrow$	.06 × $66.67 = $4	$\longleftarrow$	Counterparty
Bank		Net = 0		Counterparty

---

[21]The spread between the bank's 6 percent borrowing rate and the 8 percent lending rate is the bank's profit on the project financing.

[22]Maybe the short-term interest rate is below the five-year interest rate because investors expect interest rates to rise.

[23]Both strategies are equivalent to a series of forward contracts on LIBOR. The forward prices are $4 million each for LIBOR$_1$ × 66.67, LIBOR$_2$ × 66.67, and so on. Separately negotiated forward prices would not be $4 million for any one year, but the PVs of the "annuities" of forward prices would be identical.

TABLE 13.3

The top part shows the cash flows to a homemade fixed-to-floating interest rate swap. The bottom part shows the cash flows to a standard swap transaction.

	YEAR				
	0	1	2	3	4	5
HOMEMADE SWAP						
1. Borrow $66.67 at 6% fixed rate	+66.67	−4	−4	−4	−4	−(4+66.67)
2. Lend $66.67 at LIBOR floating rate (initially 5%)	−66.67	+.05 ×66.67	+LIBOR$_1$ ×66.67	+LIBOR$_2$ ×66.67	+LIBOR$_3$ ×66.67	+LIBOR$_4$ ×66.67 +66.67
Net cash flow	0	−4 +.05 ×66.67	−4 +LIBOR$_1$ ×66.67	−4 +LIBOR$_2$ ×66.67	−4 +LIBOR$_3$ ×66.67	−4 +LIBOR$_4$ ×66.67
STANDARD FIXED-TO-FLOATING SWAP						
Net cash flow	0	−4 +.05 ×66.67	−4 +LIBOR$_1$ ×66.67	−4 +LIBOR$_2$ ×66.67	−4 +LIBOR$_3$ ×66.67	−4 +LIBOR$_4$ ×66.67

What about the *value* of the swap at year 2? That depends on long-term interest rates. First, suppose that they do not move, so a 6 percent note issued by the bank would still trade at par. In this case the swap still has zero value. (You can confirm this by checking that the NPV of a new three-year homemade swap is zero.) But if long rates increase, say, to 7 percent, the value of a three-year note falls to

$$PV = \frac{4}{1.07} + \frac{4}{(1.07)^2} + \frac{4 + 66.67}{(1.07)^3} = \$64.92 \text{ million}$$

Now the swap is worth 66.67 − 64.92 = $1.75 million.

How do we know the swap is worth $1.75 million? Consider the following strategy:

1. The bank can enter a new three-year swap deal in which it agrees to pay LIBOR on the same notional principal of $66.67 million.
2. In return it receives fixed payments at the new 7 percent interest rate, that is, .07 × 66.67 = $4.67 per year.

The new swap cancels the cash flows of the old one, but it generates an extra $.67 million for three years. This extra cash flow is worth

$$PV = \sum_{1}^{3} \frac{.67}{(1.07)^t} = \$1.75 \text{ million}$$

Remember, ordinary interest rate swaps have no initial cost or value (NPV = 0), but their value drifts away from zero as time passes and long-term interest rates change. One counterparty wins as the other loses.

Credit Derivatives

In recent years there has been considerable growth in the use of *credit derivatives*, which protect lenders against the risk that a borrower will default. For example, bank A may be reluctant to refuse a loan to a major customer (customer X) but may be concerned about the total size of its exposure to that customer. Bank A can go ahead with the loan, but use credit derivatives to shuffle off the risk to bank B.

The most common credit derivative is known as a *default swap*. It works as follows. Bank A promises to pay a fixed sum each year to B as long as company X has not defaulted on its debts. If X defaults, B makes a large payment to A, but otherwise pays nothing. Thus you can think of B as providing A with long-term insurance against default in return for an annual insurance premium.[24]

HOW TO SET UP A HEDGE

In each of our examples of hedging the firm has offset the risk by buying one asset and selling an equal amount of another asset. For example, our farmer owned 100,000 bushels of wheat and sold 100,000 bushels of wheat futures. As long as the wheat that the farmer owns is identical to the wheat that he has promised to deliver, this strategy minimizes risk.

In practice the wheat that the farmer owns and the wheat that he sells in the futures markets are unlikely to be identical. For example, if he sells wheat futures on the Kansas City exchange, he agrees to deliver hard, red winter wheat in Kansas City in September. But perhaps he is growing northern spring wheat many miles from Kansas City; in this case the prices of the two wheats will not move exactly together.

Figure 13.2 shows how changes in the prices of the two types of wheat may have been related in the past. Notice two things about this figure. First, the scatter of points suggests that the price changes are imperfectly related. If so, it is not possible to construct a hedge that eliminates all risk. Some residual, or *basis*, risk will remain. Second, the slope of the fitted line shows that a 1 percent change in the price of Kansas wheat was on average associated with an .8 percent change in the price of the farmer's wheat. Because the price of the farmer's wheat is relatively insensitive to changes in Kansas prices, he needs to sell $.8 \times 100,000$ bushels of wheat futures to minimize risk.

Let us generalize. Suppose that you already own an asset, A (e.g., wheat), and that you wish to hedge against changes in the value of A by making an offsetting sale of another asset, B (e.g., wheat futures). Suppose also that percentage changes in the value of A are related in the following way to percentage changes in the value of B:

$$\begin{matrix} \text{Expected change} \\ \text{in value of A} \end{matrix} = a + \delta \begin{pmatrix} \text{change in} \\ \text{value of B} \end{pmatrix}$$

Delta (δ) measures the sensitivity of A to changes in the value of B. It is also equal to the *hedge ratio*—that is, the number of units of B which should be sold to hedge the purchase of A. You minimize risk if you offset your position in A by the sale of delta units of B.[25]

---

[24]Another form of credit derivative is the credit option. In this case A would pay an upfront premium and B would assume the obligation to pay A in the event of X's default.

[25]Notice that A, the item that you wish to hedge, is the dependent variable. Delta measures the sensitivity of A to changes in B.

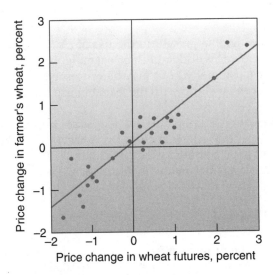

Figure 13.2

Hypothetical plot of past changes in the price of the farmer's wheat against changes in the price of Kansas City wheat futures. A 1 percent change in the futures price implies, on average, an .8 percent change in the price of the farmer's wheat.

The trick in setting up a hedge is to estimate the delta or hedge ratio. This often calls for a strong dose of judgment. For example, suppose that Antarctic Air would like to protect itself against a hike in oil prices. As the financial manager, you need to decide how much a rise in oil prices would affect firm value. Suppose the company spent $200 million on fuel last year. Other things equal, a 10 percent increase in the price of oil will cost the company an extra .1 × 200 = $20 million. But perhaps you can partially offset the higher costs by higher ticket prices, in which case earnings will fall by *less* than $20 million. Or perhaps an oil price rise will lead to a slowdown in business activity and therefore lower passenger numbers. In that case earnings will decline by *more* than $20 million. Working out the likely effect on firm *value* is even more tricky, because that depends on whether the rise is likely to be permanent. Perhaps the price rise will induce an increase in production or encourage consumers to economize on energy usage.

Sometimes in such cases some past history may help. For example, you could look at how firm value changed in the past as oil prices changed. In other cases it may be possible to call on a little theory to set up the hedge.

Using Theory to Set Up the Hedge: An Example

Potterton Leasing has just purchased some equipment and arranged to rent it out for $2 million a year over eight years. At an interest rate of 12 percent, Potterton's rental income has a present value of $9.94 million:[26]

---

[26]We ignore taxes in this example.

$$PV = \frac{2}{1.12} + \frac{2}{(1.12)^2} + \cdots + \frac{2}{(1.12)^8} = \$9.94 \text{ million}$$

Potterton proposes to finance the deal by issuing a package of $1.91 million of one-year debt and $8.03 million of six-year debt, each with a 12 percent coupon. Think of its new asset (the stream of rental income) and the new liability (the issue of debt) as a package. Does Potterton stand to gain or lose on this package if interest rates change?

To answer this question, it is helpful to go back to the concept of duration that we introduced in Chapter 10. Duration, you may remember, is the weighted-average time to each cash flow. Duration is important because it is directly related to volatility. If two assets have the same duration, their prices will be equally affected by any change in interest rates. If we call the total value of Potterton's rental income V, then the duration of Potterton's rental income is calculated as follows:

$$\text{Duration} = \frac{1}{V}\{[PV(C_1) \times 1] + [PV(C_2) \times 2] + [PV(C_3) \times 3] + \cdots\}$$

$$= \frac{1}{9.94}\left\{\left[\frac{2}{1.12} \times 1\right] + \left[\frac{2}{(1.12)^2} \times 2\right] + \cdots + \left[\frac{2}{(1.12)^8} \times 8\right]\right\}$$

$$= 3.9 \text{ years}$$

We can also calculate the duration of Potterton's new liabilities. The duration of the 1-year debt is 1 year, and the duration of the 6-year debt is 4.6 years. The duration of the package of 1- and 6-year debt is a weighted average of the durations of the individual issues:

$$\text{Duration of liability} = (1.91 / 9.94) \times \text{duration of 1-year debt}$$

$$+ (8.03 / 9.94) \times \text{duration of 6-year debt}$$

$$= (.192 \times 1) + (.808 \times 4.6) = 3.9 \text{ years}$$

Thus, both the asset (the lease) and the liability (the debt package) have a duration of 3.9 years. Therefore, both are affected equally by a change in interest rates. If rates rise, the present value of Potterton's rental income will decline, but the value of its debt obligation will also decline by the same amount. By equalizing the duration of the asset and that of the liability, Potterton has *immunized* itself against any change in interest rates. It looks as if Potterton's financial manager knows a thing or two about hedging.

When Potterton set up the hedge, it needed to find a package of loans that had a present value of $9.94 million and a duration of 3.9 years. Call the proportion of the proceeds raised by the six-year loan x and the proportion raised by the one-year loan $(1 - x)$. Then

$$\begin{matrix}\text{Duration of} \\ \text{package}\end{matrix} = (x \times \text{duration of 6-year loan}) + [(1 - x) \times \text{duration of 1-year loan}]$$

$$3.9 \text{ years} = (x \times 4.6 \text{ years}) + [(1 - x) \times 1 \text{ year}]$$

$$x = .808$$

Since the package of loans must raise $9.94 million, Potterton needs to issue $.808 \times 9.94 = \$8.03$ million of the six-year loan.

An important feature of this hedge is that it is dynamic. As interest rates change and time passes, the duration of Potterton's asset may no longer be the same as that of its liability. Thus, to remain hedged against interest rate changes, Potterton must be prepared to keep adjusting the duration of its debt.

If Potterton is not disposed to follow this dynamic hedging strategy, it has an alternative. It can devise a debt issue whose cash flows exactly match the rental income from the lease. For example, suppose that it issues an eight-year sinking fund bond; the amount of the sinking fund is $810,000 in year 1, and the payment increases by 12 percent annually. Table 13.4 shows that the bond payments (interest plus sinking fund) are $2 million in each year.

Since the cash flows on the asset exactly match those on the liability, Potterton's financial manager can now relax. Each year the manager simply collects the $2 million rental income and hands it to the bondholders. Whatever happens to interest rates, the firm is always perfectly hedged.

Why wouldn't Potterton's financial manager *always* prefer to construct matching assets and liabilities? One reason is that it may be relatively costly to devise a bond with a specially tailored pattern of cash flows. Another may be that Potterton is continually entering into new lease agreements and issuing new debt. In this case the manager can never relax; it may be simpler to keep the durations of the assets and liabilities equal than to maintain an exact match between the cash flows.

Options, Deltas, and Betas

Here's another case where some theory can help you set up a hedge. In Chapter 8 we came across options. These give you the right, but not the obligation, to buy or sell an asset. Options are derivatives; their value depends only on what happens to the price of the underlying asset.

The *option delta* summarizes the link between the option and the asset. For example, if you own an option to buy a share of Walt Disney stock, the change in the value of your investment will be the same as it would be if you held delta shares of Disney.

Since the option price is tied to the asset price, options can be used for hedging. Thus, if you own an option to buy a share of Disney and at the same time you sell delta shares of Disney, any change in the value of your position in the stock will be exactly offset by the change in the value of your option position.[27] In other words, you will be perfectly hedged—hedged, that is, for the next short period of time. Option deltas change as the stock price changes and time passes. Therefore, option-based hedges need to be adjusted frequently.

Options can be used to hedge commodities too. The miller could offset changes in the cost of future wheat purchases by buying call options on wheat (or on wheat futures). But this is not the simplest strategy if the miller is trying to lock in the future cost of wheat. She would have to check the option delta to determine how many options to buy, and she would have to keep track of changes in the option delta and reset the hedge as necessary.

It's the same for financial assets. Suppose you hold a well-diversified portfolio of stocks with a beta of 1.0 and near-perfect correlation with the market return. You want to lock in the portfolio's value at year-end. You could accomplish this by selling call options on the index, but to maintain the hedge, the option position would have to be adjusted frequently. It's simpler just to sell index futures maturing at year-end. But if you wish to lock in the price of an individual stock, you will probably hedge with options, since futures contracts trade only on market indexes.

Speaking of betas . . . what if your portfolio has a beta of .60, not 1.0? Then your hedge will require 40 percent fewer index futures contracts. And since your low-beta portfolio is probably not

---

[27]We are assuming that you hold one option and hedge by selling δ shares. If you owned one share and wanted to hedge by selling options, you would need to sell $1/\delta$ options.

TABLE 13.4								

Potterton can hedge by issuing this sinking fund bond that pays out $2 million each year

	CASH FLOWS ($ MILLIONS)							
	YEAR							
	1	2	3	4	5	6	7	8
Balance at start of year	9.94	9.13	8.23	7.22	6.08	4.81	3.39	1.79
Interest at 12%	1.19	1.10	.99	.87	.73	.58	.40	.21
Sinking fund payment	.81	.90	1.01	1.13	1.27	1.42	1.60	1.79
Interest plus sinking fund payment	2.00	2.00	2.00	2.00	2.00	2.00	2.00	2.00

perfectly correlated with the market, there will be some basis risk as well. In this context our old friend beta (β) and the hedge ratio (δ) are one and the same. Remember, to hedge A with B, you need to know δ because

$$\text{Expected change in value of A} = a + \delta(\text{change in value of B})$$

When A is a stock or portfolio, and B is the market, we estimate beta from the same relationship:

$$\text{Expected change in stock or portfolio value} = a + \beta(\text{change in market index})$$

IS "DERIVATIVE" A FOUR-LETTER WORD?

Our earlier example of the farmer and miller showed how futures may be used to reduce business risk. However, if you were to copy the farmer and sell wheat futures without an offsetting holding of wheat, you would not be *reducing* risk: You would be *speculating*.

Speculators in search of large profits (and prepared to tolerate large losses) are attracted by the leverage that derivatives provide. By this we mean that it is not necessary to lay out much money up front and the profits or losses may be many times the initial outlay.[28] "Speculation" has an ugly ring, but a successful derivatives market needs speculators who are prepared to take on risk and provide more cautious people like our farmer and miller with the protection they need. For example, if an excess of farmers wish to sell wheat futures, the price of futures will be forced down until enough speculators are tempted to buy in the hope of a profit. If there is a surplus of millers wishing to buy wheat futures, the reverse will happen. The price of wheat futures will be forced *up* until speculators are drawn in to sell.

---

[28]For example, if you buy or sell forward, no money changes hands until the contract matures, though you may be required to put up margin to show that you can honor your commitment. This margin does not need to be cash; it can be in the form of safe securities.

Speculation may be necessary to a thriving derivatives market, but it can get companies into serious trouble. For example, the Japanese company Showa Shell reported a loss of $1.5 billion on positions in foreign exchange futures. Sumitomo Bank lost over $2 billion when a rogue Sumitomo trader tried to buy enough copper to control that market.[29] The German metals and oil trading company Metallgesellschaft took a loss of about $1.3 billion from oil futures and Procter & Gamble lost $157 million on swap positions.[30] Banks also have had their share of derivative losses. In 1995 Baring Brothers, a blue-chip British merchant bank with a 200-year history, became insolvent. The reason: A trader in its Singapore office had placed very large bets on the Japanese stock market index resulting in losses of $1.4 billion.

These tales of woe have some cautionary messages for corporations. During the 1970s and 1980s many firms turned their treasury operations into profit centers and proudly announced their profits from trading in financial instruments. But it is not possible to make large profits in financial markets without also taking large risks, so these profits should have served as a warning rather than a matter for congratulation.

A Boeing 747 weighs 400 tons, flies at nearly 600 miles per hour, and is inherently very dangerous. But we don't ground 747s; we just take precautions to ensure that they are flown with care. Similarly, it is foolish to suggest that firms should ban the use of derivatives, but it makes obvious sense to take precautions against their misuse. Here are two bits of horse sense:

- *Precaution 1.* Don't be taken by surprise. By this we mean that senior management needs to monitor regularly the value of the firm's derivatives positions and to know what bets the firm has placed. At its simplest, this might involve asking what would happen if interest rates or exchange rates were to change by 1 percent. But large banks and consultants have also developed sophisticated models for measuring the risk of derivatives positions. J.P. Morgan, for example, offers corporate clients its *RiskMetrics* software to keep track of their risk.

- *Precaution 2.* Place bets only when you have some comparative advantage that ensures the odds are in your favor. If a bank were to announce that it was drilling for oil or launching a new soap powder, you would rightly be suspicious about whether it had what it takes to succeed. Conversely, when an industrial corporation places large bets on interest rates or exchange rates, it is competing against some highly paid pros in banks and other financial institutions. Unless it is better informed than they are about future interest rates or exchange rates, it should use derivatives for hedging, not for speculation.

Imprudent speculation in derivatives is undoubtedly an issue of concern for the company's shareholders, but is it a matter for more general concern? Some people believe so. They point to the huge volume of trading in derivatives and argue that speculative losses could lead to major defaults that might threaten the whole financial system. These worries have led to calls for increased regulation of derivatives markets.

Now, this is not the place for a discussion of regulation, but we should warn you about careless measures of the size of the derivatives markets and the possible losses. In April 1998 the worldwide turnover in derivatives (other than forward exchange) averaged $1.7 *trillion* a day.[31] This is a very large sum, but it tells you *nothing* about the money that was being put at risk. For example, suppose that a

---

[29]The attempt failed, and the company later agreed to pay $150 million more in fines and restitution. The trader is in jail in Japan.

[30]We should be cautious, however, not to fall into the trap of assuming that losses on derivatives positions always indicate speculation. If those derivatives form part of a hedge, there should be offsetting profits from other assets.

[31]Bank of International Settlements, *Central Bank Survey of Foreign Exchange and Derivatives Market Activity in April 1998: Preliminary Global Data*, October 19, 1998.

bank enters into a $10 million interest rate swap and the other party goes bankrupt the next day. How much has the bank lost? Nothing. It hasn't paid anything up front; the two parties simply promised to pay sums to each other in the future. Now the deal is off.

Suppose that the other party does not go bankrupt until a year after the bank entered into the swap. In the meantime interest rates have moved in the bank's favor, so it should be receiving more money from the swap than it is paying out. When the other side defaults on the deal, the bank loses the difference between the interest that it is due to receive and the interest that it should pay. But it doesn't lose $10 million.[32]

The only meaningful measure of the potential loss from default is the amount that it would cost firms showing a profit to replace their swap positions. This figure is only a small fraction of the principal amount of swaps outstanding.[33]

SUMMARY

As a manager, you are paid to take risks, but you are not paid to take *any* risks. Some are simply bad bets, and others could jeopardize the success of the firm. In these cases you should look for ways to insure or hedge.

Most businesses take out insurance against a variety of risks. Insurance companies have considerable expertise in assessing risk and may be able to pool risks by holding a diversified portfolio. Insurance works less well when the insurance policy attracts only the worst risks (*adverse selection*) or when the insured firm is tempted to skip on maintenance and safety procedures (*moral hazard*).

Insurance is generally purchased from specialist insurance companies, but sometimes firms issue specialized securities instead. CAT (catastrophe) bonds are an example.

The idea behind hedging is straightforward. You find two closely related assets. You then buy one and sell the other in proportions that minimize the risk of your net position. If the assets are *perfectly* correlated, you can make the net position risk-free.

The trick is to find the hedge ratio or delta—that is, the number of units of one asset that is needed to offset changes in the value of the other asset. Sometimes the best solution is to look at how the prices of the two assets have moved together in the past. For example, suppose you observe that a 1 percent change in the value of B has been accompanied on average by a 2 percent change in the value of A. Then delta equals 2.0; to hedge each dollar invested in A, you need to sell two dollars of B.

On other occasions a little theory can help to set up the hedge. For example, the effect of a change in interest rates on an asset's value depends on the asset's duration. If two assets have the same duration, they will be equally affected by fluctuations in interest rates.

Many of the hedges described in this chapter are static. Once you have set up the hedge, you can take a long vacation, confident that the firm is well protected. However, some hedges, such as those that match durations, are dynamic. As time passes and prices change, you need to rebalance your position to maintain the hedge.

---

[32]This does not mean that firms don't worry about the possibility of default, and there are a variety of ways that they try to protect themselves. In the case of swaps, firms are reluctant to deal with banks that do not have the highest credit rating.

[33]United States General Accounting Office, "Financial Derivatives: Actions Needed to Protect the Financial System," report to congressional requesters, May 1994. This does not mean that swaps have *increased* risk. If counterparties use swaps to hedge risk, they are *less likely* to default.

Firms use a number of tools to hedge:

1. Futures contracts are advance orders to buy or sell an asset. The price is fixed today, but the final payment does not occur until the delivery date. The futures markets allow firms to place advance orders for dozens of different commodities, securities, and currencies.

2. Futures contracts are highly standardized and are traded in huge volumes on the futures exchanges. Instead of buying or selling a standardized futures contract, you may be able to arrange a tailor-made contract with a bank. These tailor-made futures contracts are called forward contracts. Firms regularly protect themselves against exchange rate changes by buying or selling forward currency contracts. Forward rate agreements (FRAs) provide protection against interest rate changes.

3. It is also possible to construct homemade forward contracts. For example, if you borrow for two years and at the same time lend for one year, you have effectively taken out a forward loan.

4. In recent years firms have entered into a variety of swap arrangements. For example, a firm may arrange for the bank to make all the future payments on its dollar debt in exchange for paying the bank the cost of servicing a euro loan.

Instead of using derivatives for hedging, some companies have decided that speculation is more fun, and this has sometimes got them into serious trouble. We do not believe that such speculation makes sense for an industrial company, but we caution against the view that derivatives are a threat to the financial system.

Further Reading

Two general articles on corporate risk management are:
C. W. Smith and R. M. Stultz: "The Determinants of Firms' Hedging Policies," *Journal of Financial and Quantitative Analysis*, 20:391–405 (December 1985).

K. A. Froot, D. Scharfstein, and J. C. Stein: "A Framework for Risk Management," *Journal of Applied Corporate Finance*, 7:22–32 (Fall 1994).

Schaefer's paper is a useful review of how duration measures are used to immunize fixed liabilities:
S. M. Schaefer: "Immunisation and Duration: A Review of Theory, Performance and Applications," *Midland Corporate Finance Journal*, 3:41–58 (Autumn 1984).

The texts that we cited in the readings for Chapter 8 cover futures and swaps as well as options. There are also some useful texts that focus on futures and swaps. They include:
D. Duffie: *Futures Markets*, Prentice-Hall, Inc., Englewood Cliffs, N.J. 1989.

D. R. Siegel and D. F. Siegel: *Futures Markets*, Dryden Press, Chicago, 1990.

C. W. Smith, C. H. Smithson, and D. S. Wilford: *Managing Financial Risk*, 3d ed., McGraw-Hill, Inc., New York, 1990.

CIBC Wood Gundy Financial Products publishes a Yearbook *on* Managing Financial Risk. *It can be reached electronically at* www:schoolfp.cibc.com.

The Metallgesellschaft debacle makes fascinating reading. The following three papers cover all sides of the debate:
C. Culp and M. H. Miller: "Metallgesellschaft and the Economics of Synthetic Storage," *Journal of Applied Corporate Finance*, 7:62–76 (Winter 1995).

F. Edwards: "The Collapse of Metallgesellschaft: Unhedgeable Risks, Poor Hedging Strategy, or Just Bad Luck?" *Journal of Futures Markets*, 15 (May 1995).

A. Mello and J. Parsons: "Maturity Structure of a Hedge Matters: Lessons from the Metallgesellschaft Debacle," *Journal of Applied Corporate Finance*, 7 (Spring 1995).

MANAGING INTERNATIONAL RISKS

I n the last chapter we considered the risks that flow from changes in interest rates and commodity prices. But companies with substantial overseas interests encounter a variety of other hazards, including political risks and currency fluctuations. *Political risk* means the possibility that a hostile foreign government will expropriate your business without compensation or not allow profits to be taken out of the country.

To understand currency risk, you first need to understand how the foreign exchange market works and how prices for foreign currency are determined. We therefore start this chapter with some basic institutional detail about the foreign exchange market and we will look at some simple theories that link exchange rates, interest rates, and inflation. We will use these theories to show how firms assess and hedge their foreign currency exposure.

Financial managers do not need to forecast exchange rates in order to evaluate overseas investment proposals. They can simply forecast the foreign currency cash flows and discount these flows at the foreign currency cost of capital. In this chapter we will explain *why* this rule makes sense. It turns out that it is the ability to hedge foreign exchange risk that allows companies to ignore future exchange rates when making investment decisions.

We conclude the chapter with a discussion of political risk. We show that, while companies cannot restrain a determined foreign government, they can structure their operations to reduce the risk of hostile actions.

THE FOREIGN EXCHANGE MARKET

An American company that imports goods from France may need to buy euros in order to pay for the purchase. An American company exporting to France may receive euros, which it sells in exchange for dollars. Both firms make use of the foreign exchange market.

The foreign exchange market has no central marketplace. Business is conducted electronically. The principal dealers are the larger commercial banks and investment banks. A corporation that wants to buy or sell currency usually does so through a commercial bank. Turnover in the foreign exchange market is huge. In London in April 1998 $637 billion of currency changed hands each day. That is equivalent to an annual turnover of $159 trillion ($159,000,000,000,000). New York and Tokyo together accounted for a further $500 billion of turnover per day.

Table 14.1 is adapted from the table of exchange rates in the *Financial Times*. It shows exchange rates on the first day that the euro started to trade.[1] Exchange rates are generally expressed in terms of the number of units of the foreign currency needed to buy one U.S. dollar. This is termed an *indirect quote*. In the first column of Table 14.1, the indirect quote for the yen shows that you can buy 112.645 yen for $1. This is often written as ¥112.645/$.

A *direct* exchange rate quote states how many dollars you can buy for one unit of foreign currency. The euro and the British pound sterling are usually shown as direct quotes.[2] For example, Table 14.1 shows that €1 is equivalent to $1.1799 or, more concisely, $1.1799/€. If €1 buys $1.1799, then $1 must buy 1/1.1799 = €.8475. Thus the indirect quote for the euro is €.8475/$.

The exchange rates in the first column of Table 14.1 are the prices of currency for immediate delivery. These are known as **spot rates of exchange**. The spot rate for the yen is ¥112.645/$, and the spot rate for the euro is $1.1799/€.

In addition to the spot exchange market, there is a *forward market*. In the forward market you buy and sell currency for future delivery. If you know that you are going to pay out or receive foreign currency at some future date, you can insure yourself against loss by buying or selling forward. Thus, if you need one million yen in three months, you can enter into a three-month *forward contract*. The **forward rate** on this contract is the price you agree to pay in three months when the one million yen are delivered. If you look again at Table 14.1, you will see that the three-month forward rate for the yen is quoted at ¥111.300. If you buy yen for three months' delivery, you get fewer yen for your dollar than if you buy them spot. In this case the yen is said to trade at a forward *premium* relative to the dollar, because forward yen are more expensive than spot ones. Expressed as an annual rate, the forward premium is

$$4 \times \frac{112.645 - 111.300}{111.300} \times 100 = 4.8\%$$

You could also say that the dollar was selling at a 4.8 percent *forward discount*.

A forward purchase or sale is a made-to-measure transaction between you and the bank. It can be for any currency, any amount, and any delivery day. You could buy, say, 99,999 Vietnamese dong or Haitian gourdes for a year and a day forward as long as you can find a bank ready to deal. Most forward transactions are for six months or less, but banks are prepared to buy and sell the major currencies for several years forward.[3]

---

[1]The euro is the common currency of the European Monetary Union. The initial 11 members of the Union are Austria, Belgium, Finland, France, Germany, Ireland, Italy, Luxembourg, Netherlands, Portugal, and Spain.

[2]Foreign exchange dealers usually refer to the exchange rate between pounds and dollars as *cable*. In Table 14.1 cable is 1.6599.

[3]Forward and spot trades are often undertaken together. For example, a company might need the use of Japanese yen for one month. In this case it would buy the yen spot and simultaneously sell them forward. This is known as a *swap* trade, but do not confuse it with the longer-term interest rate and currency swaps described in Chapter 13.

TABLE 14.1			

Spot and forward exchange rates, January 4,1999

		FORWARD RATE*		
	SPOT RATE*	1 MONTH	3 MONTHS	1 YEAR
Europe:				
EMU (euro)	1.1799	1.1819	1.1854	1.2026
Greece (drachma)	276.920	278.345	280.745	289.77
Norway (krone)	7.5025	7.5239	7.5550	7.6075
Sweden (krona)	8.0305	8.019	7.998	7.904
Switzerland (franc)	1.3683	1.3635	1.3560	1.3242
United Kingdom (pound)	1.6599	1.6581	1.6557	1.6531
Americas:				
Canada (dollar)	1.5251	1.5250	1.5247	1.5218
Mexico	9.8400	10.085	10.4875	12.3600
Pacific:				
Australia (dollar)	1.6159	1.6151	1.6125	1.6018
Hong Kong (dollar)	7.7465	7.7473	7.7530	7.8585
Indonesia (rupiah)	8000	8225	8637.5	9950
Japan (yen)	112.645	112.155	111.300	107.495
New Zealand (dollar)	1.8838	1.8869	1.8923	1.9111
Singapore (dollar)	1.6599	1.6549	1.6474	1.6524

*Rates show the number of units of foreign currency per dollar, except for the euro and the U.K. pound, which show the number of dollars per unit of foreign currency.

Source: Financial Times, January 5, 1999.

There is also an organized market for currency for future delivery known as the currency *futures* market. Futures contracts are highly standardized; they exist only for the main currencies, and they are for specified amounts and for a limited choice of delivery dates.[4]

When you buy a forward or futures contract, you are committed to taking delivery of the currency. As an alternative, you can take out an *option* to buy or sell currency in the future at a price that is fixed today. Made-to-measure currency options can be bought from the major banks, and standardized options are traded on the options exchanges.[5]

---

[4]See Chapter 13 for a further discussion of the difference between forward and futures contracts.

[5]Some investment banks have also made one-off issues of currency warrants (i.e., long-term options to buy currency).

Finally, you can agree with the bank that you will buy foreign currency in the future at whatever is the prevailing spot rate *but subject to maximum and minimum prices*. If the value of the foreign currency rises sharply, you buy at the agreed upper limit; if it falls sharply, you buy at the lower limit.[6]

SOME BASIC RELATIONSHIPS

You can't develop a consistent international financial policy until you understand the reasons for the differences in exchange rates and interest rates. Therefore let us consider the following four problems:

- *Problem 1.* Why is the dollar rate of interest ($r_\$$) different from, say, the yen rate ($r_¥$)?
- *Problem 2.* Why is the forward rate of exchange ($f_{¥/\$}$) different from the spot rate ($s_{¥/\$}$)?
- *Problem 3.* What determines next year's expected spot rate of exchange between dollars and yen [$E(r_{¥/\$})$]?
- *Problem 4.* What is the relationship between the inflation rate in the United States ($i_\$$) and the inflation rate in Japan ($i_¥$)?

Suppose that individuals were not worried about risk and that there were no barriers or costs to international trade. In that case the spot exchange rates, forward exchange rates, interest rates, and inflation rates would stand in the following simple relationship to one another:

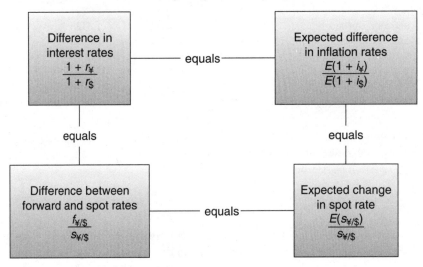

Why should this be so?

Interest Rates and Exchange Rates

It is January 1999 and you have $1 million to invest for one year. U.S. dollar deposits are offering an interest rate of about 5 percent; Japanese yen deposits are offering a meager .25 percent. Where should you put your money? Does the answer sound obvious? Let's check:

---

[6]This contract is equivalent to buying forward currency, buying a put option on the currency with an exercise price equal to the lower limit, and selling a call with an exercise price equal to the upper limit. Here's a chance to review your knowledge of options by checking this out with a position diagram. See Chapter 8 if you need a review.

- *Dollar loan.* The rate of interest on one-year dollar deposits is 5.0 percent. Therefore at the end of the year you get $1,000,000 \times 1.05 = \$1,050,000$.

- *Yen loan.* The current exchange rate is ¥112.645/\$. For \$1 million, you can buy $1,000,000 \times 112.645 =$ ¥112,645,000. The rate of interest on a one-year yen deposit is .25 percent. Therefore at the end of the year you get $112,645,000 \times 1.0025 =$ ¥112,927,000. Of course, you don't know what the exchange rate is going to be in one year's time. But that doesn't matter. You can fix today the price at which you sell your yen. The one-year forward rate is ¥107.495/\$. Therefore, by selling forward, you can make sure that you will receive $112,927,000/107.495 = \$1,050,500$ at the end of the year.

Thus, the two investments offer almost exactly the same rate of return.[7] They have to—they are both risk-free. If the domestic interest rate were different from the *covered* foreign rate, you would have a money machine.

When you make the yen loan, you receive a lower interest rate. But you get an offsetting gain because you sell yen forward at a higher price than you pay for them today. The interest rate differential is

$$\frac{1 + r_{¥}}{1 + r_{\$}}$$

And the differential between the forward and spot exchange rates is

$$\frac{f_{¥/\$}}{s_{¥/\$}}$$

Interest rate parity theory says that the difference in interest rates must equal the difference between the forward and spot exchange rates:

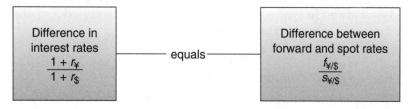

In our example,

$$\frac{1.0025}{1.05} = \frac{107.495}{112.645}$$

The Forward Premium and Changes in Spot Rates

Now let's consider how the forward premium is related to changes in spot rates of exchange. If people didn't care about risk, the forward rate of exchange would depend solely on what people expected the spot rate to be. For example, if the one-year forward rate on yen is ¥107.495/\$, that could only be because traders expect the spot rate in one year's time to be ¥107.495/\$. If they expected it to be, say, ¥120/\$, nobody would be willing to buy yen forward. They could get more yen for their dollar by waiting and buying spot.

---

[7]The minor difference in our calculated end-of-year payoffs was mostly due to rounding in the interest rates.

Therefore the *expectations theory* of exchange rates tells us that the percentage difference between the forward rate and today's spot rate is equal to the expected change in the spot rate:

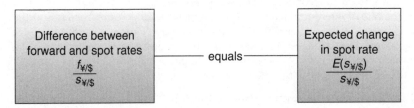

Of course, this assumes that traders don't care about risk. If they do care, the forward rate can be either higher or lower than the expected spot rate. For example, suppose that you have contracted to receive one million yen in three months, You can wait until you receive the money before you change it into dollars, but this leaves you open to the risk that the price of yen may fall over the next three months. Your alternative is to sell yen forward. In this case, you are fixing today the price at which you will sell your yen. Since you avoid risk by selling forward, you may be willing to do so even if the forward price of yen is a little *lower* than the expected spot price.

Other companies may be in the opposite position. They may have contracted to pay out yen in three months. They can wait until the end of the three months and then buy yen, but this leaves them open to the risk that the price of yen may rise. It is safer for these companies to fix the price today by *buying* yen forward. These companies may, therefore, be willing to buy forward even if the forward price of yen is a little *higher* than the expected spot price.

Thus some companies find it safer to *sell* yen forward, while others find it safer to *buy* yen forward. When the first group predominates, the forward price of yen is likely to be less than the expected spot price. When the second group predominates, the forward price is likely to be greater than the expected spot price. On average you would expect the forward price to underestimate the expected spot price just about as often as it overestimates it.

Changes in the Exchange Rate and Inflation Rates

Now we come to the third side of our quadrilateral—the relationship between changes in the spot exchange rate and inflation rates. Suppose that you notice that silver can be bought in the United States for $5.00 a troy ounce and sold in Japan for ¥675. You think you may be onto a good thing. You decide to buy silver for $5.00 and put it on the first plane to Tokyo, where you sell it for ¥675. Then you exchange your ¥675 for 675/112.645 = $5.99. You have made a gross profit of $.99 an ounce. Of course, you have to pay transportation and insurance costs out of this, but there should still be something left over for you.

Money machines don't exist—not for long, anyway. As others notice the disparity between the price of silver in Japan and the price in the United States, the price will be forced down in Japan and up in the United States until the profit opportunity disappears. Arbitrage ensures that the dollar price of silver is about the same in the two countries.

Of course, silver is a standard and easily transportable commodity, but the same forces should act to equalize the domestic and foreign prices of other goods. Those goods that can be bought more cheaply abroad will be imported, and that will force down the price of domestic products. Similarly, those goods that can be bought more cheaply in the United States will be exported, and that will force down the price of the foreign products.

This is often called *purchasing power parity*.[8] Just as the price of goods in Safeway must be roughly the same as the price of goods in A&P, so the price of goods in Japan when converted into dollars must be roughly the same as the price in the United States:

$$\text{Dollar price of goods in the USA} = \frac{\text{yen price of goods in Japan}}{\text{number of yen per dollar}}$$

Purchasing power parity implies that any differences in the rates of inflation will be offset by a change in the exchange rate. For example, if prices are rising by 2 percent in the United States, while they are declining by 2.5 percent in Japan, the number of yen that you can buy for $1 must fall by .975/1.02 − 1, or about 4.5 percent. Therefore purchasing power parity says that in order to estimate changes in the spot rate of exchange, you need to estimate differences in inflation rates:[9]

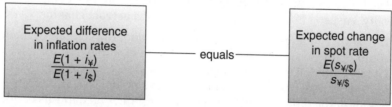

In our example,

$$\text{Current spot rate} \times \text{expected difference in inflation rates} = \text{expected spot rate}$$

112.645	× .975 / 1.02	= 107.68

Interest Rates and Inflation Rates

Now for the fourth leg! Just as water always flows downhill, so capital tends to flow where returns are greatest. But investors are not interested in *nominal* returns; they care about what their money will buy. So, if investors notice that real interest rates are higher in Japan than the United States, they will shift their savings into Japan until the expected real returns are the same in the two countries. If the expected real interest rates are equal, then the difference in money rates must be equal to the difference in the expected inflation rates:[10]

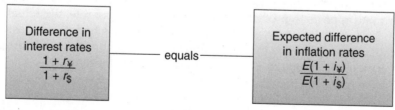

---

[8]Economists use the term *purchasing power parity* to refer to the notion that the level of prices of goods in general must be the same in the two countries. They tend to use the phrase *law of one price* when they are talking about the price of a single good.

[9]In other words, the *expected* difference in inflation rates equals the *expected* change in the exchange rate. Strictly interpreted, purchasing power parity also implies that the *actual* difference in the inflation rates always equals the *actual* change in the exchange rate.

[10]In Chapter 10 we discussed Irving Fisher's theory that over time money interest rates change to reflect changes in anticipated inflation. Here we argue that international differences in money interest rates also reflect differences in anticipated inflation. This theory is sometimes known as the *international Fisher effect*.

In Japan the real one-year interest rate is about 2.8 percent:

$$r_¥(\text{real}) = \frac{1 + r_¥}{E(1 + i_¥)} - 1 = \frac{1.0025}{.975} - 1 = .028$$

Ditto for the United States:

$$r_\$(\text{real}) = \frac{1 + r_\$}{E(1 + i_\$)} - 1 = \frac{1.05}{1.02} - 1 = .029$$

Is Life Really That Simple?

We have described above four theories that link interest rates, forward rates, spot exchange rates, and inflation rates. Of course, such simple economic theories are not going to provide an exact description of reality. We need to know how well they predict actual behavior.

1. Interest rate parity theory.   Interest rate parity theory says that the yen rate of interest covered for exchange risk should be the same as the dollar rate. In the example that we gave you earlier we used the rates of interest on dollar and yen deposits in London. Since money can be moved easily between these deposits, interest rate parity almost always holds. In fact, dealers *set* the forward price of yen by looking at the difference between the interest rates on deposits of dollars and yen.[11]

The relationship does not hold so exactly for deposits made in different domestic money markets. In these cases taxes and government regulations sometimes prevent the citizens of one country from switching out of one country's bank deposits and covering their exchange risk in the forward market.

2. The expectations theory of forward rates.   The expectations theory of forward rates does not imply that managers are perfect forecasters. Sometimes the *actual* future spot rate will jump above previous forward rates. Sometimes it will fall below. But if the theory is correct, we should find that *on the average* the forward rate is equal to the future spot rate. The theory passes this test with flying colors.[12] That is important news for the financial manager; it means that a company which always covers its foreign exchange commitments does not pay any extra for this insurance.

Although *on the average* the forward rate is equal to the expected spot rate, the forward rate does seem to provide an exaggerated estimate of the likely change in the spot rate. When the forward rate appears to predict a sharp rise in the spot rate, the actual rise turns out to be less. And when the forward rate appears to predict a sharp decline in the spot rate, the actual decline is also likely to be less.[13] This result is *not* consistent with the expectations hypothesis. Instead, it looks as if sometimes companies are prepared to give up return in order to buy forward currency and other times they are prepared to give up return in order to sell forward currency.[14]

---

[11]The forward exchange rates shown in the *Financial Times* and reproduced in Table 14.1 are simply calculated from the differences in interest rates.

[12]Of course, if we average the difference across all currencies, this has to be true. For some evidence on the average difference between the forward rate and the subsequent spot rate for dollars, see B. Cornell, "Spot Rates, Forward Rates, and Market Efficiency," *Journal of Financial Economics* 5 (1977), pp. 55–65.

[13]Many researchers have even found that, when the forward rate predicts a rise, the spot rate is more likely to fall, and vice versa. For a readable discussion of this puzzling finding, see K. A. Froot and R. H. Thaler, "Anomalies: Foreign Exchange," *Journal of Political Economy* 4 (1990), pp. 179–192.

[14]For evidence that forward exchange rates contain risk premia that are sometimes positive and sometimes negative, see, for example, E. F. Fama, "Forward and Spot Exchange Rates," *Journal of Monetary Economics* 14 (1984), pp. 319–338.

	TABLE 14.2		

Price of Big Mac hamburgers in different countries

COUNTRY	LOCAL PRICE CONVERTED TO U.S. DOLLARS	COUNTRY	LOCAL PRICE CONVERTED TO U.S. DOLLARS
Australia	$1.75	Israel	$3.38
Brazil	2.72	Japan	2.08
Canada	1.97	Mexico	2.10
China	1.20	Russia	2.00
Denmark	3.39	Sweden	3.00
Germany	2.69	Switzerland	3.87
Hong Kong	1.32	Thailand	1.30
Hungary	1.22	United Kingdom	3.05
Indonesia	1.16	United States	2.56

Source: "Big Mac Currencies," *The Economist*, April 11–17, 1998, p. 88.

We should also warn you that the forward rate does not tell you much about the future spot rate. This does not mean that the forward rate is a poor measure of managers' expectations; it just means that exchange rates are very tough to predict. Many banks and consultants produce forecasts of future exchange rates. But Richard Levich found that more often than not the forward rate provided a more accurate forecast than the currency advisory services.[15]

3. *Purchasing power parity theory.*   What about the third side of our quadrilateral—purchasing power parity theory? No one who has compared prices in foreign stores with prices at home really believes that prices are the same throughout the world. Look, for example, at Table 14.2, which shows the price of a Big Mac in different countries. Notice that at current rates of exchange a Big Mac costs $3.87 in Switzerland, while it costs only $2.56 in the United States. To equalize prices in Switzerland and the United States, the number of Swiss francs that you could buy for your dollar would have to increase by 3.87/2.56 − 1 = .51, or 51 percent.

This suggests a possible way to make a quick buck. Why don't you buy a hamburger-to-go in (say) China for the equivalent of $1.20 and take it for resale in Switzerland, where the price in dollars is $3.87? The answer, of course, is that the gain would not cover the costs. The same good can be sold for different prices in different countries because transportation is costly and inconvenient.[16]

On the other hand, there is clearly some relationship between inflation and changes in exchange rates. For example, between 1991 and 1996 prices in Brazil rose about 10,000 times. Or, to put it another way, you could say that the purchasing power of money in Brazil declined by about 99.9 percent. If exchange rates had not adjusted, Brazilian exporters would have found it impossible to sell their goods. But, of course, exchange rates did adjust. In fact, the value of the Brazilian currency declined by 99.9 percent relative to the U.S. dollar.[17]

---

[15]See R. M. Levich, "How to Compare Chance with Forecasting Expertise," *Euromoney* (August 1981), pp. 61–78.

[16]Of course, even *within* a currency area there may be considerable price variations. The price of a Big Mac, for example, differs substantially from one part of the United States to another. Even after the introduction of the euro, the price of Big Macs varied between $2.43 in Spain and $2.87 in France. See "Big Mac Currencies," *The Economist*, April 3–9, 1999, p. 90.

[17]However, by 1998 inflation in Brazil had fallen to about 4 percent.

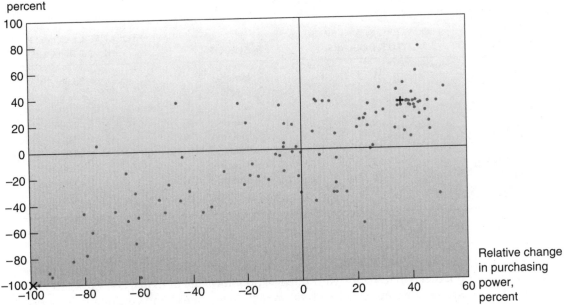

Figure 14.1

A decline in the exchange rate and a decline in a currency's purchasing power usually go hand in hand. In this diagram, each point represents the experience of a different country between 1991 and 1996. The vertical axis shows the change in the value of the foreign currency relative to the average. The horizontal axis shows the change in purchasing power relative to the average. The × at the lower left is Brazil; the + at the upper right is the United States.

Brazil is an extreme case, but in Figure 14.1 we have plotted the relative change in purchasing power for a sample of countries against the change in the exchange rate. Brazil is tucked in the bottom left-hand corner; the United States is closer to the top right. You can see that although the relationship is far from exact, large differences in inflation rates are generally accompanied by an offsetting change in the exchange rate.

Strictly speaking, purchasing power parity theory implies that the differential inflation rate is always identical to the change in the spot rate. But we don't need to go as far as that. We should be content if the *expected* difference in the inflation rates equals the *expected* change in the spot rate. That's all we wrote on the third side of our quadrilateral. Look, for example, at Figure 14.2. The solid line shows that in 1998 £1 sterling bought almost 70 percent fewer dollars than it did at the beginning of the century. But this decline in the price of sterling was largely matched by the higher inflation rate in the United Kingdom. The thin line shows that the inflation-adjusted, or *real*, exchange rate has been roughly constant.[18] If you were a financial manager called on to estimate the

---

[18]The real exchange rate is equal to the nominal exchange rate multiplied by the inflation differential. For example, suppose that the value of sterling falls from $1.54 = £1 to $1.40 = £1 at the same time that the price of goods rises 10 percent faster in the United Kingdom than in the United States. The inflation-adjusted, or real, exchange rate is unchanged at

$$\text{Initial exchange rate} \times (1 + i_£) / (1 + i_\$) = 1.40 \times 1.1 = \$1.54/£$$

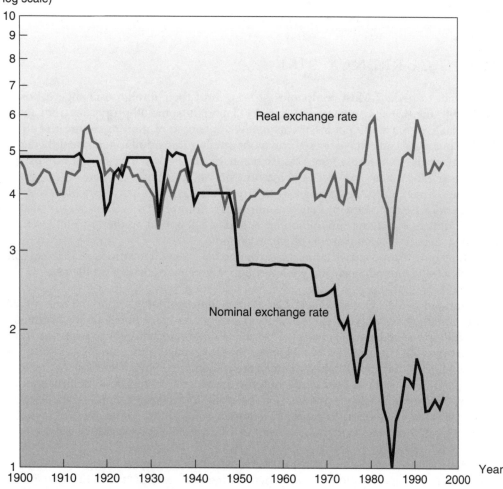

Nominal versus Real Exchange Rates

U. S. dollar/
British pound
(in log scale)

Figure 14.2

Since 1900 sterling has fallen sharply in value against the dollar. But this fall has largely offset the higher inflation rate in the U.K. The *real* value of sterling has been roughly constant.

Source: N. Abuaf and P. Jorion, "Purchasing Power Parity in the Long Run," *Journal of Finance* 45 (March 1990), pp. 157–174. We are grateful to Li Jin for extending the data to 1998.

long-term change in the value of sterling, you could not have done much better than to assume that it would offset the difference in inflation rates.

4. Equal real interest rates.   Finally we come to the relationship between interest rates in different countries. Do we have a single world capital market with the same *real* rate of interest in all countries? Does the difference in money interest rates equal the difference in the expected inflation rates?

This is not an easy question to answer since we cannot observe *expected* inflation. However, in Figure 14.3 we have plotted the average interest rate in each of 25 countries against the inflation that subsequently occurred. You can see that, in general, the countries with the highest interest rates also had the highest inflation rates. There were much smaller differences between the real rates of interest than between the nominal (or money) rates.[19]

HEDGING CURRENCY RISK

To hedge or not to hedge? Most companies at least limit their foreign exchange exposure. For example, in 1989 the British company, Enterprise Oil, bought some oil properties from Texas Eastern for $440 million. Since the payment was delayed a couple of months, Enterprise's plans for financing the purchase could have been thrown out of kilter if the dollar had strengthened during this period. Enterprise therefore covered the exchange risk by borrowing pounds, buying spot dollars, and investing the dollars in short-term instruments until the payment date.[20]

At the same time Enterprise also agreed to buy Texas Eastern's North Sea oil assets for $1.03 billion, but in this case the payment date was imprecise. Enterprise's solution was to place a floor on the cost of dollars by paying $26 million for a 90-day call option on the $1.03 billion it needed. The exercise price of the option was, of course, in pounds.

To illustrate how firms cope with foreign exchange risk, we will now look at a typical company in the United States, Outland Steel, and walk through its foreign exchange problems.

Example: Outland Steel Outland Steel has a small but profitable export business. Contracts involve substantial delays in payment, but since the company has a policy of always invoicing in dollars, it is fully protected against changes in exchange rates. Recently the export department has become unhappy with this practice and believes that it is causing the company to lose valuable export orders to firms that are willing to quote in the customer's own currency.

You sympathize with these arguments, but you are worried about how the firm should price long-term export contracts when payment is to be made in foreign currency. If the value of that currency declines before payment is made, the company may suffer a large loss. You want to take the currency risk into account, but you also want to give the sales force as much freedom of action as possible.

Notice that Outland can insure against its currency risk by selling the foreign currency forward. This means that it can separate the problem of negotiating sales contracts from that of managing the company's foreign exchange exposure. The sales force can allow for currency risk by pricing on the

---

[19]In Chapter 10 we saw that in some countries the government has issued indexed bonds promising a fixed real return. The annual interest payment and the amount repaid at maturity increase with the rate of inflation. In these cases, therefore, we can observe and compare the real rate of interest. For example, as we write this, the real interest rate promised by indexed bonds issued by the U.S. Treasury is 3.8 percent, while the rate promised by similar bonds issued by the British government is 2.2 percent. Unfortunately we are not quite comparing like with like, for the British government taxes only the regular interest payment, while the United States taxes both the regular interest payment and the increase in the amount that is repaid at maturity. A higher yield on indexed bonds in the United States is needed to compensate for the additional tax that must be paid.

[20]See "Enterprise Oil's Mega Forex Option," *Corporate Finance* 53 (April 1989), p. 13.

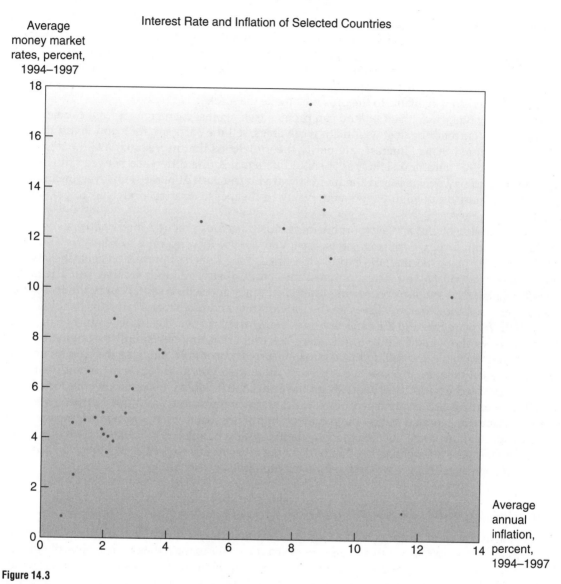

Figure 14.3

Countries with the highest interest rates generally have the highest inflation rates. In this diagram, each point represents the experience of a different country.

basis of the forward exchange rate. And you, as financial manager, can decide whether the company *ought* to hedge.

   What is the cost of hedging? You sometimes hear managers say that it is equal to the difference between the forward rate and *today's* spot rate. That is wrong. If Outland does not hedge, it will receive the spot rate at the time that the customer pays for the steel. Therefore, the cost of insurance is the difference between the forward rate and the expected spot rate when payment is received.

Insure or speculate? We generally vote for insurance. First, it makes life simpler for the firm and allows it to concentrate on its main business.[21] Second, it does not cost much. (In fact, the cost is zero on average if the forward rate equals the expected spot rate, as the expectations theory of forward rates implies.) Third, the foreign currency market seems reasonably efficient, at least for the major currencies. Speculation should be a zero-NPV game, unless financial managers have information that is not available to the pros who make the market.

Is there any other way that Outland can protect itself against exchange loss? Of course. It can borrow foreign currency against its foreign receivables, sell the currency spot, and invest the proceeds in the United States. Interest rate parity theory tells us that in free markets the difference between selling forward and selling spot should be equal to the difference between the interest that you have to pay overseas and the interest that you can earn at home. However, in countries where capital markets are highly regulated, it may be cheaper to arrange foreign borrowing rather than forward cover.[22]

Our discussion of Outland's export business illustrates four practical implications of our simple theories about forward exchange rates. First, you can use forward rates to adjust for exchange risk in contract pricing. Second, the expectations theory suggests that protection against exchange risk is usually worth having. Third, interest rate parity theory reminds us that you can hedge either by selling forward or by borrowing foreign currency and selling spot. Fourth, the cost of forward cover is not the difference between the forward rate and *today's* spot rate; it is the difference between the forward rate and the expected spot rate when the forward contract matures.

Perhaps we should add a fifth implication. You don't make money simply by buying currencies that go up in value and selling those that go down. For example, suppose that you buy Narnian leos and sell them after a year for 2 percent more than you paid for them. Should you give yourself a pat on the back? That depends on the interest that you have earned on your leos. If the interest rate on leos is 2 percentage points less than the interest rate on dollars, the profit on the currency is exactly canceled out by the reduction in interest income. Thus you make money from currency speculation only if you can predict whether the exchange rate will change by more or less than the interest rate differential. In other words, you must be able to predict whether the exchange rate will change by more or less than the forward premium or discount.

Transaction Exposure and Economic Exposure

The exchange risk from Outland Steel's export business is due to delays in foreign currency payments and is therefore referred to as *transaction exposure*. Transaction exposure can be easily identified and hedged. Since a 1 percent fall in the value of the foreign currency results in a 1 percent fall in Outland's dollar receipts, for every euro or yen that Outland is owed by its customers, it needs to sell forward one euro or one yen.[23]

---

[21]It also relieves shareholders of worrying about the foreign exchange exposure they may have acquired by purchase of the firm's shares.

[22]Sometimes governments also attempt to prevent currency speculation by limiting the amount that companies can sell forward.

[23]To put it another way, the hedge ratio is 1.0.

However, Outland may still be affected by currency fluctuations even if its customers do not owe it a cent. For example, Outland may be in competition with Swedish steel producers. If the value of the Swedish krona falls, Outland will need to cut its prices in order to compete.[24] Outland can protect itself against such an eventuality by selling the krona forward. In this case the loss on Outland's steel business will be offset by the profit on its forward sale.

Notice that Outland's exposure to the krona is not limited to specific transactions that have already been entered into. Financial managers often refer to this broader type of exposure as *economic exposure*.[25] Economic exposure is less easy to measure than transaction exposure. For example, it is clear that the value of Outland Steel is positively related to the value of the krona, so to hedge its position it needs to sell krona forward. But in practice it may be hard to say exactly how many krona Outland needs to sell.

Economic exposure is a major source of risk for many firms. When the deutschemark appreciated in value in 1991 and 1992, German luxury carmakers such as Porsche and Mercedes took a bath on their overseas sales. So did American dealers that had a franchise to sell these cars. Competitors such as Jaguar, however, benefited from their rivals' discomfiture. Thus the German and British car producers and their dealers were affected by exchange rate changes even though they may have had no fixed obligation to pay or receive dollars. They had economic exposure as well as possible transaction exposure.[26]

Most firms do not attempt to quantify economic exposure, but that does not mean that they ignore it. For example, when a company makes a major overseas investment, it often finances it by foreign currency borrowing. A subsequent fall in the value of the foreign currency may reduce the dollar value of the investment, but this is compensated by the fall in the dollar cost of servicing the foreign debt.

Currency Speculation

Outland Steel's currency exposure arose naturally from its business activity, but the risk was avoidable; it could have been hedged using either the forward markets or the loan markets. Sometimes, however, companies deliberately take on currency risk in the hope of gain. Now there is nothing wrong with that if you truly do have a forecasting edge, but we should warn you against the dangers of naive strategies.

Suppose, for example, that a company in the United States notices that the interest rate on the Swiss franc is lower than on the dollar. Does this mean that it is "cheaper" to borrow Swiss francs? Before jumping to that conclusion, you need to ask *why* the Swiss interest rate is so low. Unless the

---

[24]Of course, if purchasing power parity always held, the fall in the value of the krona would be matched by higher inflation in Sweden. The risk for Outland is that the *real* value of the krona may decline, so that when measured in dollars Swedish costs are lower than previously. Unfortunately, it is much easier to hedge against a change in the *nominal* exchange rate than against a change in the *real* rate.

[25]Financial managers also refer to *translation exposure*, which measures the effect of an exchange rate change on the company's financial statements.

[26]The German car producers could have hedged their exposure by borrowing dollars. As the deutschemark appreciated, their dollar income fell but the cost of servicing dollar loans would also have fallen. However, while borrowing dollars would have reduced the risk for German car producers, it should not have affected their decisions about where to produce and sell cars.

Swiss government is deliberately holding the rate down by restrictions on the export of capital, you should suspect that the real cost of capital is roughly the same in Switzerland as anywhere else. The nominal interest rate is low only because investors expect a low domestic rate of inflation and a strong currency. Therefore, the advantage of the low rate of interest is likely to be offset by the additional dollars required to buy the Swiss francs required to pay off the loan.

You cannot expect to make a profit simply by borrowing in countries with low nominal rates of interest and you may be taking on considerable currency exposure by doing so. If the currency subsequently appreciates *more* rapidly than investors expect, it could turn out to be very costly to buy the currency that you need to service the loan. In 1989 several Australian banks learned this lesson the hard way. They had induced their clients to borrow at the low Swiss interest rates. When the value of the Swiss franc rose sharply, the banks found themselves sued by irate clients for not having warned them of the risk of a rise in the price of Swiss francs.

EXCHANGE RISK AND INTERNATIONAL INVESTMENT DECISIONS

Suppose that the Swiss pharmaceutical company, Roche, is evaluating a proposal to build a new plant in the United States. To calculate the project's net present value, Roche forecasts the following dollar cash flows from the project:

CASH FLOWS ($ MILLIONS)

C_0	C_1	C_2	C_3	C_4	C_5
−1,300	400	450	510	575	650

These cash flows are stated in dollars. So to calculate their net present value Roche discounts them at the dollar cost of capital. (Remember dollars need to be discounted at a *dollar* rate, not the Swiss franc rate.) Suppose this cost of capital is 12 percent. Then

$$\text{NPV} = -1,300 + \frac{400}{1.12} + \frac{450}{1.12^2} + \frac{510}{1.12^3} + \frac{575}{1.12^4} + \frac{650}{1.12^5} = \$513 \text{ million}$$

To convert this net present value to Swiss francs, the manager can simply multiply the dollar NPV by the spot rate of exchange. For example, if the spot rate is 2 SFr/$, then the NPV in Swiss francs is

$$\text{NPV in francs} = \text{NPV in dollars} \times \text{SFr}/\$ = 513 \times 2 = 1{,}026 \text{ million francs}$$

Notice one very important feature of this calculation. Roche does not need to forecast whether the dollar is likely to strengthen or weaken against the Swiss franc. No currency forecast is needed, because the company can hedge its foreign exchange exposure. In that case, the decision to accept or reject the pharmaceutical project in the United States is totally separate from the decision to bet on the outlook for the dollar. For example, it would be foolish for Roche to accept a poor project in the United States just because management is optimistic about the outlook for the dollar; if Roche wishes to speculate in this way it can simply buy dollars forward. Equally, it would be foolish for Roche to reject a good project just because management is pessimistic about the dollar. The company would do much better to go ahead with the project and sell dollars forward. In that way, it would get the best of both worlds.[27]

When Roche ignores currency risk and discounts the dollar cash flows at a dollar cost of capital, it is implicitly assuming that the currency risk is hedged. Let us check this by calculating the number of Swiss francs that Roche would receive if it hedged the currency risk by selling forward each future dollar cash flow.

We need first to calculate the forward rate of exchange between dollars and francs. This depends on the interest rates in the United States and Switzerland. For example, suppose that the dollar interest rate is 6 percent and the Swiss franc interest rate is 4 percent. Then interest rate parity theory tells us that the one-year forward exchange rate is

$$s_{SFr/\$} \times (1 + r_{SFr}) / (1 + r_\$) = \frac{2 \times 1.04}{1.06} = 1.962$$

Similarly, the two-year forward rate is

$$s_{SFr/\$} \times (1 + r_{SFr})^2 / (1 + r_\$)^2 = \frac{2 \times 1.04^2}{1.06^2} = 1.925$$

So, if Roche hedges its cash flows against exchange rate risk, the number of Swiss francs it will receive in each year is equal to the dollar cash flow times the forward rate of exchange:

CASH FLOWS (MILLIONS OF SWISS FRANCS)

C_0	C_1	C_2	C_3	C_4	C_5
$-1,300 \times 2$	400×1.962	450×1.925	510×1.889	575×1.853	650×1.818
$= -2,600$	$= 785$	$= 866$	$= 963$	$= 1,066$	$= 1,182$

These cash flows are in Swiss francs and therefore they need to be discounted at the risk-adjusted Swiss franc discount rate. Since the Swiss rate of interest is lower than the dollar rate, the risk-adjusted discount rate must also be correspondingly lower. The formula for converting from the required dollar return to the required Swiss franc return is[28]

$$(1 + \text{Swiss franc return}) = (1 + \text{dollar return}) \times \frac{(1 + \text{Swiss franc interest rate})}{(1 + \text{dollar interest rate})}$$

---

[27]There is a general point here that is not confined to currency hedging. Whenever you face an investment that appears to have a positive NPV, decide what it is that you are betting on and then think whether there is a more direct way to place the bet. For example, if a copper mine looks profitable only because you are unusually optimistic about the price of copper, then maybe you would do better to buy copper futures or the shares of other copper producers rather than opening a copper mine.

[28]The following example should give you a feel for the idea behind this formula. Suppose the spot rate for Swiss francs is 2 SFr = \$1. Interest rate parity tells us that the forward rate must be $2 \times 1.04/1.06 = 1.9623$ SFr/\$. Now suppose that a share costs \$100 and will pay an expected \$112 at the end of the year. The cost to Swiss investors of buying the share is $100 \times 2 = 200$ SFr. If the Swiss investors sell forward the expected payoff, they will receive an expected $112 \times 1.9623 = 219.8$ SFr. The expected return in Swiss francs is $219.9/200 - 1 = .099$ or 9.9 percent. More simply, the Swiss franc return is $1.12 \times 1.04/1.06 - 1 = .099$.

In our example

$$(1 + \text{Swiss franc return}) = 1.12 \times \frac{1.04}{1.06} = 1.099$$

Thus the risk-adjusted discount rate in dollars is 12 percent, but the discount rate in Swiss francs is only 9.9 percent.

All that remains is to discount the Swiss franc cash flows at the 9.9 percent risk-adjusted discount rate:

$$\text{NPV} = -2,600 + \frac{785}{1.099} + \frac{866}{1.099^2} + \frac{963}{1.099^3} + \frac{1,066}{1.099^4} + \frac{1,182}{1.099^5} = 1,026 \text{ million francs}$$

Everything checks. We obtain exactly the same net present value by (a) ignoring currency risk and discounting Roche's dollar cash flows at the dollar cost of capital and (b) calculating the cash flows in francs on the assumption that Roche hedges the currency risk and then discounting these Swiss franc cash flows at the franc cost of capital.

To repeat: When deciding whether to invest overseas, separate out the investment decision from the decision to take on currency risk. This means that your views about future exchange rates should NOT enter into the investment decision. The simplest way to calculate the NPV of an overseas investment is to forecast the cash flows in the foreign currency and discount them at the foreign currency cost of capital. The alternative is to calculate the cash flows that you would receive if you hedged the foreign currency risk. In this case you need to translate the foreign currency cash flows into your own currency *using the forward exchange rate* and then discount these domestic currency cash flows at the domestic cost of capital. If the two methods don't give the same answer, you have made a mistake.

When Roche analyzes the proposal to build a plant in the United States, it is able to ignore the outlook for the dollar *only because it is free to hedge the currency risk.* Because investment in a pharmaceutical plant does not come packaged with an investment in the dollar, the opportunity for firms to hedge allows for better investment decisions.

More About the Cost of Capital

In our discussion of Roche's investment decision we did not explain how Roche estimated the cost of capital for its investment in the United States. There is no simple agreed-upon procedure for doing this but we suggest that you first estimate the cost of capital in Swiss francs and then convert it to a dollar cost.

To estimate the required return on Roche's overseas investment, you need to decide how risky an investment in the U.S. pharmaceutical business would be to a Swiss investor. For example, a good starting point might be to look at the betas of a sample of U.S. pharmaceutical companies *relative to the Swiss market index.*[29]

---

[29]When we use the beta relative to the U.S. index to estimate the returns required by U.S. investors, we are assuming that the U.S. market index is an efficient portfolio for these investors. Similarly, when we use the beta relative to the Swiss index to estimate the returns that Swiss investors require, we are assuming that the Swiss market index is an efficient portfolio for these investors. Investors do invest largely, but not exclusively, in their home markets.

Suppose that you decide that the investment's beta relative to the Swiss market is .7 and that the market risk premium in Switzerland is 8.4 percent. Then the required return on the project can be estimated as

$$\text{Required return} = \text{Swiss interest rate} + (\text{beta} \times \text{Swiss market risk premium})$$

$$= 4 + (.7 \times 8.4) = 9.9\%$$

This is the project's cost of capital measured in Swiss francs. We used it above to discount the expected *Swiss franc* cash flows if Roche hedged the project against currency risk. We cannot use it to discount the *dollar* cash flows from the project.

To discount the expected *dollar* cash flows, we need to convert the Swiss franc cost of capital to a dollar cost of capital. This means running the calculation that we did earlier in reverse:

$$(1 + \text{dollar return}) = (1 + \text{Swiss franc return}) \times \frac{(1 + \text{dollar interest rate})}{(1 + \text{Swiss franc interest rate})}$$

In our example

$$(1 + \text{dollar return}) = 1.099 \times \frac{1.06}{1.04} = 1.12$$

We used this 12 percent dollar cost of capital to discount the forecasted dollar cash flows from the project.

POLITICAL RISK

So far we have focused on the management of exchange rate risk, but managers also worry about political risk. By this they mean the threat that a government will change the rules of the game—that is, break a promise or understanding—*after* the investment is made. Of course political risks are not confined to overseas investments. Businesses in every country are exposed to the risk of unanticipated actions by governments or the courts. But in some parts of the world foreign companies are particularly vulnerable.

Some managers dismiss political risk as an act of God, like a hurricane or earthquake. But the most successful multinational companies structure their business to reduce political risk. Foreign governments are not likely to expropriate a local business if it cannot operate without the support of its parent. For example, the foreign subsidiaries of American computer manufacturers or pharmaceutical companies would have relatively little value if they were cut off from the know-how of their parents. Such operations are much less likely to be expropriated than, say, a mining operation which can be operated as a stand-alone venture.

We are not recommending that you turn your silver mine into a pharmaceutical company, but you may be able to plan your overseas manufacturing operations to improve your bargaining position with foreign governments. For example, Ford has integrated its overseas operations so that the manufacture of components, subassemblies, and complete automobiles is spread across plants in a number of countries. None of these plants would have much value on its own, and Ford can switch production between plants if the political climate in one country deteriorates.

Multinational corporations have also devised financing arrangements to help keep foreign governments honest. For example, suppose your firm is contemplating an investment of $500 million to reopen the San Tomé silver mine in Costaguana with modern machinery, smelting equipment, and shipping facilities.[30] The Costaguanan government agrees to invest in roads and other infrastructure and to take 20 percent of the silver produced by the mine in lieu of taxes. The agreement is to run for 25 years.

The project's NPV on these assumptions is quite attractive. But what happens if a new government comes into power five years from now and imposes a 50 percent tax on "any precious metals exported from the Republic of Costaguana?" Or changes the government's share of output from 20 to 50 percent? Or simply takes over the mine "with fair compensation to be determined in due course by the Minister of Natural Resources of the Republic of Costaguana?"

No contract can absolutely restrain sovereign power. But you can arrange project financing to make these acts as painful as possible for the foreign government. For example, you might set up the mine as a subsidiary corporation, which then borrows a large fraction of the required investment from a consortium of major international banks. If your firm guarantees the loan, make sure the guarantee stands only if the Costaguanan government honors its contract. The government will be reluctant to break the contract if that causes a default on the loans and undercuts the country's credit standing with the international banking system.

If possible, you should finance part of the project with a loan from the World Bank (or one of its affiliates). Include a *cross-default* clause, so that a default to any creditor automatically triggers default on the World Bank loan. Few governments have the guts to take on the World Bank.[31]

Here is another variation on the same theme. Arrange to borrow, say, $450 million through the Costaguanan Development Agency. In other words, the development agency borrows in international capital markets and relends to the San Tomé mine. Your firm agrees to stand behind the loan as long as the government keeps its promises. If it does keep them, the loan is your liability. If not, the loan is *its* liability.

Political risk is not confined to the risk of expropriation. Multinational companies are always exposed to the criticism that they siphon funds out of countries in which they do business, and, therefore, governments are tempted to limit their freedom to repatriate profits. This is most likely to happen when there is considerable uncertainty about the rate of exchange, which is usually when you would most like to get your money out.

Here again a little forethought can help. For example, there are often more onerous restrictions on the payment of dividends to the parent than on the payment of interest or principal on debt. Royalty payments and management fees are less sensitive than dividends, particularly if they are levied equally on all foreign operations. A company can also, within limits, alter the price of goods that are bought or sold within the group, and it can require more or less prompt payment for such goods.

SUMMARY

The international financial manager has to cope with different currencies, interest rates, and inflation rates. To produce order out of chaos, the manager needs some model of how they are related. We described four very simple but useful theories.

---

[30]The early history of the San Tomé mine is described in Joseph Conrad's *Nostromo*.

[31]In Chapter 11 we described how the World Bank provided the Hubco power project with a guarantee against political risk.

Interest rate parity theory states that the interest differential between two countries must be equal to the difference between the forward and spot exchange rates. In the international markets, arbitrage ensures that parity almost always holds. There are two ways to hedge against exchange risk: One is to take out forward cover; the other is to borrow or lend abroad. Interest rate parity tells us that the costs of the two methods should be the same.

The expectations theory of exchange rates tells us that the forward rate equals the expected spot rate. If you believe the expectations theory, you will generally insure against exchange risks.

In its strict form, purchasing power parity states that $1 must have the same purchasing power in every country. That doesn't square well with the facts, for differences in inflation rates are not perfectly related to changes in exchange rates. This means that there may be some genuine exchange risks in doing business overseas. On the other hand, the difference in inflation rates is just as likely to be above as below the change in the exchange rate.

Finally, we saw that in an integrated world capital market real rates of interest would have to be the same. In practice government regulation and taxes can cause differences in real interest rates. But do not simply borrow where interest rates are lowest. Those countries are also likely to have the lowest inflation rates and the strongest currencies.

With these precepts in mind we showed how you can use forward markets or the loan markets to hedge transactions exposure, which arises from delays in foreign currency payments and receipts. But the company's financing choices also need to reflect the impact of a change in the exchange rate on the value of the entire business. This is known as economic exposure.

Because companies can hedge their currency risk, the decision to invest overseas does not involve currency forecasts. There are two ways for a company to calculate the NPV of an overseas project. The first is to forecast the foreign currency cash flows and to discount them at the foreign currency cost of capital. The second is to translate the foreign currency cash flows into domestic currency assuming that they are hedged against exchange rate risk. These domestic currency flows can then be discounted at the domestic cost of capital. The answers should be identical.

In addition to currency risk, overseas operations may be exposed to extra political risk. However, firms may be able to structure the financing to reduce the chances that government will change the rules of the game.

Further Reading

There are a number of useful textbooks in international finance. Here is a small selection:

D. K. Eiteman and A. I. Stonehill: *Multinational Business Finance*, 8th ed., Addison-Wesley Publishing Company, Inc., Reading, Mass., 1997.

J. O. Grabbe, *International Financial Markets*, 3d ed., Prentice-Hall, Inc., Englewood Cliffs, N.J., 1996.

P. Sercu and R. Uppal: *International Financial Markets and the Firm*, South-Western College Publishing, Cincinnati, Ohio, 1995.

A. C. Shapiro: *Multinational Financial Management*, 5th ed., Prentice-Hall, Inc., Englewood Cliffs, N.J., 1996.

Here are some general discussions of international investment decisions and associated exchange risks:

D. R. Lessard: "Global Competition and Corporate Finance in the 1990s," *Journal of Applied Corporate Finance*, 3:59–72 (Winter 1991).

M. D. Levi and P. Sercu: "Erroneous and Valid Reasons for Hedging Foreign Exchange Exposure," *Journal of Multinational Financial Management*, 1:25–37 (1991).

A. C. Shapiro: "International Capital Budgeting," *Midland Corporate Finance Journal*, 1:26–45 (Spring 1983).

Listed below are a few of the articles on the relationship between interest rates, exchange rates, and inflation:

Forward and spot exchange rates

B. Cornell: "Spot Rates, Forward Rates and Exchange Market Efficiency," *Journal of Financial Economics*, 5:55–65 (1977).

M. D. D. Evans and K. K. Lewis: "Do Long-Term Swings in the Dollar Affect Estimates of the Risk Premia?" *Review of Financial Studies*, 8:709–742 (1995).

E. F. Fama: "Forward and Spot Exchange Rates," *Journal of Monetary Economics*, 14:319–338 (1984).

Interest-rate parity

K. Clinton: "Transaction Costs and Covered Interest Arbitrage: Theory and Evidence," *Journal of Political Economy*, 96:358–370 (April 1988).

J. A. Frenkel and R. M. Levich: "Covered Interest Arbitrage: Unexploited Profits?" *Journal of Political Economy*, 83:325–338 (April 1975).

Purchasing power parity

M. Adler and B. Lehmann: "Deviations from Purchasing Power Parity in the Long Run," *Journal of Finance*, 38:1471–1487 (December 1983).

K. Froot and K. Rogoff: "Perspectives on PPP and Long-run Real Exchange Rates," in G. Grossman and K. Rogoff (eds.), *Handbook of International Economics*, North-Holland Publishing Company, Amsterdam, 1995.

P. Jorion and R. Sweeney: "Mean Reversion in Real Exchange Rates: Evidence and Implications for Forecasting," *Journal of International Money and Finance*, 15:535–550 (1996).

K. Rogoff, "The Purchasing Power Parity Puzzle," *Review of Economic Literature*, 34:667–668 (June 1996).

FINANCIAL PLANNING

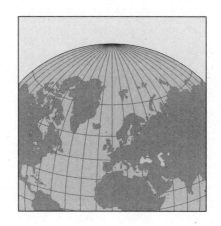

FINANCIAL ANALYSIS AND PLANNING

A camel looks like an animal designed by a committee. If a firm made all its financial decisions piecemeal, it would end up with a financial camel. Therefore, smart financial managers consider the overall effect of financing and investment decisions and ensure that they have the financial strategies in place to support the firm's plans for future growth.

Understanding the past is a necessary prelude to contemplating the future. Therefore we start the chapter with a brief review of a company's financial statements and we look at how you can use financial data to analyze a firm's overall performance and assess its current financial standing. For example, you may need to see whether your own firm's financial performance is in the ballpark of standard practice. Or you may wish to understand the policies of a competitor or check on the financial health of a customer.

Financial analysts calculate a few key financial ratios to measure the company's performance. These ratios are no substitute for a crystal ball, but they do help you to ask the right questions. For example, when the firm needs a loan from the bank, the financial manager can expect some searching questions about the firm's debt ratio and the proportion of profits that is absorbed by interest. Likewise, financial ratios may alert senior management to potential problem areas. If a division is earning a low rate of return on its capital or if its profit margins are under pressure, you can be sure that management will demand an explanation.

Growing firms need to invest in working capital, plant and equipment, product development, and so on. All this requires cash. We will, therefore, explain how firms use financial planning models to help them understand the financial implications of their business plans and to explore the consequences of alternative financial strategies. We conclude the chapter with a look at the relationship between a firm's growth plans and its need for external financing.

351

EXECUTIVE PAPER'S FINANCIAL STATEMENTS

We don't wish to discuss the finer points of accounting practice. But because we will be referring to financial statements throughout this chapter, it may be useful to review their main features. We begin with the balance sheet of the Executive Paper Corporation.

The Balance Sheet

The balance sheet in Table 15.1 provides a snapshot of Executive Paper's assets and the sources of the money that was used to buy those assets.

The items in the balance sheet are listed in declining order of liquidity. For example, you can see that the accountant lists first those assets which are most likely to be turned into cash in the near future. They include cash itself, marketable securities and receivables (that is, bills to be paid by the firm's customers), and inventories of raw materials, work in process, and finished goods. These assets are all known as *current assets.*

The remaining assets on the balance sheet consist of long-term, usually illiquid, assets such as pulp and paper mills, office buildings, and timberlands. The balance sheet does not show up-to-date market values of these long-term assets. Instead, the accountant records the amount that each asset originally cost and then, in the case of plant and equipment, deducts a fixed annual amount for depreciation. The balance sheet does not include all the company's assets. Some of the most valuable ones are intangible, such as patents, reputation, a skilled management, and a well-trained labor force. Accountants are generally reluctant to record these assets in the balance sheet unless they can be readily identified and valued.

Now look at the right-hand portion of Executive Paper's balance sheet, which shows where the money to buy the assets came from.[1] The accountant starts by looking at the liabilities, that is, the money owed by the company. First come those liabilities that need to be paid off in the near future. These *current liabilities* include debts that are due to be repaid within the next year and payables (that is, amounts owed by the company to its suppliers).

The difference between the current assets and current liabilities is known as the *net current assets* or *net working capital*. It roughly measures the company's potential reservoir of cash. For Executive Paper in 1999

$$\text{Net working capital} = \text{current assets} - \text{current liabilities}$$

$$= 900 - 460 = \$440 \text{ million}$$

The bottom portion of the balance sheet shows the sources of the cash that was used to acquire the net working capital and fixed assets. Some of the cash has come from the issue of bonds and leases that will not be repaid for many years. After all these long-term liabilities have been paid off, the remaining assets belong to the common stockholders. The company's equity is simply the total value of the net working capital and fixed assets less the long-term liabilities. Part of this equity has come from the sale of shares to investors and the remainder has come from earnings that the company has retained and invested on behalf of the shareholders.

---

[1]The British and Americans can never agree whether to keep to the left or the right. British accountants list liabilities on the left and assets on the right.

TABLE 15.1

The balance sheet of Executive Paper Corporation (figures in $ millions)

ASSETS	DEC 1998	DEC 1999	CHANGE
Current assets:			
Cash & securities	100	110	+10
Receivables	433.1	440	+6.9
Inventory	339.9	350	+10.1
Total current assets	873	900	+27
Fixed assets:			
Property, plant, and equipment	929.8	1,000	+70.2
Less accumulated depreciation	396.7	450	+53.3
Net fixed assets	533.1	550	+16.9
Total assets	1,406.1	1,450	+43.9

LIABILITIES AND SHAREHOLDERS' EQUITY	DEC 1998	DEC 1999	CHANGE
Current liabilities:			
Debt due within 1 year	96.6	100	+3.4
Payables	349.9	360	+10.1
Total current liabilities	446.5	460	+13.5
Long-term debt	400	400	0
Shareholders' equity	559.6	590	+30.4
Total liabilities & shareholders' equity	1,406.1	1,450	+43.9

Other financial information:		
Estimated replacement cost of assets	1,110	1,231
Market value of equity	598	708
Average number of shares (millions)	14.16	14.16
Share price ($)	42.25	50.00

Table 15.1 provides some other financial information about Executive Paper. For example, it shows the market value of the common stock. It is often helpful to compare the *book value* of the equity (shown in the company's accounts) with the *market value* established in the capital markets.

The Income Statement

If Executive Paper's balance sheet resembles a snapshot of the firm at a particular point in time, its income statement is like a video. It shows how profitable the firm has been over the past year.

Look at the summary income statement in Table 15.2. You can see that during 1999 Executive Paper sold goods worth $2,200 million and that the total costs of producing and selling these goods were $1,980 million. In addition to these out-of-pocket expenses, Executive Paper also made a

TABLE 15.2

The 1999 income statement of Executive Paper Corporation (figures in $ millions)

	$ MILLIONS
Revenues	2,200
Costs	1,980
Depreciation	53.3
EBIT	166.7
Interest	40
Tax	50.7
Net income	76.0
Dividends	45.6
Retained earnings	30.4
Earnings per share, dollars	5.37
Dividend per share, dollars	3.22

deduction of $53.3 million for the value of the fixed assets used up in producing the goods. Thus Executive Paper's earnings before interest and taxes (EBIT) were

$$EBIT = Total\ revenues - costs - depreciation$$

$$= 2,200 - 1,980 - 53.3 = \$166.7\ million$$

Of this sum $40 million went to pay the interest on the short- and long-term debt (remember debt interest is paid out of pretax income) and a further $50.7 million went to the government in the form of taxes. The $76 million that was left over belonged to the shareholders. Executive Paper paid out $45.6 million as dividends and reinvested the remaining $30.4 million in the business.

Sources and Uses of Funds

Table 15.3 shows the sources of funds for Executive Paper and how these funds were used. In 1999 the company generated $129.3 million from operations. This included $53.3 million of depreciation (remember depreciation is not a cash outflow) and $76 million of net income. Executive Paper did not issue any long-term debt or shares in 1999. Of the new funds, $13.5 million were used to increase net working capital, $70.2 million were invested in fixed assets, and the balance of $45.6 million was paid out to shareholders as a dividend.

FINANCIAL RATIOS

In Chapter 1 we pointed out that a large corporation is a team effort. All the players—the shareholders, lenders, directors, management, and employees—have a stake in the company's success and therefore need to monitor its progress. The company's financial statements help them to do so.

TABLE 15.3	

1999 sources and uses of funds for Executive Paper
Corporation (figures in $ millions)

	$ MILLIONS
Sources:	
Net income	76
Depreciation	53.3
Operating cash flow	129.3
Borrowing	0
Stock issues	0
Total sources	129.3
Uses:	
Increase in net working capital	13.5
Investment	70.2
Dividends	45.6
Total uses	129.3

But actual financial statements contain a huge amount of data, far more than do the simplified statements that we have provided for Executive Paper. To condense these data into a manageable form, financial analysts calculate a small number of key financial ratios. We will describe five types of financial ratios:

- Leverage ratios show how heavily the company is in debt.
- Liquidity ratios measure how easily the company can lay its hands on cash.
- Efficiency ratios measure how productively the company is using its assets.
- Profitability ratios show the return that the firm earns on its investments.
- Market value ratios show how highly the firm is valued by investors.

Leverage Ratios

When a firm borrows money, it promises to make a series of fixed payments. Because the shareholders get only what is left over after the debtholders have been paid, debt is said to create *financial leverage*. In extreme cases, if hard times come, firms with high leverage are liable to find that they cannot pay their debts. So, when a firm wishes to take out a bank loan, it can be sure that the bank will scrutinize several measures of whether the firm is borrowing too much. The bank will also insist that the firm *keep* its debt within reasonable bounds. These borrowing limits are stated in terms of financial ratios.

Debt Ratio   Financial leverage is usually measured by the ratio of long-term debt to total long-term capital. Since long-term lease agreements also commit the firm to a series of fixed payments, it makes sense to include the value of lease obligations with the long-term debt. For Executive Paper

$$\text{Debt ratio} = \frac{\text{(long-term debt + value of leases)}}{\text{(long-term debt + value of leases + equity)}}$$

$$= 400/(400 + 590) = .40$$

Another way to say the same thing is that Executive Paper has a debt-to-equity ratio of $400/590 = .68$:

$$\text{Debt–equity ratio} = \frac{\text{long-term debt + value of leases}}{\text{equity}}$$

$$= \frac{400}{590} = .68$$

Notice that this measure makes use of book (i.e., accounting) values rather than market values.[2] The market value of the company finally determines whether the debtholders get their money back, so you would expect analysts to look at the face amount of the debt as a proportion of the total market value of debt and equity. The main reason that they don't do this is that the market values are often not readily available. Does it matter much? Perhaps not; after all, the market value includes the value of intangible assets generated by research and development, advertising, staff training, and so on. These assets are not readily saleable, and if the company falls on hard times, their value may disappear altogether. For some purposes, it may be just as good to follow the accountant and ignore these intangible assets. This is just what lenders do when they insist that the borrower should not allow the book debt ratio to exceed a specified limit.

Debt ratios are sometimes defined in other ways. For example, analysts may include short-term debt or other obligations such as payables. There is a general point here. There are a variety of ways to define most financial ratios and there is no law stating how they *should* be defined. So be warned: Don't accept a ratio at face value without understanding how it has been calculated.

Times-Interest-Earned (or Interest Cover)   Another measure of financial leverage is the extent to which interest is covered by earnings before interest and taxes (EBIT) plus depreciation. For Executive Paper,[3]

$$\text{Times interest earned} = \frac{\text{(EBIT + depreciation)}}{\text{interest}}$$

$$= \frac{(166.7 + 53.3)}{40} = 5.5$$

The regular interest payment is a hurdle that companies must keep jumping if they are to avoid default. The times-interest-earned ratio measures how much clear air there is between hurdle and hurdler.

---

[2]In the case of leased assets accountants try to estimate the present value of the lease commitments. In the case of long-term debt they simply show the face value. This can sometimes be very different from present value. For example, the present value of low-coupon debt may be only a fraction of its face value. The difference between the book value of equity and its market value can be even more dramatic.

[3]The numerator of times interest earned can be defined in several ways. Sometimes depreciation is excluded. Sometimes it is just earnings plus interest, that is, earnings before interest *but after* tax. This last definition seems nutty to us, because the point of times interest earned is to assess the risk that the firm won't have enough money to pay interest. If EBIT falls below interest obligations, the firm won't have enough money to worry about taxes. Interest is paid before the firm pays taxes.

Liquidity Ratios

If you are extending credit or lending to a company for a short period, you are not just concerned with the amount of the company's debts. You also want to know whether the company will be able to lay its hands on the cash to repay you. That is why credit managers and bankers look at several measures of *liquidity*. They know that firms with poor liquidity are more likely to fail and default on their debts. Another reason that managers focus on liquid assets is that the figures are more reliable. The book value of a catalytic cracker may be a poor guide to its true value, but at least you know what cash in the bank is worth.

Liquidity ratios also have some *less* desirable characteristics. Because short-term assets and liabilities are easily changed, measures of liquidity can rapidly become out-of-date. You might not know what that catalytic cracker is worth, but you can be fairly sure that it won't disappear overnight. Also, companies often choose a slack period for the end of their financial year. For example, retailers may end their financial year in January, after the Christmas boom. At such times the companies are likely to have more cash and less short-term debt than during the busier seasons.

Current Ratio Executive Paper's current assets consist of cash and assets that can readily be turned into cash. Its current liabilities consist of payments that the company expects to make in the near future. Thus the ratio of the current assets to current liabilities measures the margin of liquidity. It is known as the *current ratio:*

$$\text{Current ratio} = \frac{\text{current assets}}{\text{current liabilities}} = \frac{900}{460} = 1.9$$

Rapid decreases in the current ratio sometimes signify trouble. However, they can also be misleading. For example, suppose that a company borrows a large sum from the bank and invests it in short-term securities. If nothing else changes, net working capital is unaffected, but the current ratio changes. For this reason it might be preferable to net off the short-term investments and the short-term debt when calculating the current ratio.

Quick (or Acid-Test) Ratio Some assets are closer to cash than others. If trouble comes, inventories may not sell at anything above fire-sale prices. (Trouble typically comes *because* customers are not buying and the firm's warehouse is stuffed full of unwanted goods.) Thus, managers often focus only on cash, short-term securities, and bills that customers have not yet paid:

$$\text{Quick ratio} = \frac{(\text{cash} + \text{short-term securities} + \text{receivables})}{\text{current liabilities}}$$

$$= \frac{110 + 440}{460} = 1.2$$

Cash Ratio A company's most liquid assets are its holdings of cash and marketable securities. That is why financial analysts also look at the cash ratio:

$$\text{Cash ratio} = \frac{(\text{cash} + \text{short-term securities})}{\text{current liabilities}} = \frac{110}{460} = .24$$

Of course lack of cash may not matter if the firm can borrow at short notice. Who cares whether the firm has actually borrowed from the bank or whether it has a guaranteed line of credit that allows it to do so whenever it chooses? None of the standard liquidity measures takes the firm's reserve borrowing power into account.

Efficiency Ratios

Financial analysts employ another set of ratios to judge how efficiently the firm is using its assets.

Sales-to-Assets (or Asset Turnover) Ratio   The sales-to-assets ratio shows how hard the firm's assets are being put to use:

$$\frac{\text{Sales}}{\text{average total assets}} = \frac{2{,}200}{(1{,}406.1 + 1{,}450)/2} = 1.54$$

Assets here are measured as the sum of current and fixed assets. A high ratio could indicate that the firm is working close to capacity. It may prove difficult to generate further business without an increase in invested capital.

Notice that since the assets are likely to change over the course of a year, we use the *average* of the assets at the beginning and end of the year. Averages are commonly used whenever a *flow* figure (in this case, sales) is compared with a *stock* or snapshot figure (total assets).

Instead of looking at the ratio of sales to *total* assets, managers sometimes look at how hard particular types of capital are being put to use. For example, they might look at the ratio of sales to fixed assets or to net working capital.

Days in Inventory   The speed with which a company turns over its inventory is measured by the number of days that it takes for the goods to be produced and sold. First convert the cost of goods sold to a daily basis by dividing by 365. Then express inventories as a multiple of the daily cost of goods sold:

$$\text{Days in inventory} = \frac{\text{average inventory}}{\text{cost of goods sold} \div 365}$$

$$= \frac{(339.9 + 350) \div 2}{(1980 \div 365)} = 63.6 \text{ days}$$

A low level of inventories is often regarded as a sign of efficiency. But don't jump to conclusions; it may simply indicate that the firm is living from hand to mouth.

Average Collection Period   The average collection period measures how quickly customers pay their bills:

$$\text{Average collection period} = \frac{\text{average receivables}}{\text{sales} \div 365}$$

$$= \frac{(433.1 + 440) \div 2}{2200 \div 365} = 72.4 \text{ days}$$

A low ratio is again believed to indicate an efficient collection department, but it sometimes results from an unduly restrictive credit policy.

Profitability Ratios

Net Profit Margin If you want to know the proportion of sales that finds its way into profits, you look at the profit margin. Thus,[4]

$$\text{Net profit margin} = \frac{(\text{EBIT} - \text{tax})}{\text{sales}} = \frac{(166.7 - 50.7)}{2{,}200} = .053, \text{ or } 5.3\%$$

Return on Assets (ROA) Managers often measure the performance of the firm by the ratio of income to total assets (income is usually defined as earnings before interest but after taxes). This is known as the firm's *return on assets* (ROA) or *return on investment* (ROI):[5]

$$\text{Return on assets} = \frac{(\text{EBIT} - \text{tax})}{(\text{average total assets})}$$

$$= \frac{(166.7 - 50.7)}{(1{,}406.1 + 1{,}450) \div 2} = .081, \text{ or } 8.1\%$$

Another measure focuses on the return on the firm's equity:

$$\text{Return on equity (ROE)} = \frac{\text{earnings available for common stockholders}}{\text{average equity}}$$

$$= \frac{76}{(559.6 + 590) \div 2} = .132, \text{ or } 13.2\%$$

It is natural for firms to compare the return that they are earning with the opportunity cost of capital. Of course, the assets in Executive Paper's books are shown at *net book value*, that is, original

---

[4]Net profit margin is sometimes measured as net income ÷ sales. This ignores the profits that are paid out to debtholders as interest and should therefore not be used to compare firms with different capital structures.

When making comparisons between firms, it makes sense to recognize that firms which pay more interest pay less tax. We suggest that you calculate the tax that the company would pay if it were all-equity-financed. To do this you need to adjust taxes by adding back interest tax shields (interest payments × marginal tax rate). Using an assumed tax rate of 40 percent,

$$\text{Net profit margin} = \frac{\text{EBIT} - (\text{tax} + \text{interest tax shields})}{\text{sales}}$$

$$= \frac{166.7 - [50.7 + (.4 \times 40)]}{2{,}200} = .045, \text{ or } 4.5\%$$

[5]When comparing the returns on total assets of firms with different capital structures, it makes sense to add back interest tax shields (see footnote 4). This adjusted ratio then measures the return that the company would have earned if it were all-equity-financed.

One other point about return on assets: Since profits are a flow figure and assets are a snapshot figure, analysts commonly divide profits by the average of assets at the start and end of the year. The reason that they do this is that the firm may raise large amounts of new capital during the year and then put it to work. Therefore part of the year's earnings is a return of new capital.

However, this measure is potentially misleading and should not be compared with the cost of capital. After all, when we defined the return that shareholders require from investing in the capital market, we divided expected profit by the initial outlay, not by an average of starting and ending values.

cost less any depreciation.[6] The assets' actual values may be less, so a low ROA does not necessarily imply that those assets could be better employed elsewhere. Nor would a high ROA mean that you could buy the same assets today and get a high return.

In a competitive industry, firms can expect to earn only their cost of capital. Therefore, a high return on assets is sometimes cited as an indication that the firm is taking advantage of a monopoly position to charge excessive prices. For example, when a public utility commission tries to determine whether a utility is charging a fair price, much of the argument will center on a comparison of the return that the utility is earning on its assets (its ROA) and the cost of capital.

Payout Ratio   The payout ratio measures the proportion of earnings that is paid out as dividends. Thus

$$\text{Payout ratio} = \frac{\text{dividends}}{\text{earnings}} = \frac{45.6}{76} = .6$$

We saw in Chapter 7 that managers don't like to cut dividends because of a shortfall in earnings. Therefore, if a company's earnings are particularly variable, management is likely to play it safe by setting a low average payout ratio. When earnings fall unexpectedly, this payout ratio is likely to rise temporarily. Likewise, if earnings are expected to rise next year, management may feel that it can pay somewhat more generous dividends than it would otherwise have done.

Market-Value Ratios

There is no law that prohibits the financial manager from introducing data which are not in the company accounts. For example, in the case of a paper company, you might want to look at the cost per ton of paper produced; for an airline you might calculate revenues per passenger mile, and so on. Managers also find it helpful to look at ratios that combine accounting and stock market data. Here are four of these market-based ratios.

Price–Earnings Ratio   The price–earnings, or P/E, ratio measures the price that investors are prepared to pay for each dollar of earnings. In the case of Executive Paper:

$$\text{P/E ratio} = \frac{\text{stock price}}{\text{earnings per share}} = \frac{50}{5.37} = 9.3$$

A high P/E ratio may indicate that investors think the firm has good growth opportunities or that its earnings are relatively safe and therefore more valuable. Of course, it may also mean temporarily depressed earnings. If a company just breaks even, reporting zero earnings, its P/E ratio is infinite.

---

[6]More careful comparisons between the return on assets and the cost of capital need to recognize the biases in accounting numbers. See, for example, E. Solomon and J. Laya, "Measurement of Company Profitability: Some Systematic Errors in the Accounting Rate of Return," in A. A. Robicheck (ed.), *Financial Research and Management Decisions,* John Wiley & Sons, Inc., New York, 1967, pp. 152–183.

Dividend Yield The stock's dividend yield is simply the expected dividend as a proportion of the stock price. Thus for Executive Paper,

$$\text{Dividend yield} = \frac{\text{dividend per share}}{\text{stock price}} = \frac{3.22}{50} = .064, \text{ or } 6.4\%$$

Remember that the return to an investor comes in two forms, dividend yield and capital appreciation. If a stock has a low dividend yield, it may indicate that investors are content with a relatively low rate of return or that they are looking for the compensation of a rapid growth in dividends and consequent capital gains.

Market-to-Book Ratio The market-to-book ratio is the ratio of the stock price to book value per share. For Executive Paper,

$$\text{Market-to-book ratio} = \frac{\text{stock price}}{\text{book value per share}} = \frac{50}{590 \div 14.16} = 1.2$$

Book value per share is just stockholders' book equity divided by the number of shares outstanding. Book equity equals common stock plus retained earnings—the net amount that the firm has received from stockholders or reinvested on their behalf.[7] Thus Executive Paper's market-to-book ratio of 1.2 means that the firm is worth 20 percent more than past and present stockholders have put into it.

Suppose that you need to estimate the value of a business that is proposing to make an initial sale of its common stock. You would probably wish to make some careful forecasts of its cash flows and discount them to find their present value. But it would also make sense to use a few market-value ratios to check that your estimate of value is in the right ballpark. For example, you may be able to identify some comparable companies whose values you already know. If the market values of these firms are well in excess of their book values and they truly have similar prospects and accounting policies, then you might reasonably conclude that your business also is worth much more than its book value. Similarly, if the comparable firms are selling at above-average price–earnings multiples, you might judge that the value of your business would also be a high multiple of its earnings.

Tobin's q The ratio of the market value of a company's debt and equity to the current replacement cost of its assets is often called *Tobin's q*, after the economist James Tobin:[8]

$$\text{Tobin's } q = \frac{\text{market value of assets}}{\text{estimated replacement cost}}$$

$$= \frac{(400 + 708)}{1,231} = .9$$

---

[7]Retained earnings are measured net of depreciation. They represent stockholders' new investment in the business over and above the amount needed to maintain the firm's existing stock of assets.

[8]J. Tobin, "A General Equilibrium Approach to Monetary Theory," *Journal of Money, Credit, and Banking* 1 (February 1969), pp. 15–29.

This ratio is like the market-to-book ratio, but there are several important differences. The numerator of q includes all the firm's debt and equity securities, not just its common stock. The denominator includes all assets, not just the firm's equity. Also these assets are entered not at original cost, as shown in the firm's books, but at what it would cost to replace them. Since inflation has driven the replacement cost of many assets well above their original cost, the Financial Accounting Standards Board (FASB) recommended procedures that would take into account the impact of inflation. Until 1985 large companies in the United States were obliged to report these current-cost adjustments. Since inflation subsided in the mid-1980s, it has become a voluntary inclusion in the firm's financial statements. Most firms no longer report the current cost of their assets, and therefore you need to adjust historic costs for inflation before you can calculate q.

Tobin argued that firms have an incentive to invest when q is greater than 1 (i.e., when capital equipment is worth more than the cost of replacing it) and that they will stop investing only when q is less than 1 (i.e., when equipment is worth less than its replacement cost). When q is less than 1, it may be cheaper to acquire assets through merger than to buy new assets.

Of course, it is possible to think of cases where the existing assets are worth much more than they cost, but there is no scope for further profitable investment. Nevertheless, a high value for q is usually a sign of valuable growth opportunities. The reverse is also true. Just because an asset is worth *less* than it would cost if bought today, you should not necessarily conclude that it can be better employed elsewhere. But companies such as Executive Paper, whose assets are valued below replacement cost, ought to be looking over their shoulders to see whether predators are threatening to take them over and redeploy the assets.

We should expect q to be higher for firms with a strong competitive advantage, and so it turns out. The companies with the highest values for q tend to be those with very strong brand images or know-how. Those with the lowest values have generally been in highly competitive and shrinking industries.[9]

Choosing a Benchmark

The left-hand columns of Table 15.4 summarize the key financial ratios for Executive Paper. In addition to the ratios that we have outlined above, we have added (and starred) a few other ratios that you may well encounter. Some are simply alternative ways to express the same result; others are variations on a theme.

Are the ratios for Executive Paper a cause for concern or congratulation? A good starting point is to compare the current year's ratios with equivalent figures for earlier years. It is also helpful to compare Executive Paper's financial position with that of other firms in the same industry. In the final column of Table 15.4 we show the equivalent ratios for a sample of paper and forest product companies.[10] For example, you can see that Executive Paper was more profitable than other companies and more liquid.

Financial ratios for different industries are published by the U.S. Department of Commerce, Dun and Bradstreet, Robert Morris Associates, and others. Table 15.5 gives the principal ratios for major industry groups. It should give you a feel for some of the differences between industries. For

---

[9]See, for example, E. B. Lindberg and S. A. Ross, "Tobin's q Ratio and Industrial Organization," *Journal of Business* 54 (January 1981), 1–33.

[10]You need to be careful when averaging financial ratios, since the average may be dominated by one outlying value. Table 15.4, therefore, reports median ratios for the sample of companies.

TABLE 15.4

Financial ratios for Executive Paper and a sample of large paper and forest product companies

		EXECUTIVE PAPER	OTHER PAPER COMPANIES
Leverage Ratios:			
Debt ratio	(Long-term debt + leases)/(long-term debt + leases + equity)	.40	.47
*Debt ratio (including short-term debt)	(Long-term debt + leases + short-term debt)/ (long-term debt + leases + short-term debt + equity)	.46	.50
Debt–equity ratio	(Long-term debt + leases)/equity	.68	.87
Times-interest-earned	(EBIT + depreciation)/interest	5.5	4.2
Liquidity Ratios:			
*Net-working-capital-to-total assets	(current assets – current liabilities)/total assets	.30	.06
Current ratio	Current assets/current liabilities	1.9	1.7
Quick ratio	(Cash + short-term securities + receivables)/ current liabilities	1.2	.91
Cash ratio	(Cash + short-term securities)/current liabilities	.2	.08
*Interval measure	(Cash + short-term securities + receivables)/ (costs from operations/365)	101.4	52.7
Efficiency Ratios:			
Sales-to-assets ratio	Sales/average total assets	1.54	.73
*Sales-to-net-working-capital	Sales/average net working capital	5.08	12.0
Days in inventory	Average inventory/(goods sold/365)	63.6	45.2
*Inventory turnover	Cost of goods sold/average inventory	5.74	8.08
Average collection period (days)	Average receivables/(sales/365)	72.4	4.26
*Receivables turnover	Sales/average receivables	5.04	8.56
Profitability Ratios:			
Net profit margin	(EBIT – tax)/sales	5.3%	4.7%
Return on assets (ROA)	(EBIT – tax)/average total assets	8.1%	4.6%
Return on equity (ROE)	Earnings available for common stockholders/ average equity	13.2%	3.7%
Payout ratio	Dividend per share/earnings per share	.6	.5
Market-Value Ratios:			
Price–earnings ratio (P/E)	Stock price/earnings per share	9.3	19.4
Dividend yield	Dividend per share/stock price	6.4%	2.2%
Market-to-book ratio	Stock price/book value per share	1.2	1.5
Tobin's q	Market value of assets/ estimated replacement cost	.9	NA

*This ratio is an extra bonus not discussed in this chapter.

TABLE 15.5			

Financial ratios for major industry groups, second quarter, 1998

	ALL MANUFACTURING CORPORATIONS	FOOD AND KINDRED PRODUCTS	PRINTING AND PUBLISHING
Debt ratio*	.36	.43	.39
Net-working-capital-to-total assets	.08	.05	.06
Current ratio	1.32	1.23	1.34
Quick ratio	.68	.56	.88
Sales-to-total assets	1.04	1.23	.82
Net profit margin (%)[†]	5.35	6.41	7.07
Return on total assets (%)	5.58	7.86	5.80
Return on equity (%)[††]	16.83	18.09	12.20
Dividend payout ratio	.48	.57	.45

*Long-term debt includes capitalized leases and deferred income taxes.

[†]Reflects operating income only.

[††]Reflects nonoperating as well as operating income.

Source: U.S. Department of Commerce, *Quarterly Report for Manufacturing, Mining and Trade Corporations,* second quarter 1998.

example, you can see that retailers carry much more working capital than manufacturing companies, generate a higher ratio of sales to assets, but earn a lower profit margin on these sales.

Accounting Rules and Definitions

When comparing financial ratios, it is important to remember that accountants in the United States still have a fair degree of leeway in reporting earnings and book values. For example, accountants have discretion in the way they treat intangible assets such as patents, trademarks, or franchises. Some believe that including these items on the balance sheet provides the best measure of the company's value as a going concern. Others take a more conservative approach and exclude intangible assets. They reason that, if the firm were liquidated, these assets would be largely valueless.

Even bigger differences arise in international comparisons. For example, in the United States firms generally maintain one set of accounts that is sent to investors and a different set of accounts

CHEMICAL AND ALLIED PRODUCTS	PETROLEUM AND COAL PRODUCTS	MACHINERY EXCEPT ELECTRICAL	ELECTRICAL AND ELECTRONIC EQUIPMENT	RETAIL TRADE
.38	.35	.29	.23	.35
.03	−.03	.17	.12	.16
1.14	.85	1.57	1.45	1.55
.56	.44	.91	.82	.49
.76	.85	1.19	1.02	2.06
7.18	4.71	3.11	5.88	3.23
5.45	4.02	3.71	5.99	6.66
20.78	14.39	15.47	12.23	12.57
.61	.67	.31	.34	.44

that is used to calculate their tax bill. That would not be allowed in most countries. On the other hand, standards in the United States are more stringent in other regards. For instance, German firms can smooth reported profits by tucking money away in hidden reserve accounts and untucking it again on a rainy day.

When Daimler-Benz AG, producer of the Daimler-Benz automobile, decided to list its shares on the New York Stock Exchange in 1993, it was required to revise its accounting practices to conform to U.S. standards. While it reported a modest profit in the first half of 1993 using German accounting rules, it reported a loss of $592 million under the more revealing U.S. rules, primarily because of differences in the treatment of reserves.

As you can imagine, these variations in accounting practice can lead to problems when comparing the financial ratios of firms in different countries. For example, because German companies are able to hide money in reserve accounts, the equity in their balance sheet is usually understated and the companies appear much more highly levered than their counterparts in the United States.

Rajan and Zingales found that, when they adjusted for accounting differences, debt ratios in Germany were on average *below* those in the United States.[11]

The DuPont system

Some of the profitability and efficiency ratios that we described above can be linked in useful ways. These relationships are often referred to as the **DuPont system,** in recognition of the chemical company that popularized them.

The first relationship links the return on assets (ROA) with the firm's sales-to-assets ratio and its profit margin:

$$\text{ROA} = \frac{\text{EBIT} - \text{tax}}{\text{assets}} = \underset{\underset{\substack{\text{sales-to-} \\ \text{assets ratio}}}{\Uparrow}}{\frac{\text{sales}}{\text{assets}}} \times \underset{\underset{\substack{\text{profit} \\ \text{margin}}}{\Uparrow}}{\frac{\text{EBIT} - \text{tax}}{\text{sales}}}$$

All firms would like to earn a higher return on assets, but their ability to do so is limited by competition. If the expected return on assets is fixed by competition, firms face a trade-off between the sales-to-assets ratio and the profit margin. Thus we find that fast-food chains, which turn over their capital frequently, also tend to operate on low profit margins. Classy hotels have relatively high margins, but this is offset by lower sales-to-assets ratios.

Firms often seek to increase their profit margins by becoming more vertically integrated; for example, they may acquire a supplier or one of their sales outlets. Unfortunately, unless they have some special skill in running these new businesses, they are likely to find that any gain in profit margin is offset by a decline in the sales-to-assets ratio.

The return on equity (ROE) can be broken down as follows:

$$\text{ROE} = \frac{\text{EBIT} - \text{tax} - \text{interest}}{\text{equity}}$$

$$= \underset{\underset{\substack{\text{leverage} \\ \text{ratio}}}{\Uparrow}}{\frac{\text{assets}}{\text{equity}}} \times \underset{\underset{\substack{\text{sales-to-} \\ \text{assets} \\ \text{ratio}}}{\Uparrow}}{\frac{\text{sales}}{\text{assets}}} \times \underset{\underset{\substack{\text{profit} \\ \text{margin}}}{\Uparrow}}{\frac{\text{EBIT} - \text{tax}}{\text{sales}}} \times \underset{\underset{\substack{\text{``debt} \\ \text{burden''}}}{\Uparrow}}{\frac{\text{EBIT} - \text{tax} - \text{interest}}{(\text{EBIT} - \text{tax})}}$$

Notice that the product of the two middle terms is the return on assets. This depends on the firm's production and marketing skills and is unaffected by the firm's financing mix.[12] However, the first and fourth terms do depend on the debt–equity mix. The first term measures the ratio of total assets to equity, while the last term measures the extent to which profits are reduced by interest. If

---

[11]R. G. Rajan and L. Zingales, "What Do We Know About Capital Structure? Some Evidence from International Data," *Journal of Finance* 50 (December 1995), pp. 1421–1460.

[12]There is a complication here because the amount of tax paid does depend on the financing mix. We suggested in footnote 4 that it would be better to add back any interest tax shields when calculating the firm's profit margin.

the firm is leveraged, the first term is greater than 1.0 (assets are greater than equity) and the fourth term is less than 1.0 (part of the profits are absorbed by interest). Thus leverage can either increase or reduce the return on equity.

The Uses of Financial Ratios

Before we leave the topic of financial ratios, we should remind you how frequently they are referred to in financial decisions.

Consider, for example, leverage ratios. Whenever a company ponders an issue of bonds, the financial manager needs to consider whether the new borrowing is prudent and its leverage is within the ballpark of standard practice. That involves looking at the debt and times-interest-earned ratios. If the firm decides to go ahead with the issue, the interest rate will depend on the bond's rating. In deciding on this rating, the bond-rating companies, such as Moody's and Standard and Poor's, must satisfy themselves about the creditworthiness of the company and its ability to service the new debt. Therefore they also pay close attention to the standard leverage ratios. The lenders too are interested in bond quality; they don't want to lend to a triple-A borrower today only to find a few years later that they own a junk bond. So, to ensure that the firm keeps its borrowing within prudent limits, the bond contract will specify a maximum debt ratio. Thus, the firm that is issuing the bonds, the bond-rating companies, and the investors that buy the bonds all need to measure the firm's leverage. To do so, they use a few key financial ratios.

Or consider the standard efficiency ratios. If the firm is reviewing its operations to identify which activities should be expanded or shut down, one of the first measures that the manager will look at is the return that each business is earning on its assets. Of course, differences in these returns may reflect how well each business is being run. So those divisional managers whose businesses are earning more than their cost of capital are likely to get a pat on the back; those whose divisions are earning inadequate returns are likely to face some tough questions or worse. In this way each division's return on assets is linked formally or informally to the firm's reward system. A high return on assets is likely to be welcomed by the company's shareholders, but it may also draw criticism from consumers' groups or regulators that the firm is charging excessive prices. Naturally, such conclusions are seldom cut and dried. There is plenty of room for argument as to whether the return on assets is properly measured or whether it exceeds the cost of capital.

FINANCIAL PLANNING

Executive Paper's financial statements not only help management to understand the past, but they also provide the starting point for developing a financial plan for the future.

Financial plans begin with the firm's product development and sales objectives. For example, Executive Paper's corporate staff might ask each division to submit three alternative business plans covering the next five years:

1. A *best-case* or aggressive growth plan calling for heavy capital investment and new products, increased market share of existing markets, or entry into new markets.
2. A *normal growth* plan in which the division grows with its markets but not significantly at the expense of its competitors.
3. A plan of *retrenchment* designed to minimize required capital outlays. This is planning for lean economic times.

Of course, the planners might also look at the opportunities and costs of moving into a wholly new area where the company can exploit its existing strengths. Often they may recommend entering the market for strategic reasons, that is, not because the *immediate* investment has positive net present value but because it establishes the firm in the market and creates *options* for possibly valuable follow-up investments. In other words, there is a two-stage decision. At the second stage (the follow-up project) the financial manager faces a standard capital budgeting problem. But at the first stage projects may be valuable primarily for the options they bring with them.[13]

To see the financial consequences of the business plan, Executive Paper's financial manager needs to translate them into forecasts of future cash flows. If the likely operating cash flow is insufficient to cover the planned dividend payments and investment in net working capital and fixed assets, then the firm needs to ensure that it can raise the balance by borrowing or by the sale of additional shares.

When they prepare a financial plan, wise managers don't look just at the most likely financial consequences. They also plan for the unexpected. Some do so by working through the consequences of the plan under the most likely set of circumstances and they then use *sensitivity analysis* to vary the assumptions one at a time. Others look at the consequences of a business plan under several plausible scenarios.[14] For example, one scenario might envisage high interest rates leading to a slowdown in world economic growth and lower commodity prices. The second scenario might involve a buoyant domestic economy, high inflation, and a weak currency.

FINANCIAL PLANNING MODELS

Suppose that management's plans call for a 20 percent annual growth in Executive Paper's sales and profits over the next five years. Can the company realistically expect to finance this out of retained earnings and borrowing, or should it plan for an issue of equity? Spreadsheet programs are tailor-made for questions such as these. Let's investigate.

The basic sources and uses relationship tells us that

External capital required

= operating cash flow

– investment in net working capital

– investment in fixed assets

– dividends

Thus there are four steps to finding how much extra cash Executive Paper will need and the implications for its debt ratio:

Step 1:   Project next year's operating cash flow (depreciation provision plus net income) assuming the planned 20 percent increase in revenues. This gives the total sources of funds in the absence of

---

[13]The importance of these real options to strategic decisions is emphasized in S. C. Myers, "Finance Theory and Financial Strategy," *Interfaces* 14 (January–February 1984), pp. 126–137.

[14]For a description of the use of different planning scenarios in the Royal Dutch/Shell group, see P. Wack, "Scenarios: Uncharted Waters Ahead," *Harvard Business Review* 63 (September–October 1985) and "Scenarios: Shooting the Rapids," *Harvard Business Review* 64 (November–December 1985).

any new issue of securities. Look, for example, at the second column of Table 15.6, which provides a forecast of operating cash flow in year 2000 for Executive Paper.

Step 2:   Project what additional investment in net working capital and fixed assets will be needed to support this increased activity and how much of the net income will be paid out as dividends. The sum of these expenditures gives you the total *uses* of funds. The second column of Table 15.7 provides a forecast of uses of funds for Executive Paper.

Step 3:   Calculate the difference between the projected operating cash flow (from Step 1) and the projected uses (Step 2). This is the cash that will need to be raised from new sales of securities. For example, you can see from Table 15.7 that Executive Paper will need to issue $157.5 million of debt if it is to expand at the planned rate and not sell more shares.

Step 4:   Finally, construct a pro forma balance sheet that incorporates the additional assets and the increase in debt and equity. This is done in the second column of Table 15.8. Executive Paper's equity increases by the additional retained earnings (net income less dividends), while long-term debt is increased by the $157.5 million new issue.

TABLE 15.6

Latest and pro forma income statements for Executive Paper (figures in $ millions)

	1999	2000	2004
Revenues	2,200	2,640	5,474
Costs (90% of revenues)	1,980	2,376	4,927
Depreciation (10% of fixed assets at start of year)	53.3	55.0	114
EBIT	166.7	209.0	433.4
Interest (10% of long-term debt at start of year)	40	40	125.8
Tax (40% of pretax profit)	50.7	67.6	123.0
Net income	76.0	101.4	184.5
Operating cash flow	129.3	156.4	298.5

TABLE 15.7

Latest and pro forma statements of sources and uses of funds for Executive Paper (figures in $ millions)

	1999	2000	2004
Increase in net working capital (NWC) assuming NWC = 20% of revenues	13.5	88	182.5
Investment in fixed assets (FA) assuming FA = 25% of revenues	70.2	165	342.1
Dividend (60% of net income)	45.6	60.8	110.7
Total uses of funds	129.3	313.8	635.3
External capital required = Total uses of funds − operating cash flow	0	157.5	336.8

TABLE 15.8			

Latest and pro forma balance sheets for Executive Paper (figures in $ millions)

	1999	2000	2004
Net working capital (20% of revenues)	440	528	1,095
Net fixed assets (25% of revenues)	550	660	1,369
Total net assets	990	1,188	2,464
Long-term debt	400	557.5	1,595
Equity	590	630.5	869
Total long-term liabilities and equity	990	1,188	2,464

Once you have set up the spreadsheet, it is easy to run out your projections for several years. The final columns in Tables 15.6–15.8 show the pro forma income statement, sources and uses of funds, and balance sheet for the year 2004 assuming Executive Paper continues to fund a 20 percent annual growth rate solely from retained earnings and new debt issues. Over the five-year period Executive Paper would need to borrow an additional $1.2 billion and by year 2004 the company's long-term debt ratio would have increased to 65 percent. Most financial managers would regard this as sailing too close to the wind, and the debt ratio would probably be above the limit set by the company's banks and bondholders.

The obvious solution for Executive Paper is to issue a mix of debt and equity, but there are other possibilities that the financial manager may want to explore. One option may be to hold back dividends during this period of rapid growth, but it turns out that even a complete dividend freeze would still leave Executive Paper needing to raise just under $1 billion of new funds. An alternative might be to investigate whether the company could economize on net working capital. For example, we have seen that on average Executive Paper's customers take 72 days to pay their bills. Simply cutting the average payment delay by one third would release about $400 million more cash to support the planned growth.

We stated earlier that financial planning is not just about exploring how to cope with the most likely outcomes. It is also concerned with ensuring the firm is prepared for unlikely ones. For example, the paper industry has high fixed costs and is notoriously exposed to economic downturn. Executive Paper's financial manager would certainly wish to check that the firm could cope with a cyclical decline in sales and profit margins. Sensitivity or scenario analysis can help the manager to do so.

Pitfalls in Model Design

The Executive Paper model that we have developed is too simple for practical application. You probably have already thought of several ways to improve it—by keeping track of the outstanding shares, for example, and printing out earnings and dividends per share. Or you might want to distinguish between short-term lending and borrowing opportunities, now buried in working capital.

The model that we developed for Executive Paper is known as a *percentage of sales model.* Almost all the forecasts for the company are proportional to the forecasted level of sales. However, in reality many variables will *not* be proportional to sales. For example, important components of working capital such as inventory and cash balances will generally rise less rapidly than sales. In addition, fixed assets such as plant and equipment are typically not added in small increments as sales increase. Executive Paper's plant may well be operating at less than full capacity, so that the company can initially increase output without *any* additions to capacity. Eventually, however, if sales continue to increase, the firm may need to make a large new investment in plant and equipment.

But beware of adding too much complexity: There is always the temptation to make a model bigger and more detailed. You may end up with an exhaustive model that is too cumbersome for routine use. The fascination of detail, if you give in to it, distracts attention from crucial decisions like stock issues and dividend policy.

There Is No Finance in Financial Planning Models

Why do we say there is no finance in these corporate financial models? The first reason is that they usually incorporate an accountant's view of the world. They are designed to forecast accounting statements. They do not emphasize the tools of financial analysis: incremental cash flow, present value, market risk, and so on.[15]

This may not matter as long as everyone recognizes the financial forecasts for what they are. However, you sometimes hear managers stating corporate goals in terms of accounting numbers. They may say, "Our objective is to achieve an annual sales growth of 20 percent," or "We want a 25 percent return on book equity and a profit margin of 10 percent." On the surface such objectives don't make sense. Shareholders want to be richer, not to have the satisfaction of a 10 percent profit margin. Also, a goal that is stated in terms of accounting ratios is not operational unless it is translated back into what the statement means for business decisions. For example, what does a 10 percent profit margin imply—higher prices, lower costs, increased vertical integration, or a move into new, high-margin products?

So why do managers define objectives in this way? In part such goals may be a mutual exhortation to try harder, like singing the company song before work. But we suspect that managers are often using a code to communicate real concerns. For example, the goal to increase sales rapidly may reflect managers' belief that increased market share is needed to achieve scale economies, or a target profit margin may be a way of saying that the firm has been pursuing sales growth at the expense of margins. The danger is that everyone may forget the code and the accounting targets may be seen as goals in themselves.

The second reason for saying that there is no finance in these planning models is that they produce no signposts pointing toward optimal financial decisions. They do not even tell us which alternatives are worth examining. For example, we saw that Executive Paper is planning to grow its sales and earnings per share. But is that good news for the shareholders? Well, not necessarily; it depends on the opportunity cost of the additional capital that Executive Paper needs to invest. If the new investment earns more than the cost of capital, it will have a positive NPV and add to shareholder wealth. But, suppose that it earns less than the cost of capital. In this case Executive Paper's investment makes shareholders worse off, even though the company is recording steady growth in earnings per share. Executive's planning model tells it how much

---

[15]Of course, there is no reason that the manager can't use the output to calculate the present value of the firm (given some assumption about growth beyond the planning period), and this is sometimes done.

money the firm must raise to fund the planned growth, but it cannot say whether that growth contributes to shareholder value.

The capital that Executive Paper needs to raise depends on its decision to pay out two-thirds of its earnings as a dividend. But the financial planning model does not tell us whether this dividend payment makes sense or what mixture of equity or debt the company should issue. In the end the management has to decide. We would like to tell you exactly how to make the choice, but we can't. There is no model that encompasses all the complexities encountered in financial planning.

As a matter of fact, there never will be one. This bold statement is based on Brealey and Myers's Third Law:

- *Axiom:* The number of unsolved problems is infinite.
- *Axiom:* The number of unsolved problems that humans can hold in their minds is at any time limited to 10.
- *Law:* Therefore in any field there will always be 10 problems which can be addressed but which have no formal solution.

Brealey and Myers's Third Law implies that no model can find the best of all financial strategies.[16]

GROWTH AND EXTERNAL FINANCING

We started this chapter by noting that financial plans force managers to be consistent in their goals for growth, investment, and financing. Before leaving the topic of financial planning, we should look at some general relationships between a firm's growth objectives and its financing needs.

Recall that in 1999 Executive Paper started the year with fixed assets and net working capital of $960 million. It plowed back $30.4 million. So assets increased by 30.4/960 or 3.17 percent. Thus Executive Paper grew by 3.17 percent without needing to raise additional capital. The growth rate that the company can achieve without additional external funds is known as the *internal growth rate.* For Executive Paper

$$\text{Internal growth rate} = \frac{\text{retained earnings}}{\text{assets}} = 3.17\%$$

We can gain more insight into what determines this internal growth rate by multiplying the top and bottom of the expression for internal growth by *net income* and *equity* as follows:

$$\text{Internal growth rate} = \frac{\text{retained earnings}}{\text{net income}} \times \frac{\text{net income}}{\text{equity}} \times \frac{\text{equity}}{\text{assets}}$$

$$= \text{plowback ratio} \times \text{return on equity} \times \frac{\text{equity}}{\text{assets}}$$

Executive Paper plows back 40 percent of net income and earns a return of 13.6 percent on the equity with which it began the year. At the start of 1999 equity finances 58.3 percent of Executive Paper's assets. Therefore,

$$\text{Internal growth rate} = .40 \times .136 \times .583 = .0317, \text{ or } 3.17\%$$

---

[16]It is possible to build linear programming models that help search for the best strategy subject to specified assumptions and constraints. These models can be more effective in screening alternative financial strategies.

Notice that if Executive Paper wishes to grow faster than this without raising equity capital, it would need to (1) plow back a higher proportion of its earnings, (2) earn a higher return on equity (ROE), or (3) have a lower debt-to-equity ratio.[17]

Instead of focusing on how rapidly the company can grow without *any* external financing, Executive Paper's financial manager may be interested in the growth rate that can be sustained without additional *equity* issues. Of course, if the firm is able to raise enough debt, virtually any growth rate can be financed. It makes more sense to assume that the firm has settled on an optimal capital structure which it will maintain as equity is increased by the retained earnings. Thus the firm issues only enough debt to keep the debt–equity ratio constant. The *sustainable growth rate* is the highest growth rate the firm can maintain without increasing its financial leverage. It turns out that the sustainable growth rate depends only on the plowback rate and the return on equity:

$$\text{Sustainable growth rate} = \text{plowback ratio} \times \text{return on equity}$$

For Executive Paper,

$$\text{Sustainable growth rate} = .4 \times .136 = .0543, \text{ or } 5.43\%$$

These simple formulas remind us that financial plans need to be consistent. Firms may grow rapidly in the short term by relying on debt finance, but such growth cannot be maintained without incurring excessive debt levels.

SUMMARY

Managers use financial statements to monitor their own company's performance, to help understand the policies of a competitor, or to check on the health of a customer. But there is a danger of being overwhelmed by the sheer volume of data. That is why managers use a few salient ratios to summarize the firm's leverage, liquidity, efficiency, profitability, and market valuation. We have described some of the more popular financial ratios.

We offer the following general advice to users of these ratios:

1. Financial ratios seldom provide answers, but they do help you to ask the right questions.
2. There is no international standard for financial ratios. A little thought and common sense are worth far more than blind application of formulas.
3. You need a benchmark for assessing a company's financial position. Compare financial ratios with the company's ratios in earlier years and with the ratios of other firms in the same business.

Understanding the past is the first step to being prepared for the future. Most firms prepare a financial plan that describes the firm's strategy and projects its future consequences by means of pro forma balance sheets, income statements, and statements of sources and uses of funds. The plan establishes financial goals and is a benchmark for evaluating subsequent performance.

The plan is the end result, but the process that produces the plan is valuable in its own right. First, planning forces the financial manager to consider the combined effects of all the firm's investment and financing decisions. This is important because these decisions interact and should

---

[17]Notice that the internal growth rate does not stay constant over time. As the firm plows back earnings, the debt-to-equity ratio declines and the internal growth rate increases.

not be made independently. Second, planning requires the manager to consider events that could upset the firm's progress and to devise strategies to be held in reserve for counterattack when unhappy surprises occur.

There is no theory or model that leads straight to *the* optimal financial strategy. Consequently, financial planning proceeds by trial and error. Many different strategies may be projected under a range of assumptions about the future. The dozens of separate projections that may be made during this trial-and-error process generate a heavy load of arithmetic. Firms have responded by developing corporate financial planning models to forecast the financial consequences of different strategies. We showed how you can use a simple spreadsheet model to analyze Executive Paper's strategies. But remember there is no finance in these models. Their primary purpose is to produce accounting statements.

Further Reading

There are some good general texts on financial statement analysis. See, for example:
G. Foster: *Financial Statement Analysis*, 2d ed., Prentice-Hall, Inc., Englewood Cliffs, N.J., 1986.

K. G. Palepu, V. L. Bernard, and P. M. Healy, *Business Analysis and Valuation: Using Financial Statements*, South-Western College Publishing, Cincinnati, OH, 1996.

Three classic articles on the application of financial ratios to specific problems are:
W. H. Beaver: "Financial Ratios as Predictors of Failure," *Empirical Research in Accounting: Selected Studies,* supplement to *Journal of Accounting Research*, 1966, pp. 77–111.

W. H. Beaver, P. Kettler, and M. Scholes: "The Association between Market-Determined and Accounting-Determined Risk Measures," *Accounting Review,* 45:654–682 (October 1970).

J. O. Horrigan: "The Determination of Long Term Credit Standing with Financial Ratios," *Empirical Research in Accounting: Selected Studies*, supplement to *Journal of Accounting Research*, 1966, pp. 44–62.

Corporate planning has an extensive literature of its own. Good books and articles include:
G. Donaldson: "Financial Goals and Strategic Consequences," *Harvard Business Review,* 63:57–66 (May–June 1985).

G. Donaldson: *Strategy for Financial Mobility,* Harvard Business School Press, Boston, 1986.

A. C. Hax and N. S. Majluf: *The Strategy Concept and Process—A Pragmatic Approach,* 2d ed., Prentice-Hall, Inc., Englewood Cliffs, N.J., 1996.

The links between capital budgeting, strategy, and financial planning are discussed in:
S. C. Myers: "Finance Theory and Financial Strategy," *Interfaces,* 14:126–137 (January–February, 1984).

Here are three references on corporate planning models:
W. T. Carleton, C. L. Dick, Jr., and D. H. Downes: "Financial Policy Models: Theory and Practice," *Journal of Financial and Quantitative Analysis,* 8:691–709 (December 1973).

W. T. Carleton and J. M. McInnes: "Theory, Models and Implementation in Financial Management," *Management Science,* 28:957–978 (September 1982).

S. C. Myers and G. A. Pogue: "A Programming Approach to Corporate Financial Management," *Journal of Finance,* 29:579–599 (May 1974).

SHORT-TERM FINANCIAL PLANNING

Most of this book is devoted to long-term financial decisions such as the choice of capital structure. Such decisions are called *long-term* for two reasons. First, they usually involve long-lived assets or liabilities. Second, they are not easily reversed and therefore may commit the firm to a particular course of action for several years.

Short-term financial decisions generally involve short-lived assets and liabilities, and usually they *are* easily reversed. Compare, for example, a 60-day bank loan for $50 million with a $50 million issue of 20-year bonds. The bank loan is clearly a short-term decision. The firm can repay it two months later and be right back where it started. A firm might conceivably issue a 20-year bond in January and retire it in March, but it would be extremely inconvenient and expensive to do so. In practice, such a bond issue is a long-term decision, not only because of the bond's 20-year maturity but because the decision to issue it cannot be reversed on short notice.

A financial manager responsible for short-term financial decisions does not have to look far into the future. The decision to take the 60-day bank loan could properly be based on cash-flow forecasts for the next few months only. The bond issue decision will normally reflect forecasted cash requirements 5, 10, or more years into the future.

Managers concerned with short-term financial decisions can avoid many of the difficult conceptual issues encountered elsewhere in this book. In a sense, short-term decisions are easier than long-term decisions, but they are not less important. A firm can identify extremely valuable capital investment opportunities, find the precise optimal debt ratio, follow the perfect dividend policy, and yet founder because no one bothers to raise the cash to pay this year's bills. Hence the need for short-term planning.

In this chapter, we will review the major classes of short-term assets and liabilities, show how long-term financing decisions affect the firm's short-term financial planning problem, and describe how financial managers trace changes in cash and working capital. We will also describe how managers forecast month-by-month cash requirements or surpluses and how they develop short-term investment and financing strategies.

THE COMPONENTS OF WORKING CAPITAL

Short-term or *current* assets and liabilities are collectively known as **working capital.** Table 16.1 gives a breakdown of current assets and liabilities for all manufacturing corporations in the United States in 1998. Note that total current assets were $1,319.9 billion and current liabilities were $996.8 billion. **Net working capital** (current assets less current liabilities) was $323.1 billion.

One important current asset is *accounts receivable.* When one company sells goods to another company or a government agency, it does not usually expect to be paid immediately. These unpaid bills, or *trade credit*, make up the bulk of accounts receivable. Companies also sell goods on credit to the final consumer. This *consumer credit* makes up the remainder of accounts receivable. We will discuss the management of receivables in Chapter 17. You will learn how companies decide which customers are good or bad credit risks and when it makes sense to offer credit.

Another important current asset is *inventory.* Inventories may consist of raw materials, work in process, or finished goods awaiting sale and shipment. Firms *invest* in inventory. The cost of holding inventory includes not only storage cost and the risk of spoilage or obsolescence but also the opportunity cost of capital, that is, the rate of return offered by other, equivalent-risk investment opportunities.[1] The benefits of holding inventory are often indirect. For example, a large inventory of finished goods (large relative to expected sales) reduces the chance of a "stockout" if demand is unexpectedly high. A producer holding a small finished-goods inventory is more likely to be caught short, unable to fill orders promptly. Similarly, large inventories of raw materials reduce the chance that an unexpected shortage would force the firm to shut down production or use a more costly substitute material.

Bulk orders for raw materials lead to large average inventories but may be worthwhile if the firm can obtain lower prices from suppliers. (That is, bulk orders may yield quantity discounts.) Firms are often willing to hold large inventories of finished goods for similar reasons. A large inventory of finished goods allows longer, more economical production runs. In effect, the production manager gives the firm a quantity discount.

The task of inventory management is to assess these benefits and costs and to strike a sensible balance. In manufacturing companies the production manager is best placed to make this judgment. Since the financial manager is not usually directly involved in inventory management, we will not discuss the inventory problem in detail.

The remaining current assets are cash and marketable securities. The cash consists of currency, demand deposits (funds in checking accounts), and time deposits (funds in savings accounts). The principal marketable security is commercial paper (short-term, unsecured notes sold by other firms). Other securities include U.S. Treasury bills and state and local government securities.

---

[1]How risky are inventories? It is hard to generalize. Many firms just assume inventories have the same risk as typical capital investments and therefore calculate the cost of holding inventories using the firm's average opportunity cost of capital. You can think of many exceptions to this rule of thumb however. For example, some electronics components are made with gold connections. Should an electronics firm apply its average cost of capital to its inventory of gold?

TABLE 16.1

Current assets and liabilities for U.S. manufacturing corporations, second quarter 1998 (figures in $ billions)

CURRENT ASSETS*		CURRENT LIABILITIES*	
Cash	112.3	Short-term loans	181.4
Marketable securities	88.2	Accounts payable	295.3
Accounts receivable	479.1	Accrued income taxes	38.3
Inventories	465.1	Current payments due on	
		long-term debt	60.3
Other current assets	175.3	Other current liabilities	421.5
Total	1,319.9	Total	996.8

*Net working capital (current assets – current liabilities) is $1,319.9 – $996.8 = $323.1 billion.

Source: U.S. Department of Commerce, *Quarterly Financial Report for Manufacturing, Mining and Trade Corporations,* Second Quarter, 1998, p. 4.

In choosing between cash and marketable securities, the financial manager faces a task like that of the production manager. There are always advantages to holding large "inventories" of cash—they reduce the risk of running out of cash and having to raise more on short notice. On the other hand, there is a cost to holding idle cash balances rather than putting the money to work in marketable securities. In Chapter 18 we will tell you how the financial manager collects and pays out cash and decides on an optimal cash balance.

We have seen that a company's principal current asset consists of unpaid bills from other companies. One firm's credit must be another's debit. Therefore it is not surprising that a company's principal current liability consists of *accounts payable,* that is, outstanding payments to other companies.

To finance its investment in current assets, a company may rely on a variety of short-term loans. Commercial banks are by far the largest source of such loans, but an industrial firm may also borrow from other sources. Another way of borrowing is to sell commercial paper.

Many short-term loans are unsecured, but sometimes the company may offer its inventory or receivables as security. For example, a firm may decide to borrow short-term money secured by its accounts receivable. When its customers have paid their bills, it can use the cash to repay the loan. An alternative procedure is to *sell* the receivables to a financial institution and let it collect the money. In other words, some companies solve their financing problem by borrowing on the strength of their current assets; others solve it by selling their current assets. In Chapter 19 we will look at the varied and ingenious methods of financing current assets.

LINKS BETWEEN LONG-TERM AND SHORT-TERM FINANCING DECISIONS

All businesses require capital, that is, money invested in plant, machinery, inventories, accounts receivable, and all the other assets it takes to run a business efficiently. Typically, these assets are not purchased all at once but obtained gradually over time. Let us call the total cost of these assets the firm's *cumulative capital requirement.*

Most firms' cumulative capital requirement grows irregularly, like the wavy line in Figure 16.1. This line shows a clear upward trend as the firm's business grows. But there is also seasonal variation around the trend: In the figure the capital requirements peak late in each year. Finally, there would be unpredictable week-to-week and month-to-month fluctuations, but we have not attempted to show these in Figure 16.1.

The cumulative capital requirement can be met from either long-term or short-term financing. When long-term financing does not cover the cumulative capital requirement, the firm must raise short-term capital to make up the difference. When long-term financing *more* than covers the cumulative capital requirement, the firm has surplus cash available for short-term investment. Thus the amount of long-term financing raised, given the cumulative capital requirement, determines whether the firm is a short-term borrower or lender.

Lines *A, B,* and *C* in Figure 16.1 illustrate this. Each depicts a different long-term financing strategy. Strategy *A* always implies a short-term cash surplus. Strategy *C* implies a permanent need for short-term borrowing. Under *B,* which is probably the most common strategy, the firm is a short-term lender during part of the year and a borrower during the rest.

What is the *best* level of long-term financing relative to the cumulative capital requirement? It is hard to say. There is no convincing theoretical analysis of this question. We can make practical observations, however. First, most financial managers attempt to "match maturities" of assets and

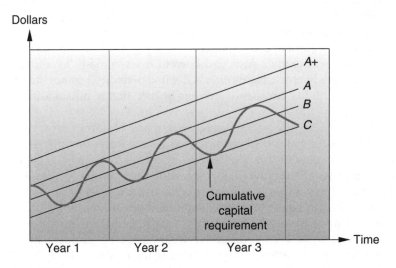

Figure 16.1

The firm's cumulative capital requirement (heavy line) is the cumulative investment in plant, equipment, inventory, and all other assets needed for the business. In this case the requirement grows year by year, but there is seasonal fluctuation within each year. The requirement for short-term financing is the difference between long-term financing (lines A^+, A, B, and C) and the cumulative capital requirement. If long-term financing follows line C, the firm always needs short-term financing. At line B, the need is seasonal. At lines A and A^+, the firm never needs short-term financing. There is always extra cash to invest.

liabilities. That is, they finance long-lived assets like plant and machinery with long-term borrowing and equity. Second, most firms make a permanent investment in net working capital (current assets less current liabilities). They finance this investment from long-term sources.[2]

The Comforts of Surplus Cash

Many financial managers would feel more comfortable under strategy A than strategy C. Strategy A^+ (the highest line) would be still more relaxing. A firm with a surplus of long-term financing never has to worry about borrowing to pay next month's bills. But is the financial manager paid to be comfortable? Firms usually put surplus cash to work in Treasury bills or other marketable securities. This is at best a zero-NPV investment for a taxpaying firm.[3] Thus we think that firms with a *permanent* cash surplus ought to go on a diet, retiring long-term securities to reduce long-term financing to a level at or below the firm's cumulative capital requirement. That is, if the firm is on line A^+, it ought to move down to line A, or perhaps even lower.

TRACING CHANGES IN CASH AND WORKING CAPITAL

Table 16.2 compares 1998 and 1999 year-end balance sheets for Dynamic Mattress Company. Table 16.3 shows the firm's income statement for 1999. Note that Dynamic's cash balance increased by $1 million during 1999. What caused this increase? Did the extra cash come from Dynamic Mattress Company's additional long-term borrowing, from reinvested earnings, from cash released by reducing inventory, or from extra credit extended by Dynamic's suppliers? (Note the increase in accounts payable.)

The correct answer is "all the above," as well as many other activities and actions taken by the firm during the year. All we can say is that *sources* of cash exceeded *uses* by $1 million.

Financial analysts often summarize sources and uses of cash in a statement like the one shown in Table 16.4. The statement shows that Dynamic *generated* cash from the following sources:

1. It issued $7 million of long-term debt.
2. It reduced inventory, releasing $1 million.
3. It increased its accounts payable, in effect borrowing an additional $7 million from its suppliers.
4. By far the largest source of cash was Dynamic's operations, which generated $16 million. See Table 16.3, and note: Income ($12 million) understates cash flow because depreciation is deducted in calculating income. Depreciation is *not* a cash outlay. Thus, it must be added back in order to obtain operating cash flow.

Dynamic *used* cash for the following purposes:

1. It paid a $1 million dividend. (*Note:* The $11 million increase in Dynamic's equity is due to retained earnings: $12 million of equity income, less the $1 million dividend.)

---

[2]In a sense this statement is true by definition. If net working capital (current assets less current liabilities) is positive, it must be financed by long-term debt or equity. Our point is that firms *plan* it that way.

[3]If there is a tax advantage to borrowing, as most people believe, there must be a corresponding tax *dis*advantage to lending, and investment in Treasury bills has a negative NPV. See Chapter 6.

TABLE 16.2

Year-end balance sheets for 1998 and 1999 for Dynamic Mattress Company (figures in $ millions)

	1998	1999
Current assets:		
Cash	4	5
Marketable securities	0	5
Inventory	26	25
Accounts receivable	25	30
Total current assets	55	65
Fixed assets:		
Gross investment	56	70
Less depreciation	−16	−20
Net fixed assets	40	50
Total assets	95	115
Current liabilities:		
Bank loans	5	0
Accounts payable	20	27
Total current liabilities	25	27
Long-term debt	5	12
Net worth (equity and retained earnings)	65	76
Total liabilities and net worth	95	115

TABLE 16.3

Income statement for 1999 for Dynamic Mattress Company (figures in $ millions)

Sales	350
Operating costs	−321
	29
Depreciation	−4
	25
Interest	−1
Pretax income	24
Tax at 50%	−12
Net income	12

Note: Dividend = $1 million; retained earnings = $11 million.

TABLE 16.4

Sources and uses of cash for 1999 for Dynamic Mattress Company (figures in $ millions)

Sources:	
Issued long-term debt	7
Reduced inventories	1
Increased accounts payable	7
Cash from operations:	
Net income	12
Depreciation	4
Total sources	31
Uses:	
Repaid short-term bank loan	5
Invested in fixed assets	14
Purchased marketable securities	5
Increased accounts receivable	5
Dividend	1
Total uses	30
Increase in cash balance	1

2. It repaid a $5 million short-term bank loan.[4]
3. It invested $14 million. This shows up as the increase in gross fixed assets in Table 16.2.
4. It purchased $5 million of marketable securities.
5. It allowed accounts receivable to expand by $5 million. In effect, it lent this additional amount to its customers.

Tracing Changes in Net Working Capital

Financial analysts often find it useful to collapse all current assets and liabilities into a single figure for net working capital. Dynamic's net-working-capital balances were (in millions):

	CURRENT ASSETS	LESS	CURRENT LIABILITIES	EQUALS	NET WORKING CAPITAL
Year-end 1998	$55	–	$25	=	$30
Year-end 1999	$65	–	$27	=	$38

---

[4]This is principal repayment, not interest. Sometimes interest payments are explicitly recognized as a use of funds. If so, operating cash flow would be defined *before* interest, that is, as net income plus interest plus depreciation.

	1998	1999

TABLE 16.5

Condensed year-end balance sheets for 1998 and 1999 for Dynamic Mattress Company (figures in $ millions)

	1998	1999
Net working capital	30	38
Fixed assets:		
Gross investment	56	70
Less depreciation	−16	−20
Net fixed assets	40	50
Total assets	70	88
Long-term debt	5	12
Net worth	65	76
Long-term liabilities and net worth*	70	88

*When only *net* working capital appears on a firm's balance sheet, this figure (the sum of long-term liabilities and net worth) is often referred to as *total capitalization*.

Table 16.5 gives balance sheets which report only net working capital, not individual current asset or liability items.

"Sources and uses" statements can likewise be simplified by defining *sources* as activities which contribute to net working capital and *uses* as activities which use up working capital. In this context working capital is usually referred to as *funds*, and a *sources and uses of funds statement* is presented.

In 1998, Dynamic contributed to net working capital by

1. Issuing $7 million of long-term debt.
2. Generating $16 million from operations.

It used up net working capital by

1. Investing $14 million.
2. Paying a $1 million dividend.

The year's changes in net working capital are thus summarized by Dynamic Mattress Company's sources and uses of funds statement, given in Table 16.6.

Profits and Cash Flow

Now look back to Table 16.4, which shows sources and uses of *cash*. We want to register two warnings about the entry called *cash from operations*. It may not actually represent real dollars—dollars you can buy beer with.

First, depreciation may not be the only noncash expense deducted in calculating income. For example, most firms use different accounting procedures in their tax books than in their reports to

TABLE 16.6	
Sources and uses of funds (net working capital) for 1999 for Dynamic Mattress Company (figures in $ millions)	

Sources:	
Issued long-term debt	7
Cash from operations:	
Net income	12
Depreciation	4
	23
Uses:	
Invested in fixed assets	14
Dividend	1
	15
Increase in net working capital	8

shareholders. The point of special tax accounts is to minimize current taxable income. The effect is that the shareholder books overstate the firm's current cash tax liability,[5] and after-tax cash flow from operations is therefore understated.

Second, income statements record sales when made, not when the customer's payment is received. Think of what happens when Dynamic sells goods on credit. The company records a profit at the time of sale, but there is no cash inflow until the bills are paid. Since there is no cash inflow, there is no change in the company's cash balance, although there is an increase in working capital in the form of an increase in accounts receivable. No net addition to cash would be shown in a sources and uses statement like Table 16.4. The increase in cash from operations would be offset by an increase in accounts receivable.

Later, when the bills are paid, there is an increase in the cash balance. However, there is no further profit at this point and no increase in working capital. The increase in the cash balance is exactly matched by a decrease in accounts receivable.

That brings up an interesting characteristic of working capital. Imagine a company that conducts a very simple business. It buys raw materials for cash, processes them into finished goods, and then sells these goods on credit. The whole cycle of operations looks like this:

---

[5]The difference between taxes reported and paid to the Internal Revenue Service shows up on the balance sheet as an increased deferred tax liability. The reason why a liability is recognized is that accelerated depreciation and other devices used to reduce current taxable income do not eliminate taxes; they only delay them. Of course, this reduces the present value of the firm's tax liability, but still the ultimate liability has to be recognized. In the sources and uses statements an increase in deferred taxes would be treated as a source of funds. In the Dynamic Mattress example we ignore deferred taxes.

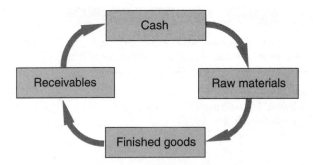

If you draw up a balance sheet at the beginning of the process, you see cash. If you delay a little, you find the cash replaced by inventories of raw materials and, still later, by inventories of finished goods. When the goods are sold, the inventories give way to accounts receivable, and finally, when the customers pay their bills, the firm draws out its profit and replenishes the cash balance.

There is only one constant in this process, namely, working capital. The components of working capital are constantly changing. That is one reason why (net) working capital is a useful summary measure of current assets and liabilities.

The strength of the working-capital measure is that it is unaffected by seasonal or other temporary movements between different current assets or liabilities. But the strength is also its weakness, for the working-capital figure hides a lot of interesting information. In our example cash was transformed into inventory, then into receivables, and back into cash again. But these assets have different degrees of risk and liquidity. You can't pay bills with inventory or with receivables, you must pay with cash.

CASH BUDGETING

The past is interesting only for what one can learn from it. The financial manager's problem is to forecast *future* sources and uses of cash. These forecasts serve two purposes. First, they alert the financial manager to future cash needs. Second, the cash-flow forecasts provide a standard, or budget, against which subsequent performance can be judged.

Preparing the Cash Budget: Inflow

There are at least as many ways to produce a quarterly cash budget as there are to skin a cat. Many large firms have developed elaborate corporate models; others use a spreadsheet program to plan their cash needs. The procedures of smaller firms may be less formal. But there are common issues that all firms must face when they forecast. We will illustrate these issues by continuing the example of Dynamic Mattress.

Most of Dynamic's cash inflow comes from the sale of mattresses. We therefore start with a sales forecast by quarter[6] for 2000:

---

[6]Most firms would forecast by month instead of by quarter. Sometimes weekly or even daily forecasts are made. But presenting a monthly forecast would triple the number of entries in Table 16.7 and subsequent tables. We wanted to keep the examples as simple as possible.

TABLE 16.7

To forecast Dynamic Mattress's collections on accounts receivable, you have to forecast sales and collection rates (figures in $ millions)

	FIRST QUARTER	SECOND QUARTER	THIRD QUARTER	FOURTH QUARTER
1. Receivables at start of period	30	32.5	30.7	38.2
2. Sales	87.5	78.5	116	131
3. Collections:				
Sales in current period (80%)	70	62.8	92.8	104.8
Sales in last period (20%)	15*	17.5	15.7	23.2
Total collections	85	80.3	108.5	128.0
4. Receivables at end of period				
4 = 1 + 2 − 3	32.5	30.7	38.2	41.2

*Sales in the fourth quarter of the previous year were $75 million.

	FIRST QUARTER	SECOND QUARTER	THIRD QUARTER	FOURTH QUARTER
Sales ($ millions)	87.5	78.5	116	131

But sales become accounts receivable before they become cash. Cash flow comes from *collections* on accounts receivable.

Most firms keep track of the average time it takes customers to pay their bills. From this they can forecast what proportion of a quarter's sales is likely to be converted into cash in that quarter and what proportion is likely to be carried over to the next quarter as accounts receivable. Suppose that 80 percent of sales are "cashed in" in the immediate quarter and 20 percent are cashed in in the next. Table 16.7 shows forecasted collections under this assumption.

In the first quarter, for example, collections from current sales are 80 percent of $87.5, or $70 million. But the firm also collects 20 percent of the previous quarter's sales, or .2(75) = $15 million. Therefore total collections are $70 + $15 = $85 million.

Dynamic started the first quarter with $30 million of accounts receivable. The quarter's sales of $87.5 million were *added* to accounts receivable, but collections of $85 million were *subtracted*. Therefore, as Table 16.7 shows, Dynamic ended the quarter with accounts receivable of $30 + 87.5 − 85 = $32.5 million. The general formula is

$$\text{Ending accounts receivable} = \text{beginning accounts receivable}$$

$$+ \text{sales} - \text{collections}$$

	TABLE 16.8			

Dynamic Mattress's cash budget for 2000 (figures in $ millions)

	FIRST QUARTER	SECOND QUARTER	THIRD QUARTER	FOURTH QUARTER
Sources of cash:				
Collections on accounts receivable	85	80.3	108.5	128
Other	0	0	12.5	0
Total sources	85	80.3	121	128
Uses of cash:				
Payments on accounts payable	65	60	55	50
Labor, administrative, and other expenses	30	30	30	30
Capital expenditures	32.5	1.3	5.5	8
Taxes, interest, and dividends	4	4	4.5	5
Total uses	131.5	95.3	95	93
Sources minus uses	−46.5	−15.0	+26	+35
Calculation of short-term financing requirement:				
1. Cash at start of period	5	−41.5	−56.5	−30.5
2. Change in cash balance (sources less uses)	−46.5	−15.0	+26	+35
3. Cash at end of period*				
1 + 2 = 3	−41.5	−56.5	−30.5	+4.5
4. Minimum operating cash balance	5	5	5	5
5. Cumulative short-term financing required†				
5 = 4 − 3	46.5	61.5	35.5	.5

*Of course, firms cannot literally hold a negative amount of cash. This is the amount the firm will have to raise to pay its bills.

†A negative sign would indicate a cash *surplus*. But in this example the firm must raise cash for all quarters.

The top section of Table 16.8 shows forecasted sources of cash for Dynamic Mattress. Collection of receivables is the main source, but it is not the only one. Perhaps the firm plans to dispose of some land or expects a tax refund or payment of an insurance claim. All such items are included as "other" sources. It is also possible that you may raise additional capital by borrowing or selling stock, but we don't want to prejudge that question. Therefore, for the moment we just assume that Dynamic will not raise further long-term finance.

Preparing the Cash Budget: Outflow

So much for the incoming cash. Now for the outgoing cash. There always seem to be many more uses for cash than there are sources. For simplicity, we have condensed the uses into four categories in Table 16.8.

1. *Payments on accounts payable*. You have to pay your bills for raw materials, parts, electricity, etc. The cash-flow forecast assumes all these bills are paid on time, although Dynamic could probably delay payment to some extent. Delayed payment is sometimes called *stretching your payables*. Stretching is one

source of short-term financing, but for most firms it is an expensive source, because by stretching they lose discounts given to firms that pay promptly. This is discussed in more detail in Chapter 17.

2. *Labor, administrative, and other expenses.* This category includes all other regular business expenses.

3. *Capital expenditures.* Note that Dynamic Mattress plans a major capital outlay in the first quarter.

4. *Taxes, interest, and dividend payments.* This includes interest on presently outstanding long-term debt but does not include interest on any additional borrowing to meet cash requirements in 2000. At this stage in the analysis, Dynamic does not know how much it will have to borrow, or whether it will have to borrow at all.

The forecasted net inflow of cash (sources minus uses) is shown in the box in Table 16.8. Note the large negative figure for the first quarter: a $46.5 million forecasted *outflow.* There is a smaller forecasted outflow in the second quarter, and then substantial cash inflows in the second half of the year.

The bottom part of Table 16.8 (below the box) calculates how much financing Dynamic will have to raise if its cash-flow forecasts are right. It starts the year with $5 million in cash. There is a $46.5 million cash outflow in the first quarter, and so Dynamic will have to obtain at least $46.5 − 5 = $41.5 million of additional financing. This would leave the firm with a forecasted cash balance of exactly zero at the start of the second quarter.

Most financial managers regard a planned cash balance of zero as driving too close to the edge of the cliff. They establish a *minimum operating cash balance* to absorb unexpected cash inflows and outflows. Also, banks usually require firms to maintain a minimum average cash balance as partial compensation for services the bank provides to the firm. This is described in more detail in Chapter 18. We will assume that Dynamic's minimum operating cash balance is $5 million. That means it will have to raise the full $46.5 million cash outflow in the first quarter and $15 million more in the second quarter. Thus its cumulative financing requirement is $61.5 million in the second quarter. This is the peak, fortunately: The cumulative requirement declines in the third quarter by $26 million to $35.5 million. In the final quarter Dynamic is almost out of the woods: Its cash balance is $4.5 million, just $.5 million shy of its minimum operating balance.

The next step is to develop a *short-term financing plan* that covers the forecasted requirements in the most economical way possible. We will move on to that topic after two general observations:

1. The large cash outflows in the first two quarters do not necessarily spell trouble for Dynamic Mattress. In part, they reflect the capital investment made in the first quarter: Dynamic is spending $32.5 million, but it should be acquiring an asset worth that much or more. In part, the cash outflows reflect low sales in the first half of the year; sales recover in the second half.[7] If this is a predictable seasonal pattern, the firm should have no trouble borrowing to tide it over the slow months.

2. Table 16.8 is only a best guess about future cash flows. It is a good idea to think about the *uncertainty* in your estimates. For example, you could undertake a sensitivity analysis, in which you inspect how Dynamic's cash requirements would be affected by a shortfall in sales or by a delay in collections. The trouble with such sensitivity analyses is that you are changing only one item at a time, whereas in practice a downturn in the economy might affect, say, sales levels *and* collection rates. An alternative but more complicated solution is to build a model of the cash budget and then to simulate to determine the probability of cash requirements significantly above or below the forecasts shown in Table 16.8.[8] If cash requirements are difficult to predict, you may wish to hold additional cash or marketable securities to cover a possible unexpected cash outflow.

---

[7] Maybe people buy more mattresses late in the year when the nights are longer.

[8] In other words, you could use Monte Carlo simulation.

THE SHORT-TERM FINANCING PLAN

Dynamic's cash budget defines its problem: Its financial manager must find short-term financing to cover the firm's forecasted cash requirements. There are dozens of sources of short-term financing, but for simplicity we start by assuming that there are just two options.

Options for Short-Term Financing

1. *Unsecured bank borrowing:* Dynamic has an existing arrangement with its bank allowing it to borrow up to $41 million at an interest cost of 11.5 percent per year or 2.875 percent per quarter. The firm can borrow and repay whenever it wants so long as it does not exceed the credit limit. Dynamic does not have to pledge any specific assets as security for the loan. This kind of arrangement is called a *line of credit.*[9]

   When a company borrows on an unsecured line of credit, it is generally obliged to maintain a *compensating balance* on deposit at the bank. In our example, Dynamic has to maintain a balance of 20 percent of the amount of the loan. In other words, if the firm wants to raise $100, it must actually borrow $125, because $25 (20 percent of $125) must be left on deposit in the bank.

2. *Stretching payables:* Dynamic can also raise capital by putting off paying its bills. The financial manager believes that Dynamic can defer the following amounts in each quarter:

	FIRST QUARTER	SECOND QUARTER	THIRD QUARTER	FOURTH QUARTER
Amount deferrable ($ millions)	52	48	44	40

That is, $52 million can be saved in the first quarter by *not* paying bills in that quarter. (Table 16.8 assumes these bills *are* paid in the first quarter.) If deferred, these payments *must* be made in the second quarter. Similarly, $48 million of the second quarter bills can be deferred to the third quarter, and so on.

Stretching payables is often costly, however, even if no ill will is incurred. The reason is that suppliers often offer discounts for prompt payment. Dynamic loses this discount if it pays late. In this example we assume the lost discount is 5 percent of the amount deferred. In other words, if a $100 payment is delayed, the firm must pay $105 in the next quarter.

The First Financing Plan

With these two options, the short-term financing strategy is obvious: Use the line of credit first, if necessary up to the $41 million credit limit. If cash requirements exceed the credit limit, stretch payables.

Table 16.9 shows the resulting financing plan. In the first quarter the plan calls for borrowing the full amount available under the line of credit ($41 million) and stretching $3.6 million of payables (see lines 1 and 2 in the table). In addition, the firm sells the $5 million of marketable

---

[9]Lines of credit are discussed in more detail in Chapter 19.

TABLE 16.9

Dynamic Mattress's first financing plan (figures in $ millions)

	FIRST QUARTER	SECOND QUARTER	THIRD QUARTER	FOURTH QUARTER
New borrowing:				
1. Line of credit	41	0	0	0
2. Stretching payables	3.6	20	0	0
3. Total	44.6	20	0	0
Repayments:				
4. Line of credit	0	0	4.8	36.2
5. Stretched payables	0	3.6	20	0
6. Total	0	3.6	24.8	36.2
7. Net new borrowing	44.6	16.4	−24.8	−36.2
8. Plus securities sold	5*	0	0	0
9. Less securities bought	0	0	0	0
10. Total cash raised	49.6	16.4	−24.8	−36.2
Interest payments:				
11. Line of credit	0	1.2	1.2	1.0
12. Stretching payables	0	.2	1.0	0
13. Less interest on marketable securities	−.1*	0	0	0
14. Net interest paid	−.1	1.4	2.2	1.0
15. Additional funds for compensating balance†	3.2	0	−1.0	−2.2
16. Cash required for operations‡	46.5	15	−26	−35
17. Total cash required	49.6	16.4	−24.8	−36.2

*Dynamic held $5 million in marketable securities at the end of 1999. The yield is assumed to be 2.4 percent per quarter.

†Twenty percent of the amount borrowed on the line of credit in excess of $25 million. Dynamic's $5 million minimum operating cash balance serves as compensating balance for loans up to $25 million.

‡From Table 16.8.

securities it held at the end of 1999 (line 8). Thus, under this plan it raises $49.6 million in the first quarter (line 10).

Why raise $49.6 million when Table 16.8 shows a cash requirement of only $46.5 million? The major reason is that the $41 million borrowed under the line of credit require a compensating balance of 20 percent of $41 million, or $8.2 million. Dynamic can cover part of this with its $5 million minimum balance, but $3.2 million still have to be raised (line 15).

In the second quarter, the plan calls for Dynamic to maintain line-of-credit borrowing at the upper limit and stretch $20 million in payables. This raises $16.4 million after payment of the $3.6 million of payables stretched in the first quarter.

Again, the amount of cash raised exceeds the amount required for operations ($16.4 versus $15 million). In this case, the difference is the interest cost of the first quarter's borrowing: $1.2 million for the line of credit and $.2 million for the stretched payables (lines 11 and 12.)[10]

In the third and fourth quarters the plan calls for Dynamic to pay off its debt. In turn, this releases cash tied up by the compensating balance requirement of the line of credit.

Evaluating the First Plan   Does the plan shown in Table 16.9 solve Dynamic's short-term financing problem? No: the plan is feasible, but Dynamic can probably do better. The most glaring weakness of this first plan is its reliance on stretching payables, an extremely expensive financing device. Remember that it costs Dynamic 5 percent *per quarter* to delay paying bills—20 percent per year at simple interest. The first plan would merely stimulate the financial manager to search for cheaper sources of short-term borrowing. Perhaps the $41 million limit on the line of credit could be increased, for example.

The financial manager would ask several other questions as well. For example:

1. Does the plan yield satisfactory current and quick ratios?[11] Its bankers may be worried if these ratios deteriorate.[12]

2. Are there intangible costs of stretching payables? Will suppliers begin to doubt Dynamic's creditworthiness?

3. Does the plan for 2000 leave Dynamic in good financial shape for 2001? (Here the answer is yes, since Dynamic will have paid off all short-term borrowing by the end of the year.)

4. Should Dynamic try to arrange long-term financing for the major capital expenditure in the first quarter? This seems sensible, following the rule of thumb that long-term assets deserve long-term financing. It would also reduce the need for short-term borrowing dramatically. A counterargument is that Dynamic is financing the capital investment *only temporarily* by short-term borrowing. By year-end, the investment is paid for by cash from operations. Thus Dynamic's initial decision not to seek immediate long-term financing may reflect a preference for ultimately financing the investment with retained earnings.

5. Perhaps the firm's operating and investment plans can be adjusted to make the short-term financing problem easier. Is there any easy way of deferring the first quarter's large cash outflow? For example, suppose that the large capital investment in the first quarter is for new mattress-stuffing machines to be delivered and installed in the first half of the year. The new machines are not scheduled to be ready for full-scale use until August. Perhaps the machine manufacturer could be persuaded to accept 60 percent of the purchase price on delivery and 40 percent when the machines are installed and operating satisfactorily.

6. Dynamic may also be able to release cash by reducing the level of other current assets. For example, it could reduce receivables by getting tough with customers who are late paying their bills. (The cost is

---

[10]The interest rate on the line of credit is 11.5 percent per year, or 11.5/4 = 2.875 percent per quarter. Thus the interest due is .02875(41) = 1.2, or $1.2 million. The "interest" cost of the stretched payables is actually the 5 percent discount lost by delaying payment. Five percent of $3.6 million is $180,000, or about $.2 million.

[11]These ratios are discussed in Chapter 15.

[12]We have not worked out these ratios explicitly, but you can infer from Table 16.9 that they would be fine at the end of the year but relatively low in midyear, when Dynamic's borrowing is high.

that in the future these customers may take their business elsewhere.) Or it may be able to get by with lower inventories of mattresses. (The cost is that it may lose business if there is a rush of orders that it cannot supply.)

Short-term financing plans are developed by trial and error. You lay out one plan, think about it, and then try again with different assumptions on financing and investment alternatives. You continue until you can think of no further improvements.

Trial and error is important because it helps you understand the real nature of the problem the firm faces. The process of financial planning entails not just choosing a plan but understanding what can go wrong with it and what will be done if conditions change unexpectedly.[13]

We cannot trace through each trial and error in Dynamic Mattress's search for the best short-term financing plan. The reader may be buried in numbers already. Instead we will wrap up this chapter by looking at Dynamic's second try.

The Second Financing Plan

The second financing plan, shown in Table 16.10, reflects two significant new assumptions.

1. A commercial finance company[14] has offered to lend Dynamic up to 80 percent of its accounts receivable at an interest rate of 15 percent per year, or 3.75 percent per quarter. In return, Dynamic is to pledge accounts receivable as security for the loan. This is clearly cheaper than stretching payables. It appears much more expensive than the bank line of credit, but remember that the line of credit requires a 20 percent compensating balance, whereas every dollar borrowed against receivables can be spent.

2. The financial manager is uncomfortable with the first plan, which includes no cushion of marketable securities. The second plan calls for a $2.5 million marketable securities portfolio held throughout the year.

A comparison of Tables 16.9 and 16.10 shows that the second plan is broadly similar to the first, except that borrowing against receivables replaces stretching payables and the firm holds $2.5 million of marketable securities. The second plan is also cheaper than the first. This can be seen by comparing net interest paid (line 14) under the two plans.

	FIRST QUARTER	SECOND QUARTER	THIRD QUARTER	FOURTH QUARTER	TOTAL
First plan	−.1	1.4	2.2	1.0	4.5
Second plan	−.1	1.3	2.0	1.0	4.2

Over the year the second plan saves $4.5 − 4.2 = $.3 million, or about $300,000 of interest.[15]

---

[13]This point is even more important in *long-term* financial planning. See Chapter 15.

[14]Commercial finance companies are nonbank financial institutions that specialize in lending to businesses.

[15]These are pretax figures. We simplified this example by forgetting that each dollar of interest paid is a tax-deductible expense.

TABLE 16.10

Dynamic Mattress's second financing plan (figures in $ millions)

	FIRST QUARTER	SECOND QUARTER	THIRD QUARTER	FOURTH QUARTER
New borrowing:				
1. Line of credit	41	0	0	0
2. Secured borrowing (receivables pledged)	6.1	16.4	0	0
3. Total	47.1	16.4	0	0
Repayments:				
4. Line of credit	0	0	2.0	36.7
5. Secured borrowing	0	0	22.4	0
6. Total	0	0	24.4	36.7
7. Net new borrowing	47.1	16.4	−24.4	−36.7
8. Plus securities sold	2.5*	0	0	0
9. Less securities bought	0	0	0	0
10. Total cash raised	49.6	16.4	−24.4	−36.7
Interest payments:				
11. Line of credit	0	1.2	1.2	1.1
12. Secured borrowing	0	.2	.8	0
13. Less interest on marketable securities	−.1*	−.1	−.1	−.1
14. Net interest paid	−.1	1.3	2.0	1.0
15. Additional funds for compensating balance[†]	3.2	0	−.4	−2.8
16. Cash required for operations[‡]	46.5	15	−26	−35
17. Total cash required	49.6	16.4	−24.4	−36.7

Note: There are minor inconsistencies in this table because of rounding.

*Dynamic held $5 million in marketable securities at the end of 1999.

[†]Twenty percent of the amount borrowed on the line of credit in excess of $25 million. Dynamic's $5 million minimum operating cash balance serves as compensating balance for loans up to $25 million.

[‡]From Table 16.8.

A Note on Short-Term Financial Planning Models

Working out a consistent short-term plan requires burdensome calculations.[16] Fortunately much of the arithmetic can be delegated to a computer. Many large firms have built *short-term financial planning models* to do this. Smaller companies like Dynamic Mattress do not face so much detail and complexity and find it easier to work with a spreadsheet program on a personal computer. In

---

[16]If you doubt that, look again at Table 16.9 or 16.10. Notice that the cash requirements in each quarter depend on borrowing in the previous quarter, because borrowing creates an obligation to pay interest. Also, borrowing under a line of credit may require additional cash to meet compensating balance requirements; if so, that means still more borrowing and still higher interest charges in the next quarter. Moreover, the problem's complexity would have been tripled had we not simplified by forecasting per quarter rather than by month.

either case the financial manager specifies forecasted cash requirements or surpluses, interest rates, credit limits, etc., and the model grinds out a plan like those shown in Tables 16.9 and 16.10. The computer also produces balance sheets, income statements, and whatever special reports the financial manager may require.

Smaller firms that do not want custom-built models can rent general-purpose models offered by banks, accounting firms, management consultants, or specialized computer software firms.

Most of these models are *simulation* programs.[17] They simply work out the consequences of the assumptions and policies specified by the financial manager. *Optimization* models for short-term financial planning are also available. These models are usually linear programming models. They search for the *best* plan from a range of alternative policies identified by the financial manager.

As a matter of fact, we used a linear programming model developed by Pogue and Bussard[18] to generate Dynamic Mattress's financial plans. Of course, in that simple example we hardly needed a linear programming model to identify the best strategy. It was obvious that Dynamic should always use the line of credit first, turning to the second-best alternative (stretching payables or borrowing against receivables) only when the limit on the line of credit was reached. The Pogue–Bussard model nevertheless did the arithmetic quickly and easily.

Optimization helps when the firm faces complex problems with many interdependent alternatives and restrictions for which trial and error might never identify the *best* combination of alternatives.

Of course the best plan for one set of assumptions may prove disastrous if the assumptions are wrong. Thus the financial manager has to explore the implications of alternative assumptions about future cash flows, interest rates, and so on. Linear programming can help identify good strategies, but even with an optimization model the financial plan is still sought by trial and error.

SUMMARY

Short-term financial planning is concerned with the management of the firm's short-term, or current, assets and liabilities. The most important current assets are cash, marketable securities, inventory, and accounts receivable. The most important current liabilities are bank loans and accounts payable. The difference between current assets and current liabilities is called (net) working capital.

Current assets and liabilities are turned over much more rapidly than the other items on the balance sheet. Short-term financing and investment decisions are more quickly and easily reversed than long-term decisions. Consequently, the financial manager does not need to look so far into the future when making them.

The nature of the firm's short-term financial planning problem is determined by the amount of long-term capital it raises. A firm that issues large amounts of long-term debt or common stock, or which retains a large part of its earnings, may find that it has permanent excess cash. In such cases there is never any problem paying bills, and short-term financial planning consists of managing the firm's portfolio of marketable securities. We think that firms with permanent cash surpluses ought to return the excess cash to their stockholders.

---

[17]Short-term financial planning models rarely include uncertainty explicitly. The models referred to here are built and used in the same way as the long-term financial planning models described in Chapter 15.

[18]G. A. Pogue and R. N. Bussard, "A Linear Programming Model for Short-Term Financial Planning under Uncertainty," *Sloan Management Review,* 13 (Spring 1972), pp. 69–99.

Other firms raise relatively little long-term capital and end up as permanent short-term debtors. Most firms attempt to find a golden mean by financing all fixed assets and part of current assets with equity and long-term debt. Such firms may invest cash surpluses during part of the year and borrow during the rest of the year.

The starting point for short-term financial planning is an understanding of sources and uses of cash.[19] Firms forecast their net cash requirements by forecasting collections on accounts receivable, adding other cash inflows, and subtracting all forecasted cash outlays.

If the forecasted cash balance is insufficient to cover day-to-day operations and to provide a buffer against contingencies, you will need to find additional finance. It may make sense to raise long-term finance if the deficiency is permanent and large. Otherwise, you may choose from a variety of sources of short-term finance. For example, you may be able to borrow from a bank on an unsecured line of credit, you may borrow on the security of your receivables or inventory, or you may be able to finance the deficit by not paying your bills for a while. In addition to the explicit interest costs of short-term financing, there are often implicit costs. For example, the firm may be required to maintain a compensating balance at the bank, or it may lose its reputation as a prompt payer if it raises cash by delaying payment on its bills. The financial manager must choose the financing package that has lowest total cost (explicit and implicit costs combined) and yet leaves the firm with sufficient flexibility to cover contingencies.

The search for the best short-term financial plan inevitably proceeds by trial and error. The financial manager must explore the consequences of different assumptions about cash requirements, interest rates, limits on financing from particular sources, and so on. Firms are increasingly using computerized financial models to help in this process. The models range from simple spreadsheet programs that merely help with the arithmetic to linear programming models that help to find the best financial plan.

Further Reading

Here are some general textbooks on working-capital management:

G. W. Gallinger and P. B. Healey: *Liquidity Analysis and Management*, 2d. ed., Addison-Wesley Publishing Company, Inc., Reading, MA, 1991.

N. C. Hill and W. L. Sartoris, *Short-Term Financial Management: Text and Cases*, 3d. ed., Prentice-Hall, Inc., Englewood Cliffs, NJ, 1995.

K. V. Smith and G. W. Gallinger: *Readings on Short-Term Financial Management*, 3d ed., West Publishing Company, New York, 1988.

J. H. Vander Weide and S. F. Maier: *Managing Corporate Liquidity: An Introduction to Working Capital Management*, John Wiley & Sons, Inc., New York, 1985.

F. C. Scherr: *Modern Working Capital Management: Text and Cases*, Prentice-Hall, Inc., Englewood Cliffs, NJ, 1989.

Pogue and Bussard present a linear programming model for short-term financial planning:

G. A. Pogue and R. N. Bussard: "A Linear Programming Model for Short-Term Financial Planning under Uncertainty," *Sloan Management Review*, 13:69–99 (Spring 1972).

---

[19]We pointed out earlier that sources and uses of *funds* are often analyzed rather than sources and uses of cash. Anything that contributes to working capital is called a *source of funds;* anything that diminishes working capital is called a *use of funds*. Sources and uses of funds statements are relatively simple because many sources and uses of cash are buried in changes in working capital. However, in forecasting, the emphasis is on cash flow: You pay bills with cash, not working capital.

PART SEVEN

SHORT-TERM FINANCIAL MANAGEMENT

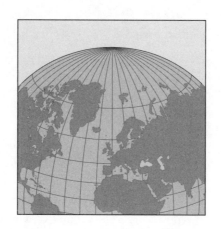

CREDIT MANAGEMENT

Chapter 16 provided an overall idea of what is involved in short-term financial management. Now it is time to get down to detail.

When companies sell their products, they sometimes demand cash on or before delivery, but in most cases they allow some delay in payment. If you turn back to the balance sheet in Table 16.1, you can see that for the average manufacturing company, *accounts receivable* constitute on the average about one-third of its current assets. Receivables include both trade credit and consumer credit. The former is by far the larger and will, therefore, be the main focus of this chapter.

Companies that do not pay for their purchases immediately are effectively borrowing money from their suppliers. Such "debts" show up as *accounts payable* in the purchasing companies' balance sheets. Table 16.1 shows that payables are the most important source of short-term finance, almost twice as large as short-term loans from banks and other institutions.

Management of trade credit requires answers to five sets of questions:

1. On what terms do you propose to sell your goods or services? How long are you going to give customers to pay their bills? Are you prepared to offer a cash discount for prompt payment?

2. What evidence do you need of indebtedness? Do you just ask the buyer to sign a receipt, or do you insist on some more formal IOU?

3. Which customers are likely to pay their bills? To find out, do you examine customers' past records or past financial statements? Or do you rely on bank references?

4. How much credit are you prepared to extend to each customer? Do you play safe by turning down any doubtful prospects? Or do you accept the risk of a few bad debts as part of the cost of building up a large regular clientele?

5. How do you collect the money when it becomes due? How do you keep track of payments? What do you do about reluctant payers or deadbeats?

We will discuss each set of questions in turn.

TERMS OF SALE

Not all sales involve credit. For example, if you are producing goods to the customer's specification or incurring substantial delivery costs, then it may be sensible to ask for cash before delivery (CBD). If you are supplying goods to a wide variety of irregular customers, you may prefer cash on delivery (COD).[1] If your product is expensive and custom-designed, you may require **progress payments** as work is carried out. For example, a large, extended consulting contract might call for 30 percent payment after completion of field research, 30 percent more on submission of a draft report, and the remaining 40 percent when the project is finally completed.

When we look at transactions that do involve credit, we find that each industry seems to have its own particular usage with regard to payment terms.[2] These norms have a rough logic. For example, firms selling consumer durables may allow the buyer a month to pay, while those selling perishable goods, such as cheese or fresh fruit, typically demand payment in a week. Similarly, a seller will generally allow more extended payment if its customers are in low-risk businesses, if their accounts are large, if the customers need time to ascertain the quality of the goods, and if the goods are not quickly resold.

In order to induce customers to pay before the final date, it is common to offer a cash discount for prompt settlement. For example, shoe manufacturers commonly require payment within 30 days but offer a 5 percent discount to customers who pay within 10 days. These terms are referred to as "5/10, net 30." Toy manufacturers generally sell goods on terms of 2/30, net 50; their customers receive a 2 percent discount for payment within 30 days and must pay in full within 50 days.

Cash discounts are often very large. For example, a customer who buys on terms of 5/10, net 30 may decide to forgo the cash discount and pay on the thirtieth day. This means that the customer obtains an extra 20 days' credit but pays about 5 percent more for the goods. This is equivalent to borrowing money at a rate of 155 percent per annum.[3] Of course, any firm that delays payment beyond the due date gains a cheaper loan but damages its reputation for creditworthiness.

You can think of the terms of sale as fixing both the price for the cash buyer and the rate of interest charged for credit. For example, suppose that a firm reduces the cash discount from 5 to 4 percent. That would represent an *increase* in the price for the cash buyer of 1 percent but a *reduction* in the implicit rate of interest charged the credit buyer from just over 5 percent per 20 days to just over 4 percent per 20 days.

For many items that are bought on a recurrent basis, it is inconvenient to require separate payment for each delivery. A common solution is to pretend that all sales during the month in fact occur at the end of the month (EOM). Thus goods may be sold on terms of 8/10, EOM, net 60. This

---

[1]Some goods *can't* be sold on credit—a glass of beer, for example.

[2]Standard credit terms in different industries are reported in *Handbook of Credit Terms*, Dun and Bradstreet, New York, 1970. They are analyzed in B. Wilner, "Paying Your Bills: An Empirical Study of Trade Credit," unpublished working paper, University of Michigan, Ann Arbor, November 1995.

[3]The cash discount allows you to pay $95 rather than $100. If you do not take the discount, you get a 20-day loan, but you pay 5/95 = 5.26 percent more for your goods. The number of 20-day periods in a year is 365/20 = 18.25. A dollar invested for 18.25 periods at 5.26 percent per period grows to $(1.0526)^{18.25} = \$2.55$, a 155 percent return on the original investment. If a customer is happy to borrow at this rate, it's a good bet that he or she is desperate for cash (or can't work out compound interest). For a discussion of this issue, see J. K. Smith, "Trade Credit and Information Asymmetry," *Journal of Finance* 42 (September 1987), pp. 863–872.

arrangement allows the customer a cash discount of 8 percent if the bill is paid within 10 days of the end of the month; otherwise, the full payment is due within 60 days of the invoice date.[4] When purchases are subject to seasonal fluctuations, manufacturers often encourage customers to take early delivery by allowing them to delay payment until the usual order season. This practice is known as "season dating."

COMMERCIAL CREDIT INSTRUMENTS

The terms of sale define when payment is due but not the nature of the contract. Repetitive sales to domestic customers are almost always made on *open account* and involve only an implicit contract. There is simply a record in the seller's books and a receipt signed by the buyer.

If an order is very large and there is no complicating cash discount, the customer may be asked to sign a *promissory note.* This is just a straightforward IOU, worded along the following lines:

New York
April 1, 2000

Sixty days after date I promise to pay to the order of the XYZ Company one thousand dollars ($1,000.00) for value received.

Signature

Such an arrangement is not common,[5] but it has two advantages. First, as long as the note is payable to "order" or to "bearer," the holder may sell it or use it as a security for a loan. Second, the note prevents any argument about the existence of the debt.

If you want a clear commitment from the buyer, it is more useful to have it *before* you deliver the goods. In this case the simplest procedure is to arrange a **commercial draft.**[6] It works as follows: The seller draws a draft ordering payment by the customer and sends this draft to the customer's bank together with the shipping documents. If immediate payment is required, the draft is termed a *sight draft;* otherwise, it is known as a *time draft.* Depending on whether it is a sight or a time draft, the customer either pays up or acknowledges the debt by adding the word *accepted* and his or her signature. The bank then hands the shipping documents to the customer and forwards the money or the **trade acceptance** to the seller.[7] The latter may hold the trade acceptance to maturity or use it as security for a loan.

If the customer's credit is for any reason suspect, the seller may ask the customer to arrange for his or her bank to accept the time draft. In this case, the bank guarantees the customer's debt. These **bankers' acceptances** are often used in overseas trade; they have a higher standing and greater negotiability than trade acceptances.

---

[4]Terms of 8/10, prox., net 60 would entitle the customer to a discount if the bill is paid within 10 days of the end of the following (or "proximo") month.

[5]In some countries, such as Japan, sales on open account are rare and promissory notes tend to be the rule.

[6]Commercial drafts are sometimes known by the more general term *bills of exchange.*

[7]You often see the terms of sale defined as "SD-BL." This means that the bank will hand over the bill of lading in return for payment on a sight draft.

The exporter who requires greater certainty of payment can ask the customer to arrange for an *irrevocable letter of credit.* In this case the customer's bank sends the exporter a letter stating that it has established a credit in his or her favor at a bank in the United States. The exporter then draws a draft on the customer's bank and presents it to the bank in the United States together with the letter of credit and the shipping documents. The bank in the United States arranges for this draft to be accepted or paid and forwards the documents to the customer's bank.

If you sell goods to a customer who proves unable to pay, you cannot get your goods back. You simply become a general creditor of the company, in common with other unfortunates. You can avoid this situation by making a *conditional sale,* whereby title to the goods remains with the seller until full payment is made. The conditional sale is common practice in Europe. In the United States it is used only for goods that are bought on an installment basis. In this case, if the customer fails to make the agreed number of payments, then the goods can be immediately repossessed by the seller.

CREDIT ANALYSIS

Firms are not allowed to discriminate between customers by charging them different prices. Neither may they discriminate by offering the same prices but different credit terms.[8] You *can* offer different terms of sale to different *classes* of buyers. You can offer volume discounts, for example, or discounts to customers willing to accept long-term purchase contracts. But as a rule, if you have a customer of doubtful standing, you should keep to your regular terms of sale and protect yourself by restricting the volume of goods that the customer may buy on credit.

There are a number of ways by which you can find out whether customers are likely to pay their debts. The most obvious indication is whether they have paid promptly in the past. However, beware of the customer who establishes a high credit limit on the basis of a series of small payments and then disappears, leaving you with a large unpaid bill.

If you are dealing with a new customer, you will probably arrange for a credit agency to undertake a credit check. Dun and Bradstreet is by far the largest of such agencies: Its database contains information on more than 10 million companies. Credit agencies usually report the experience that other firms have had with the customer; you may also be able to get this information by checking with a credit bureau or by contacting the firms directly.

Your bank can also do a credit check. It will contact the customer's bank and ask for information on the customer's average bank balance, access to bank credit, and general reputation.

In addition to checking with your customer's bank, it might make sense to check what everybody else in the financial community thinks about your customer's credit standing. Does that sound expensive? It isn't if your customer is a public company. You just look at the Moody's or Standard and Poor's rating for the customer's outstanding bonds.[9] You can also compare prices of these bonds to prices of other firms' bonds. (Of course, the comparisons should be between bonds of similar maturity, coupon, etc.) Finally, you can look at how the customer's stock price has been behaving recently. A sharp fall in price doesn't mean that the company is in trouble, but it does suggest that prospects are less bright than they formerly were.

---

[8]Price discrimination, and by implication credit discrimination, is prohibited by the Robinson-Patman Act.

[9]See Chapter 10.

Financial Ratio Analysis

We have suggested a number of ways to check whether your customer is a good risk. You can ask your collection manager, a specialized credit agency, a credit bureau, a banker, or the financial community at large. But if you don't like relying on the judgment of others, you can do your own homework. Ideally this would involve a detailed analysis of the company's business prospects and financing, but this approach is usually too expensive. Therefore credit analysts concentrate on the company's financial statements, using rough rules of thumb to judge whether the firm is a good credit risk. The rules of thumb are based on *financial ratios*. Chapter 15 described how these ratios are calculated and interpreted.

Numerical Credit Scoring

When the firm has a small, regular clientele, the credit manager can easily handle the investigation process informally. But when the company is dealing directly with consumers, some streamlining is essential. In these cases it may make sense to use a mechanical scoring system to prescreen credit applications.

For example, if you apply for a credit card or bank loan, you will be asked various questions about your job, home, and financial position. The information that you provide is used to calculate an overall credit score. Applicants who do not make the grade on the score are likely to be refused credit or subjected to more detailed analysis.

Banks and the credit departments of industrial firms also use mechanical credit scoring systems to cut the costs of assessing commercial credit applications. One bank claimed that by introducing a credit scoring system, it reduced the cost of loan appraisal by two-thirds. It cited the case of an application for a $5,000 credit line from a small business. A clerk entered information from the loan application into a computer and checked the firm's deposit balances with the bank, as well as the owner's personal and business credit files. Immediately the loan officer could see the applicant's score: 240 on a scale of 100 to 300, well above the bank's cutoff figure. All that remained for the bank to do was to check that there was nothing obviously suspicious about the application. "We don't want to lend to set up an alligator farm in the desert," said one bank official.[10]

Suppose you want to devise a scoring system that will help you decide whether to extend credit to small businesses. You suspect that there is an above-average probability that firms with a low return on assets and a low current ratio will default on their debts.[11] To test this, you take a sample of past loans and construct a scatter diagram showing for each borrower the return on assets and the current ratio (see Figure 17.1). Those businesses that repaid their loans are shown by a black x; the ones that defaulted are shown in blue. Now try to draw a straight dividing line between the two groups. You can't completely separate them, but the line in our diagram keeps the two groups as far apart as possible. (Note that there are only three black x's below the line and three blue +'s above it.) This line tells us that if we wish to *discriminate*

---

[10]Quoted in S. Hansell, "Need a Loan? Ask the Computer; 'Credit Scoring' Changes Small-Business Lending," *The New York Times,* April 18, 1995, sec. D, p. 1.

[11]The current ratio is the ratio of current assets to current liabilities. It is commonly used as a measure of the company's ability to lay its hands on cash. See Chapter 15.

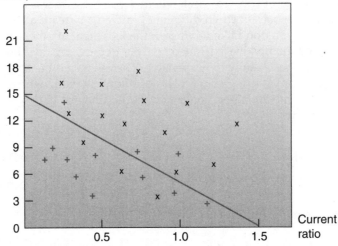

Figure 17.1

The black x's represent a hypothetical group of firms that subsequently repaid their loans; the blue +'s represent those that defaulted. The sloping line discriminates between the two groups on the basis of return on assets and current ratio. The line represents the equation

$$Z = \text{return on assets} + 10(\text{current ratio})$$
$$= 15$$

Firms that plot above the line have Z scores greater than 15.

between the good and the bad risks, we should give ten times as much weight to the current ratio as we give to return on assets. The index of creditworthiness is

$$\text{Index of creditworthiness} = Z = \text{return on assets, percent} + 10 \text{ (current ratio)}$$

You minimize the degree of misclassification if you predict that applicants with Z scores over 15 will pay their debts and that those with Z scores below 15 will not pay.[12] In practice we do not need to consider only two variables, nor do we need to estimate the equation by eye. *Multiple-discriminant analysis* (MDA) is a straightforward statistical technique for calculating how much weight to put on each variable in order to separate the creditworthy sheep from the impecunious goats.[13]

---

[12]The quantity 15 is an arbitrary constant. We could just as well have used 150, in which case the Z score is

$$Z = 10(\text{return on assets, percent}) + 100(\text{current ratio})$$

[13]MDA is not the only statistical technique that you can use for this purpose. Probit and logit are two other potentially useful techniques. These estimate the probability of some event (e.g., default) as a function of observable attributes.

TABLE 17.1			

Recent Z scores for a sample of large firms. Firms with a high Z score have lower default risk.

COMPANY	Z SCORE	COMPANY	Z SCORE
Bethlehem Steel	2.5	Hewlett-Packard	14.3
Boeing	5.9	IBM	3.1
Coca-Cola	32.1	Merck	36.4
Exxon	11.6	Wal-Mart	8.1

Edward Altman has used MDA to predict bad business risks. Altman's object was to see how well financial ratios could be used to determine which firms would go bankrupt during the period 1946–1965. MDA gave him the following index of creditworthiness:[14]

$$Z = 3.3\left(\frac{EBIT}{total\ assets}\right) + 1.0\left(\frac{sales}{total\ assets}\right) + .6\left(\frac{market\ value\ equity}{book\ value\ of\ debt}\right)$$

$$+ 1.4\left(\frac{retained\ earnings}{total\ assets}\right) + 1.2\left(\frac{working\ capital}{total\ assets}\right)$$

This equation did a good job at distinguishing the bankrupt and nonbankrupt firms. Of the former, 94 percent had Z scores of *less* than the cutoff score the year before they went bankrupt. In contrast, 97 percent of the nonbankrupt firms had Z scores *above* the cutoff.[15]

Updated and refined versions of Altman's Z-score model are regularly used by banks and industrial companies. We wish we could show you one of these recent versions, but they are all top secret: A company with a superior method for identifying good and bad borrowers has a significant leg up on the competition.[16] Yet, despite the age of Altman's original model, it continues to be very much alive and used. In Table 17.1, we have used the model to compute Z scores for a small sample of large companies. Of course, the probability of most large firms entering bankruptcy is remote.

Credit scoring systems should carry a health warning. When you construct a risk index, it is tempting to experiment with many different combinations of variables until you find the equation that would have worked best in the past. Unfortunately, if you "mine" the data in this way, you are likely to find that the system works less well in the future than it did previously. If you are misled by the past successes into placing too much faith in your model, you may refuse credit to a number of potentially good customers. The profits that you lose by turning away these customers could

---

[14]EBIT is earnings before interest and taxes. E. I. Altman, "Financial Ratios, Discriminant Analysis and the Prediction of Corporate Bankruptcy," *Journal of Finance* 23 (September 1968), pp. 589–609.

[15]This equation was fitted with hindsight. The equation did slightly less well when used to *predict* bankruptcies after 1965.

[16]When a British bank laid off a number of employees, one unhappy staff member decided that the best way to retaliate was to leak details of the bank's credit scoring system to the press. See V. Orvice, "Would You Get a Loan?" *Daily Mail*, March 16, 1994, p. 29.

more than offset the gains that you make from avoiding a few bad eggs. As a result, you could be worse off than if you had pretended that you could not tell one customer from another and extended credit to all of them.

Does this mean that you should not use credit scoring systems? Not a bit. It simply implies that it is not sufficient to have a good credit scoring system; you also need to know how much to rely on it. That is the topic of the next section.

THE CREDIT DECISION

Let us suppose that you have taken the first three steps toward an effective credit operation. In other words, you have fixed your terms of sale; you have decided whether to sell on open account or to ask your customers to sign IOUs; and you have established a procedure for estimating the probability that each customer will pay up. Your next step is to work out which of your customers should be offered credit.

If there is no possibility of repeat orders, the decision is relatively simple. Figure 17.2 summarizes your choice. On one hand, you can refuse credit. In this case you make neither a profit nor a loss. The alternative is to offer credit. Suppose that the probability that the customer will pay up is p. If the customer does pay, you receive additional revenues (REV) and you incur additional costs; your net gain is the present value of REV − COST. Unfortunately, you can't be certain that the customer will pay; there is a probability $(1 - p)$ of default. Default means you receive nothing and incur the additional costs. The *expected* profit from each course of action is therefore as follows:

	EXPECTED PROFIT
Refuse credit	0
Grant credit	pPV(REV − COST) − $(1 - p)$PV(COST)

You should grant credit if the expected profit from doing so is greater than the expected profit from refusing.

Consider, for example, the case of the Cast Iron Company. On each nondelinquent sale Cast Iron receives revenues with a present value of $1,200 and incurs costs with a value of $1,000. Therefore the company's expected profit if it offers credit is

$$p\text{PV(REV − COST)} - (1 - p)\text{PV(COST)} = p \times 200 - (1 - p) \times 1,000$$

If the probability of collection is 5/6, Cast Iron can expect to break even:

$$\text{Expected profit} = \frac{5}{6} \times 200 - \left(1 - \frac{5}{6}\right) \times 1,000 = 0$$

Therefore Cast Iron's policy should be to grant credit whenever the chances of collection are better than 5 out of 6.

When to Stop Looking for Clues

We told you earlier where to *start* looking for clues about a customer's creditworthiness, but we never said anything about when to *stop*. Now we can work out how your profits would be affected by more detailed credit analysis.

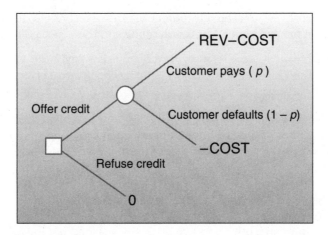

Figure 17.2

If you refuse credit, you make neither profit nor loss. If you offer credit, there is a probability p that the customer will pay and you will make REV – COST; there is a probability $(1 – p)$ that the customer will default and you will lose COST.

Suppose that Cast Iron Company's credit department undertakes a study to determine which customers are most likely to default. It appears that 95 percent of its customers have been prompt payers and 5 percent have been slow payers. However, customers with a record of slow payment are much more likely to default on the next order than those with a record of prompt payment. On the average 20 percent of the slow payers subsequently default, but only 2 percent of the prompt payers do so.

Suppose Cast Iron reviews a sample of 1,000 customers, none of whom has defaulted yet. Of these, 950 have a record of prompt payment, and 50 have a record of slow payment. On the basis of past experience Cast Iron should expect 19 of the prompt payers to default in the future and 10 of the slow payers to do so:

CATEGORY	NUMBER OF CUSTOMERS	PROBABILITY OF DEFAULT	EXPECTED NUMBER OF DEFAULTS
Prompt payers	950	.02	19
Slow payers	50	.20	10
All customers	1,000	.029	29

Now the credit manager must make a decision: Should the company refuse to give any more credit to customers that have been slow payers in the past?

If you are aware that a customer has been a slow payer, the answer is clearly "yes." Every sale to a slow payer has only an 80 percent chance of payment ($p = .8$). Selling to a *slow* payer, therefore, gives an expected *loss* of $40:

$$\text{Expected profit} = p\text{PV}(\text{REV} – \text{COST}) – (1 – p)\text{PV}(\text{COST})$$

$$= .8(200) – .2(1,000) = -\$40$$

But suppose that it costs \$10 to search through Cast Iron's records to determine whether a customer has been a prompt or slow payer. Is it worth doing so? The expected payoff to such a check is

$$\begin{aligned}\text{Expected payoff} \\ \text{to credit check}\end{aligned} = \begin{aligned}&\text{(probability of identifying a slow payer} \\ &\times \text{gain from not extending credit}) - \text{cost of credit check}\end{aligned}$$

$$= (.05 \times 40) - 10 = -\$8$$

In this case checking isn't worth it. You are paying \$10 to avoid a \$40 loss 5 percent of the time. But suppose that a customer orders 10 units at once. Then checking is worthwhile because you are paying \$10 to avoid a *\$400* loss 5 percent of the time:

$$\text{Expected payoff to credit check} = (.05 \times 400) - 10 = \$10$$

The credit manager therefore decides to check customers' past payment records only on orders of more than five units. You can verify that a credit check on a five-unit order just pays for itself.

Our illustration is simplistic, but you have probably grasped the message: You don't want to subject each order to the same credit analysis. You want to concentrate your efforts on the large and doubtful orders.

Credit Decisions with Repeat Orders

So far we have ignored the possibility of repeat orders. But one of the reasons for offering credit today is that you may get yourself a good, regular customer by doing so.

Figure 17.3 illustrates the problem.[17] Cast Iron has been asked to extend credit to a new customer. You can find little information on the firm, and you believe that the probability of payment is no better than .8. If you grant credit, the expected profit on this customer's order is

$$\text{Expected profit on initial order} = p_1 \times \text{PV(REV} - \text{COST)} - (1 - p_1) \times \text{PV(COST)}$$

$$= (.8 \times 200) - (.2 \times 1{,}000) = -\$40$$

You decide to refuse credit.

This is the correct decision if there is no chance of a repeat order. But look again at the decision tree in Figure 17.3. If the customer does pay up, there will be a reorder next year. Because the customer has paid once, you can be 95 percent sure that he or she will pay again. For this reason any repeat order is very profitable.

$$\text{Next year's expected profit on repeat order} = p_2\text{PV(REV}_2 - \text{COST}_2) - (1 - p_2)\,\text{PV(COST}_2)$$

$$= (.95 \times 200) - (.05 \times 1{,}000) = \$140$$

Now you can reexamine today's credit decision. If you grant credit today, you receive the expected profit on the initial order *plus* the possible opportunity to extend credit next year:

$$\begin{aligned}\text{Total expected profit} = \ &\text{expected profit on initial order} \\ &+ \text{probability of payment and repeat order} \\ &\times \text{PV(next year's expected profit on repeat order)}\end{aligned}$$

$$= -40 + .80 \times \text{PV(140)}$$

---

[17]Our example is adapted from H. Bierman, Jr., and W. H. Hausman, "The Credit Granting Decision," *Management Science* 16 (April 1970), pp. B519–B532 .

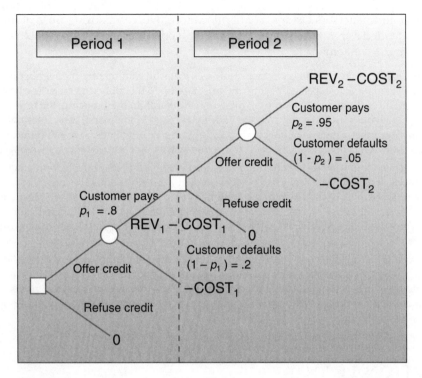

Figure 17.3

In this example there is only a .8 probability that your customer will pay in period 1; but if payment is made, there will be another order in period 2. The probability that the customer will pay for the second order is .95. The possibility of this good repeat order more than compensates for the expected loss in period 1.

At any reasonable discount rate, you ought to extend credit. For example, if the discount rate is 20 percent,

$$\text{Total expected profit (present value)} = -40 + \frac{.8(140)}{1.2} = \$53.33$$

In this example you should grant credit even though you expect to take a loss on the order. The expected loss is more than outweighed by the possibility that you will secure a reliable and regular customer.

Some General Principles

Sometimes the credit manager faces clear-cut choices. In such circumstances it may be possible to estimate fairly precisely the consequences of a more liberal or a more stringent credit policy. But real-life situations are generally far more complex than our simple examples. Customers are not all good or all bad. Many of them pay consistently late; you get your money, but it costs more to collect and you lose a few months' interest. Then there is the question of risk: You may be able to measure the revenues and costs, but at what rate do you discount them?

Like almost all financial decisions, credit allocation involves a strong dose of judgment. Our examples are intended as reminders of the issues involved rather than as cookbook formulas. Here are the basic things to remember.

1. *Maximize profit.* As credit manager, you should not focus on minimizing the number of bad accounts; your job is to maximize expected profit. You must face up to the following facts: The best that can happen is that the customer pays promptly; the worst is default. In the best case, the firm receives the full additional revenues from the sale less the additional costs; in the worst, it receives nothing and loses the costs. You must weigh the chances of these alternative outcomes. If the margin of profit is high, you are justified in a liberal credit policy; if it is low, you cannot afford many bad debts.

2. *Concentrate on the dangerous accounts.* You should not expend the same effort on analyzing all credit applications. If an application is small or clear-cut, your decision should be largely routine; if it is large or doubtful, you may do better to move straight to a detailed credit appraisal. Most credit managers don't make credit decisions on an order-by-order basis. Instead, they set a credit limit for each customer. The sales representative is required to refer the order for approval only if the customer exceeds this limit.

3. *Look beyond the immediate order.* The credit decision is a dynamic problem. You cannot look only at the present. Sometimes it may be worth accepting a relatively poor risk as long as there is a likelihood that the customer will become a regular and reliable buyer. New businesses must, therefore, be prepared to incur more bad debts than established businesses. This is part of the cost of building up a good customer list.

COLLECTION POLICY

It would be nice if all customers paid their bills by the due date. But they don't—and since you may also occasionally "stretch" your payables, you can't altogether blame them.

The credit manager keeps a record of payment experiences with each customer. Thus the manager knows that company Alpha always takes the discount and that company Omega generally takes 90 days to pay. In addition, the manager monitors overdue payments by drawing up a schedule of the aging of receivables. This may look roughly like Table 17.2.

When a customer is in arrears, the usual procedure is to send a statement of account and to follow this at intervals with increasingly insistent letters or telephone calls. If none of these has any

TABLE 17.2				
Schedule of the aging of receivables (figures in dollars)				
CUSTOMER'S NAME	AMOUNT NOT YET DUE	1 MONTH OVERDUE	MORE THAN 1 MONTH OVERDUE	TOTAL OWED
Alpha	10,000	0	0	10,000
Beta	0	0	5,000	5,000
⋮	⋮	⋮	⋮	⋮
Omega	5,000	4,000	21,000	30,000
Total	200,000	40,000	58,000	298,000

effect, most companies turn the debt over to a collection agency or an attorney. The fee for such services is usually between 15 and 40 percent of the amount collected.

There is always a potential conflict of interest between the collection department and the sales department. Sales representatives commonly complain that they no sooner win new customers than the collection department frightens them off with threatening letters. The collection manager, on the other hand, bemoans the fact that the sales force is concerned only with winning orders and does not care whether the goods are subsequently paid for.

There are also many instances of cooperation between sales managers and the financial managers who worry about collections. For example, the specialty chemicals division of a major pharmaceutical company actually made a business loan to an important customer that had been suddenly cut off by its bank. The pharmaceutical company bet that it knew its customer better than the customer's bank did. The bet paid off. The customer arranged alternative bank financing, paid back the pharmaceutical company, and became an even more loyal customer. It was a nice example of financial management supporting sales.

It is not common for suppliers to make business loans to customers in this way, but they lend money indirectly whenever they allow a delay in payment. Trade credit can be an important source of short-term funds for indigent customers that cannot obtain a bank loan. But that raises an important question: If the bank is unwilling to lend, does it make sense for you, the supplier, to continue to extend trade credit? Here are two possible reasons why it may make sense: First, as in the case of our pharmaceutical company, you may have more information than the bank does about the customer's business. Second, you need to look beyond the immediate transaction and recognize that your firm may stand to lose some profitable future sales if the customer goes out of business.[18]

Factoring and Credit Insurance

A large firm has some advantages in managing its accounts receivable. There are potential economies of scale in record keeping, billing, and so on. Also debt collection is a specialized business that calls for experience and judgment. The small firm may not be able to hire or train a specialized credit manager. However, it may be able to obtain some of these economies by farming out part of the job to a **factor.**

Factoring works as follows: The factor and the client agree on credit limits for each customer and on the average collection period. The client then notifies each customer that the factor has purchased the debt. Thereafter, for any sale, the client sends a copy of the invoice to the factor, the customer makes payment directly to the factor, and the factor pays the client on the basis of the agreed average collection period regardless of whether the customer has paid. There are, of course, costs to such an operation, and the factor typically charges a fee of 1 to 2 percent of the value of the invoice.[19]

This factoring arrangement, known as *maturity factoring,* provides assistance with collection and insurance against bad debts. Generally, the factor is also willing to advance 70 to 80 percent of

---

[18]Of course, banks also need to recognize future opportunities to make profitable loans to the firm. The question therefore is whether suppliers have a *greater* stake in the continued prosperity of the firm. For some evidence on the determinants of the supply and demand for trade credit, see M. A. Petersen and R. G. Rajan, "Trade Credit: Theories and Evidence," *Review of Financial Studies* 10 (1997), pp. 661–692.

[19]Many factors are subsidiaries of commercial banks. Their typical client is a relatively small manufacturing company selling on a repetitive basis to a large number of industrial or retail customers.

the value of the accounts at an interest cost of 2 or 3 percent above the prime rate. Factoring that provides collection, insurance, and finance is generally termed *old-line factoring.*[20]

Factoring is most common in industries such as clothing and toys. These industries are characterized by many small producers and retailers that do not have long-established relationships with each other. Because a factor may be employed by a number of manufacturers, it sees a larger proportion of the transactions than any single firm and therefore is better placed to judge the creditworthiness of each customer.[21]

If you don't want help with collection but do want protection against bad debts, you can obtain credit insurance. The credit insurance company obviously wants to be certain that you do not throw caution to the winds by extending boundless credit to the most speculative accounts. It therefore generally imposes a maximum amount that it will cover for accounts with a particular credit rating. Thus it may agree to insure up to a total of $100,000 of sales to customers with the highest Dun and Bradstreet rating, up to $50,000 to those with the next-highest rating, and so on. You may claim not only if the customer actually becomes insolvent but also if an account is overdue. Such a delinquent account is then turned over to the insurance company, which makes vigorous efforts to collect.

Most governments have established agencies to insure export credits. In the United States this insurance is provided by the *Export–Import Bank (Ex–Im Bank)* in association with a group of insurance companies known as the *Foreign Credit Insurance Association (FCIA).* Banks are much more willing to lend against export credits which have been insured.

SUMMARY

Credit management involves five steps. The first is to establish normal terms of sale. This means that you must decide the length of the payment period and the size of any cash discounts. In most industries these conditions are standardized.

The second step is to decide the form of the contract with your customer. Most domestic sales are made on open account. In this case the only evidence that the customer owes you money is the entry in your ledger and a receipt signed by the customer. Particularly if the customer is located in a foreign country, you may require a more formal contract. We looked at three such devices—the promissory note, the trade acceptance, and the letter of credit.

The third step is to assess each customer's creditworthiness. There are a variety of sources of information—your own experience with the customer, the experience of other creditors, the assessment of a credit agency, a check with the customer's bank, the market value of the customer's securities, and an analysis of the customer's financial statements. Firms that handle a large volume of credit information often use a formal system for combining the data from various sources into an overall credit score. Such numerical scoring systems help separate the borderline cases from the obvious sheep or goats. We showed how you can use statistical techniques such as multiple-discriminant analysis to give an efficient measure of default risk.

---

[20]Under an arrangement known as *with-recourse factoring*, the company is liable for any delinquent accounts. In this case the factor provides collection, but not insurance.

[21]This point is made in S. L. Mian and C. W. Smith, Jr., "Accounts Recievable Management Policy: Theory and Evidence," *Journal of Finance* 47 (March 1992), pp. 169–200.

When you have made an assessment of the customer's credit standing, you can move to the fourth step in credit management, which is to establish sensible credit limits. The job of the credit manager is not to minimize the number of bad debts; it is to maximize profits. This means that you should increase the customer's credit limit as long as the probability of payment times the expected profit is greater than the probability of default times the cost of the goods. Remember not to be too shortsighted in reckoning the expected profit. It is often worth accepting the marginal applicant if there is a chance that the applicant may become a regular and reliable customer.

The fifth, and final, step is to *collect*. Doing so requires tact and judgment. You want to be firm with the truly delinquent customer, but you don't want to offend the good one by writing demanding letters just because a check has been delayed in the mail. You will find it easier to spot troublesome accounts if you keep a careful record of the aging of receivables.

These five steps are interrelated. For example, you can afford more liberal terms of sale if you are very careful about whom you grant credit to. You can accept higher-risk customers if you are very active in pursuing any late payers. A good credit policy is one that adds up to a sensible whole.

Further Reading

A standard text on the practice and institutional background of credit management is:
R. H. Cole and L. Mishler: *Consumer and Business Credit Management,* 11th ed., McGraw-Hill, New York, 1998.

For a more analytical discussion of credit policy, see:
S. Mian and C. W. Smith: "Extending Trade Credit and Financing," *Journal of Applied Corporate Finance,* 7:75–84 (Spring 1994).

M. A. Peterson and R. G. Rajan, "Trade Credit: Theories and Evidence," *Review of Financial Studies,* 10:661–692 (1997).

Altman's paper is the classic on numerical credit scoring:
E. I. Altman: "Financial Ratios, Discriminant Analysis and the Prediction of Corporate Bankruptcy," *Journal of Finance,* 23:589–609 (September 1968).

CASH MANAGEMENT

C ash pays no interest. So why do individuals and corporations hold billions of dollars in cash and demand deposits? Why, for example, don't you take all your cash and invest it in interest-bearing securities? The answer of course is that cash gives you more *liquidity* than securities. You can use it to buy things. It is hard enough getting New York cab drivers to give you change for a $20 bill, but try asking them to split a Treasury bill.

In equilibrium all assets in the same risk class are priced to give the same expected marginal benefit. The benefit from holding Treasury bills is the interest that you receive; the benefit from holding cash is that it gives you a convenient store of liquidity. In equilibrium the marginal value of this liquidity is equal to the marginal value of the interest on an equivalent investment in Treasury bills. This is just another way of saying that Treasury bills are investments with zero

net present value; they are fair value relative to cash.

Does this mean that it does not matter how much cash you hold? Of course not. The marginal value of liquidity declines as you hold increasing amounts of cash. When you have only a small proportion of your assets in cash, a little extra can be extremely useful; when you have a substantial holding, any additional liquidity is not worth much. Therefore, as financial manager you want to hold cash balances up to the point where the marginal value of the liquidity is equal to the value of the interest forgone.

If that seems more easily said than done, you may be comforted to know that production managers must make a similar trade-off. Ask yourself why they carry inventories of raw materials. They are not obliged to do so; they could simply buy materials day by day, as needed. But then they would pay higher prices for ordering in small lots, and they would risk production delays if the materials were not delivered on time. That is why they order more than the firm's immediate needs.[1]

But there is a cost to holding inventories. Interest is lost on the money that is tied up in inventories, storage must be paid for, and often there is spoilage and deterioration. Therefore production managers try to strike a sensible balance between the costs of holding too little inventory and those of holding too much.

That is all we are saying you need to do with cash. Cash is just another raw material that you require to carry on production. If you keep too small a proportion of your funds in the bank, you will need to make repeated small sales of securities every time you want to pay your bills. On the other hand, if you keep excessive cash in the bank, you are losing interest. The trick is to hit a sensible balance.

The trade-off between the benefits and costs of liquidity is one essential part of cash management. The other part is making sure that the collection and disbursement of cash are as efficient as possible. To understand this, we will have to look closely at the relationships between firms and their banks. Most of the latter part of this chapter is devoted to the mechanics of cash collection and disbursement and the services offered by banks to assist firms in cash management.

INVENTORIES AND CASH BALANCES

Let us take a look at what economists have had to say about managing inventories and then see whether some of these ideas may help us to manage cash balances. Here is a simple inventory problem.

Everyman's Bookstore experiences a steady demand for *Principles of Corporate Finance* from customers who find that it makes a serviceable bookend. Suppose that the bookstore sells 100 copies of the book a year and that it orders Q books at a time from the publishers. Then it will need to place $100/Q$ orders per year:

$$\text{Number of orders per year} = \frac{\text{sales}}{Q} = \frac{100}{Q}$$

Just before each delivery, the bookstore has effectively no inventory of *Principles of Corporate Finance*. Just *after* each delivery it has an inventory of Q books. Therefore its *average* inventory is midway between 0 books and Q books:

$$\text{Average inventory} = \frac{Q}{2} \text{ books}$$

For example, if the store increases its regular order by one book, the average inventory increases by 1/2 book.

---

[1]Not much more, in many manufacturing operations. "Just-in-time" assembly systems provide for a continuous stream of parts deliveries, with no more than two or three hours' worth of parts inventory on hand. Financial managers likewise strive for just-in-time cash management systems, in which no cash lies idle anywhere in the company's business. This ideal is never quite reached because of the costs and delays discussed in this chapter. Large corporations get close, however.

TABLE 18.1

How order cost varies with order size

ORDER SIZE, NUMBER OF BOOKS	NUMBER OF ORDERS PER YEAR	TOTAL ORDER COSTS ($)
1	100	$200
2	50	100
3	33	66
4	25	50
10	10	20
100	1	2

There are two costs to holding this inventory. First, there is the carrying cost. This includes the cost of the capital that is tied up in inventory, the cost of shelf space, and so on. Let us suppose that these costs work out to a dollar per book per year. Adding one more book to each order therefore increases the average inventory by 1/2 book and the carrying cost by $1/2 \times \$1.00 = \$.50$. Thus the marginal carrying cost is a constant $.50:

$$\text{Marginal carrying cost} = \frac{\text{carrying cost per book}}{2} = \$.50$$

The second type of cost is the order cost. Imagine that each order placed with the publisher involves a fixed clerical and handling expense of $2. Table 18.1 illustrates what happens to order costs as you increase the size of each order. You can see that the bookstore gets a large reduction in costs when it orders two books at a time rather than one, but thereafter the savings from increases in order size steadily diminish. In fact, the *marginal* reduction in order cost depends on the *square* of the order size:[2]

$$\text{Marginal reduction in order cost} = \frac{\text{sales} \times \text{cost per order}}{Q^2} = \frac{\$200}{Q^2}$$

Here, then, is the kernel of the inventory problem: As the bookstore increases its order size, the number of orders falls but the average inventory rises. Costs that are related to the number of orders decline; those that are related to inventory size increase. It is worth increasing order size as long as

---

[2]Let T = total order cost, S = sales per year, and C = cost per order. Then

$$T = \frac{SC}{Q}$$

Differentiate with respect to Q:

$$\frac{dT}{dQ} = -\frac{SC}{Q^2}$$

Thus, an *increase* of dQ reduces T by SC/Q^2.

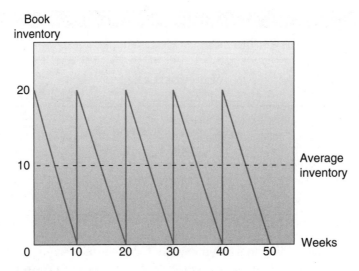

Figure 18.1

Everyman's Bookstore minimizes inventory costs by placing five orders per year for 20 books per order. That is, it places orders at about 10-week intervals.

the decline in order cost outweighs the increase in carrying cost. The optimal order size is the point at which these two effects exactly offset each other. In our example this occurs when $Q = 20$:

$$\text{Marginal reduction in order cost} = \frac{\text{sales} \times \text{cost per order}}{Q^2} = \frac{\$200}{20^2} = \$.50$$

$$\text{Marginal carrying cost} = \frac{\text{carrying cost per book}}{2} = \$.50$$

The optimal order size is 20 books. Five times a year the bookstore should place an order for 20 books, and it should work off this inventory over the following 10 weeks. Its inventory of *Principles of Corporate Finance* will therefore follow the sawtoothed pattern in Figure 18.1.

The general formula for optimum order size is found by setting marginal reduction in order cost equal to marginal carrying cost and solving for Q:

$$\text{Marginal reduction in order cost} = \text{marginal carrying cost}$$

$$\frac{\text{Sales} \times \text{cost per order}}{Q^2} = \frac{\text{carrying cost}}{2}$$

$$Q^2 = \frac{2 \times \text{sales} \times \text{cost per order}}{\text{carrying cost}}$$

$$Q = \sqrt{\frac{2 \times \text{sales} \times \text{cost per order}}{\text{carrying cost}}}$$

In our example,

$$Q = \sqrt{\frac{2 \times 100 \times 2}{1}} = \sqrt{400} = 20$$

The Extension to Cash Balances

William Baumol was the first to notice that this simple inventory model can tell us something about the management of cash balances.[3] Suppose that you keep a reservoir of cash that is steadily drawn down to pay bills. When it runs out, you replenish the cash balance by selling Treasury bills. The main carrying cost of holding this cash is the interest that you are losing. The order cost is the fixed administrative expense of each sale of Treasury bills. In these circumstances your inventory of cash also follows a sawtoothed pattern as in Figure 18.1.

In other words, your cash management problem is exactly analogous to the problem of optimum order size faced by Everyman's Bookstore. You just have to redefine variables. Instead of books per order, Q becomes the amount of Treasury bills sold each time the cash balance is replenished. Cost per order becomes cost per sale of Treasury bills. Carrying cost is just the interest rate. Total cash disbursements take the place of books sold. The optimum Q is

$$Q = \sqrt{\frac{2 \times \text{annual cash disbursements} \times \text{cost per sale of Treasury bills}}{\text{interest rate}}}$$

Suppose that the interest rate on Treasury bills is 8 percent, but every sale of bills costs you $20. Your firm pays out cash at a rate of $105,000 per month or $1,260,000 per year. Therefore the optimum Q is

$$Q = \sqrt{\frac{2 \times 1,260,000 \times 20}{.08}}$$

$$= \$25,100, \text{ or about } \$25,000$$

Thus your firm would sell approximately $25,000 of Treasury bills four times a month—about once a week. Its average cash balance will be $25,000/2, or $12,500.

The Cash Management Trade-off

Baumol's model implies that, if interest rates are high, the firm should hold smaller average cash balances and therefore make smaller and more frequent sales of Treasury bills (that is, lower Q).[4] On the other hand, if the firm uses up cash at a high rate or incurs high costs in selling securities, it should hold larger cash balances.

Baumol's model of cash balances is unrealistic in one important respect: It assumes that the firm is steadily using up its cash inventory. But that is not what usually happens. In some weeks the firm may collect some large unpaid bills and therefore receive a *net inflow* of cash. In other weeks it may pay its suppliers and so incur a net *outflow* of cash. Some of these cash flows can be forecasted with confidence; in other cases the amount of the flow or its timing is uncertain.

Economists and management scientists have developed a variety of more elaborate and realistic models that allow for the possibility of both cash inflows and outflows. But no model will ever succeed in capturing all the intricacies of the firm's cash requirements or provide a substitute for

---

[3]W. J. Baumol, "The Transactions Demand for Cash: An Inventory Theoretic Approach," *Quarterly Journal of Economics* 66 (November 1952), pp. 545–556.

[4]Note that the interest rate is in the denominator of the expression for optimal Q. Thus, increasing the interest rate reduces the optimal Q.

the judgment of the cash manager. The importance of Baumol's model and its many offspring is that they all highlight the basic trade-off that the cash manager needs to make between the fixed costs of selling securities and the carrying costs of holding cash balances. Since there are economies of scale in buying or selling securities, the firm should wait and place a sufficiently large order rather than place a series of smaller orders.

Baumol's model helps us understand why small and medium-sized firms hold significant cash balances. But for very large firms, the transaction costs of buying and selling securities become trivial compared with the opportunity cost of holding idle cash balances.

Suppose that the interest rate is 8 percent per year, or roughly $8/365 = .022$ percent per day. Then the daily interest earned by $1 million is $.00022 \times 1,000,000 = \$220$. Even at a cost of $50 per transaction, which is generously high, it pays to buy Treasury bills today and sell them tomorrow rather than to leave $1 million idle overnight.

A corporation with $1 billion of annual sales has an average daily cash flow of $1,000,000,000/ 365, about $2.7 million. Firms of this size end up buying or selling securities once a day, every day, unless by chance they have only a small positive cash balance at the end of the day.

Why do such firms hold any significant amounts of cash? There are basically two reasons. First, cash may be left in non-interest-bearing accounts to compensate banks for the services they provide. Second, large corporations may have literally hundreds of accounts with dozens of different banks. It is often better to leave idle cash in some of these accounts than to monitor each account daily and make daily transfers between them.

One major reason for the proliferation of bank accounts is decentralized management. You cannot give a subsidiary operating autonomy without giving its managers the right to spend and receive cash.

Good cash management nevertheless implies some degree of centralization. You cannot maintain your desired inventory of cash if all the subsidiaries in the group are responsible for their own private pools of cash. And you certainly want to avoid situations in which one subsidiary is investing its spare cash at 8 percent while another is borrowing at 10 percent. It is not surprising, therefore, that even in highly decentralized companies there is generally central control over cash balances and bank relations.

CASH COLLECTION AND DISBURSEMENT SYSTEMS

We have talked loosely about a firm's cash balance; it is now time to be more precise about how cash enters and exits the corporation and how the available cash balance is computed. The first necessary step is understanding *float*.

Float

Suppose that the United Carbon Company has $1 million on demand deposit with its bank. It now pays one of its suppliers by writing and mailing a check for $200,000. The company's ledgers are immediately adjusted to show a cash balance of $800,000. But the company's bank won't learn anything about this check until it has been received by the supplier, deposited at the supplier's bank, and finally presented to United Carbon's bank for payment.[5] During this time United Carbon's

---

[5]Checks deposited with a bank are cleared through the Federal Reserve clearing system, through a correspondent bank, or through a clearinghouse of local banks.

bank continues to show in its ledger that the company has a balance of $1 million. The company obtains the benefit of an extra $200,000 in the bank while the check is clearing. This sum is often called *payment,* or *disbursement float.*

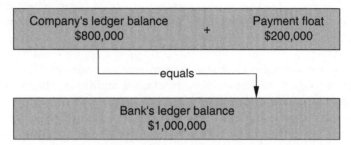

Float sounds like a marvelous invention, but unfortunately it can also work in reverse. Suppose that in addition to paying its supplier, United Carbon *receives* a check for $100,000 from a customer. It deposits the check, and both the company and the bank increase the ledger balance by $100,000:

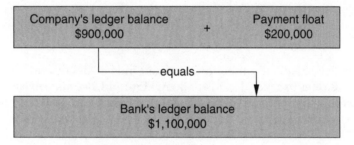

But this money isn't available to the company immediately. The bank doesn't actually have the money in hand until it has sent the check to, and received payment from, the customer's bank. Since the bank has to wait, it makes United Carbon wait too—usually one or two business days. In the meantime, the bank will show that United Carbon has an *available balance* of $1 million and an *availability float* of $100,000:

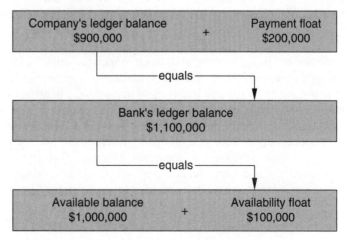

Notice that the company gains as a result of the payment float and loses as a result of the availability float. The difference is often termed the *net float*. In our example, the net float is $100,000. The company's available balance is therefore $100,000 greater than the balance shown in its ledger.

As financial manager you are concerned with the available balance, not with the company's ledger balance. If you know that it is going to be a week or two before some of your checks are presented for payment, you may be able to get by on a smaller cash balance. This game is often called *playing the float*.

You can increase your available cash balance by increasing your net float. This means that you want to ensure that checks paid in by customers are cleared rapidly and those paid to suppliers are cleared slowly. Perhaps this may sound like rather small beer, but think what it can mean to a company like Ford. Ford's daily sales average about $350 million. Therefore if it can speed up the collection process by one day, it frees $350 million, which is available for investment or payment to Ford's stockholders.

Some financial managers have become overenthusiastic in managing the float. In 1985 E. F. Hutton pleaded guilty to 2,000 separate counts of mail and wire fraud. Hutton admitted that it had created nearly $1 billion of float by shuffling funds between its branches, and through various accounts at different banks. These activities cost the company a $2 million fine and its agreement to repay the banks any losses they may have incurred.

Managing Float

Float is the child of delay. Actually there are several kinds of delay, and so people in the cash management business refer to several kinds of float. Figure 18.2 summarizes.

Of course the delays that help the payer hurt the recipient. Recipients try to speed up collections. Payers try to slow down disbursements.

Speeding Up Collections

Many companies use **concentration banking** to speed up collections. In this case customers in a particular area make payment to a local branch office rather than to company headquarters. The local branch office then deposits the checks into a local bank account. Surplus funds are transferred to a *concentration account* at one of the company's principal banks.

Concentration banking reduces float in two ways. First, because the branch office is nearer to the customer, mailing time is reduced. Second, since the customer's check is likely to be drawn on a local bank, the time taken to clear the check is also reduced. Concentration banking brings many small balances together in one large, central balance, which can then be invested in interest-paying assets through a single transaction. For example, when Amoco streamlined its U.S. bank accounts in 1995, it was able to reduce its daily bank balances in non-interest-bearing accounts by almost 80 percent.[6]

Often concentration banking is combined with a **lock-box system.** In a lock-box system, you pay the local bank to take on the administrative chores. The system works as follows. The company rents a locked post office box in each principal region. All customers within a region are instructed to send their payments to the post office box. The local bank, as agent for the company, empties the box at regular intervals and deposits the checks in the company's local account. Surplus funds are transferred periodically to one of the company's principal banks.

---

[6]"Amoco Streamlines Treasury Operations," *The Citibank Globe*, November/December 1998.

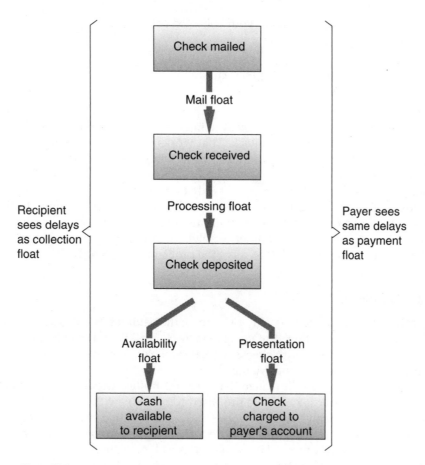

Figure 18.2

Delays create float. Each heavy arrow represents a source of delay. Recipients try to reduce delay to get available cash sooner. Payers prefer delay because they can use their cash longer. *Note:* The delays causing availability float and presentation float are equal on average but can differ from case to case.

How many collection points do you need if you use a lock-box system or concentration banking? The answer depends on where your customers are and on the speed of the U.S. mail. For example, suppose that you are thinking of opening a lock box. The local bank shows you a map of mail delivery times. From that and knowledge of your customers' locations, you come up with the following data:

- Average number of daily payments to lock box: 150
- Average size of payment: $1,200
- Rate of interest *per day:*   .02 percent
- Saving in mailing time: 1.2 days
- Saving in processing time: .8 day

On this basis, the lock box would increase your collected balance by

$$150 \text{ items per day} \times \$1,200 \text{ per item} \times (1.2 + .8) \text{ days saved} = \$360,000$$

Invested at .02 percent per day, $360,000 gives a daily return of

$$.0002 \times \$360,000 = \$72$$

The bank's charge for operating the lock-box system depends on the number of checks processed. Suppose that the bank charges $.26 per check. That works out to $150 \times .26 = \$39$ per day. You are ahead by $72 - 39 = \$33$ per day, plus whatever your firm saves from not having to process the checks itself.

Our example assumes that the company has only two choices. It can do nothing, or it can operate the lock box. But maybe there is some other lock-box location, or some mixture of locations, that would be still more effective. Of course, you can always find this out by working through all possible combinations, but it may be simpler to solve the problem by linear programming. Many banks offer linear programming models to solve the problem of locating lock boxes.[7]

Controlling Disbursements

Speeding up collections is not the only way to increase the net float. You can also do so by slowing down disbursements. One tempting strategy is to increase mail time. For example, United Carbon could pay its New York suppliers with checks mailed from Nome, Alaska, and its Los Angeles suppliers with checks mailed from Vienna, Maine.

But on second thought you will realize that such post office tricks are unlikely to give more than a short-run payoff. Suppose you have promised to pay a New York supplier on February 29. Does it matter whether you mail the check from Alaska on the 26th or from New York on the 28th? Of course, you could use a remote mailing address as an excuse for paying late, but that's a trick easily seen through. If you have to pay late, you may as well mail late.[8]

There are effective ways of increasing presentation float, however. For example, suppose that United Carbon pays its suppliers with checks written on a New York City bank. From the time that the check has been deposited by the supplier, there will be an average lapse of little more than a day before it is presented to United Carbon's bank for payment. The alternative is that United Carbon pays its suppliers with checks mailed to *arrive* on time but written on a bank in Helena, Montana; Midland, Texas; or Wilmington, Delaware. In these cases, it may take three or four days before each check is presented for payment. United Carbon, therefore, gains several days of additional float.[9]

Some firms even maintain disbursement accounts in different parts of the country. The computer looks up each supplier's zip code and automatically produces a check on the most distant bank.

---

[7]See, for example, A. Kraus, C. Janssen, and A. McAdams, "The Lock-Box Location Problem," *Journal of Bank Research* 1 (Autumn 1970), pp. 50–58.

[8]Since the tax authorities look at the date of the postmark rather than the date of receipt, companies have been tempted to use a remote mailing address to pay their tax bills. But the tax authorities have reacted by demanding that large tax bills be paid by electronic transfer.

[9]Remote disbursement accounts are described in I. Ross, "The Race Is to the Slow Payer," *Fortune*, April 18, 1983, pp. 75-80.

The suppliers won't object to these machinations because the Federal Reserve guarantees a maximum clearing time of two days on all checks cleared through the Federal Reserve system. The Federal Reserve does object and has been trying to prevent remote disbursement.

A New York City bank receives several check deliveries each day from the Federal Reserve system as well as checks that come directly from other banks or through the local clearinghouse. Thus, if United Carbon uses a New York City bank for paying its suppliers, it will not know at the beginning of the day how many checks will be presented for payment. It must either keep a large cash balance to cover contingencies or be prepared to borrow. However, instead of having a disbursement account with, say, J.P. Morgan in New York, United Carbon could open a *zero-balance* account with Morgan's affiliated bank in Wilmington, Delaware. Because it is not in a major banking center, this affiliated bank receives almost all check deliveries in the form of a single, early-morning delivery from the Federal Reserve. Therefore, it can let the cash manager at United Carbon know early in the day exactly how much money will be paid out that day. The cash manager then arranges for this sum to be transferred from the company's concentration account to the disbursement account. Thus by the end of the day (and at the start of the next day), United Carbon has a zero balance in the disbursement account.

United Carbon's Wilmington account has two advantages. First, by choosing a remote location, the company has gained several days of float. Second, because the bank can forecast early in the day how much money will be paid out, United Carbon does not need to keep extra cash in the account to cover contingencies.

Electronic Funds Transfer

Many cash payments involve pieces of paper, such as a dollar bill or a check. But the use of paper transactions is on the decline. For consumers it is being replaced by credit or debit cards. In the case of companies, payments are increasingly made electronically.

Electronic payment systems may be of two kinds—a *gross* settlement system or a *net* settlement system. With gross settlement each payment is settled individually; with net settlement all payment instructions are accumulated and then at the end of the day any imbalances are settled.

In the United States there are two systems for making large-value electronic payments—Fedwire (a gross system) and CHIPS (a net system). Fedwire is operated by the Federal Reserve system and connects over 10,000 financial institutions in the United States to the Fed and thereby to each other. Suppose Bank A instructs the Fed to transfer $1 million from its account with the Fed to the account of Bank B. Bank A's account is debited immediately and Bank B's account is credited at the same time. Fedwire is therefore an example of a *real-time gross settlement (RTGS)* system. Most developed countries operate RTGS systems for large-value payments. For example, *Target*, the central settlement system for cross-border euro payments, is an RTGS system.

Real-time gross settlement suffers from a potential problem. If Bank A needs to pay Bank B, B needs to pay C, and C needs to pay A, there is a risk that the system could gridlock unless each bank kept a large reserve with the Fed. (A might not be able to pay B until it has been paid by C, C can't pay A until paid by B, and B in turn is awaiting payment by A.) To oil the wheels, therefore, the Fed takes on the credit risk by paying the receiving bank even if there are insufficient funds in the account of the payer. Since each payment is final and guaranteed by the Fed, each receiving bank can be sure that it has the money and can give its customer immediate access to the funds.

Cross-border high-value payments in dollars are handled by CHIPS, which is a privately owned system connecting 115 large domestic and foreign banks. CHIPS accumulates payment instructions throughout the day, and at the end of the day each bank settles up the net payment using Fedwire. This means that, if the bank receiving payments makes the funds available to its customers during the day, it would be at risk if the paying bank goes belly up during the day. Banks control this risk by imposing intraday credit limits on their exposure to each other.

Fedwire and CHIPS provide same-day settlement and are used to make high-value payments. Bulk payments such as wages, dividends, and payments to suppliers generally travel through the *Automated Clearinghouse (ACH)* system and take two to three days.[10] In this case the company simply needs to provide a computer file of instructions to its bank, which then debits the corporation's account and forwards the payments to the ACH system. The ACH system is the largest payment system in the United States and in 1997 handled 3.4 billion payments with a value of nearly $11 trillion.

For companies that are "wired" to their banks, customers, and suppliers, these electronic payment systems have at least three advantages:

- Record keeping and routine transactions are easy to automate when money moves electronically. Campbell Soup's Treasury Management Department discovered that it could handle cash management, short-term borrowing and lending, and bank relationships with a total staff of seven. The company's domestic cash flow was about $5 billion.[11]

- The marginal cost of transactions is very low. For example, it costs less than $10 to transfer huge sums of money using Fedwire and only a few cents to make an ACH transfer.

- Float is drastically reduced. Wire transfers generate no float at all. This can result in substantial savings. For example, cash managers at Occidental Petroleum found that one plant was paying out about $8 million per month three to five days early to avoid any risk of late fees if checks were delayed in the mail. The solution was obvious: The plant's managers switched to paying large bills electronically; that way they could ensure they arrived exactly on time.[12]

International Cash Management

Cash management in domestic firms is child's play compared with that in large multinational corporations operating in dozens of countries, each with its own currency, banking system, and legal structure.

A single, centralized cash management system is an unattainable ideal for these companies, although they are edging toward it. For example, suppose that you are the treasurer of a large multinational company with operations throughout Europe. You could allow the separate businesses to manage their own cash but that would be costly and would almost certainly result in each one accumulating little hoards of cash. The solution is to set up a regional system. In this case the company establishes a local concentration account with a bank in each country. Then any surplus cash is swept daily into central multicurrency accounts in London or another European banking center. This cash is then invested in marketable securities or used to finance any subsidiaries that have a cash shortage.

---

[10]Credit transfers (party making payment initiates transaction) settle in three days and debit transfers (receiver of payment initiates transaction) settle in two days.

[11]J. D. Moss, "Campbell Soup's Cutting-Edge Cash Management," *Financial Executive* 8 (September/October 1992), pp. 39–42.

[12]R. J. Pisapia, "The Cash Manager's Expanding Role: Working Capital," *Journal of Cash Management* 10 (November/December 1990), pp. 11–14.

Payments also can be made out of the regional center. For example, to pay wages in each European country, the company just needs to send its principal bank a computer file with details of the payments to be made. The bank then finds the least costly way to transfer the cash from the company's central accounts and arranges for the funds to be credited on the correct day to the employees in each country.

Most large multinationals have several banks in each country, but the more banks they use, the less control they have over their cash balances. So development of regional cash management systems favors banks that can offer a worldwide branch network. These banks also can afford to invest the several billion dollars that are needed to set up computer systems for handling cash payments and receipts in many different countries.

BANK RELATIONS

Much of the work of cash management—processing checks, transferring funds, running lock boxes, helping keep track of the company's accounts—is done by banks. And banks provide many other services not so directly linked to cash management, for example, handling payments and receipts in foreign currency, executing the purchase or sale of Treasury securities, or acting as a custodian for securities. Of course, banks also lend money or give firms the *option* to borrow under a line of credit.[13]

All these services have to be paid for. Banks demand fees for processing checks, operating lock boxes, or standing by ready to lend. These fees can be paid directly, by paying a monthly charge based on services provided, or indirectly, by letting money sit in non-interest-bearing bank accounts.

Banks like demand deposits. After setting aside a portion of the deposits in a reserve account with the Federal Reserve Bank, they can relend these deposits and earn interest on them. Banks would, therefore, be prepared to pay interest to attract demand deposits, but the government prohibits them from doing so.

One thing that governments never learn is that it is very difficult to legislate prices. Although they stop banks from offering money in payment for demand deposits, they do not stop them from offering services to attract deposits. Therefore, if a firm keeps a sufficiently large balance with the bank, the bank will process the firm's checks without charge, it will operate a lock-box system—it will provide all kinds of advice and services.

Thus firms can pay for bank services by maintaining interest-free demand deposits. These deposits generate *earnings credits,* which are used to pay for bank services. The earnings credits are interest by another name.[14]

Demand deposits earmarked to pay for bank services are termed *compensating balances.* There has been a steady trend toward direct fees for bank services and away from compensating balances. But some banks still request them, for example, in exchange for a line of credit. In some cases *you* may request them. Suppose you had other reasons for keeping a working balance in a certain bank, perhaps to support local operations. This money may also serve as a compensating

---

[13]See Chapter 19.

[14]Under this system of indirect rewards the bank will insist that you maintain a specified average level of balances over the month. Therefore you don't want to allow your cash inventory to run down to zero before replenishing it.

balance. In other words, it may be more efficient to let the money sit in the bank and generate earnings credits than to pay the costs of frequent transfers into or out of interest-bearing securities.

What Happens If Money Pays Interest?

The prohibition on paying interest on demand deposits is breaking down. The United States is closing in on other countries in which interest is paid routinely on corporate checking accounts.[15] But even where explicit interest-bearing checking accounts are the norm, firms and individuals still face a trade-off between liquidity and forgone interest, because checking accounts offer lower interest rates than direct investment in securities. (Otherwise, banks lose money, and in the long run they cannot offer a money-losing service.) Thus, the less money kept in a checking account, the more interest earned. Yet low balances in checking accounts mean frequent sales or purchases of securities and thus frequent transaction costs. This is the same problem we started the chapter with.

SUMMARY

Cash provides liquidity, but it doesn't pay interest. Securities pay interest, but you can't use them to buy things. As financial manager you want to hold cash up to the point where the marginal value of liquidity is equal to the interest that you could earn on securities.

Cash is just one of the raw materials that you need to do business. It is expensive keeping your capital tied up in large inventories of raw materials when it could be earning interest. Why do you hold inventories at all? Why not order materials as and when you need them? The answer is that it is also expensive to keep placing many small orders. You need to strike a balance between holding too large an inventory of cash (and losing interest on the money) and making too many small adjustments to your inventory (and incurring additional administrative and transaction costs). If interest rates are high, you want to hold relatively small inventories of cash. If your cash needs are variable and your costs are high, you want to hold relatively large inventories.

We might add that you have the alternative of borrowing to cover a cash deficiency. Again, you face a trade-off. Since banks charge a high interest rate on borrowing, you want to keep sufficiently large liquid funds so that you don't need to keep borrowing. On the other hand, by having large liquid balances, you are also not earning the maximum return on your cash.

The cash shown in the company ledger is not the same as the available balance in your bank account. The difference is the net float. When you have written a large number of checks awaiting clearance, the available balance will be larger than the ledger balance. When you have just deposited a large number of checks which have not yet been collected by the bank, the available balance will be smaller. If you can predict how long it will take checks to clear, you may be able to play the float and get by on a smaller cash balance.

You can also *manage* the float by speeding up collections and slowing down payments. One way to speed collections is to use concentration banking. Customers make payments to a regional office which then pays the checks into a local bank account. Surplus funds are transferred from the local account to a concentration bank. An alternative technique is lock-box banking. In this case customers

---

[15]In these countries, bank services are almost always paid by fee rather than indirectly by compensating balances.

send their payments to a local post office box. A local bank empties the box at regular intervals and clears the checks. Concentration banking and lock-box banking reduce mailing time and the time required to clear checks.

Large-value payments are almost always made electronically. In the United States there are two large-value systems—Fedwire (for dollar payments within the country) and CHIPS (for cross-border payments). Bulk payments, such as wages and dividends, are usually made by means of the Automated Clearinghouse (ACH) system.

Banks provide many services. They handle checks, manage lock boxes, provide advice, obtain references, and so on. Firms either pay cash for these services or pay by maintaining sufficient cash balances with the bank.

In many cases you will want to keep somewhat larger balances than are needed to pay for the tangible services. One reason is that the bank may be a valuable source of ideas and business connections. Another reason is that you may use the bank as a source of short-term funds. Leaving idle cash at your bank may be implicit compensation for the willingness of the bank to stand ready to advance credit when needed. A large cash balance may, therefore, be good insurance against a rainy day.

Further Reading

Baumol was the pioneer in applying inventory models to cash management. Miller and Orr extend the Baumol model to handling uncertain cash flows, and Mullins and Homonoff review tests of inventory models for cash management.

W. J. Baumol: "The Transactions Demand for Cash: An Inventory Theoretic Approach," *Quarterly Journal of Economics,* 66:545–556 (November 1952).

M. H. Miller and D. Orr: "A Model of the Demand for Money by Firms," *Quarterly Journal of Economics,* 80:413–435 (August 1966).

D. Mullins and R. Homonoff: "Applications of Inventory Cash Management Models," in S. C. Myers (ed.), *Modern Developments in Financial Management,* Frederick A. Praeger, Inc., New York, 1976.

The next three articles analyze the design of lock-box and concentration banking systems:

A. Kraus, C. Janssen, and A. McAdams: "The Lock-Box Location Problem," *Journal of Bank Research,* 1:50–58 (Autumn 1970).

G. Cornuejols, M. L. Fisher, and G. L. Nemhauser: "Location of Bank Accounts to Optimize Float: An Analytic Study of Exact and Approximate Algorithms," *Management Science,* 23:789–810 (April 1977).

S. F. Maier and J. H. Vander Weide: "What Lock-Box and Disbursement Models Really Do," *Journal of Finance,* 37:361–371 (May 1983).

The following article provides a useful description of electronic payments systems in the United States:

G. R. Junker, B. J. Summers, and F. M. Young: "A Primer on the Settlement of Payments in the United States," *Federal Reserve Bulletin,* 77:847–858 (November 1991).

Specialized "how-to" texts on cash management include:

J. E. Finnerty: *How to Manage Corporate Cash Effectively,* American Management Association, New York, 1991.

C. R. Malburg: *The Cash Management Handbook,* Prentice-Hall, Englewood Cliffs, N.J., 1992.

J. G. Kallberg and K. L. Parkinson: *Corporate Liquidity: Management and Measurement,* Richard D. Irwin, Homewood Ill., 1993.

SHORT-TERM LENDING AND BORROWING

I f a company has a temporary cash surplus, it can invest in short-term securities. If it has a temporary deficiency, it can replenish cash by selling securities or by borrowing on a short-term basis. Chapter 18 discussed when to make such changes. But you need to know more than that. There is an elaborate menu of short-term securities; you should be familiar with the most popular entrées. Similarly there are many kinds of short-term debts, and you should know their distinguishing characteristics. That is why we have included the present chapter on short-term lending and borrowing. You will encounter little in the way of new theory, but there is a good deal of interesting institutional material.

SHORT-TERM LENDING

The Money Market

The market for short-term investments is generally known as the **money market.** The money market has no physical marketplace. It consists of a loose agglomeration of banks and dealers linked together by telex, telephones, and computers. But a huge volume of securities is regularly traded on the money market, and competition is vigorous.

Most large corporations manage their own money-market investments, buying and selling through banks or dealers. Small companies sometimes find it more convenient to hire a professional investment-management firm or to put their cash into a money-market fund. This is a mutual fund that invests only in short-term securities. In return for a fee, money-market funds provide professional management and a diversified portfolio of high-quality, short-term securities. We discussed money-market funds in Chapter 5.

In Chapter 11 we pointed out that there are two main markets for long-term dollar bonds. There is the domestic market in the United States and there is an international market. Similarly, in this chapter we shall see that in addition to the domestic money market, there is also an international market for short-term dollar investments. Since this market is based largely in Europe, it has traditionally been known as the *eurodollar* market. However, now that the European single currency has been called the euro, the term "eurodollar" is potentially confusing and we will just refer to "international dollars."

An international dollar is not some strange bank note; it is simply a dollar deposit in a bank outside the United States. For example, suppose that an American oil company buys crude oil from an Arab sheik and pays for it with a $1 million check drawn on Chase Manhattan Bank. The sheik then deposits the check into his account at Barclays Bank in London. As a result, Barclays has an asset in the form of a $1 million credit in its account with Chase Manhattan. It also has an offsetting liability in the form of a dollar deposit. That dollar deposit is placed in Europe; it is, therefore, an international dollar deposit.[1]

We will describe the principal domestic and international dollar investments shortly, but bear in mind that there is also an international market for investments in other currencies. For example, if a U.S. corporation wishes to make a short-term investment in yen, it can do so in the Tokyo money market or it can make an international yen deposit in London.

If we lived in a world without regulation and taxes, the interest rate on an international dollar loan would have to be the same as the rate on an equivalent domestic dollar loan, the rate on an international yen loan would have to be the same as that on a domestic yen loan, and so on. However, the international loan markets thrive because individual governments attempt to regulate domestic bank lending. For example, between 1963 and 1974 the U.S. government controlled the export of funds for corporate investment. Therefore, companies that wished to expand abroad were forced to borrow dollars outside the United States. This demand tended to push the interest rate on these loans above the domestic rate. At the same time the government limited the rate of interest that banks in the United States could pay on domestic deposits; this also tended to keep the rate of interest that you could earn on dollar deposits in Europe above the rate on domestic dollar deposits. By early 1974 the restrictions on the export of funds had been removed, and for large deposits the interest rate ceiling had also been abolished. In consequence, the difference between the interest rate on international dollar deposits and domestic deposits narrowed, but it did not disappear: Banks are not subject to Federal Reserve requirements on international dollar deposits and are not obliged to insure these deposits with the Federal Deposit Insurance Corporation. On the other hand, depositors are exposed to the (very low) risk that a foreign government could prohibit banks from repaying international dollar deposits. For these reasons international dollar investments continue to offer slightly higher rates of interest than domestic dollar deposits.

The U.S. government has become increasingly concerned that its regulations are driving banking business overseas to foreign banks and the overseas branches of American banks. In an attempt to attract some of this business back to the States, the government in 1981 allowed U.S. and foreign banks to establish so-called *international banking facilities* (IBFs). An IBF is the financial equivalent of a free-trade zone; it is physically situated in the United States, but it is not required to maintain reserves with the Federal Reserve and depositors are not subject to any U.S. tax.[2] However, there

---

[1]The sheik could equally well deposit the check with the London branch of a U.S. bank or a Japanese bank. He would still have made an international dollar deposit.

[2]For these reasons dollars held on deposit in an IBF are also classed as international dollars.

are tight restrictions on what business an IBF can conduct. In particular, it cannot accept deposits from domestic United States corporations or make loans to them.

Banks in London lend dollars to one another at the *London interbank offered rate* (LIBOR). LIBOR is a benchmark for pricing many types of short-term loans in the United States and overseas. For example, a corporation in the United States may issue a floating-rate note with interest payments tied to LIBOR.

Valuing Money-Market Investments

When we value long-term debt, it is important to take default risk into account. Almost anything may happen in 30 years; even today's most respectable company may get into trouble eventually. This is the basic reason why corporate bonds offer higher yields than Treasury bonds.

Short-term debt is not risk-free either. When Penn Central failed, it had $82 million of short-term commercial paper outstanding. After that shock, investors became much more discriminating in their purchases of commercial paper, and the spread between interest rates on high- and low-quality paper widened dramatically.

Such examples of failure are exceptions that prove the rule; in general, the danger of default is less for money-market securities issued by corporations than for corporate bonds. There are two reasons for this. First, the range of possible outcomes is smaller for short-term investments. Even though the distant future may be clouded, you can usually be confident that a particular company will survive for at least the next month. Second, for the most part only well-established companies can borrow in the money market. If you are going to lend money for only one day, you can't afford to spend too much time in evaluating the loan. Thus you will consider only blue-chip borrowers.

Despite the high quality of money-market investments, there are often significant differences in yield between corporate and U.S. government securities. For example, in January 1999 the rate of interest on three-month commercial paper was about .4 percentage points higher than the rate on Treasury bills. Why is this? One answer is the risk of default on commercial paper. Another is that the investments have different degrees of liquidity or "moneyness." Investors prefer Treasury bills because they are easier to turn into cash on short notice. Securities that can be converted quickly and cheaply into cash offer relatively low yields.

Calculating the Yield on Money-Market Investments

Many money-market investments are pure discount securities. This means that they don't pay interest: The return consists of the difference between the amount you pay and the amount you receive at maturity. Unfortunately, it is no good trying to persuade the Internal Revenue Service that this difference represents a capital gain. The IRS is wise to that one and will tax your return as ordinary income.

Two features make it difficult to work out the yield on money-market securities. One is the fact that rates are often quoted on a discount basis; the other is that they are usually quoted on a 360-day year. For example, in January 1999, 91-day Treasury bills were issued at a discount of 4.36 percent. This is a rather complicated way of saying that the price of a 91-day bill was $100 - 91/360 \times 4.36 = \$98.898$. For each $98.898 that you invested in January, the government agreed to pay $100 to you 91 days later. The return over the 91 days was therefore $(100 - 98.898)/98.898 = 1.11$ percent, equivalent over a 365-day year to a yield of 4.47 percent simple interest and 4.55 percent if interest was compounded annually.[3] Notice that the yield is higher than the discount. When you read that Treasury bills are at a discount of 4.36 percent, it is very easy to slip into the mistake of thinking that this is their yield.[4]

MONEY-MARKET INVESTMENTS

Table 19.1 summarizes the principal money-market investments. We will describe each in turn, but you should note that in the United States the volume of business in three of these investments is much larger than in the others. These three are Treasury bills, commercial paper, and repurchase agreements.

U.S. Treasury Bills

The first item in Table 19.1 is U.S. Treasury bills. These mature in three months, six months, or one year.[5] Both three-month and six-month bills are issued every week and one-year bills are generally issued every month. Sales are by auction. You can enter a competitive bid and take your chance of receiving an allotment at your bid price. Alternatively, if you want to be sure of getting your bills, you can enter a noncompetitive bid. Noncompetitive bids are filled at the *average* price of the successful competitive bids. You don't have to participate in the auction in order to invest in Treasury bills. There is also an excellent secondary market in which billions of dollars of bills are bought and sold every day.

Federal Agency Securities

Agencies of the federal government such as the Federal Home Loan Bank (FHLB) and the Federal National Mortgage Association ("Fannie Mae") borrow both short and long term. The short-term debt consists of discount notes, which are similar to Treasury bills. They are very actively traded and are often held by corporations. Their yields are slightly above those on comparable Treasury securities. One reason for the slightly higher yields is that agency debt is not quite as marketable as Treasury issues. Another is that most agency debt is backed not by the "full faith and credit" of the U.S. government but only by the agency itself. It is possible that the government would allow one of its agencies to default on its debt, but most investors regard this risk as exceedingly remote.

---

[3]Money-market dealers calculate yields on bills of six months or less on the basis of simple interest, using either a 360-day year (the so-called *money-market yield*) or a 365-day year (the *equivalent bond yield*). In other words, they multiply the 91-day yield by either 360/91 or 365/91. This is often confusing and not, in principle, the right way to do it. The compound rate is better

$$(1.0111)^{365/91} - 1 = .0455, \text{ or } 4.55\%$$

[4]For more detail on how to calculate yields on money-market investments, see M. Stigum, *Fixed Income Calculations, Vol. 1: Money Market Paper and Bonds* (Homewood, IL: Dow Jones-Irwin, Inc., 1994).

[5]So-called three-month bills actually mature 91 days after issue, and six-month bills mature 182 days after issue.

TABLE 19.1

Money-market investments in the United States

INVESTMENT	BORROWER	MATURITIES WHEN ISSUED	MARKETABILITY	BASIS FOR CALCULATING INTEREST	COMMENTS
Treasury bills	U.S. government	3-month, 6-month, and 1-year	Excellent secondary market	Discount	3-month and 6-month bills auctioned weekly; 1-year bills auctioned monthly
Federal agency discount notes	FHLB, "Fannie Mae," "Sallie Mae," "Freddie Mac," etc.	Typically 3 to 6 months	Very good secondary market	Discount	Sold through dealers
Tax-exempt municipal notes	Municipalities, states, school districts, etc.	3 months to 1 year	Good secondary market	Usually interest-bearing; interest at maturity	Tax anticipation notes (TANs), revenue anticipation notes (RANs), bond anticipation notes (BANs), etc.
Tax-exempt variable-rate demand bonds (VRDBs)	Municipalities, states, state universities, etc.	20 to 40 years	Good secondary market	Variable interest rate	Long-term bonds but with put options to demand repayment
Negotiable certificates of deposit (CDs)	Commercial banks, savings and loans	Usually 1 to 3 months; also longer-maturity variable-rate CDs	Poor secondary market	Interest-bearing with interest at maturity	Receipt for time deposit
Commercial paper (CP)	Industrial firms, finance companies, and bank holding companies; also municipalities	Maximum 270 days; usually 60 days or less	Dealers or issuer will repurchase paper	Discount	Unsecured promissory note; may be placed through dealer or directly with investor
Medium-term notes (MTNs)	Largely finance companies and banks; also industrial firms	Minimum 270 days; usually less than 10 years	Dealers will repurchase notes	Interest-bearing; usually fixed rate	Unsecured promissory note; placed through dealer
Bankers' acceptances (BAs)	Major commercial banks	1 to 6 months	Fair secondary market	Discount	Demands to pay that have been accepted by a bank
Repurchase agreements (repos)	Dealers in U.S. government securities	Overnight to about 3 months; also open repos (continuing contracts)	No secondary market	Repurchase price set higher than selling price; difference quoted as repo interest rate	Sales of government securities by dealer with simultaneous agreement to repurchase

Short-Term Tax-Exempts

Short-term notes are also issued by municipalities, states, and agencies such as state universities and school districts.[6] These are slightly more risky than Treasury bills and not as easy to buy or sell.[7] Nevertheless they have one particular attraction—the interest is not subject to federal income tax.[8]

Pretax yields on tax-exempts are substantially lower than those on comparable taxed securities. But if your company pays tax at the standard 35 percent corporate rate, the lower gross yield of the municipals may be more than offset by the savings in tax.

Tax-exempt issues also include variable-rate demand bonds (VRDBs). These are long-term securities, whose interest payments are linked to the level of short-term interest rates. Whenever the interest rate is reset, investors have the right to sell the bonds back to the issuer for their face value. This ensures that on these reset dates the price of the bonds cannot be less than their face value. Therefore, although VRDBs are long-term bonds, their prices are very stable and they compete with short-term tax-exempt notes as a home for spare cash.

Bank Time Deposits and Certificates of Deposit

When you make a time deposit with a bank, you are lending money to the bank for a fixed period. If you need the money before maturity, the bank will usually allow you to withdraw it but will exact a penalty in the form of a reduced rate of interest.

Wouldn't it be nice if you could avoid that penalty by selling your loan to another would-be lender? You can if you have $1 million or more to invest.[9] In this case, when the bank borrows, it issues a **negotiable certificate of deposit (CD).** A CD is simply evidence of a time deposit with a bank. However, if you decide that you need the money before maturity, you don't have to ask the bank: You just sell your CD to another investor. When the loan matures, the new owner of the CD presents it to the bank and receives payment.

CDs typically have a maturity of between 30 days and three months, but banks also issue longer-term CDs with a variable interest rate. The supply of CDs in the United States expanded rapidly until the mid-1980s, but since then it has fallen away as banks found more attractive ways to raise funds.[10]

We pointed out earlier that, instead of depositing dollars with a bank in the United States, a corporation can deposit them overseas with a foreign bank or the foreign branch of a U.S. bank. These deposits pay a fixed rate of interest, and either they are for a fixed term that may vary from

---

[6]Some of these notes are *general obligations* of the issuer; others are *revenue securities,* and in these cases payments are made from rent receipts or other user charges.

[7]Defaults on tax-exempts are rare but not unknown. For example, in 1983 the municipal utility Washington Public Power Supply System (unfortunately known as WPPSS) defaulted on $2.25 billion of bonds. The 1994 default of Orange County is described in Chapter 4.

[8]This advantage is partly offset by the fact that Treasury securities are free of state and local taxes.

[9]Banks also sell nonnegotiable CDs to individuals. Most of these pay a fixed rate of interest, but there are also some quirky CDs. Peterson Bank sold a World Soccer CD which paid double interest if the United States won the World Cup, and Bank of Boulder sold CDs that paid interest in the form of sporting rifles and shotguns.

[10]One disadvantage with any time deposit is that the bank has to set aside part of the money as a reserve with the Federal Reserve Bank. This cash does not earn interest. The reserve is therefore equivalent to a tax on the deposit.

one day to several years or they are for an undefined term but may be called at one or more days' notice. Since a time deposit is an illiquid investment, the London branches of the major banks also issue negotiable international dollar CDs.

Commercial Paper

A bank is an intermediary which borrows short-term funds from one group of firms or individuals and relends the money to another group. It makes its profit by charging the borrower a higher rate of interest than it offers the lender.

Sometimes it is convenient to have a bank in the middle. It saves lenders the trouble of looking for borrowers and assessing their creditworthiness, and it saves borrowers the trouble of looking for lenders. Depositors do not care whom the bank lends to: They need only satisfy themselves that the bank as a whole is safe.

There are also occasions on which it is *not* worth paying an intermediary to perform these functions. Large, well-known companies can bypass the banking system by issuing their own short-term unsecured notes. These notes are known as **commercial paper.**

Financial institutions, such as bank holding companies and finance companies,[11] also issue commercial paper, sometimes in very large quantities. For example, GE Capital Corporation has $71 billion of commercial paper in issue. Often such firms set up their own marketing department and sell their issues directly to investors. Other companies sell through dealers who receive a fee for marketing the issue.

Commercial paper has a maximum maturity of nine months, though most paper is for 60 days or less. Most buyers of commercial paper hold it to maturity, but the company or dealer that sells the paper is usually prepared to repurchase it earlier.

The majority of commercial paper is issued by high-grade, nationally known companies.[12] Companies generally support their issue of commercial paper by arranging a backup line of credit with a bank, which guarantees that they can find the money to repay the paper. The risk of default is, therefore, small.

Commercial paper is very popular with major companies. By cutting out the intermediary, they are able to borrow at rates that may be 1 to 1 1/2 percent below the prime rate charged by banks. Even after allowing for a dealer's commission and the cost of any backup line of credit, this is still a substantial saving. Banks have felt the competition from commercial paper and have been prepared to reduce their rates to blue-chip customers. As a result, "prime rate" doesn't mean what it used to. It once meant the rate banks charged their most creditworthy customers. Now the prime customers often pay less than the prime rate.

---

[11]A *bank holding company* is a firm that owns a bank and also nonbanking subsidiaries. Thus a bank holding company might hold a bank (the major part of its business) and also a leasing company, a management consulting company, etc. *Finance companies* are firms that specialize in lending to businesses or individuals. They include independent firms such as Household Finance as well as subsidiaries of nonfinancial corporations, such as General Motors Acceptance Corporation (GMAC). In their lending finance companies compete with banks. However, they raise funds not by attracting deposits, as banks do, but by issuing commercial paper and other, longer-term securities.

[12]Moody's and Standard and Poor's publish quality ratings for commercial paper. For example, Moody's provides three ratings, from P–1 (denoting Prime 1, the highest-grade paper) to P–3. Investors rely on these ratings, along with other information, when they compare the quality of different firms' paper. Most are reluctant to buy low-rated paper.

As an alternative to issuing commercial paper in the United States, companies can also sell commercial paper in the international capital market. This is known as *eurocommercial paper* or *ECP*.[13]

Medium-Term Notes

New issues of securities do not need to be registered with the SEC as long as they mature within 270 days. So by limiting the maturity of commercial paper issues, companies can avoid the delays and expenses of registration. However, in 1982 the SEC introduced shelf registration, which permits companies to file a single registration statement for a series of similar issues.[14] This encouraged large blue-chip companies to make regular issues of unsecured **medium-term notes (MTNs).**

You can think of MTNs as a hybrid between corporate bonds and commercial paper. Like bonds, they are relatively long-term instruments; their maturity is never less than 270 days and may be as long as 30 years.[15] On the other hand, like commercial paper, MTNs are not underwritten but are sold on a regular basis either through dealers or, occasionally, directly to investors. Borrowers, such as finance companies that are always needing cash, welcome the flexibility of MTNs. For example, a company may tell its dealers the amount of money that it needs to raise that week, the range of maturities that it can offer, and the maximum interest rate that it is prepared to pay. It is then up to the dealers to find the buyers.

Just as there is both a domestic and an international market for commercial paper, so there are two parallel markets for medium-term notes. The international MTN market is younger than that in the United States, but it has grown rapidly.

We have described MTNs in this chapter because of their resemblance to short-term commercial paper. However, buyers of MTNs tend to be long-term investors who want to nail down a fixed rate of interest for a number of years. Unlike most other money-market investments, MTNs are not commonly used as a temporary home for spare cash.[16]

Bankers' Acceptances

A **banker's acceptance (BA)** begins life as a written demand for the bank to pay a given sum at a future date. The bank then agrees to this demand by writing "accepted" on it. Once accepted, the draft becomes the bank's IOU and is a negotiable security, which can be bought and sold through money-market dealers.

A banker's acceptance may arise in one of two ways. We have already seen in Chapter 17 that an acceptance may be arranged to finance exports or imports. Later in this chapter we shall see that acceptances are also occasionally used in connection with inventory financing.

---

[13]For a general discussion of commercial paper, see M. A. Post, "The Evolution of the U.S. Commercial Paper Market since 1980," *Federal Reserve Bulletin* 78 (December 1992), pp. 879–891; and T. K. Hahn, "Commercial Paper," *Economic Quarterly* (Federal Reserve Bank of Richmond) 79 (Spring 1993), pp. 45–67.

[14]We described shelf registration in Chapter 3.

[15]Walt Disney Company has even used its MTN shelf registration to issue a 100-year bond. See L. E. Crabbe, "Medium Term Notes," in F. J. Fabozzi and T. D. Fabozzi (eds.), *Handbook of Fixed Income Securities*, 4th ed. (Homewood, IL: Dow Jones-Irwin, Inc., 1995).

[16]A few MTNs have floating interest rates and offer investors the right to demand early repayment. These are used as a parking lot for short-term cash.

Acceptances by the large U.S. banks generally mature in one to six months and involve very low credit risk.[17]

Repurchase Agreements

Repurchase agreements, or *repos,* are effectively secured loans to a government security dealer. They work as follows: The investor buys part of the dealer's holding of Treasury securities and simultaneously arranges to sell them back again at a later date at a specified higher price. The borrower (the dealer) is said to have entered into a *repo;* the lender (who buys the securities) is said to have a *reverse repo.*

Repos sometimes run for several months, but more frequently they are just overnight (24-hour) agreements. No other domestic money-market investment offers such liquidity. Corporations can treat overnight repos almost as if they were interest-bearing demand deposits.

Suppose that you decide to invest cash in repos for several days or weeks. You don't want to keep renegotiating agreements every day. One solution is to enter into an *open repo* with a security dealer. In this case there is no fixed maturity to the agreement; either side is free to withdraw at one day's notice. Alternatively, you may arrange with your bank to transfer any excess cash automatically into repos.

For many years repos appeared to be not only very liquid instruments but also very safe. This reputation took a knock in 1982 when two money-market dealers went bankrupt. Each case involved heavy use of repos. One dealer, Drysdale Securities, had been in existence for only three months and had total capital of $20 million. However, it went bankrupt, owing Chase Bank $250 million. It's not easy to run up debts that fast, but Drysdale did it.

Ever since the Drysdale collapse lawyers have been trying to sort out the legal status of the repo. Is it, as the name implies, a promise to repurchase the bond at an agreed price, or is it, as some lawyers argue, a loan secured by a bond?[18]

FLOATING-RATE PREFERRED STOCK—AN ALTERNATIVE TO MONEY-MARKET INVESTMENTS

There is no law preventing firms from making short-term investments in long-term securities. If a firm has $1 million set aside for an income tax payment, it could buy a long-term bond on January 1 and sell it on April 15, when the taxes must be paid. However, the danger in this strategy is obvious: What happens if bond prices fall by 10 percent between January and April? There you are, with a $1 million liability to the Internal Revenue Service, bonds worth only $900,000, and a very red face. Of course, bond prices could also go up, but why take the chance? Corporate treasurers entrusted with excess funds for short-term investment are naturally averse to the price volatility of long-term bonds.

---

[17]For further information, see "Recent Developments in the Bankers' Acceptance Market," *Federal Reserve Bulletin* 72 (January 1986), pp. 1–12; and R. K. LaRoche, "Bankers' Acceptances," *Economic Quarterly* (Federal Reserve Bank of Richmond) 79 (Winter 1993), pp. 75–85.

[18]To reduce the risk of repos, it is common to value the security at less than its market value. This difference is known as a *haircut.*

We saw earlier how municipalities devised variable-rate demand bonds, which investors could periodically sell back to the issuer. The prices of these bonds are nearly immune to fluctuations in interest rates. In addition, the interest on municipal loans has the attraction of being tax-exempt. So a municipal variable-rate demand bond offers a safe, tax-free, short-term haven for your $1 million of cash.

Common stock and preferred stock also have an interesting tax advantage for corporations, since firms pay tax on only 30 percent of dividends received from other corporations. For each $1 of dividends received, the firm gets to keep $1 - .30 \times .35 = \$.895$. Thus the effective tax rate is only 10.5 percent. This is higher than the zero tax rate on the interest from municipal debt but much lower than the rate that the company pays on other debt interest.

Suppose you consider putting that $1 million in some other corporation's preferred shares.[19] The 10.5 percent tax rate is very tempting. On the other hand, since preferred dividends are fixed, the prices of preferred shares change when long-term interest rates change. A $1 million investment in preferred shares could be worth only $900,000 on April 15, when taxes are due. Wouldn't it be nice if someone invented a preferred share that was insulated from fluctuating interest rates?

Well, there are such securities, and you can probably guess how they work: Specify a dividend payment which goes up and down with the general level of interest rates.[20] The prices of these securities are less volatile than those of fixed-dividend preferreds.

Varying the dividend payment on preferred stock doesn't quite do the trick. For example, if investors become more concerned about the risk of preferred stock, they might demand a higher relative return and the price of the stock could fall. So investment bankers added another wrinkle to floating-rate preferred. Instead of being tied rigidly to interest rates, the dividend can be reset periodically by means of an auction which is open to all investors. Existing shareholders can enter the auction by stating the minimum dividend they are prepared to accept; if this turns out to be higher than the rate that is needed to sell the issue, the shareholders sell the stock to the new investors at its face value. Alternatively, shareholders can simply enter a noncompetitive bid, keeping their shares and receiving whatever dividend is set by the other bidders. The result is similar to the variable-rate demand note: Because auction-rate preferred stock can be resold at regular intervals for its face value, its price cannot wander far in the interim.[21]

Why would any firm want to *issue* floating-rate preferreds? Dividends must be paid out of *after-tax* income, whereas interest comes out of before-tax income. Thus, if a taxpaying firm wants to issue a floating-rate security, it would normally choose to issue floating-rate debt in order to generate interest tax shields.

However, there are plenty of firms that are not paying taxes. These firms cannot make use of the interest tax shield. Moreover, they have been able to issue floating-rate preferreds at yields *lower* than what they would have to pay on a floating-rate debt issue. (The corporations buying the

---

[19]Preferred shares are usually better short-term investments for a corporation than common shares. The preferred shares' expected return is virtually all dividends; most common shares are expected to generate capital gains, too. The corporate tax on capital gains is usually 35 percent. Corporations therefore have a strong incentive to like dividends and dislike capital gains.

[20]Usually there are limits on the maximum and minimum dividends that can be paid. Thus if interest rates leap to 100 percent, the preferred dividend would hit a ceiling of, say, 15 percent. If interest rates fall to 1 percent, the preferred dividend would hit a floor at, say, 5 percent.

[21]See M. J. Alderson, K. C. Brown, and S. L. Lummer, "Dutch Auction Rate Preferred Stock," *Financial Management* 16 (Summer 1987), pp. 68–73.

preferreds are happy with these lower yields because 70 percent of the dividends they receive escape tax.)

Floating-rate preferreds were invented in Canada in the mid-1970s, when several billion dollars' worth were issued before the Canadian tax authorities cooled off the market by limiting the dividend tax exclusion on some types of floating-rate issues. They were reinvented in the United States in May 1982, when Chemical New York Corporation, the holding company for Chemical Bank, raised $200 million. The securities proved so popular that over $4 billion of floating-rate preferreds were issued by the following spring. Then the novelty wore off, and the frequency of new issues slowed down. It was back to business as usual, with one important exception: There was one more item on the menu of investment opportunities open to corporate money managers.

SHORT-TERM BORROWING

You now know where to invest your surplus cash. But suppose that you have the opposite problem and face a temporary cash deficit. Where can you find the short-term funds?

We have in part already answered that question. Remember that all those money-market investments that we discussed above must be *issued* by someone. So your firm may be able to raise short-term money by issuing commercial paper or discounting a banker's acceptance or (in the case of a bank) issuing CDs. But there are also other possible sources of cash that we have not yet discussed. In particular, you may take out a loan from a bank or finance company.

Obviously, if you approach a bank for a loan, the bank's lending officer is likely to ask searching questions about your firm's financial position and its plans for the future. Also, the bank will want to monitor the firm's subsequent progress. There is a good side to this. Other investors know that banks are hard to convince, and, therefore, when a company announces that it has arranged a large bank facility, the share price tends to rise.[22]

Credit Rationing

Before we discuss the different types of bank loans, we should notice an interesting general point. The more that you borrow from the bank, the higher is the rate of interest that you will be required to pay. However, there may come a stage at which the bank will refuse to lend you more, no matter how high an interest rate you are prepared to pay.

This takes us back to our discussion in Chapter 6 of the games that borrowers can play with lenders. Suppose that Henrietta Ketchup is a budding entrepreneur with two possible investment projects offering the following payoffs:

	INVESTMENT	PAYOFF	PROBABILITY OF PAYOFF
Project 1	−12	+15	1.0
Project 2	−12	$\begin{cases} +24 \\ 0 \end{cases}$	.5 .5

---

[22]See C. James, "Some Evidence on the Uniqueness of Bank Loans," *Journal of Financial Economics* 19 (1987), pp. 217–235.

Project 1 is surefire and very profitable; project 2 is risky and a rotten project. Ms. Ketchup now approaches her bank and asks to borrow the present value of $10 (the remaining money she will find out of her own purse). The bank calculates that the payoff will be split as follows:

	EXPECTED PAYOFF TO BANK	EXPECTED PAYOFF TO MS. KETCHUP
Project 1	10	5
Project 2	$(.5 \times 10) + (.5 \times 0) = +5$	$.5 \times (24 - 10) = +7$

If Ms. Ketchup accepts project 1, the bank's debt is certain to be paid in full; if she accepts project 2, there is only a 50 percent chance of payment and the expected payoff to the bank is only $5. Unfortunately, Ms. Ketchup will prefer to take project 2, for if things go well, she gets most of the profit, and if they go badly, the bank bears most of the loss. Unless the bank can specify in the fine print which project must be undertaken, it will not lend to Ms. Ketchup the present value of $10. Suppose, however, that the bank agrees to lend the present value of $5. Then the payoffs would be

	EXPECTED PAYOFF TO BANK	EXPECTED PAYOFF TO MS. KETCHUP
Project 1	+5	+10
Project 2	$(.5 \times 5) + (.5 \times 0) = +2.5$	$.5 \times (24 - 5) = +9.5$

By rationing Ms. Ketchup to a smaller loan, the bank has now made sure that she will not be tempted to speculate with its money.[23]

Bank Loans

We have so far referred to bank loans as if they were a standard product, but in practice they come in a variety of flavors.[24]

Commitment   Companies sometimes wait until they need the money before they apply for a bank loan, but most commercial bank loans are made under commitment. In this case the company establishes a line of credit that allows it to borrow from the bank up to an established limit.[25] Sometimes this line of credit is an *evergreen credit* with no fixed maturity, but more commonly it takes the form of a *revolving credit* with a fixed maturity of up to three years.

---

[23]You might think that if the bank suspects Ms. Ketchup will undertake project 2, it should raise the interest rate on its loan. In this case Ms. Ketchup will not want to take on project 2 (they can't *both* be happy with a lousy project). But Ms. Ketchup also would not want to pay a high rate of interest if she is going to take on project 1 (she would do better to borrow less money at the risk-free rate). So, simply raising the interest rate is not the answer. If you find this surprising, imagine that you offered to lend someone a large sum at 100 percent. Would you be happier if he accepted or declined?

[24]The results of a survey of the terms of business lending by banks in the United States are published quarterly in the *Federal Reserve Bulletin.*

[25]Banks do not want the company to use a line of credit to cover its need for long-term finance. So they often require the company to clean up its short-term bank loans for at least one month during the year.

Revolving credit agreements are relatively expensive, for, in addition to the interest on any borrowings, the company is required to pay a commitment fee on the unused amount. In exchange for this extra cost, the firm receives a valuable option: It has guaranteed access to the bank's money at a fixed spread over the general level of interest rates. This amounts to a put option, because the firm can sell its debt to the bank on fixed terms even if its own creditworthiness deteriorates.

Maturity   The majority of bank loans are for only a few months. For example, a company may need a short-term *bridge loan* to finance the purchase of new equipment or the acquisition of another firm. In this case the loan serves as interim financing until the purchase is completed and long-term financing is arranged. Often a short-term loan may be needed to finance a temporary increase in inventories. Such a loan is described as *self-liquidating;* in other words, the sale of goods provides the cash to repay the loan.

Banks are not the only source of short-term debt. We noted above that large companies often bypass the banking system and issue their own short-term debt in the form of commercial paper. But companies are conscious of the value of good bank relationships and they know that when times are hard and money is tight, banks will give priority to their regular customers. Thus few firms bypass the banking system entirely, even in good times when commercial paper is cheap and easy to sell.

When firms need medium-term financing, they can raise it directly from investors by selling medium-term notes (MTNs) or short-dated bonds. Alternatively, they can take out a *term loan* from a bank. A term loan typically has a maturity of four to five years. Usually the loan is repaid in level amounts over this period, although there is sometimes a large final balloon payment or just a single bullet payment at maturity. Banks can accommodate the repayment pattern to the anticipated cash flows of the borrower. For example, the first repayment might be delayed for a year pending completion of a new factory. The term loan may often be renegotiated in midstream, that is, before maturity. Banks are usually willing to do this if the borrower is an established customer, remains creditworthy, and has a sound business reason for making the change.[26]

Rate of Interest   Short-term bank loans are often made at a fixed rate of interest, which is often quoted as a discount. For example, if the interest rate on a one-year loan is stated as a discount of 5 percent, the borrower receives 100 − 5 = \$95 and undertakes to pay \$100 at the end of the year. The return on such a loan is not 5 percent, but 5/95 = .0526, or 5.26 percent.

Except for very short-term loans, the interest rate on bank loans is usually linked to the general level of interest rates. The most common benchmarks are the London Interbank Offered Rate (LIBOR), the federal funds rate,[27] or the bank's prime rate. Thus, if the rate is set at "1 percent over LIBOR," the borrower may pay 5 percent in the first three months when LIBOR is 4 percent, 6 percent in the next three months when LIBOR is 5 percent, and so on.

In addition to bearing the interest cost, the borrower is often obliged to maintain a minimum interest-free demand deposit with the bank. This compensating balance is commonly set at 10 to 20 percent of the amount of the loan, so the true interest rate, calculated on the money the firm can actually use, may be significantly higher than the quoted interest rate.

---

[26]Term loans typically allow the borrower to repay early, but in many cases the loan agreement specifies that the firm must pay a penalty for early repayment.

[27]The federal funds rate is the rate at which banks lend excess reserves to each other.

International Bank Loans   Instead of taking out a loan with a bank in the United States, a company may arrange an international dollar loan with a bank in London or another major international center. Sometimes these international loans involve huge sums of money and in these cases they are arranged by a lead bank and then parceled out among a syndicate of banks. For example, when Eurotunnel needed to arrange over $10 billion of borrowing to construct the tunnel between Britain and France, it used a syndicate of more than 200 major banks.

Loan Participations and Assignments   The large money-center banks in the United States have more demand for loans than they can satisfy; for smaller banks it is the other way round. As a result, a lead bank may arrange a loan and then sell a large portion of it to other institutions.

These loan sales generally take one of two forms: *assignments* or *participations.* In the first case a portion of the loan is transferred with the agreement of the borrower to the new lenders. In the second case the lead bank provides a "certificate of participation" which states that it will pay over a proportion of the cash flows from the loan. In such cases the borrower may not be aware that the sale has occurred. These loan participations differ from the syndicated loans that we described earlier; with a syndicated loan each bank has a separate loan agreement with the borrower.[28]

Participation loans hit the headlines in 1982 when Penn Square National Bank went belly up. One reason for consternation was that Penn Square had sold more than $200 million of its loan portfolio to Chase Bank. To make matters worse, the borrowers had deposited money with Penn Square, and the receiver claimed that the losses on these deposits should be deducted from the amount of the borrowers' debt. This reduced the cash flows to be paid over to Chase. Since the Penn Square collapse, banks and their lawyers have been more careful about the fine print in loan participations.

Security   Banks often ask firms to provide security for loans, particularly if they are concerned about the firm's credit risk. Since the bank is lending on a short-term basis, this security consists of liquid assets such as receivables, inventories, or securities. Sometimes the bank will accept a floating lien against receivables and inventory. This gives it a general claim against those assets, but it does not specify them in detail, and it sets few restrictions on what the company can do with the assets. More commonly, banks will require specific collateral. We will look first at how loans may be secured by receivables and then we will discuss how inventory can be used as security.

Loans Secured by Receivables.   If the bank is satisfied with the credit standing of your customers and the soundness of your product, it may be willing to lend you as much as 80 percent of accounts receivable. In return, you pledge your receivables as collateral for the loan. If you fail to repay your debt, the bank can collect the receivables and apply the proceeds to repaying the debt. If the proceeds are insufficient, you are liable for any deficiency. The loan is therefore said to be *with recourse.*

When you pledge receivables, you must keep the bank up to date on credit sales and collections. When you deliver goods to your customers, you send the bank a copy of the invoice, together with a form of assignment which gives the bank the right to the money your customers owe you. Then you can borrow up to the agreed proportion of this collateral.

Each day, as you make new sales, your collateral increases and you can borrow more money. Each day also customers pay their bills. This money is placed in a special collateral account under the bank's control and is periodically used to reduce the size of the loan. Therefore, as the firm's business fluctuates, so does the amount of the collateral and the size of the loan.

---

[28]The syndicated loan agreement may allow each bank in the syndicate to transfer its portion of the loan.

A few receivables loans are on a notification basis. In this case the bank informs your customer of the lending arrangement and asks that the money be paid directly to the bank. Firms generally do not like their customers to know they are in debt, and therefore the loans are usually made without notification.

Receivables loans can be obtained not only from commercial banks but also from finance companies which specialize in lending to businesses. The loans are flexible and the collateral may enable the firm to increase its debt capacity. However, it can be costly for borrower and lender alike to supervise and record changes in the collateral. Therefore the rate of interest on receivables financing is generally high, and there may be an additional service charge on the loan.

We discussed factoring in Chapter 17. Don't confuse factoring with lending against receivables. Factors *buy* your receivables and, if you wish, advance a portion of the money. They are, therefore, responsible for collecting the debt and suffer any losses if the customers don't pay. When you pledge your receivables as collateral for a loan, *you* remain responsible for collecting the debt and *you* suffer if a customer is delinquent.

If it moves, an investment banker will try to turn it into a security. We saw in Chapter 11 how companies have repackaged mortgages (or David Bowie's royalties) and then resold them as asset-backed bonds. Receivables and other short-term loans may also be packaged into securities. For example, in March 1998 Chrysler Financial Corporation set up a separate company to which it sold $1.1 billion of vehicle loans. To pay for these loans, the new company issued five classes of asset-backed notes. As the bills were repaid, the senior notes were paid off first, until eventually the most junior notes were repaid. Of course, holders of the junior notes were compensated by a higher rate of interest.

Loans Secured by Inventory.   Banks and finance companies also lend on the security of inventory, but they are choosy about the collateral they will accept. They want to make sure that they can identify and sell the inventory if you default. Automobiles and other standardized, nonperishable commodities are good collateral for a loan; work in process and ripe Camemberts are poor collateral.

The procedure for lending against inventories depends on where the goods are stored. If you place goods in a public warehouse, the warehouse company provides a **warehouse receipt** and will then release the goods only on the instructions of the holder of the receipt. Because the holder of the receipt controls the inventory, the receipt can be used as collateral for a loan. Notice, however, that the warehouse receipt only identifies the goods and where they are stored. It doesn't guarantee the grade of the goods, nor does it provide insurance against fire, theft, and other hazards. Therefore the lender will also need to be satisfied on all these matters.

Lenders want to make sure that goods are not released without their permission. Therefore the law states that a warehouse receipt can be issued only by a bona fide warehouse company independent of the company that owns the goods. That is fine if the goods are stored in a large public warehouse, but what if they need to be kept on the borrower's premises? The answer is that you establish a **field warehouse.** In other words, you arrange for a warehouse company to lease your warehouse or storage area. The warehouse company puts up signs stating that a field warehouse is being operated. It then remains responsible for storing your pledged goods and releases them only on the instructions of the holder of the warehouse receipt.

When you borrow from a bank, generally you sign an IOU and the bank hands you the money. Sometimes warehouse loans involve a somewhat more complicated arrangement. In exchange for your IOU the bank signs a banker's acceptance that matures on the same date. In other words, in exchange for your IOU the bank gives you not cash but *its* IOU. The advantage of this strange procedure is that the banker's acceptance is marketable whereas your promissory note is not. Therefore, you can sell your acceptance to the bank whenever you want the cash, and the bank can, if it chooses, resell the acceptance to another institution.

The important feature of warehouse loans is that the goods are physically segregated and under the control of an independent warehouse company. Suppose, however, that you are an automobile dealer who needs to finance an inventory of new cars. You can't put the cars in a warehouse; you need to keep them in a showroom under your control. The common solution is to enter into a **floor-planning** arrangement. Under this arrangement the finance company buys the cars from the manufacturer and you hold them in trust for the finance company. As evidence of this, you sign a *trust receipt* that identifies the cars involved. You are free to sell the cars, but when you do so, the proceeds are used to redeem the trust receipt. To make sure that the collateral is properly maintained, the finance company will make periodic inspections of the inventory.

The fact that liquid assets are easily saleable does not always make them good collateral. It also means that the lender has to make sure that the borrower doesn't suddenly sell the assets and run off with the money. If you want to make your hair stand on end, read the story of the great salad oil swindle. Fifty-one banks and companies made loans of nearly $200 million to the Allied Crude Vegetable Oil Refining Corporation. Warehouse receipts issued by a field warehousing company were taken as security. Unfortunately, the cursory inspections by the employees of the field warehousing company failed to uncover the fact that, instead of containing salad oil, Allied's storage tanks were filled with seawater and sludge. When the fraud was discovered, the president of Allied went to jail, the field warehousing company entered bankruptcy, and the 51 lenders were left out in the cold, looking for their $200 million. Lenders have been more careful since then, but no doubt they'll be caught by some new scam sooner or later.[29]

SUMMARY

If you have more cash than you currently need, you can invest the surplus in the money market. The principal money-market investments in the United States are

- U.S. Treasury bills
- Short-term tax-exempts
- Certificates of deposit
- Commercial paper
- Bankers' acceptances
- Repurchase agreements

If none of these catches your fancy, you can make a short-term investment in the international debt markets. For example, you can make a dollar deposit with a bank in London. This is known as a eurodollar deposit.

---

[29]See N. C. Miller, *The Great Salad Oil Swindle* (London: Gollancz, 1966). More recently, in Australia the National Safety Council in Victoria went bankrupt after taking out large bank loans on the collateral of nonexistent receivables and inventories (thereby showing that old scams *can* still work). The story of the NSC is told in T. Sykes, *The Bold Riders* (St. Leonards, NSW, Australia; Allen & Unwin, 1994), Chap. 7.

INTEREST RATES

Friday, January 8, 1999

MONEY RATES

The key U.S. and foreign annual interest rates below are a guide to general levels but don't always represent actual transactions.

PRIME RATE: 7.75% (effective 11/18/98). The base rate on corporate loans posted by at least 75% of the nation's 30 largest banks.

DISCOUNT RATE: 4.50% (effective 11/17/98). The charge on loans to depository institutions by the Federal Reserve Banks.

FEDERAL FUNDS: 5% high, 4 1/2% low, 4 1/4% near closing bid, 4 5/8% offered. Reserves traded among commercial banks for overnight use in amounts of $1 million or more. Source: Prebon Yamane (U.S.A.) Inc.

CALL MONEY: 6.50% (effective 11/18/98). The charge on loans to brokers on stock exchange collateral. Source: Telerate.

COMMERCIAL PAPER placed directly by General Electric Capital Corp.: 4.83% 30 to 104 days; 4.82% 105 to 149 days; 4.78% 150 to 210 days; % days; 4.73% 211 to 270 days.

EURO COMMERCIAL PAPER placed directly by General Electric Capital Corp.: 3.12% 30 days; 3.12% two months; 3.10% three months; 3.09% four months; 3.08% five months; 3.07% six months.

DEALER COMMERCIAL PAPER: High-grade unsecured notes sold through dealers by major corporations: 4.80% 30 days; 4.80% 60 days; 4.80% 90 days.

CERTIFICATES OF DEPOSIT: 4.62% one month; 4.68% two months; 4.74% three months; 4.96% six months; 4.98% one year. Average of top rates paid by major New York banks on primary new issues of negotiable C.D.s, usually on amounts of $1 million and more. The minimum unit is $100,000. Typical rates in the secondary market: 4.97% one month; 4.95% three months; 4.95% six months.

BANKERS ACCEPTANCES: 4.79% 30 days; 4.78% 60 days; 4.78% 90 days; 4.77% 120 days; 4.76% 150 days; 4.74% 180 days. Offered rates of negotiable, bank-backed business credit instruments typically financing an import order.

LONDON LATE EURODOLLARS: 5%–4 7/8% one month; 5%–4 7/8% two months; 5 1/32%–4 29/32% three months; 5 1/32%–4 29/32% four months; 5 1/16%–4 15/16% five months; 5 1/16%–4 15/16% six months.

LONDON INTERBANK OFFERED RATES (LIBOR): 5.00000% one month; 5.03781% three months; 5.05656% six months; 5.09047% one year. British Bankers' Association average of interbank offered rates for dollar deposits in the London market based on quotations at 16 major banks. Effective rate for contracts entered into two days from date appearing at top of this column.

INTEREST RATES

Friday, January 8, 1999

MONEY RATES, cont.

EURO LIBOR: 3.2200% one month; 3.19750% three months; 3.16375% six months; 3.13750% one year. British Bankers' Association average of interbank offered rates for euro deposits in the London market based on quotations at 16 major banks. Effective rate for contracts entered into two days from date appearing at top of this column.

EURO INTERBANK OFFERED RATES (EURIBOR): 3.217% one month; 3.196% three months; 3.166% six months; 3.139% one year. European Banking Federation-sponsored rate among 57 Euro zone banks.

FOREIGN PRIME RATES: Canada 6.75%; Germany 3.19% (eff. 01/08/99); Japan 1.500%; Switzerland 3.00%; Britain 6.00%. These rate indications aren't directly comparable; lending practices vary widely by location.

TREASURY BILLS: Results of the Monday, January 4, 1999, auction of short-term U.S. government bills, sold at a discount from face value in units of $10,000 to $1 million: 4.38% 13 weeks; 4.42% 26 weeks.

OVERNIGHT REPURCHASE RATE: 4.55%. Dealer financing rate for overnight sale and repurchase of Treasury securities. Source: Telerate.

FEDERAL HOME LOAN MORTGAGE CORP. (Freddie Mac): Posted yields on 30-year mortgage commitments. Delivery within 30 days 6.78%, 60 days 6.83%, standard conventional fixed-rate mortgages; 5.625%, 2% rate capped one-year adjustable rate mortgages. Source: Telerate.

FEDERAL NATIONAL MORTGAGE ASSOCIATION (Fannie Mae): Posted yields on 30 year mortgage commitments (priced at par) for delivery within 30 days 6.74%, 60 days 6.80%, standard conventional fixed rate-mortgages; 5.60%, 6/2 rate capped one-year adjustable rate mortgages. Source: Telerate.

MERRILL LYNCH READY ASSETS TRUST: 4.66%. Annualized average rate of return after expenses for the past 30 days; not a forecast of future returns.

Figure 19.1

Short-term interest rates on January 8, 1999.

No two of these securities are exactly the same. If you want to make effective use of your cash, you need to be aware of the differences in their liquidity, risk, and yield. Remember also that the interest rate on money-market investments is often quoted as a discount. The compound return is always higher than the rate of discount. Table 19.1 summarizes the main features of money-market instruments. Figure 19.1 shows money-market rates for January 8, 1999, as reported in *The Wall Street Journal*.

Most corporations making short-term investments of excess cash buy one or more of the instruments described in Table 19.1. But there are many alternatives, including floating-rate preferreds. These are attractive for two reasons. First, corporations pay tax on only 30 percent of the dividends received. Second, the dividend moves up and down with changes in interest rates, so the prices of floating-rate preferred shares are more or less stabilized.

For many companies surplus cash is not a worry; their problem is how to finance a temporary cash deficiency. Bank loans constitute one of the main sources of short-term funds. Often firms arrange a revolving line of credit with a bank that allows them to borrow up to an agreed amount whenever they need financing.

The interest rate on very short-term bank loans is generally fixed for the life of the loan, but in other cases the rate floats with the general level of short-term interest rates. In addition to charging interest, banks often require their customers to keep an interest-free compensating balance. This adds to the cost of a bank loan. Of course, the amount that the bank charges for a loan must be sufficient to cover not only the opportunity cost of capital for the loan but also the costs of running the loan department. As a result, large regular borrowers have found it cheaper to bypass the banking system and issue their own short-term unsecured debt, that is, to issue commercial paper.

Most bank loans are intended to tide the firm over a temporary shortage of cash and are therefore repaid in only a few months. However, banks also make *term loans* that sometimes extend for five years or more. In addition to borrowing from their domestic banks, companies may borrow dollars (or any other currency) from overseas banks or the foreign branches of U.S. banks. These international bank loans often involve huge sums of money and in this case they may be *syndicated* among a group of major banks.

If you ask to borrow more and more from a bank, you will eventually be asked to provide security for the loan. Sometimes this security consists of a floating lien on receivables and inventories, but usually you will be asked to pledge specific assets. When you borrow against receivables, the bank is informed of all sales of goods and the resulting accounts receivable are pledged to the bank. As customers pay their bills, the money is paid into a special collateral account under the bank's control.

Similarly, when you borrow against stocks of raw materials, the bank may insist that the goods be held by an independent warehouse company. As long as the bank holds the warehouse receipt for these goods, they cannot be released without the bank's permission. Loans secured on finished goods are usually made under a floor-planning arrangement. In this case you will be required to sign a trust receipt promising that you are merely holding the goods in trust for the lender.

You may also find that there comes a point at which the bank will not increase its lending no matter how high a rate of interest you are prepared to pay. Banks know that the more they lend, the more they are encouraging you to gamble with their money. Your aims and the bank's are more likely to coincide if your borrowing is kept to a responsible level.

Further Reading

For a detailed description of the money market and short-term lending opportunities, see:
M. Stigum: *The Money Market: Myth, Reality and Practice*, 3d ed., Richard D. Irwin, Inc., Homewood, Ill., 1990.

F. J. Fabozzi: *Fixed Income Securities*, Frank J. Fabozzi Associates, New Hope, Pa., 1997.

Texts on bank management usually include a discussion of lending practices. See, for example:
G. H. Hempel, A. B. Coleman, and D. G. Somonson: *Bank Management*, 4th ed., John Wiley & Sons, New York, 1993.

J. F. Sinkey, Jr.: *Commercial Bank Financial Management in the Financial Services Industry*, 5th ed., Prentice-Hall, Inc., Englewood Cliffs, N.J., 1998.

PRESENT VALUE TABLE

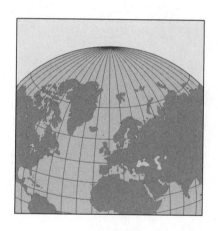

Cumulative probability [$N(d)$] that a normally distributed variable will be less than d standard deviations above the mean

d	0	0.01	0.02	0.03	0.04	0.05	0.06	0.07	0.08	0.09
0	.5000	.5040	.5080	.5120	.5160	.5199	.5239	.5279	.5319	.5359
0.1	.5398	.5438	.5478	.5517	.5557	.5596	.5636	.5675	.5714	.5753
0.2	.5793	.5832	.5871	.5910	.5948	.5987	.6026	.6064	.6103	.6141
0.3	.6179	.6217	.6255	.6293	.6331	.6368	.6406	.6443	.6480	.6517
0.4	.6554	.6591	.6628	.6664	.6700	.6736	.6772	.6808	.6844	.6879
0.5	.6915	.6950	.6985	.7019	.7054	.7088	.7123	.7157	.7190	.7224
0.6	.7257	.7291	.7324	.7357	.7389	.7422	.7454	.7486	.7517	.7549
0.7	.7580	.7611	.7642	.7673	.7704	.7734	.7764	.7794	.7823	.7852
0.8	.7881	.7910	.7939	.7967	.7995	.8023	.8051	.8078	.8106	.8133
0.9	.8159	.8186	.8212	.8238	.8264	.8289	.8315	.8340	.8365	.8389
1	.8413	.8438	.8461	.8485	.8508	.8531	.8554	.8577	.8599	.8621
1.1	.8643	.8665	.8686	.8708	.8729	.8749	.8770	.8790	.8810	.8830
1.2	.8849	.8869	.8888	.8907	.8925	.8944	.8962	.8980	.8997	.9015
1.3	.9032	.9049	.9066	.9082	.9099	.9115	.9131	.9147	.9162	.9177
1.4	.9192	.9207	.9222	.9236	.9251	.9265	.9279	.9292	.9306	.9319
1.5	.9332	.9345	.9357	.9370	.9382	.9394	.9406	.9418	.9429	.9441
1.6	.9452	.9463	.9474	.9484	.9495	.9505	.9515	.9525	.9535	.9545
1.7	.9554	.9564	.9573	.9582	.9591	.9599	.9608	.9616	.9625	.9633
1.8	.9641	.9649	.9656	.9664	.9671	.9678	.9686	.9693	.9699	.9706
1.9	.9713	.9719	.9726	.9732	.9738	.9744	.9750	.9756	.9761	.9767
2	.9772	.9778	.9783	.9788	.9793	.9798	.9803	.9808	.9812	.9817
2.1	.9821	.9826	.9830	.9834	.9838	.9842	.9846	.9850	.9854	.9857
2.2	.9861	.9864	.9868	.9871	.9875	.9878	.9881	.9884	.9887	.9890
2.3	.9893	.9896	.9898	.9901	.9904	.9906	.9909	.9911	.9913	.9916
2.4	.9918	.9920	.9922	.9925	.9927	.9929	.9931	.9932	.9934	.9936
2.5	.9938	.9940	.9941	.9943	.9945	.9946	.9948	.9949	.9951	.9952

E.g.: If $d = .22$, $N(d) = .5871$ (i.e., there is a .5871 probability that a normally distributed variable will be less than .22 standard deviations above the mean)

GLOSSARY*

A

Abnormal return Part of return that is not due to systematic influences, e.g., marketwide price movements.

Absolute priority Rule in bankruptcy proceedings whereby senior creditors are required to be paid in full before junior creditors receive any payment.

Accelerated depreciation Any *depreciation* method that produces larger deductions for depreciation in the early years of a project's life.

Accounts payable (*payables, trade debt*) Money owed to suppliers.

Accounts receivable (*receivables, trade credit*) Money owed by customers.

Accrued interest Interest that has been earned but not yet paid.

ACH *Automated Clearing House.*

Acid-test ratio *Quick ratio.*

Adjusted present value (*APV*) *Net present value* of an asset if financed solely by equity, plus the *present value* of any financing side effects.

ADR *American depository receipt.*

Adverse selection A situation in which a pricing policy causes only the less desirable customers to do business, e.g., a rise in insurance prices that leads only the worst risks to buy insurance.

Agency theory Theory of the relationship between a principal, e.g., a shareholder, and an agent of the principal, e.g., the company's manager.

Aging schedule Record of the length of time that *accounts receivable* have been outstanding.

All-or-none underwriting An arrangement whereby a security issue is canceled if the *underwriter* is unable to resell the entire issue.

American depository receipt (*ADR*) A security issued in the United States to represent shares of a foreign company.

American option *Option* that can be exercised any time before the final exercise date (cf. *European option*).

Amex American Stock Exchange.

Amortization (1) Repayment of a loan by installments; (2) allowance for *depreciation*.

Annual percentage rate (*APR*) Annual interest rate calculated using *simple interest.*

Annuity Investment that produces a level stream of cash flows for a limited number of periods.

Annuity due *Annuity* whose payments occur at the start of each period.

Annuity factor *Present value* of $1 paid for each of t periods.

Anticipation Arrangements whereby customers who pay before the final date may be entitled to deduct a normal rate of interest.

Appraisal rights A right of shareholders in a *merger* to demand the payment of a fair price for their shares, as determined independently.

Appropriation request Formal request for funds for a capital investment project.

APR *Annual percentage rate.*

APT Arbitrage pricing theory.

APV *Adjusted present value.*

Arbitrage Purchase of one security and simultaneous sale of another to give a risk-free profit.

"Arbitrage" or "risk arbitrage" Often used loosely to describe the taking of offsetting positions in related securities, e.g., at the time of a takeover bid.

Articles of incorporation Legal document establishing a corporation and its structure and purpose.

Asian currency units Dollar deposits held in Singapore or other Asian centers.

Asian option *Option* based on the average price of the asset during the life of the option.

*Italicized words are listed elsewhere in the glossary.

Ask price (*offer price*) Price at which a dealer is willing to sell (cf. *bid price*).

Asset-backed securities Securities issued by a special purpose company that holds a package of low-risk assets whose cash flows are sufficient to service the *bonds.*

Auction-rate preferred A variant of *floating-rate preferred* stock where the dividend is reset every 49 days by auction.

Authorized share capital Maximum number of shares that a company can issue, as specified in the firm's articles of incorporation.

Automated Clearing House (*ACH*) Private electronic system run by banks for high-volume, low-value payments.

Availability float Checks deposited by a company that have not yet been cleared.

Aval Bank guarantee for debt purchased by *forfaiter.*

B

BA *Banker's acceptance.*

Backwardation Condition in which *spot price* of commodity exceeds price of *future.*

Balloon payment Large final payment (e.g., when a loan is repaid in installments).

Banker's acceptance (*BA*) Written demand that has been accepted by a bank to pay a given sum at a future date (cf. *trade acceptance*).

Barrier option *Option* whose existence depends on asset price hitting some specified barrier (cf. *down-and-out option, down-and-in option*).

Basis point (*bp*) 0.01 percent.

Basis risk Residual risk that results when the two sides of a hedge do not move exactly together.

Bearer security Security for which primary evidence of ownership is possession of the certificate (cf. *registered security*).

Bear market Widespread decline in security prices (cf. *bull market*).

Benefit-cost ratio One plus *profitability index.*

Best-efforts underwriting An arrangement whereby *underwriters* do not commit themselves to selling a security issue but promise only to use best efforts.

Beta Measure of *market risk.*

Bid price Price at which a dealer is willing to buy (cf. *ask price*).

Bill of exchange General term for a document demanding payment.

Bill of lading Document establishing ownership of goods in transit.

Blue-chip company Large and creditworthy company.

Blue-sky laws State laws covering the issue and trading of securities.

Boilerplate Standard terms and conditions, e.g., in a debt contract.

Bond Long-term debt.

Bookbuilding The procedure whereby *underwriters* gather nonbinding indications of demand for a new issue.

Book entry System whereby only one global certificate is issued for *bond* and evidence of ownership is receipt showing interest in this certificate.

Book runner The managing *underwriter* for a new issue. The book runner maintains the book of securities sold.

Bought deal Security issue where one or two *underwriters* buy the entire issue.

bp *Basis point.*

Bracket A term signifying the extent of an *underwriter's* commitment in a new issue, e.g., major bracket, minor bracket.

Break-even analysis Analysis of the level of sales at which a project would just break even.

Bridging loan Short-term loan to provide temporary financing until more permanent financing is arranged.

Bull-bear bond *Bond* whose *principal* repayment is linked to the price of another security. The bonds are issued in two *tranches:* In the first the repayment increases with the price of the other security; in the second the repayment decreases with the price of the other security.

Bulldog bond *Foreign bond* issue made in London.

Bullet payment Single final payment, e.g., of a loan (in contrast to payment in installments).

Bull market Widespread rise in security prices (cf. *bear market*).

Buy-back *Repurchase agreement.*

C

Cable The exchange rate between U.S. dollars and sterling.

Call option Option to buy an asset at a specified *exercise price* on or before a specified exercise date (cf. *put option*).

Call premium (1) Difference between the price at which a company can call its *bonds* and their *face value;* (2) price of an *option.*

Call provision Provision that allows an issuer to buy back the *bond* issue at a stated price.

Cap An upper limit on the interest rate on a *floating-rate note.*

Capital budget List of planned investment projects, usually prepared annually.

Capitalization Long-term debt, plus *preferred stock,* plus *net worth.*

Capital lease *Financial lease.*

Capital market Financial market (particularly the market for long-term securities).

Capital rationing Shortage of funds that forces a company to choose between worthwhile projects.

Capital structure Mix of different securities issued by a firm.

CAPM Capital asset pricing model.

CAR Cumulative *abnormal return.*

CARDs (Certificates for Amortizing Revolving Debt) *Pass-through securities* backed by credit card *receivables.*

CARs (Certificates of Automobile Receivables) *Pass-through securities* backed by automobile *receivables.*

Cascade Rational herding in which each individual deduces that previous decisions by others may have been based on extra information.

Cash and carry Purchase of a security and simultaneous sale of a *future,* with the balance being financed with a loan or *repo.*

Cash budget Forecast of sources and uses of cash.

Cash-deficiency arrangement Arrangement whereby a project's shareholders agree to provide the operating company with sufficient *net working capital.*

CAT bond *Catastrophe bond.*

Catastrophe bond (*CAT bond*) *Bond* whose payoffs are linked to a measure of catastrophe losses such as insurance claims.

CD *Certificate of deposit.*

CEDEL A centralized clearing system for *eurobonds.* Also *Euroclear.*

Certainty equivalent A certain cash flow that has the same future value as a specified risky cash flow.

Certificate of deposit (*CD*) A certificate providing evidence of a bank time deposit.

CFO Chief financial officer.

Chaebol A Korean conglomerate.

CHIPS *Clearing House Interbank Payments System.*

Clean price (*flat price*) *Bond* price excluding *accrued interest* (cf. *dirty price*).

Clearing House Interbank Payments System (*CHIPS*) An international wire transfer system for high-value dollar payments operated by a group of major banks.

Closed-end mortgage Mortgage against which no additional debt may be issued (cf. *open-end mortgage*).

CMOs *Collateralized mortgage obligations.*

Collar An upper and lower limit on the interest rate on a *floating-rate note.*

Collateral Assets that are given as security for a loan.

Collateralized mortgage obligations (*CMOs*) A variation on the mortgage *pass-through security,* in which the cash flows from a pool of mortgages are repackaged into several *tranches* of *bonds* with different maturities.

Collateral trust bonds *Bonds* secured by *common stocks* or other securities that are owned by the borrower.

Collection float Customer-written checks that have not been received, deposited, and added to the company's available balance (cf. *payment float*).

Commercial draft (*bill of exchange*) Demand for payment.

Commercial paper Unsecured *notes* issued by companies and maturing within nine months.

Commitment fee Fee charged by bank on an unused *line of credit.*

Common stock Security representing ownership of a corporation.

Compensating balance Non-interest-bearing demand deposits to compensate banks for bank loans or services.

Competitive bidding Means by which public utility *holding companies* are required to choose their *underwriter* (cf. *negotiated underwriting*).

Completion bonding Insurance that a construction contract will be successfully completed.

Compound interest Reinvestment of each interest payment on money invested to earn more interest (cf. *simple interest*).

Compound option Option on an *option.*

Concentration banking System whereby customers make payments to a regional collection center. The collection center pays the funds into a regional bank account and surplus money is transferred to the company's principal bank.

Conditional sale Sale in which ownership does not pass to the buyer until payment is completed.

Conglomerate merger *Merger* between two companies in unrelated businesses (cf. *horizontal merger, vertical merger*).

Consol Name of a perpetual *bond* issued by the British government. Sometimes used as a general term for *perpetuity*.

Contingent claim Claim whose value depends on the value of another asset.

Contingent project Project that cannot be undertaken unless another project is also undertaken.

Continuous compounding Interest compounded continuously rather than at fixed intervals.

Controller Officer responsible for budgeting, accounting, and auditing in a firm (cf. *treasurer*).

Convenience yield The extra advantage that firms derive from holding the commodity rather than the *future*.

Conversion price *Par value* of a *convertible bond* divided by the number of shares into which it may be exchanged.

Conversion ratio Number of shares for which a *convertible bond* may be exchanged.

Convertible bond *Bond* that may be converted into another security at the holder's option. Similarly convertible *preferred stock*.

Correlation coefficient Measure of the closeness of the relationship between two variables.

Cost company arrangement Arrangement whereby the shareholders of a project receive output free of charge but agree to pay all operating and financing charges of the project.

Cost of capital *Opportunity cost of capital*.

Coupon (1) Specifically, an attachment to the certificate of a *bearer security* that must be surrendered to collect interest payment; (2) more generally, interest payment on debt.

Covariance Measure of the comovement between two variables.

Covenant Clause in a loan agreement.

Credit derivative Contract for *hedging* against loan default or changes in credit risk (see *default swap, credit option*).

Credit option Similar to a long-term insurance policy against loan default.

Credit scoring A procedure for assigning scores to borrowers on the basis of the risk of default.

Cross-default clause Clause in a loan agreement stating that the company is in default if it fails to meet its obligation on any other debt issue.

Cum dividend *With dividend*.

Cum rights *With rights*.

Cumulative preferred stock Stock that takes priority over *common stock* in regard to dividend payments. Dividends may not be paid on the common stock until all past *dividends* on the *preferred stock* have been paid.

Cumulative voting Voting system under which a stockholder may cast all of his or her votes for one candidate for the board of directors (cf. *majority voting*).

Current asset Asset that will normally be turned into cash within a year.

Current liability Liability that will normally be repaid within a year.

Current ratio *Current assets* divided by *current liabilities*—a measure of liquidity.

D

DCF *Discounted cash flow*.

Debenture Unsecured *bond*.

Decision tree Method of representing alternative sequential decisions and the possible outcomes from these decisions.

Default swap *Credit derivative* in which one party makes fixed payments while the payments by the other party depend on the occurrence of a loan default.

Defeasance Practice whereby the borrower sets aside cash or *bonds* sufficient to service the borrower's debt. Both the borrower's debt and the offsetting cash or bonds are removed from the balance sheet.

Delta *Hedge ratio*.

Depository transfer check (*DTC*) Check made out directly by a local bank to a particular company.

Depreciation (1) Reduction in the book or market value of an asset; (2) portion of an investment that can be deducted from taxable income.

Derivative Asset whose value derives from that of some other asset (e.g., a *future* or an *option*).

Diff *Differential swap*.

Differential swap (*diff, quanto swap*) Swap between two *LIBOR* rates of interest, e.g., yen LIBOR for dollar LIBOR. Payments are in one currency.

Dilution Diminution in the proportion of income to which each share is entitled.

Direct lease *Lease* in which the *lessor* purchases new equipment from the manufacturer and leases it to the *lessee* (cf. *sale and lease-back*).

Direct quote For foreign exchange, the number of U.S. dollars needed to buy one unit of a foreign currency (cf. *indirect quote*).

Dirty price *Bond* price including *accrued interest*, i.e., the price paid by the bond buyer (cf. *clean price*).

Discount bond Debt sold for less than its *principal* value. If a discount bond pays no interest, it is called a "pure" discount, or *zero-coupon*, bond.

Discounted cash flow (*DCF*) Future cash flows multiplied by *discount factors* to obtain *present value*.

Discount factor *Present value* of $1 received at a stated future date.

Discount rate Rate used to calculate the *present value* of future cash flows.

Discriminatory price auction Auction in which successful bidders pay the price that they bid (cf. *uniform price auction*).

Disintermediation Withdrawal of funds from a financial institution in order to invest them directly (cf. *intermediation*).

Dividend Payment by a company to its stockholders.

Dividend reinvestment plan (*DRIP*) Plan that allows shareholders to reinvest dividends automatically.

Dividend yield Annual *dividend* divided by share price.

Double-declining-balance depreciation Method of *accelerated depreciation*.

Double-tax agreement Agreement between two countries that taxes paid abroad can be offset against domestic taxes levied on foreign *dividends*.

Down-and-in option *Barrier option* that comes into existence if asset price hits a barrier.

Down-and-out option *Barrier option* that expires if asset price hits a barrier.

DRIP *Dividend reinvestment plan.*

Drop lock An arrangement whereby the interest rate on a *floating-rate note* or *preferred stock* becomes fixed if it falls to a specified level.

DTC *Depository transfer check.*

Dual-currency bond *Bond* with interest paid in one currency and *principal* paid in another.

Duration The average number of years to an asset's *discounted cash flows*.

E

EBIT Earnings before interest and taxes.

Economic exposure Risk that arises from changes in real exchange rates (cf. *transaction exposure, translation exposure*).

Economic income Cash flow plus change in *present value*.

Economic rents Profits in excess of the competitive level.

Economic Value Added (*EVA*) A measure of *residual income* implemented by the consulting firm Stern Stewart.

ECU (European Currency Unit) A basket of different European currencies. One ECU became convertible into one euro.

Efficient market Market in which security prices reflect information instantaneously.

Efficient portfolio Portfolio that offers the lowest risk (*standard deviation*) for its *expected return* and the highest expected return for its level of risk.

Employee stock ownership plan (*ESOP*) A company contributes to a trust fund that buys stock on behalf of employees.

EPS Earnings per share.

Equipment trust certificate Form of *secured debt* generally used to finance railroad equipment. The trustee retains ownership of the equipment until the debt is repaid.

Equity (1) *Common stock* and *preferred stock*. Often used to refer to common stock only. (2) *Net worth*.

Equivalent annual cash flow *Annuity* with the same *net present value* as the company's proposed investment.

ESOP *Employee stock ownership plan.*

Euribor *Euro Interbank Offered Rate.*

Euro Interbank Offered Rate (*Euribor*) The interest rate at which major international banks in Europe lend euros to each other.

Eurobond *Bond* that is marketed internationally.

Euroclear A centralized clearing system for *eurobonds*. Also *CEDEL*.

Eurodollar deposit Dollar deposit with a bank outside the United States.

European option *Option* that can be exercised only on final exercise date (cf. *American option*).

EVA *Economic Value Added.*

Evergreen credit *Revolving credit* without maturity.

Exchange of assets Acquisition of another company by purchase of its assets in exchange for cash or shares.

Exchange of stock Acquisition of another company by purchase of its stock in exchange for cash or shares.

Ex dividend Purchase of shares in which the buyer is not entitled to the forthcoming *dividend* (cf. *with dividend, cum dividend*).

Exercise price (*striking price*) Price at which a *call option* or *put option* may be exercised.

Expected return Average of possible returns weighted by their probabilities.

Ex rights Purchase of shares in which the buyer is not entitled to the rights to buy shares in the company's *rights issue* (cf. *with rights, cum rights, rights on*).

Extendable bond *Bond* whose maturity can be extended at the option of the lender (or issuer).

External finance Finance that is not generated by the firm: new borrowing or an issue of stock (cf. *internal finance*).

Extra dividend *Dividend* that may or may not be repeated (cf. *regular dividend*).

F

Face value *Par value.*

Factoring Arrangement whereby a financial institution buys a company's *accounts receivable* and collects the debt.

Fair price provision *Appraisal* rights.

FASB Financial Accounting Standards Board.

FCIA Foreign Credit Insurance Association.

FDIC Federal Deposit Insurance Corporation.

Federal funds Non-interest-bearing deposits by banks at the Federal Reserve. Excess reserves are lent by banks to each other.

Fedwire A wire transfer system for high-value payments operated by the Federal Reserve System (cf. *CHIPS*).

Field warehouse Warehouse rented by a warehouse company on another firm's premises (cf. *public warehouse*).

Financial assets Claims on *real assets*.

Financial engineering Combining or dividing existing instruments to create new financial products.

Financial lease (*capital lease, full-payout lease*) Long-term, noncancelable *lease* (cf. *operating lease*).

Financial leverage (*gearing*) Use of debt to increase the *expected return* on *equity*. Financial leverage is measured by the ratio of debt to debt plus equity (cf. *operating leverage*).

Fiscal agency agreement An alternative to a bond *trust deed*. Unlike the trustee, the fiscal agent acts as an agent of the borrower.

Flat price *Clean price.*

Float See *availability float, payment float*.

Floating lien General *lien* against a company's assets or against a particular class of assets.

Floating-rate note (*FRN*) *Note* whose interest payment varies with the short-term interest rate.

Floating-rate preferred *Preferred stock* paying dividends that vary with short-term interest rates.

Floor planning Arrangement used to finance inventory. A finance company buys the inventory, which is then held in trust by the user.

Foreign bond A *bond* issued on the domestic *capital market* of another country.

Forex Foreign exchange.

Forfaiter Purchaser of promises to pay (e.g., *bills of exchange* or *promissory notes*) issued by importers.

Forward cover Purchase or sale of forward foreign currency in order to offset a known future cash flow.

Forward exchange rate Exchange rate fixed today for exchanging currency at some future date (cf. *spot exchange rate*).

Forward interest rate Interest rate fixed today on a loan to be made at some future date (cf. *spot interest rate*).

Forward rate agreement (*FRA*) Agreement to borrow or lend at a specified future date at an interest rate that is fixed today.

FRA *Forward rate agreement.*

Free cash flow Cash not required for operations or for reinvestment.

FRN *Floating-rate note.*

Full-payout lease *Financial lease.*

Full-service lease (*rental lease*) *Lease* in which the *lessor* promises to maintain and insure the equipment (cf. *net lease*).

Fundamental analysis Security analysis that seeks to detect misvalued securities by an analysis of the firm's business prospects (cf. *technical analysis*).

Funded debt Debt maturing after more than one year (cf. *unfunded debt*).

Future A contract to buy a commodity or security on a future date at a price that is fixed today. Unlike forward contracts, futures are generally traded on organized exchanges and are *marked to market* daily.

G

GAAP Generally accepted accounting principles.

Gearing *Financial leverage.*

General cash offer Issue of securities offered to all investors (cf. *rights issue*).

Golden parachute A large termination payment due to a company's management if they lose their jobs as a result of a merger.

Goodwill The difference between the amount paid for a firm in a *merger* and its book value.

Gray market Purchases and sales of *eurobonds* that occur before the issue price is finally set.

Greenmail Situation in which a large block of stock is held by an unfriendly company, forcing the target company to repurchase the stock at a substantial premium to prevent a takeover.

Greenshoe option *Option* that allows the *underwriter* for a new issue to buy and resell additional shares.

Growth stock *Common stock* of a company that has an opportunity to invest money to earn more than the *opportunity cost of capital* (cf. *income stock*).

H

Haircut An additional margin of *collateral* for a loan.

Harmless warrant *Warrant* that allows the user to purchase a *bond* only by surrendering an existing bond with similar terms.

Hedge ratio (*delta, option delta*) The number of shares to buy for each *option* sold in order to create a safe position; more generally, the number of units of an asset that should be bought to hedge one unit of a liability.

Hedging Buying one security and selling another in order to reduce risk. A perfect hedge produces a riskless portfolio.

Hell-or-high-water clause Clause in a *lease* agreement that obligates the *lessee* to make payments regardless of what happens to the *lessor* or the equipment.

Highly leveraged transaction (*HLT*) Bank loan to a highly leveraged firm (formerly needed to be separately reported to the Federal Reserve Board).

HLT *Highly leveraged transaction.*

Holding company Company whose sole function is to hold stock in other companies or subsidiaries.

Horizontal merger Merger between two companies that manufacture similar products (cf. *vertical merger, conglomerate merger*).

Horizontal spread The simultaneous purchase and sale of two *options* that differ only in their exercise date (cf. *vertical spread*).

Hurdle rate Minimum acceptable rate of return on a project.

I

IBF *International Banking Facility.*

IMM *International Monetary Market.*

Immunization The construction of an asset and a liability that are subject to offsetting changes in value.

Imputation tax system Arrangement by which investors who receive a *dividend* also receive a tax credit for corporate taxes that the firm has paid.

Income bond *Bond* on which interest is payable only if earned.

Income stock *Common stock* with high *dividend yield* and few profitable investment opportunities (cf. *growth stock*).

Indenture Formal agreement, e.g., establishing the terms of a *bond* issue.

Indexed bond *Bond* whose payments are linked to an index, e.g., a consumer price index. (see *TIPs*)

Index fund Investment fund designed to match the returns on a stockmarket index.

Indirect quote For foreign exchange, the number of units of a foreign currency needed to buy one U.S. dollar (cf. *direct quote*).

Industrial revenue bond (*IRB*) Bond issued by local government agencies on behalf of corporations.

Initial public offering (*IPO*) A company's first public issue of *common stock.*

In-substance defeasance *Defeasance* whereby debt is removed from the balance sheet but not canceled (cf. *novation*).

Intangible asset Nonmaterial asset, such as technical expertise, a trademark, or a patent (cf. *tangible asset*).

Integer programming Variant of *linear programming* whereby the solution values must be integers.

Interest cover *Times interest earned.*

Interest equalization tax Tax on foreign investment by residents of the United States (abolished 1974).

Interest-rate parity Theory that the differential between the *forward exchange rate* and the *spot exchange rate* is equal to the differential between the foreign and domestic interest rates.

Intermediation Investment through a financial institution (cf. *disintermediation*).

Internal finance Finance generated within a firm by *retained earnings* and *depreciation* (cf. *external finance*).

Internal growth rate The maximum rate of firm growth without *external finance* (cf. *sustainable growth rate*).

Internal rate of return (*IRR*) *Discount rate* at which investment has zero *net present value.*

International Banking Facility (*IBF*) A branch that an American bank establishes in the United States to do eurocurrency business.

International Monetary Market (*IMM*) The financial futures market within the Chicago Mercantile Exchange.

Interval measure The number of days that a firm can finance operations without additional cash income.

In-the-money option An *option* that would be worth exercising if it expired immediately (cf. *out-of-the-money option*).

Inverse FRN *Floating-rate note* whose payments rise as the general level of interest rates falls and vice versa.

Investment banker *Underwriter.*

Investment-grade bond *Bond* rated at least Baa by Moody's or BBB by Standard and Poor's.

Investment tax credit Proportion of new capital investment that can be used to reduce a company's tax bill (abolished 1986).

IPO *Initial public offering.*

IRB *Industrial revenue bond.*

IRR *Internal rate of return.*

IRS Internal Revenue Service.

ISDA International Swap and Derivatives Association.

ISMA International Securities Market Association.

Issued share capital Total amount of shares that are in issue (cf. *outstanding share capital*).

J

Junior debt *Subordinated debt.*

Junk bond Debt that is rated below an *investment-grade bond.*

K

Keiretsu A network of Japanese companies organized around a major bank.

L

LBO *Leveraged buyout.*

Lease Long-term rental agreement.

Legal capital Value at which a company's shares are recorded in its books.

Legal defeasance *Novation.*

Lessee User of a leased asset (cf. *lessor*).

Lessor Owner of a leased asset (cf. *lessee*).

Letter of credit Letter from a bank stating that it has established a credit in the company's favor.

Letter stock Privately placed *common stock,* so-called because the *SEC* requires a letter from the purchaser that the stock is not intended for resale.

Leverage See *financial leverage, operating leverage.*

Leveraged buyout (*LBO*) Acquisition in which (1) a large part of the purchase price is debt-financed and (2) the remaining *equity* is privately held by a small group of investors.

Leveraged lease *Lease* in which the *lessor* finances part of the cost of the asset by an issue of debt secured by the asset and the lease payments.

Liabilities, total liabilities Total value of financial claims on a firm's assets. Equals (1) total assets or (2) total assets minus *net worth.*

LIBOR *London interbank offered rate.*

Lien Lender's claims on specified assets.

Limited liability Limitation of a shareholder's losses to the amount invested.

Limited partnership *Partnership* in which some partners have *limited liability* and general partners have unlimited liability.

Linear programming (*LP*) Technique for finding the maximum value of some equation subject to stated linear constraints.

Line of credit Agreement by a bank that a company may borrow at any time up to an established limit.

Liquid asset Asset that is easily and cheaply turned into cash—notably cash itself and short-term securities.

Liquidating dividend *Dividend* that represents a return of capital.

Liquidator Person appointed by unsecured creditors in the United Kingdom to oversee the sale of an insolvent firm's assets and the repayment of debts.

Liquidity premium (1) Additional return for investing in a security that cannot easily be turned into cash; (2) difference between the *forward interest rate* and the expected *spot interest rate*.

Liquid yield option note (*LYON*) Zero-coupon, callable, putable, *convertible bond*.

Load-to-load Arrangement whereby the customer pays for the last delivery when the next one is received.

Lock-box system Form of *concentration banking*. Customers send payments to a post office box. A local bank collects and processes the checks and transfers surplus funds to the company's principal bank.

London interbank offered rate (*LIBOR*) The interest rate at which major international banks in London lend to each other. (LIBID is London interbank bid rate; LIMEAN is mean of bid and offered rate.)

Long hedge Purchase of a *hedging* instrument (e.g., a *future*) to hedge a short position in the underlying asset (cf. *short hedge*).

Lookback option *Option* whose payoff depends on the highest asset price recorded over the life of the option.

LP *Linear programming*.

LYON *Liquid yield option note.*

M

MACRS *Modified accelerated cost recovery system.*

Maintenance margin Minimum margin that must be maintained on a *futures* contract.

Majority voting Voting system under which each director is voted upon separately (cf. *cumulative voting*).

Management buyout (*MBO*) *Leveraged buyout* whereby the acquiring group is led by the firm's management.

Margin Cash or securities set aside by an investor as evidence that he or she can honor a commitment.

Marked-to-market An arrangement whereby the profits or losses on a *futures* contract are settled up each day.

Market capitalization rate *Expected return* on a security.

Market risk (*systematic risk*) Risk that cannot be diversified away.

Maturity factoring *Factoring* arrangement that provides collection and insurance of *accounts receivable*.

MBO *Management buyout.*

MDA *Multiple-discriminant analysis.*

Medium-term note (*MTN*) Debt with a typical maturity of 1 to 10 years offered regularly by a company using the same procedure as *commercial paper*.

Merger (1) Acquisition in which all assets and liabilities are absorbed by the buyer (cf. *exchange of assets, exchange of stock*); (2) more generally, any combination of two companies.

MIP (**Monthly income preferred security**) *Preferred stock* issued by a subsidiary located in a tax haven. The subsidiary relends the money to the parent.

Mismatch bond *Floating-rate note* whose interest rate is reset at more frequent intervals than the rollover period (e.g., a note whose payments are set quarterly on the basis of the one-year interest rate).

Modified accelerated cost recovery system (*MACRS*) Schedule of *depreciation* deductions allowed for tax purposes.

Money center bank A major U.S. bank that undertakes a wide range of banking activities.

Money market Market for short-term safe investments.

Money-market fund *Mutual fund* that invests solely in short-term safe securities.

Monte Carlo simulation Method for calculating the probability distribution of possible outcomes, e.g., from a project.

Moral hazard The risk that the existence of a contract will change the behavior of one or both parties to the contract; e.g., an insured firm may take fewer fire precautions.

Mortgage bond *Bond* secured against plant and equipment.

MTN *Medium-term note.*

Multiple-discriminant analysis (*MDA*) Statistical technique for distinguishing between two groups on the basis of their observed characteristics.

Mutual fund Managed investment fund whose shares are sold to investors.

Mutually exclusive projects Two projects that cannot both be undertaken.

N

Naked option *Option* held on its own, i.e., not used for *hedging* a holding in the asset or other options.

NASD National Association of Security Dealers.

Negative pledge clause Clause under which the borrower agrees not to permit an exclusive *lien* on any of its assets.

Negotiated underwriting Method of choosing an *underwriter*. Most firms may choose their *underwriter* by negotiation (cf. *competitive bidding*).

Net lease *Lease* in which the *lessee* promises to maintain and insure the equipment (cf. *full-service lease*).

Net present value (*NPV*) A project's net contribution to wealth—*present value* minus initial investment.

Net working capital *Current assets* minus *current liabilities*.

Net worth Book value of a company's *common stock*, surplus, and *retained earnings*.

Nominal interest rate Interest rate expressed in money terms (cf. *real interest rate*).

Nonrefundable debt Debt that may not be called in order to replace it with another issue at a lower interest cost.

Normal distribution Symmetric bell-shaped distribution that can be completely defined by its mean and *standard deviation*.

Note Unsecured debt with a maturity of up to 10 years.

Novation (*legal defeasance*) *Defeasance* whereby the firm's debt is canceled (cf. *in-substance defeasance*).

NPV *Net present value.*

NYSE New York Stock Exchange.

O

Odd lot A trade of less than 100 shares (cf. *round lot*).

Off-balance-sheet financing Financing that is not shown as a liability in a company's balance sheet.

Offer price *Ask price.*

OID debt *Original issue discount debt.*

Old-line factoring *Factoring* arrangement that provides collection, insurance, and finance for *accounts receivable*.

On the run The most recently issued (and, therefore, typically the most liquid) government *bond* in a particular maturity range.

Open account Arrangement whereby sales are made with no formal debt contract. The buyer signs a receipt, and the seller records the sale in the sales ledger.

Open-end mortgage Mortgage against which additional debt may be issued (cf. *closed-end mortgage*).

Open interest The number of currently outstanding *futures* contracts.

Operating lease Short-term, cancelable *lease* (cf. *financial lease*).

Operating leverage Fixed operating costs, so-called because they accentuate variations in profits (cf. *financial leverage*).

Opportunity cost of capital (hurdle rate, cost of capital) *Expected return* that is forgone by investing in a project rather than in comparable financial securities.

Option See *call option, put option.*

Option delta *Hedge ratio.*

Original issue discount debt (*OID debt*) Debt that is initially offered at a price below *face value*.

OTC *Over-the-counter.*

Out-of-the-money option An *option* that would not be worth exercising if it matured immediately (cf. *in-the-money option*).

Outstanding share capital *Issued share capital* less the *par value* of shares that are held in the company's treasury.

Oversubscription privilege In a *rights issue*, arrangement by which shareholders are given the right to apply for any shares that are not taken up.

Over-the-counter (*OTC*) Informal market that does not involve a securities exchange. Specifically used to refer to the NASDAQ dealer market for *common stocks*.

P

Partnership Joint ownership of business whereby general partners have unlimited liability.

Par value (*face value*) Value of a security shown on the certificate.

Pass-through securities *Notes* or *bonds* backed by a package of assets (e.g., mortgage pass-throughs, *CARs*, *CARDs*).

Path-dependent option *Option* whose value depends on the sequence of prices of the underlying asset rather than just the final price of the asset.

Payables *Accounts payable.*

Payback period Time taken for a project to recover its initial investment.

Pay-in-kind bond (*PIK*) *Bond* that allows the issuer to choose to make interest payments in the form of additional bonds.

Payment float Company-written checks that have not yet cleared (cf. *availability float*).

Payout ratio *Dividend* as a proportion of earnings per share.

PBGC Pension Benefit Guarantee Corporation.

P/E ratio Share price divided by earnings per share.

PERC (Preferred equity redemption cumulative stock) *Preferred stock* that converts automatically into equity at a stated date. A limit is placed on the value of the shares that the investor receives.

Perpetuity Investment offering a level stream of cash flows in perpetuity (cf. *consol*).

PIK *Pay-in-kind bond.*

PN *Project note.*

Poison pill An issue of securities that is convertible, in the event of a *merger*, into the shares of the acquiring firm or must be repurchased by the acquiring firm.

Poison put A *covenant* allowing the *bond*holder to demand repayment in the event of a hostile *merger.*

Pooling of interest Method of accounting for *mergers.* The consolidated balance sheet of the merged firm is obtained by combining the balance sheets of the separate firms.

Position diagram Diagram showing the possible payoffs from a *derivative* investment.

Postaudit Evaluation of an investment project after it has been undertaken.

Preemptive right Common stockholder's right to anything of value distributed by the company.

Preferred stock Stock that takes priority over common stock in regard to *dividends.* Dividends may not be paid on *common stock* unless the dividend is paid on all preferred stock (cf. *cumulative preferred stock*). The dividend rate on preferred is usually fixed at time of issue.

Prepack *Prepackaged bankruptcy.*

Prepackaged bankruptcy (*prepack*) Bankruptcy proceedings intended to confirm a reorganization plan that has already been agreed to informally.

Present value Discounted value of future cash flows.

Present value of growth opportunities (*PVGO*) *Net present value* of investments the firm is expected to make in the future.

PRIDE Similar to a *PERC* except that as the equity price rises beyond a specified point, the investor shares in the stock appreciation.

Primary issue Issue of new securities by a firm (cf. *secondary issue*).

Prime rate Benchmark lending rate set by U.S. banks.

Principal Amount of debt that must be repaid.

Principal–agent problem Problem faced by a principal (e.g., shareholder) in ensuring that an agent (e.g., manager) acts on his or her behalf.

Privileged subscription issue *Rights issue.*

Production payment Loan in the form of advance payment for future delivery of a product.

Profitability index Ratio of a project's *NPV* to the initial investment.

Pro forma Projected.

Project finance Debt that is largely a claim against the cash flows from a particular project rather than against the firm as a whole.

Project note (*PN*) *Note* issued by public housing or urban renewal agencies.

Promissory note Promise to pay.

Prospectus Summary of the *registration* statement providing information on an issue of securities.

Proxy vote Vote cast by one person on behalf of another.

Public warehouse (*terminal warehouse*) Warehouse operated by an independent warehouse company on its own premises (cf. *field warehouse*).

Purchase fund Resembles a *sinking fund* except that money is used only to purchase bonds if they are selling below their *par value.*

Put option *Option* to sell an asset at a specified *exercise price* on or before a specified exercise date (cf. *call option*).

PVGO *Present value of growth opportunities.*

Q

q Ratio of the market value of an asset to its replacement cost.

QIBs *Qualified Institutional Buyers.*

Quadratic programming Variant of *linear programming* whereby the equations are quadratic rather than linear.

Qualified Institutional Buyers (*QIBs*) Institutions that are allowed to trade unregistered stock among themselves.

Quanto swap *Differential swap.*

Quick ratio (*acid-test ratio*) Measure of liquidity: (*current assets* – inventory) divided by *current liabilities.*

R

Range forward A *forward exchange rate* contract that places upper and lower bounds on the cost of foreign exchange.

Real assets *Tangible assets* and *intangible assets* used to carry on business (cf. *financial assets*).

Real estate investment trust (*REIT*) Trust company formed to invest in real estate.

Real interest rate Interest rate expressed in terms of real goods, i.e., *nominal interest rate* adjusted for inflation.

Receivables *Accounts receivable.*

Receiver A bankruptcy practitioner appointed by secured creditors in the United Kingdom to oversee the repayment of debts.

Record date Date set by directors when making dividend payment. *Dividends* are sent to stockholders who are registered on the record date.

Recourse Term describing a type of loan. If a loan is with recourse, the lender has a general claim against the parent company if the *collateral* is insufficient to repay the debt.

Red herring Preliminary *prospectus.*

Refunding Replacement of existing debt with a new issue of debt.

Registered security Security whose ownership is recorded by the company's *registrar* (cf. *bearer security*).

Registrar Financial institution appointed to record issue and ownership of company securities.

Registration Process of obtaining *SEC* approval for a public issue of securities.

Regression analysis In statistics, a technique for finding the line of best fit.

Regular dividend *Dividend* that the company expects to maintain in the future.

Regulation A issue Small security issues that are partially exempt from *SEC registration* requirements.

REIT *Real estate investment trust.*

Rental lease *Full-service lease.*

Repo *Repurchase agreement.*

Repurchase agreement (*RP, repo, buy-back*) Purchase of Treasury securities from a securities dealer with an agreement that the dealer will repurchase them at a specified price.

Residual income After-tax profit less the *opportunity cost of capital* employed by the business (see also *Economic Value Added*).

Residual risk *Unique risk.*

Retained earnings Earnings not paid out as *dividends.*

Return on equity Usually, equity earnings as a proportion of the book value of equity.

Return on investment (*ROI*) Generally, book income as a proportion of net book value.

Revolving credit Legally assured *line of credit* with a bank.

Rights issue (*privileged subscription issue*) Issue of securities offered to current stockholders (cf. *general cash offer*).

Rights on *With rights.*

Risk premium Expected additional return for making a risky investment rather than a safe one.

ROI *Return on investment.*

Roll-over CD A package of successive *certificates of deposit.*

Round lot A trade of 100 shares (cf. *odd lot*).

RP *Repurchase agreement.*

R squared (R^2) Square of the *correlation coefficient*—the proportion of the variability in one series that can be explained by the variability of one or more other series.

Rule 144a *SEC* rule allowing *qualified institutional buyers* to buy and trade unregistered securities.

S

Sale and lease-back Sale of an existing asset to a financial institution that then *leases* it back to the user (cf. *direct lease*).

Salvage value Scrap value of plant and equipment.

Samurai bond A yen *bond* issued in Tokyo by a non-Japanese borrower (cf. *bulldog bond, Yankee bond*).

SBIC Small Business Investment Company.

Seasoned issue Issue of a security for which there is an existing market (cf. *unseasoned issue*).

Season datings Extended credit for customers who order goods out of the peak season.

SEC Securities and Exchange Commission.

Secondary issue (1) Procedure for selling blocks of *seasoned issues* of stock; (2) more generally, sale of already issued stock.

Secondary market Market in which one can buy or sell *seasoned issues* of securities.

Secured debt Debt that, in the event of default, has first claim on specified assets.

Securitization Substitution of tradable securities for privately negotiated instruments.

Security market line Line representing the relationship between *expected return* and *market risk.*

Self-liquidating loan Loan to finance *current assets.* The sale of the current assets provides the cash to repay the loan.

Self-selection Consequence of a contract that induces only one group (e.g., low-risk individuals) to participate.

Semistrong-form efficient market Market in which security prices reflect all publicly available information (cf. *weak-form efficient market* and *strong-form efficient market*).

Senior debt Debt that, in the event of bankruptcy, must be repaid before *subordinated debt* receives any payment.

Sensitivity analysis Analysis of the effect on project profitability of possible changes in sales, costs, and so on.

Serial bonds Package of *bonds* that mature in successive years.

Series bond *Bond* that may be issued in several series under the same *indenture.*

Shark repellant Amendment to company charter intended to protect it against takeover.

Shelf registration A procedure that allows firms to file one *registration* statement covering several issues of the same security.

Shogun bond Dollar *bond* issued in Japan by a nonresident.

Short hedge Sale of a *hedging* instrument (e.g., a *future*) to *hedge* a long position in the underlying asset (cf. *long hedge*).

Short sale Sale of a security the investor does not own.

Sight draft Demand for immediate payment (cf. *time draft*).

Signal Action that demonstrates an individual's unobservable characteristics (because it would be unduly costly for someone without those characteristics to take the action).

Simple interest Interest calculated only on the initial investment (cf. *compound interest*).

Simulation *Monte Carlo simulation.*

Sinker *Sinking fund.*

Sinking fund (*sinker*) Fund established by a company to retire debt before maturity.

Skewed distribution Probability distribution in which an unequal number of observations lie below and above the mean.

Special dividend (*extra dividend*) *Dividend* that is unlikely to be repeated.

Specific risk *Unique risk.*

Spin-off Distribution of shares in a subsidiary to the company's shareholders so that they hold shares separately in the two firms.

Spot exchange rate Exchange rate on currency for immediate delivery (cf. *forward exchange rate*)

Spot interest rate Interest rate fixed today on a loan that is made today (cf. *forward interest rate*).

Spot price Price of asset for immediate delivery (in contrast to forward or futures price).

Spread Difference between the price at which an *underwriter* buys an issue from a firm and the price at which the underwriter sells it to the public.

Standard deviation Square root of the *variance*—a measure of variability.

Standard error In statistics, a measure of the possible error in an estimate.

Standby agreement In a *rights issue*, agreement that the *underwriter* will purchase any stock not purchased by investors.

Step-up bond *Bond* whose *coupon* is stepped up over time (also step-down bond).

Stock dividend *Dividend* in the form of stock rather than cash.

Stock split "Free" issue of shares to existing shareholders.

Straddle The combination of a *put option* and a *call option* with the same *exercise price.*

Straight-line depreciation An equal dollar amount of *depreciation* in each period.

Striking price *Exercise price* of an *option.*

Stripped bond *Bond* that can be subdivided into a series of *zero-coupon bonds.*

Strong-form efficient market Market in which security prices reflect instantaneously *all* information available to investors (cf. *weak-form efficient market* and *semistrong-form efficient market*).

Structured debt Debt that has been customized for the buyer, often by incorporating unusual *options.*

Subordinated debt (*junior debt*) Debt over which *senior debt* takes priority. In the event of bankruptcy, subordinated debtholders receive payment only after senior debt is paid off in full.

Sum-of-the-years'-digits depreciation Method of *accelerated depreciation.*

Sunk costs Costs that have been incurred and cannot be reversed.

Supermajority Provision in a company's charter requiring a majority of, say, 80 percent of shareholders to approve certain changes, such as a *merger.*

Sushi bond A *eurobond* issued by a Japanese corporation.

Sustainable growth rate Maximum rate of firm growth without increasing financial leverage (cf. *internal growth rate*).

Swap An arrangement whereby two companies lend to each other on different terms, e.g., in different currencies, or one at a fixed rate and the other at a floating rate.

Swaption *Option* on a *swap.*

Swingline facility Bank borrowing facility to provide finance while the firm replaces U.S. *commercial paper* with eurocommercial paper.

Systematic risk *Market risk.*

T

Take-up fee Fee paid to *underwriters* of a *rights issue* on any stock they are obliged to purchase.

Tangible asset Physical asset, such as plant, machinery, and offices (cf. *intangible assets*).

Tax-anticipation bill Short-term bill issued by the U.S. Treasury that can be surrendered at *face value* in payment of taxes.

T-bill *Treasury bill.*

Technical analysis Security analysis that seeks to detect and interpret patterns in past security prices (cf. *fundamental analysis*).

TED spread Difference between *LIBOR* and U.S. *treasury bill* rate.

Tender offer General offer made directly to a firm's shareholders to buy their stock.

Tenor Maturity of a loan.

Terminal warehouse *Public warehouse.*

Term loan Medium-term, privately placed loan, usually made by a bank.

Term structure of interest rates Relationship between interest rates on loans of different maturities (cf. *yield curve*).

Throughput arrangement Arrangement by which shareholders of a pipeline company agree to make sufficient use of pipeline to enable the pipeline company to service its debt.

Tick Minimum amount the price of a security may change.

Time draft Demand for payment at a stated future date (cf. *sight draft*).

Times interest earned (*interest cover*) Earnings before interest and tax, divided by interest payments.

TIPS (Treasury Inflation Protected Securities) U.S. Treasury *bonds* whose *coupon* and *principal* payments are linked to the Consumer Price Index.

Tombstone Advertisement listing the *underwriters* to a security issue.

Trade acceptance Written demand that has been accepted by an industrial company to pay a given sum at a future date (cf. *banker's acceptance*).

Trade credit *Accounts receivable.*

Trade debt *Accounts payable.*

Tranche Portion of a new issue sold at a point in time different from the remainder or that has different terms.

Transaction exposure Risk to a firm with known future cash flows in a foreign currency that arises from possible changes in the exchange rate (cf. *economic exposure, translation exposure*).

Transfer agent Individual or institution appointed by a company to look after the transfer of securities.

Translation exposure Risk of adverse effects on a firm's financial statements that may arise from changes in exchange rates (cf. *economic exposure, transaction exposure*).

Treasurer Principal financial manager (cf. *controller*).

Treasury bill (*T-bill*) Short-term discount debt maturing in less than one year, issued regularly by the government.

Treasury stock *Common stock* that has been repurchased by the company and held in the company's treasury.

Trust deed Agreement between trustee and borrower setting out terms of *bond*.

Trust receipt Receipt for goods that are to be held in trust for the lender.

U

Underpricing Issue of securities below their market value.

Underwriter (*investment banker*) Firm that buys an issue of securities from a company and resells it to investors.

Unfunded debt Debt maturing within one year (cf. *funded debt*).

Uniform price auction Auction in which all successful bidders pay the same price (cf. *discriminatory price auction*).

Unique risk (*residual risk, specific risk, unsystematic risk*) Risk that can be eliminated by diversification.

Unseasoned issue Issue of a security for which there is no existing market (cf. *seasoned issue*).

Unsystematic risk *Unique risk.*

V

Value additivity Rule that the value of the whole must equal the sum of the values of the parts.

Value-at-risk model (*VAR model*) Procedure for estimating the probability of portfolio losses exceeding some specified proportion.

Vanilla issue Issue without unusual features.

Variable rate demand bond (*VRDB*) Floating rate *bond* that can be sold back periodically to the issuer.

Variance Mean squared deviation from the expected value—a measure of variability.

Variation margin The daily gains or losses on a *futures* contract credited to the investor's margin account.

VAR model *Value-at-risk model.*

Venture capital Capital to finance a new firm.

Vertical merger *Merger* between a supplier and its customer (cf. *horizontal merger, conglomerate merger*).

Vertical spread Simultaneous purchase and sale of two options that differ only in their *exercise price* (cf. *horizontal spread*).

VRDB *Variable rate demand bond.*

W

WACC *Weighted-average cost of capital.*

Warehouse receipt Evidence that a firm owns goods stored in a warehouse.

Warrant Long-term *call option* issued by a company.

Weak-form efficient market Market in which security prices instantaneously reflect the information in the history of security prices. In such a market security prices follow a random walk (cf. *semistrong-form efficient market* and *strong-form efficient market*).

Weighted-average cost of capital (*WACC*) *Expected return* on a portfolio of all the firm's securities. Used as *hurdle rate* for capital investment.

White knight A friendly potential acquirer sought out by a target company threatened by a less welcome suitor.

Wi. When issued.

Winner's curse Problem faced by uninformed bidders. For example, in an *initial public offering* uninformed participants are likely to receive larger allotments of issues that informed participants know are overpriced.

With dividend (*cum dividend*) Purchase of shares in which the buyer is entitled to the forthcoming *dividend* (cf. *ex dividend*).

Withholding tax Tax levied on *dividends* paid abroad.

With rights (*cum rights, rights on*) Purchase of shares in which the buyer is entitled to the rights to buy shares in the company's *rights issue* (cf. *ex rights*).

Working capital *Current assets* and *current liabilities*. The term is commonly used as synonymous with *net working capital*.

Workout Informal arrangement between a borrower and creditors.

Writer *Option* seller.

Y

Yankee bond A dollar *bond* issued in the United States by a non-U.S. borrower (cf. *bulldog bond, Samurai bond*).

Yield curve *Term structure of interest rates.*

Yield to maturity *Internal rate of return* on a bond.

Z

Zero-coupon bond *Discount bond* making no *coupon* payments.

Z score Measure of the likelihood of bankruptcy.

INDEX

About the Authors

Richard A. Brealey is Emeritus Professor of Finance at London Business School. He is the former president of the European Finance Association and a former director of the American Finance Association. He is a fellow of the British Academy and has served as a special advisor to the Governor of the Bank of England and director of a number of financial institutions. Other books written by Professor Brealey include *Introduction to Risk and Return from Common Stocks.*

Stewart C. Myers is the Gordon Y Billard Professor of Finance at MIT's Sloan School of Management. He is past president of the American Finance Association and a research associate of the National Bureau of Economic Research. His research has focused on financing decisions, valuation methods, the cost of capital, and financial aspects of government regulation of business. Dr. Myers is a director of The Brattle Group Inc. and is active as a financial consultant.

The Brattle Group

The Brattle Group, Inc. is an economic, environmental and management consulting firm with offices in Cambridge (Massachusetts), Washington, London, and San Francisco. The firm specializes in the practical application of financial economics. It annually sponsors the Brattle Prizes for the best papers published in *The Journal of Finance* on the topic of corporate finance.